CAREER OPPORTUNITIES IN TELEVISION AND CABLE

ALLAN TAYLOR

JAMES ROBERT PARISH

Foreword by
NAT SEGALOFF

✔Checkmark Books
An imprint of Infobase Publishing

To Linda and Virgil Barnes
for their constant support and enthusiasm

Career Opportunities in Television and Cable

Copyright © 2007 by Allan Taylor and James Robert Parish

Checkmark Books
An imprint of Infobase Publishing
132 West 31st Street
New York NY 10001

Library of Congress Cataloging-in-publication Data
Taylor, T. Allan.
Career opportunities in television and cable / by Allan Taylor and James Robert Parish.
    p. cm.
Includes bibliographical references and index.
ISBN 0-8160-6312-5 (hc : alk. paper)—ISBN 0-8160-6313-3 (pb : alk. paper)
1. Television—Vocational guidance. 2. Cable television—Vocational guidance. I. Parish, James Robert. II. Title.
HE8700.4.T39 2006
384.55023'73—dc22   22005037889

Checkmark Books are available at special discounts when purchased in bulk quantities for businesses, associations, institutions, or sales promotions. Please call our Special Sales Department in New York at (212) 967-8800 or (800) 322-8755.

You can find Facts On File on the World Wide Web at http://www.factsonfile.com

Cover design by Cathy Rincon

Printed in the United States of America

VB Hermitage 10 9 8 7 6 5 4 3 2 1

This book is printed on acid-free paper.

CONTENTS

FOREWORD

by Nat Segaloff, writer, teacher, journalist, broadcaster, and television producer

The television industry today is changing its structure with confusing speed. Telephone companies now own cable franchises, movie studios own broadcast and cable networks, and all of them are fighting over who gets to provide Internet access while satellites hover watchfully above. The FCC (Federal Communications Commission) has abdicated its regulatory duty in an effort to spur innovation, marginal voices are being pushed aside, and the consumer is caught in the middle. Critics charge that there may be more TV channels, but they contain less diversity of content; supporters argue that, since anybody can start a personal blog on the Internet, that makes up for the networks abandoning their responsibility to keep the public informed. About the only thing that hasn't changed since Philo Taylor Farnsworth invented television in 1927 (at the age of 15!) is that somebody still has to make the programs. That's what this book is about.

Getting a job in the creative end of television is a little like trying to wrangle an invitation to someone else's dinner party: You can drop hints, send notes, and make phone calls, but crashing it seldom works—except for those times it does, making it one of the few instances in which the exception proves the rule. The trick is to be innovative but not *too* innovative, because that means taking a risk, and the television industry is all about minimizing risk. Whether you become a floor director or an account executive, a writer or a program manager, when the TV industry tells you it wants fresh ideas, what it really means is that it wants *old* ideas packaged in a *new* way. The proof lies in what gets on the air and what doesn't; how many times have you said to yourself, "That show is so good it's bound to get canceled"? And it usually does!

Yes, quality is important, but what fuels a commercial medium (and don't think that PBS isn't commercial in its own way) is the number of people watching it. It's the job of people fortunate enough to work in television to attract those viewers.

As the most powerful form of communication devised since the printing press, television not only has to stay *ahead* of the curve, it must *be* the curve. Those who are faint of heart need not apply. Television faces ever-growing challenges. It is, after all, an industry that's under constant attack from politicians, government agencies, pressure groups, critics, and even its own viewers. Rising costs and dwindling budgets are driving production away from American shores. Cable, satellite, and Internet delivery systems are slicing the income pie into ever-shrinking slivers. Finally, cheap video equipment has turned every consumer into a producer, creating the impression that anyone can make a TV show.

* * * *

I broke into TV in the late 1970s by what I later learned was the traditional manner: dumb luck. As a former publicist living in Boston, I knew all the broadcast station executives from having placed touring celebrities on their local talk shows (which barely exist anymore thanks to syndicated programming). I left publicity when Clark Smidt, a visionary CBS radio executive (he created the "soft rock" format), asked me to be his on-air entertainment critic. Because I have, as the insult goes, "a face made for radio," I never even considered television. Nevertheless, Russell Manker, another friend from my PR days, dared me to audition for a show that Westinghouse television was just starting called *Evening Magazine*.

Not thinking I had any chance of landing the gig, I arrogantly entered the audition room, sat on the edge of the desk rather than behind it (forcing the camera crew to adjust angles), looked squarely into the lens, and talked until someone said, "cut." Fortunately, live radio had given me the experience of ad-libbing.

And that's when dumb luck came into play. *Evening Magazine,* it turned out, was designed to put "real people" rather than anchors on the tube. My being a "mustachioed Jewish male"—that's how Russell Manker's boss described me when he gave me the job—was just what they were looking for. I did 200 *Evening* segments over the next two years, wheedling my way into producing them too (for free; I'm sure that's why they allowed me to do it). Thus, I learned at their expense. *Evening* was the first non-news show to use portable video equipment, and, as the franchise spread into some 100 cities under the name *P.M. Magazine,* its success brought hundreds of new faces into the industry.

Mine, however, was not to be among them. One day, the same executive who hired me told me I was fired because, according to a focus group Westinghouse had held in Ohio, "We seem to have an overabundance of mustachioed Jewish males." The window had been open for two years, however, and I'd climbed through it. I kept my moustache and called around to people I had met while in front of the camera to see if there were any jobs behind it. After *Evening* I began writing and producing for television stations throughout New England while continuing to work in radio and newspapers and to teach. I called it *freelancing;* I later learned it was called *synergy.* By any name, it was a constant struggle.

Contrary to popular opinion, on the local level, only the news anchors bring in the large salaries, and then only if they're in the top 20 markets. Everyone else, whether in front of or behind the camera (with the notable exception of management and sales), seldom gets rich.

So why work in television if not for the money? Because there's the chance of doing something that actually improves people's lives. If you can inform a viewer about a new medical procedure, or locate a lost child, or lift someone's burden with a laugh, then you've made the world better. On the other hand, if you exploit someone's tragedy, if you pass along lies, if you sell people harmful products, or if you stop the flow of information, then you have caused harm. (It always surprises me that a medium that's so ready to attack others for ethical breaches has no consistent ethical standard for itself.)

When, for example, I created a one-hour special for a major cable network about three communities that came together to heal themselves after hate crimes had occurred in their midst, I ran against programming executives who wanted to exploit the hate rather than the healing. "We have to be balanced," they insisted, ignoring the fact that the healers (civic leaders, students, ministers, parents) were the balance to the haters (KKK, skinheads, racists), and not the other way around. When I was unable to change their minds, I walked off the show, although, to my shame, my contract prevented me from removing my name. When it aired, people were hurt. Worse, it won some kind of humanitarian award (I never bothered to collect it). I'm still not sure what lesson this teaches.

On the other hand, I found a pleasing level of intelligence at A&E network, for whom I made several early episodes in their flagship *Biography* series. The job came from Gary Grossman, a fellow Boston journalist who had just opened a Los Angeles video production company with former *Entertainment Tonight* anchor Robb Weller. Weller/Grossman Productions had just landed a contract from A&E to produce *Biography,* but only if they could deliver a "wish list" of celebrity subjects. The late comic actor John Belushi's name was on the list, and since one of my best friends in college had married John's widow, I phoned them for permission. They not only gave us the go-ahead, it turned out that they had taped a trove of private video interviews with John's family and colleagues, and voila! Instant *Biography.*

Gary, Robb, and I followed the Belushi show with a look at talk master Larry King, a celebration of ventriloquist Shari Lewis and her friend Lamb Chop, and I still, er, marvel that I got to know comic book innovator Stan Lee while producing his *Biography.* No television job lasts forever, however. When A&E began cutting the number of independent producers who made its *Biography*s, I moved on to producing programming for The Learning Channel, HBO, USA Networks, and the Food Network. I also spent time writing books, producing audiobooks, and doing charitable work.

As a medium, television is all about impressions; as a career, it's all about relationships. It's hard to break in, but once you do you can work with some of the most talented and stimulating people in the world—as well as some of the most crass and obtuse. The thing to remember (even while others forget) is that whatever level you may be on, you are dealing with a public trust. As Edward R. Murrow once cautioned, television can "teach . . . illuminate . . . even inspire. Otherwise it is merely lights and wires in a box."

The outcome depends upon who's inside that box.

Nat Segaloff is a writer, teacher, journalist, and broadcaster who has produced programming for A&E, HBO, The Learning Channel, and USA. He resides in Los Angeles.

INDUSTRY OUTLOOK

The business of television is extremely fast-paced and continues to experience a rapid growth in the 21st century. Change has been the rule in the American television industry since its commercial inception in 1939. It was then that the National Broadcasting Company (NBC), a network of radio stations owned by the Radio Corporation of America (RCA), aired a televised speech by President Franklin D. Roosevelt to commemorate the opening of the New York's World Fair. Since then, the industry has been marked by constant change based on technological innovations and global expansion. Nonetheless, traditional approaches to its processes and deeply rooted customs—some dating back to the time when radio ruled the airwaves—continue to influence parts of the television industry. Other technological trends, such as the introduction of digital television and digital techniques in television production and the industry's convergence with the Internet, are making new rules and, once again, fast-altering the TV business.

The roots of the invention called television extend back to 1876, when Alexander Graham Bell first demonstrated his telephone to an astonished public. Bell's invention opened up the possibilities of a future filled with electronic communication media. Other inventors supplied pieces of what would become television. German physicist Karl Braun developed in 1897 the cathode ray oscilloscope, which would later be applied to the scanning system of television. Guglielmo Marconi discovered how to reproduce radio waves; Reginald Fessenden found out how to send radio signals on modulating waveforms; and Lee DeForest discovered how to amplify and generate waves. Other inventors became fascinated with the idea of wireless transmission of visual images. In 1923, Valdimir Zworykin, a Russian scientist and immigrant who had come to the United States after World War I, patented the iconoscopic camera, a television tube in which a beam of high-velocity electrons scans a photoemissive mosaic. Zworykin subsequently became director of David Sarnoff's RCA electronics research laboratory. In 1927, American inventor Philo Taylor Farnsworth put together an electric scanning system similar to Zworykin's iconosope. Throughout the 1930s, RCA and Farnsworth battled over television-related patents, with the result that Farnsworth was reimbursed by RCA with royalty payments for his patents. Then Farnsworth devised the television camera called a Kinescope, which converted the captured image into an electronic signal. Thus, no one person invented television.

By the mid-1940s, the Columbia Broadcasting System (CBS) and the DuMont network had joined National Broadcasting Corporation (NBC) as broadcasters. Allen B. DuMont, who had earlier developed the kinescope tube, marketed the first modern home television receiver (set) in 1939, and in August 1940, Peter Goldmark announced his invention of a color TV system. However, World War II interrupted all commercial television development activity. At the end of the war, there were only 7,000 TV receivers in the United States. Only five cities had TV stations: New York City, Philadelphia, Chicago, Los Angeles, and Schenectady (N.Y.), the last of which was the site of General Electric's experimental TV station, WGY, which had done its first broadcast of a dramatic program in 1928.

In 1941, the Federal Communications Commission (FCC) allocated various spectrums for use by the companies involved with television broadcasting (the future networks) and approved commercial television service. In the years after World War II, with the advent of full-fledged network broadcast schedules, the sales of television sets increased steadily. By 1965, 96 percent of American households had at least one set, and 22 percent had more than one. Today, it is estimated that there are nearly a billion television sets in use worldwide.

* * * *

Television began as a live medium, completely unlike motion picture filming, with its painstaking postproduction methods. In the early days, television sound was of limited quality, and a program, once transmitted, was lost forever unless the network happened to Kinescope the particular show. (The unsophisticated Kinescope process, which focused its camera on a TV screen to film a show as it was being aired, was the only medium then available for recording transmitted television shows.)

By the mid-1950s, magnetic tape was already being used to capture sound, but the greater quantity of information carried by the television visual signal demanded something new. Charles Ginsburg of Ampex Corporation developed the first practical videotape recorder (VTR). The system used a rapidly rotating recording head to apply high-frequency signals onto a reel of magnetic tape.

The VTR revolutionized television broadcasting because it was so much less expensive than film and did not require the developing process. This development had two significant consequences. First, recordings could be edited using the best takes, which meant viewers no longer had to witness the mistakes made in live transmissions. Second, music and sound effects could be mixed into the original taped sound. Thus, production values improved, and the postproduction process became an accepted part of television production.

In 1956, CBS became the first network to employ VTR technology. However, while simple mechanical edits of videotape could be performed, the process was still complex, difficult, and limited. That situation changed with the introduction in 1967 of timecode editing, which identified each individual frame of video with accurate clock time. With the introduction of computer technology in the digitizing of video images, the entire process of television editing underwent yet another revolutionary change in the 1980s. By 2005, computer-based editing of both video and audio signals of a television production has almost completely replaced traditional tape and film editing.

* * * *

Understanding broadcast television and cable as a business requires knowing how the players interact. The broadcast networks consist of sports, entertainment, and news divisions. Their programming is fed to television stations the networks own and operate (the *O&Os*) and to affiliate stations. The networks produce their own programming, as well as acquire entries from television studios, production companies, and syndicators. Most of the networks generally pay their affiliated stations to distribute their programming, thus allowing local broadcasters to transmit the networks' programming at relatively little cost. The networks make their profit from the advertising they sell on the programs.

Public television produces programming and buys it from independent producers and, of course, has little to no commercial advertising. Low-power television (LPTV) stations are designed to provide the opportunity for small rural communities to establish their own stations. They often are operated like a cross between a local newspaper and an FM radio station: They generally operate with limited power, covering a distance of less than 20 miles. Some may be operated as nonprofit organizations, while others may depend on local advertising revenue or, in some cases, scramble their television signal and charge viewers a monthly subscription fee.

Cable television networks produce programming, obtain shows from syndicators, and deal with cable system operators (the companies that install and maintain local cable hookups) and satellite systems. In addition to advertising revenue, cable networks are paid per-subscriber monthly fees by local cable system owners/satellite systems. Subscription cable networks, such as HBO, Showtime, and Cinemax, where the subscriber pays an additional monthly charge beyond the "basic" monthly fee, share part of their subscribers' fees with the local cable system or satellite system.

A network is generally divided into two main divisions: the broadcast group and the television group. The broadcast group typically is in charge of the operation and profitability of the network's O&Os and manages television advertising sales, video and cable enterprises, and radio stations owned by the network. The television group distributes programming to the network's affiliated stations. It also produces or licenses news, sports, and entertainment programming. As a result, networks maintain large staffs in their in-house production units. The television group is also responsible for broadcast operations and engineering, providing technical and logistical support for its various components. Networks have an information and publicity staff as well to handle public relations for both its programming and its other operations. The FCC now allows networks to be involved in cable and video operations, which may take the form of a financial interest in a cable TV network and/or supplying programming to either domestic or foreign cable networks and to video networks.

At an individual television station, whether it is a network O&O, an affiliate station, or an independent station, the job opportunities are generally in one of the following groupings: management; sales and marketing; programming; news, sports, and weather; and engineering.

The top level of a station is its management staff, which makes the key decisions and does the most worrying. Networks and stations make their money selling airtime. Additionally, network affiliates receive affiliate compensation from the networks. Stations and network sales forces sell three types of advertising airtime: *Network TV sales* are aired on all stations affiliated with a network (50 percent of network sales are for prime-time programs, whereas 20 percent are for sports programs). *Spot TV sales* are from sponsors that, for whatever reason, decide to advertise only in selected markets. *Local TV sales* are from local businesses that are highly selective in choosing their markets. At O&Os and network affiliates, most programming is supplied by the network, though news shows are produced locally at the station. Likewise, independent stations and public TV stations get much of their programming from outside sources, such as syndicators, but do produce some shows in-house. Programming at TV stations encompasses both planning and production of programs and usually also includes liaison with the networks and syndicators.

The scope of TV news is now so wide that, for just one network, it involves more than a thousand people and a budget of more than $1 million a day. In addition, local stations carry area news programs for as much as four hours a day. At even the smallest stations, there is an average of six people handling the news operation.

* * * *

Today's television technology is totally unlike that of early broadcasting. These days, engineering personnel work with electronic news-gathering equipment that relays information and visuals from the field without requiring any intervening film editing at the station. Satellite transmissions put together news packages and entertainment programming from all parts of the world quickly and efficiently. Video compression allows a single satellite channel to carry up to a dozen television programs. A network facility may employ 100 engineering and technical personnel, while a large-market station may have nearly 200 people in this capacity. Small stations employ engineers and assistants, maintenance people, and often minicam operators and electronic news-gathering crews as part of their engineering and technical team.

Until about 1995, television networks did not produce prime-time programming other than news and sports. They licensed, instead, the largest portion of their programming from independent production firms and from studios that created these shows and contracted with the performers, directors, and technical crew in the making of such fare. Today, the networks are allowed by federal regulation to produce their own shows, and most of them own studios for that purpose. This change means that more projects can be developed, which translates into more jobs for more people in the creative areas of television programming. Networks and independent production operations are both responsible for all phases of production. Often these companies form partnerships, for both financial reasons and for availability of physical facilities, with television studios (who may produce their own series as well).

* * * *

In the coming decade, the television industry will undergo an even greater transformation than it experienced in the prior 10 years. In order to make sense of the rapidly developing new technology driving the television industry, it is important to understand the components of this high-tech revolution. *Broadband* is a descriptive term of evolving digital technologies that offer the public a signal-switching facility that provides integrated access to voice, high-speed data, video-on-demand services, and interactive information delivery systems. For example, Comcast, the largest cable system provider in the United States (with more than 21.5 million subscribers), offers to its broadband customers high-speed Internet access, an improved picture on their television sets, voice services, and a personalized e-mail home page on the Yahoo portal.

Broadband represents a convergence of telecommunications (including television) and computer technology. Digital television is the broadcasting technology for transmitting and receiving digital television signals. Digital signals offer clearer resolution and better sound quality than analog signals. High-definition television (HDTV) is a digital television format that offers approximately twice the vertical and horizontal screen resolution of non-HDTV television sets.

This is a resolution similar to that of a high-focus movie screen. It also provides audio quality approaching that of the highest quality of compact discs on the market today. Cable networks presently are leading the way in providing high-definition television to the public, though the networks are catching on that this is a hot new popular item.

Digital cable's biggest rival is satellite broadcasting (which are broadcast signals from a relay station for audio and video transmission orbiting in space to a satellite station on earth, such as the parabolic dish attached to customers' homes) and is a key growth area, with more than 30 million subscribers today.

Another digital television format is standard-definition television (SDTV). It provides superior picture quality; the resolution is similar to what is obtainable from a DVD product. Because SDTV's compressed digital signal is smaller than a compressed HDTV signal, a broadcaster can transmit up to five SDTV programs simultaneously. Finally, another device, the digital video recorder (DVR), records television shows onto a hard drive instead of tapes or discs. A DVR, using digital technology, is capable of pausing a live television broadcast and allowing a viewer to rewind or use slow-motion to replay the action of live TV, zapping over ads, and auto-recording any television show from a display of TV listings. The latter's effect on the network's advertising revenue is yet to be determined, but it will be considerable. Some advertisers are looking at placing their products all over the set of a television production instead of running ads. Such corporations as AOL Time Warner, and Toshiba are looking to use the technology of DVR in television sets, while preventing consumers from making, storing, or sharing copies of programming. Obviously, in this fast-track game of telecommunications, no one company remains ahead of the pack for long.

* * * *

So where does all of television's new technology take us, and how does it affect the industry's present job market? For the entertainment industry and television in particular, the sending, receiving, and storing of information (including images and sounds from television productions) will continue to be a major focus and concern. The data storage capacity and quality of video need to improve as the technology of data compression and transmission leaps forward.

How data is configured and stored is pivotal to the new digital world, and a universal standard for storage and compression may become a key factor in closing the gap in resolution and clarity between film and video, as well as becoming accepted worldwide. Data have an advantage in that the disk or tape on which data are stored improves and change often, but the method by which data are stored, written, or configured should change little over time.

With a way to store content (such as a television production, a film, or a book) in a digital format with computer access that one hopes will be universally acceptable soon, there are endless possibilities—and no foreseeable limits to sending, receiving, and storing this digitized data.

For the job market in the industry, obviously technology is going to play a tremendous part in the continued good health of the entire television business. This is certainly going to change the way television technicians and engineers are going to work and how productions will be accomplished. It may well increase the demand for more television programming to be made available in all kinds of intriguing new formats. This means job growth as the technology pushes the industry forward, much like the impact that the development of the computer and the Internet has had on society as a whole.

ACKNOWLEDGMENTS

First and foremost, we want to thank our editor, James Chambers, at Facts On File, Inc. Jim has been an unfailing, enthusiastic, and concerned editor, and his aid is gratefully acknowledged. We also want to thank our agent, Stuart Bernstein, for his help and suggestions on this project. In addition, we, of course, want to thank Nat Segaloff for the informative and delightful foreword to this book.

We also wish to thank the following individuals and organizations for their assistance with this project: Mark Allen, Gregory Baker, Larry Billman (Academy of Dance on Film), Stephen Cole, Ernest Cunningham, Jane Klain (Museum of Television & Radio), Frederick Levy, Paul Meyers, Kimberly O'Quinn, Seth Oster (Screen Actors Guild), Jonathan Rosenthal, Brad Schreiber, Nat Segaloff, Joan Singleton, Chris Vine (National Association of Broadcasters), Steven Whitney, and Mike Wilcox.

HOW TO USE THIS BOOK

Purpose

The 100 careers described in *Career Opportunities in Television and Cable* make it one of the most inclusive directories of television jobs available in a single volume. In many cases, these careers are involved in some of the most exciting technological developments in today's high-tech world. Whether our current environment is labeled the "information age" or the "electronic era," there is no doubt that the television industry is a major component in our ever-expanding digital economy.

The tremendous number of electronic devices that affect, influence, and, to some degree, define our lives represents a new entertainment and information society that is vital and dynamic. Within the television industry the underlying factor behind the equipment and processes is people. Television is often portrayed as a high-paying, glamorous business. The talented performers who appear on our television screens every day become a part of our lives. However, for every performer we see onscreen, there are hundreds of individuals working behind the scenes who make those on-camera appearances possible. The continual expansion of the television and cable industries relies on trained engineers; talented programming, production, and marketing/promotional professionals; skilled craftspeople; persevering clerical workers; and aggressive managers.

The purpose of *Career Opportunities in Television and Cable* is to serve as a guide to the most common occupations within the industry. By consulting this volume, high school and college students interested in a career in television can learn who does what within the vast industry. Those who are currently employed in a professional capacity within the TV business will also find the information contained in this book helpful as they expand and/or redefine their career paths.

In *Career Opportunities in Television and Cable* jobs are not merely summarized in a few paragraphs but are explained in detail, including duties, alternate titles, salary ranges, employment and advancement prospects (with a Career Ladder detailing typical routes to and from the position), prerequisites (including education and training, experience, and skills requirements), organizations to join, and helpful tips for entering the job arena under discussion. This volume is geared to assist both those seeking to start a career in the television industry and to those experienced members of that industry who are looking to make career changes within their profession.

Many of the jobs detailed in this volume are available to individuals with appropriate education credentials (typically at least a high school diploma and some college work or a bachelor's degree) and from none up to five years or more of experience. These are principally entry- and mid-level posts within the TV field. Other jobs described herein require more training and/or education, as well as more years of experience within the field, and these are both mid-level and high-end posts.

Sources of Information

Research for this book includes the authors' own experiences, interviews with professionals in assorted positions within the television industry, and facts, reports, surveys, and other data obtained from job data banks, professional associations, trade unions/guilds, the federal government, and educational institutions.

The job descriptions provided are based on representative samples of actual job posts, employment documents, research studies, salary surveys, and tables of organization from many sources in the communications industry. Thus, the career descriptions detailed are not theoretical; they represent current practice and reflect the actual structure of jobs in the industry.

How the Book Is Organized

The 100 job profiles in *Career Opportunities in Television and Cable* are organized into 13 sections, reflecting different aspects of the television industry: Advertising; Arts and Design; Cable/Satellite Television; Directing; Education; Engineering; Management and Administration; News; Performing; Producing; Programming, Public Relations, and Marketing; Technical Production; and Writing.

To better reflect the scope and responsibilities of actual TV jobs, the Technical Production section is further broken down into specific components: Camera; Editing; Hair, Makeup, and Wardrobe; Lighting and Electrical; Location and Transportation; Management (Technical); Music; Props and Set Maintenance; Sound; and Special Effects and Visual Effects. An Introduction provides an overview of the television industry, both broadcast and cable, and the career opportunities available in the industry.

The careers discussed in this book are the most frequent job positions found within the television industry. Job titles, however, are not universally consistent, and their definitions will vary and often overlap from setting to setting. While most of the job positions describe functions in broadcasting, many are also found in other television-related operations.

For example, a producer or a camera operator may work with programs produced for cable television or a health care communications firm as well as for commercial or public broadcasting. Each job description notes when there are opportunities for a position in other related areas.

The Job Profile

Each job profile starts with a Career Profile, a brief description of the position's major duties, any alternate job titles for the position, salary ranges, employment prospects, opportunities for promotion, and the job prerequisites insofar as education and training, job experience, special skills, and personality traits are concerned. A Career Ladder graphically illustrates a typical career path to and from the position described, including the positions below and above each job. The rest of the profile is in an extended narrative format with more detailed information on the job that contains the following:

- Position description, including typical major responsibilities and duties, working hours and conditions, and optional duties that may or may not be part of the given job
- Salary ranges from entry-level to top earnings, including the factors (such as individual skills or geographic location) that often affect how much a particular position may pay, and indicating any minimum wage levels set by union/guild regulations
- Employment expectations or job forecast, indicating how difficult the post may be to obtain
- Possibilities and suggestions for advancement, and whether such work progression is unusually difficult
- Education required and any special training necessary for the particular job (including any licensing or certification requirements)
- Necessary and/or useful experience, skills, and personal attributes that enhance the potential for success in the job
- Union/guild requirements for holding the particular job and/or professional associations related to the job that may be useful
- Tips and practical suggestions for obtaining that initial job in this job category

The Appendixes

Four Appendixes offer further resources for individuals seeking any of the 100 job positions described in *Career Opportunities in Television and Cable*. Appendix I, "Educational Institutions," lists colleges, universities, and educational institutions, in every state and the District of Columbia, that offer undergraduate degrees (both two- and four-year programs) in acting and communications, as well other specialties, such as radio and television, broadcast journalism, broadcasting, cinematography and film/video production, communications technology, dance, film/video arts, media studies, playwriting/screenwriting, and telecommunications technology. The listing does *not* include every institution that offers courses or degrees in communications, nor, generally, institutions that offer graduate degrees in communications (since such an educational prerequisite is not that prevalent a requirement for jobs in the television industry). The listings provide each institution's address, telephone number, fax number, e-mail address, and Web site, as well as the major programs, specialties, and courses of particular relevance to the television industry.

Appendix II, "Major Trade Periodicals, Newsletters, and Other Publications," offers a useful resource list of magazines, newsletters, directories, and annuals concerned with television and telecommunications in general. (Note that books are not included in this Appendix, but are part of the Bibliography.)

Appendix III, "Professional, Industry, and Trade Associations, Guilds, and Unions," is organized into two sections. The first lists unions and guilds that have members within the television industry and are involved in labor negotiations in the industry. The second section lists professional associations related to the television and telecommunications industries. For each entry, the address, telephone number, fax number, e-mail, and Web site are provided.

Appendix IV, "Useful Web Sites," offers a wide range of Internet resources in many categories that are useful for job searching, trade news gathering, and networking, as well as a list of general search engines that will help in researching the industry.

A Glossary of terms relevant to the television industry includes technical terminology, buzz words, and names used frequently in the industry. The Glossary is followed by a Bibliography, which includes sources used in researching this book. In those instances in which online sources are cited, it may be necessary to check the particular Web site to determine whether new updates on the topic are now available. Also included with these sources is an expansive list of current useful books on careers in television and on the expanding technological innovations now pervasive throughout the industry.

The Index provides a quick source for locating particular job titles (including cross-references to alternate job names), organizations cited in the text (but not the Appendixes), and other relevant information appearing in the chapters of this volume.

Last, please keep in mind that the Internet is in a constant state of flux, and Web sites sometimes change their Web address or, on occasion, cease to exist. If a URL stated in this book—each of which were verified as this volume was written—does not produce the desired Web site, it may be necessary to do a search engine query using the name of the Web site to locate its new home.

ADVERTISING

ACCOUNT EXECUTIVE—SALES

CAREER PROFILE

Duties: Sell advertising time locally, regionally, or nationally for a television station

Alternate Title(s): Advertising Salesperson

Salary Range: $30,000 to $80,000 or more

Employment Prospects: Very Good

Advancement Prospects: Good

Prerequisites:

Education and Training—High school diploma, minimum; some college or undergraduate degree in marketing or advertising preferable

Experience—Minimum of one to two years in retail or print advertising sales useful

Special Skills and Personality Traits—Highly competitive spirit; initiative; meticulousness; organizational ability; persistent; personable and persuasive

CAREER LADDER

```
┌─────────────────────────────────┐
│     Assistant Sales Manager     │
└─────────────────────────────────┘

┌─────────────────────────────────┐
│    Account Executive—Sales      │
└─────────────────────────────────┘

┌─────────────────────────────────┐
│ Salesperson; Advertising Salesperson │
│        in Print Medium          │
└─────────────────────────────────┘
```

Position Description

A commercial television station's advertising Account Executive is responsible for selling advertising airtime to businesses or advertising agencies acting on behalf of businesses, and, in so doing, generating income for the station. Account Executives at most stations are assigned specific territories or responsibilities. Some focus on local sales, some on nationwide sales, and others on obtaining specific sponsors for particular programs.

Through the late 1960s, television advertisements were 60 seconds long; now they are mostly 30 seconds and even more commonly only 15 seconds, allowing for more advertisements in the break from regular programming. There are several methods by which advertisers buy time on network programs, namely by sponsorship, spot buying, or upfront buying. Sponsorship can be full-program, whereby a single sponsor will buy most or all of the commercial time available within a given program, or the sponsorship can be a participating one in which several sponsors share some form of exclusive sponsorship within a show or series. In spot, or "scatter," buying, an advertiser buys television time as a package of commercials whose cumulative impact, it is hoped, will cover the desired demographics for successful ad impact. In upfront buying, the networks offer advertisers available time slots (or "avails") at a discount months before the network's season begins.

The Account Executive is the person in charge of matching the station's available advertising air time (as set by the program scheduling of the network) with a client's stated needs as put forth by the client's advertising agency. The Account Executive explains to potential customers the size and type of audience for specific planned programs or series and how these viewers can be reached with particular advertising formats. Therefore, an Account Executive must understand many different kinds of products and merchandising techniques. In addition, Account Executives must be very familiar with the station's programming (syndicated, network, and local), its audience's viewing habits, and ratings of all the programming. They need to evaluate all research data and devise sales presentations, including charts, graphs, ratings records, and other types of audience research data in order to interest advertising clients in buying time for their ads.

At larger stations, the Account Executive works with and sells to the advertising agency representing the client. The agency usually prepares and produces the television commercial and delivers it to the station. In some other instances, the Account Executive may work directly with the advertiser in creating and preparing commercial spots and announcements, using the station's production facilities.

Primarily, Account Executives serve as the continuous link and liaison between the advertising client and the television station in all advertising and program matters. They have to work closely with the sales coordinator and the traffic-continuity specialist in ensuring the proper scheduling for the advertising spots within the larger programming schedules of the station. As such, they will attend regular sales staff meetings in order to exchange ideas, submit reports, and receive new assignments from the senior sales management staff.

Salaries

Salaries for Account Executives vary considerably according to the size of the market being covered by the station's programming and are dependent on the individual's experience and background. The top 100 television markets generally offer a chance for better income, although some stations in the smaller markets may pay higher wages due to special competitive or geographic circumstances. According to a salary survey taken in 2005 by Broadcast Employment Services on television salaries in 2004, earnings of Account Executives ranged from a low of $10,000 to a high of $176,000, with a mean average salary of $63,687. At the smaller market stations, the salaries ranged from $10,000 to $75,000, with a mean average of $39,710, whereas the top 100 market stations had a range from $22,000 to $176,000 and a mean average salary of $69,350.

Unlike assistant sales managers, most Account Executives are paid a straight commission on the advertising they land for the station (or a "draw" against commissions) as opposed to a regular salary. While many commissions are paid after the advertising client is billed for the airtime, some are not paid until after the income is actually received by the television station. Because of commissions, the income for an Account Executive may vary from year to year and even from month to month. Most television stations offer Account Executives the chance to contribute to life and medical insurance plans, and almost all stations provide them with appropriate expense accounts.

Employment Prospects

The opportunities for employment and promotion in the field are quite good. It is estimated that television advertisements account for one-fifth to one-fourth of all U.S. advertising expenditures (or roughly the same amount expended on advertising in magazines). Most small stations employ at least two to five Account Executives to handle the extensive load of advertising clients, and it is not unusual for major market television stations to have 15 or more Account Executives on staff.

Thus, there is a steady need in commercial television for competent and effective Advertising Executives. It has long been the case that television station management has found it more difficult to find qualified salespeople than other TV and media specialists.

Also, there tends to be a brisk turnover of sales personnel, leaving the stations with plenty of openings, particularly in the fall for the coming season. Thus, the wide-ranging outlook of employment as an advertising Account Executive for a television station or network is better than many other occupations within the medium.

Advancement Prospects

Most Account Executives actively seek advancement to become either an assistant sales manager or a general sales manager. Aggressive and successful Account Executives typically move to higher administrative sales positions within their own television station or switch to parallel positions at larger market stations. Some may even move on to become general sales managers at smaller stations.

The skills required for a solid Account Executive in broadcast television are easily transferable to other media firms, such as cable and satellite TV systems, which have greatly increased time available for advertising in their programming. In most instances, the personality of a successful Account Executive demands further job advancement to higher positions of sales authority and higher salaries in the development of their career.

Education and Training

While a basic minimum of high school education is usually required for the position of Account Executive, the ability of that person to sell is often more important than the specifics of formal schooling. However, having some college or a full college education is a clear sign that such individuals are seriously motivated about their career.

Employers at most major television market stations seek candidates who have undergraduate degrees in advertising, business administration, or marketing. This is especially the case if the Account Executive will be handling national sales, which entails more competitive and complicated sales environments.

Experience, Skills, and Personality Traits

At least one year of sales experience in a retail field or in newspaper or other print advertising is considered extremely helpful for aspiring television Account Executives. In addition, some experience or background in television production and programming can be quite beneficial in negotiating a position as Account Executive.

An Account Executive must have an extroverted and outgoing personality, as well as be able to relate well with others.

They will need initiative and determination in their pursuit of advertising accounts. They should have a good appearance and proper manners, coupled with a highly competitive drive. They will need to exhibit self-confidence and imagination when making sales presentations and be skilled at communicating their business ideas in conversation and/or in writing. Above all, such individuals must thrive on selling and be geared to be high achievers in making money for both their television station (or network) and themselves.

Unions and Associations

There are no specific unions or professional organizations that represent television Account Executives. However, they might want to belong to one or more of the general advertising associations in America, such as the American Advertising Federation or the American Marketing Association.

Tips for Entry

1. While in college, take courses in marketing or advertising, or consider making one of these subjects your major.
2. Read the important trade publications (e.g., *Advertising Age* and *Adweek*) for insight into broadcast advertising.
3. Internship programs run by some ad agencies and advertisers are another good entry point. Search the *Standard Advertising Register* and the *Standard Directory of Advertising Agencies* for such agencies or client companies and find out about their internship and hiring practices. Experience in an advertising agency will greatly enhance your abilities as a successful television Account Executive.
4. If you have had any experience in creating commercials, collect these ads on tape or disc, as well as their storyboards (if you had a part to play in their creation), to add to your portfolio.

ADVERTISING COPYWRITER

CAREER PROFILE

Duties: Write copy for television commercials

Alternate Title(s): None

Salary Range: $30,000 to $75,000 or more

Employment Prospects: Fair

Advancement Prospects: Fair

Prerequisites:

Education and Training—Undergraduate degree in advertising, English, journalism, or mass communication

Experience—Some advertising or writing background essential

Special Skills and Personality Traits—Excellent writing abilities; solid comprehension of human motivations; originality

CAREER LADDER

```
┌─────────────────────────────────────────┐
│  Senior Copywriter; Creative Director    │
└─────────────────────────────────────────┘

┌─────────────────────────────────────────┐
│         Advertising Copywriter           │
└─────────────────────────────────────────┘

┌─────────────────────────────────────────┐
│   Junior (or Assistant) Copywriter;      │
│              Secretary                    │
└─────────────────────────────────────────┘
```

Position Description

Advertising Copywriters work in the creative department of advertising agencies. They conceptualize and write the announcements, dialogue, expository material, special effects, and voice-overs heard in television commercials. For this work, they need more that just a mastery of the English language. They also must have a complete understanding of the overall advertising campaign for the client, a clear perception of the potential audience for the promotion, and familiarity with the client's marketing philosophy concerning the product being advertised.

In large advertising agencies, copywriters usually report to a senior copywriter or copy executive, who, in turn, reports to an advertising or creative director. In smaller firms, copywriters may report directly to the advertising or creative director.

The copywriter does not become involved with an ad plan or campaign until after the market research concerning the product or service has been completed and the media and market approach has been determined. At this juncture the copywriter becomes involved, drawing on all this data in order to create the advertising copy. They will confer with the account executive to establish the overall thrust of the commercial message, as well as become totally familiar with the product (or service), its competition, and the intended audience. By working with the art director of the agency, copywriters develop the advertising concept of the product (or service) that will ensure an imaginative, informational, and integrated commercial that will attract potential customers and motivate them to respond.

In addition to the writing of the final copy of the ad, copywriters also prepare the material for the storyboard (a preliminary treatment that roughly represents the frame-by-frame action of a television commercial). They also devise slogans and enticing phrases for clients' products or services to assure audience recognition and acceptance, as well as create copy for brochures and other promotional pieces used in the advertising campaign.

Good copywriters use the English language and modern idioms of expression to satisfy the advertising needs of the agency's clients and to stimulate consumer buying impulses and product acceptance. Thus, besides being writers, they are also salespeople, wordsmiths, and artists.

Salaries

Salaries for Advertising Copywriters diverge considerably depending on the geographical location of the agency, the local competition, and the expertise of the writer. Generally, college-trained beginners (usually starting as junior or assistant copywriters) can expect to start between $20,000 and $25,000 per year.

Advertising Age reported in 2003 that the average salary of copywriters depended a great deal on the amount of experience they had. Those with two to four years of experience had a mean average of $41,426, that is, $40,680 base pay plus a $746 bonus. Those with four to six years of experience had a mean average of $55,188, that is, $54,304 base pay plus an $885 bonus. Those with six to eight years experience had a mean average of $65,967, that is, $64,041 plus a $1,196 bonus. The high average salary for those with two to four years of experience was $46,284, while that of a copywriter with four to six years in the field was $60,453, and that of those with six to eight years was $75,574.

In its follow-up surveys of advertising agency salaries in 2004, *Advertising Age* indicated that the mean average total salary (including bonus) for copywriters was $61,000 and that they could expect a projected raise of 4 percent at most agencies in 2005. This survey also made clear that salaries varied from region to region, but not necessarily by the agency's size or annual revenues. For example, the mean average 2004 salary for Advertising Copywriters based in the East was $73,000, whereas for the Midwest it was $53,000, for the South it was $55,000, and for the West it was $61,000, but salaries remained the same for all agencies in each region, regardless of size.

Employment Prospects

There are 47,000 advertising and public relations services establishments in the United States, with nearly 19,000 of those writing copy and preparing creative work for television commercials. Many advertising agencies have multiple offices, and in larger agencies there will be several copywriters on staff, which opens up significant employment possibilities. However, while there are many aspiring writers, few have the necessary training and understanding of television production, the talent to create imaginative but concise copy, and the marketing insights requisite for the work. A good writer who has training or experience in these areas and a knack for writing advertising copy will have a tremendous advantage.

Copywriting is often thought of as an entry-level position in the advertising industry. However, many copywriters find the job amenable and remain in their posts for years. Those who display a particular flair for the creative side of advertising are often promoted to more advanced agency positions in the creative department, while others shift to larger agencies or markets (for position or salary reasons), thus opening up new job opportunities for beginning copywriters. Clerical or secretarial positions at advertising agencies are often a good springboard to copywriter positions.

Advancement Prospects

Copywriters who show creativity, have an instinct for advertising, and display their grasp for the broader concepts of creating a commercial, ad plan, or campaign should have no trouble advancing within the industry. Advertising professionals often pursue highly mobile careers, sometimes by moving upward within a single company, but more often by joining another agency at a higher salary with accompanying greater job responsibility and prestige. At larger agencies the career path for a copywriter is to become the creative director, a position that is responsible for the entire creative output of the agency. In addition, there is an industry trend for television stations, networks, and cable TV systems to employ copywriters within their own sales departments.

Education and Training

It is practically a requirement for copywriters to have a bachelor's degree. While a degree in advertising is advantageous for employment, English and journalism studies and even a broad liberal arts education are just as important to aspiring copywriters. Coursework that includes mass communications, television writing and/or production, marketing, and psychology is desirable. In addition, art courses in design and color provide excellent background in preparing effective, coordinated advertising.

Experience, Skills, and Personality Traits

Writing experience beyond that undertaken as part of a college education is highly recommended, such as working on school newspapers, yearbooks, and literary magazines, as well as community or Internet newspapers and journals. Working on campus radio and television stations can provide practical experience. Any project involving selling, persuasion, marketing, or distribution will supply insights into advertising skills. A copywriter must have an excellent command of English, including contemporary vocabulary, and must be able to visualize ideas. A knowledge of print production, including typography, basic design, and layout, is necessary, and proficiency in word processing and desktop publishing are required technical skills. Above all, a copywriter must be imaginative, self-motivated, willing to experiment with novel and/or unusual uses of language and presentation of ideas, and able to work well under pressure.

Unions and Associations

There is no union that specifically represents or negotiates on behalf of Advertising Copywriters. Some copywriters may want to maintain membership in the Writers Guild of America (WGA) or such advertising associations as the American Advertising Federation (AAF) or the American Marketing Association (AMA).

Tips for Entry

1. Read trade publications, such as *Advertising Age* and *AdWeek,* and explore Web sites to learn of new trends in advertising, as well as find possible job prospects.

2. When seeking employment, make use of the *Standard Advertising Register* or the *Standard Directory of Advertising Agencies,* available at most libraries, to target your prospects by getting the names and titles of key people and the size of the agencies you are looking at. Find examples of their current campaigns to verify that you are in synch with their advertising approaches and techniques.

3. Consider journalism as a possible career entry point for advertising copywriting.

4. Keep your résumé constantly updated with examples of your work showing your initiative, marketing creativity, and writing skills.

·ASSISTANT SALES MANAGER

CAREER PROFILE

Duties: Assist the general sales manager in local/national advertising sales for a television station

Alternate Title(s): Local Sales Manager; National Sales Manager

Salary Range: $30,000 to $185,000 or more

Employment Prospects: Good

Advancement Prospects: Good

Prerequisites:

Education and Training—Minimum requirement of high school diploma and some college; undergraduate degree in advertising or marketing preferable

Experience—Minimum of three to four years in television advertising sales

Special Skills and Personality Traits—Ability to motivate others; analytical mind; leadership qualities; supervisory abilities

CAREER LADDER

```
+---------------------------+
|   General Sales Manager   |
+---------------------------+

+---------------------------+
|  Assistant Sales Manager  |
+---------------------------+

+---------------------------+
|  Advertising Salesperson  |
+---------------------------+
```

Position Description

The Assistant Sales Manager at a commercial television station assists the general sales manager in every aspect of the station's advertising sales activities. It is the job of the Assistant Sales Manager to relieve the general sales manager of much of the burdensome details and personnel management so that the senior person can focus on long-range sales planning. The assistant helps the general sales manager plan budgets, set and monitor sales quotas for each advertising salesperson, and assign these salespersons to particular accounts. The assistant also aids in the planning of the weekly staff sales meetings and conducts weekly and quarterly performance reviews with each of the sales staff to discuss goals and budgets. Thus, the Assistant Sales Manager has to be an experienced professional salesperson who understands both the advertising business and the market of the station.

Assistant Sales Managers are usually also responsible for one particular account area, such as local, national, or spot sales, in addition to their regular duties. In many large-market stations, there may be two or more Assistant Sales Managers, often with titles that reflect their differing responsibilities, such as local sales manager and national sales manager. An Assistant Sales Manager who is responsible for local sales activities usually oversees several local accounts and advertising salespersons, keeping these salespersons informed about station policies and sales procedures.

Assistant Sales Managers may specialize on certain type of on-air programs, such as news, special events, or sports. In some stations, they will deal with difficult accounts or in soliciting new business. They are often assigned direct consumer response sales, or they may concentrate on persuading advertisers who are traditionally print-oriented to buy ads on television. At some of the larger stations, the Assistant Sales Manager is put in charge of supervising the servicing of all accounts once they are sold.

Although Assistant Sales Managers are generally supervisors, they may also actively sell airtime and may be responsible for continued sales to their own accounts. In most cases, they oversee all advertising proposals and contracts and maintain advertiser, agency, and prospect files for the general sales manager. In addition, they analyze the rating statistics, monitor all available advertising airtime, and prepare competitive products studies, internal sales analyses, and sales reports for specific clients.

Salaries

Most Assistant Sales Managers are paid on a salary-plus-commission, salary-plus-bonus, or salary-bonus-commission basis. Commissions range from 10 to 25 percent, with the majority at the rate of 15 percent of the advertising income received by the station. In almost all cases, advertising salespersons are allowed to retain their sales accounts and commissions when promoted to Assistant Sales Manager. When they accept the administrative duties that come with the elevated position, their initial employment contract is renegotiated to provide for a larger base salary and smaller commissions. In a few cases, the commission rate, instead, is raised, and the Assistant Sales Manager is given a modest salary increase.

According to a salary survey conducted in 2005 by Broadcast Employment Services of 2004 annual salaries of national and local sales managers within the television industry, salaries ranged from a low of $30,000 to $185,000, with a mean average salary of $92,180. In addition, most Assistant Sales Managers have expense accounts, as well as company-paid life insurance and group health plans. A clear majority of them also participate in company pension plans.

Employment Prospects
Nearly 10 to 15 percent of the staffs of local television stations work within the sales department, making employment for beginning salespersons much easier than most other positions at the station. In general, however, only the brightest, most energetic and successful within sales are ever promoted to Assistant Sales Manager. The relative scarcity of good salespersons and the high turnover rate in sales create frequent openings, but the competition for these openings is severe.

Assistant Sales Managers are usually chosen from those salespersons within the station who have the best sales record and the most experience. Some, of course, are recruited from other stations where they already have been successful in specific sales areas.

Advancement Prospects
Advancement opportunities are generally good. Most Assistant Sales Managers actively seek the position of general sales manager and, ultimately, that of general manager for the station. The chances of promotion at commercial stations, however, are limited by the number of TV stations on the air, and only the most capable are able to make the transition. Some Assistant Sales Managers move to smaller-market stations as general sales managers or to network or syndicated program sales positions. As cable television systems expand their advertising sales departments, another

avenue for experienced Assistant Sales Managers has opened up. The skills and experience gained in television time sales is readily transferable to other media-related industries as well.

Education and Training
A high school diploma, along with some college work, is usually required for this position. Many stations prefer to hire only salespeople who have an undergraduate degree in advertising, communications, or marketing. Coursework in business administration is also helpful. In general, however, the ability to generate sales effectively and consistently is more crucial than a specific college degree.

Experience, Skills, and Personality Traits
To be promoted to Assistant Sales Manager, a salesperson should have three to five years of experience along with a consistent and successful track record in television advertising sales, as well as an expertise within a particular sales area.

Assistant Sales Managers must be able to analyze data quickly and to motivate other sales employees. They also need a highly competitive drive and need to demonstrate initiative. Above all, supervisory and leadership skills are essential as they oversee, in most cases, less experienced salespeople.

Unions and Associations
There are no specific unions for Assistant Sales Managers since they are considered management. They might want to belong to one or more of the general advertising associations, such as the American Advertising Federation, the Advertising Council, or the American Marketing Association.

Tips for Entry
1. While in college, take courses in marketing or advertising, and consider making one or both of these subjects your major.
2. Work in a paid or internship capacity in a sales department of a local television or cable company to learn the specifics of selling advertising time for television.
3. Consider obtaining employment with an advertising agency in order to become involved in creating television commercials, begin building a portfolio of your work, and establish a contact list of people in the business.

DIRECTOR OF DEVELOPMENT

CAREER PROFILE

Duties: Fund-raise and sell services for a public television station

Alternate Title(s): Director of Marketing; Vice President of Development; Chief of Development

Salary Range: $32,000 to $135,000 or more

Employment Prospects: Poor

Advancement Prospects: Fair

Prerequisites:

Education and Training—Undergraduate degree in advertising, communications, marketing, or public relations

Experience—Minimum of three to five years in fund-raising, promotion, or publicity

Special Skills and Personality Traits—Charm and good interpersonal skills; excellent writing ability; organizational skills; sales talent

CAREER LADDER

General Manager

Director of Development

Director of Publicity and Promotion

Position Description

A Director of Development handles all fund-raising for a public television station (PTV). The responsibilities of the position range from designing, planning, executing, and evaluating marketing and management strategies and campaigns to soliciting and increasing operating and capital funds from the station's viewers and sponsors (as well as from corporations and private donors). In addition, the Director of Development is often, in actuality, in charge of all promotion and advertising for the station.

The position of Director of Development is unique to public (nonprofit) television stations, and no such parallel job exists at commercial TV, cable TV, or multichannel multipoint distribution stations (MMDS). (This post is also not found at education, government, or health media centers. Fund-raising activities at all these nonprofit agencies is usually handled by an employee of the parent organization.)

The position of Director of Development is a blend of promotion, public relations, and sales. The product being promoted is the public television station's programming and services to the community and to local area firms. A Director of Development encourages corporations to underwrite particular programs or specific time spans of the broadcast day by enlisting the companies to donate funds to the sta-

tion. In return, the sponsoring corporation receives an on-screen credit before or after the program or on-air time span and is acknowledged in the station's program guide and other promotional pieces. As all public television stations are nonprofit organizations, such gifts provide tax advantages to the participating corporations.

The Director of Development also prompts financial contributions from individual viewers in the form of on-the-air auctions of merchandise donated by local companies, or during specific pledge weeks in which special programs are broadcast and viewers are encouraged to become station members. Membership costs vary, and premiums (such as umbrellas, tote bags, books, and special VCR or DVD versions of programs shown on the station) are offered to encourage viewers toward both membership and fund-giving. Extensive direct-mail campaigns are also used to attract potential members.

Another method of fund-raising used by Directors of Development is to encourage individuals to leave a portion of their estates to the PTV station. Directors also write grant proposals for the funding of specific programs or series by local, state, or federal agencies. At the same time, Directors of Development often work out the complicated arrangements for finding and obtaining funds from an assortment of sources for the production of special programs or series for national broadcast by the Public Broadcasting Service (PBS). The director also may design and institute fund-raising campaigns to replace technical equipment and/or facilities at the station.

As a logical result of all these fund-raising activities, the Director of Development is responsible for projecting the amount of money that can be raised in any given time period for the support of the station's operating and capital budgets. This authority also includes being in charge of the budget for the development department and overall supervision of its staff.

As the tasks of the Director of Development are so strongly tied to those of promotion and publicity, the director is frequently put in charge of those functions as well at a PTV station. Thus, the Director of Development will supervise the activities of the director of publicity/promotion and any assistants. The Directors of Development will also speak at public and community functions on behalf of the station as well as maintain membership in and participate with community groups. Moreover, he or she will organize and supervise volunteers assisting in the station's fund-raising activities and often will make on-the-air appearances in order to solicit funds. The Director of Development usually reports to the general manager of the station.

Salaries

In line with the extensive responsibilities and magnitude of the job, Directors of Development in noncommercial public television are usually well paid. Yearly salaries ranged from a low of $32,000 to a high of $135,000 or more. The median range for an experienced Director of Development was approximately $71,000. Salaries are highest at the larger-market community-leased stations.

Employment Prospects

The opportunities for negotiating a position as Director of Development for a public television station are relatively poor, due to the low number of PTV stations licensed in the United States. Such a job opening occurs only when there is the occasional turnover in the position. Most Directors of Development tend to stay within this lucrative field and move only from station to station. Sometimes, the assistants in charge of specific fund-raising activities, such as underwriting or managing volunteers, will be able to transition into the job of Director of Development, but this is rare. Some opportunities exist for qualified personnel from other nonprofit organizations to fill this position within the public television industry.

Advancement Prospects

Due to the importance and responsibility of Directors of Development and their resultant exposure to management problems and working out of solutions, many of them seek and eventually obtain the position of general manager at the smaller PTV stations. Other directors migrate to larger PTV stations as Directors of Development at higher salaries. Some directors may promote their career by achieving fund-raising posts at larger nonprofit organizations at the state or national level.

Education and Training

As a minimum, an undergraduate degree in advertising, communications, marketing, or public relations is required for this position. Graduate work or a degree (such as an M.B.A.) is even more preferable. It is recommended that any candidate also take courses in photography, printing, speech, and writing.

Experience, Skills, and Personality Traits

A minimum of three to five years of experience in marketing and communications in a multifaceted organization, as well as five years or more of successful working experience in fund-raising, marketing, public relations, and publicity in a nonprofit environment is usually considered essential for this key position. The working background should include that of customer service and customer relationship management, database marketing, direct response incentives, marketing research, and online and product marketing.

A candidate for Director of Development must be well organized and resourceful, as well as poised, articulate, and equipped to deal with a wide range of individuals in relatively sophisticated environments. In addition, a candidate needs to have hands-on experience with the budget process, and have effective verbal and written communication skills. Above all, a Director of Development must possess charm and enthusiasm and be personable, persuasive, and a good salesperson.

Unions and Associations

While there are no specific unions or organizations that represent Directors of Development, many of them belong to one of the general umbrella organizations of American advertising, such as the American Advertising Federation or the American Marketing Association. They may also belong to ProMax International, Inc., in order to share their mutual concerns with other members and to advance their own careers.

Tips for Entry

1. Read trade publications such as *Advertising Age, Adweek, Promo Magazine,* and others to learn of new trends, marketing opportunities, and job prospects in publicity or promotion in the television industry.
2. Consider volunteering, interning, or working for a nonprofit organization in order to understand the differences between it and a for-profit operation.
3. Volunteer to work on fund-raising for a local community, state, or national organization (or political campaign) to gain insight into the fund-raising processes.

GENERAL SALES MANAGER

CAREER PROFILE

Duties: Produce all advertising sales revenue for a television station

Alternate Title(s): Advertising Sales Manager; Sales Director

Salary Range: $35,000 to $200,000

Employment Prospects: Fair

Advancement Prospects: Good

Prerequisites:

Education and Training—Undergraduate degree in advertising, business administration, or marketing

Experience—Minimum of five to eight years of experience in broadcast advertising sales

Special Skills and Personality Traits—Assertiveness; excellent interpersonal skills; leadership qualities; organizational talent; perseverance; self-confidence

CAREER LADDER

```
┌─────────────────────────────────┐
│    Station General Manager      │
└─────────────────────────────────┘

┌─────────────────────────────────┐
│     General Sales Manager       │
└─────────────────────────────────┘

┌─────────────────────────────────┐
│     Assistant Sales Manager     │
└─────────────────────────────────┘
```

Position Description

The General Sales Manager at a commercial television station is responsible for generating the advertising revenue for the station to pay for programming, salaries, technical equipment, and its operations. The General Sales Manager must deal with a limited inventory of airtime available for advertising and must work closely with the station's program manager and general manager in allocating available advertising airtime to those programs that are able to attract the highest-paying or most consistent advertisers.

A General Sales Manager is in charge of all daily advertising sales activities and the station's sales staff, who number anywhere from 12 to 18 employees or more (especially in the larger-market stations). The General Sales Manager administers and coordinates all local, regional, and national advertising programming and spot commercial sales accounts with clients, advertising agencies, and the station's national sales representative. The manager's duties include developing the station's overall advertising sales plan and targets, previewing programs and the advertisements slotted to be used with the programs, and directly supervising all sales efforts to ensure their effectiveness.

The General Sales Manager reports to the station's general manager, and together they establish the operation's advertising policies and procedures. A General Sales Man-

ager must understand the local market and the regional competition in order to establish competitive advertising rates. In addition, a General Sales Manager must appreciate national markets and deal with their national representatives and the rates other national competition (such as other networks) have set. The General Sales Manager also is responsible for developing audiovisual and statistical sales tools to assist the station salespersons in their work.

General Sales Managers must be sensitive to ever-changing economic factors that may affect advertising decisions; merchandising, barter, and trade agreements; as well as the latest programming trends and audience demographics and psychographics at both the local and national levels. They must work closely with advertising agencies, advertising reps, and local clients to ensure a continuing and profitable relationship between them and the station. They have to monitor the Arbitron and Nielsen ratings of television programs and any research studies of the station's audience. They need to ensure that the commercial time sold by the station conforms to the guidelines set by the National Association of Broadcasters, the regulations set by the Federal Trade Commission, and the policies set by the station. They supervise all commercial scheduling and copywriting, and it is recommended that they service top agency accounts in order to keep tabs on the selling scene.

Salaries

The General Sales Manager in a local commercial television station is typically the second-highest paid staff member, commensurate with the amount of responsibility this job entails. According to statistics compiled in 2005 by the Broadcast Employment Services (available at http://www.tvjobs.com), annual salaries may range from a low of $32,000 to a high of $201,000 depending on the size of the market the station serves. At the high end of the scale, the average low for a yearly salary was $90,000 and the high was $201,000, with the median being $127,500. These figures do not include other compensation, such as commissions or bonuses.

Employment Prospects

Getting a position as a General Sales Manager at a commercial television station is much more limited than for most other management positions at the station, as the competition is fierce and there is little turnover in the coveted post. Most General Sales Managers are promoted from within the television station organization, usually after having first served as assistant sales managers. Some may be recruited from the sales force at one of the larger-market stations or even from the competition within the local community. Others may come from advertising sales forces or from print or other media.

Advancement Prospects

Opportunities for promotion of General Sales Managers tend to be good. They typically move to the position of general manager of the station, though some individuals may advance by transferring to larger markets, advertising rep firms, group-owned stations, or even into top advertising sales management at a television network.

The skills of a General Sales Manager at a commercial television station are easily applicable to such a position at a cable TV system. While such opportunities are solid, the compensation levels are not as high as in the commercial sector.

Education and Training

While the ability to sell effectively and consistently is paramount for a General Sales Manager, a degree is also considered very important. An undergraduate degree in advertising, business administration, or marketing will provide an excellent background for entering into sales positions with television stations and, eventually, for advancement to a higher management position, such as General Sales Manager. In some larger markets, many General Sales Managers also have a master's degree in business administration

Experience, Skills, and Personality Traits

It is expected that General Sales Managers are profit-oriented administrators with proven track records. Most stations require their General Sales Managers to have five to 10 years of television advertising sales experience, to display a talent to organize and motivate a sales staff, and to develop the station's sales efforts. General Sales Managers must have an instinctive feel for organization and logistics and an outgoing and positive personality. They need to have strong written and oral presentation skills and should enjoy involvement with community endeavors.

Successful General Sales Managers must be able to analyze research data easily and apply this data constructively in station planning procedures. They must be well seasoned in marketing, merchandising, and retailing. Their enthusiasm for actual sales procedures must be contagious with their staff. As a group, General Sales Managers are ambitious, efficient at controlling expenses and meeting budgets, and poised and persistent in their pursuit of sales for the station.

Unions and Associations

There are no specific unions or professional organizations that represent General Sales Managers. However, they might find value in belonging to one or more of the general advertising associations in the United States, such as the American Advertising Federation, the Advertising Council, or the American Marketing Association.

Tips for Entry

1. While in college, take courses in advertising, business administration, or marketing and consider making one or two of these your major.
2. Enroll in an internship program with a local television station to become familiar with procedures and methodologies used in a station environment.
3. As a way of starting out in the advertising side of the television industry, apply for a job as a junior salesperson at a TV station in a city with a population of about 100,000, where you will gain experience in selling to local retailers and business establishments.
4. If unable to obtain a television salesperson's job at first, try for a similar position at a local newspaper or radio station, and from there move into the television arena in the same city.

MARKET RESEARCHER

CAREER PROFILE

Duties: Acquire and analyze information essential to advertising and marketing decisions

Alternate Title(s): Research Analyst; Research Specialist; Researcher/Planner

Salary Range: $29,000 to $80,000 or more

Employment Prospects: Good

Advancement Prospects: Fair

Prerequisites:

Education and Training—Undergraduate degree in advertising, business administration, market research, or mass communication; graduate degree may be required

Experience—Some experience in a research department of a company outside the advertising industry, such as an educational institution or a firm specializing in research studies

Special Skills and Personality Traits—Analytical aptitude; computer literacy; detail-oriented; solid communication skills (both verbal and written); statistical knack

CAREER LADDER

```
┌─────────────────────────────────────┐
│   Senior Analyst; Project Director   │
└─────────────────────────────────────┘

┌─────────────────────────────────────┐
│          Market Researcher           │
└─────────────────────────────────────┘

┌─────────────────────────────────────┐
│          Junior Researcher           │
└─────────────────────────────────────┘
```

Position Description

Market Researchers in an advertising agency are concerned with the potential sales of a product or service. They obtain and examine information on which profit-making advertising and marketing decisions are made. They analyze statistical data on past sales to predict future sales, compile data on competitors, and analyze prices, sales, and methods of advertising, marketing, and distribution. Most of the commercials seen on television are purchased for the advertiser by an agency only after a considerable amount of research has been done before the actual production of the advertisement.

Research data may derive from government agencies, interviews and focus group discussions, questionnaires, research done at such institutions as private and public libraries, trade associations, and magazines, or on the Internet. The objective of advertising research is to establish who will buy a particular product (or service) and why. Research will also examine the potential market and will help to resolve how a new product (or service) can best be showcased to the public, or how an existing product (or service) can be presented more attractively to increase its usage by the public and create an upsurge in sales and new demand.

Research at a large advertising firm may be conducted by an entire research department, with a director supervising several project directors and Market Researchers. At a smaller company, all these responsibilities may be held by one or two people. In addition, research duties at the smaller agencies may be added to the responsibilities of other staff members or, more often, subcontracted by the agency to an outside independent research organization.

There are three areas of concentration in advertising research, and a Market Researcher may work in all of them or, in the larger agencies, specialize in a single one. The first concerns the target markets for which the advertising is to appeal. Data has to be gathered to determine who are the likely consumers for the product (or service), how they think, how they will probably react to a particular on-air commercial message, and what kind of advertising techniques will most capture their attention.

The second concentration of research focuses on the product (or service) to be promoted. It becomes the task of the Market Researcher to understand the full range of what the product (or service) does and how its use will affect potential buyers. In addition, the Market Researcher must determine what the impact of packaging and pricing will have on consumers, how to attract buyers of the product (or service), why consumers might, or might not, purchase it, and how the other agencies handling competing products or services treat these questions.

The third research area focuses on the effectiveness of the advertising. This is mainly follow-up work, done after the television commercials have already appeared. It weighs the specific ad campaign efficacy and creates guidelines for future advertising of the client's products (or services). In the process, the viewers' degree of product (or service) awareness before and after the advertising has to be calculated, as well as the buyers' motivations and the direct results, in sales, of the advertising.

A good Market Researcher has to think and write clearly, take a clever approach to assigned projects, devise a successful research procedure, interpret information compiled from all facets of the study, and analyze and verbalize the results. The researcher must be logical, concise, and direct in communicating research conclusions that provide sound analysis of the client's obstacles in marketing the product (or service). Similarly, it is key for Market Researchers to have a sound understanding of human behavior and motivation in interpreting how they apply to the client's current and future advertising campaigns.

In this process, Market Researchers need to scrutinize already-published research and statistical data relating to comparable products, markets, consumer preferences, and buying trends. They must be resourceful in finding the most useful method of gathering the needed research. They will prepare appropriate questionnaires to be used and will supervise both field and telephone research. Finally, they must provide suggestions for the agency's media and creative departments.

Salaries

According to the U.S. Bureau of Labor Statistics in its 2004 annual survey, annual salaries for Market Researchers at advertising agencies ranged from a low of $29,000 to a high of $100,000, with median yearly earnings of $53,810. The middle percentage of Market Researchers earned annually between $38,760 and $76,310. As with so many other job positions, Market Researchers with five or more years of successful experience in the field can anticipate incomes at the high end of these ranges.

Employment Prospects

There is an usual amount of turnover among advertising research people, thus opening up a flow of available job positions in the research area. While some smaller firms contract all their research services with outside firms, most agencies have Market Researchers as permanent staff members. In addition, many television stations in the major markets employ Market Researchers to support their advertising sales staff. According to the Bureau of Labor Statistics, employment of Market Researchers is expected to grow faster than the average for all occupations through 2012.

As in the past, many advertising agencies consider the position of Market Researcher to be an entry-level job. Thus, this position is frequently filled by young college graduates. In some instances, however, more seasoned professionals (even with advanced degrees) may be required by some agencies.

Advancement Prospects

Opportunities for advancement for Market Researchers are only fair, primarily due to the heavy competition. A smart, dedicated, and winning Market Researcher, however, can now and then move up to the position of research director at a larger advertising agency, though usually only after four to six years of experience. At smaller companies, promotion to more responsible positions in other areas of the agency may be feasible.

Some Market Researchers move or return to independent research firms at higher pay to advance their careers. Others may use their skills after several years of experience to obtain similar posts in the sales departments of major-market television stations, on television network staffs, or in the cable industry.

Education and Training

As a bare minimum, an undergraduate degree from an accredited college or university is obligatory for any applicant seeking a Market Researcher position at an advertising agency. A degree in business administration or market research with a solid liberal arts background or a degree in advertising or mass communication with some marketing and statistical analysis coursework is preferable. In addition, Market Researchers need to take social science courses, such as economics, psychology, and sociology.

In some cases, a master's degree in business administration is an additional requirement. An M.B.A. also helps to guarantee advancement to more responsible positions within the agency.

Experience, Skills, and Personality Traits

Analytical experience in research procedures and design is considered useful for this job, and computer literacy is expected. Some actual experience, either with an independent research firm or in the research department of a company in some unrelated area, would also be useful, as some industry sources indicate that they want to hire marketing or advertising people who have experience in research, not researchers who happen to work in advertising. Because this post may be an entry-level one, part-time work in an agency or research firm while in college can provide valuable firsthand knowledge of advertising, marketing, and research techniques.

Market Researchers have to be skilled at statistical interpretation and possess the patience and persistence to carry out heavily detailed projects. They will have to spend long hours on independent study and problem solving. At the same time, they must be able to work well with others, as they will often oversee interviews with a wide variety of individuals. Communication skills are also extremely important. They must be able to present their findings, both orally and in writing, in a clear, concise, and logical manner. Finally, they must be able to work under the pressure of deadlines and tight schedules.

Unions and Associations

There are no unions that serve as a representative or bargaining agent for Market Researchers. However, membership in such groups as the Advertising Council, the Advertising Research Foundation, and the American Marketing Association can provide professional guidance and support.

Tips for Entry

1. While in college, take courses in mathematics, research techniques, sampling theory, statistics, and survey design, as these skills will be extremely important to you as a Market Researcher.
2. Investigate available internships with research firms or advertising agencies to gain experience while getting your degree and to establish personal relationships with future contacts.
3. Take extensive computer courses, so that your knowledge of Word, Excel, PowerPoint, and Internet browsers is excellent, as these may be requirements in your job hunt.

SALES COORDINATOR

CAREER PROFILE

Duties: Coordinate all advertising activities for a television station

Alternate Title(s): Order Processor; Traffic/Sales Assistant

Salary Range: $24,000 to $55,000

Employment Prospects: Good

Advancement Prospects: Good

Prerequisites:

Education and Training—Minimum of a high school diploma; some business or secretarial training desirable

Experience—General office and retail sales work required

Special Skills and Personality Traits—Detail-oriented; excellent keying capabilities; solid mathematics skills; organizational ability; sales talent

CAREER LADDER

```
┌─────────────────────────────┐
│   Advertising Salesperson   │
└─────────────────────────────┘

┌─────────────────────────────┐
│     Sales Coordinator       │
└─────────────────────────────┘

┌─────────────────────────────┐
│         Secretary           │
└─────────────────────────────┘
```

Position Description

At most commercial television stations in middle to major markets, the Sales Coordinator supervises all traffic within the advertising sales department and helps in the organization of the activities of the advertising salespersons. Major tasks include keeping track of all commercial advertising matters, maintaining a schedule of available airtime for advertisements, and writing advertising orders. Individuals who undertake this post also serve as a general assistant to the sales department team.

The Sales Coordinator has to keep up to date on the shifting status of all actual and potential advertising sales to appear on airtime, all the scheduled commercials, makegoods (advertising time supplied gratis by a station to advertisers whose commercials were preempted by, say, national news or were broadcast incorrectly), exceptions, and cancellations. The coordinator organizes and maintains a master scheduling board, either as a bulletin board or, in most cases, on a computer, which displays the current lineup of all sales traffic for use by the advertising department. Thus, one of the primary responsibilities of the Sales Coordinator is to keep the traffic continuity department apprised of all sales activities and to coordinate with the production department all dubbing of commercials for clients, the commercial production schedules, and all other client production services.

Moreover, the Sales Coordinator updates the master sales files and schedules, the advertising order control sheets, and the contracts for the advertising salespersons. In some instances the Sales Coordinator also serves as a telephone solicitor of advertising sales for the station, and will act as a backup for advertising salespersons when they are absent from the office. Sales Coordinators also verify for accuracy all sales contracts against work orders, control sheets, and the clients' time orders, and shift all prelog schedules to assist in clearing and changing commercial airtime availabilities. In addition, this person also researches competitive product and media reports for general use by the sales department. The Sales Coordinator usually reports to the assistant sales manager or in some cases directly to the general sales manager.

Salaries

According to industry data, the salaries for Sales Coordinators are relatively low, reflecting the position's proximity to an entry-level job position. Starting annual salaries may be as low as $24,000 at smaller-market stations for employees with little or no experience, and as high as $30,000 yearly at major-market stations. For individuals with some experience and seniority, annual salaries may range from $35,000 to more than $50,000. Sales Coordinators are frequently promoted to their jobs from within the station, thus carrying with them their previous seniority and some modest income increase.

Employment Prospects

The position of Sales Coordinator is often the first promotion for a secretary in the sales department of a commercial television station. In other instances, the position may be an entry-level one.

Television salespersons tend to be highly mobile. According to industry studies, some 30 to 40 percent of them transition into other positions each year. In addition, many major-market stations employ two or more Sales Coordinators to handle the large load of duties demanded by a larger client base. Their tasks may be divided according to specific areas, such as national versus local sales, but they perform essentially the same work.

The opportunity for employment at a commercial television station as a Sales Coordinator, or promotion to that position, is good. Likewise, job opportunities as Sales Coordinators for cable television systems are improving as these systems escalate their advertising sales.

Advancement Prospects

The knowledge of advertising procedures and practices gained while in the position of a Sales Coordinator will often lead to quick advancement in a television sales career. While competition for other positions is stiff, prospects for moving into a more responsible position within the sales department are good for a bright and alert Sales Coordinator. Those individuals who display their capabilities of working well with clients and providing good assistance in the servicing of accounts are often promoted into a direct selling position as an advertising salesperson. They will also have to demonstrate their aggressiveness and persistence, qualities needed as an advertising salesperson.

For those Sales Coordinators not specifically sales oriented, they may become specialists in "co-op" (cooperative) advertising, in which they help to organize the complex deals between local advertisers and national manufacturers to share advertising costs. Co-op coordinators with commercial stations tend to have a higher salary (due to the intricacies and sensitivity of their jobs) than other Sales Coordinators.

Education and Training

At the bare minimum, a high school diploma is needed for this post. Many employers require further education at a business or secretarial school, and some demand a bachelor's degree in business administration, communications, or marketing. Most employers now require previous computer and various software program training or experience for this position.

Experience, Skills, and Personality Traits

General office work experience is helpful in obtaining this type of position, as is some background in sales at a retail level. Many employers tend to advance the smartest and most competent of secretaries to this position.

Proficiency with word processing and spreadsheet software has become almost required for employment in this position. Knowledge of Microsoft Excel, Word, and Power-Point is extremely helpful. In addition, Sales Coordinators need to be extremely precise and detail-oriented, as well as highly organized, with the ability to multitask, prioritize, and problem solve in a deadline-driven environment. They must possess solid people skills and strong verbal and written communication talents.

Unions and Associations

There are no unions or professional associations that represent Sales Coordinators. However, they may find it useful to join one or more of the umbrella advertising or marketing associations, such as the American Advertising Federation or the American Marketing Association.

Tips for Entry

1. While in high school or college take additional computer courses to increase your facility with such software as Microsoft Excel and PowerPoint and, even such programs as Photoshop and Quark.
2. Look for internship programs at advertising agencies to gain familiarity with and insight into advertising procedures and practices. This is also an excellent way to begin establishing contacts in the advertising industry.
3. Consider a part-time sales position in a retail firm during high school or college years to gain hands-on selling and marketing experience.

TRAFFIC-CONTINUITY SPECIALIST

CAREER PROFILE

Duties: Schedule programs and commercials and develop logs; write station identifications and announcements

Alternate Title(s): Continuity Copywriter; Traffic Assistant

Salary Range: $17,000 to $50,000 or more

Employment Prospects: Good

Advancement Prospects: Good

Prerequisites:

Education and Training—High school diploma required; some college preferable, with degree useful

Experience—Knowledgeable in computer operations; writing experience

Special Skills and Personality Traits—Computer literacy; detail-oriented; good writing skills; organizational ability; precise and thorough

CAREER LADDER

```
┌─────────────────────────────────────────┐
│   Operations Manager; Advertising       │
│   Salesperson; Sales Coordinator        │
└─────────────────────────────────────────┘

┌─────────────────────────────────────────┐
│      Traffic-Continuity Specialist      │
└─────────────────────────────────────────┘

┌─────────────────────────────────────────┐
│          School; Secretary              │
└─────────────────────────────────────────┘
```

Position Description

The Traffic-Continuity Specialist is one of the most important and indispensable staff members at a television station. While the specific duties may differ from large- to small-market stations and even between public and commercial stations, this position is essential to daily operations, as this individual is responsible for the detailed scheduling of all programming for the station, including programs, station breaks, commercials, and public service announcements.

The Traffic-Continuity Specialist prepares the daily operational Federal Communications Commission (FCC) log, which lists the minute-by-minute broadcasting operation, both analog and digital, from sign-on to sign-off. In many situations the Traffic-Continuity Specialist writes on-air promotional copy for the station announcers to use during station breaks and whenever a bridge is needed as a transition between shows.

At commercial stations the Traffic-Continuity Specialist typically reports to the general sales manager but may, in some instances, report to the program manager instead. The Traffic-Continuity Specialist maintains a full and continuous record of all available commercial airtime, advising the sales department when airtime is open and when this time is sold and scheduled. The specialist also guarantees that there is a reasonable time break between advertised products of a related nature, and that all commercials conform both to the

regulations set by the FCC and the Federal Trade Commission (FTC) and to the station's standards.

Commercial stations now rely on computer networks to deal with the complex, ever-changing traffic information involved in advertising sales and scheduling. Traffic-Continuity Specialists ensure that media assignments are made to enable all programs to be recorded in a timely fashion and that all shows scheduled for broadcast are recorded into the automation systems and readied for air. They perform quality control and routing of incoming shows and troubleshoot any program discrepancies. They assemble and process all audio and video information into the station's operating log and schedule announcers for the recording station's breaks and any pronouncements or live announcements. In tandem with the programming or the production department, they create slide, film, or videotape spots to accompany the audio for local station identifications.

Many midsize and major-market stations separate the duties of continuity and traffic. For them, the continuity copywriter is responsible for preparing written copy, whereas the traffic assistant is involved largely in scheduling and has *no* writing responsibilities. In these cases, both positions are generally supervised by a director of continuity/traffic.

In public television, the Traffic-Continuity Specialist usually reports to the program manager and seldom has any responsibility for making available commercial airtime. In this case, the specialist compiles all program information, creates and distributes the FCC log to engineering and operations personnel, writes the station identifications (or IDs), and usually writes and schedules all public service announcements and any of the station's promotional spots.

Salaries

As Traffic-Continuity Specialists are usually considered to be support personnel, their salaries, despite the importance of their responsibilities, tend to be low. In commercial television at stations with the top 50 market ranges, annual salaries for traffic specialists ranged from a low of $17,000 to a high of $90,000, with a mean average yearly salary of $35,763. In the next lowest 50 market range stations, the annual salaries ranged from $14,000 to $42,000, with a mean average of $24,312 yearly. In public television, salaries of Traffic-Continuity Specialists were generally lower than in commercial television.

Employment Prospects

Traffic-Continuity Specialist is often an entry-level position at both commercial and public television stations. With high turnover and promotion rates for this position, many opportunities are available for newcomers. In addition, traffic-continuity posts are available at most cable TV systems, as well as at multichannel multipoint distribution service (MMDS) operations and at low-power television (LPTV) stations.

Most of the larger-market stations employ three or more people in their traffic/continuity departments, with each being assigned specific responsibilities. In some instances, secretaries and clerical staff in the programming department may be promoted to the position of a Traffic-Continuity Specialist. Thus, the circumstances for employment for this job are good.

Advancement Prospects

Chances for advancement to other positions at a television station are also good. As a Traffic-Continuity Specialist, an individual has the opportunity to learn many of the fundamental aspects of broadcasting, providing an excellent background for many jobs at the station such as an advertising salesperson or sales coordinator or even eventually the most responsible position as operations manager.

Education and Training

The minimum educational requirement for the position of Traffic-Continuity Specialist is a high school diploma.

Many employers, particularly in major market stations, prefer some college education or even an undergraduate degree in advertising or mass communication. Any courses in broadcasting, copywriting, or marketing are also useful.

Experience, Skills, and Personality Traits

As this position is frequently an entry-level job, many employers do not require extensive television experience. However, some broadcast background is a bonus, and some stations require two to three years of work experience beyond education.

Stations look for clever, alert young people who are very detail oriented and have solid organizational skills. Candidates should have strong computer skills, as most stations use computerized systems for traffic and continuity. Applicants must possess strong verbal, interpersonal, and written communication abilities (as they will need to create good copy for promotional announcements and station breaks), combined with good math skills and a demonstrable ability to think and work in a logical manner.

Traffic-Continuity Specialists need to be able to work well in a team environment but be self-motivated to work independently. They must be flexible and able to shift priorities as needed. Above all, they must be able to cope with daily deadline pressures, handle a multiplicity of tasks simultaneously, and effectively prioritize their workload.

Unions and Associations

There are no unions that serve as collective bargaining agents or representatives for Traffic-Continuity Specialists. Specialists with an eye on their future in the industry may want to belong to umbrella associations for the industry, such as the Corporation for Public Broadcasting or the National Association of Broadcasters.

Tips for Entry

1. Take computer courses during schooling to enhance your technical skills, as television stations now rely on computer networks to deal with the complex information related to traffic continuity.
2. Investigate intern programs at local television stations to gain hands-on experience in the television business.
3. Gain writing experience by working on high school or college publications or through an intern program at an advertising agency to acquire copywriting experience.

ARTS AND DESIGN

ART DIRECTOR

CAREER PROFILE

Duties: Create, contour, and coordinate the visual components of a TV production and the overall visual style of a TV station or media center

Alternate Title(s): Graphic Arts Manager; Graphic Arts Supervisor; Senior Artist

Salary Range: $17,000 to $100,000 or more

Employment Prospects: Fair

Advancement Prospects: Fair

Prerequisites:

Education and Training—Minimum of an undergraduate degree in commercial art, design, or fine arts

Experience—Minimum of five years as a graphic artist in television production

Special Skills and Personality Traits—Administrative skills; creativity; good communication abilities; sense of aesthetics and spatial design; technical aptitude

CAREER LADDER

```
┌─────────────────────────────────────┐
│      Production Designer;            │
│      Art Director (Ad Agency);       │
│      Owner (Art/Design Company)      │
└─────────────────────────────────────┘

┌─────────────────────────────────────┐
│            Art Director              │
└─────────────────────────────────────┘

┌─────────────────────────────────────┐
│  Graphic Artist; Production Assistant│
└─────────────────────────────────────┘
```

Position Description

The Art Director is accountable for directing the full realization of the production designer's ideas for a TV production. As Art Director David Lazan points out, "I facilitate the designer's vision. I'm in charge of managing the art department, budgets and crew . . . [and] logistics. It's both a design and a management position."

The Art Director works in tandem with the production designer in analyzing and interpreting the script to determine the art direction requirements within the department's budget. Besides studying the final script and working with the production designer, the producer, and the director, the Art Director researches and studies the project from the perspective of the scenery and sets in relationship to the story and its characters. Storyboards, layouts, and rough sketches of the production must be prepared. The Art Director is then responsible for creating the sets and scenery for the production by either constructing new sets and/or modifying existing scenery. The Art Director works with the props department, the set dresser, and the construction coordinator in the completion of the sets. The Art Director oversees the finished look of the sets in conjunction with the director prior to shooting. While filming is being done on one set,

the Art Director will be working ahead on the next set or location as the script requires, monitoring all the functions of the art department during the shoot.

The Art Director must be knowledgeable about all the assorted techniques available for creating scenic visual looks, including the use of computer-digitized images to create set environments. In these instances, the Art Director will work with visual effects supervisors and artists who specialize in digital design to be incorporated into the overall visual effect of a set.

As manager of the art department the Art Director is responsible for budgets and crew, including set designers, graphic designers, illustrators, and construction personnel. All ordering, installing, operating, and maintaining of art equipment and supplies are the ultimate responsibility of the Art Director. Budgets and scheduling must be coordinated with other departments, as well as the special logistics of the production. Thus, this is both a design and a management position as well as a highly creative post. In many lower-budget productions, the positions of Art Director and production designer may be merged into one individual.

In addition to all the work directly related to TV production, the Art Director often supervises the graphics and visual representation of a station in its promotional material. This includes advertising rate cards and displays, booklets and pamphlets, promotion/publicity brochures, business stationery, and Web sites.

Salaries

Art Directors are moderately compensated in the television field, and their salary depends greatly on the market range of the television station. According to the Broadcast Employment Services survey of earnings in 2004, salaries for Art Directors in commercial television ranged from a low of $17,000 annually to a high of $105,000, with the mean yearly salary being $51,733 and the median annual salary being $46,000. Art Directors who belong to Local 800, the Art Directors Union, have a five-day minimum rate salary of $2,189.78 for the first six months they work in the industry. Thereafter, for the second six months, the minimum salary for a five-day period goes up to $2,433.84, and thereafter rises to $2,670.24. In public television, Art Directors usually are paid a bit lower on the average, according to the Corporation for Public Broadcasting (CPB).

Employment Prospects

Generally, prospects for employment as an Art Director are fair. An Art Director at a television station must have considerable knowledge and experience in all phases of commercial art and television production. With fewer than 1,600 operating television stations in the United States, the opportunities are not limitless. Some very small stations use only freelance graphic artists as required.

While some cable television systems employ Art Directors in full-time positions, others, as well as multichannel multipoint distribution services (MMDS) and low-power TV (LPTV) stations, only occasionally employ Art Directors for specific projects. Another avenue for part-time, project-by-project employment of Art Directors is with some of the full-service production and postproduction facilities.

Advancement Prospects

The possibilities for Art Directors moving up the career ladder in television are fair. Their next logical career step is usually to become a production designer. It might be said that being an Art Director is like being a production designer in training. All production designers need to have this type of art direction background in order to be effective in their field. Art Directors handle the nuts and bolts of set construction; production designers provide the portrait of what the set is to be.

At smaller television stations Art Directors may find that the next logical step is to move to similar positions in larger markets, thus gaining greater responsibility and a larger salary, making the transition to production designer more likely. In some cases, Art Directors may decide to form their own commercial art/design firms or join independent television production agencies that create artwork for specific clients.

Education and Training

Most Art Directors have undergraduate degrees in commercial art, design, fine arts, or even theater arts. Courses in architecture, drafting, and illustration, along with some liberal arts background, are helpful. A year or two of training at a commercial art school is usually a requisite for gaining an entry post as graphic artist, the first step toward the position of Art Director.

Experience, Skills, and Personality Traits

Most employers expect their Art Directors to have had at least five years of experience in television production artwork. In addition, wide exposure to assorted art forms, such as drawing, layout, scenic design, and sculpture, is usually expected. In addition, some administrative experience is helpful.

Art Directors must possess excellent communication and management skills. They will need to manage a diverse team of creative subordinates as well as work considerably with other production and technical people, as well as talent, promotion, and public relations personnel. They must be well organized and have the talent to administer a budget. Some experience with computer graphics is often another requirement in obtaining a position as Art Director.

Unions and Associations

Many Art Directors are represented by the International Alliance of Theatrical Stage Employees (IATSE). Some are members of the National Association of Broadcast Employees and Technicians AFL-CIO (NABET). However, there are also some Art Directors in both commercial and public television who are not represented by a union. Many commercial television Art Directors are members of the Broadcast Designers Association International in order to share their mutual professional concerns.

Tips for Entry

1. Take courses in architecture or industrial design and study theatrical design, lighting, and filmmaking.
2. During college, volunteer to work on student, music video, commercial, or nonunion film or television productions to gain both experience and contacts, or try to become an apprentice to Art Directors, set designers, or production designers as a production assistant for the art department.
3. Take a job as an illustrator or storyboard artist in a television art department. Remember to be patient, as persistence and experience is essential to be able to grab the right opportunity for advancement when it occurs.

GRAPHIC ARTIST AND GRAPHIC DESIGNER

CAREER PROFILE

Duties: Design and create visual art and related visual material for television productions; create sets and choose props

Alternate Title(s): Staff Artist's Illustrator; Television Artist; Staff Designer

Salary Range: $19,000 to $70,000 or more

Employment Prospects: Good

Advancement Prospects: Fair to Good

Prerequisites:

Education and Training—Minimum of an associate's degree in commercial art or scenic design; an undergraduate art degree is preferable

Experience—Minimum of one to two years as a commercial artist or designer

Special Skills and Personality Traits—Creativity; design abilities; talent for illustration; versatility

CAREER LADDER

```
┌─────────────────────────────────────┐
│           Art Director              │
└─────────────────────────────────────┘

┌─────────────────────────────────────┐
│ Graphic Artist and Graphic Designer │
└─────────────────────────────────────┘

┌─────────────────────────────────────┐
│       Art School or College;        │
│        Commercial Artist            │
└─────────────────────────────────────┘
```

Position Description

A Graphic Artist at a commercial or public television station designs and implements an assortment of visual art forms to be used in a television production, under the direction of the art director or production designer. These forms might include the creation of charts, graphs, maps, three-dimensional objects, or title cards, as well as some facets of the set design and construction. The Graphic Artist will operate various types of art equipment, such as airbrushes, dry mount machines, electronic paint and animation editing systems, and digital video effects (DVC) devices.

A Graphic Designer in a commercial or public television station environment works with the art director and the production designer in creating the sets and choosing needed props. Most of the work, done in preproduction, involves analyzing and interpreting the script in order to determine the art director's requirements. From this study, the Graphic Designer creates and designs backdrops, set pieces, and props for the television production, all under the direction of the art director or production designer.

Graphic Artists and Designers are principally illustrators of concepts and ideas. They are required to translate the thoughts and perceptions of the production designer and the art director into finished art and designs that enhance the visual image of a program and thereby communicate these ideas directly to the viewer.

Graphic Artists and Designers work in a variety of artistic expressions to accomplish their tasks, including cartooning, decorative background painting, realistic renderings of objects, model-making, and sculpting. Graphic Artists and Designers frequently use computer graphics equipment, usually in association with videotape engineers and editors. This computer-controlled gear generates pictures and effects such as shading or airbrushing. Animation, graphs, and charts can also be developed electronically. Computer graphics are used extensively to produce commercial art today.

Salaries

According to surveys done by the Broadcast Employment Services, Graphic Artists and Graphic Designers may earn annual salaries ranging from a low of $19,000 to a high of

$75,000 or more. The median annual salary is $30,000. In public television, salaries for Graphic Artists and Graphic Designers tend to be lower, as do those from the smaller-market commercial television stations.

Employment Prospects

Graphic Artist and Graphic Designer are typically entry-level jobs in the art departments of television stations. The chances for employment are good. Most small-market stations (and public television stations) with art departments employ at least two Graphic Artists and/or Designers, whereas major-market stations might have five or more in house in their art department. Part-time positions are also usually available. Graphic Artist positions can be found at cable TV systems as well as commercial networks, and even in instructional and closed circuit television (ITV and CCTV). Instead of maintaining their own art department, a number of television stations use freelancers to work on a project-by-project basis (such as elaborate graphics work for an awards show), or contract an established outside graphics firm to supply the needed graphics work, either on a long-term contract or per-project basis. Such companies are another good starting point for beginner Graphic Artists and Graphic Designers.

Advancement Prospects

The opportunities for advancement for creative and hard-working Graphic Artists and Designers at a commercial or public TV station are only fair. The relative scarcity of art director positions and the intense competition for such positions tends to limit potential advancement. In addition, the specific duties, skills, and talents of Graphic Artists and Designers generally do not prove easily transferable to many other production or technical positions within the station, other than those within the art department.

On the other hand, such particularized skills and talents do lead to positions in other TV- or entertainment-related industries. The experience gained in television art and design can be put to excellent advantage in obtaining posts in advertising agencies, postproduction houses (for television or film), and public relations firms. Another pathway for advancement is to move to a parallel position at a larger station for a higher salary or attempt to negotiate a job as an art director with one of the smaller-market television stations. Moving on to project management in television is yet another possibility.

Education and Training

Most television stations require a minimum of a high school diploma and at least an associate's degree in commercial art

and/or design when hiring either a Graphic Artist or a Graphic Designer. Some employers prefer an undergraduate degree in commercial or fine art or in design, as well as experience in art and/or design.

Experience, Skills, and Personality Traits

An extensive background in television art or design is not considered essential, but some middle- and major-market television stations require at least a year of experience within the television business.

For Graphic Artists, facility in an assortment of commercial art techniques and styles, as well as versatility in print art, are often a prerequisite for employment. The Graphic Artist's portfolio should contain a diversity of projects, all demonstrating a clean and clear style. Experience with basic art equipment and computer-generated graphic systems is required. In addition, some film animation skills are helpful when working with video animation.

For Graphic Designers, a talent for drawing and drafting, as well as a demonstrable ability at architectural design, are requirements for employment. Some experience with the drawing of blueprints and actual construction, painting, and finishing of projects is helpful. For both positions, the ability to work rapidly and meet deadlines is a basic requirement.

Unions and Associations

Some Graphic Artists and Designers belong to and are represented by the National Association of Broadcast Employees and Technicians AFL-CIO (NABET). In most instances, however, neither Graphic Artists nor Designers in commercial and public television are members of a union. Many artists and designers in public and commercial television belong to the Broadcast Designers Association International in order to share mutual concerns and to add to their skills and knowledge of their particular area in the industry.

Tips for Entry

1. Broaden your educational background by taking liberal arts courses in history or the social sciences to provide background to handle design or artistic challenges posed by television productions.
2. Consider working in commercial art or design firms to gain experience and build a portfolio of your work.
3. During college volunteer to work on student, music video, commercial, or nonunion film or television productions both to gain experience and to establish useful industry contacts.

MATTE ARTIST

CAREER PROFILE

Duties: Paint backgrounds or other illustrations (manually or digitally) as needed for television productions

Alternate Title(s): Mattematician; Production Illustrator

Salary Range: $25,000 to $85,000

Employment Prospects: Good

Advancement Prospects: Fair

Prerequisites:

Education and Training—Undergraduate degree in art or film helpful, but not essential

Experience—Background as a commercial artist; work with computer graphics

Special Skills and Personality Traits—Artistic; creative; excellent manual dexterity and strong visual interpretive talents; good interpersonal abilities; passion for artistic expression and a vivid imagination; sound computer skills

CAREER LADDER

```
Storyboard Artist; Art Director;
Production Designer
```

```
Matte Artist
```

```
Art Department Production Assistant
```

Position Description

Matte Artists construct backgrounds (either with traditional artists' tools or, increasingly, with computer graphic software) that are then integrated with the live action being captured by the cameras for a project. Theirs is the art of creating scenes (for film, videotape, or digital format) that would otherwise be too expensive to build as a set, too impractical to go on location to obtain, or outright impossible to locate (such as those required for science fiction productions, surreal scenes, or large panoramic historical productions). Matte paintings can be as simple as adding snow to an existing shot and thus changing the season, altering a scene from day to night, or extending existing outdoor sets by digitally "adding" buildings behind those already filmed. Or it can be an extremely complex, multiplaned, full-frame matte painting. In all cases, the goal of the Matte Artist is to generate a scene that looks as real as if it had actually existed and been captured on film. Ideally, the human eye and brain should not be able to notice the difference between art and reality. This type of creativity takes a special skill with design and composition, as well as an acute sense of shadows and light, depth of field, and the perception of the human eye.

Matte painting used to be done by printing images onto glass and then photographically compositing these images with filmed elements. Today, most matte painting is done digitally in a computer paint program and combined with live action elements in a computer program. This digital process allows for a much broader range of realistic manipulation (such as moving clouds, smoke trails, and other such effects). As Craig Barron, cofounder of Matte World Digital and coauthor of the book *The Invisible Art* (a history of matte painting as told by many of the painters who created the genre), says, "The computer graphic techniques we use are constantly changing. There are no rules; we do what it takes to produce a realistic illustration. Most filmmakers still call what we do matte shots. . . . It's more accurate to say we are involved in environment creation."

Salaries

By union contract (Local 790 of the International Alliance of Theatrical Stage Employees), the minimum hourly wage for a Matte Artist is $48.71. According to the U.S. Department of Labor's *Occupational Outlook Handbook, 2004–05 Edition,* median annual earnings of salaried multimedia artists (which includes Matte Artists) were $43,980 in 2002. The middle 50 percent earned between $33,970 and $61,120 per year. The lowest 10 percent earned less than $25,830 and the highest 10 percent earned more than $85,160.

Employment Prospects

Although technological change in the television industry moves most artistic creative activity toward the use of computer graphics, Matte Artists are still needed—even if their paint is now a pixel and their canvas is a computer. Thus, having these new skills as well as more traditional artistic creativity, prospects for employment of Matte Artists remain good.

Advancement Prospects

Matte Artists frequently advance their careers to become storyboard artists. Some may move on to become art directors or production designers, though the competition for these higher-paying positions is tough.

Education and Training

For Matte Artists, a bachelor of arts degree is helpful, but not required. Art training is always a plus, as is an understanding of television and film production. Courses in illustration and graphic design are useful, and classes in computer graphics are almost obligatory. Matte painting is often a skill acquired on the job while working as an assistant to established Matte Artists.

Experience, Skills, and Personality Traits

Beyond their visual ingenuity, Matte Artists must have an acute sense of design and composition and an eye for light, shade, and colors. They need strong interpersonal skills and should be amenable to taking instruction from directors, set designers, and other members of the production crew. They need to be conversant with computer graphics software and have a passion for their work, as it can be very demanding and tightly scheduled.

Unions and Associations

Membership in the International Alliance of Theatrical Stage Employees (IATSE) union can help to guarantee minimum wages and provide support. Membership in film and television industry associations, such as Women in Film (WIF) or the Broadcast Designers Association, may be helpful for networking purposes.

Tips for Entry

1. In order to improve your artistic skills, draw at least four days a week, and keep a sketchbook of all your work.
2. Along with your art education, be sure to take computer courses to become thoroughly familiar with computer graphics software.
3. Take time to watch movies, television shows, and commercials carefully. Develop your own background sketches for scenes (or commercials) you have seen in film or on television.
4. As a creative artist, observe the background of everyday scenes. Using computer graphics, experiment with methods of illustrating such backgrounds.

PRODUCTION DESIGNER

CAREER PROFILE

Duties: Conceive and create the style of television productions, establishing and planning the visual design

Alternate Title(s): Broadcast Designer

Salary Range: $22,000 to $125,000

Employment Prospects: Fair

Advancement Prospects: Poor

Prerequisites:

Education and Training—Minimum of an undergraduate degree in commercial art, fine arts, or design

Experience—Minimum of five years as a graphic artist and/or two to three years as an art director

Special Skills and Personality Traits—Creativity; excellent basic design abilities; good communication skills; supervisory and administrative abilities

CAREER LADDER

```
+---------------------------+
|    Production Manager      |
+---------------------------+

+---------------------------+
|    Production Designer     |
+---------------------------+

+---------------------------+
|       Art Director         |
+---------------------------+
```

Position Description

A Production Designer in the television industry has the overall responsibility for creating the style of a production and establishing and planning the visual design of the total project. It is a very creative and conceptual role and a key art position in the production team. Production Designers provide an integrated whole, an environment in which the on-camera action will take place. They also usually decide which scenes will be shot at existing locations and which can be on the soundstage.

In the crew for most television productions, the art director reports to the Production Designer. The latter conceptualizes the overall design, while the art director oversees the execution of that artistic vision into a physical reality. Sometimes, in smaller television productions, the two positions may be merged into one post, with the individual reporting directly to the producer.

In preproduction, the Production Designer will meet with the producer and director to determine their project goals and communicate their expectations for the production. Next, the Production Designer devises an appropriate visual concept within set budgetary parameters. The Production Designer presents sketches and/or models of the proposed design to the producer and director. Once these are approved, the designer will work with (and frequently hire) the art director (if such a position is required) and the craftsmen (including set designer, costume designer, and property master) to construct the set, purchase or rent furniture and props, and oversee the realization of the design.

While most of Production Designers' work is accomplished during the preparation phase of the production, their involvement may extend into the actual production stage as well. During this part of the production, the Production Designer will work closely with the director, the production manager, and the cinematographer (or director of photography) to help determine the final "look" of the production.

Salaries

While salaries may vary from production to production as well as according to the individual's standing within the television community, compensation of Production Designers tends to be higher than that of art directors. According to Broadcast Employment Services, annual salaries for Production Designers in television ranged from a low of $22,000 to a high of $125,000. The median annual salary is $41,000. On small productions with minimal budgets (usually nonunion), beginner Production Designers may earn little or nothing but the experience of the work and the establishment of a credit to advance to higher-paid positions on later productions.

Employment Prospects

Overall, the chance for employment as a Production Designer is fair for those individuals who have had design experience as an art director or a graphic designer in the film or television industries. The progression route for future Production Designers is often from a trainee graphic artist to an assistant art director to becoming an art director and then from there to the position as Production Designer. As a Production Designer is also a supervisor of the various art and design functions in the preproduction phase of a television show, some management experience is necessary (and that can be gained as an art director or an assistant art director).

Advancement Prospects

Advancement for a Production Designer is difficult. While this position requires a thorough knowledge of production and has management requirements as well, the opportunity for promotion within a television station to production manager or other supervisory jobs (such as producer or director) is seldom available. Production Designers who have reached the top of their position after years of experience and have reached top salary levels rarely want to go on to some other type of job.

Education and Training

An undergraduate degree in commercial art, fine arts, or design is the usual background for beginners in the art departments of television stations. Some liberal arts background in literature, history, and theater is also recommended, as are courses in drafting and design. Many Production Designers have studied architecture and environmental design or theatrical set design as well. Most Production Designers start in graphic design positions within the art department of a television station, gaining experience and production training in that job, and then move upward from that position.

Experience, Skills, and Personality Traits

Production Designers must possess innate creativity and basic design skills and be good communicators of ideas, able to explain what they visualize and how it is to be accomplished. They must be skilled environmental designers, have a thorough understanding of filmmaking, and be able to manage the multiple components and people of the artistic part of a production. They need the ability to draw plans and sketch the design of scenes based on their conceptualization of words written on a page, and provide the script with their own strong visual creative sense. As Production Designer Ernest Roth states, "You really have to love architecture, interior design, and art in general. I think you have the ability to control how people see something when they come into a space . . . They say I arrange things, I can take your eye from right to left or left to right, or up to down, just by the color and texture and the way things are angled."

Unions and Associations

Membership in the International Alliance of Theatrical Stage Employees (IATSE) is sometimes required on major television productions. Such membership is also beneficial for industry networking. At a few of the major-market stations, Production Designers may be represented by United Scenic Artists for bargaining purposes. In both commercial and public television, many Production Designers may not be represented by a union. Many commercial television Production Designers may be members of the Broadcast Designers Association International in order to share mutual professional concerns and to network.

Tips for Entry

1. A broad educational background is helpful, but you need to have an inborn artistic sense and enhance it by training in the aesthetic use of color, shapes, and light.
2. Volunteer to work on student films or low-budget movies to gain practical experience, build your résumé, and make contacts for future projects.
3. Consider enrolling in film or television school to add to your educational background.
4. Offer to work for free for a Production Designer so that you can observe the process at hand or, if you are working as a production assistant on a television (or film) project, offer to help the art department while keeping within the strictures of union and guild guidelines.

SET DESIGNER

Duties: Design and decorate the sets and scenery for television productions

Alternate Title(s): Scenic Designer

Salary Range: $17,000 to $65,000 or more

Employment Prospects: Poor

Advancement Prospects: Poor

Prerequisites:

Education and Training—Undergraduate degree in art or design; master's degree in theater arts helpful

Experience—Minimum of three to five years in theatrical and/or television set design

Special Skills and Personality Traits—Artistic flair; creativity; good interpersonal skills; graphic arts talent; knowledge of television production

```
┌──────────────────────────────────────┐
│   Set or Scenic Designer for         │
│   Major Theater or Film Productions  │
└──────────────────────────────────────┘

┌──────────────────────────────────────┐
│            Set Designer              │
└──────────────────────────────────────┘

┌──────────────────────────────────────┐
│   Assistant Set Designer;            │
│   Production Assistant               │
└──────────────────────────────────────┘
```

Position Description

Set Designers for a television production design the sets and scenery, supervise their construction, and decide how they will be decorated and dressed (all the necessary finishing touches needed for an effective set). Their duties usually include the conception, design, and supervision of the creation (or acquisition) of backdrops, exterior and interior sets, furniture to be used, and all the decorative and functional details of the sets and scenery.

They first study the script and then confer with the art director, production designer, director, and producer to understand the purpose or thrust of the production and the place, time, and atmosphere of the show's action. They conduct research to settle on the fashion and architectural styles appropriate for the current production. They then produce preliminary sketches, illustrations, and perspectives to draft the plans and elevations of the sets to be constructed. Increasingly, 3-D modeling software programs are used to render more lifelike the drawings of the set that the director and/or cinematographer can then take advantage of to walk through specific camera and lighting angles. In some cases (usually larger productions), three-dimensional scale models may be constructed to guide in the finalizing of the set construction plans of the actual sets in consultation with producers, writers, and the director.

In the actual construction, the Set Designer must envision the set as it will appear from the various camera angles, including close-ups and long shots. Working in conjunction with the director's concept of the layout, the Set Designer takes into account the activity and physical movement that the sets and the scenery must make possible. During the pre-production stages, a floor plan is created that indicates where each set will be situated, where major equipment (such as lighting and cameras) will be positioned, where permanent lighting fixtures and outlets are located, and where scenery and furniture will be placed.

Set Designers are usually employed by networks and independent production companies, rather than individual television stations. Often they work directly for the art director or the production designer and, if there are many sets, may be assigned to one or only a few of them. On large-scale projects and made-for-television films (and miniseries), there may be several set designers working on the show, each designing one or more individual sets under the control of the art director or the production designer.

During the design phase of the project, Set Designers typical work at a drafting board or at a computer in an art studio. While overseeing construction they will be found in carpentry and scene shops, and will be in the television studio during setup and production. Set Designers may supervise one or more assistants, scenic artists, set dressers, a propmaster, and others related to the production on a project-by-project basis. They will be working directly with both the costume people and lighting director. During this process, they must keep an inventory of backdrops, furniture, scenery, and sets and at the end must oversee the dismantling of the sets.

Salaries

According to the U.S. Bureau of Labor Statistics, median annual salaries for Set Designers in 2002 were $33,870. The middle 50 percent earned yearly between $24,780 and $46,350. The lowest 10 percent earned less than $17,830 annually, and the highest 10 percent earned more than $63,280. The Web site of Interior Design Schools (http://www.interior-design-school.net) indicates that in 2004, entry-level set designers earned from $1,000 to $10,000 per production. In contrast to this, the middle range for Set Designers was $15,000 to $20,000 per production, and the highly experienced Set Designer could expect to earn up to $80,000 per production.

Senior Set Designers who belong to Local 847, the union for Set Designers and model builders are entitled by contract to an hourly rate of $35.62 for an eight-hour day, or a weekly rate (five eight-hour days) of $1,349.23. For junior Set Designers, the hourly rate drops to $32,28, and the weekly rate to $1,228.36.

Employment Prospects

The job outlook for Set Designers fluctuates greatly depending on how many new television productions are started from season to season. This seasonal nature of work results sometimes in periods of unemployment. Most hiring is for onetime-only jobs, but a Set Designer may occasionally get continuing employment on a weekly series or a daily soap opera, which often use several different sets in each show's installment.

While most employment is still confined to major productions in New York City and Hollywood or at one of the top 20 major-market commercial or public television stations, television productions now occur in virtually every state due to the increased flexibility of sophisticated equipment and the financial incentives and advantageous currency exchange rates offered by various municipalities and countries competing to host film and television production.

Aspiring Set Designers must be willing to work hard and start at the bottom, often as unpaid volunteers, as those with a keen understanding of the technology and applications involved will have a distinct advantage over other aspiring candidates. Nonetheless, even after being an assistant Set Designer for years, it will be hard to negotiate the first critical job as a full Set Designer, whether for a specific television project or as a staff member on a program. Solid personal contacts in the industry and a high degree of talent will make it easier to get that first job and subsequent regular work. As veteran Set Designer Todd Chernawsky states, "Many people's first jobs find them. You'll offer to help someone on a project and they will hire you for their next one, or you impress someone else who is also helping out and they hire or recommend you for a job. It's all about networking."

Advancement Prospects

This is a highly competitive field, and advancement opportunities are generally poor. Beginning designers usually receive on-the-job training and normally need from three to five years of training before they will even be considered for any higher-level position. A few individuals may be able to move into more responsible, higher-paying set design work on a regular staff basis. Others may find it better to advance by contracting for the larger and more frequent projects, particularly at networks. Many of the more experienced Set Designers progress in their professional standing by broadening their work base to include employment on major theatrical and motion picture productions along with their television work. During the customary spells of unemployment endemic to this industry position, some Set Designers may find that their diverse skills can translate to other creative jobs, such as visual merchandiser, stylist, exhibition designer, and stage manager.

Education and Training

A bachelor's degree in art and design, radio/TV production, theater arts, or architectural design is required for most entry-level design positions. The curriculum in schools that offer a bachelor of fine arts degree usually includes art and art history, designing and sketching, principles of design, and specialized studies for each of the design disciplines. Courses in stagecraft, television production, drafting, and architecture are also essential, as well as study in drawing, painting, sculpture, and the graphic arts. Familiarity with computer-aided design software is increasingly important. In addition, a liberal arts education or a program that includes training in business or project management is recommended. In some instances, a master's degree in theater arts can be of additional help.

Experience, Skills, and Personality Traits

A minimum of three to five years in television and/or theatrical set designing on a professional level is typically required of any aspiring Set Designer. Some beginners start as "journeyman" set design artists before they move to the top position. Most Set Designers have devoted a considerable amount of time as apprentices in either theater, film, or television, working in an assortment of backstage jobs such as scene painters, carpenters, or other craft positions.

Set Designers must be creative, imaginative, and persistent. They need to possess an artistic flair and style and have fine graphic arts skills. They must be able to communicate their ideas in writing, in clear visual presentations, and verbally. They are expected to have good budgeting and planning skills and be knowledgeable in research techniques. They should have a broad historical and cultural background and a technical expertise in set and scenery construction as well as prop building. A knowledge of television production techniques is a requirement, and they must be able to understand the relationship between time, space, and movement. As this type of work is a collaborative effort, they must have the ability to work well with others and be able to handle stress during long work hours and tight deadlines.

Unions and Associations

For bargaining purposes, Set Designers may find membership in the United Scenic Artists, Local 829, to be advanta-geous, particularly as membership is recognized nationally as having attained a solid professional standing in the field. Many designers also join graphic design and visual arts associations in order to share ideas, make contacts, and advance their careers. Others are members of the International Alliance of Theatrical Stage Employees (IATSE).

Tips for Entry

1. Be sure to broaden your educational experience beyond a fine arts or design program to include a basic liberal arts background to provide the perspective you will need in creating sets.
2. Take courses in computer-aided design (CAD), as this will be invaluable in your career growth.
3. Be flexible about working in any type of entry-level position in the art department of a production to get your foot in the door.

STORYBOARD ARTIST

CAREER PROFILE

Duties: Create illustrations of a script that help the television production crew and director to visualize the production

Alternate Title(s): Production Illustrator

Salary Range: $25,000 to $85,000

Employment Prospects: Good

Advancement Prospects: Fair

Prerequisites:

Education and Training—Undergraduate degree in art and/or film helpful, but not essential

Experience—Background as a commercial artist or graphic designer; work with computer graphics

Special Skills and Personality Traits—Artistic; creative; excellent manual dexterity and strong visual interpretive talents; good interpersonal abilities; sound computer skills; vivid imagination

CAREER LADDER

```
┌─────────────────────────────────────┐
│  Art Director; Production Designer   │
└─────────────────────────────────────┘

┌─────────────────────────────────────┐
│          Storyboard Artist           │
└─────────────────────────────────────┘

┌─────────────────────────────────────┐
│ Art Department Production Assistant  │
└─────────────────────────────────────┘
```

Position Description

Working under the direction of the producer, director, or production designer, the Storyboard Artist illustrates the sequence of scenes as described by the words of the script of a television production or commercial. Storyboards are usually hand-drawn images (though there are computer programs that make possible interactive storyboards) representing the proposed sequence of events, designed to become the foundation for the continuity of the project's action and dialogue. From their reading of the script, artists create these boards, translating that script into a visual form. They render the action and storyline, as laid out by the writer, in sequential images, taking into account scene detail, character, continuity, camera angles, special effects, and all other pertinent elements needed for the production. According to veteran Storyboard Artist Mike Harris, "A storyboard is very similar to drawing a comic strip or book. You take a sequence of events and make them visually exciting."

The primary purpose of these illustrations is to help all personnel involved in the project to visualize each sequence of the script. This visual aid also can serve as a guide to placing actors and cameras on the television set, to knowing what part of the set or location is going to be shot at any one time, and to depict other details necessary for the making of the show or commercial. Another type of storyboard, one usually more finished and slicker than those used for preproduction purposes, is used as a presentation device to sell the concept of the script (or commercial) to potential financial backers.

While a lot of television news programming is immediate in its planning and execution, with little time to produce a shot-by-shot scheme (or storyboard) of how the end product is to look and feel, much commercial television magazine and documentary production, as well as made-for-television films and series, find storyboard guidelines necessary. Many of these productions have multidisciplinary production teams that may be split between different filming sites, and carefully coordinated planning is essential. Storyboarding provides everyone with a common point of reference and will verify and validate the structure and content of the forthcoming production.

Most television productions (films, series, documentaries) employ one Storyboard Artist, full time or part time. Some larger productions may require a team of Storyboard Artists, especially if many special effects will be used. In those instances, Storyboard Artists may be required to draw something that does not exist outside the mind of the scriptwriter or director. These storyboard drawings need to be more detailed and are accomplished mostly through computer software, sometimes with the end result being three-dimensional storyboards and computer-generated images for use in the production.

Salaries

By union contract (Local 790 of the International Alliance of Theatrical Stage Employees), the minimum day rate for a Storyboard Artist is $425.87. According to the U.S. Department of Labor's *Occupational Outlook Handbook, 2004–05 Edition,* median annual earnings of salaried multimedia artists (which includes Storyboard Artists) were $43,980 in 2002. The middle 50 percent earned between $33,970 and $61,120 per year. The lowest 10 percent earned annually less than $25,830, and the highest 10 percent earned more than $85,160.

Employment Prospects

More and more television productions (in particular, made-for-TV features and series) are using Storyboard Artists to keep firm track of their storylines, as well as relying heavily on computer graphics and special effects in both their planning and production stages. Thus, prospects for employment are good. Some Storyboard Artists supplement their income by creating cartoons and illustrations for newspapers, magazines, and online publications.

Advancement Prospects

Storyboard Artists' next career level is usually that of either an art director or a production designer. However, this step is relatively difficult due to the number of strong candidates vying to fill a limited number of openings in either of these two positions.

Education and Training

For Storyboard Artists, a bachelor of arts degree is helpful, but not required. Art training is always a plus, as is an understanding of television and film production. Additionally, courses in illustration and graphic design are useful, and classes in computer graphics may be a requirement. Sometimes Storyboard Artists acquire their skills while working as an assistant to an established Storyboard Artist. Many Storyboard Artists have worked previously in advertising.

Experience, Skills, and Personality Traits

Storyboard Artists must be visually creative and able to tell stories with drawings, indicate motions of people per the script, and, through their drawings, help the creative and production crews to visualize scenes as they will unfold before the camera. They need to be skilled in both quick sketching and in creating more detailed, finished drawings. Communication and people skills are essential, as Storyboard Artists must be comfortable taking instruction and criticism from the director or scriptwriter. They must be both enthusiastic and energetic, as they may be called on to produce multiple drawings in a very short time or to redraw ones they had already finished.

Unions and Associations

Membership in the International Alliance of Theatrical Stage Employees (IATSE) union can help to guarantee minimum wages and provide support. In New York, independent Storyboard Artists may be represented by the United Scenic Artists, Local 829. Film and television industry associations, such as Women in Film (WIF) or the Broadcast Designers Association, may be helpful for networking purposes.

Tips for Entry

1. To improve your artistic skills, draw at least four days a week, and keep a sketchbook of all your work.
2. Along with your art education, be sure to take computer courses to become familiar with computer graphics software.
3. Take time to watch movies, television shows, and commercials carefully. Experiment by creating storyboards for some of the productions you have watched.
4. As a creative artist, observe cars and ships in motion, youngsters at play, and adults as they move about their daily lives, and think about how you would draw or pictorialize these actions.

CABLE/SATELLITE TELEVISION

CHIEF TECHNICIAN

CAREER PROFILE

Duties: Supervise all on-site technical installation, operation, and transmission at a cable TV system or multichannel multipoint distribution service (MMDS) firm

Alternate Title(s): Chief Engineer; Technical Operating Manager

Salary Range: $30,000 to $75,000 or more

Employment Prospects: Good

Advancement Prospects: Good

Prerequisites:

Education and Training—High school diploma and additional technical training are basic requirements; college degree in electrical engineering, physics, or allied field preferable; requires certification

Experience—Five to seven years in broadcast or cable TV engineering

Special Skills and Personality Traits—Administrative abilities; design skills; leadership qualities; technical aptitude

CAREER LADDER

```
┌─────────────────────────────────────────┐
│  Chief Engineer (or Chief Technician at  │
│      large system or station);           │
│       Director of Engineering            │
└─────────────────────────────────────────┘

┌─────────────────────────────────────────┐
│            Chief Technician              │
└─────────────────────────────────────────┘

┌─────────────────────────────────────────┐
│               Technician                 │
└─────────────────────────────────────────┘
```

Position Description

A Chief Technician is responsible for the day-to-day supervision of the technical staff of a cable television system or a MMDS. The technical staff may vary from three to more than 30 employees depending on the size of the markets covered by the system.

In MMDS companies, a Chief Technician is sometimes termed a chief engineer. In contrast, in cable television, the title of chief engineer is almost synonymous with that of general manager, as it usually entails the broader responsibilities of administrative duties and planning and developing new services. Some smaller cable systems and MMDS companies contract with outside professional engineering firms to provide the services of a Chief Technician.

Typically, the Chief Technician is the senior and most expert associate of the engineering staff (particularly in the absence of a chief engineer or general manager), and is accountable for all engineering aspects of the operation, including the construction and installation of amplifiers, antenna towers, satellite receiving stations (dishes), signal processing equipment, and the electronic control center called the head end. If the system is the origin of local programming, the Chief Technician is responsible for the selection and acquisition of all television production equipment and supervises its installation and operation. The Chief Technician also is in charge of aligning the assorted electronic elements of incoming satellite or microwave signals, processing them, and retransmitting them to subscribers' homes. At a cable television system, the Chief Technician is also in charge of obtaining needed permits from local electrical and telephone utility companies for the use of their poles or underground facilities. The Chief Technician has to settle on the number of connections for each pole, create a diagram of the layout of the cable system, and oversee the connection, installation, and servicing of the system's equipment installed in subscribers' homes.

Chief Technicians also evaluate and purchase all technical and technical transmission equipment as well as manage the preventive maintenance program for all such equipment. They are responsible for designing and installing systems to deliver any new program services, such as interactive (two-way) communications, teletext, and data transmissions.

They must be familiar with all aspects of digital transmission as well. They prepare all necessary technical applications, such as construction permits, proof of performance tests, and license renewals of modifications to meet the regulations of the Federal Communications Commission (FCC). In the process, they have to ensure that the system complies with all federal, state, and local utility and safety regulations. Beyond their regular engineering duties, Chief Technicians sometimes serve as the system or station manager of a small facility, and may be the owner or part owner of the operation, or they may be assigned to a particular locality by the parent company or multiple system operator (MSO).

Salaries

Generally, while the salaries for Chief Technicians in cable TV or MMDS operations tend to be somewhat less that those of their peers in the broadcast industry, they are, nevertheless, still relatively high. Chief Technicians' annual salaries at cable systems ranged from $30,000 to as much as $75,000 or more, according to surveys done by the Broadcast Employment Services.

Employment Prospects

The opportunities for qualified engineers to obtain this post are good. The rapid growth of the telecommunications system in general and cable systems in particular during the last decade has created a general shortage of engineering and technical personnel. Experienced and capable engineers who have a proven record of accomplishment should find few obstacles in becoming employed by cable systems, particularly if they have some experience in managing a small business. Technicians employed at television or cable stations who pursue further study (in both technology and business administration) and who demonstrate the necessary leadership skills are sometimes promoted to the position of Chief Technician.

Advancement Prospects

It is the growing need for qualified engineering personnel in cable TV systems, MMDS stations, and even regular television stations that creates good opportunities for advancement, even with the heavy competition for higher management positions. Some Chief Technicians in cable television look for promotion to new and larger systems or to posts as chief engineers of regional or systemwide operations as a means of advancing their careers. In MMDS operations, some obtain the position of director of engineering within the parent company, giving them responsibility for the planning and construction of other stations. Still other Chief Technicians may find career advancement by joining manufacturing companies as design engineers, field service managers, or construction/engineering managers.

Education and Training

A high school diploma and one or two years of training in electronics and engineering are the bare minimum requirements for this job. Most systems or stations prefer candidates for this position to have some college education or even an undergraduate degree in electrical engineering, physics, or a related science degree. Chief Engineers for MMDS station operations are required to have a Restricted Radio Telephone Operator permit from the FCC. Many other cable and MMDS employers require certification from a study program from one of the industry groups, such as the Society of Broadcast Engineers (SBE).

Experience, Skills, and Personality Traits

A background of at least five to seven years of experience in broadcast electronics or a closely related field involving highly complex electronic transmission equipment is a basic requirement for this position. Solid experience with all types and models of technical gear, a thorough understanding of the principles of electronics and their applications to the television industry, and experience with and understanding of FCC rules and regulations are additional requirements for this job.

Chief Technicians must combine their technical design skills with hands-on experience dealing with electronics systems. They must be able to supervise and lead other technicians, be extremely budget conscious, and be an organized and capable administrator.

Unions and Associations

There are no unions that serve as bargaining agents for Chief Technicians or chief engineers in cable systems or MMDS stations. Some Chief Technicians may find it beneficial to belong to the Society of Cable Telecommunication Engineers (SCTE) to share common concerns with their peers and to aid in the advancement of their careers. Others may join the Society for Motion Picture and Television Engineers (SMPTE) or the Society of Broadcast Engineers for the same purposes.

Tips for Entry

1. While in high school or college look for intern programs with electronics firms to gain practical experience in the application of your studies.
2. Consider further training beyond high school from a technical school or college to give you needed education and training to apply for a technician position.
3. Look into study programs given by such industry groups as the Society of Broadcast Engineers to obtain a certification that will aid in your employment search or advancement.

CUSTOMER SERVICE REPRESENTATIVE

CAREER PROFILE

Duties: Coordinate customer installation and service requests and complaints at a cable TV system or multi-channel multipoint distribution service (MMDS) company; turn customer inquiries into orders

Alternate Title(s): None

Salary Range: $30,000 to $50,000 or more

Employment Prospects: Good

Advancement Prospects: Good

Prerequisites:

Education and Training—Minimum of high school diploma; some college preferred

Experience—Minimum of one to two years of office work

Special Skills and Personality Traits—Ability with details; aptitude for numbers; computer literacy; good organizational skills; sales talent; service orientation

CAREER LADDER

```
┌─────────────────────────────────────┐
│          Office Manager              │
└─────────────────────────────────────┘

┌─────────────────────────────────────┐
│   Customer Service Representative    │
└─────────────────────────────────────┘

┌─────────────────────────────────────┐
│        Clerk; Secretary;             │
│   High School / Business School      │
└─────────────────────────────────────┘
```

Position Description

A Customer Service Representative's job is to serve, sell, and satisfy customers. The representative coordinates all customer requests for service with the sales, marketing, and engineering staffs of a cable television system or an MMDS station. A representative's obligation is to help sustain successful and profitable rapport and understanding with current and potential subscribers. A Customer Service Representative usually reports to the office manager in small organizations and to the marketing director in larger ones. In either case, this is seldom a supervisory position.

Customer Service Representatives process all requests and complaints concerning information on prices and services from subscribers and must ensure that they are dealt with promptly. They are also responsible for converting a casual inquiry into a firm sale, or to upgrading an installation request into a higher-priced service. It is the Customer Service Representatives' job to explain the benefits and costs of the various program services offered by the cable system or the MMDS station. They must be able to discourage disconnect requests through the use of standard sales strategies. At some systems or stations, Customer Service Representatives are also actively involved in telemarketing to potential new customers.

At smaller systems or stations, a Customer Service Representative may deal with as many as 2,000 to 3,000 subscriber

orders during a given year. In addition, in many of the smaller operations, this individual is assigned the tasks of a billing clerk (invoicing subscribers), a work order control clerk (seeing that installation and service calls are expedited), or a service dispatcher (scheduling technicians to make installation and service calls on customers). Today, most of these activities are initiated and controlled by computer input by the service representative. In smaller systems and stations, where there are few or no sales personnel, the Customer Service Representative position is critical to the maintenance of the subscriber base and also to its future growth.

In larger companies, most representatives concentrate on providing over-the-counter, telephone responses, and e-mail communications to queries from potential customers or requests from current subscribers. Larger systems or stations usually have more than one Customer Service Representative on staff, and sometimes up to five or more.

In addition to performing public relations, sales, and service roles, Customer Service Representatives ensure the timely fulfillment of subscribers' orders and requests. They are also essential in minimizing the disconnect rate of an operation. By exhibiting a friendly and persuasive manner, they can often dissuade discontented customers from canceling their subscription to the service. In addition, Customer Service Representatives maintain accurate records of all calls and of dispatcher and work orders. They process all phone-in, over-the-counter, or Web site orders from new customers and assign them to the appropriate salesperson. Finally, they prepare the preliminary invoices for monthly billings to subscribers and often contact delinquent accounts for payment.

Salaries

Recompense for Customer Service Representatives in cable TV systems and MMDS stations tend to be mid-level to high in comparison to salaries of other employees. Some cable systems offer commissions on sales, bonus plans, or incentive sales plans during the year, which can add greatly to the basic salary. Customer Service Representatives are often paid by the hour. Experienced representatives can earn from $30,000 to $50,000 yearly according to authoritative sources within the cable TV industry. Salaries in MMDS stations tend to be comparable to those in cable TV systems.

Employment Prospects

The position of Customer Service Representative is often a beginner's post. Many clerks and secretaries who have proved their attentiveness and organizational abilities are elevated to this position. Due to the increasing number of both telecommunication companies and the expansion of the cable TV industry as well as the relatively high turnover rate in this job, there are many opportunities for employment. Recent high school or business school graduates should find it comparatively easy to gain employment in Customer Service Representative jobs in the industry. Part-time positions are also sometimes available at either MMDS or cable operations.

Advancement Prospects

Opportunities for advancement are reasonably solid for enterprising individuals who have gained experience. People can learn a lot about the fundamental aspects of customer service, telecommunications operations, and general office functions while acting as Customer Service Representatives. As they gain this work experience, they can anticipate being promoted to more responsible jobs in various intermediate supervisory positions. After several years of experience, they may even be able to move into the post of office manager within the Cable TV company or the MMDS station, or move to a competing firm into such a position. Still others may be able to trade on their learned experience to win more responsible jobs at higher salaries in nonmedia service-related industries.

Education and Training

The minimum requirement for this position is a high school diploma. Individuals with business or vocational school training (and, preferably, a diploma) will be at a distinct advantage. Courses in computer operations and training or experience in information management information systems can be very helpful.

Experience, Skills, and Personality Traits

Although this position is often considered an entry-level job, one or more years of experience in an office environment is usually required of candidates. A working knowledge of standard office equipment is needed and know-how with computers and word processors is essential. Background in direct customer contact, as gained by working in credit card companies or for an airline, is very helpful as well.

Most Customer Service Representatives tend to be bright young people who have a natural instinct for details and an ability to work successfully with numbers. These people are well organized and capable of dealing on a daily basis with a variety of tasks and all types of people. Some may even be homemakers who have reentered the job market.

Interpersonal skills in managing and coordinating internal logistics and communications between departments are necessary, as well as a service-oriented and pleasing personality. Customer Service Representatives have to possess excellent manners on the telephone, in person, and on the Internet, always being tactful and courteous when dealing with subscribers and potential customers. They also must be able to reinforce given sales strategies during their various contacts with customers. Being able to sell or resell a service is mandatory for this position.

Unions and Associations

Although there are no unions or professional organizations that represent Customer Service Representatives at cable TV systems or at MMDS companies, individuals in this position might want to belong to general umbrella associations, such as the American Marketing Association, for job contacts and information.

Tips for Entry

1. Consider additional vocational school training in business or management beyond high school in order to gain an edge in your employment search.
2. Be sure to include computer courses in your curriculum, as these skills will be necessary in your career as a Customer Service Representative as well as any advanced management position in the television industry.
3. Look for any possible intern programs at your local television stations, cable or otherwise, to acquire practical experience in television production and management.
4. Perfect your interpersonal and organizational skills by joining in high school extracurricular groups in some sort of administrative capacity.

DIRECTOR OF LOCAL ORIGINATION

CAREER PROFILE

Duties: Produce and schedule programming at a cable television system

Alternate Title(s): Director of Public Access; Manager of Local Origination; Production Director

Salary Range: $26,000 to $50,000 or more

Employment Prospects: Fair

Advancement Prospects: Poor

Prerequisites:

Education and Training—Undergraduate degree in communications or radio-television production

Experience—Minimum of three to five years in television production

Special Skills and Personality Traits—Creativity; good organizational abilities; administrative and leadership qualities

CAREER LADDER

```
┌─────────────────────────────────┐
│       Production Manager         │
└─────────────────────────────────┘

┌─────────────────────────────────┐
│  Director of Local Origination   │
└─────────────────────────────────┘

┌─────────────────────────────────┐
│       Producer; Director         │
└─────────────────────────────────┘
```

Position Description

A Director of Local Origination is the person in charge of local productions originated by a cable television system. Being the manager of a cable system's production schedule, a Director of Local Origination has a post similar to that of a production manager at a commercial or public television station. The scope of duties, however, is typically narrower at a cable TV station. This job is also parallel to that of a supervisor of media services at a corporate television center.

The position of Director of Local Origination includes creating and monitoring budgets for all local productions, as well as keeping track of the costs for capital equipment, expenses, materials, and supplies. The director works with the marketing team to determine the requirements of the community through studies conducted by that staff or by personal surveys to develop appropriate local programs. The chief task of the director is to control all phases of the creation of programs, from the conception of the idea to the writing of the script through the actual technical production of the show. These programs can include entertainment or talent shows, local newscasts, public affairs programs, remote coverage of community events, sports events, and talk shows. For any of the programs that are sponsored, the Director of Local Origination is responsible for overseeing the production of commercials that will be shown with the program.

In some of the larger cable television systems, two separate individuals oversee the locally produced fare. The director of public access is in charge of the operation of channels that are allocated for use by the public. This person must assist, supervise, and train volunteers in the production of programs for these channels. Many cable TV systems also offer governmental or educational access channels. If the studio facilities are involved, there may be a third individual, the director of governmental or educational access, who participates in the technical production and supervision and training of volunteers interested in using the facilities. The second main individual, the Director of Local Origination, in these cases concentrates on productions that are conceived, developed, and produced by the cable system's full-time staff. In most midsize and small cable television systems, these two (or three) positions are usually combined into one, the Director of Local Origination, who then oversees the production of all community-developed shows.

The Director of Local Origination often writes the scripts of the programs to be produced and then oversees the design of the sets (usually simple) and art and graphics for both the remote and in-studio productions. The director will schedule rehearsals, production dates, and availability of personnel for all the locally produced programs, as well as coordinate the availability of equipment and facilities needed by the production. Additionally, the director will monitor standards of quality in all these local productions and will implement research and feedback mechanisms to evaluate the effectiveness of these productions.

Salaries

Annual salaries for Directors of Local Origination are relatively low, ranging from $26,000 to a high of $50,000 or more. While some positions at the larger-market stations may command salaries exceeding $75,000, the median annual salary for this position is $44,000, according to studies made by Broadcast Employment Services. Salaries are highest at the larger cable TV systems in the larger urban areas, such as New York and Los Angeles.

Employment Prospects

The opportunities for employment in this post are only fair. A local community sometimes grants a franchise to a cable TV system to produce programs about or of particular interest to that community. Most such cable franchises require that the cable TV system provide for local educational, governmental, or access programming, with the signal originating from the local system control center. Sometimes, however, many of these originations are quite simple, being character-generated community bulletin boards, slide or one-camera shows, or playbacks of programs produced by outside agencies and then transmitted over access, educational, or governmental channels.

As a result, the job market for this position is usually limited to the systems that have local origination or nonautomatic origination capabilities, as well as to the usual nonprofit or public organizations (agencies, groups, schools) that produce programs for transmission over the access channels of the local cable system. Nevertheless, local origination brings community goodwill, visibility, and occasional income to a cable system. As the cable systems continue to expand, jobs (and that of the Director of Local Origination) in the production of such localized programming will only increase.

Advancement Prospects

Opportunities for promotion within the local cable system tend to be extremely limited, since most systems are run as distributors rather than creators of programming. Thus, the skills and talents of production personnel are not usually transferable to engineering, management, or sales positions. Some Directors of Local Origination advance their careers by moving on to larger cable television systems, gaining both more responsibility and higher salaries. Others may join corporate television centers or educational, health, or governmental television operations in similar supervisory positions, but at higher salaries. Some may be able to transfer their experience and skills to production supervisory jobs at public TV or commercial stations.

Education and Training

While it may not be considered essential, most Directors of Local Origination have undergraduate degrees in communications or radio-TV production. Some may have graduate degrees in the same. It is highly recommended that applicants have taken courses in television production, particularly gaining experience with a range of up-to-date equipment.

Experience, Skills, and Personality Traits

Most Directors of Local Origination have had some prior television production experience. Many of them have been camera operators, directors, or producers. Generally, Directors of Local Origination are expected to have had three to five years of experience in television production.

Directors of Local Origination must have excellent organizational abilities as well as leadership qualities. They must exhibit some creativity and be able to work with and manage people in a variety of complex tasks. They must be able to supervise the transformation of creative ideas and concepts into visually exciting cable programs.

Unions and Associations

There are no unions that represent Directors of Local Origination. Some individuals in this position may want to belong to specific groups such as the Association of Local Television Stations, the Cable Telecommunication Association, or the larger umbrella organizations supporting the industry, such as the National Association of Broadcasters or the Corporation for Public Broadcasting.

Tips for Entry

1. During your years of technical education, look for intern programs at local television stations (commercial or cable) to gain on-site experience in television production.
2. Apply for production positions, such as camera operators or production assistants, at commercial or public television stations to get the experience necessary for a Director of Local Origination.
3. Get to know your local community, its businesses and groups, by volunteering your services and by belonging to area associations to gain contacts and knowledge about local needs that you will translate into television programming that will satisfy those requirements.

INSTALLER

CAREER PROFILE

Duties: Install receiving equipment for cable or multichannel multipoint distribution service (MMDS) operation or direct broadcast satellite (DBS) service at customers' homes or offices

Alternate Title(s): None

Salary Range: $18,000 to $38,000

Employment Prospects: Excellent

Advancement Prospects: Good

Prerequisites:

Education and Training—High school diploma and technical school training

Experience—School training in technical equipment

Special Skills and Personality Traits—Good interpersonal skills; mechanical ability; physical strength; technical knowledge

CAREER LADDER

```
┌─────────────────────────┐
│       Technician        │
└─────────────────────────┘

┌─────────────────────────┐
│        Installer        │
└─────────────────────────┘

┌─────────────────────────┐
│     Technical School    │
└─────────────────────────┘
```

Position Description

An Installer makes certain that the signal and programming of a telecommunications operation (whether cable or satellite) are received properly in the homes of its subscribers. This is the typical entry-level technical post available at MMDS stations, cable television systems, and DBS operations.

While Installers usually work with subscribers in private homes, they also connect their companies' equipment in apartment houses, hotels, and office buildings. Many small cable and satellite companies contract with special firms that provide installation services. At many of the larger operations, Installers are full-time employees of the cable franchise, the MMDS license holder, or the DBS service. Nevertheless, virtually all systems use contract Installers at one time or another. In particular, Installers working for independent contractors often perform the initial construction work for a cable system, such as digging trenches, relocating telephone poles, and stringing cable between poles.

For cable systems, Installers prepare the customer's home for the reception of the television signal by running wire from a telephone pole or an underground terminal and attaching it to the connector box(es) and television set(s) within the home. An Installer may even perform some of the duties of a technician in checking the equipment to be used.

For MMDS operations, Installers attach a special antenna, called a dish receiver, to the roof of the subscriber's house, test and adjust it to receive the system's signal, and then connect it to the descrambling receiver now attached by wires to the television set(s) in the customer's home. DBS Installers work in a similar manner.

All Installers are responsible for explaining and demonstrating the operation of the system to subscribers as well as detailing for them the available channels and programs. They also perform minor repairs and adjustments at subscribers' homes. As cable television Installers, they may add or delete program services by adjusting customers' cable connections and disconnecting the equipment when requested. For smaller operations, they may even collect payment for installation or service calls when done.

Installers who are employed full time by media companies receive their assignments from the customer service representatives or the dispatcher at the company's main office. However, they report directly to the chief technician or chief engineer, or other designated technical supervisor. Installers who work for independent companies typically receive their assignments from a supervisor working closely with the chief technician of the media company or, in the case of a DBS operation, the retail manager.

Salaries

Installers working directly for cable television, DBS, or MMDS operations are usually paid on an hourly basis. According to authoritative sources within the cable TV industry, hourly rates ranged from $9 an hour for beginners to $19 an hour for experienced Installers with seniority. This amounted to an annual salary range from $18,000 to $38,000 for, generally, a 40-hour, 50-week work cycle. Most Installers also work overtime hours, which are usually paid at a time-and-a-half rate.

Employment Prospects

Opportunities for entry-level positions of Installers are excellent. The continued growth of cable television systems and the ongoing expansion of satellite operations (particularly as they offer customers such newer products as cable Internet access and video-on-demand services) will help to ensure continuous job positions for Installers, as is also true for technicians. It should be noted that the disconnect rate (churn) in many established cable systems can be as high as 33 percent annually. New customers to replace those who have moved away or disconnected to change to satellite operations require new installations (in both cases) and the services of an Installer. Thus, the demand for Installers is constant.

Small companies or systems employ from three to five Installers, whereas at large cable systems and MMDS stations, an installation staff of 25 or more individuals is not uncommon. Nonetheless, the greatest immediate opportunity for beginning Installers remains with independent contracting firms.

Advancement Prospects

Opportunities for advancement to technician positions are good for industrious and responsible employees. Many Installers seek additional electronics training and technical improvement to make the transition to becoming technicians in cable television or satellite operations. Others might move to supervisory construction positions at new systems owned by the parent multiple system operator (MSO), while others might best advance their career by joining competing companies or other independent contractors who offer higher salaries.

Education and Training

A high school diploma and some post–high school education at a technical school are usually required. Training can also be obtained while serving in the military. In addition, many major MSOs and cable television trade associations offer training sessions and seminars.

Experience, Skills, and Personality Traits

Little previous professional experience is usually required for beginning Installers. Newcomers will learn skills on the job from experienced Installers, technicians, and supervisors. Interest and schooling in electronics and in the repair, maintenance, and operation of electronic equipment are key for this post. MMDS operations often require more technical education in broadcast engineering than is usually required for an Installer in a cable system.

Installers must have manual dexterity, mechanical aptitude, and some technical ability with electronic equipment. Candidates should be strong physically, have good health, and have no fear of heights. Since there is close interaction with customers, Installers also have to be courteous and like working with the public. Installers employed by independent contractors must be willing to travel and live away from their homes for periods of time because such companies move freely from city to city.

Unions and Associations

There are no national unions or professional organizations that represent Installers in cable television, DBS, or MMDS operations. Some local and state utility and construction unions, however, do represent them in specific locations.

Tips for Entry

1. Build electronic equipment from hobby kits. Work, volunteer, or intern for a local radio or television station to become familiar with the equipment Installers use.
2. Be sure to participate in group activities in high school, as Installers are in constant touch with the public and need to know how to handle such situations.
3. Upon getting a job as an Installer and gaining some experience, consider joining one of the technical associations as a career advancement move and to make useful industry contacts.

MARKETING DIRECTOR

CAREER PROFILE

Duties: Develop and coordinate all marketing activities for a cable television system or multichannel multipoint distribution service (MMDS) station

Alternate Title(s): Marketing Manager

Salary Range: $27,000 to $80,000

Employment Prospects: Good

Advancement Prospects: Good

Prerequisites:

Education and Training—Undergraduate degree in advertising, communications, or marketing required; graduate degree in business administration preferable

Experience—Minimum of three to four years of experience in telecommunications sales or marketing

Special Skills and Personality Traits—Aggressiveness; leadership abilities; organizational skills; outgoing personality; promotional talent

CAREER LADDER

```
┌─────────────────────────────┐
│       System Manager        │
└─────────────────────────────┘

┌─────────────────────────────┐
│     Marketing Director      │
└─────────────────────────────┘

┌─────────────────────────────┐
│       Sales Manager         │
└─────────────────────────────┘
```

Position Description

A Marketing Director of a cable television system or MMDS operation is in charge of advertising, marketing (including all commercial sales and telemarketing), promotion, publicity, and direct sales to subscribers. The primary goal of a Marketing Director is to get and retain as many customers as is feasible for the organization. Responsibilities include the development of sales campaigns that will reach the largest possible percentage of the potential subscribers in the area covered by the system or station. The challenge is not just in signing on new subscribers, but also retaining their loyalty (and their subscription payments) by guaranteeing their customer satisfaction. The objective is to gain and retain subscribers for the system or station without increasing the overhead.

The Marketing Director is charged with selecting, training, and supervising the sales staff, which may consist of two to more than 20 individuals depending on the size of the system or station. The Marketing Director coordinates and monitors all sales activities, as well as creates and develops sales tools, which may include printed brochures, billboard advertising displays, and Web site ads, to bolster sales efforts.

Marketing Directors also establish advertising rates, discounts, and special offers for program services, all in consultation with the system manager; recommend and research potential new subscriber services, such as pay-per-view programming, home security, and interactive customer response systems; design and monitor research to determine subscriber satisfaction; and create incentive sales plans for sales managers and salespersons.

The Marketing Director also may perform programming duties. With the cooperation of the systems manager, the Marketing Director may research and select the types of basic and premium pay television services the system or the station will offer its subscribers. The person in this position may also pick programs from existing national satellite services, negotiate with pay-TV program companies, or deal directly with suppliers to obtain particular shows.

Marketing Directors generally report directly to systems managers, but not all companies employ Marketing Directors. Systems that have 10,000 or more subscribers are likely to have Marketing Directors. At smaller operations, the marketing chores are handled either by the system manager alone or are divided between the system manager and the sales manager.

Salaries

According to Broadcast Employment Services salary surveys, annual salaries for marketing persons at cable systems in 2004 ranged from $27,000 at a smaller cable television operation to $35,000 yearly at a medium-sized operation to $80,000 for experienced directors with seniority at systems with a large number of subscribers. The mean average annual salary for marketing people in the industry was $45,000.

At systems with a larger market, additional benefits of a company car, a bonus or profit-sharing plan, a reasonable expense account, and a health and pension plan are often provided. In a few instances, the Marketing Director is also paid a commission on overall yearly sales that go above budgetary quotas. Salaries at MMDS operations tended to be slightly lower than those at cable systems.

Employment Prospects

Opportunities for employment at a cable TV system or an MMDS station for Marketing Directors are good. The position is not an entry-level job and usually requires experience in telecommunications marketing from three to five or seven years. In addition, there usually is considerable turnover in this post. As this industry has grown, so have the opportunities at new systems and stations for aggressive and qualified individuals. With this industry expansion there is much more emphasis placed on marketing and providing services to customers. To retain subscribers, more sophisticated marketing techniques are being used. This creates a real need for qualified personnel to lead such efforts. In some cases, talented, experienced sales managers from smaller systems move on to larger systems as Marketing Directors.

Advancement Prospects

While opportunities for advancement are good, the competition is stiff. By their very nature, most Marketing Directors are ambitious and seek new challenges and opportunities in telecommunications. When they achieve a successful sales record and high profits for one company, they frequently move to a similar, but higher-paying, position with a different operation. Still others may become system managers at their company or in similar or smaller markets. Successful Marketing Directors may also move into more responsible marketing or programming positions at the headquarters of cable TV multiple system operations (MSOs), or join one of the larger pay television services, such as Home Box Office (HBO) or the Discovery Channel.

Education and Training

An undergraduate degree in advertising, communications, or marketing is required at all companies. At the large urban organizations, a master of business administration (M.B.A.) is an additional requirement. Courses in sales management can be useful. As an additional needed tool, training in computer science is necessary, since customer service and billing operations are totally computerized, as well as most management information systems (such as tracking and service subscriber lists).

Experience, Skills, and Personality Traits

At the smaller systems or stations a minimum of three years of previous experience in marketing or telecommunication sales is usually sufficient. At the larger systems, this experience requirement may extend to five to seven years. Much of this experience can be gained in the position of a sales manager at the smaller operations.

Marketing Directors have to be aggressive and capable of providing leadership and motivation to a diverse group of salespersons. Candidates for this position must be well organized and have some background in sales. A flair for promotion and publicity, along with a good instinct for logistics, research, and statistics, are additional necessary traits. Above all, they need to be outgoing and have a positive personality.

Unions and Associations

While there are no unions that represent Marketing Directors, many individuals in this position belong to such industry associations as the National Cable Television Association (NCTA), Cable and Telecommunications: A Marketing Society, or the Cable Telecommunication Association. Some female Marketing Directors (as well as women in other positions in the industry) may find it worthwhile to belong to Women in Cable and Telecommunications (WICT).

Tips for Entry

1. While earning your degree in advertising, communications, or marketing, be sure that you include courses in sales management as well.
2. Take computer classes as a matter of course, and look at intern programs with companies that may be able to combine actual experience in sales and involvement with computer systems.
3. Check out intern programs with local television or cable satellite stations to gain hands-on experience with television production processes.

SALES MANAGER

CAREER PROFILE

Duties: Responsible for all sales at a cable television system or multichannel multipoint distribution service (MMDS) company

Alternate Title(s): Sales Director

Salary Range: $50,000 to $130,000

Employment Prospects: Good

Advancement Prospects: Good

Prerequisites:

Education and Training—High school diploma essential; college degree in advertising, business administration, or communications preferable

Experience—Minimum of two to three years in sales

Special Skills and Personality Traits—Administrative and leadership qualities; high initiative and persistence; dependability; organizational talents; sales knack

CAREER LADDER

```
┌─────────────────────────────┐
│     Marketing Director      │
└─────────────────────────────┘

┌─────────────────────────────┐
│       Sales Manager         │
└─────────────────────────────┘

┌─────────────────────────────┐
│        Salesperson          │
└─────────────────────────────┘
```

Position Description

A Sales Manager is responsible for all of the sales activities of a cable television system or MMDS operation. This sales thrust is devoted to convincing from 3,000 (low market stations) to 300,000 or more (larger urban stations) potential individual customers to purchase the company's various program services.

The Sales Manager typically reports directly to the marketing director or, in smaller systems that do not have a marketing director, to the system manager. The Sales Manager hires and instructs all the salespersons employed by the company. Depending on the size of the company, a Sales Manager may have a staff of three to more than 20 salespersons who telemarket (sell by phone), sell in the field, or sell company services over the Internet. Part of the responsibility of the Sales Manager is to assign these individuals to particular areas or accounts and directly oversee their daily activities. The Sales Manager will work with newly hired individuals to ensure they understand fully the company's services and policies and work with them to develop methods on how to sell these services effectively to potential subscribers. The Sales Manager will interact directly with each salesperson to develop a selling technique that is appropriate.

In addition, the Sales Manager informs all salespersons of any changes in discounts, organizational policies, prices, and special offers and implements and monitors incentive sales plans for the salespersons. Besides maintaining records on each salesperson's progress and activities, the Sales Manager also recommends price adjustments and new program services to the marketing director.

Sales Managers often participate in consumer sales on an individual or company basis. In so doing, Sales Managers actively sell to and service individual current subscribers as well as new subscribers, at times initiating bulk sales to apartment houses or multiunit buildings. Sales Managers are supposed to spend more than half of their time aggressively selling program services to potential subscribers.

Working with the marketing director or system manager, Sales Managers outline sales campaigns and set forth the goals and quotas for specific geographic areas as well as for individual time periods. They devise strategies for reaching potential customers and convincing them to subscribe. They also develop methods of persuading current customers to purchase additional program services. Through their continuous contact with the public, Sales Managers can assess the effectiveness of the company's sales strategies, advertising, and displays and then make recommendations to the marketing director (or the system manager).

Salaries

Sales Managers at cable television organizations and MMDS companies usually are paid in any or all of three ways: with a relatively small salary, a commission on each sale, and a "bonus" payment for each commissionable sale made by salespersons in their department. The actual annual salary for Sales Managers in cable TV ranged from $50,000 to $130,00 or more during 2004, according to surveys conducted by Broadcast Employment Services. Salaries at MMDS companies tended to be comparable to those at cable TV organizations. In addition, Sales Managers often receive health insurance and vacation benefits, along with a company car and/or travel allowance.

Employment Prospects

Opportunities for employment are good at both cable systems and MMDS companies. With the extensive growth of the cable industry has come an increased awareness on the part of system managers and station owners of the importance of increasing the subscriber base.

While the position of Sales Manager is hardly an entry-level post, there is constant need for qualified people with good leadership and sales abilities for this demanding position. Along with the increasing number of media operations opening each year, there is also a considerable turnover in existing sales positions. Many experienced and highly successful salespersons are promoted to this more responsible (and higher-paying) position. Aggressive individuals with some door-to-door (or "outside") sales experience should be able to find jobs as Sales Managers if they also have demonstrable management, organizational, and leadership talents.

Advancement Prospects

There tends to be a high turnover rate in the cable television industry (particularly in sales), and some Sales Managers may find that they can attain more responsible sales or marketing positions within the industry (such as by moving from smaller stations to larger, more diversified companies). The competition is fierce, however, for the higher administrative positions within both the sales departments and the administrative side of the industry. Advancement is achieved only by those with initiative and strong managerial abilities who, in addition, obtain further education and training.

Being naturally ambitious and upwardly mobile, most Sales Managers often seek higher-paying jobs, either by moving to the position of marketing director (or, in some instances, systems manager) within their parent organization (whereby they are assigned to new systems or stations), or by moving to larger-market cable or telecommunications organizations. Other Sales Managers may choose to apply their sales and managerial experience to companies in a nonmedia field.

Education and Training

A high school diploma is essential and some college education is generally required. Courses in business administration, interpersonal relations, marketing, and psychology will prove to be extremely helpful. At the large multiple system operator (MSO) companies, a college degree is frequently required. Nonetheless, even more important than the specifics of post–high school education, the ability to motivate, lead, and train a sales staff is vital. Thus, leadership and management capabilities are paramount qualities needed in a winning Sales Manager.

Experience, Skills, and Personality Traits

This position is not an entry-level post. A bare minimum of two to three years of sales experience with a consistent and reliable performance record is a major requirement, as well as one to two years of sales management experience. A thorough knowledge of cable or MMDS services and allied sales operations are usually an additional requirement.

Successful candidates must be capable of being aggressive sales persons as well as managers in order to lead by example. They need to be dependable, enthusiastic, persistent, and highly persuasive. Above all, they must be well organized, be consistent in their management techniques, and have a true love of and demonstrable talent for sales work.

Unions and Associations

There are no unions or professional organizations that represent Sales Managers in cable television or MMDS operations. Some may belong to regional associations or societies or one or more of the umbrella national associations, such as the American Advertising Federation or the American Marketing Association, in order to share in industry concerns and to advance their careers.

Tips for Entry

1. While earning your college degree (and even during your high school years), look into internship programs with advertising or marketing firms to gain an understanding of sales organizations and practices.
2. Volunteer or look for intern programs to work at local television stations to obtain practical knowledge of the operations of the industry.
3. Attend advertising or marketing conferences and trade shows in order to network with advertising, marketing, and salespeople. Likewise, look for television industry trade shows to talk with salespeople there and to gain networking contacts.

SYSTEM MANAGER

CAREER PROFILE

Duties: Manage the physical plant and operations of a cable television system or multichannel multipoint distribution service (MMDS) station

Alternate Title(s): General Manager; Station Manager

Salary Range: $35,000 to $150,000 or more

Employment Prospects: Fair

Advancement Prospects: Fair

Prerequisites:

Education and Training—Undergraduate degree; graduate degree in business administration or communications often required

Experience—Minimum of three to five years in business management, preferably within the telecommunications industry

Special Skills and Personality Traits—Good judgment; leadership qualities; organizational skills; sense of responsibility; technical knowledge

CAREER LADDER

```
┌─────────────────────────────────────────┐
│  System Manager (Large System or         │
│  Station); District or Regional Manager  │
└─────────────────────────────────────────┘

┌─────────────────────────────────────────┐
│          System Manager                  │
└─────────────────────────────────────────┘

┌─────────────────────────────────────────┐
│  Marketing Director; Sales Manager;      │
│  Chief Technician; Chief Engineer        │
└─────────────────────────────────────────┘
```

Position Description

System Managers (sometimes called general managers) of a cable television system or MMDS station are responsible for the full management of the operation. They set and implement policy, administer all income and expenses, and are involved in programming, sales, and the technical operation itself.

As the chief operations officer of a small (or moderately-sized) telecommunications firm, a System Manager is charged with managing a program service that may reach from 2,000 to more than 300,000 subscribers or more. In cable television, this person is usually referred to as the System Manager, whereas in MMDS operations this position is known as the station manager. Regardless, the functions of both are similar, and their responsibilities parallel those of a general manager at a commercial or public full-power television station.

The most important aspects of the job are safeguarding the system's (or the station's) valuable license and overseeing the company's revenue growth. For the former the System Manager is tasked with maintaining positive relations with community institutions, civic groups, and local governmental agencies, as well as judiciously supervising the system's or station's news and other local programming. (It should be

noted that network programming is rarely inflammatory, whereas syndicated programs, for example, talk shows, may demand closer scrutiny.) The second major duty requires the System Manager to have a thorough understanding of the syndication marketplace as well as an ability to pick the right shows for the station's marketplace and schedule them in appropriate time periods. Generally, the System Manager determines the types of basic program and pay-TV services to be offered to the system's subscribers, the number of channels to be used, and the fees associated with these services. If a cable system sells advertising, the System Manager, working closely with the sales department, sets rates for the commercials, supervises salespersons in selling the commercials, and then sets the time period for them.

In addition, the System Manager provides forecasts for monthly and annual income and expenses, and both evaluates and approves all marketing and sales efforts. It is usual for the System Manager to hire all employees and monitor their performance. Finally, System Managers must handle customer complaints and any billing or payment disagreements.

A cable system or an MMDS broadcast station operates in compliance with Federal Communications Commission (FCC) regulations as well as other federal, state, and local laws, and it is the duty of the System Manager to see that the operation conforms to these regulations. System Managers have to keep up-to-date about access charges, construction laws, and tariffs and must interact directly with local utility companies and government agencies to provide a public service to the community. Thus, a System Manager is the company's most visible representative within the community and thus is responsible for all customer relations.

In some cases, a System Manager is an owner or part-owner of the operation. In other instances, the manager is a salaried employee who reports to a board of directors. In many companies the System Manager is one of the management team that represents a group owner. Sometimes, a System Manager may also act as the local manager for one or more of the company's systems in any given geographic area.

Salaries

Salaries for System Managers are based largely on the size of the operation, the number of subscribers, and, to a lesser extent, the operation's geographic location. Salaries in cable TV systems can range from an annual low of $35,000 to $40,000 in the smaller systems to as much as $150,000 or more in major markets, according to studies made by Broadcast Employment Services. Station managers at MMDS companies tend to be paid somewhat less than in the cable industry. Many such firms offer excellent benefit plans, including health and pension plans, profit sharing, and sometimes a company car. Most companies offer bonus plans and basic expense accounts as well.

Employment Prospects

Prospects for bright, conscientious, and experienced individuals are fair. While many additional cable and MMDS operations are starting up and providing opportunities, this position is never an entry-level post and demands years of experience for most candidates to become eligible. In some cases, a talented marketing director, chief technician, or chief engineer (from broadcasting) can be elevated into the position of System Manager.

Advancement Prospects

As with employment, opportunities for career advancement are fair, but the competition is intense. Many System Managers relocate to larger, competing systems or stations in other markets with more responsibilities and higher salaries. Some successful managers may be transferred within their own organizations to larger existing systems or to other communities to establish new franchises or licenses. In other instances, System Managers may be promoted to district or regional manager positions within a multiple system operator (MSO), or they may elevate into middle management positions at their parent companies' headquarters.

Education and Training

As in most management positions in telecommunications, an undergraduate degree is required, and an advanced degree is considered desirable. Most System Managers for national MSOs have undergraduate degrees in business administration or marketing. Some of them have graduate degrees in communications, computer science, or electrical engineering.

Experience, Skills, and Personality Traits

A minimum of three to five years in general business management, preferably in telecommunications, is a blanket requirement for this position. Some System Managers have been chief technicians in cable systems or MMDS stations or chief engineers at broadcast station. The engineering experience thus gained is valuable as background for most System Managers. Some others in this job may originate from a marketing and sales background, which is becoming a crucial part of the job of a System Manager.

Applicants for this job should be self-motivated, with solid initiative and leadership abilities. Excellent organizational skills, an appreciation for profits, a strong sense of responsibility, and sound business judgment are other attributes of successful System Managers. They also must boast strong social skills and poise to function effectively with a wide range of community leaders and agencies, as well as to handle situations arising from their company's subscriber base.

Unions and Associations

There are no unions that act as bargaining agents for System Managers. Most cable companies belong to the National Cable Television Association (NCTA), and most System Managers represent their company in this association. They may also belong to a state or regional cable association, such as the Cable Telecommunications Association or the National Cable Television Institute, in order to share mutual concerns and advance their career. Managers of MMDS companies often belong to the Wireless Cable Association to share mutual industry concerns.

Tips for Entry

1. While getting your undergraduate degree, investigate intern programs at local radio or television stations to gain practical knowledge of their operations.
2. Include psychology and sociology courses in your educational program to improve your people skills and knowledge of human interactions.
3. Seriously consider an advanced degree in business, communications, or computer science to gain an edge in your application for a lower management position, and be willing to work several years to get the experience needed for a higher management job such as System Manager.

TECHNICIAN

CAREER PROFILE

Duties: Maintain and service technical equipment at a cable TV system or multichannel multipoint distribution service (MMDS) station

Alternate Title(s): Bench Technician; Maintenance Technician; Plant Technician; Service Technician; Trunk Technician

Salary Range: $19,000 to $50,000

Employment Prospects: Excellent

Advancement Prospects: Good

Prerequisites:

Education and Training—High school diploma and technical school training; college degree frequently required

Experience—Minimum of six months to a year of on-the-job training

Special Skills and Personality Traits—Analytical skills; careful; curious; dependable; technical aptitude

CAREER LADDER

```
┌─────────────────────────┐
│   Chief Technician      │
└─────────────────────────┘

┌─────────────────────────┐
│      Technician         │
└─────────────────────────┘

┌─────────────────────────┐
│       Installer         │
└─────────────────────────┘
```

Position Description

A Technician (sometimes called a plant technician in cable television) is the individual who maintains, repairs, and installs equipment at a cable or satellite system or MMDS station. Technicians usually report to a chief technician or a chief engineer. In smaller operations Technicians may perform an assortment of technical duties. In larger companies Technicians often focus on one of a number of technical areas.

In cable television, the technical priority is on the electronic and physical connection of subscribers' homes to the central originating point of the system (sometimes referred to as the head end) by either coaxial or fiber cable. In such systems, Technicians are responsible for maintaining equipment at both ends as well as the cable itself and all the support equipment along its route. As MMDS stations transmit their signals over the air to be caught by a satellite dish at the subscribers' end, their operations are somewhat simpler than for cable systems. Technicians for MMDS stations are responsible for the transmission equipment as well as the subscribers' receiving devices. In either case, the Technician must understand fully the television spectrum and have a complete knowledge of amplifiers as well as be capable of

conducting electronic calculations through the use of sophisticated equipment.

In addition to these duties, Technicians service the television production equipment (such as audio consoles, cameras, program switches, and the like). They also have to maintain videotape and satellite equipment.

When the Technician's responsibility is divided up among several people (as in larger cable or MMDS operations), these positions include that of a bench technician, who diagnoses and repairs broken or malfunctioning subscriber converter boxes as well as readying equipment for installation in homes and repairing testing devices. A maintenance technician will repair damaged cable between the support poles (usually telephone poles) as well as fix equipment damaged by bad weather or accidents. Such a technician for an MMDS station will concentrate on repairing amplifiers, pay-TV signal scrambling units, testing equipment, and transmitting antennas.

Another specialized position is that of a service technician, who repairs malfunctions in subscribers' equipment, fixes signal amplifiers, and electronically scans the system to spot potential problems. His or her counterpart at MMDS stations repairs faulty receiving antennas and subscriber descrambling units. Finally, a trunk technician for a cable company rectifies troubles in the main cable lines that transmit the signal and in amplifiers that enhance that signal, as well as wires and maintains the electronic components in the field.

Salaries

According to surveys made by Broadcast Employment Services, salaries for Technicians in the cable television industry in 2004 ranged from $19,000 annually for beginners to $50,000 or more for experienced individuals, with the average annual salary being $32,125. In general, of the specialized technical positions, bench, service, and trunk technicians earn higher incomes than maintenance technicians. The salary level for Technicians at MMDS stations tends to be comparable to those at cable television systems.

Salaries at cable television systems and MMDS companies have risen due mainly to the growing need for Technicians in their organizations, and are now getting closer to similar positions in the broadcast field.

Employment Prospects

The opportunities for employment for Technicians in the cable television industry and at MMDS stations is excellent and is expected to grow about as fast as the average for all occupations through the year 2012. As noted by the U.S. Department of Labor's *Occupational Outlook Handbook,* employment of Technicians in the cable and pay television part of the broadcasting industry should elevate as these systems and companies expand to provide such products as cable Internet access and video-on-demand services for their subscribers. Many small- and medium-sized cable systems and MMDS stations employ five or more Technicians, whereas larger operations may have more than 30 on their staff. Also, besides openings at new systems and stations, there is usually a fairly high turnover in Technician positions, with the result that qualified Technicians are always in demand. Many installers complete additional study and training courses to qualify for promotion to Technician positions.

Advancement Prospects

The prospect of advancement for qualified, enterprising individuals is good. Beginner Technicians frequently start their careers in small stations and, once they have learned skills on the job from experienced Technicians and supervisors, move on to larger operations. As raiding of trained and qualified Technicians by competing companies always occurs, most operations promote from within the organization to fill the resultant vacancies. Some major MSO cable systems pay bright Technicians to attend classes that will qualify them for higher-paying posts. Experienced and highly capable Technicians with back-

ground in all technical areas can be expected to be promoted to chief technicians.

Education and Training

A high school diploma and some technical or electronics trade school training are basic requirements for beginner Technicians. Given the ever-increasing sophistication of the technologies used in the broadcast industry, a college degree is often preferable. Such a degree is a requirement of chief engineers at most large television operations. Some larger MSOs train in-house.

The Federal Communications Commission (FCC) no longer demands the licensing of broadcast Technicians, as the Telecommunications Act of 1996 eliminated this requirement. However, certification by the Society of Broadcast Engineers is a mark of competence and experience and can be gained after successful testing by the society.

Experience, Skills, and Personality Traits

Candidates for beginning Technician positions should have six months to a year of actual on-the-job experience in the technical position being sought. Technicians must be reliable and diligent individuals who have an inquisitive mind, a basic understanding of electronics and physics, manual dexterity, and an aptitude for working with electrical, electronic, and mechanical systems and equipment. They must be able to read and interpret schematic diagrams and be excellent problem solvers and troubleshooters. They must have no fear of heights, since roof or pole climbing and bucket truck aerial work are nearly everyday tasks.

Unions and Associations

There are no national trade unions that act as bargaining agents for Technicians at cable television systems or MMDS operations. Some local and state utility and technical organizations may represent Technicians in particular geographic areas.

Technicians often belong to such associations as the Society for Broadcast Engineers (SBE) and the Society for Motion Picture and Television Engineers (SMPTE). In addition, the Society of Cable Telecommunications Engineers (SCTE) has a program leading to certification as a professional cable television engineer.

Tips for Entry

1. While in high school, be sure to take courses in mechanics, physics, and electronics.
2. Look for work in college radio and television stations to gain hands-on experience.
3. Building electronic equipment from hobby kits is another good way of learning how to read schematics and gaining dexterity with your hands.

DIRECTING

ASSISTANT DIRECTOR

CAREER PROFILE

Duties: Assist the director in television productions

Alternate Title(s): Associate Director

Salary Range: $11,000 to $85,000 or more

Employment Prospects: Fair

Advancement Prospects: Fair

Prerequisites:

Education and Training—Undergraduate degree in mass communications, radio-television, or theater

Experience—Minimum of two years as a television station unit manager, floor manager, or production assistant

Special Skills and Personality Traits—Detail-oriented; comprehension of television production; organizational skills

CAREER LADDER

```
┌─────────────────────────────────────┐
│     Director; Associate Producer     │
└─────────────────────────────────────┘

┌─────────────────────────────────────┐
│          Assistant Director          │
└─────────────────────────────────────┘

┌─────────────────────────────────────┐
│   Floor Manager; Production Assistant;│
│            DGA Trainee                │
└─────────────────────────────────────┘
```

Position Description

The Assistant Director (or AD) supports the director in coordinating the production elements of a television show or a made-for-television film, making certain that performers, equipment, sets, and staff are prepared and in place for rehearsals and shooting. The Assistant Director functions as the director's right hand prior to, during, and following the production, coordinating all deadlines. Usually the Assistant Director is responsible to a production manager at the television station and is assigned to a director on a project basis.

For major productions or films for network television, Assistant Directors come in pairs, a First Assistant Director, and a Second Assistant Director, usually engaged by the independent production company. First Assistant Directors work with the unit production manager to establish and then execute the shooting schedule. Their specialty is knowing the time required to get a shot and then achieving it. They are the people managers within the creative environment, staying close to the camera(s) and the actual shooting. Second Assistant Directors support First Assistant Directors but generally are more involved in logistics and paperwork. They also help move extras around in crowd scenes. In all situations, the Assistant Director's job is to organize the preproduction steps of the project.

Most importantly, Assistant Directors have to ensure that all prerecorded segments, slides, inserts, and electronic titles (which are produced by a Chyron generator) have been assembled and timed in the preproduction stage. Additionally, they aid in the development and preparation of scripts and time rehearsals, blocking the movements of performers and camera shots and prompting performers.

For shoots outside of the station, the Assistant Director scouts locations and works with the unit manager (or second unit director) in arranging transportation, lodging, facilities, and necessary personnel. During rehearsals in the studio, Assistant Directors take extensive notes and transmit the director's requirements to the team.

During rehearsals and the actual production shoot, Assistant Directors are generally in the control room and are in charge of the timing of the assorted elements of the live program or film segment, and relay time cues to the floor manager and other production personnel. On location, Assistant Directors usually direct background action and supervise extras and crowds used as backdrop. They generally are the ones to secure minor cast contracts and releases from extras. If there is no technical director present, Assistant Directors are charged with presetting and readying camera shots and cueing preshot inserts. They will sometimes help the director in the postproduction editing. In addition, Assistant Directors prepare production reports (including actual time spent filming each scene, breaks, and down time due to equipment or personnel problems).

Salaries

Annual earnings in 2004 for Assistant Directors ranged from a low of $11,000 to a high of $85,000, with an average of $37,450, according to a salary survey by Broadcast Employment Services. The smaller-market stations, both commercial and public, with relatively simple news, interview, and entertainment programs, generally paid only low yearly salaries, ranging from $11,000 to $22,000, with an average annual salary of $15,750. Experienced Assistant Directors working for major-market stations command much higher salaries, ranging from $25,000 to $85,000 annually, with a mean average of $43,846.

Those Assistant Directors who fall under the contract union guidelines for freelance live and tape television set by the Directors Guild of America (DGA) had minimum weekly salary rates in 2005 of $3,385 for studio work and $4,738 for distant location work. Their studio workweek is for five days, whereas their location work is for seven days per these union guidelines. These Assistant Directors will work on two or more projects a year as contract personnel and usually are *not* part of the regular station staff.

Employment Prospects

The Assistant Director job is a highly desired post in most commercial and public television stations, as well as in independent production companies, because it often leads to higher production positions. Thus, the competition for such openings among production personnel and trainees is intense.

Most major television productions require more than one Assistant Director on a project-by-project basis (whether it be a television series or a made-for-television feature). Only the larger-market stations and networks (and some of the larger independent production companies) hire Assistant Directors as full-time staff. Since many quality Assistant Directors move on to be directors or producers at smaller-market stations, openings for this position for qualified individuals are often available. However, because of the competition, employment prospects remain only fair.

Advancement Prospects

Assistant Directors are prone to view the job as a stepping-stone to becoming a director or an associate producer, and some of them may obtain such an assignment at smaller-market stations or independent production companies. However, due to competition, only the best Assistant Directors are likely to be elevated. Therefore, prospects for advancement for Assistant Directors are only fair.

Education and Training

Assistant Directors usually need to have an undergraduate degree in mass communications, radio-TV, or theater to even be considered for the job. At some of the smaller-mar-

ket stations, having such a degree may not be a requirement, but employers favor applicants who have had some post–high school training in television production or in the theater. At the large-market stations and networks, however, such a degree is necessary.

On most large-scale network television productions, the Directors Guild of America operates a formal, on-site training program for individuals wanting to become Assistant Directors. The trainees work under the supervision of the unit production manager and the Assistant Directors and provide managerial and administrative support to the actors, crew, and production personnel, as well as assist the Assistant Directors in running the set. By contract, those enrolled in the training program are paid weekly rates from $558 to $686 depending on the length of the production.

Experience, Skills, and Personality Traits

Most employers in major market stations or independent production companies require a minimum of two to three years of experience in production positions (usually as unit managers or floor managers) for advancement to Assistant Director. In some cases, experienced and successful production assistants may be elevated to this post.

In addition to having a sound background in all aspects of television production, Assistant Directors must be familiar with such technical equipment as production switchers and Chyron Infinits (the electronic character generator that makes the words that appear on the screen). In addition, they must be highly organized and quite detail oriented to handle the complex elements involved in working on a television program, series, or telefilm. Above all, they must be inventive and capable of dealing with a variety of other creative and technical people within a stressful environment.

Unions and Associations

For Assistant Directors working at the smaller-market stations or on many regular television programs, there is no union or professional organization that represents them. However, for most major made-for-television films, specials, extended series, and other major productions, the Directors Guild of America does represent them and sets up contract guidelines for their work and earnings.

Tips for Entry

1. While in high school or college, become involved in any aspect of filmmaking available to you, such as creating student films with a video or digital camera, to learn the process.
2. Accept any entry-level job on a television production to understand how the television production process works and to make industry contacts.
3. The Directors Guild of America training program is a great entry into becoming an Assistant Director.

DIRECTOR

CAREER PROFILE

Duties: Integrate all creative and technical components of a television production into a completed program

Alternate Title(s): None

Salary Range: $10,000 to $160,000 or more

Employment Prospects: Fair

Advancement Prospects: Good

Prerequisites:

Education and Training—Undergraduate degree in mass communications or radio-television

Experience—Minimum of two years in television production

Special Skills and Personality Traits—Creativity; motivational talents; organizational and leadership abilities; technical knowledge of television production

CAREER LADDER

```
┌─────────────────────────────────┐
│            Producer             │
└─────────────────────────────────┘

┌─────────────────────────────────┐
│            Director             │
└─────────────────────────────────┘

┌─────────────────────────────────┐
│ Assistant Director; Unit Manager;│
│          Floor Manager          │
└─────────────────────────────────┘
```

Position Description

The function of the Director is a vital one in any television production. It is the Director's duty to create from an idea or a script a convincing, coherent, and fascinating program, series episode, or film—and to accomplish it effectively and within budget. Working within a pressure-filled environment filled with crucial deadlines, a Director must be the unifying element during all phases of executing the program. Most Directors spend about half their time planning and the other half rehearsing, shooting, and/or editing. It is the Director's concept that is seen on the television set. If the program is successful, it is primarily due to the Director's talent, ingenuity, and vision.

Yet, to get that success, the Director must collaborate with a large team, including scriptwriters, casting directors, actors, set designers, and cinematographers. Directors are involved in equipment and engineering decisions as well as the production's design elements. These encompass selection of the sets, costumes, choreography, and music as well as conclusions reached about sound and lighting and how many cameras the production requires. Directors interpret the script, convey their concept of the production to set and costume designers, audition and select cast members, review the script with the performers, conduct rehearsals, and direct the cast and the crew during the production.

Working with a floor plan, Directors plot camera shots, equipment placement, and the blocking of the performers for each scene. In short, Directors coordinate all the elements, facilities, and people during rehearsal and the actual production and instruct the studio or location crew and talent through to the conclusion of the production.

During planning, rehearsals, and shooting of dramatic or comedy television series, Directors usually spend the first two days going over the script with cast members, plotting camera angles, screening the edited version of the previous week's show, and, on the second day, working with the performers on the set. The third day is a camera rehearsal where performances and camera angles are integrated, and the fourth day is typically one more rehearsal and then two (or three) takes of the entire show. During this process Directors oversee the production and the engineering personnel from a control room, communicating with the set via headphones. The fifth day is devoted to screening and working with the editor in selecting the best reading of each line in the script for the final version to be broadcast. At this point, Directors must ensure that all the preplanned creative and technical elements are combined into a polished production.

If a single Director handles an entire series or shares it with one or more other Directors, a season-long contract with the station or network is common. Most television sitcoms work with several Directors who are paid per episode and may be guaranteed a particular number of installments per season. For TV soap operas, the same routine is used but compressed to produce five shows weekly. Several Directors may share duties on a single daytime drama series, shooting one or two days and prepping on the others. As soaps run for years, principal Directors are typically hired as staff. In made-for-television films, of course, Directors work directly on the set during the shoot.

For news programs and documentaries, the Director's role is somewhat different. It is the producer who usually determines what stories and events will be covered and what prerecorded footage is utilized. The Director reviews the script, screens as many of the edited taped stories as possible, prepares for any live interview segments, and then organizes these pre-edited pieces and studio elements into a unified broadcast.

Talk shows are generally recorded or broadcast live, one per day (or in some cases of a condensed schedule, two or even three per day). Rehearsal usually precedes the recording or live broadcast by an hour or so. Directors for talk shows are usually hired for the entire television season and are paid a weekly salary as freelancers. Game shows are usually recorded in batches of three to five half hours per day, typically for several weeks running. Then the staff prepares more game material for the next group. Typically, a Director is paid per week of completed programs on a freelance contract.

Directors are employed as staff members by all networks and virtually every television station. A Director is usually assigned to a producer for a particular program, series episode, or film, but sometimes assumes the producer's job as well. At some smaller stations, one or two staff Directors may handle all locally produced programs. At others, a single Director may be responsible for a continuing program or series, or may specialize in one particular format, such as news or sports. Independent production companies also employ staff Directors or hire freelancers for specific projects.

Salaries

Annual earnings for Directors of television productions in 2004 ranged from a low of $10,000 to a high of $171,000, with an average salary of $34,326, according to a salary survey by Broadcast Employment Services (BES). The smaller-market stations, both commercial and public, generally paid low yearly salaries to Directors, ranging from $12,000 to $37,000, with an average of $19,309. In the largest-market stations and networks, per-year salaries for Directors ranged from $10,000 to $171,000, with an average of $45,316, according to the same BES salary survey for 2004.

The Directors Guild of America (DGA) sets minimum rates for member Directors for both motion pictures and television work. Their rates are based on the length and type of program on which the Director is working, and on whether it is a non–prime time production or a nonnetwork production. For network prime time shows of a half-hour duration, for example, Directors must have a minimum one-time fee of $19,361 for a guaranteed seven days of employment on the project, according to the DGA contract covering the year from July 1, 2004, to June 30, 2005. For a two-hour show, the rate jumps to $92,056 with a guaranteed employment of 42 days. For a nonnetwork or network non–prime time two-hour production, the rate drops to $34,429, with a guarantee for 24 days of employment. Separate guidelines are in place for shows of durations between these two, as well as the making of trailers, promos for shows, and other types of programs. The guild also has guidelines for overtime, holidays, time off, and other member benefits.

Employment Prospects

Most commercial and public stations employ two to six or more Directors. The job requires considerable experience. Thus, the competition is always strong. Most Directors in television are promoted after working several years as assistant directors, floor managers, or second unit directors. The increased number of independent production companies and expansion of cable television operations provide further employment opportunities for Directors. Therefore, despite the intense rivalry among candidates for this position, overall chances of becoming a Director are fair.

Advancement Prospects

Some television Directors regard their position to be the crown of their successful career. However, a considerable number of other Directors become producers or accept more responsibility as producers-directors. Directors looking to become producers or producers-directors usually obtain one of these positions at a smaller-market station at more salary, or they may move into comparable positions at independent production firms. Some Directors specialize in a particular program genre, becoming experts at directing news, sport, variety, or cultural shows, and, for their expertise, they generally command higher salaries. Thus, in general, chances for advancement to higher-paying directing jobs or producing positions are good.

Education and Training

An undergraduate degree in communications or radio-TV is usually required for being signed on as a Director. Many Directors have some education in theater or film and even a degree from a film school, while others may come from the journalism field. A broad educational background, typically in liberal arts, is extremely useful for Directors, who must work on productions involving a wide range of subjects, styles, and formats.

The job of Director is not an entry-level one, and very few Directors are hired as such straight out of college, film school, or broadcast training school. Training to become a television Director is as fixed in its parameters as it is for theatrical feature films, and many Directors work in both fields. Training can be gained from workshops and seminars that the Directors Guild of America conducts for its members.

Experience, Skills, and Personality Traits

Directors have to know exactly what they are doing, which means they must be seasoned in nearly all aspects of filmmaking and television production. Many Directors gain such know-how while working as a production crew member, such as camera operator, floor manager, unit production manager, or, eventually, assistant director. They also have to have an innate respect for the script. As veteran director Mel Damski points out, "I think the best way to become a director is through screenwriting. . . . Many directors come from cinematography, from acting, and from the stage. There are a lot of different ways to approach it. The important thing is you've got to understand the story. If people go into directing thinking it's all about getting sexy shots and clever angles, they are going to miss the boat."

Directors need to have a mix of creative talent, outstanding technical knowledge about film and television production, good organizational skills, and the ability to motivate people. They have to be self-confident and have a clear vision of their production. They must have fast reflexes to give instructions to numerous people working in a variety of tasks under severe time constraints. Above all, they must act decisively under tremendous pressure, be creative and flexible, and have an excellent eye for the composition of images that will appear in the final product.

Unions and Associations

Directors who work for the networks, most major-market stations, and independent production companies are usually members of, and are represented by, the Directors Guild of America (DGA). Other than the DGA, there is no union or professional organization that represents Directors.

Tips for Entry

1. During your educational years, get involved in any aspect of moviemaking available to you, such as creating student films.
2. Consider internship programs at television stations to learn the specifics of television production.
3. Join the Directors Guild of America, as their training programs are probably the best preparation, other than a film school education, for becoming a television Director.

EDUCATION

DIRECTOR OF INSTRUCTIONAL TELEVISION (ITV)

CAREER PROFILE

Duties: Administer an instructional television operation at an educational institution

Alternate Title(s): Assistant Director of Media; Director of ETV; Director of Instructional Services; Director of ITV and Telecommunications

Salary Range: $25,000 to $75,000 or more

Employment Prospects: Fair

Advancement Prospects: Fair

Prerequisites:

Education and Training—Master's degree in education or telecommunications; doctorate degree desirable

Experience—Minimum of two years in classroom teaching and instructional television

Special Skills and Personality Traits—Excellent language abilities; good administrative and leadership qualities; interpersonal skills; sound educational judgment

CAREER LADDER

```
┌─────────────────────────────────────┐
│     Director of Media Services       │
└─────────────────────────────────────┘

┌─────────────────────────────────────┐
│  Director of Instructional Television │
└─────────────────────────────────────┘

┌─────────────────────────────────────┐
│  Instructional Television Specialist; │
│        Teacher; Producer             │
└─────────────────────────────────────┘
```

Position Description

A Director of Instructional Television (ITV) is charged with the administration and operation of an instructional television fixed service (ITFS) station, a closed circuit television (CCTV) system, and the Internet connectivity at a school, school district, college, or university. An ITV operation provides educational television programs and services to students in a classroom environment to complement and enrich their regular curriculum. ITV operations at many school-owned operations also encompasses in-service teacher training.

There are several categories (or types) of ITV. One concerns learning over a distance. Via video and DVD or television, a teacher, in real time, can conduct "live" instruction to classes far away from the actual classroom. In such instances, videoconferencing, e-mail, and chat room messaging technologies allow for two-way response from these separated students and the teacher, thus improving their interaction. However, due to its generalized content, such fare tends not to hold the interest of the class as a whole and is limited to discussions of unique events or highly specific subject areas.

Another type of ITV uses broadcast programming by taking existing video or DVD programs and bringing them into the classroom via television or videotape or DVD for teaching purposes. The problem is finding available material that is concentrated enough, or having to take only segments of preexisting programs, to cover the specific area of study and maintain classroom attention.

The third major type of ITV involves programming that has been designed specifically for the classroom setting. These programs can be viewed passively via preproduced programs distributed by videocassette or DVD or by video-based broadcast, cable, or satellite to the students or classes concerned. In contrast, interactive ITV can provide opportunities for student-teacher interaction via two-way television with two-way audio, allowing all students to view and interact with the teacher. Thus, instructional television is effective in illustrating a step-by-step process, can transport students to new environments and different times or places, can illustrate (as through animation) complex concepts, and is valuable in introducing, summarizing, and reviewing concepts. It should be noted that ITV programming can easily be applied to many business environments and that there are production firms devoted to providing such material to both educational institutions and business operations.

Some ITV operations are analogous to, although usually smaller than, public television broadcast stations but, unlike them, are frequently involved with Internet-based instruction. The Director of ITV has a similar post to that of a general manager of such a station or the system manager at a cable television system. Directors of ITV oversee the operation and its schedule in accordance with the regulations of the Federal Communications Commission (FCC) and with the policies of the educational institution for which they work.

Directors of ITV are professional educators as much as they are media or television managers. They are dedicated to the use of television and video programming to enhance classroom instruction and efficiency. They team with teachers and heads of departments to identify curriculum areas and courses that would benefit from the use of ITV programming.

Based on the size and range of the operation, a Director of ITV may oversee from four to 10 people. The smaller operations usually include only technical and operations staff, and the Director of ITV is responsible for selecting, renting, or acquiring prerecorded instructional programs for transmission. At larger operations (usually two- and four-year colleges and universities or larger school districts), the Director of ITV is often tasked with the actual production and transmission of original programming. In these instances, directors hire and supervise a staff, which includes engineering, operation, and production individuals, as well as instructors who appear in the shows. As a facet of their duties, directors develop and control a budget for operational expenses, chart and develop research methods to test the effectiveness of instructional television in their specific educational environments, and spread awareness of ITV operations both within the academic system in which they operate and with the public at large.

A Director of ITV may report to a director of media services. Generally, however, Directors of ITV are chiefs of a separate department within the educational institution and are accountable to an assistant superintendent of a school system or a vice president of academic affairs at a school or university.

Public television stations (PTVs) also use directors of instructional services, who, in this instance, are then in charge of all the station's ITV projects. They also supervise the use of the station's educational television schedule and coordinate the acquisition of the station's ITV programs with the schools using the offerings.

Salaries

According the U.S. Department of Labor's *Occupational Outlook Handbook,* in 2002 median annual earnings of instructional coordinators, which Directors of ITV operations

are, were $47,350. The middle 50 percent of these individuals earned between $34,450 and $62,460, whereas the lowest 10 percent earned less that $25,880. The highest 10 percent of instructional coordinators, those usually highly experienced, full-time persons at institutions of higher education, earned more than $76,820. As is typical in the education environment, salaries are based on a combination of the individual's academic degree(s), seniority, and experience. Thus, in general, Directors of ITV at four-year and community colleges tend to earn more than those at the individual lower grades and high schools or school districts. At PTV stations, salaries for this position ranged annually from $23,000 to $95,000 for persons with many years of experience in this position, and the median yearly salary was $48,600.

Employment Prospects

Opportunities for employment as a Director of ITV are only fair. The use of ITV programming in its traditional methodologies has declined somewhat at both the school and college levels with the increased commitment toward computer literacy and the use of Internet resources. This new emphasis in the use of media tools has shifted toward bolstering computer-assisted instruction. In some cases, Director of ITV positions have expanded their scope of responsibilities to include overseeing computer-assisted and Internet instruction.

In many school districts, Directors of ITV have other media, teaching, or curriculum duties. Full-time positions as just Directors of ITV operations are usually available only at colleges, universities, some of the larger school districts, and at some PTV stations. While there has been some lessening of public television programming devoted to instruction, the explosion of cable and satellite stations now available has opened up further possibilities in the area of public television programming. Nonetheless, the number of positions available at PTV stations is limited, and there is little turnover in the field.

Advancement Prospects

Chances for professional advancement for Directors of ITV are only fair. There is little turnover in higher positions of administration, and competition is fierce for these posts. Many Directors of ITV regard their positions as the summit of their successful career. Some, however, may become directors of media services for their own school districts, colleges, or universities, even with the little turnover in such positions. Others may relocate to larger systems in other areas or join health or government media operations as a career advance.

Education and Training

A master's degree is an absolute requirement for this job, whether at a school, community college, or PTV station, and a doctorate is usually necessary for employment at four-year colleges and universities. Most Directors of ITV have had extensive schooling in educational media development, design, and use as well as in television production and telecommunications. Additional coursework in curriculum design, educational psychology, and instruction methodologies is typically mandatory.

Experience, Skills, and Personality Traits

It is key for Directors of ITV to have a solid background in classroom teaching, particularly in school systems that require actual participation in classroom instruction. Thus, candidates for this position should have at least three to four years of classroom teaching and some instructional television experience.

Directors of ITV must have sound educational judgment as well as superior speaking and writing abilities. Directors also must possess excellent interpersonal skills to deal with colleagues and subordinates. They need to be both organized and persuasive and possess strong administrative and leadership talents.

Unions and Associations

There are no national unions that represent Directors of ITV for bargaining purposes. However, as teachers or faculty members, they are represented by the American Association of University Professors (AAUP), or the American Federation of Teachers (AFT), or the National Education Association (NEA). Many Directors also find it useful to belong to the Association for Educational Communications and Technology (AECT), in particular, to its Division of Telecommunication.

Tips for Entry

1. Take courses in education and psychology to enhance your background in television production and communications.
2. Consider working for or interning at a public television station to understand the techniques used in educational programming.
3. Consider subscribing to the *Interactive TV Today* newsletter for information on the business of interactive television as used in both education and business. The newsletter's Web site is http://www.itvt.com.

INSTRUCTIONAL TELEVISION (ITV) SPECIALIST

CAREER PROFILE

Duties: Coordinate the use of instructional television programs at a school, school district, or public broadcasting station

Alternate Title(s): Education-Utilization Specialist; ITV Coordinator; School Services Assistant (public television)

Salary Range: $20,000 to $40,000

Employment Prospects: Fair

Advancement Prospects: Fair

Prerequisites:

Education and Training—Undergraduate degree in education minimum requirement; master's degree in media preferable

Experience—Minimum of one to three years of experience in classroom teaching or as a media librarian

Special Skills and Personality Traits—Good interpersonal and communication skills; leadership qualities; organizational abilities

CAREER LADDER

```
┌─────────────────────────────────────────┐
│   Director of Instructional Television   │
└─────────────────────────────────────────┘

┌─────────────────────────────────────────┐
│   Instructional Television Specialist    │
└─────────────────────────────────────────┘

┌─────────────────────────────────────────┐
│   Elementary/Secondary School Teacher;   │
│            Media Librarian               │
└─────────────────────────────────────────┘
```

Position Description

An Instructional Television (ITV) Specialist maximizes the effective use of televised programs and telecommunication resources in a school district or a regional educational agency. Specialists also work at individual elementary and secondary schools, where they collaborate with classroom teachers to map out and help implement techniques to make the learning process more incisive and effective with the use of instructional television programming.

ITV Specialists are employed directly by a school district or a school system. They interact largely with elementary and middle (junior high) school teachers. Sometimes they are assigned to function at a public television station, and some of them may become full-time employees of the station. ITV Specialists are not employed in institutions of higher education.

Usually based at a school district office or administrative headquarters, ITV Specialists allocate most of their workday to their work in schools and classrooms, helping teachers gain full use of television programs in an educational setting. They conduct training programs for teachers on the use of instructional television, either by televised sessions or in person. They seek to instill a team-teaching approach in which an instructor appearing in an ITV prerecorded program will supplement what the classroom teacher has taught by presenting informative and highly visualized television presentations of the coursework.

ITV Specialists also prepare and distribute lesson guides, manuals, and other materials for use by the classroom teacher. The teacher then prepares the students for the TV lesson, oversees the actual viewing of the program, answers questions and leads discussions, makes assignments, and gives periodic tests on the material. In this process, ITV Specialists help classroom teachers and curriculum specialists to acquire, preview, and select appropriate ITV fare. They develop the scheduling of ITV transmissions with classroom teachers and administrators, and they conduct research and evaluations as to the extent and effectiveness of the use of ITV programs in the classroom.

Some large school districts may employ more than one ITV Specialist, assigning each to specific geographic locales or grade levels. In smaller systems, the tasks of an ITV Specialist may be combined with the duties of other media employees, such as the media librarian.

ITV Specialists usually report to a director of instructional television or a director of media services of the school district or system. The position of ITV Specialist is seldom a supervisory job.

Salaries

Earnings for ITV Specialists range from about $20,000 annually for relatively inexperienced individuals to $40,000 or more yearly for those with experience and seniority, according to professional estimates. As in other educational environments, salaries are based on the level of academic achievement, teaching status, and seniority. Individuals with a master's degree and substantial experience in a school system usually earn more, particularly in large urban systems. At public television stations, ITV Specialists usually earn higher salaries than those of their peers in school systems.

Employment Prospects

It is generally the larger school districts and systems that employ full-time ITV Specialists. Many smaller districts combine their duties with those of either the audiovisual or the media librarian. There is not much turnover in the field.

However, it is estimated by the Bureau of Labor Statistics that employment of instructional coordinators is expected to grow faster than the average for all occupations through the year 2012. The Bureau's *Occupational Outlook Handbook* goes on to state that instructional coordinators, such as ITV Specialists, will be instrumental in training the teacher workforce to improve the quality of education, and that the demand for these workers will increase. Nonetheless, in the short term, budget cuts at many school districts and systems may negatively affect employment to some extent.

Advancement Prospects

Most ITV Specialists are professional teachers who seek or are assigned to this position. Their career progress often is reliant on them increasing their fields of competence or enhancing their administrative abilities in the system.

There is only a fair chance of advancement to the next level, the more responsible position of director of ITV, and the competition for these jobs is heavy. Those ITV Specialists who look to make this career advancement need to investigate further education, as doctoral degrees are often mandatory for directors of ITV. ITV Specialists may advance their careers by moving to larger school systems and from there to colleges, universities, or community colleges. Some specialists may find job opportunities in national educational organizations, which occasionally employ specialists in ITV.

Education and Training

An undergraduate degree in education is an absolute requirement, and a master's degree in media or telecommunications is preferable. In addition, coursework in curriculum design, educational psychology, and media and television production are necessary to obtain this position. Some in-service training or seminars in ITV use are frequently required. This position usually requires basic teaching credentials.

Experience, Skills, and Personality Traits

One to three years of classroom teaching and some hands-on work in television, video, or other media production and/or use are preferable as experience for this job. This experience may be gained by employment at an organization producing ITV programs or in a classroom where extensive use is made of such ITV and media programs. Work as a media librarian with ITV responsibilities for at least one or two years is also considered sufficient background by most school district employers.

ITV Specialists must be keen believers in the use of television and video and DVD programs in the educational process. They need to have superior interpersonal and communication skills. They should exhibit leadership qualities and be very well organized. Above all, they must love to teach.

Unions and Associations

There are no unions that serve as representatives or bargaining agents for ITV Specialists. As teachers, however, they may be represented by the American Federation of Teachers (AFT) or the National Education Association (NEA). Many ITV Specialists find it useful to belong to the Association for Educational Communications and Technology (AECT) and its Division of Telecommunications, and the Association of Visual Communicators (AVC) to share with their peers mutual concerns and to maintain contacts that may be useful in the advancement of their careers.

Tips for Entry

1. While in college, seek work at a college publication, television station, or radio station to hone your technical and interpersonal skills in a work environment.
2. Take additional coursework in television and media production if possible, or seek an intern program that will enable you to gain this experience.
3. Check out industry publications, such as the newsletter available from *Interactive TV Today* (which can be found on the Web site http://www.itvt.com) for information about technical developments in the field, trends, and business opportunities that are shaping the industry.

ENGINEERING

ASSISTANT CHIEF ENGINEER

CAREER PROFILE

Duties: Responsible for day-to-day operation, maintenance, and scheduling of a television station's equipment and facilities

Alternate Title(s): Assistant Director of Engineering

Salary Range: $35,000 to $85,000

Employment Prospects: Fair

Advancement Prospects: Good

Prerequisites:

Education and Training—Undergraduate degree in electrical engineering or allied field is required; advanced engineering degree is desirable; training in broadcast equipment; Federal Communications Commission (FCC) license; certification

Experience—Five to seven years as an engineering supervisor

Special Skills and Personality Traits—Administrative and organizational abilities; leadership talents; technical abilities

Special Requirements—A restricted radio telephone operators permit from the FCC is required, as well as certification from one of the engineering industry certification study programs.

CAREER LADDER

```
┌─────────────────────────────┐
│      Chief Engineer          │
└─────────────────────────────┘

┌─────────────────────────────┐
│  Assistant Chief Engineer    │
└─────────────────────────────┘

┌─────────────────────────────┐
│  Engineering Supervisor      │
└─────────────────────────────┘
```

Position Description

As the second in command within the engineering department of a commercial or public television station, the Assistant Chief Engineer reports directly to the chief engineer and is tasked with the daily operation of the station and scheduling its engineering employees. Under the direction of the chief engineer, the Assistant Chief Engineer also puts into operation the department's budget and policies.

In gearing up for a new television show, the Assistant Chief Engineer advises program and production personnel on the technical aspects of the planned offering, and then puts into operation the technical support system needed. Assistant Chief Engineers also assist the chief engineer in developing technical designs and specifications and are accountable for (or oversee the creation of) the documentation needed for the installation or modification of equipment.

Also, the Assistant Chief Engineer aids in the determination of the satellite or land connecting services needed for program distribution, orders them from carriers, and keeps up with the latest broadcast equipment specifications, their vendors, their prices, and the availability of such equipment. Assistant Chief Engineers are the pivotal coordinators who mesh personnel and schedules to meet the continuously changing demands of television operations. They must anticipate all possible contingencies in the studio and at the transmitter and create policies and procedures to minimize any technical downtime. They oversee equipment replacement and modification and assist in installing new equipment. Usually the Assistant Chief Engineer purchases engineering supplies, conducts transmission tests, and inventories materials.

In fulfilling these duties, Assistant Chief Engineers generate, process, update, and keep records and documentation of all service quality issues that relate to local channels and their programming. They interact with site and station engineers and supervisors to troubleshoot and remedy issues of local channel quality and other technical difficulties. Assistant Chief Engineers are typically the station's experts in computerized engineering equipment, directly supervising its installation and integration into the operation's engineering system. They also train employees in these tasks.

The Assistant Chief Engineer supervises the master control, editing, and transmitting operations and conducts test to ensure that the station is functioning in accordance with Federal Communications Commission (FCC) regulations. Finally, the Assistant Chief Engineer always serves as a backup for other engineering supervisory personnel.

Salaries

Earnings for Assistant Chief Engineers are comparatively good in broadcasting. At commercial television stations, they may range from $35,000 annually at those serving smaller markets to $85,000 or more at larger-market stations. Public television salaries are somewhat lower, ranging from $25,000 annually at small-market stations to $65,000 or more at larger-market stations.

Employment Prospects

Opportunities for employment as Assistant Chief Engineers (or advancement to that post) in commercial or public television are only fair. There is little turnover in this post, and in the smaller-market stations the engineering supervisor in charge of transmission of programs usually takes on the duties of an Assistant Chief Engineer. In bigger-market stations, positions do open up, but the competition is strong.

Positions in cable television, satellite, and multichannel multipoint distribution service (MMDS) operations do become available, and many educational, governmental, and health production units need management-level technical workers who have some broadcasting experience. The increased call for engineering personnel in all areas of broadcast and nonbroadcast operations expands this market for ambitious and qualified people.

Advancement Prospects

Most Assistant Chief Engineers seek advancement to the position of chief engineer. Some move to a smaller-market station to assume a more responsible role and receive a higher salary. Still others join independent production organizations or take positions as chief technicians in cable, satellite, or MMDS companies. Another option is to become chief engineer at a low-power television (LPTV) station. Because of the relative lack of experienced engineering professionals with broadcasting backgrounds, Assistant Chief Engineers have a good chance of advancement.

Education and Training

Nearly every Assistant Chief Engineer must have an undergraduate degree in electrical engineering, physics, or a related science. Some training by equipment manufacturers or at technical schools is necessary.

Special Requirements

Assistant Chief Engineers must have a restricted radio telephone operators permit from the FCC (though the FCC has relaxed this requirement for most other types of broadcast engineers). They are also required to have completed a study program and received a certificate from one of the industry certification programs, such as those operated by the International Society of Certified Electronics Technicians (ISCET) or the Society of Broadcast Engineers (SBE).

Experience, Skills, and Personality Traits

A minimum of five years of experience encompassing all aspects of broadcast technology (mainly, but not always, in the position of an engineering supervisor) is usually required of all aspiring Assistant Chief Engineers. To achieve that position, an individual needs to have a thorough understanding of current television systems and components of UHF television transmitters and associated maintenance, experience and training with video, audio, and RF signal processing equipment, both analog and digital, as well as a complete familiarity with computer networking. Also, a full comprehension of FCC technical regulations is mandatory.

The applicant also must possess supervisory and leadership capabilities, needs to be well organized and budget conscious, and must be capable of working and dealing with a wide variety of staff and vendors.

Unions and Associations

Assistant Chief Engineers are usually considered part of management and, as such, are not represented by any union. However, at some time in their career they most likely belonged to either the International Brotherhood of Electrical Workers (IBEW) or the National Association of Broadcast Employees and Technicians (NABET). In addition, most Assistant Chief Engineers belong to one or more of the professional television engineering societies, such as the Society of Broadcast Engineers or the Society of Motion Picture and Television Engineers (SMPTE).

Tips for Entry

1. While the best college degree for this position is that of an electrical engineer, it is also key to be computer literate and to have good communication skills.
2. Look for internship programs at local television stations or college television stations to learn the basics about television broadcasting.
3. Start in a small-market station or a nonunionized facility or begin with a production firm to gain experience in production and engineering.

AUDIO ENGINEER AND VIDEO ENGINEER

CAREER PROFILE

Duties: Operate electronic video and audio equipment at a television station, production center, or facilities company

Alternate Title(s): Audio Technician; Sound Technician; Video Technician

Salary Range: $17,000 to $65,000

Employment Prospects: Good

Advancement Prospects: Good

Prerequisites:

Education and Training—High school diploma required; technical school training necessary; bachelor's degree preferable; certification recommended

Experience—Minimum of one year as an engineering technician

Special Skills and Personality Traits—Quick reflexes; technical ability; versatility

Special Requirements—A certification from one of the engineering industry certification study programs may be required.

CAREER LADDER

```
┌─────────────────────────────────────────┐
│      Engineering Supervisor;             │
│  Technical Director; Cable Technician    │
└─────────────────────────────────────────┘

┌─────────────────────────────────────────┐
│          Audio/Video Engineer            │
└─────────────────────────────────────────┘

┌─────────────────────────────────────────┐
│         Engineering Technician           │
└─────────────────────────────────────────┘
```

Position Description

Audio/Video Engineers are tasked with the operation of all electronic controls of audio and video equipment employed in a television station's studio or on-location production. They both set up and operate such equipment as microphones, sound speakers, video screens, projectors, video monitors, recording equipment, connecting wires and cables, sound and mixing boards, and related electronic equipment. Audio/Video Engineers are also employed at corporate television media centers; education, government, and health agencies; concerts; sports events; meetings and conventions; presentations and news conferences; and production facilities firms. Most television engineering departments cross-train personnel to handle both audio and video jobs, but Audio/Video Engineers typically focus on and are more experienced in one of the two functions.

Audio Engineers are in charge of the sound part of a production, which includes voices, music, and special effects. They operate audio and computer equipment to record, enhance, mix, and edit sound, which includes location sound for film, video, and DVD shoots, studio sound recording, and audio postproduction. They set up, test, and operate this equipment in accordance with the acoustical demands of the studio or location. They select, place, and adjust microphones and instruct performers on the proper use of microphones. During production, Audio Engineers monitor audio signals to detect any quality deviations or malfunctions and operate controls to preserve correct sound levels. They prerecord all required material demanded by the script and during production cue in where this prerecorded material is to be used. During videotape or digital editing of a major show, such prerecorded elements, such as music, applause, or other sound effects, may be added to the program, and some portions of the material may be modified to improve the overall sound quality. Audio Engineers also must log and manage all the audio production notes (to be employed in the postproduction process).

Video Engineers are in charge of the quality of the visualization of the production, which includes cameras and lights. They are responsible for the setting up and aligning of cameras and during production controlling their brightness, color, and depth levels. Due to the sensitivity of the equipment, continuous monitoring is necessary to ensure that the best possible image is being captured (and/or broadcast). Besides cameras, Video Engineers handle video recorders, video switches, time base correctors, monitors, character generators, and other assorted video production equipment. Video Engineers must be able to set up video production systems, both remote and at the studio, and guarantee acceptable quality control in the technical setup of the studio, mobile truck, master control playback, and editing and portable equipment.

Working in either specialty, the Audio Engineer and Video Engineer positions are crucial in the production process. Each contributes essential elements to the overall technical quality of the production by providing professional expertise in the use of specialized electronic equipment. They also are in charge of the maintenance of and any necessary repair to the audio and video equipment.

Audio Engineers and Video Engineers usually report to an engineering supervisor who makes the necessary work shift and project assignments. During rehearsals and actual production, Audio and Video Engineers report to the technical director. It is this person with whom they interact to achieve any special sound or visual effects required by the production.

During a studio production, Audio and Video Engineers are based in a control room. For on-location programs or productions, they work in a remote truck that contains all the necessary equipment. During the postproduction phase, Audio and Video Engineers are usually found in the editing area (or bay) or in the control room of the editing suite.

Salaries

According to the *Occupational Outlook Handbook* of the U.S. Department of Labor, median annual earnings of audio and video equipment technicians were $31,110. The middle 50 percent earned yearly between $22,670 (typically employees at small-market stations with one or two years of experience) and $43,950. The lowest 10 percent earned less than $17,710 yearly, and the highest 10 percent earned more than $61,420 (generally experienced engineers with seniority at major-market stations). These figures included both commercial and public television operations. It should be noted that an engineer with a certification from the Society of Broadcast Engineers tends to get a higher salary.

Employment Prospects

Of the 93,000 broadcast and sound engineering and radio operators employed in 2002, 42,000 of them were audio and video equipment technicians, according to the *Occupational Outlook Handbook*. Of these technicians, about 71 percent of these individuals worked in broadcasting. Most television stations employ eight or more Audio and Video Engineers. At least two are assigned to studio productions, one special-

izing in audio and the other in video. Complex studio or on-location productions require several more individuals, particularly in the video area. The explosion of cable television productions has added to the need for qualified people in both video and audio areas. In addition, corporate business, education, government, and health production operations produce television or video programs that require Audio and Video Engineers, as do independent production and postproduction facilities. Altogether, employment opportunities for qualified Audio and Video Engineers are good.

Advancement Prospects

Qualified Audio and Video Engineers are in demand. Those with several years of experience, especially with the latest digital technologies, have good opportunities to obtain engineering posts with greater responsibilities and higher salaries. Some are promoted to engineering supervisors at their own stations, while some move to larger-market stations (or networks) as technical directors. In addition, chances for employment in middle management engineering jobs at production centers of corporations as well as educational, health, and governmental production studios are good. The burgeoning industries of cable television and multichannel multipoint distribution service (MMDS) operations are another source of employment. Another advancement avenue for engineers can be to higher-paying positions at production and postproduction facilities in New York and Los Angeles.

Education and Training

A high school diploma and some training at a technical or vocational school is usually the bare minimum requirement to obtain a job as an engineering technician, from which the applicant may be promoted to an Audio/Video Engineer position at a television station. Many stations require a bachelor's degree in broadcasting, electronics, or the equivalent, and two to three years of related work experience in broadcast television production or electronic repair and maintenance of broadcast television equipment. Other audio/video specialists who are employed at corporate television centers or in education, governmental, or health agencies may have a bachelor's degree in mass communications with no formal education in engineering, but have gained their experience through on-the-job training.

Special Requirements

Some stations may insist that applicants have studied and received a certificate from one of the programs offered by the Society of Broadcast Engineers (SBE) or the Society of Cable Telecommunication Engineers (SCTE).

Experience, Skills, and Personality Traits

A minimum of two to three years of experience as an engineering technician is typically required for promotion to the position of Audio/Video Engineer. This individual must be thoroughly familiar with all audio and video equipment used in television production and must be capable of handling routine maintenance as well as troubleshooting and correcting system problems when they occur.

Most technical directors and engineering supervisors seek technicians who are versatile but display a particular skill in the operation of computerized audio or video equipment. Audio personnel must possess a discriminating "ear" for detail in all areas of sound, and video personnel must have an "eye" for lighting and color mix in video projection. Both jobs call for quick reflexes and strong communication skills, both verbal and written. Both positions involve considerable pressure, so candidates for these posts must be even-tempered and flexible in order to function smoothly in collaboration with artists and producers of each production.

Unions and Associations

Many Audio/Video Engineers in commercial television (and even public television) are members of the National Association of Broadcast Employees and Technicians AFL-CIO (NABET) or of the International Brotherhood of Electrical Workers (IBEW). Some may also belong to such associations as the Society of Broadcast Engineers and the Society of Cable Telecommunication Engineers, or for Audio Engineers, the Audio Engineering Society (AES).

Tips for Entry

1. During your formal education (high school and technical or vocational school), an internship at a television station is a good way to acquire experience and knowledge of the broadcast environment.
2. As both sound and video technology is always changing, continuing education is a must.
3. A business management course somewhere in your educational background would be a good idea, as you will be required to keep logs, notes, and other documentation on work done with each production.

CHIEF ENGINEER

CAREER PROFILE

Duties: Oversee all engineering and technical operations at a television station

Alternate Title(s): Director of Engineering; Vice President of Engineering

Salary Range: $30,000 to $120,000 or more

Employment Prospects: Fair

Advancement Prospects: Fair

Prerequisites:

Education and Training—Undergraduate degree in electrical engineering required; advanced engineering degree preferred; training in broadcast equipment; certification; Federal Communications Commission (FCC) license

Experience—Minimum of five to six years as an assistant chief engineer

Special Skills and Personality Traits—Excellent administrative and organizational abilities; leadership qualities; technical expertise

Special Requirements—A restricted radio telephone operators permit from the FCC is required, as well as certification from one of the engineering industry certification study programs.

CAREER LADDER

```
┌─────────────────────────────────┐
│  General Manager; Engineering   │
│  Management (TV Network)        │
└─────────────────────────────────┘

┌─────────────────────────────────┐
│       Chief Engineer            │
└─────────────────────────────────┘

┌─────────────────────────────────┐
│   Assistant Chief Engineer      │
└─────────────────────────────────┘
```

Position Description

The Chief Engineer is accountable for all of a television station's technical facilities, equipment, and services required to conduct its broadcast and programming business. Chief Engineers report to the station's general manager and are responsible for the administration and supervision of all engineering and operations personnel, as well as for keeping the station on the air without technical interruptions during broadcast times.

Chief Engineers are responsible for all long-range planning of the station's technical facilities, of systems design, and of the budget and purchasing of technical equipment. They have to make certain that all station operations comply with Federal Communications Commission (FCC) regulations and all relevant local, state, and federal laws.

As they are an essential part in the design, construction, and installation of all engineering equipment, Chief Engi-

neers must have in-depth knowledge of digital and analog technologies used in a broadcast environment as well as a thorough understanding of computer and networking technologies. They diagnose causes of transmitter malfunctions and map out preventive maintenance programs for the station facilities to ensure the optimal and effective use of the station's equipment. They coordinate and negotiate any use of outside telecommunications facilities with appropriate utility companies or private agencies and prepare all necessary technical applications, including FCC construction authorization permits, licenses, and the renewal or modification of licenses.

One of the primary functions of the Chief Engineer is managing personnel involved in the complex environment of television engineering. Engineering departments at commercial and public television stations tend to have the largest number of employees, ranging from 10 to more than

75 at major-market facilities. The Chief Engineer interviews, hires, and trains employees; plots work schedules and assigns and directs the work; appraises performances, rewarding and disciplining where needed; addresses complaints and resolves difficulties; and develops and maintains effectual working relationships with the station's other departments.

Chief Engineers must have strong project management skills and have a progressive capacity for thinking and planning for the station's electronic future. Budgeting and planning for new equipment is one of their major tasks. They need to be able to work independently, efficiently, and safely while coping with substantial pressure.

Salaries

Despite their many work obligations, Chief Engineers are paid only moderately compared to other management personnel in broadcast television. Salaries can range from as low as $30,000 annually at the smallest-market stations to $120,000 or more yearly at the largest-market stations. According to a study done by Broadcast Employment Services, in 2004 the average annual salary of engineering technical management in commercial and cable television stations was $66,936. Salaries in public television, generally, are somewhat lower than those in commercial television.

Employment Prospects

Employment opportunities for Chief Engineers are somewhat limited. While there is demand for qualified personnel, a minimum of five years of experience in all aspects of broadcast engineering is essential. Because of the amount of technical expertise necessary for this post, it is often viewed as the climax to a career in engineering, and, as such, there is little turnover for this job.

In contrast, the expansion of cable and satellite systems as well as multichannel multipoint distribution service (MMDS) companies has produced a steady availability of Chief Engineer jobs to be filled, albeit at lower salaries than at commercial stations. In addition, there are other opportunities in educational, health, and governmental production organizations and in the low-power television (LPTV) stations. Altogether, the lack of qualified broadcast engineers provides a potential job market for ambitious and diligent individuals who have the necessary education and experience.

Advancement Prospects

Many Chief Engineers view their position as a successful culmination to their career path. Some, however, may advance that professional standing by moving on to the same position at a higher salary at a larger-market station or by joining one of the large cable television operations. Others may transfer to networks or large production companies to advance both their salary and their careers. A few may be able to move into the position of general managers at smaller-market stations.

Education and Training

Most Chief Engineers have degrees in electrical engineering, physics, or a related science. Some of them may have undertaken graduate work or even earned a graduate degree. All must have had some technical training in broadcast engineering at a school or technical center.

Special Requirements

Chief Engineers must have a restricted radio telephone operators permit from the FCC (though the FCC has relaxed this requirement for most other types of broadcast engineers). They are also required to have completed a study program and received a certificate from one of the industry certification programs, such as those operated by the International Society of Certified Electronic Technicians (ISCET), the Society of Broadcast Engineers (SBE), or other industry groups.

Experience, Skills, and Personality Traits

Chief Engineers must have considerable experience with all types and models of electronic gear, as well as a thorough understanding of the principles of electronics. Television equipment tends to break down, even during transmission, and Chief Engineers have to be ready to act quickly to ensure no interruption of the transmission. They must be able to scan and decipher schematic drawings rapidly in order to solve problems and reach solutions quickly. Their engineering and mechanical skills must be exemplary, as well as their understanding of computer network and operating systems. They need to have a complete understanding of advanced electronics, transmitters, microwaves, translators, and the entire broadcast transmission process. Most television stations require a Chief Engineer to have at least five years of experience as an assistant chief engineer.

In addition, Chief Engineers need a thorough understanding of FCC regulations and must be well informed on all state-of-the-art television equipment. They will have to design assorted technical systems using interrelated components to upgrade the engineering facilities at the station. They must possess both leadership qualities and management skills, as they must administer and keep to budgets. They need to maintain effective working relationships with both their own staff and that of other departments and have good verbal and written communication skills, particularly as they are tasked with preparing reports to upper management and ownership.

Unions and Associations

Chief Engineers are considered to be part of the management of a television station, and, as such, are not represented by any union or bargaining agent. In previous positions, some of them may have been members of the International Brotherhood of Electrical Workers (IBEW) or the National Association of Broadcast Employees and Technicians AFL-CIO (NABET). Upon becoming Chief Engineers, however, most become inactive in such organizations. Many Chief Engineers belong to the Society of Broadcast Engineers or the Society of Motion Picture and Television Engineers (SMPTE) to share mutual concerns with their peers and increase their technical knowledge of broadcast engineering.

Tips for Entry

1. While getting your degree in electrical engineering or an allied field, consider an internship with a local television station to become familiar with the processes of television broadcasting.
2. Explore working in a production company in order to gain some management experience, as this will be required of you when you advance to Chief Engineer.
3. Think about going on for an advanced degree in engineering, as some broadcast organizations will require such educational background for the post of Chief Engineer.

ENGINEERING SUPERVISOR

CAREER PROFILE

Duties: Supervise engineering staff at a television station or production facilities

Alternate Title(s): Broadcast Supervisor/Engineer; Engineering Coordinator; Supervising Engineer

Salary Range: $30,000 to $65,000

Employment Prospects: Fair

Advancement Prospects: Fair

Prerequisites:

Education and Training—High school diploma; one to two years of training in technical or vocational school; undergraduate degree in engineering preferable; certification usually needed

Experience—Minimum of two to three years as an audio/video, maintenance, master control, transmitter, or videotape/digital engineer

Special Skills and Personality Traits—Excellent supervisory talents; good leadership qualities; technical aptitude

Special Requirements—A restricted radio telephone operators permit from the Federal Communications Commission (FCC), as well as a technical certificate from one of the industry certification groups, may be required.

CAREER LADDER

```
┌─────────────────────────────────────┐
│      Assistant Chief Engineer        │
└─────────────────────────────────────┘

┌─────────────────────────────────────┐
│      Engineering Supervisor          │
└─────────────────────────────────────┘

┌─────────────────────────────────────┐
│  Audio/Video, Maintenance, Master    │
│      Control, Transmitter, or        │
│     Videotape/Digital Engineer       │
└─────────────────────────────────────┘
```

Position Description

An Engineering Supervisor directs the daily operation of electronic and technical equipment and the work of operating engineers at a television station or production facility. In smaller-market operations, one or two Engineering Supervisors direct the full engineering staff. In middle-market and major-market stations, there may be four or more Engineering Supervisors to direct the activities of audio/video, maintenance, master control, transmitter, and videotape engineers. In some small- or middle-market stations, the Engineering Supervisor often acts as the assistant chief engineer.

The major duty of this job is to guarantee that all engineering work is performed in a timely manner and according to standard, and that all electronic equipment is properly maintained and operated by the engineering team. An Engineering Supervisor is accountable for the safe, efficient, and effective operation of this equipment. Engineering Supervisors often serve as technical directors of productions for the station. They test and calibrate the equipment to guarantee that the station conforms to Federal Communications Commission (FCC) regulations and guidelines. They supervise preventive and emergency maintenance and repair of all hardware and review all discrepancy and technical reports to spot and correct technical problems. In addition, they supervise the installation of new component parts and/or equipment, especially any computerized electronic gear.

The Engineering Supervisor frequently administers the performance of five or more engineers and acts as the daily manager of the various shifts. The supervisor is responsible for all personnel policies and evaluations and scheduling assignments within each shift. Depending on the size of the station and of the department, the Engineering Supervisor may also be the individual who actually runs the equipment. Usually, however, the person serves as both a manager and a technical backup for all the station's engineering operations.

Salaries

In keeping with their technical and management responsibilities, Engineering Supervisors are relatively well paid. Salaries in commercial television ranged from $30,000 annually at smaller-market stations to $65,000 or more in major markets for individuals with experience and seniority, with a median annual salary of $51,300, according to industry sources.

Employment Prospects

The opportunities for employment as an Engineering Supervisor are only fair. The position is not an entry-level job and requires considerable experience and knowledge of sophisticated electronic and computerized broadcast equipment. While most stations employ four or more Engineering Supervisors, the competition for these jobs is severe. Only the more diligent, competent, and experienced engineers from within the department can advance to this position.

However, positions similar to those in commercial television are available at the larger cable television and satellite systems and at multichannel multipoint distribution service (MMDS) companies. Some similar supervisory positions can be found at educational, governmental, and health television production organizations, as well as in the corporate television industry. In addition, supervisory positions are sometime open at organizations where the equipment is less sophisticated, and the Engineering Supervisor often becomes the de facto chief engineer. Production and postproduction facilities also have openings for Engineering Supervisors.

Advancement Prospects

Prospects for advancement to the position of assistant chief engineer or, in some cases, directly to chief engineer in a station's management hierarchy, are only fair. Those who want to advance must keep abreast of all the new technologies in the field.

Enterprising Engineering Supervisors who are alert, bright, and dedicated and who have earned a reputation in a specific area (such as digital editing, transmission operations, or videotape recording) have the best chance for promotional opportunities. Some supervisors use their technical and people skills to obtain higher-paying positions at larger-market stations, while others may advance by assuming more responsibilities at smaller stations. Some experienced Engineering Supervisors may find career advancement by obtaining better positions at higher salaries in the cable television industry or at production and postproduction facilities companies, which are always in need of qualified engineers and supervisors.

Education and Training

The bare minimum of a high school education and at least two years of training at a technical school is required for the position of Engineering Supervisor. Far more preferable is a bachelor's degree in electrical engineering, physics, or a related field.

Special Requirements

At this level of management, Engineering Supervisors often are required to obtain a restricted radio telephone operators permit from the FCC, as well as a technical certificate from one of the industry certification groups.

Experience, Skills, and Personality Traits

Most candidates for the position of Engineering Supervisor are anticipated to have had two to three years of experience as an audio/video, maintenance, master control, transmitter, or videotape/digital engineer. As they will be supervising individuals in these assorted positions, an Engineering Supervisor needs to have a complete familiarity with these specialties, as well as other broadcast engineering functions. They need to be completely familiar with computerized electronic equipment and should have a reputation for skilled and successful troubleshooting.

They also must have the talent to supervise other engineers in the installation, operation, and maintenance of sophisticated electronic equipment. They need to be able to deal with a wide assortment of technical roadblocks and quickly determine effective solutions. Above all, they must be extremely well organized and resourceful. If working at a facilities company, Engineering Supervisors also have to have good interpersonal skills, as they will be interacting with clients.

Unions and Associations

In most cases, Engineering Supervisors are considered management and, as such, are not represented by any union. Others may be represented by the International Brotherhood of Electrical Workers (IBEW). Some supervisors may find it easier to advance their careers by joining such associations as the Society of Broadcast Engineers (SBE) and the Society of Motion Picture and Television Engineers (SMPTE).

Tips for Entry

1. Every bit of experience is important in building your résumé, so look for intern programs while in high school, technical school, and college to further your experience within the broadcast industry.
2. While intensifying your expertise in a particular television engineering field, also broaden your experience to include all other types of engineering needed at the television station or system in which you work.
3. Join the umbrella organizations of the industry, such as the Society of Broadcast Engineers, in order to make networking contacts and keep apprised of job opportunities throughout the field.

ENGINEERING TECHNICIAN

CAREER PROFILE

Duties: Perform assorted engineering tasks at a television station or production facility

Alternate Title(s): Broadcast Technician; Operating Engineer; Operator Technician; Technical Engineer; Technician

Salary Range: $15,000 to $70,000

Employment Prospects: Good

Advancement Prospects: Good

Prerequisites:

Education and Training—High school diploma; some technical school; associate degree in electronics or related area sometimes required

Experience—Familiarity with electronic and technical equipment

Special Skills and Personality Traits—Mechanical aptitude; problem-solving and analytical skills

CAREER LADDER

```
┌─────────────────────────────────────┐
│        Audio/Video, Maintenance,     │
│   Master Control, Transmitter, or    │
│         Videotape Engineer           │
└─────────────────────────────────────┘

┌─────────────────────────────────────┐
│        Engineering Technician        │
└─────────────────────────────────────┘

┌─────────────────────────────────────┐
│      High School / Technical School  │
└─────────────────────────────────────┘
```

Position Description

The position of Engineering Technician is typically the entry-level job in the engineering branch at a commercial or public television station. Engineering Technicians can also be found working for educational, health, and governmental organizations engaged in television productions, at the larger independent production and postproduction facilities companies, and at low-power television (LPTV) stations.

Engineering Technicians perform a range of technical tasks in one or more units of the television operation. They are responsible for or contribute to the design, development, construction, installation, maintenance, and repair of electronic systems and equipment used at the television station. They install components and systems, collating and summarizing test data in the process. They also handle such hardware as audio switchers and mixers, audio and video testing devices, cameras, lighting equipment, microphones, slide and film projectors, transmission equipment, video and audio tape recorders, and video switchers and their special effects boards. In some cases, they may set up, operate, and maintain equipment that regulates the signal strength, clarity, and range of sounds and colors of the television broadcast, operating the control panels that pick the source of that material. In addition, they collate the engineering records,

including the Federal Communications Commission (FCC) program and transmitter logs, as well as facilities utilization forms and testing and monitoring reports. They regularly maintain an inventory of engineering supplies and replacement parts.

Engineering Technicians typically report to a technical director or an engineering supervisor. When they have shown particular talents, they are often trained to become specific types of engineers used by the station, such audio/video, maintenance, master control, transmitter, or videotape engineers/editors. In any station where camera operators are considered part of the engineering department, Engineering Technicians may be trained for that post as well.

The average television station employs several Engineering Technicians in assorted capacities. Supervisors cross-train them as a rule so that each such person can gain experience in as many technical areas of the station as possible. As the responsibilities of the engineering department are diverse, Engineering Technicians can function in almost any area of the station or production/facilities center. As such, during a production, they may be assigned to the studio, the videotape room, the transmitter, the master control shop, the maintenance shop, or an on-location site outside the station. They may be switched from one camera or studio to another, from film to live programming, or from network to local programming.

Salaries

Earnings for Engineering Technicians are fairly good, particularly considering that their position is usually an entry-level one. According to the U.S. Department of Labor's *Occupational Outlook Handbook,* median annual earnings of Engineering Technicians (sometimes referred to as broadcast technicians) in 2002 were $27,760. The middle 50 percent earned yearly between $18,800 and $45,200. The lowest 10 percent earned less than $14,600 annually and the highest 10 percent earned more than $70,000.

Salaries in public television tend to be lower, according to industry observers. However, salaries for technicians at business television centers and at educational, governmental, and health media operations were comparable to those earned by technicians in commercial television.

Employment Prospects

There are usually more starter engineering positions available than there are qualified candidates to fill them. The average commercial or public television station employs more than 12 Engineering Technicians, and many major-market stations may have 60 or more on their payroll. Opportunities abound also at production and postproduction/facilities houses and at business, educational, governmental, and health media operations. Thus, the opportunities for bright, capable, electronically and mechanically oriented newcomers are definitely good. Most beginner technicians begin their careers in small stations and, once experienced, move on to larger ones. Large operations usually only hire technicians with experience.

Advancement Prospects

The opportunities for advancement to other engineering positions at a station are also good. Any Engineering Technician showing application and thoroughness can anticipate being promoted to one of the station's engineering specialties, such as audio/video, maintenance, master control, transmitter, or videotape engineer/editor after a year or two of gaining experience and knowledge of the ins and outs of broadcast technology.

With additional seasoning, beginning Engineering Technicians can move further up the career ladder to become engineering supervisors or even assistant chief engineers. While some may be promoted within the station to more responsible and higher-paying posts, others may choose to move to better-paying jobs at larger-market stations. However, competition is always stiff at bigger operations. Other technicians seek promotion opportunities in cable television, multichannel multi-

point distribution service (MMDS) operations, or at the larger production and postproduction facilities companies.

Education and Training

A high school diploma and some electronics training at a technical or vocational school is a basic requirement for employment. Some television and cable stations operate intern programs to help train prospective employees. Other stations require an associate degree in electronics or in a related area. Candidates who have studied for and passed a certificate program from an industry organization, particularly with an emphasis on digital technologies, are especially sought by employers. Some stations offer to pay tuition and expenses for courses or seminars to help technicians keep abreast of developments in the field.

Experience, Skills, and Personality Traits

Most stations do not insist on extensive experience for the position of Engineering Technician, as most beginners will acquire proficiency on the job from experienced technicians and supervisors. An interest in and understanding of electronics and repair of mechanical and audiovisual equipment is a plus. A general knowledge of television production technologies and techniques as well as a basic grasp of physics and an ability to read schematic drawings are also helpful, as is a gift for mathematics.

Employers seek alert, ambitious, and diligent people who have a love of electronics and who enjoy working with technical equipment. They need to demonstrate strong problem-solving, analytical, and oral communication skills as well.

Unions and Associations

Many Engineering Technicians in commercial television are represented by the National Association of Broadcast Employees and Technicians AFL-CIO (NABET) or the International Brotherhood of Electrical Workers (IBEW). Some public television employees may be represented by one of these unions, but most of them work at nonunion stations.

Tips for Entry

1. After high school, the best way to prepare for a broadcast Engineering Technician job is to get training in electronics or broadcast technology at a technical school or community college.
2. Find intern programs at local (or college) television stations to acquire a hands-on understanding of broadcast technology and techniques.
3. Take high school courses in math, physics, and electronics in preparation.
4. Set your sights at building electronic equipment from hobby kits as useful experience.

MAINTENANCE ENGINEER

CAREER PROFILE

Duties: Install, maintain, repair, and perform preventive maintenance on all standard technical broadcast equipment at a television station or production facility

Alternate Title(s): Maintenance Technician

Salary Range: $35,000 to $85,000

Employment Prospects: Excellent

Advancement Prospects: Good

Prerequisites:

Education and Training—High school diploma; one to two years of technical school training; certification

Experience—Minimum of one to two years as an engineering technician

Special Skills and Personality Traits—Computer skills; good communication skills; intuition and curiosity; technical aptitude; troubleshooting and problem-solving abilities

Special Requirements—A certificate from an engineering industry organization and a Federal Communications Commission (FCC) general class license or an FCC restricted radio telephone operator permit may be required.

CAREER LADDER

Engineering Supervisor

Maintenance Engineer

Engineering Technician

Position Description

Maintenance Engineers are tasked with the maintenance and repair of all broadcast-related equipment (down to a component level) at a television station, in the field, or at a production facilities operation. They also frequently assist in the installation of new hardware. Under the direction of the engineering supervisor, they perform preventive maintenance on such equipment as audio consoles, cable and cable modems, cameras, computers and other digital devices, film chains, generators, microphones, microwave and satellite apparatus, routers, switchers, video equipment, and videotape recorders. Maintenance Engineers also design, modify, and repair component parts, systems, and elements used in all production and transmission equipment.

Maintenance Engineers are on-the-spot problem solvers and troubleshooters, coping with both minor and major repair problems and often reconstructing existing equipment to upgrade it to conform to present standards and up-to-date technology. They may have to execute bench repairs, modula-

tor repairs, and microwave line maintenance. They conduct system tests, such as chart recording, return loss bridge, signal/noise, signal/hum, and summation sweep, along with performing monthly, semiannual, and annual tests. They store and maintain all test equipment used, as well as keep an inventory of parts and supplies needed to repair all equipment. They keep complete records of all equipment maintenance and propose replacement of equipment that is outdated or that cannot be repaired. In addition, they are usually required to produce, compile, update, and manage computer-aided design (CAD) drawings and other engineering documentation.

In addition, Maintenance Engineers must ensure that the equipment meets all design specifications and the Federal Communications Commission (FCC) rules and guidelines. They are required to conduct FCC testing on a regular basis, as well as guarantee that there is as little downtime as possible. They must have a good working knowledge of personal computers, basic computer networking, and common computer operating systems.

Maintenance Engineers typically work in the engineering shop, which is often adjacent to the station's master control room. They may also function in the field at a transmitter location and may be required to carry heavy loads and climb transmitter poles to accomplish needed repair and replacement of transmission equipment and cables. They may also operate in the shop area of a production or postproduction facilities firm. Maintenance Engineers are usually employed for a regular shift, but also must be able to work a flexible schedule and a variety of shifts, as they are often called on to do major and complex repairs that require immediate attention, no matter what the hour.

Salaries

Salaries of Maintenance Engineers tend to be higher than those for their peers who are involved in audio, video, or transmitter engineering. According to the U.S. Department of Labor's *Occupational Outlook Handbook,* median hourly earnings of electronics repairers in 2002 were $19.77, with lows from $11.71 to highs of $27.08. In a salary study made by Broadcast Employment Services, annual earnings for Maintenance Engineers ranged from a low of $37,000 to a high of $83,000, with the median average salary being $54,900.

Employment Prospects

Opportunities for Maintenance Engineers in all quarters of television, telecommunications, and video are excellent. Qualified Maintenance Engineers are not easy to find and are in steady demand. Most commercial and public television stations employ five or more such people who are experienced electronic troubleshooters who can labor both at the station and in the field. There is a similar demand for Maintenance Engineers at production and postproduction facilities companies.

Television equipment of today consists of hundreds of complex, interrelated components with many computer elements (particularly with the digital equipment that is now commonly used at most television stations).The ability to determine which element (or combination of elements) in the system has malfunctioned and how best to repair it in as short a time as possible is a highly prized talent. Thus, corporate, educational, governmental, and health production organizations are constantly looking for capable Maintenance Engineers, as are multichannel multipoint distribution service (MMDS) companies, cable TV systems, and low-power television (LPTV) stations. Frequently, as engineering technicians increase their experience and their training with additional study, they can become maintenance engineers.

Advancement Prospects

Creative, inventive, and successful Maintenance Engineers have several opportunities to advance their career. Many of them assume more responsible positions at smaller-market stations or move up at their own stations by becoming engineering supervisors in charge of all equipment maintenance and, eventually, assistant chief engineers, In addition, there are prospects for advancement to engineering supervisor jobs at MMDS companies, or in such nonprofit settings as educational, health and governmental agencies. On the other hand, many private corporations that operate media centers also have a strong need for trained and experienced engineering supervisors. Finally, those Maintenance Engineers who have become familiar with the latest equipment used in broadcast technology are good candidates for finding openings with production and postproduction facilities companies that, of necessity, must utilize state-of-art equipment.

Education and Training

A high school diploma and at least two years of training in electronics at a vocational or technical school is the bare minimum education needed for this post. From two to five years of work as an engineering technician in the broadcast industry is a big plus.

Special Requirements

In addition, many stations recommend or require a certificate from an industry organization such as the International Society of Certified Electronics Technicians (ISCET) or the Society of Broadcast Engineers (SBE). In some cases, they may also demand a Federal Communications Commission (FCC) general class license or an FCC restricted radio telephone operator permit, as well as a master's degree in computer science.

Experience, Skills, and Personality Traits

A minimum of two to four years of television maintenance experience is expected of engineering technicians to be promoted to the position of Maintenance Engineer. A thorough knowledge of the repair of broadcast equipment, an understanding of all aspects in the operations of a television station, and a solid comprehension of digital and analog engineering test equipment, such as oscilloscopes, signal level meters, spectrum analyzers, and wave form and vector scopes, are required. A familiarity with computer networking, systems, and technologies is another requirement. An ability to read and interpret schematic diagrams is recommended, as is a familiarity with assorted types of drill motors, hand tools, sanders, shop grinders, and similar equipment employed in repair work.

A probing and logical mind is extremely useful, as is the ability to analyze electronic problems. Maintenance Engineers need to be self-motivated and to appreciate the necessity of accurate documentation of all work performed. Excellent verbal and written communication skills and the capacity to work well in a broadcast team environment under strict time deadlines are also important. Good Maintenance

Engineers are excellent problem solvers who combine experience and intuition when troubleshooting malfunctions in complex electronic gear and computer hardware.

Unions and Associations

Many Maintenance Engineers in commercial television are members of the National Association of Broadcast Employees and Technicians AFL-CIO (NABET) or the International Brotherhood of Electrical Workers (IBEW). In public television, most Maintenance Engineers are not represented by a union except in the major-market stations.

Associations of interest for Maintenance Engineers include the Institute of Electrical and Electronics Engineers, Inc. (IEEE), the International Society of Certified Electronic Technicians, the Society of Broadcast Engineers, and the Society of Motion Picture and Television Engineers (SMPTE).

Tips for Entry

1. While in school, take as many computer courses as possible to acquire an understanding of computer technology and computer networking.
2. Investigate intern programs with local television stations to gain experience and a general appreciation of all aspects of the operation of a broadcast station, its environment, and its technologies.
3. Be prepared to spend two to four years or more as a broadcast technician to gain the expertise and intuition expected of a Maintenance Engineer.

MASTER CONTROL ENGINEER

CAREER PROFILE

Duties: Coordinate and monitor all audio and video inputs for broadcasting at a television station or network center

Alternate Title(s): Air Operator; Master Control Operator

Salary Range: $20,000 to $60,000 or more

Employment Prospects: Fair

Advancement Prospects: Fair

Prerequisites:

Education and Training—High school diploma; technical training in electronics; Federal Communications Commission (FCC) license may be required

Experience—At least one year as an engineering technician

Special Skills and Personality Traits—Decision-making ability; knowledge of broadcast audio and video equipment; quick reflexes; sound judgment

CAREER LADDER

Operations Manager; Engineering Supervisor; Technical Director; Audio/Video Engineer

Master Control Engineer

Engineering Technician

Position Description

Master Control Engineers are responsible for the integration of all audio and video input from a mixture of sources at a television station and the delivery of their signals, by way of the master control switchers and processing equipment, to the broadcasting transmitter. As the key person handling this coordination, the Master Control Engineer is charged with guaranteeing that all transmissions from the station follow the rules and regulations set down by the Federal Communications Commission (FCC).

Master Control Engineers coordinate the video and audio portions of programming that come from the studio, the networks, prerecorded segments, satellites, electronic news gathering (ENG) crews, and other sources. They verify by checking the television programming log what times programs and station breaks are to air and that all the scheduled program elements are ready prior to broadcast. They cue and roll the film, videotape, and digital programs, intermingling the video and audio inputs from their various sources. They double-check video and color monitors and fine tune video, audio, and color levels to specifications. They are also responsible for assuring the seamless rollover from one show to another and the control of the switching to and from station breaks. This requires that they integrate the broadcasting of commercials, public service messages, slides, and promotional tapes, as well as cue announcers as to when they are on air.

Master Control Engineers are also tasked with dealing with all emergencies. By monitoring the on-air transmission, they can ascertain any problems, such as loss of audio or video signals, program overruns and underruns, as well as sudden equipment malfunctions. They then press buttons to access and transmit technical difficulties signs or station identifications to the viewing audience. They must determine the cause and area of the problem and inform engineering personnel of the situation so that broadcast interruptions are kept to a bare minimum. One of their other duties is to record onto the television programming log the actual time a program or station break was aired. In addition, they prepare reports describing any problems encountered during transmission and the reason(s) for same. In the job of assuring the smooth broadcast of all of the station's programming, the Master Control Engineer interacts with the operations manager, videotape engineer/editors, the film/tape librarian, announcers, and the traffic/continuity supervisor.

The Master Control Engineer post is more of an operational job than a technical one. It encompasses the synchronization of the activities and work output of many individuals, as well as the mixing and merging of a varied group of electronic equipment. The Master Control Engineer is a mixture of a logistician and a conductor, with the major duty being the caliber of the station's on-air look and its public image as a well-oiled professional enterprise.

Salaries

Master Control Engineers do not earn as much as many of their peers in the broadcasting industry. During 2004, annual salaries ranged from $35,000 to $50,000 in commercial television, according to industry sources. In public television, the yearly salaries may be as low as $20,000 and may go as high as $60,000 for individuals with experience and seniority in major-market community stations.

Employment Prospects

Most television stations employ three or more Master Control Engineers in eight-hour day and night shifts. In the larger, more complex major-market station operations, there may be two or more engineers assigned to each of the three shifts. Prospects in this arena are fair for smart, attentive, and qualified engineering technicians who demonstrate sound judgment in the operation of television equipment to advance to becoming Master Control Engineers. Part-time weekend and holiday work adds a boost to engineers' income as well.

Master Control Engineers can also be found at some educational, governmental, and health operations that regularly transmit programming. They are also used at videoconferencing origination companies, at all the large national cable and satellite program services, and at the headquarters of satellite news networks.

Advancement Prospects

Opportunities for advancement are only fair. Many Master Control Engineers move to smaller-market stations into positions as operations managers, or become engineering supervisors at their own stations. Others may be able to move up the career ladder to become technical directors or audio/video engineers, usually at higher salaries. A few who have gained additional required skills through experience and further course work may become maintenance engineers.

Education and Training

Most engineering supervisors require a bare minimum of a high school education and one to two years of technical training at a technical or vocational school for hiring (or promoting) individuals to the post of Master Control Engineer. As television equipment has become both more sophisticated and automated, some stations require less of a background in engineering than before. Some Master Control Engineers are recent college graduates with communications or broadcasting education backgrounds and with little engineering training per se.

Special Requirements

Often, a restricted radio telephone operator permit from the FCC is required, as well as a certificate from one of the industry certification programs, such as those given by the International Society of Certified Electronic Technicians, (ISCET), the Society of Broadcast Engineers (SBE), or other industry groups.

Experience, Skills, and Personality Traits

A minimum of one year as an engineering technician is usually required for a promotion to the position of Master Control Engineer. Some major-market stations may expect more engineering experience than that. Usually, experience in operating broadcast video servers, tape machines, satellite receivers, and a good understanding of computer operations is desirable.

Master Control Engineers must possess a working knowledge of the limitations and operating characteristics of a wide assortment of audio and video equipment. They need to be continuously alert and capable of making decision rapidly. They must have very good reflexes and demonstrate sound judgment at all times.

Unions and Associations

Some Master Control Engineers in commercial television are members of the National Association of Broadcast Employees and Technicians AFL-CIO (NABET), while others may be represented by the International Brotherhood of Electrical Workers (IBEW). Most personnel at public television stations do not belong to a union.

Tips for Entry

1. Training and background requirements for this position mean that taking an electronics curriculum at a vocational or technical school or earning a degree from a college with a broadcast engineering program is a necessity.

2. Be sure to include computer courses with your technical training, as you will need familiarity with computer technology and applications in your work.

3. Find intern work at a television station to become familiar with its wide assortment of audio and video equipment.

TECHNICAL DIRECTOR

Duties: Oversee the technical quality of a television production; responsible for the operation of the production control room

Alternate Title(s): Switcher

Salary Range: $24,000 to $86,000 or more

Employment Prospects: Fair

Advancement Prospects: Good

Prerequisites:

Education and Training—High school diploma and some technical training minimum; college degree or alternate technical training in telecommunications often required

Experience—Minimum of two to three years as an audio/video engineer, lighting director, or camera operator

Special Skills and Personality Traits—Understanding of television production and engineering processes; good interpersonal abilities; leadership qualities; patience; quick reflexes

```
┌─────────────────────────────────────┐
│  Engineering Supervisor; Unit Manager; │
│         Assistant Director           │
└─────────────────────────────────────┘

┌─────────────────────────────────────┐
│          Technical Director          │
└─────────────────────────────────────┘

┌─────────────────────────────────────┐
│   Audio/Video Engineer; Camera       │
│     Operator; Lighting Director      │
└─────────────────────────────────────┘
```

Position Description

As a vital component in the production of a television show, the chief duty of Technical Directors is to supervise (along with the director of photography and the video operator) the technical quality of the program. They prepare, set up, operate, and adjust audio and visual broadcast equipment master controls to assure the proper transmission of the television signals. During production, they work the production switcher, the unit that controls the choice of camera images and special effects that are broadcast or fed into the videotape recorders to be broadcast later.

All public and commercial television stations employ Technical Directors, as do most large-scale production and postproduction facilities firms. They function in a studio, usually in the production control room, or in a remote truck when on location for a production. A few educational, governmental, and health organizations involved in larger televised or videotaped productions also employ Technical Directors.

The Technical Director works directly with the director and is the principal link between that person and the technical crew assigned to the production. Technical Directors usually supervise from three to 10 engineers and assistants, depending on the size of and needs of the particular production. At television facilities that do not employ a lighting director, Technical Directors often must handle the duties of this position.

During the preproduction and planning phases the Technical Director studies the requirements of the production, consulting with the director of photography and the video operator on such concerns as filter options and lens choices, and then makes suggestions to the director. During rehearsals and actual production, the Technical Director is close by and works in tandem with the director in the control room. The Technical Director transmits directives (via headphones) to camera operators about the positioning of cameras as well as oversees the other studio and control room technical personnel. Following the director's instructions about switching from one camera shot to another and/or selecting other picture inputs, such as film or videotape, to interrupt the live action, the Technical Director operates the production switcher, implementing the director's choices for special electronic effects and transitions. Switchers can be as simple as a four-camera router (switching from one to the other), or as complex as a digital state-of-the-art component allowing for picture manipulation with computer-generated effects.

In addition, the Technical Director provides technical leadership during any production emergencies and also prepares reports on the facilities used in a production for the engineering supervisor or assistant chief engineer. Usually, the Technical Director also assigns and trains studio and control room crew members and checks their performance.

Normally, the Technical Director reports to an engineering supervisor and is assigned to a specific production. During the actual production time, the Technical Director reports to and works closely with the director. In smaller stations where there is no staff Technical Director, the duties of this post are often divided between an engineering supervisor and an assistant director. In some midsize television facilities, where there is no need for the technical and supervisory abilities of a Technical Director, the tasks are handled by a switcher who reports to the production manager for assignment, but to the director during actual production. In some instances in the smallest stations, directors may handle their own switching during the production.

Salaries

According to a 2004 salary survey by Broadcast Employment Services, annual salaries for Technical Directors generally ranged from $24,000 to $85,000 or higher. Yearly salaries at the smaller stations may vary anywhere from $17,000 to $25,000, whereas at the larger-market stations, such salaries may extend from $45,000 to $85,000 or more. The mean average annual salary of all positions studied was $38,341.

Employment Prospects

The job of Technical Director is not an entry-level one. Some experience, usually two to three years, in television engineering and, specifically, studio engineering is a general prerequisite. While some major-market commercial and public television stations with heavy production schedules may employ five or more Technical Directors, most operations, even large ones, typically have only two or three on staff. In the smallest stations, there may be none. In addition, the competition for this job among television engineering personnel is stiff, so employment opportunities are only fair. Technical Directors are also used by the television networks as well as the major production and postproduction facilities companies, but they generally only hire seasoned people with solid studio engineering resumes.

Advancement Prospects

Technical Directors usually want to advance to the position of engineering supervisor or, in some of the major production organizations, to a unit manager. Since a large part of the job of a technical director is the positioning of cameras and the preparation of shots, many of them use their expertise to move into director positions, frequently by first becoming assistant directors. Some Technical Directors move to smaller-market stations where they have a higher salary and more responsibility for technical and production work. Technical Directors tend to view their position as a transitional one that will aid them in moving up to more responsible engineering or production positions. Thus, opportunities tend to be good for ambitious and successful Technical Directors with initiative.

Education and Training

Minimum requirements for this position are a high school diploma and some technical education at a vocational school. In some instances, the completion of a college-level program or industry recognized training in telecommunications might be required. It is useful for candidates to have had courses in television production techniques, as well as some engineering education.

Experience, Skills, and Personality Traits

Most engineering supervisors require a minimum of two to three years of experience in an engineering and production position in the studio environment, such as an audio/video engineer, a camera operator, or a lighting director. Above all, experience in both professional studio and remote television production is vital.

Technical Directors must have a thorough knowledge of media production and equipment used in television productions, postproduction, and master control equipment, usually including digital television devices and editing procedures and their equipment. They need to be able to set up and operate this equipment. In addition, they must be very familiar with Federal Communications Commission (FCC) rules and regulations pertaining to technical operations and safety practices related to the operation—both in the studio and in the field—of this technical equipment.

In addition, Technical Directors must be able to respond swiftly to orders given to them and make decisions rapidly in highly pressured situations. They need to exhibit skill and patience, diplomacy, and a positive attitude, as well as a knack to lead and to cooperate with other crew members. They also need to be aware that their job requires constant learning and training.

Unions and Associations

Technical Directors in commercial television are usually part of the engineering staff, and, as such, they are represented by the International Brotherhood of Electrical Workers (IBEW) or by the National Association of Broadcast Employees and Technicians AFL-CIO (NABET). In public television, Technical Directors are usually not represented by any union, nor are switchers who work in either commercial or public television.

Tips for Entry

1. While in high school or, later, in vocational school, seek out intern programs at local television stations to get firsthand experience with television production procedures.

2. Get hired as an engineering technician to learn the television production business from the ground up and as a necessary work experience to qualify you for a specific engineering position.

3. Understanding that a team spirit and a cooperative, politic attitude must pervade a television station's engineering and production crews, some beginner courses in sociology and psychology might be useful.

TRANSMITTER ENGINEER

CAREER PROFILE

Duties: Operate and maintain a television transmitter

Alternate Title(s): Broadcast Engineer; Broadcast Technician; Field Service Technician; Transmitter Technician

Salary Range: $14,000 to $65,000 or more

Employment Prospects: Good

Advancement Prospects: Good

Prerequisites:

Education and Training—High school diploma; some technical training; certification; bachelor's degree and Federal Communications Commission (FCC) license preferable

Experience—Two to three years as an engineering technician

Special Skills and Personality Traits—Mechanical skills; perseverance; technical knack

Special Requirements—An FCC general class radio telephone license and/or an engineer certification from the Society of Broadcast Engineers may be required

CAREER LADDER

```
┌─────────────────────────────┐
│   Engineering Supervisor    │
└─────────────────────────────┘

┌─────────────────────────────┐
│   Transmitter Engineer      │
└─────────────────────────────┘

┌─────────────────────────────┐
│   Engineering Technician    │
└─────────────────────────────┘
```

Position Description

Transmitter Engineers (or broadcast technicians, as they are commonly known) are involved in all phases of the direct transmission of a television signal to the viewing audience. (It should be noted that the terms *engineer, operator,* and *technician* often are used interchangeably to describe this and other such engineering posts.) They set up, operate, and maintain the hardware that regulates the signal strength, clarity, and range of sounds and colors of television broadcasts. They are responsible for monitoring the Federal Communications Commission (FCC) licensed analog and digital transmitters, keeping them operational within the obligatory FCC specifications and on the frequency that the commission has assigned to the station. In co-owned radio-TV stations, a Transmitter Engineer may also operate the AM or FM transmitter for the radio signals as well.

Transmitter Engineers have a critical task in the daily operations of the broadcasting industry. Their primary duty is to ensure that the television signal is transmitted uninterruptedly from the station to the public. They monitor signal emission and any spurious radiation discharged outside the licensed transmission frequency to make certain that the sig-

nal is not infringing on frequencies assigned to other stations. They give the final authorization before the actual transmission of the station's broadcast signal. They check indicators on their control panels to monitor and log the outgoing signals and adjust them as necessary (to regulate sound fidelity, quality, and volume and image brightness and contrast) to maintain a constant sound modulation and to guarantee that the transmitted signal is sharp and clear. As such, they are accountable for the actual broadcasting of a TV signal, and they oversee the continual monitoring of the studio-transmitter link (STL) microwave signal to assure continuous signals for retransmission. In addition, they constantly monitor all incoming and outgoing transmissions, including those from studio, satellite, network, or regional broadcasts.

In some instances, the transmitter is located within the station's facilities in a metropolitan area or suburb. In other circumstances, the transmitter tower and antenna are situated in a remote location (usually on high terrain) away from the main studio. Transmitter Engineers work at either location, under the guidance of the engineering supervisor in charge of the transmitter, and the supervisor may assign them to various shifts during the broadcast day or night.

Transmitter Engineers also take care of the daily maintenance of the transmitters, antennas, and associated equipment by employing test equipment, such as oscilloscopes, voltmeters, and ammeters. They test and measure transmitter and antenna output according to FCC mandates and conduct daily inspections of building, tower, and antenna lights to certify continuous operation. They adjust and reposition the equipment associated with microwave receiving and transmitting parabolas located on transmission towers, as well as regulate and reposition the satellite transmission-receiving unit and its associated apparatuses.

Transmitter Engineers maintain hour-by-hour and program-by-program transmission logs as demanded by the FCC. They develop, plan, and prepare schematic drawings of prototype or experimental components and devices to improve existing transmitter equipment and direct, coordinate, or install equipment modifications to avert interruptions in the transmitting operations. In addition, they keep an inventory of supplies and parts for all the electronic components and systems associated with the station's transmission.

Salaries

Salaries for Transmitter Engineers in commercial television range from $14,000 yearly for beginning personnel to more than $65,000 or more for experienced individuals. According to the U.S. Department of Labor's *Occupational Outlook Handbook,* in 2002 median annual earnings of Transmitter Engineers were $27,760. The middle 50 percent earned between $18,860 and $45,200 per year. The lowest 10 percent earned less than $14,600, and the highest 10 percent earned more than $65,970. In a study of TV job salaries conducted by Broadcast Employment Services, in 2004 the yearly salaries for Transmitter Engineers ranged from $14,000 to $85,000, with a mean average salary being $50,000. Salaries in public television tended to be similar, but slightly higher at the low end of the scale, and with a slightly lower mean average salary, approximately $44,000 per year.

Employment Prospects

The potential for employment is good. It is expected that employment of broadcast and sound engineering technicians (engineers) will grow about as fast as the average for all occupations through the year 2012. In 2002 there were 35,000 Transmitter Engineers employed.

The need for qualified applicants for this position is very real, particularly with the advent and installation of digital and high-definition television (HDTV) transmission capabilities. Most television stations employ at least three, and usually more, full-time Transmitter Engineers for various shifts and specific duties. Alert and enterprising engineering technicians and other types of broadcast personnel with broadcast experience should find opportunities exist to further their career by becoming Transmitter Engineers. Such positions are located in virtually all cities, but the highest paying and most specialized jobs are concentrated in New York City, Los Angeles, Chicago, and Washington, D.C.— the originating centers for most network and news programs. In addition, there are job opportunities for Transmitter Engineers at multichannel multipoint distribution service (MMDS) companies and at low-power television (LPTV) stations.

Advancement Prospects

While opportunities are good for qualified and ambitious Transmitter Engineers to upgrade to more responsible positions within the engineering department, the competition for such advancement is stiff. All engineering supervisors in charge of transmitters, assistant chief engineers, and even chief engineers have typically worked as Transmitter Engineers at some time in their careers. Because of their particular experience in broadcast technology, many Transmitter Engineers find a ready berth at MMDS and LPTV operations.

Education and Training

As a basic requirement, aspiring Transmitter Engineers need a high school diploma and, usually, an associate degree in electronics, computer networking, or broadcast technology. In some cases, four to six years of broadcast engineering experience may be substituted for such a degree.

Special Requirements

While the FCC no longer demands the licensing of broadcast technicians (a result of the Telecommunications Act of 1996 eliminating this requirement), many stations and networks still require an FCC general class radio telephone license and/or an engineer certification from the Society of Broadcast Engineers (SBE) in order to be hired as a Transmitter Engineer. A valid driver license is usually an additional requirement.

Experience, Skills, and Personality Traits

Transmitter Engineers usually have from two to four years of experience as engineering technicians, with some of that as on-the-job experience including work at transmitters. They must be familiar with the specialized electronic equipment used to keep a television station on the air. Considerable know-how with standard engineering test equipment is also a requirement, as well as the ability to read schematic drawings. They must exhibit manual dexterity and a talent for working with electrical, electronic, and mechanical systems and equipment.

Above all, Transmitter Engineers must have good written and verbal skills. Most employers are seeking conscientious, technically adept individuals who are good with details and at solving problems. They must be self-motivated and agreeable to taking the lead on assigned projects and diligent in their pursuit of their exacting duties.

Unions and Associations

Nearly all Transmitter Engineers at commercial television stations belong to and are represented by the National Association of Broadcast Employees and Technicians AFL-CIO (NABET) or by the International Brotherhood of Electrical Workers (IBEW). While the majority of such workers in public television are not members of either union, some engineering employees at major-market community-owned public television stations do belong to one of them.

Tips for Entry

1. Take courses in computer technology, electronics, math, and physics while in high school as preliminary to additional vocational education training.

2. Look for internship programs at local television stations or, if in college, in campus radio and television stations, to gain firsthand experience in broadcasting.

3. Building electronic equipment from hobby kits or even operating a "ham" (amateur) radio are good experience in developing manual dexterity and an aptitude for working with electronic equipment and mechanical systems.

VIDEOTAPE (AND DIGITAL) ENGINEER

CAREER PROFILE

Duties: Operate videotape (and/or digital editing) machines at a television station or a production facilities center

Alternate Title(s): Digital Editor; Digital Operator; Operating Technician; Videotape Editor; Videotape Operator

Salary Range: $14,000 to $74,000

Employment Prospects: Good

Advancement Prospects: Good

Prerequisites:

Education and Training—High school diploma; some technical training in electronics or broadcasting technology

Experience—Minimum of one to two years as an engineering technician

Special Skills and Personality Traits—Creativity; good interpersonal aptitude; technical knack

Special Requirements—A Federal Communications Commission (FCC) general class radio telephone license and/or an engineer certification from an industry association, such as the Society of Broadcast Engineers, may be required.

CAREER LADDER

```
┌─────────────────────────────────┐
│     Engineering Supervisor      │
└─────────────────────────────────┘

┌─────────────────────────────────┐
│ Videotape (and Digital) Engineer│
└─────────────────────────────────┘

┌─────────────────────────────────┐
│     Engineering Technician      │
└─────────────────────────────────┘
```

Position Description

The Videotape (and Digital) Engineer sets up and operates a wide scope of machines that record, play back, and edit programs at television stations. The actual editing is usually done in postproduction, or by camera operators, or, in the case of news programs, electronic news gathering (ENG) operators. Videotape (and Digital) Engineers are also employed at postproduction facilities companies, where their primary function is editing, rather than operating (and they are frequently known as film/tape editors, even though they may work with videotape and digital materials as well).

Television photography and editing have improved incredibly with the use of videotape (and now the increasing use of digitally stored materials). Film consumes time for developing and processing before it is available for editing and then broadcast transmission. Today, with videotape and the ever-advancing digital technology, film is increasingly becoming obsolete for day-to-day television broadcasts. The greatest advantage of using videotape or digitized footage is that it can be played back immediately without the need for laborious processing.

Responsibilities of Videotape (and Digital) Engineers include the evaluation of videotapes and satellite feeds, the duplication (or dubbing) of taped material, and the assembling of videotape segments for production use and broadcast. In addition to setting up the machines, they align, adjust, clean, and monitor all video machines prior to operating them and file any necessary technical and malfunction reports with the station's engineering supervisor.

Videotape (and Digital) Engineers record programs being produced in studios at their stations or those from networks and other sources outside the station. They monitor the audio and visual quality of the recordings, working closely with the master control engineer and other audio-video engineers. (At some of the smallest stations, the functions of a Videotape [and Digital] Engineer may be taken by the master control engineer.) If the job includes editing, they work with producers, associate producers, directors, assistant directors, and reporters in editing various pretaped segments into a finished program (though most editing for made-for-television features and some programs is done in a separate postproduction phase). They may also provide dubbing services for the programming and sales departments and for the promotion and publicity departments of the station.

Videotape (and Digital) Engineers are among the busiest individuals in the engineering department during the broadcast day, as they have to juggle various requirements among the machines and have to determine priorities necessary for a smooth and professional operation.

Salaries

According to the U.S. Department of Labor's *Occupational Outlook Handbook,* median annual earnings in 2002 for television, video, and motion picture camera operators (which include Videotape [and Digital] Engineers) were $32,720. Salaries ranged from $14,710 (the lowest 10 percent) to more than $65,070 (the highest 10 percent). In a study by Broadcast Employment Services, yearly salaries for video editors and technicians in 2004 ranged from a low of $14,000 (for beginners and some personnel at smaller stations) to a high of $74,000 (for those with seniority at larger stations). The mean average annual salary was $37,725.

Employment Prospects

The majority of productions in present day television environments are prerecorded onto videotape or a digital format. As a result, the need for Videotape (and Digital) Engineers is constant. Such editing, whether accomplished at the station's studio or in a postproduction facility, has become almost an art form unto itself.

Most stations usually employ three or more Videotape (and Digital) Engineers and, if a large station, may have as many as 15 on staff to cover all shifts and contingencies in program scheduling. Opportunities also are available at corporate, educational, and governmental organizations that are involved in production. Most cable television stations, as well as multichannel multipoint distribution service (MMDS) operations, also have need for Videotape (and Digital) Engineers. As noted above, production and postproduction facilities houses, where the emphasis is on the editing process rather than operating the equipment, have a need for Videotape (and Digital) Engineers as well.

Advancement Prospects

The chances of advancement from this position are generally good. Seasoned and talented Videotape (and Digital) Engineers may look for advancement by becoming engineering supervisors. Others may move to smaller stations for more senior positions within the engineering departments. Some may use their skills and experience to advance to more responsible positions within large advertising agencies that operate their own production and engineering units. Likewise, some may move to a network or seek more responsible engineering positions at MMDS or cable television operations.

Education and Training

Most employers require at least a high school education and some post–high school technical or vocational training

before employing or promoting personnel to this post. Today's sophisticated editing devices have made it easier to operate them once the systems have been learned. Many Videotape (and Digital) Engineers may have worked previously in film production or have an art background.

Special Requirements

In addition, many stations recommend or require a certificate from an industry organization such as the International Society of Certified Electronics Technicians (ISCET) or the Society of Broadcast Engineers (SBE). In some cases, they may also demand a Federal Communications Commission (FCC) general class license even though this is no longer a necessity for most broadcast technicians.

Experience, Skills, and Personality Traits

This position is rarely an entry-level one. Most Videotape (and Digital) Engineers are promoted after a year or two as engineering technicians or some other type of engineer at the station or facility. A thorough knowledge of and experience with all types of relevant equipment is necessary, as well as a familiarity with computerized editing machinery. In addition, a basic engineering knowledge of other types of technical equipment used in television production is helpful.

Videotape (and Digital) Engineers must have, above all, a solid technical aptitude and be capable of working with broadcast equipment. They must also have some people skills, as they may have to work with an assortment of nonengineering personnel if they edit productions. As they need to be creative in assembling prerecorded segments into a polished program, they must have an understanding of the aesthetics of editing. They have to be able to work under tremendous stress and pressure in the busy daily routines.

Unions and Associations

Most Videotape (and Digital) Engineers in commercial television are members of the International Brotherhood of Electrical Workers (IBEW) or the National Association of Broadcast Employees and Technicians AFL-CIO (NABET). In public television, some individuals at large community-owned stations may be members of one of these unions.

Tips for Entry

1. During high school take courses in electronics and physics as building blocks upon which you will add your technical and vocational training afterward.
2. Look for intern programs (or work part time) at a television studio, as this is a great way of gaining experience, knowledge, and networking contacts.
3. Be prepared to start out in a low-key position, such as a dubber or video helper, before moving into a more responsible position as engineering technician, from which your career can move steadily forward.

MANAGEMENT AND ADMINISTRATION

ACCOUNTANT

CAREER PROFILE

Duties: Assist the business manager in billings, payroll, and accounts receivable and payable at a television station, media center, cable system, or LPTV station

Alternate Title(s): Assistant Business Manager

Salary Range: $25,000 to $62,000 or more

Employment Prospects: Good

Advancement Prospects: Fair

Prerequisites:

Education and Training—Minimum of undergraduate degree in accounting or related field

Experience—Minimum of two years of accounting work

Special Skills and Personality Traits—Accuracy; analytical mind; computer skills; dependability; detail oriented; mathematical affinity

Special Requirements—Certification as a certified public accountant (CPA) or a certified management accountant (CMA) may be required

CAREER LADDER

```
┌─────────────────────────────────────────┐
│  Business Manager; Public Accountant     │
└─────────────────────────────────────────┘

┌─────────────────────────────────────────┐
│              Accountant                  │
└─────────────────────────────────────────┘

┌─────────────────────────────────────────┐
│  Bookkeeper; Business School/College     │
└─────────────────────────────────────────┘
```

Position Description

Accountants in a commercial or public television station are responsible for particular financial transactions. They usually report directly to the business manager and in the discharge of their duties work with the general sales manager and with staff advertising salespersons. Accountants work also at cable systems, multiple system operators (MSOs), low-power television (LPTV) stations, production/facilities companies, and other related media businesses. They are also employed in a number of educational and health media organizations.

At a station, Accountants usually oversee the accounting and business team, which includes bookkeepers and billing clerks, accounts receivable/payable employees, and payroll clerks. While the specific duties of Accountants may vary from one station to another, typically they are responsible for examining invoices, vouchers, payroll timesheets, and purchase orders for correctness before the business manager gives approval on these items. They review network accounts and agency and client accounts and payments and continually screen department budgets to balance expenses with budgeted resources.

Some large-market stations may maintain three or more Accountants on staff, each with specific tasks and authority. At top-market operations, Accountants sometimes are given full responsibility for billing and accounts receivable. At smaller facilities, Accountants' duties are broader and cover most of the activities of the business department, including the direct supervision of clerical and support personnel, as well as the control of office supplies, furniture, and other equipment.

One of the major tasks of Accountants is to develop and enhance methods of cost accounting in defined financial areas so that the business manager can scrutinize more effectively any problem areas. Accountants systematically gather and maintain financial data that provide a basis on which management can itemize income and expenses. In addition, they prepare data and summaries of financial reports for the business manager and maintain records for Federal Communications Commission (FCC) reports, income tax returns, and insurance claims.

Most Accountants have to be skilled in computer technology and word processing techniques. With the aid of accounting software packages, Accountants can summarize transactions in standard formats for financial records and organize data in special layouts geared to financial analysis, greatly reducing the amount of wearisome manual labor previously associated with data management and record-keeping. Other Accountants have particular capabilities in such areas as assets and liabilities, inventory assessment, and profit and loss statements, and, as such, are often assigned particular responsibilities in those fields.

Salaries

Wages for Accountants in both commercial and public television tend to be relatively low, ranging from between $25,000 and $30,000 annually at small-market stations to $60,000 or more a year in major markets. Salaries are inclined to increase proportionately with certification, a master's degree, or specialized expertise. For example, according to a salary survey conducted by the National Association of Colleges and Employers, bachelor's degree candidates in accounting received starting offers averaging $40,647 per year in 2003, whereas master's degree candidates in accounting were initially offered yearly incomes of $42,241.

According to a 2003 salary survey conducted by Robert Half International, a staffing services firm specializing in accounting and finance, accountants with up to one year of experience earned between $29,500 and $40,500 annually. Those with one to three years of experience earned between $34,000 and $49,500 yearly, whereas senior accountants earned between $41,000 and $61,500 per year.

Employment Prospects

Despite the keen competition, prospects for obtaining or being promoted to the position of Accountant at a commercial or public television station remain good. The majority of Accountants are generally not recruited from outside the station unless specific skills, such as specialized computer experience or tax proficiency, are required. Nonetheless, employment openings for recent college graduates with accounting or related degrees are good due to the need for qualified accountants in commercial and public television, as well as at cable systems and other television industry companies. According to the U.S. Department of Labor's *Occupational Outlook Handbook,* employment of Accountants is expected to grow about as fast as the average for all occupations through the year 2012.

Advancement Prospects

The top promotion for an Accountant at a television station is to the post of business manager. The opportunities for such a move, however, are somewhat limited because of the job stability of that position, lack of openings, and the high competition. Some Accountants may have the chance to become business managers at smaller stations or join commercial production firms or other media-related organiza-tions in some parallel capacity. Still others may use their experience and expertise to move into a top financial post in an unrelated business such as public accountant.

Education and Training

An undergraduate degree in business administration or accounting is usually the bare minimum required for this job. Some of the larger stations may prefer in addition a master's degree in accounting or a master's degree in business administration with a concentration in accounting. Business managers habitually seek individuals who have computer science training.

Taking courses in bookkeeping, human resources, or personnel management is also helpful. The Association to Advance Collegiate Schools of Business (AACSB) can provide information on colleges and universities that have accredited accounting programs.

Special Requirements

Accountants usually are required to study and pass the exam and requirements for certification as a certified public accountant (CPA) licensed by a state board of accountancy, or a certified management accountant (CMA) given by the Institute of Management Accountants.

Experience, Skills, and Personality Traits

Many Accountants are relatively young—between the ages of 25 and 35—and the promotion to Accountant may be their first career advancement. Often, they have worked as bookkeepers for at least two years in the station's business department and have completed additional coursework and training in accounting while working. In today's work environment, all successful candidates for advancement must have training and experience in computer business programs. Some of the larger stations and media organizations sometimes hire promising college graduates directly into accounting positions.

Accountants should be intelligent and vigilant, accurate and dependable, detail oriented but also aggressive in the pursuit of their duties. They need to have outstanding interpersonal and communication abilities, as they will be working in tandem with people from different backgrounds. Most have a particular specialty in accounting, business, computer science, or law. Successful Accountants are fact finders and problem solvers who bring fresh concepts and techniques to handling the array of financial matters dealt with in the business department.

Unions and Associations

There are no unions that serve as bargaining agents for Accountants. However, many individuals belong to the Broadcast Cable Financial Management Association (BCFMA), which is devoted to developing new concepts of financial management for the industry. The Public Telecommunications Financial Management Association (PTFMA) provides a similar function for Accountants in public television.

Tips for Entry

1. Take courses in computer science and word processing as applied to business situations to give yourself an advantage when seeking a position as bookkeeper or Accountant.

2. Intern at a college television facility or a local television station to become familiar with the television environment and gain experience in production as background for your future job as an Accountant for such a station.

3. Aside from your general accounting expertise, decide on and study more about a specialty, such as assets and liabilities, inventory assessment, or profit and loss statements to enhance your chances to be hired.

BOOKKEEPER

CAREER PROFILE

Duties: Maintain financial records and ledgers at a television station, media center, cable system, or LPTV station

Alternate Title(s): None

Salary Range: $23,000 to $42,000

Employment Prospects: Good

Advancement Prospects: Good

Prerequisites:

Education and Training—Minimum of an associate's degree in business

Experience—Minimum of one year of bookkeeping experience

Special Skills and Personality Traits—Capacity to work quickly under stress; accuracy; computer literacy; good communication skills; mathematical knack; reliability

CAREER LADDER

Accountant

Bookkeeper

Business School/College; Bookkeeper (at another TV station or company)

Position Description

A Bookkeeper's main responsibility is to update and maintain journals, ledgers, and financial accounting records (which include tabulating expenditures, receipts, accounts payable and receivable, and profit and loss) for use by a television station's management in its daily operation and budget forecasting. Based on the size of the operation and the market, television stations and non-broadcast organizations may employ from two to 10 or more Bookkeepers. Generally, they report to the business manager or at larger stations to an accountant.

Bookkeepers are assigned to defined areas of responsibility, such as keeping the station's advertising billing accounts and files or preparing all payroll elements (including overtime compensation, payroll and Society Security deductions, time sheets, and records of vacation and sick leave). Some Bookkeepers may be based in accounts payable, where they post bills received by the station. (These include telephone bills, power and lighting bills, subscriptions, invoices for videotapes, and other normal operational expenses.) The Bookkeeper records all these bills, matches them with purchase orders or vouchers, and verifies their accuracy with the department head who purchased the items or services. As a matter of course, Bookkeepers keep precise backup records of all invoices or bills and all related documents for reference. In addition, they keep an ongoing file of past-due accounts receivable or payable for use by the business manager or accountant, as well as manage an inventory file of equipment, facilities, and supplies used or purchased by the station.

Some Bookkeepers are assigned to handle the day-to-day accounts of a particular department, such as engineering or programming. Typically at most stations, the programming department is the most expensive group in terms of salaries, program purchases, licensing fees, line charges, production expenses, shipping costs, and other show-related outlays. For this reason, a Bookkeeper is often assigned specifically to monitor all income and expenses related to this department. At some small operations, Bookkeepers may work in all areas of accounting, including accounts payable and receivable, advertising billings, and payroll. Where Bookkeepers are tasked with these assignments, they may also be required to write letters, make phone calls to clients, customers, or vendors, and interact with colleagues.

In today's world, computers are prevalent in every business; they are a basic tool in the operation of all television stations. Bookkeeping functions are routinely done on a computer using tailored accounting software. Instead of manually posting information to general ledgers, they now post charges to accounts on computer spreadsheets and databases. Thus, Bookkeepers must be very familiar with computer technology and software.

Salaries

Wages for this position tend to be somewhat low in commercial television. The Bureau of Labor Statistics' *Occupational Outlook Handbook* indicates that in 2002 Bookkeepers generally had a mean average hourly earning of $13.16, which translates to roughly $28,000 in annual wages. Higher salaries are usually paid to beginners who have a graduate degree in accounting and to Bookkeepers who have been with the station for a time.

Bookkeeper salaries vary depending on the region of the country, scope of the market area serviced by the television station, and size of the station (or media center) itself. The level of technical expertise required and the complexity and uniqueness of a Bookkeeper's tasks also affect earnings.

Employment Prospects

This is usually an entry-level position, and job opportunities at a television station or in a related media or video operation are good. Most commercial, public, and cable stations employ two or more Bookkeepers, presenting good promise for job positions for smart business school graduates.

Positions open up frequently as the station's Bookkeepers are promoted regularly within the station or move to other television or media positions to advance their careers. Bookkeeping skills are readily transferable to related jobs at multichannel multipoint distribution service (MMDS) operations, low-power TV (LPTV) stations, or to nonmedia business organizations. While slower than average growth is expected in the employment of Bookkeepers and accounting clerks through 2012 (in part due to labor-saving chores increasingly being handled by computer programs), the large size of this occupation ensures plentiful job openings, including many opportunities for temporary or part-time work. Specialization is important, but Bookkeepers who can fulfill a wider range of accounting activities may be in greater demand.

Advancement Prospects

Although chances for advancement to higher positions within the business department are good, the competition is always heavy. Once a beginner Bookkeeper learns the job or becomes a specialist in one or more accounting disciplines within the department, promotion is a distinct likelihood. The job upgrade may be to a specific bookkeeping responsibility with a higher salary or to the post of a Bookkeeper in charge of a single departmental area within the station.

With further training and education, some Bookkeepers can advance to the position of accountant after putting in their apprenticeship time in other areas of the business department. Still other Bookkeepers may move their career along by joining advertising agencies or other media-related organizations. Some may use their acquired business and accounting expertise to assume more responsible (and higher-salaried) positions outside the television industry altogether.

Education and Training

It is considered essential that a newly hired Bookkeeper have, as a minimum, an associate's degree in business, with the major emphasis of study in bookkeeping and accounting. An undergraduate degree in accounting or in business administration with a major in accounting is sometimes required at major- or middle-market stations. Courses in computer science and software are highly recommended, as is some education in personnel management. The important aspect, however, is that the applicant's educational background be well grounded in accounting and bookkeeping.

Some Bookkeepers, particularly those who hope to, or presently do, handle all the recordkeeping for a television station or department, may find it useful to become certified. The "certified bookkeeper" designation, awarded by the American Institute of Professional Bookkeepers, will help to assure employers that individuals have all the skills and knowledge demanded by the job. For certification, candidates must have at least two years of bookkeeping experience, pass three tests, and adhere to a code of ethics.

Experience, Skills, and Personality Traits

While some stations recruit experienced Bookkeepers from other stations or media companies, extensive experience is not a prerequisite for this position. Nonetheless, some experience working in the bookkeeping department of a business, even part time during school or college, is helpful. While many Bookkeepers are young, there are also older individuals who have been in the position for a number of years.

Successful Bookkeepers need to be able to work rapidly under pressure and be precise, alert, and reliable. Most important, they must be good at and enjoy working with figures and must understand accounting software.

Unions and Associations

There are no unions or professional organizations that represent Bookkeepers in commercial or public television.

Tips for Entry

1. Include courses in computer science and software in your technical or college education, as this education will both help you gain a job and make it easier for you to become a successful Bookkeeper.
2. While completing your education, explore possible intern work or part-time employment in an accounting or bookkeeping department to gain an understanding of these processes.
3. Certification may help to your chances of advancement but also broadens your bookkeeping abilities beyond one or two specialties, as this generalization of knowledge is critical in positions of higher responsibility in television business departments.

BUSINESS MANAGER

CAREER PROFILE

Duties: Manage all financial activities and planning for a television station or production/facility company

Alternate Title(s): Controller; Treasurer; Vice President of Business Affairs

Salary Range: $35,000 to $100,000 or more

Employment Prospects: Fair

Advancement Prospects: Good

Prerequisites:

Education and Training—Undergraduate degree in accounting, business administration, finance, or management

Experience—Minimum of five years in business and accounting, preferably in the television industry or a related field

Special Skills and Personality Traits—Analytical talent; interpersonal skills; knack for details; management ability; thorough knowledge of computer operations; understanding of business and finance

Special Requirements—Certification as a certified public accountant (CPA) may be useful.

CAREER LADDER

```
+-----------------------------+
|      General Manager        |
+-----------------------------+

+-----------------------------+
|      Business Manager       |
+-----------------------------+

+-----------------------------+
|         Accountant          |
+-----------------------------+
```

Position Description

Business Managers of a television station handle all financial transactions, which include accounts receivable and payable, general ledgers, journals, and vouchers. They are tasked with all financial planning and developing business plans and goals. They oversee the activities of the business department (which generally includes accountants, bookkeepers, billing and payroll clerks, benefits personnel, and other support staff), and they hire all necessary personnel. Business Managers supervise the preparation of all billings and the development and analysis of the financial statements and records of the station's assorted activities.

Business Managers are also employed at production/facilities companies and low-power television (LPTV) stations. At a television station, the Business Manager is the primary aide to the general manager. The Business Manager develops short- and long-range plans, goals, and budgets and modifies and interprets financial data in reports on a weekly, quarterly, and yearly basis. It is these reports that the general manager and the station's ownership use to make financial and business projections.

Business Managers develop and supervise all accounting policies and practices, including the value appraisal of plant, equipment, programming, and other assets for the preparation of reports to the Internal Revenue Service and for the corporate balance sheets. Business Managers generate all profit and loss and cash flow statements and monitor all departmental expenditures. They assist the sales manager and the general manager in setting realistic advertising rates for the station and in establishing credit policies that result in maximum sales results (while reducing the number of late payments and defaults).

In addition, Business Managers direct the management of the station's physical plant (including equipment and furniture). They oversee the station's personnel policies and provide accurate data and records for union negotiations concerning labor contracts and arbitration matters that arise.

Salaries

Annual earnings for Business Managers at commercial television stations are reasonably high, commensurate with their important responsibilities. According to the U.S. Department of Labor's *Occupational Outlook Handbook,* financial managers generally had median annual earnings of $73,340 in 2002. The middle 50 percent earned between $52,490 and $100,660 yearly. The lowest 10 percent had annual earnings of less than $39,000, while the top 10 percent earned more than $142,000 per year. In the Association for Financial Professionals' 14th annual compensation survey of 2002, it was found that financial managers generally had an average total compensation (which included bonuses and deferred compensations) of $84,500 yearly. In a selective survey of 2004 salaries conducted by Broadcast Employment Services, it was found that Business Managers in television earned per-year salaries ranging from a low of $33,000 to a high of more than $100,000, resulting in a mean average salary of those surveyed of $52,200.

Salaries for business or financial officers in public television were similar to those in commercial television. Many financial managers in both public and commercial television receive additional compensation in the form of bonuses and deferred compensation in the form of stock options.

Employment Prospects

Opportunities for employment as Business Manager of a television station are apt to be limited. In smaller-market television stations, both commercial and public, the Business Manager is usually someone who has been promoted from within the business department of the station. Thus, this person has an intimate knowledge of the specifics of that station's particular financial methods and operations.

In major-market commercial and public stations, Business Managers are somewhat less likely to be promoted from within the ranks of the business department. Sometimes they are recruited from other stations or associated media businesses or are brought in by the corporate ownership to improve the station's financial condition. Opportunities for individuals outside the station's business department are thus, to an extent, limited, and the competition for such prestigious jobs is heavy.

Advancement Prospects

Some Business Managers are able to rise to the post of general manager at their own stations, or they join a smaller-market station, which may be owned by the parent corporation, in that elevated capacity. The financial skills and experience achieved as a Business Manager of a television station are readily transferable to other television-related operations, such as multichannel multipoint distribution service (MMDS) companies or production/facilities firms.

Since the majority of Business Managers at television stations were initially trained in communications, most of them regard the position as a broad-based financial management job and, thus, very applicable to many fields in both public and private enterprise. As a result, many Business Managers unable to rise to the level of general managers seek nonmedia business opportunities to further their careers.

Education and Training

Business Managers in both commercial and public television must have an undergraduate degree in accounting, business administration, economics, or management to be hired for the job. In larger-market stations, with their added scope of responsibilities, a master's degree in business administration or finance is often compulsory to be hired or promoted from within the business department.

Continuing education is vital for financial managers, who must cope with the growing complexity of global interactions, changes in federal and state laws and regulations that might affect television production, and the proliferation of new and complex financial instruments to measure financial success. Many have extensive education or degrees in computer science. Generally, however, an academic background in accounting is the primary requirement of Business Managers.

Special Requirements

Many Business Managers of television stations find it useful to be certified public accountants (CPAs), and some may have law degrees in addition to their undergraduate business education.

Experience, Skills, and Personality Traits

Business Managers are inclined to be heavily detail-obsessed fact-finders who usually see things in black and white and are very "bottom-line" oriented regarding expenditures and budgets. They are primarily concerned with maximum productivity. Most have extensive experience with and skills in computer science. They must have excellent communication abilities to explain to their associates the complex financial data with which they are involved. In addition, they must have good interpersonal talents in personnel management and the ability to deal fairly and effectively with a wide range of people. Some television employers require candidates for Business Managers also to have experience in labor negotiations along with some knowledge of law.

At the majority of stations, potential Business Managers are required to have between five and seven years of seasoning in business and accounting, preferably in television broadcasting or in a related media field. The managers' personal accuracy, integrity, and dependability are crucial elements, as well as a realistic viewpoint toward television as a business. Profit orientation and the time value of money are critical qualifications for this job.

Unions and Associations

There are no unions that act as representatives or bargaining agents. Business Managers are frequently considered to be management and thus not eligible for any union membership. Many managers, however, belong to the Broadcast Cable Financial Management Association (BCFMA), an organization devoted to developing new concepts of financial management. In public television, the Public Telecommunications Financial Management Association (PTFMA) provides a similar forum.

Tips for Entry

1. While pursuing your business education, add psychology and sociology courses to enhance your understanding of human behavior and your capability to deal effectively with people.

2. Comprehension of computer science and financial software are critical to this position, so take every opportunity to expand your knowledge base of these areas.

3. Explore potential intern programs with local television stations to gain firsthand awareness of the procedures and production techniques of the industry.

GENERAL MANAGER

CAREER PROFILE

Duties: Manage the overall operation of a television station

Alternate Title(s): Station Manager; Vice President/ General Manager

Salary Range: $40,000 to $310,000

Employment Prospects: Poor

Advancement Prospects: Fair

Prerequisites:

    Education and Training—Undergraduate degree in advertising, business, or communications; master's degree usually required

    Experience—Minimum of 10 to 12 years in television management

    Special Skills and Personality Traits—Extensive broadcasting knowledge; leadership qualities; sound business judgment

CAREER LADDER

General Manager (larger station); Network Executive; Program Syndication Executive

General Manager

Program Manager; Business Manager; General Sales Manager

Position Description

The General Manager (GM) is accountable for the management and operation of a television station. Duties encompass all business and financial matters, which include budgeting, forecasting, expenses, income, profitability, and short- and long-range planning. Above all, the General Manager is charged with establishing and maintaining the station's image. In addition, the General Manager must run the station in compliance with all federal, state, and local laws, including Federal Communications Commission (FCC) regulations.

If the station is affiliated with a network, the General Manager is duty-bound to uphold the policies of the affiliation agreement and to be in constant contact with network officials. The person in this post is also obligated to support all relationships with advertisers, ad agencies, community leaders, contributors, program suppliers, and any other necessary outside station contacts.

A General Manager is frequently a corporate officer who in commercial broadcasting reports directly to the station's chief executive officer or owner or, if at a public television station, to a board of directors. In turn, seven major departments of the station—business, engineering, news, production, programming, promotion and publicity, and sales and marketing—report to the General Manager. General Managers hire the

department heads and establish their goals, check their performance, and approve their budgets. Although they have the daily responsibility of running their departments, General Managers still oversee each department's range of activities.

In business matters the General Manager approves all financial transactions and reports, whereas in engineering the General Manager approves the investment in new equipment and facilities. In news the formats of the news programs and editorial policies must be authorized, and in production program budgets must be monitored and modified when necessary. For programming, the General Manager approves what programming is prepared locally, decides which syndicated programs are acquired, determines what kind of programs should be aired in the future, and evaluates the schedule in response to audience ratings, the competition, and the station's policies. Finally, in the realm of advertising sales the General Manager settles advertising policies, evaluates the ad rates of the station in comparison with its competition, helps identify potential advertisers, and tracks income. In addition, General Managers often deliver editorials on the air and represent the station at industry conferences.

All these responsibilities of the General Manager are similar in commercial and public television broadcasting, with the exception of the generation of income. In commercial television, the General Manager is fully in charge of producing advertising revenues and, as such, must continuously monitor and evaluate the effectiveness of the sales department. On the other hand, in public television, the General Manager prepares and defends budgets submitted to legislatures or other public entities and solicits funds from the viewing public, corporations, and foundations. Additionally, public television General Managers frequently find themselves supervising the rental of the station's facilities and other profit-making ventures in order to bolster the stations' income. At commercial low-power television (LPTV) stations, the General Manager has responsibilities similar to those at full-power stations, just on a much smaller scale.

Salaries

In keeping with the extensive demands of the position, General Managers are paid well. According to salary surveys conducted by Broadcast Employment Services, in 2004 salaries for General Managers at commercial stations ranged annually from $55,000 to $400,000 for middle- and major-market stations, with a median yearly average being $115,300. For smaller and LPTV stations, annual salaries ranged from $22,000 to $50,000. These salaries did not include bonuses and other compensations. Most General Managers can anticipate being paid by a salary-plus-bonus arrangement and have an expense account, a company profit-sharing plan, a fully paid pension plan, and company-paid life and medical insurance.

General Managers at public television and LPTV stations usually are less generously paid than their for-profit counterparts. In addition, most General Managers of noncommercial stations contribute to their medical insurance, life insurance, and pension plans and, of course, do not participate in any profit-sharing plans.

Employment Prospects

Opportunities for employment as General Managers in both commercial and public broadcasting are extremely limited. It is the peak career position for most managers. When, on rare occasions, posts open up due to incumbents' retirement, promotion from within the stations' management personnel may be likely but also highly competitive. Chances for such a position at LTPV stations, usually located in rural areas, are better, but at reduced levels of responsibility and pay.

Advancement Prospects

Most General Managers have reached the crest of their career in this post. Many of them are between 45 and 60 years of age. Some younger candidates may be able to be promoted to the more responsible position of General Manager at the larger stations or become network executives

involved in sales or network relations with their affiliated stations. Some may even become managers in program syndication operations or establish their own advertising agencies or consulting firms.

Education and Training

Generally, the minimum requirement for a General Manager is an undergraduate degree in advertising, communications, or journalism. Marketing and business degrees are also suitable. Many General Managers also have a master's degree in business administration or at least have taken graduate level business courses. Some General Managers also possess a law degree. The position requires a fairly extensive background in the business of the broadcasting industry, usually gained as years in subsidiary management positions within the business department of one or more television stations.

Experience, Skills, and Personality Traits

At least 10 to 12 years of supervisory work in assorted television positions are a mandatory background for the position of General Manager. In commercial television, General Managers frequently come from the ranks of the sales or business departments. In public broadcasting, they usually have a middle management background in programming or fund-raising and development. Usually, a General Manager's background encompasses a successful record of accomplishment as a program manager, a business manager, a general sales manager, or, in some cases, a news director.

Essential qualities of General Managers include an ability to inspire people, a deep and extensive knowledge of the broadcasting industry and its procedures, self-confidence and determination, sound business judgment, and a strong sense of responsibility and integrity. They need to be able to communicate clearly and persuasively. They must have analytical minds able to assess quickly large amounts of information and data, as well as a capacity to consider and evaluate the interrelationships of numerous factors before making business decisions for the station.

Unions and Associations

There are no unions that serve as bargaining agents or representatives for General Managers. Some of them belong to the National Association of Television Program Executives (NATPE), the International Radio and Television Society (IRTS), or the National Academy of Television Arts and Sciences (NATAS). Most of them are active in a range of network affiliate committees and boards. In public television, General Managers are regularly members of regional networks and associations.

Tips for Entry

1. As a program manager, a business manager, a general sales manager, or news director for a station, consider

getting a master's degree in business administration to bolster your career advance.

2. If you are employed in public television, volunteer to help in fund-raising activities to gain experience in this vital area of the management of a public television station.

3. Taking on different managerial posts within the different departments of a television station will give you the needed extensive familiarity with the broadcasting environment and procedures.

RECEPTIONIST AND OFFICE CLERK

CAREER PROFILE	CAREER LADDER

Duties: Greet customers and visitors and render clerical and secretarial support at a television station or media organization

Alternate Title(s): None

Salary Range: $14,000 to $35,000

Employment Prospects: Excellent

Advancement Prospects: Good

Prerequisites:

Education and Training—High school diploma

Experience—Part-time office work

Special Skills and Personality Traits—Familiarity with office equipment; good personal skills; word processing ability

---

Various positions in the Business Department

Receptionist and Office Clerk

High School; Business School; College

Position Description

Receptionists have an obligation to make a good first impression as they greet customers, vendors, and visitors at a communications company or television station and determine what their needs are. Usually, Receptionists also answer telephones and route calls to the proper staff individual. Increasingly, Receptionists are using multiline telephone systems, personal computers, and fax machines. While some stations may have automated answering systems or voice mail, Receptionists are still relied on to take messages and inform other employees of the arrival of visitors and customers or any cancellations of appointments. They arrange appointments, screen telephone calls, take messages, and help any unscheduled visitors or customers. They may provide temporary identification cards and arrange staff escorts for visitors or customers.

In addition, Receptionists are frequently responsible for the coordination of all mail into and out of the office, the opening and sorting of that mail, the collection and distribution of parcels, and arranging for express mail or other types of mail services. They may also be responsible for such word processing duties as keying correspondence or reports, addressing envelopes, creating labels and lists, and forwarding incoming e-mails to appropriate department personnel. Receptionists are employed at nearly every public and commercial television station. They are also part of the staff of most other organizations related to the broadcasting industry.

Office Clerks are tasked with various administrative and clerical duties. They help to maintain the rapid flow of written communications among the departments. They act as information managers for the station or media operation, planning and scheduling meetings and appointments, making travel arrangements, organizing and maintaining files (which may contain correspondence, rough drafts, orders, invoices and business records), and may conduct research.

Office Clerks may work in specific sections of a media operation, while others may be part of a pool of such personnel shared among the departments. Beginning clerks often process and print mailing labels, orders and invoices, and form letters as well as operate copying machines, calculators, and other office equipment. More experienced clerks often transcribe rough handwritten drafts, which may be difficult to read or that may contain considerable amounts of technical information or budgetary detail, into report forms that can be circulated as required within departments. They may also be required to plan and key onto a computer file complicated statistical tables, combining and managing materials from different sources, into reports and prepare the master copies to be reproduced on office copying machines. As support to managers and department heads, they may also be called on to use personal computers to create spreadsheets, compose correspondence, manage databases, and create presentations, reports, and documents.

In some large media firms, word processing centers handle the transcription and keyboarding for many departments. In these cases, Office Clerks may work in that center. However, most media companies are moderate or small in size and without a full word processing center. In such cases, Office Clerks may work in a single location but do work for many individuals from various departments.

Salaries

According to the *Occupational Outlook Handbook* of the U.S. Department of Labor's Bureau of Labor Statistics, the median annual earnings of full-time general Office Clerks were $22,280, with the middle 50 percent earning between $17,630 and $28,190. The lowest 10 percent earned less than $14,260, and the highest 10 percent earned more than $34,890. In contrast, the *Handbook* indicates that in 2002 median annual earnings of general secretaries were about $25,290. In a salary survey of Receptionists done by Broadcast Employment Services, it was found that in 2004 their salaries ranged from a low of $10,000 yearly to a high of $27,000, with a median salary being $24,000.

Employment Prospects

The job prospects for these positions are excellent. They are almost always considered entry-level jobs, and, as such, they are fine opportunities for beginners to get into the industry as well as for those individuals returning to the job market. Every commercial and public television station employs at least one Receptionist, and most of them have three to five staff Office Clerks. Some of the larger stations may have as many as 15 such individuals in these clerical support jobs. Opportunities also exist at production/facilities companies, corporate television centers, cable TV systems, and at educational, governmental, and health media centers.

Employment of Receptionists and Office Clerks is expected to grow as fast or faster than the average for all occupations through 2012, according to the Bureau of Labor Statistics, due to the high turnover rate of these posts. While these positions are affected by growing technology adopted in the office workplace, many of the tasks are interpersonal in nature and, as such, are not easily automated, thus ensuring a continued demand.

Advancement Prospects

The chances for advancement for bright, attentive, and personable individuals are good. The responsibilities of these positions are such that they require persons in them to learn thoroughly the assorted facets of media operations, giving them both background and training for other positions in the field. Many Receptionists and Office Clerks use their positions to scout out other job openings.

Some of them are promoted to a production secretary or production assistant position, while others may become bookkeepers or desk assistants. Individuals with a talent for sales work may advance to jobs as sales coordinators or traffic continuity specialists. Some may move into jobs in nonbroadcast firms that still deal in media communications.

Education and Training

The minimum requirement for the positions of Receptionist or Office Clerk is a high school diploma. While these are entry-level administrative support positions, some employers may prefer or even require some previous office or business experience, as well as basic computer skills, keyboarding abilities, and other general office skills. Other employers may require some formal training at a community or junior college or at a postsecondary vocational school. They may require some education in communications or even an undergraduate degree in media or television in order to train a beginner candidate for more responsible positions. Some employers may require new support staff to attend classes or participate in online education in order to learn how to operate new office technologies, such as information storage systems, scanners, the Internet, and updated software packages.

Experience, Skills, and Personality Traits

Most employers do not require extensive business experience for these positions. However, employers increasingly are requiring candidates to have fairly extensive knowledge of software applications, such as word processing, spreadsheets, and database management. Good grammar, punctuation, spelling—beyond word processing aids—as well as solid oral communication skills are important for these positions. A basic familiarity with standard office equipment and procedures is an asset. As these individuals often interact with both staff and visitors, employers look for candidates with good customer service and interpersonal skills. Also, applicants must be detail oriented and flexible.

Unions and Associations

There are no unions or professional associations that represent Receptionists or Office Clerks.

Tips for Entry

1. During high school or afterward, take computer courses in word processing, spreadsheets, and database management to give you an edge for this entry-level position into the television industry.
2. Consider additional course work after high school in business office skills or business administration, and seek part-time work to use these skills.
3. Take psychology and sociology courses in high school to further your understanding of human behavior and to increase your interpersonal skills.

NEWS

ASSISTANT NEWS DIRECTOR

CAREER PROFILE

Duties: Supervise day-to-day newsroom operations and oversee the scheduling of assignments for news coverage

Alternate Title(s): Assignment Editor; Desk Editor; Television Managing Editor

Salary Range: $28,000 to $100,000 or more

Employment Prospects: Fair

Advancement Prospects: Good

Prerequisites:

   Education and Training—Undergraduate degree in journalism, mass communications, or political science

   Experience—Two to five years as a reporter and in other positions in the news department

   Special Skills and Personality Traits—Good communication skills; leadership qualities; objectivity; organizational abilities; sound news judgment

CAREER LADDER

```
┌─────────────────────────────┐
│       News Director         │
└─────────────────────────────┘

┌─────────────────────────────┐
│   Assistant News Director   │
└─────────────────────────────┘

┌─────────────────────────────┐
│         Reporter            │
└─────────────────────────────┘
```

Position Description

The majority of commercial television stations and many public television operations as well as large cable systems and newsgathering organizations employ Assistant News Directors. The national cable and broadcast networks have Assistant News Directors as well, as do most local TV stations. While responsibilities may vary from one station to another, nearly every Assistant News Director supervises the daily functioning of the newsroom and usually is accountable for the selection and assigning of commentators, news writers, and reporters to cover specific news and special events.

In managing the daily operation of the television newsroom, Assistant News Directors coordinate wire service reports, network news feeds, and taped or filmed inserts to be used in the broadcast with stories from individual news writers and reporters. They monitor all the assignments and news activities leading to each newscast and schedule work shifts so that the newsroom is properly staffed at all times. At some stations, the Assistant News Director also designates the technical crews to be used for each news assignment and selects the producer for each newscast segment.

Assistant News Directors scrutinize news reports, weigh their significance, and decide on the coverage that will be given them in the broadcast. They evaluate finished news stories, review any film inserts and taped reports, and select the significant stories for use on a newscast. They check for any reportorial mistakes or misinterpretations to ensure credible and balanced news reporting on the station's newscast. They work closely with specialty reporters, such as investigative consumer reporters and medical journalists, in the preparation of their stories and the reporting of them on the station's newscasts. Assistant News Directors must make sure that the station's news direction and vision as established by the news director and the general manager are adhered to on a daily basis. Most important, it is the Assistant News Director who sets the tenor, decides the substance, and is ultimately responsible for the visual elements and accuracy of all news products. As such, Assistant News Directors often have direct supervisory control over the video and film news units.

Assistant News Directors report to and confer with news directors and assist them in overseeing newsroom personnel, including hiring, firing, and any corrective actions that need to be taken. The assistant usually assumes complete supervision of the news staff when the news director is away from the station and often when fast-breaking stories are developing. Frequently, Assistant News Directors are expected to collaborate with the news director on editorial direction, strategic initiatives for the station, and product and talent development.

Today's television newsroom's computer systems instantly transmit news assignments and their stories to and from field reporters, indicating the whereabouts of a news crew that is nearest to a "breaking" story. Such systems constantly monitor all the logistics of newsgathering teams, allowing the Assistant News Director to assign quickly needed news personnel to stories in the field. An additional duty of the Assistant News Director is to develop procedures (and recommend the purchase of any needed news equipment) to improve and strengthen the technical aspects of news gathering so as to improve the speed, flexibility, and efficiency of the news operation.

Salaries

According to the Radio-Television News Directors Association (RTNDA), in 2003 the annual salaries for Assistant News Directors ranged from a minimum of $22,000 to a maximum of $170,000. Assistant News Directors working in the smallest television markets had a median yearly salary of $35,500, and those working in the largest television markets had a median salary of $100,000. The average annual salary was $64,000. Interestingly, a 2004 annual salary survey of Assistant News Directors conducted by Broadcast Employment Services indicated that earnings ranged from a low of $28,000 to a high of $81,000, with a median salary being $46,000, and the mean average salary being $49,966.

Employment Prospects

Most major-market television stations employ more than one Assistant News Director, with each one responsible for a specific news area, and nearly every television station and network has this position in its staff lineup as well. However, there are many ambitious and able reporters competing for advancement to this position at commercial, public, and cable stations of all sizes, so opportunities for employment remain generally only fair.

Advancement Prospects

Television newscast shows are more popular and have higher ratings than ever before. Cable networks are greatly expanding their news broadcasts to meet the competition of their rivals. In addition, with the presence of such all-news cable television networks as CNN (as well as online news services), the opportunities for advancement for Assistant News Directors are good.

For one thing, the relatively high turnover rate of news directors provides for the possibility of direct promotion to that position. The wire services, such as Associated Press (AP), United Press International (UPI), and Reuters News

Service, government, information, and public relations fields also represent possible career advancement for people who have had management experience in broadcast news. Another area for potential career advancement is that of magazine or newspaper management positions.

Education and Training

An undergraduate degree in journalism, mass communications, or political science is an absolute requirement for the position of Assistant News Director. Equally vital is a strong liberal arts background, including both history courses (which contribute a sense of perspective to news events) and English courses (which improve language skills). Many employers also look for some educational background in business administration or economics. Training in and knowledge of journalism and television production are pluses.

Experience, Skills, and Personality Traits

Assistant News Director is not an entry-level position. It is typically filled by promotion from within the ranks of the news department at a television station. Several years of experience (from two to five or more) as a reporter and in various other newsroom positions are usually expected for such a promotion to occur. Some Assistant News Directors are recruited from another television station (usually in a smaller market) or from print journalism. In the latter case, some experience in broadcast news is usually required.

The job of an Assistant News Director is both demanding and challenging. It calls for an inquiring mind, strong organizational, interpersonal, and communication talents, and the ability to direct, coach, and manage a news staff. Assistant News Directors have to possess the awareness and initiative of a good reporter, a strong command of current events (including local news, national news, world news, cultural affairs, and sports), and an eye for creative live coverage of news events. They must have great news judgment, even when under tremendous pressure, and a knack for coordinating many work-related activities on a tight schedule.

A knowledge of television production, copyediting procedures, journalism ethics, journalism law, news photography, news tape editing processes, news equipment and operations, and computers as applied to news production are additional requirements. An understanding of nonlinear editing techniques and electronic newsgathering (ENG) technology and procedures is a helpful bonus.

Unions and Associations

If their duties involve any news writing or reporting on the air, Assistant News Directors may be members of the American Federation of Television and Radio Artists (AFTRA) or the Writers Guild of America (WGA). This is more likely to be the case of jobs with large-market stations or at the network level. In some cases, due to their duties in selecting and assigning commentators, news writers, and reporters, Assistant News Directors may be member of the International Alliance of Theatrical and Stage Employees (IATSE).

Assistant News Directors may find it beneficial to become members of the Radio-Television News Directors Association. An additional professional association that might prove useful is the Society of Professional Journalists.

Tips for Entry

1. While in high school and college, work on your language skills, both writing and public speaking.

2. Become computer literate, both in searching for information and knowing about the Internet and Web construction. Become adept with things digital.

3. Participate on your school newspaper and look into part-time or freelance work in news announcing or production at a local radio or television station, on or off campus.

4. When working as a reporter, learn all you can about television production, how news footage is edited, and how newscasts are assembled. This will help to prepare you for the more exacting work of an Assistant News Director.

DESK ASSISTANT AND RESEARCHER

CAREER PROFILE

Duties: Provide clerical and general assistance to the news department of a television station; support television staff with background research for news programs

Alternate Title(s): News Desk Assistant; News Assistant

Salary Range: $9,000 to $55,000

Employment Prospects: Good; Fair

Advancement Prospects: Good; Fair

Prerequisites:

Education and Training—High school diploma required, some college or business school or college degree preferred; undergraduate degree in communications, English, or journalism

Experience—None necessary, but any news-related work is helpful; media background preferred

Special Skills and Personality Traits—Accurate and detail-oriented; clerical and organizational abilities; computer skills; writing aptitude

CAREER LADDER

News Writer; Production Assistant; Reporter

Desk Assistant and Researcher

High School / Business School / College

Position Description

The Desk Assistant is a multitask helper in a television news department who performs routine office and clerical tasks while learning the trade. The position is almost always an entry-level apprenticeship for individuals with specific interest in a broadcast news career. The usual employers of Desk Assistants are the medium and large stations and networks, where staffs are sufficiently large enough to warrant the need for such clerical backup. Desk Assistants may work part or full time, all hours of the day or night as needed, any days of the week and even on holidays.

In their performance of broad office duties, Desk Assistants answer telephones, take messages for staff members, open and distribute mail, deliver newspapers and magazines, order office supplies, and file scripts and correspondence. They are also usually responsible for monitoring copy from wire service printer terminals and distributing it to the desks of news writers, editors, and reporters. As Desk Assistants are considered to be general messengers, they are expected to fill requests for information and deliver film or videotape to and from editors and reporters, the newsroom library, the videotape storage room, labora-

tories, and studios. They are frequently involved in logging incoming and outgoing news film and tape and making sure it is delivered to the proper location for shipment or use at the station. On occasion, they are even dispatched to a local airport, bus terminal, or train depot to ship or retrieve news film and videotape. Also as part of their messenger status, they may have to pick up food for newsroom personnel and distribute packages both inside and outside the station.

Their job may also include assisting producers to assemble news programs for broadcast and aiding production assistants with script preparation. "Breaking script," as it is called, is done for every news broadcast. This process includes word processing updated sections of the script for a newscast, special report, or documentary and then distributing the scripts to all the appropriate staff members. Desk Assistants may also be required to transcribe the audio portion of a film or videotape interview into a text format so that a reporter or producer can select the segments to be included in the final news production. They generally are assigned to assist studio and control room personnel during production and even may accompany a reporter to an on-location assignment to be on hand to rush film or videotape back to the home plant or to a laboratory for development.

In larger stations and at networks, the Desk Assistant may be assigned on a regular basis to a specific news show or special news unit. In most stations, however, Desk Assistants are involved in the full newsroom operation. As such, this post provides a wonderful introduction to the news profession and an invaluable chance to become acquainted with all facets of television news.

A Researcher in the news department is also an entry-level job, though some of the bigger stations as well as the networks may have separate levels of junior and senior Researchers. The primary duties of Researchers are to help news directors and editors, news writers, and reporters by amassing background information on stories to be aired. A 30-minute news broadcast may contain from 15 to 30 different (or interlinked) stories, and an individual Researcher may work on several stories for each broadcast.

Most of the research work is done by telephone or on the Internet, previewing and checking sources to uncover the best ones for a reporter to interview as well as verifying specific data pertaining to stories. The Researcher then prepares summary reports of the findings for reporters or news writers to use. Researchers need to be able to review a lot of information quickly, sift out the most important data, and then summarize this information in as concise a manner as possible. Other work of Researchers may consist of deeper background searching for information for feature stories to be aired later. As Theresa Collington Moore, a news researcher for WRSP-TV says, "Facts are better than adjectives when it comes to strengthening a story, a pitch, a lead, a tag or an argument. Managers are more inclined to accept a story idea when it's not just a cool idea but a cool idea that can be illustrated with the use of supporting fact-based information. . . . The fact is, research takes time, and reporters and producers often are focused on their daily turns. Spending the time it takes to debunk or confirm everything they hear on the street is not an option for them. That's where a Researcher comes in."

Researchers rely on television or newspaper archives or such online research sites as NewsLab (http://www.newslab.org), Nielsen Media Research (http://www.nielsenmedia.com), World News Connection (http://www.fedworld.gov), or other Internet-based reference sources. Researchers may also generate ideas for stories. They must maintain contact with news sources as well as continuously monitor magazines, newspapers, and Internet news sites. They have to be familiar with such online research tools as Lexis-Nexus (http://www.lexis-nexus.com) national database, Factiva (http://www.factiva.com), and other public records databases as well as census tools, mapping tools, and people finders. At some stations, Researchers may be assigned to specific geographic areas or to particular subject areas, such as business, education, or government. At smaller- or medium-sized stations, the positions of Desk Assistant and Researcher may be combined into one. However, the larger stations and networks may require their senior Researchers to have a library background and a master of library science (M.L.S.) degree.

As noted above, researchers may also assist reporters or news writers in collecting audio and visual materials for stories, searching library files, or contacting other stations to acquire film or videotape footage. They are expected to do follow-up work on pieces for possible further development as well as their regular work, and, in some cases, they may be loaned to the station's marketing department, where they track ratings on various new shows.

Salaries

Entry-level positions in television tend have low salaries. According to the 2004 salary survey of the previous year made by the Radio-Television News Directors Association (RTNDA), Desk Assistants earned annual salaries ranging from a low of $9,000 (entry-level salary) to a high of $55,000, with an average salary being $22,700. Median annual salaries at the smaller-market stations were $15,000, whereas the larger- (and larger-staffed) market stations had median yearly salaries ranging from $18,000 to $34,500. Seniority, the size of the station and its market, and geographical differences all affect the scale of salaries. As in most other news positions, the larger the market or the larger the station's staff, the higher the salaries.

Researchers are frequently recompensed on a weekly or hourly rate, with extra pay for overtime. Some Researchers may be used only part time. Beginner Researchers may earn from $11,000 to $15,000 or more annually, while seasoned Researchers with more than three years of experience can earn up to $40,000 or more, including overtime, according to industry sources. The best-paid positions are generally found at the larger-market stations and with the networks.

Employment Prospects

Opportunities for entry-level positions in television are good. Desk Assistant jobs are most likely to be found at middle- and large-market stations, though small facilities also hire for this post. Despite the tough competition, the demand for filling this position is generally steady due to the relatively rapid turnover in the job as Desk Assistants are promoted or decide to pursue careers in other fields. In addition, the growth of cable television news has expanded opportunities for beginners, as has the increase in the number of low power television stations (LPTV) and online news services.

The position of Researcher is normally regarded to be an entry-level job in the news department of a television station or network. However, some of the larger stations and the networks may insist on a certain degree of experience and even in some cases additional educational background in library science. Competition for these positions is also strenuous, but the increasing need for news research will help to guarantee a job market for this position. Part-time positions are also a viable option, as they often can evolve into full-time positions.

Advancement Prospects

The Desk Assistant is an outstanding training ground for nearly every type of position in the news department of a television station, from production to newswriting to reporting. To achieve that promotion, Desk Assistants need to demonstrate a thorough knowledge of news broadcast operations, reliable news judgment, and solid writing and speaking skills. They must show high motivation by seeking assignments beyond the normal range of Desk Assistants' duties. With the necessary skills, they may progress to become news writers or reporters, while others may move into news production as production assistants. Still others may find advancement opportunities in cable TV news or at newspapers, wire services, or news magazines.

While obtaining a full-time position as a Researcher in the news department of a television station may be somewhat problematic, once established, a Researcher will find advancement opportunities are often good. With the experience of several years as a Researcher, an individual may move up the career ladder to reporting the news, writing scripts for the news, or assisting in the production of the news, special features, documentaries, or other television programs.

Education and Training

While a college degree is not essential for the post of Desk Assistant, it will be necessary for higher positions within broadcast journalism. For this reason, some Desk Assistants work part time while completing their college work. Whatever their major may be, aspiring broadcast journalists should include courses in broadcasting, communications, English, history, journalism, political science, and other social sciences. Initially, a year or two of business school education may be a substitute for a college degree, but the degree will become necessary for advancement.

Much the same type of education requirements apply to a Researcher. A strong liberal arts background, with some courses in library science and broadcast journalism, and a thorough familiarity with computer research tools, software, and the Internet are useful educational areas to delve into for this position.

Experience, Skills, and Personality Traits

Experience in any type of news-related job is helpful. Such jobs might include working on a community newspaper or a school publication or an internship at a local radio or television station. Clerical and office skills, word processing, writing, and organizational abilities are important. Initiative, an inquisitive mind, and enthusiasm are also helpful traits. Desk Assistants aspiring to newswriting or reporting positions must have or acquire good journalistic research and writing skills, as well as possess both ambition and self-motivation.

For Researchers also, any experience in a news-related environment, such as working on school or community publications or interning at local radio or television stations, is useful. Working part time in a library or research facility would be beneficial. Researchers have to be skillful at gathering information rapidly. They need to be comfortable interviewing over the telephone or through e-mail, able to use computer software to search for information, and be extremely detail oriented and well organized. They must be able to work under considerable deadline pressure and be equipped to produce clearly written and concise reports and/or summaries of their research findings. They must have good news judgment and be very knowledgeable about resources for information.

Unions and Associations

At network owned and operated stations and some other major-market stations, Desk Assistants and Researchers are represented for bargaining purposes by the National Association of Broadcast Employees and Technicians AFL-CIO (NABET). At most television news outlets, however, they are not represented by any one union.

Both Desk Assistants and Researchers may find it beneficial to belong to the American Federation of Television and Radio Artists, the Society of Professional Journalists, or the Writers Guild of America. Researchers who are expanding their education to a library science degree may also want to belong to the American Library Association.

Tips for Entry

1. While in school and college, become actively involved with your campus radio or television stations to gain broadcast experience, and work on any school publication to acquire journalistic know-how.
2. Participate in internship programs at local independent, cable, or network affiliated stations.
3. Take an office part-time job during school to acquire needed clerical and office skills.
4. Cultivate your speaking abilities (by English, drama, or speech courses) and your computer skills, as both will be essential in your career as a broadcast journalist.
5. A summer job in a research facility, such as a library, will add to your understanding of the dimensions and demands of the research process.

NEWS ANCHOR

Duties: Host news or other current events programs; report the news and introduce reports on the air; interview guests; serve as the focal point for a newscast

Alternate Title(s): Anchor; TV Newscaster

Salary Range: $15,000 to $110,000 or more

Employment Prospects: Poor

Advancement Prospects: Poor

Prerequisites:

Education and Training—Undergraduate degree in communications, English, journalism, or political science with emphasis on liberal arts; graduate degree may in some cases be required.

Experience—Many years as a news correspondent, reporter, or in other television newsroom positions

Special Skills and Personality Traits—Ability to communicate with authority; attractive on-camera look; capacity for working under pressure; excellent interpersonal skills; good voice and diction; integrity; agreeable persona

Anchor (large station or network)

News Anchor

Reporter; Correspondent

Position Description

The main responsibilities of News Anchors are to conduct regularly scheduled newscasts, host the broadcasting of special events such as elections and news-breaking events, present news stories, and introduce prerecorded news or live transmissions from on-the-scene reporters. They also report on some of the major news stories, initiate lead-ins for other pieces covered by reporters in or out of the studio, provide voice-over commentary for filmed or taped material of a particular story or event, interview any guests who appear on the show, and serve as the pivotal personalities around whom the entire newscast revolves. These individuals are highly visible in a community, sometime becoming public personalities or celebrities. As such, the job of anchorperson is a coveted one within the broadcasting business. Understandably, rivalry for any desirable openings is intense. Anchors earn their jobs by putting in many years of hard work as reporters or correspondents and becoming knowledgeable about politics, social trends, and other issues of great public concern.

This position often appears to be highly lucrative, glamorous, and easy. In fact, it is sometimes high paying (in the large-market stations and networks generally), occasionally glamorous, and almost never easy. As Peter Jennings, the late ABC network anchor, said: "If your concentration wavers for just a second, you're going to miss something. The job of the anchorperson then is to sit there and knit the whole thing together and give it perspective and give it context and know what questions to ask and know who to bring in, who to put onstage. And when to get them onstage, and when to get them offstage. And to not get in the way of those dimensions of the story that don't need a lot of clutter." Sometimes, News Anchors at large stations or networks specialize in a particular type of news, such as entertainment, finance, sports, or weather. In some small-market stations, anchors may only read accounts of the day's stories and introduce background reports provided by their affiliated network or by a television news service. In other smaller- and most medium-sized stations, anchors often do the legwork necessary to research and write news stories or construct the stories from wire service copy, network feeds, or Internet sources. In larger-market stations (and on the networks), support staff usually performs these functions, and the anchor's primary job is to host the show, read the news copy, and conduct interviews. Nevertheless, even at stations with large news teams (and at the network level), the News Anchor frequently writes or rewrites some of the material to be used on the air.

Prior to broadcast time, News Anchors review the contents of the broadcast with the news director and staff. At large stations (and at the networks) anchors have the deciding voice in the content of the broadcast and the time to be devoted to each of the various stories. Most of the network news shows (and even those of medium-sized and large stations) provide time for anchors to question reporters and exchange conversation and banter. Some of this, of course, is orchestrated, and some of it is spontaneous.

A top-market station might have as many as eight or nine News Anchors to cover its full news line-up. Local stations usually have a two-anchor team that may handle both morning and evening news, whereas large-market stations typically have three teams of anchors who divide up the broadcasting day. In addition, anchors sometime report from locations outside the studio, usually in the case of a breaking major story or news event. They may also do the primary coverage on-site for conferences and conventions and work on documentaries or specials to be broadcast separately from the daily and weekly newscasts.

With the continuous escalation of news coverage by public, commercial, and cable television stations and the constant involvement of stations in rating wars to grab viewers' attention, the anchor has become one of the most important elements of a newscast. An attractive and popular individual can bring more viewers to the newscast each day, thus increasing the station's consumer audience and helping to guarantee increased revenues from advertising.

Salaries

The salary range for News Anchors is an extremely wide one, with smaller-market stations paying near the lower end of the scale and the major networks near the top. Some major network personalities earn more than a $1 million a year. According to a study made in 2004 of 2003 broadcasting salaries by the Radio-Television News Directors Association (RTNDA), annual salaries for television News Anchors ranged from a minimum of $10,000 to a maximum of $400,000. Their average salary for that year was $72,200, and the median yearly income was $59,500. At the largest-market stations, the median annual salary was $115,000, whereas at the smaller-market stations it was $30,000.

In a separate survey taken in 2005 about 2004 salaries by Broadcast Employment Services for their http://www. TVJobs.com Web site, it was found that annual salaries for News Anchors ranged from a low of $15,000 to a high of $400,000, with a mean average of $57,782 and a median income of $45,000. Broadcast Employment Services also found that for entry-level anchors, the yearly salaries ranged

from a low of $16,000 to a high of $65,000, with the mean average being $25,459.

Employment Prospects

The position of News Anchor at any television station or network is an extremely appealing post and is frequently considered to be the highest point in a broadcaster's career. It is well paid, extremely visible, and usually accompanied by substantial benefits. The contest for these positions is very intense. Only a very small percentage of television reporters or correspondents ever become News Anchors. The typical small television station hires only two anchors, whereas major-market stations and networks may have 10 to 15 anchors on staff.

The success of News Anchors is frequently judged by television ratings in their time slot within their market. This continuous emphasis on ratings guarantees high turnover in some anchor positions as anchors fail to meet the ratings standards or are hired away by competing local stations or higher-paying stations in larger markets (or by the networks). The proliferation of cable and satellite television systems offering news programs (and the continuous broadcast of such by the CNN cable network), help increase the chance of employment as an anchor. Job openings continue to be better for minorities and women as stations seek to maintain a balance in this highly visible position.

Advancement Prospects

As the position of News Anchor is the highest position for a reporter or correspondent to achieve, the only real occasion for advancement for an anchor at a station is to shift upward to a larger-market station (with the result of higher pay) or to a national network (with higher pay, greater prestige, and more national visibility). Again, the rivalry is extremely severe, making advancement potentials generally quite poor.

Education and Training

An undergraduate degree in communications, journalism, political science, or one of the liberal arts is a basic requirement for an aspiring anchor, and a graduate degree is often preferable. News directors generally recommend a strong liberal arts education and an emphasis on courses in English, speech, government, sociology, and the humanities.

Experience, Skills, and Personality Traits

Reporters and correspondents typically devote many years to working in the field before becoming eligible for promotion to a News Anchor position. Then more years of newsroom experience at smaller- or medium-market stations are necessary before moving up to the larger-market stations or networks. This includes news writing and reporting in all content areas of a newscast to gain the broadest experience possible.

Anchors need to possess excellent writing abilities, good interpersonal skills, and solid news judgment. A large part of the success of an anchor is based on the person's on-air look, demeanor, and delivery. Anchors must have a pleasing on-camera appearance (good grooming) and personality, as well as speak in a clear and confident manner. Their presentation needs to convey authority, and they must demonstrate a knowledge of issues, names, geography, and history and have the ability to put all of these and the current stories being covered into perspective for the television viewer. Their command of diction, grammar, storytelling, syntax, and tone needs to be exemplary. As hosts of newscasts, they need to be able to process new information fast, be skillful in the interviewing process, and be sensitive to the ethical problems of unconfirmed information as well as any words that might convey the wrong message to viewers or thoughtlessly add pain to any already traumatized victims who might be interviewed. Finally, anchors must be adroit at multitasking and be able to ad-lib convincingly and think spontaneously as news events or other unexpected things occur live during the broadcast.

Unions and Associations

When represented by a union, News Anchors may be members of the American Federation of Television and Radio Artists (AFTRA) or the Writers Guild of America (WGA). They may also find it beneficial to belong to the Radio-Television News Directors Association, which is very active in promoting the profession of broadcast news, the National Association of Broadcasters, or the Society of Professional Journalists.

Tips for Entry

1. While in college, become actively involved in your campus radio and television stations and consider participating in any internship programs at local independent, cable, or network-affiliated stations.
2. Read everything you can about what's going on in the world, and consider combining your liberal arts education with a graduate program in journalism or broadcasting to gain the technical skills you will need.
3. After beginning work at a television station, be willing to be employed in a variety of newsroom positions to gain needed television experience.
4. Try using newspaper stories to practice ad-libbing live, presenting the story without a script.

NEWS DIRECTOR

Duties: Assign news coverage; determine the station's policies toward news; supervise entire news operation of a television station

Alternate Title(s): News Editor; Vice President of News

Salary Range: $16,000 to $260,000 or more

Employment Prospects: Poor

Advancement Prospects: Fair

Prerequisites:

Education and Training—Undergraduate degree in communications, journalism, or liberal arts; graduate degree in journalism, mass communications, political science, or the social sciences

Experience—Several years in other television news positions or news work in print journalism or radio

Special Skills and Personality Traits—Excellent news judgment; imagination; inquisitive mind; objectivity and integrity; solid managerial and administrative abilities

General Station Manager; News VP
(large station or network)

News Director

Assistant News Director;
Executive Producer

Position Description

The News Director is the senior decision maker in charge of a television station's news department and is accountable for a television station's entire news operations. News Directors are the final authority for the choice of all news, documentaries, interviews, and special events programs broadcast by a station.

They determine what stories and events will be covered, how the pieces are to be presented, and which reporters will be assigned to handle them. In so doing, they must rely on their strong journalistic instincts, assessing the significance of a story and deciding how best to use the station's on-hand reporting talent and technical resources. They edit and review all scripts and news file reports. In overseeing every aspect of the news department (from the photographers to the anchors to the production team), they have the final accountability for and authority over what appears on the air.

An average television station has a staff of 20 to 30 individuals. Larger stations typically have 50 to 85 and may even employ up to 130 or more reporters, anchorpersons, sportscasters, weather reporters, news reporters, film-video-digital camera operators, and cinematographers/videographers along with other professionals and support personnel. Therefore, News Directors have to be able to supervise and communicate with a highly varied news team that often has individuals with strong personalities. They are the final arbiter in all newsroom personnel matters, making the position more of a management one than one pertaining just to journalism.

As a part of their duties, News Directors develop and administer the budget for the department. At small stations, they may also take part in the gathering and reporting of news, and they may even serve as talk show hosts. They monitor the progress of any extensive investigative research and reporting and of coverage of special events. They review and approve all news footage to be broadcast as well as edited news copy to be used.

News Directors typically coordinate the technical operations of the news production (and are sometimes termed news producers), resolving any production or technical problems at the station. This aspect of their job also involves assigning camera crews to stories and camera operatives to work in the studio. In addition, they coordinate all news department activities with the traffic/continuity and programming departments and frequently supervise the station's public affairs offerings.

News Directors report directly to station general managers or, in the case of large stations or networks, to the vice president of news. They are often on duty for extremely long hours and work under great pressure. They need to make many quick decisions as to what major stories need to be covered immediately. An additional point of pressure on them is that the security of their jobs is heavily dependent on station ratings.

Salaries

Earnings of News Directors vary considerably, depending on the station's size, its geographical location, and the level of its local news coverage. Annual salaries ranged from a low of $16,000 to a high of $260,000, according to the 2003 salary study done by the Radio-Television News Directors Association (RTNDA). The study indicated that the average yearly base salary was $78,900. The larger the market, or the larger the news staff, the higher the salaries tended to be. News Directors in the smallest markets ranked number 150 onward had an average median salary of $50,000 per year. Those in the top 25 markets averaged $100,000. In stations with staffs of 10 or less, News Directors' annual salaries had a median average of $39,000. In stations of 51 or more staff, News Directors' salaries averaged a median of $126,000 yearly. Public television salaries for News Directors were comparable or slightly less.

While these salaries are very respectable, News Directors generally are paid less than the superstar anchorpersons of both local and network news. News Directors at midsize and small stations, however, often act as anchorpersons. In a survey of News Directors and their 2004 salaries done by Broadcast Employment Services, it was found that the annual salaries ranged from $16,000 to $185,000, with a mean average being $56,738. In a parallel survey by Broadcast Employment Services of News Directors who also act as anchors, it was found that the annual salaries ranged from $14,000 to $400,000, with a mean average of $58,049.

Employment Prospects

Although the U.S. Department of Labor's Bureau of Labor Statistics projects slower than average growth (about 10 percent) in television jobs through the year 2012, competition will remain strong for News Director posts, particularly in the highly desirable major cities and the larger markets and networks. The news profession is filled with individuals who are capable, ambitious, and aggressive, making the competition for this highly coveted position fierce. Only exceptionably talented people become News Directors. Often, a successful assistant news director or executive producer is promoted to this top position.

However, the necessity of high ratings in the extremely competitive television marketplace combined with the economic value of news to a television station's income create a continuing search for new formats, ideas, different on-air personalities, and fresh News Directors. Thus, there is a high turnover rate among News Directors. An additional source for this job position is the growth of alternative media sources, such as cable television, satellite radio, and Internet journalism Web sites.

Advancement Prospects

Although there is a fairly high turnover rate among News Directors, there are few positions of higher authority or wage earnings to which they may advance. Some move on to print journalism or new media journalism (such as Internet Web sites devoted to news). Some become news vice presidents at very large television stations or networks, and some are even promoted to the top general management position of station manager (though that position is more often filled by someone from the sales department of the station).

For many newspersons, the position of News Director is the culmination of their news career. Because of the limited number of possible further career upward moves for most News Directors, chances for advancement from this position are considered to be only fair.

Education and Training

The minimum educational requirement for a newsroom supervisory position such as News Director is an undergraduate degree in communications, English, journalism, or political science. A solid liberal arts educational background with additional courses in economics, history, law, and sociology is recommended. Many News Directors also have a graduate degree.

Experience, Skills, and Personality Traits

Television News Directors must have several years of experience in lower-level news department positions (such as reporters, assistant news directors, or executive producers) before they can achieve a promotion to the position. Previous experience in radio news, in print journalism, or as a wire service reporter is also good training. Large operations, with all the attendant additional responsibilities, usually require more hands-on newsroom experience than smaller stations.

Energy, experience, imagination, and enterprise are all necessary for this position, and they need to be effective administrators. News Directors must have an extremely sound news judgment, good communication skills, an inquisitive mind, objectivity, a willingness to shoulder responsibilities, and an ability to make swift decisions. They must comprehend relevant Federal Communications Commission (FCC) regulations and understand the intricacies of the Freedom of Information Act, as well as applicable copyright and libel laws.

Unions and Associations

Being part of the management team, News Directors are not represented by any union for bargaining purposes. The primary membership association for News Directors and other news professionals is the Radio-Television News Directors Association. This organization sets standards for its members, encourages college students who are preparing for a broadcast news career, operates a placement service, and acts as a lobby presence in securing and protecting the right to report the news. Other useful associations for News Directors include the Academy of Television Arts and Sciences, the National Academy of Television Arts and Sciences, and, above all, the Society of Professional Journalists.

Tips for Entry

1. A solid liberal arts educational background with a major in journalism may be the best scholastic preparation for the eventual position of a News Director.
2. While in college, become actively involved in a campus radio or television station, work on any school publication to gain journalistic experience, and investigate potential internship programs at local independent, cable, or network-affiliated stations.
3. While working in various newsroom positions, anticipate your additional management responsibilities as a News Director by getting an advanced degree in business or management.

NEWS WRITER

CAREER PROFILE

Duties: Write and edit news stories and continuity material for newscasts

Alternate Title(s): Senior Editor

Salary Range: $13,000 to $90,000

Employment Prospects: Good

Advancement Prospects: Good

Prerequisites:

Education and Training—Undergraduate degree in communications or journalism, with a strong liberal arts background

Experience—Occasionally entry-level with no experience required; minimum of one year as a newsroom desk assistant, or in a similar or related writing position

Special Skills and Personality Traits—Ability to write clearly and concisely; computer skills; good news judgment and talent for research; speed, exactness, and facility to meet deadlines

CAREER LADDER

Reporter; Executive Producer

News Writer

College; Desk Assistant; Researcher

Position Description

A News Writer writes and edits news pieces, commentaries, continuity (transitional phrases or sentences), introductions, and descriptions that become the verbal portions of a newscast. It is a hectic job, demanding swiftness, good reportorial skills, sound news judgment, and the knack of writing for the ear rather than the eye.

At most television stations, News Writers do not write copy for advertising or commercials; they write primarily for newscasts. Even then, they do not prepare all the news stories as often, the reporter who gathers the information for the story and delivers the report on the air has written or has assisted in writing the story. Just as often reporters in the field ad-lib their reports from their notes and add voice-over narrative (which they have also written) in the editing process at the studio. Therefore, the writer usually concentrates on reportorial content for the anchorpersons and in-studio reporters. A writer also provides voice-over narrative copy for tape, film, or digital inserts and transitional copy (continuity) between stories and between the on-camera appearances of the reporters. Sometimes, a News Writer may be asked to follow through on a particular story and act as a producer or a reporter. On any given day, a News Writer may work on a few big stories or may write many small ones.

If needed, News Writers may be consigned to any shift, including holidays. They start their day by reviewing (and later rewriting) press releases and news stories from wire and satellite news services such as CNN and the Associated Press. They also review newspapers and stories aired on previous newscasts, study Internet sites, and review any relevant telephone interviews already done by reporters. It is also part of their job to verify all the facts for the news broadcasts and to get any additional relevant details needed. News Writers typically undertake their own research, corroborating other news sources and investigating conflicting reports, such as differences in the number of injuries reported in an accident. They interview sources by telephone or e-mail and rewrite the information they have collected, as well as research information in the station's library and on the Internet. They generally participate at one or more editorial meetings each day in which decisions are made as to what stories will be covered and who will be responsible for tracking and updating breaking stories. In some cases, News Writers may be assigned to coordinate footage and graphics to be used during newscasts, even working with artists, producers, or representatives of other television stations.

News Writers must be able to use language effectively and write succinct story scripts that are both easy for the newscaster to read and simple enough for viewers to understand easily. News writing differs from other forms of writing in that the writer must compose brief, descriptive sentences using correct adjectives and adverbs. An additional constraint is that these pieces must fit onto a teleprompter screen. These scripts are constricted by time (an average news story seldom runs more than 90 seconds and may be as short as 10 seconds for a special newsbreak). Because television is a visual medium, the writing of a news story is usually done after the visual material has been selected and edited. The News Writer then must match words to video images. At the same time, transitional "lead-ins" and "lead-outs" must be provided for on-camera interviews that are incorporated into the story. Thus, timing becomes crucial. To help them, News Writers may preview tapes of what is going to be shown, or they are given "shot sheets" in which visuals and time lengths are provided. The News Writer must measure and match the beat and meter of a phrase with the speech patterns and pace of the reporter or anchorperson who will be delivering the news on the air.

Other duties of News Writers frequently include assisting assignment editors, producers, or reporters with assorted tasks (for example, monitoring police beat calls). They may also work on making news digests, news documentaries, or other special programs. They may be required to supervise tape editing for news reports and even to write promotional stories about upcoming broadcasts. They usually work under the direct supervision of an assistant news director, a news editor, or a news director (depending on the size of the station staff). They must be accurate, thorough, and capable of writing under the pressure of instant deadlines. Overtime is a constant requirement, with 10- to 12-hour shifts not uncommon.

Salaries

News Writers generally earn less than the more visible on-air members of the news team. In its study of 2003 television news salaries, the Radio-Television News Directors Association found that the annual salaries of News Writers may range from a low of $14,000 to a high of $80,000, and the average salary was $29,700. In a recent study of salaries of television News Writers in 2004, Broadcast Employment Services found that those surveyed had yearly salaries ranging from $13,000 to $80,000, with a mean average salary of the group being $33,809.

Employment Prospects

Prospects for News Writers are generally good. Large television stations usually employ several News Writers, and the expansion of news coverage (with the increased length and frequency of newscasts) and the growing prestige of all-news cable television networks indicate ample opportunities for writers. However, the networks and major-market large stations usually hire only seasoned News Writers (with three to five years or more of experience), who have worked their way up from the smaller venues. For beginners, local and regional cable and independent stations are a good starting point.

Advancement Prospects

News Writers have the potential of advancing to such posts as full-time reporters or news editors, but only after they have proven their worth to the station. Such opportunities may open up at the station level, in cable TV news, or with one of the wire services. Some experienced News Writers may look to gain experience from production assignments to move on to a position as a producer at their own station or in a larger-market station.

Education and Training

An undergraduate degree in journalism or mass communication is almost a necessity. However, News Writers must be able to deal with a large array of subjects and need to have a solid historical perspective on the news events about which they are writing. Thus, a broad education in economics, English, history, liberal arts, political science, and the social sciences may prove to be just as beneficial as a degree in broadcast journalism or communications. Nonetheless, understanding the technical side of the broadcasting business through courses in broadcasting techniques and production methodologies is equally vital.

Experience, Skills, and Personality Traits

At small station outlets, News Writers are frequently entry-level individuals with little or no broadcasting experience. A candidate with at least one year as a desk assistant or a similar news function, however, stands a better chance for employment. This experience could be acquired outside of television broadcasting, but a familiarity with television news is helpful. In contrast, large stations and networks demand extensive experience and proven talents from their newly hired News Writers.

News Writers need to have a crisp journalistic writing style and the ability to translate complex ideas into meaningful copy. They have to be able to compress important data into story scripts that will be heard, not seen. They seldom have time to revise, and any revisions usually have to be done on the spot. As researchers, they have to be detail oriented but also work under the pressure of regular deadlines. Above all, News Writers need to be exceedingly adaptable and versatile, as they must be able to absorb many different topics and issues and, in turn, make them understandable to the average television viewer.

Unions and Associations

News Writers in the larger station markets and the networks are members of such unions as the American Federation of Television and Radio Artists (AFTRA), the National Association of Broadcast Employees and Technicians AFL-CIO (NABET), or the Writers Guild of America (WGA). Major professional associations that promote professional growth and offer support include the Academy of Television Arts and Sciences, the National Academy of Television Arts and Sciences, the Radio-Television News Directors Association (RTNDA), and the Society of Professional Journalists.

Tips for Entry

1. While in college, become actively involved with your campus radio and television stations to gain firsthand broadcast experience, and work on any school publication to achieve concrete practical writing experience.

2. Look into internship programs at local independent, cable, or network-affiliated stations.

3. As the skills of a News Writer are usually learned on the job, acquire all the writing experience possible. Even writing publicity materials for local businesses would be helpful.

4. Broaden your educational background to gain the breadth that a good News Writer must possess. Add a foreign language to your skills as it may become helpful on the job.

REPORTER

Duties: Gather news from various sources; analyze and prepare news and feature stories for broadcast; do on-air broadcasting

Alternate Title(s): Correspondent; Newscaster

Salary Range: $13,000 to $180,000

Employment Prospects: Fair

Advancement Prospects: Fair

Prerequisites:

Education and Training—Undergraduate degree in communications, journalism, or political science with strong liberal arts background

Experience—Minimum of two years as a news writer or researcher in television, radio, or print journalism

Special Skills and Personality Traits—Excellent reporting, speaking, and writing abilities; comfortable on camera and in the interviewing process; inquisitive mind and self-motivation; perseverance and dependability; solid news judgment

Assistant News Director; News Anchor

Reporter

College; News Writer; Researcher

Position Description

A television Reporter's main duty as a working journalist is to dig up news from diverse sources and prepare stories for broadcast. This process includes interviewing sources, researching facts, organizing material, sometimes writing the script, working with video (or digital) editors in the studio, and, finally, delivering the news piece(s) on air. At the major-market station and network level, a Reporter assigned to an area outside the studio or overseas usually is termed a correspondent. In some operations, Reporters serve as their own producers for particular assignments.

The daily tasks of Reporters vary noticeably from one site to another. At a small facility that does not employ a news writer, Reporters write the stories before delivering them on the air. In larger stations (and networks) with several Reporters and one or more news writers on staff, each Reporter may specialize in a particular subject area. In these cases, news writers aid Reporters in developing pieces for on-air presentation.

Reporters are always working against time, not only against the clock for scheduled news programs for which their story (or stories) must be ready to be aired, but also against the limited time they have to present the given piece on air. Most major newsstories normally run for about two minutes of airtime, while many items are allotted only 90 seconds or less in which to be presented.

Reporters are usually assigned stories (and a set time length) by an assignment editor or a news director. Editors often rely on the Reporter's news sense and instincts to determine the focus or emphasis of a particular entry as well as its length. Many Reporters at large stations or the networks specialize in particular fields, such as business and economics, consumer concerns, crime and the police, entertainment, health, politics, science and technology, or sports. Such Reporters usually have more say over the stories they generate than do those who cover general news events. Some Reporters also serve as anchorpersons and vice versa, particularly in the smaller stations.

Assembling data for stories includes interviewing people either by phone, in person, or by e-mail. While some stations have researchers or assistants to handle background fact checking and news writers to prepare the actual stories, most Reporters undertake all these tasks themselves. In addition, Reporters go on location with a camera crew and direct the shooting of the story. Their on-air report may include parts of one or more prerecorded interviews, a voice-over for the visual images, and a stand-up summary.

Reporters also generate ideas for potential stories for approval by, typically, the news director. After developing such story ideas, Reporters must hunt for extra information to bolster the piece and then deliver these stories with accuracy and a sense of urgency. Generally, Reporters are delegated to either a day or evening shift. They may also work on special features or investigative pieces that may take weeks before the story is ready to air. In addition, some Reporters may prepare special report series to be presented on a succession of programs. They must have strong conversational and writing skills, as well as the knack to ad-lib when required. They need to understand complex subject matter and to generate compelling and informative stories.

Salaries

While Reporters' salaries have increased in recent years, they are still paid substantially less than the top anchors. There is also a wide variance in Reporters' earnings between small local stations and the top market stations and networks.

In its 2003 television news salaries survey, the Radio-Television News Directors Association found that overall annual earnings for Reporters ranged from a low of $10,700 to a high of $400,000, and that the median yearly salary was $28,000 and the average annual salary was $33,700.

In an extensive survey of 2004 annual salaries of reporters, Broadcast Employment Services (BES) found that salaries ranged from a low of $13,000 to a high of $180,000, with a median salary of $26,000 and a mean average annual salary of $29,560. In the top 50 largest-market stations (usually with staffs of 50 or more), the low annual salary was $14,000, the high was $180,000, the median yearly salary was $38,000, and the mean average annual salary was $43,068. In contrast, in the smallest-market stations (with, generally, one to 10 employees), the low annual salary was $13,000, the high was $53,000, the median was $18,000, and the mean average yearly salary was $19,884. In a complimentary study of the 2004 earnings of entry-level reporters, BES found that the low salary was $10,000, the high was $65,000, the median salary was $18,000, and the mean average salary was $18,905.

The best salaries are offered in the East, with the lowest in the Midwest (except for the larger cities such as Chicago) and the South. Reporters who develop specialty areas have a distinct advantage in the job market.

Employment Prospects

Although a Reporter position is sometimes considered an entry-level job at the smaller-market stations, most Reporters have had experience as television news writers or researchers. Market size is an important determinant in the size of television salaries and the availability of jobs, even more so for Reporters than for production personnel. Although most midsize- and large-market stations, as well as networks, employ several Reporters, there tend to be more job applicants for these positions than are available at any one time. For beginners, the best places to seek employment as a Reporter remain in suburban and small town local television stations (which, of course, will also have the lower salaries), from which they can move upward to a larger-market city. At the same time, there tends to be a high turnover rate in this position, which provides opportunities for employment as a replacement Reporter.

Advancement Prospects

The U.S. Bureau of Labor Statistics projects slower growth in the employment of news analysts, Reporters, and correspondents than the average for all occupations through 2012. In the case of television, this slow expansion is due largely to the consolidation of local television ownerships, as well as the constant competition for viewers from large cable networks and news data available on the Internet.

Most Reporters aspire to become an anchorperson, a position with higher salary and attendant glamour. However, competition for the limited number of positions available (most anchorpersons are reluctant to vacate their job) is extremely severe. Yet it is possible to progress by moving to a larger-market station as a Reporter, and thus to a higher salary and more prestige. In other instances, some Reporters turn their ambitions to off-camera jobs, such as assistant news director.

Education and Training

Most television station employers prefer applicants with an undergraduate degree in communications, journalism, or political science, with considerable coursework in all the liberal arts, as television Reporters must have a broad knowledge of many disciplines. Specialized degrees in such areas as business, health, or political science may become advantageous for career advancement. As reporting and photojournalism are so tightly bound together, knowledge of news photography and digital editing procedures are extremely valuable skills for entry-level applicants. Internships with news organizations (television, radio, print, or Internet) provide good experience for those who want to be television Reporters. Many Reporters acquire their first hands-on experience in a real news operation as interns. A bonus to such work is that an aspiring Reporter can begin to develop a networking base of professional contacts.

Experience, Skills, and Personality Traits

Most large TV stations (and networks) hire only Reporters with three or more years of experience in a television news department, usually as a desk assistant, a researcher, or a news writer. Some applicants may be hired right out of college at small stations or cable operations where they may be required to shoot the news film, edit it, and then deliver it on the air. However, most Reporters have had some kind of journalistic experience before they are permitted to go on the air as broadcast Reporters. Some Reporters become television Reporters after having a successful career in print journalism.

Broadcast employers look for intelligent, attentive individuals who are both inquisitive and diligent. Reporters should have a well-modulated voice, first-rate delivery (and the ability to ad-lib when necessary), good pronunciation and command of English, and a well-groomed appearance. They must be dependable and exhibit tact in their interviewing and objectivity in their reporting. They need to understand and explain complex issues and data and have a working knowledge of many subjects. Primarily, television Reporters need the same skills as do all journalists—a capacity to function under heavy pressure, accuracy, perceptive news judgment, and strong self-motivation.

Unions and Associations

Most television Reporters are union members of the American Federation of Television and Radio Artists (AFTRA), the National Association of Broadcast Employees and Technicians (NABET), or the Writers Guild of America (WGA). While some small stations may not be unionized, most reporting, photography, producing, tape-editing, and even writing jobs are off limits except to union members.

Other valuable professional associations include the Academy of Television Arts and Sciences, the Association for Women in Communications, the International Radio and Television Society, the National Academy of Television Arts and Sciences, the Radio-Television Correspondents' Gallery (only for congressional Reporters), the Radio-Television News Directors Association (RTNDA), and the Society of Professional Journalists.

Tips for Entry

1. Besides writing courses, obtain as much journalistic experience as you can during college on the campus newspaper or other publications.
2. Experience in public speaking, debate, or dramatic arts will help prepare you for on-air reporting.
3. Learn to use a computer effectively, understanding the Internet, and become proficient with things digital.
4. Read and observe all you can about all types of people and activities, and become a well-informed listener and viewer of broadcast news programs.

SPORTSCASTER

CAREER PROFILE

Duties: Report on athletic and sports events on regularly scheduled television newscasts; provide play-by-play coverage for sports events broadcast by the station

Alternate Title(s): Sports Director; Sports Reporter

Salary Range: $14,000 to $325,000 or more

Employment Prospects: Poor

Advancement Prospects: Poor

Prerequisites:

Education and Training—Undergraduate degree in journalism or mass communications with extensive exposure to the sports scene

Experience—Some newsroom and preferably sports desk experience in television, radio, or print journalism

Special Skills and Personality Traits—Extensive knowledge of all sports; outgoing and pleasing personality; strong writing and verbal abilities

CAREER LADDER

```
┌─────────────────────────────────┐
│       Sports Director           │
│  (large station or network)     │
└─────────────────────────────────┘

┌─────────────────────────────────┐
│         Sportscaster            │
└─────────────────────────────────┘

┌─────────────────────────────────┐
│   Desk Assistant; News Writer   │
└─────────────────────────────────┘
```

Position Description

A Sportscaster's duties and responsibilities are similar to those of a reporter, but in the highly specialized area of the sports world. At small stations, a Sportscaster often combines the positions of sports director, anchor, talk show host, producer, and reporter. In this situation, Sportscasters usually have autonomy in choosing, preparing, and delivering the sports news for each broadcast. At major-market stations (and networks) there are usually several staff Sportscasters, each specializing in a particular sport or event or acting in the differing positions or anchor, host, and reporter. All of them report to the sports director of the station (who may also be the sports producer and/or anchor).

While Sportscasters report the outcomes of local games and athletic contests and events, they also cover such general sports topics as national baseball news, local players who appear headed for major prominence in the field, legislation that affects the athletic scene, professional players' contracts, any record-breaking events, and more. Generally, the Sportscaster is required to cover any happening that involves or affects the sports scene.

Sportscasters gather and edit sports information, using their knowledge to discriminate between the hype of industry publicity and the facts of the events to be reported. Sportscasters spend a significant amount of time outside the station tracking down leads and stories and verifying facts. In their preparation of copy for newscasts, Sportscasters review information available from national networks, syndicated sports clips, wire stories on national and international sports news, and Internet sources. They select the visual material to be used. They interview local and visiting sports personalities and represent the television station at community events and in conjunction with special station projects.

In addition, Sportscasters provide play-by-play narrative and/or color commentary (informative analysis of the action) coverage for games and other sports events covered by the station. They maintain continuous contact and encourage good relationships with local and regional sports figures (such as athletic directors, coaches, and players and their organizations). They also generate story ideas and originate and develop special sports commentaries, features, and documentaries.

Salaries

Sportscasters' salaries vary widely depending on the station's market size, the number of sports staff at the station, and the amount of duties and responsibilities they carry. According to the 2003 salary survey made by the Radio-Television News Directors Association, national annual salaries for sports reporters ranged from a low of $16,000 to a high of $125,000, with an average salary being $32,600. For sports anchors, the annual salaries ranged from a low of $10,000 to a high of $200,000, with an average being $51,600. In its 2004 study of annual newsroom salaries, Broadcast Employment Services found that annual salaries for sports reporters ranged from a low of $11,000 to a high of $130,000, with an average salary being $30,020, whereas annual salaries for sports anchors ranged from a low of $12,000 to a high of $400,000, with an average income of $45,073.

At smaller-market stations, Sportscasters' annual salaries can run from a low of $11,000 to a high of $35,000 or more, dependent on whether the individual is both anchor and reporter, let alone sports director as well. At major-market stations and networks, Sportscasters' yearly pay may range between a low of $18,000 to as much as $325,000 or more for the popular Sportscasters at network stations.

Employment Prospects

Competition for sportscasting jobs in commercial television is fierce, and employment prospects tend to be poor. The position demands an extensive background knowledge in worldwide sports, as well as solid reporting and writing skills. It is not an entry-level position but must be earned after years in a television newsroom environment. However, the high level of interest in sports in this country and technological advancements in satellite transmission have created more opportunities for expanding coverage of sports by both commercial and cable television stations, opening up more need for sports reporting.

Advancement Prospects

Sportscasting, whether at commercial, cable, or public television stations, is seldom a stepping-stone to higher-salaried positions within the news department. Sportscasters may achieve promotion to a sports director position at their own or a larger-market station (or a network), but these posts become available infrequently. Expertise and specialization in a particular sport are usually key components in such promotion.

Education and Training

Employers usually require Sportscasters to have an undergraduate degree in journalism, mass communications, or a related field, with coursework in speech, writing, sociology, and psychology. They need to be both articulate and knowledgeable about all aspects of sports and must have well-honed writing skills.

Experience, Skills, and Personality Traits

With the necessity of understanding basic newsroom operations, most Sportscasters gain this general experience as desk assistants or news writers before moving into sports writing. Both writing and speaking experience in television or radio is a requirement. They also need to be knowledgeable about sports journalism ethics, slander, and libel laws and work harmoniously with the public and coworkers.

Sportscasters need to be enthusiastic and have a broad experience in a wide range of athletic endeavors. They have to be vigorous, innovative, and self-motivated and be able to dig up compelling and informative sports stories. They need an appealing voice and diction, a personal style, and a distinctive on-air personality. In some cases, they may need to have photographic experience, as they will be required to be both a Sportscaster and a photojournalist.

Unions and Associations

Some television Sportscasters at networks and network-owned stations in major markets may be union members of the American Federation of Television and Radio Artists (AFTRA), the National Association of Broadcast Employees and Technicians (NABET), or the Writers Guild of America (WGA). At smaller-market stations, however, Sportscasters are not usually represented by any union. Sportscasters may find it beneficial to hold membership in the Radio-Television News Directors Association (RTNDA), the Society of Professional Journalists, or other journalism organizations.

Tips for Entry

1. Besides enrolling in writing courses, get as much journalistic experience as you can during college, such as working on the campus newspaper or other publications.
2. Experience in public speaking, debate, or dramatic arts will help prepare you for on-air reporting.
3. While in college, seek internships at local television stations or even an unpaid position in a large-market station to acquire experience in news operations. You can also develop a networking base of professional contacts, which can later help you acquire a job and advance your career.

WEATHER REPORTER

CAREER PROFILE

Duties: Provide weather conditions and forecasts as a feature of regularly scheduled television newscasts

Alternate Title(s): Meteorologist; Weathercaster

Salary Range: $12,000 to $200,000 or more

Employment Prospects: Poor

Advancement Prospects: Poor

Prerequisites:

    Education and Training—Undergraduate degree in meteorology required at most midsize and all major-market stations and networks

    Experience—General newsroom background and some public speaking

    Special Skills and Personality Traits—Good communication and interpersonal skills; distinctive style; agreeable appearance and manner; strong organizational abilities

CAREER LADDER

```
┌─────────────────────────────┐
│     Weather Reporter        │
│ (large station or network)  │
└─────────────────────────────┘

┌─────────────────────────────┐
│      Weather Reporter       │
└─────────────────────────────┘

┌─────────────────────────────┐
│     Announcer; Reporter     │
└─────────────────────────────┘
```

Position Description

Weather reporting is a self-contained section of daily broadcasts at television stations. There are essentially two types of TV Weather Reporters, those who are trained, certified meteorologists, and those who are not. The smaller-market stations often use the latter, who may not even be college graduates, as all they do is read the National Weather Service statistics on the air. At some local stations, the news anchor covers the weather, or reporters assigned to traffic combine the weather report with other coverage. At larger stations, however, Weather Reporters usually are trained meteorologists familiar with the latest weather-measuring technology and the use of sophisticated devices in preparing reports.

Weather Reporters are supervised by either the news director or the assistant news director. They are tasked with gathering information from assorted sources about weather conditions, both locally and nationally, on a daily basis. They prepare national summaries of current weather events and pull together the weather graphics needed for each newscast. They also provide forecasts of future weather probabilities. These forecasts are usually presented for the following five days or a week and attempt to predict trends and changes in weather patterns, both locally and nationally.

Weather Reporters collect data from national satellite weather services, local and regional government weather agencies, wire services, reports from field reporters, and Internet sites. At larger stations and the networks, the weather department often maintains specialized equipment (such as barometers, hygrometers, and thermometers), as well as sophisticated computer hardware and software (such as the WSI Weather Producer, Baron's VIPIR system, and the Millennium system) to gauge and measure local weather conditions and predict changes during the next several days. Some weather departments are actually independent companies based at the stations. They provide weather data for the stations and often for local radio stations and print journalism.

Weather Reporters have an assortment of visual devices to illustrate weather conditions during the newscast, including radarscopes to reflect storm conditions and dials and charts that indicate temperature, humidity, wind velocity, barometric pressure, and pollen count. They also use computer graphics to add color and movement to maps, transparent plastic overlays, and satellite photographs of the continental United States to pictorialize weather patterns. They work with the production crew and news director in setting up, altering, and modifying the weather visuals for a newscast.

Salaries

The salaries of Weather Reporters vary greatly with the size of the station and its market, its geographic location, the value that management places on weather reports, and the qualifications of the individual holding the position. Weather Reporters with a distinctive style and popularity with viewers may earn annual salaries of $300,000 or more.

In its 2003 salary study of news operations, the Radio-Television News Directors Association (RTNDA) found that wages of weathercasters ranged from a yearly low of $10,000 to a high of $215,000, giving an overall average of $58,700 for the position. Furthermore, in the largest-market stations (top 50), the median annual salary was $86,750, whereas the smallest-market stations had a median average salary of $30,000.

In its 2004 survey of annual salaries of Weather Reporters, Broadcast Employment Services found that salaries ranged from $12,000 to $240,000, with average earnings being $54,340. For larger-market stations (top 50), the yearly pay range was from $28,000 to $240,000, with a mean average salary being $67,320. For the smallest-market stations (with the smallest staff), the range was from $12,000 to $51,000, with an average income being $24,775.

Employment Prospects

Because most television stations employ no more than one or two Weather Reporters, prospects for employment in this field are limited. Some stations have only one full-time Weather Reporter, with an announcer filling in on the early morning and weekend reports. Others use only a weekend Weather Reporter on a permanent basis. Many major-market stations have more than two Weather Reporters on staff, particularly if they also operate AM or FM radio stations. Cable systems also employ Weather Reporters on a regular basis, and opportunities exist in such specialized cable operations as the Weather Channel, which broadcasts continuous weather reports, specials, and commentary throughout the day. While this job may be considered an entry-level position with the smallest stations (which seldom require certifications), most mid-size and larger stations (and networks) require at least one to two years of experience in a commercial television newsroom and usually certification as a Weather Reporter.

Advancement Prospects

For a professional Weather Reporter, the most likely career progression is to switch to a larger-market station or, if possible, a network. With the expansion of specialized cable network news (especially the Weather Channel), some Weather Reporters have found this area a means to advance their vocation. For those announcers who are assigned the job of weather reporting, a good performance on their part can pave the way for advancement within the news department. In general, however, most successful Weather Reporters remain in that post, and their chances of advancement to another market or to a different television career are strictly limited.

Education and Training

Educational requirements are similar from station to station and from market to market. At most television stations (and at all networks), an undergraduate degree in meteorology is a must. In addition, most midsize and larger-market stations and the networks require candidates to have a certification from the American Meteorological Society (AMS) and sometimes an additional seal of certification from the National Weather Association (NWA). Courses in journalism, mass communication, and public speaking are also beneficial.

Experience, Skills, and Personality Traits

As the weather section of the newscast is usually delivered by Weather Reporters without a script and with almost constant eye contact with the camera, strong communication skills are a prerequisite for any Weather Reporter. They must be able to project a professional presence on camera and be able to ad-lib with style, wit, and enthusiasm. News directors seek articulate, dynamic, and good-looking individuals who have well-modulated voices and good diction. Weather Reporters need to be able to relate to and attract a viewing audience, usually by developing their own unique on-air personalities.

In addition, Weather Reporters have to be conversant with the production of weather graphics and the use of computer weather software and satellite information systems. They must possess excellent writing, editing, and interviewing abilities, have good organizational know-how, and be capable of working under pressure and deadlines.

Unions and Associations

Some Weather Reporters are members of the American Federation of Television and Radio Artists (AFTRA), but most are not represented by this or any other union. Some weathercasters may find it beneficial to belong to the Radio-Television News Directors Association for career information and advancement. For meteorologists, membership in AMS or NWA is a mark of prestige for their career.

Tips for Entry

1. During college, experience in public speaking, debate, or dramatic arts will help prepare you for your on-air reporting as a Weather Reporter.
2. While in college, seek internships at local television stations, where you can obtain experience working in an actual news operation and observe how professional newscasters perform their jobs.
3. Learn to use a computer effectively and become familiar with graphics software, particularly that designed for use with weather forecasting.

PERFORMING

CHOREOGRAPHER

CAREER PROFILE

Duties: Create any dance routines used in a television production

Alternate Title(s): Musical Stage Coordinator

Salary Range: $14,000 to $58,000 or more

Employment Prospects: Poor

Advancement Prospects: Poor

Prerequisites:

Education and Training—Training as a professional dancer and as a Choreographer; understanding of television production techniques and the creative, technical, and visual demands and possibilities of the medium as related to dance

Experience—Extensive dance experience; previous work choreographing for contemporary street and club dance, the stage, music videos, or film

Special Skills and Personality Traits—Creativity related to dance or staged sequences; dancing ability; organizational and teamwork skills; patience; teaching skills to explain dance and movement sequences to other dancers, performers, and directors

CAREER LADDER

```
+---------------------------+
|         Director          |
+---------------------------+

+---------------------------+
|       Choreographer       |
+---------------------------+

+---------------------------+
|          Dancer           |
+---------------------------+
```

Position Description

Choreographers are the artists responsible for creating any dance sequences and musical or specialized movement used in television productions (and music videos, movies, and theatrical musicals). Often, they are older dancers with years of experience in the theater, film, and/or television. Through their performance as dancers, they develop reputations for creativity and organizational skills that lead to opportunities to choreograph productions.

Choreographers may be involved with any or all of the various styles of dancing. They must be able to replicate popular dance styles, classic forms, or have an individual dance language of their own. These include classical and contemporary ballet, modern dance, jazz, tap, ballroom, social, and ethnic dance, as well as such "specialized" movements as mime, aerial, gymnastics, water, ice, combat, and so on. Choreographers often begin during the preproduction of musical scenes to work out any complicated dance or movement sequences and shots with the director. In addition,

they discuss with producers, musical directors, art directors, costume designers, and photography directors the requirements of the particular performance and often assist in choosing specific dancers needed for the dance sequences. In some cases, they also seek and teach dance "doubles," those dancers who, like stunt doubles, have to perform the dance steps called for by the script in place of the actor due to the technical difficulty of the dance or to stand in for an unavailable actor during the process of camera blocking.

Choreographers have to plan each movement of the dancers and actors and ensure they are well rehearsed and comfortable with the movement. They may have to use a form of dance notation to record the movements they create. They understand the importance of creating appropriate and effective movement for television studio–based filming, as well as shows with a live studio audience, where the dynamics and energy of the dancers are central to a successful production.

Another type of choreography is that employed for combat and fight scenes. A fight scene is a sequence in a production that is intended to simulate combat with varying degrees of realism. Essentially, these movements are a form of carefully choreographed dance performed by actors or stuntpersons. These complex pantomimes demand careful choreography to avoid injury while simulating realistic combat.

Salaries

Salaries vary greatly depending on the budget for musical, specialized movement, or dance scenes, or how many fight scenes need to be staged, or the reputation of the Choreographer. The U.S. Department of Labor's *Occupational Outlook Handbook* found that median annual earnings of salaried choreographers were $29,470 in 2002. The middle 50 percent earned between $19,590 and $43,720. The lowest 10 percent earned less than $14,000 annually, and the highest 10 percent earned more than $57,590.

In a study of choreography as a career, the Minnesota Department of Education found that in 2004 the median wage for Choreographers was $2,460 per month (that is, $14.17 per hour) and that half of all Choreographers earned between $1,630 and $3,640 per month ($9.42 and $21,02 per hour). Furthermore, Choreographers can earn $10,000 for two weeks of work on a television program, but the number of such large productions is limited. Many Choreographers find it necessary to work in assorted media to enhance their income.

Employment Prospects

Opportunities for employment are only as good as the number of television productions that use dance and specialized movement in some form. Most choreographers active in the television industry also work on related projects, such as music videos, motion pictures, live musicals, and concerts, and often teach in dance schools in order to supplement their income from television productions. In order to be considered for work in either film or television, Choreographers must have agents or managers. Choreographers are usually chosen by their previous credits (in many cases music videos).

Advancement Prospects

Reputation is as important as recommendations or any word-of-mouth praise for any advancement for a television Choreographer. Being associated with a critically acclaimed television show or popular music video can greatly advance a career. Continuous success as a Choreographer, along with an accumulated knowledge of camera and editing techniques, can also translate into an opportunity to direct an entire production, leading to a career as a director.

Education and Training

Most successful Choreographers have originally been dancers and often start choreographing while still perform-

ing. Majoring in dance in college or graduate school, followed by education and training as a Choreographer at a dance school, are often requirements for working as a Choreographer in a television production. Studying privately with famous dancers and Choreographers or assisting Choreographers on music videos or live musicals are other ways to train and gain the necessary education. They also need to research and know all popular street and club social dances. In addition, learning about television production techniques will help Choreographers looking for work in television. Training as an actor, acrobat, or martial artist also can be helpful.

Experience, Skills, and Personality Traits

Working as a professional dancer is the best background for a career as a Choreographer, as well as working with other Choreographers on projects other than television productions, such as live concerts, stage musicals, or music videos. Choreographers need to enjoy a high level of social interaction, as they supervise, coach, and train dancers. They need to be enthusiastic and patient and have the ability to work and concentrate for long periods. They must be able to communicate to other dancers their vision for the dance sequence. For this reason, they need to be highly articulate in teaching and directing dances and actors to perform properly the choreography and/or staging. They need to be aware of any changes in the movement sequences as rehearsals proceed and be able to envision new ideas or other creative ways to produce the overall effect they and the director desire. Their skill in creating dance routines is due as much to innate talent and knowledge of dance as it is to their experience.

Unions and Associations

The Society of Stage Directors and Choreographers is the only union that represents Choreographers, and only those who work in live theater. The society's attempts to include Choreographers who work in any type of filmed media have failed as of the present day. Thus, Choreographers who work in film, television, or music videos are still without a union. Some Choreographers who are also dancers may be covered by union contracts. Dancers who appear on live or prerecorded television programs are represented by the American Federation of Television and Radio Artists (AFTRA); those who perform in films and on television may be represented by the Screen Actors Guild (SAG).

Tips for Entry

1. Besides your formal rigorous dance training, obtain a broad, general education, including music, literature, history, and the visual arts, as they will be helpful in your interpretation of dramatic episodes, ideas, and feelings.

2. Dance for any performing arts opportunities you find available to gain the experience you need as background for your career as a Choreographer.

3. Continually research and learn about all popular social dances (such as break dance, hip hop, krumping, and salsa), as contemporary television production continually use such forms. As a Choreographer, use assistants who specialize in these fields of dance.

4. Since most Choreographers are self-employed freelancers, you may find it useful to take business, accounting, and computer courses to help manage your career.

EXTRAS

CAREER PROFILE

Duties: Appear in television productions in the background or in crowd scenes

Alternate Title(s): Background Actors; Supporting Artists; Walk-ons (nonspeaking)

Salary Range: $73 to $204 per day

Employment Prospects: Good

Advancement Prospects: Poor

Prerequisites:

Education and Training—Actor training is not necessary, but it is helpful.

Experience—Usually on-the-job training

Special Skills and Personality Traits—Availability to work early in the morning and long hours for all-day shoots; flexible schedule and availability on short notice; patience; persistence

CAREER LADDER

```
┌─────────────────────────────┐
│     Performing Artist       │
└─────────────────────────────┘

┌─────────────────────────────┐
│           Extra             │
└─────────────────────────────┘

┌─────────────────────────────┐
│  Amateur Actor/Performer    │
└─────────────────────────────┘
```

Position Description

Extras are those union or nonunion actors who populate crowd scenes, both indoors and outside, on television productions (and in films). Generally, Extras do not have speaking parts, but some of them may be given speaking parts, for which they receive higher pay.

While it may seem that to be a member of a crowd scene is quite easy, it really is not. In addition to the time that they might have to devote to getting into costume or having special makeup applied, Extras have to be available on very short notice and then be willing to wait lengthy periods of time for their scene to be shot. They have to take direction from directors (or their assistants) on take after take. Their efforts are usually uncredited and in many cases even unseen, as their recorded footage may not make the production's final cut due to the director's or editor's artistic choice and time constraints. For these reasons, Extras must enjoy the (anonymous) work and take pleasure in being part of a television production. It is also good exposure to work with the crew of a television project, and it may provide an entrance point for further acting work and eventually speaking parts.

If the television production is a signatory of the Screen Actors Guild (SAG) or the American Federation of Television and Radio Artists (AFTRA), there are guidelines for minimum wages depending on the length and type of the scenes needed and the time spent in both rehearsal and actual production. If Extras are employed in a television serial (either single or multiple appearances in any one calendar week), there are additional minimum wage advisements, as well as guidelines as to what constitutes a speaking part and how important their characters are in their interaction with the principal actors. In addition, if an Extra does not speak on camera but portrays a major role, his or her salary must be upgraded. Thus, despite required membership dues, belonging to either or both of these unions can be extremely beneficial for Extras, whether they hope to advance in their acting career or take background acting work as a supplement to their regular vocation.

Salaries

Most Extras also have other part-time or full-time jobs or are students, as the Extra work is sporadic and usually short-term. Depending on the type of production (a single appearance on a program or single or multiple appearances on a series), Extras may earn a minimum wage (per union guidelines) of from $72 to $204 per eight-hour day (plus provided meals or snacks), depending on the program length. For programs other than serials and variety shows, the minimum wage guideline for Extras ranges from $90 to $100, depending on whether any special abilities are demanded of the Extra. Few Extras can earn a solid living from their work, but it is a way of getting involved in television productions and being noticed, not to mention the thrill of being part of a television show or film. There is also the potential of making industry contacts on the set.

Employment Prospects

Most employment opportunities for Extras exist only in Hollywood and New York, where most television production is done. While some on-location shoots for made-for-television films or commercials do require Extras, and usually a lot, during the actual filming, they are not anywhere near as prevalent as in motion picture productions. (To find out if a film or commercial is being made in a city or town other than Hollywood or New York, the local film commission for the area should be contacted.)

Advancement Prospects

Most Extra parts are nonspeaking, but there is always the prospect of moving up to a part with a few spoken words or lines of dialogue. In addition, some Extras develop professional reputations as people with a special ability or a unique feature that guarantees their being requested for certain crowd scenes or situations. For those Extras looking to advance into steady television acting, they need to be distinctive, but in a positive way.

Education and Training

Some acting training may be useful, particularly if Extras are using their appearance in a production as a stepping-stone to actual acting jobs, but most Extras are technically just supposed to blend into the background as part of the "crowd on the street" or "faces in the crowd." Thus, for this position there is no formal training required.

Experience, Skills, and Personality Traits

Extras need to have a flexible schedule to be available to take on jobs on short notice. They need to be extremely patient, as they will probably have to sit around for hours at a time waiting until they are needed for one or more scenes. They have to be comfortable with their anonymous role, as they will not be listed in the credits. They need to be cooperative, agreeable to taking orders, and willing to dress in whatever costume is needed and have any special makeup applied or changes made in their hair style to fit the specific background or walk-on parts they are hired to play.

Unions and Associations

It is not strictly necessary to be a dues-paying member of an acting union, either the Screen Actors Guild or the American Federation of Television and Radio Artists or both, in order to get a job as an Extra. However, it helps, particularly in guaranteeing minimum wages for specific work. In addition, for those who make a profession of being background artists, they can become members of the Screen Extras Guild (SEG).

Tips for Entry

1. If you know anyone who is working on a television production or a made-for-TV film, alert them that you are willing to work as an Extra.
2. If you are planning to do Extra work on a regular basis, it might be advantageous to belong to one or more of the principal unions covering actors, SAG, AFTRA, or SEG.
3. Research what information and services are offered by the Extras Casting Guild (ECG), established in 2001, a company that can help you find casting agencies that are hiring Extras, mostly in Southern California. There is a minimum membership requirement of 3 months to join. Check out their Web site at http://www.extrascastingguild.com.

PERFORMING ARTISTS (INCLUDING ACTORS, DANCERS, SINGERS)

CAREER PROFILE

Duties: Act, sing, dance, or otherwise perform in a television production

Alternate Title(s): Performers; Talent

Salary Range: $13,000 to $125,000 or more

Employment Prospects: Poor

Advancement Prospects: Poor to Fair

Prerequisites:

Education and Training—High school graduate; post–high school training in acting, dancing, singing, or performing arts; undergraduate theater arts degree helpful

Experience—Extensive amateur or professional performance work in theater or film

Special Skills and Personality Traits—Assertiveness; commitment; imagination and creativity; perseverance; poise; talent

CAREER LADDER

```
┌─────────────────────────────────┐
│   Featured Performer; Star;      │
│      Director; Producer          │
└─────────────────────────────────┘

┌─────────────────────────────────┐
│       Performing Artist          │
└─────────────────────────────────┘

┌─────────────────────────────────┐
│   Performer (other media);       │
│  Amateur Actor/Singer/Dancer;    │
│  College or Professional School  │
└─────────────────────────────────┘
```

Position Description

Television Performing Artists present themselves on camera to entertain or inform the viewer. They can be actors, singers, dancers, comedians, emcees, jugglers, magicians, pantomimists, talk or game show hosts, ventriloquists, or any number of other types of talents. Primary performers on television are actors who play featured or supporting roles in daytime soaps, dramatic programs, made-for-TV movies, miniseries, situation comedies, television specials, and variety shows. They may also be singers or dancers appearing in specials. Many entertainers get their first jobs as extras or walkons in dramatic productions or comedy series and sketches, and may continue this type of work even when they begin to get speaking parts in shows. They may break into the business by doing commercials in speaking or nonspeaking roles.

Performers can appear in programs for commercial and public television stations and networks, independent production companies, cable television systems that create original fare for their viewers, advertising agencies (for commercials), and, on occasion, business, governmental, health, or educational institutions involved in television projects. They will find themselves working in rehearsal halls, studios, and sometimes on location. Although they are usually cast and employed by a producer, they report directly to the director or his or her assistants during rehearsals and production.

As is true within the film industry, hard work and luck are two key factors in determining whether performers become famous in their television careers. Also important is having enough basic talent, training that capitalizes on that gift, and a shrewd and well-informed manager or talent agent who helps them make the best career choices. There are always far more people who want to become actors (or singers, or dancers) than there are places for them in either television or theatrical features. Nonetheless, there are always jobs for character and supporting actors as well as a need for individuals to fill lesser roles in projects, such as backup singers or members of dance groups.

When appearing in a television production, Performing Artists use the skills and techniques of the theater but play to a camera rather than to a live audience. The performers' (re)actions and movements must conform to the camera's mobility and stay within the type of camera shots that the director demands. They are required to attend scheduled readings of the script, camera run-throughs, sessions devoted to the blocking of their movements (known as position placement), and other scheduled rehearsals. Performers are expected to follow instructions, regardless of whether this expectation is explicitly written into their contract. Most performers agree to this authority, take the instructions, add their own creativity, and work hard to achieve the desired effect. Ultimately, of course, performers should be comfortable with the words, the style, and the presentation in which they participate. Although films make similar demands upon Performing Artists, television offerings are usually made in such tight time constraints that performers must learn their assignments much more quickly to accommodate the medium's faster tempo and condensed production schedule.

Most performers also work in television commercials. These often represent an especially important source of income (especially if the talent's contract calls for residuals to be paid for each showing of the ad), and they provide a good form of industry exposure. In addition, most Performing Artists do not limit themselves to just television, but also perform in theater, films, nightclubs and comedy clubs, theme parks, and occasionally industrial shows or music videos. They may also do voice-over work, where they are the narrator (of, say, a documentary), or the voice of an animated character in a television commercial or an animated film, or the reader for a books-on-DVD or tape enterprise, or a background singer for a TV ad. Most important, Performers frequently attend performing arts classes to hone further their craft.

Salaries

Most Performing Artists are employed on a project-by-project and often a day-to-day basis. Union pay scales for performers are quite complicated and are related to the type and length of a program and to the importance of the part. Performers generally are members of the American Federation of Television and Radio Actors (AFTRA) or the Screen Actors Guild (SAG), or both. AFTRA wage guidelines are computed by the length of the show being produced (and sometimes by the amount of five-minute segments in which the performer appears, which is simply an agreed-upon arrangement hammered out during a past contract negotiation). SAG wage guidelines, however, are based on the role being played and the number of days it requires to complete the given part. While SAG minimum wage earning scales are concerned primarily with film actors, and AFTRA scales concern television and video actors, there are also a lot of exceptions and overlaps. The joint AFTRA/SAG contract jurisdiction statement says that AFTRA covers "employment of performers in network and nationally syndicated television programs primarily in the formats of news, host-type shows, sports events, variety shows, 'book' musicals with a primary music emphasis, and dramatic soap operas. . . . Other programs produced for prime time exhibition (e.g., situation comedy and dramatic programs produced on videotape) may be subject to either AFTRA or SAG jurisdiction."

According to SAG minimum wage scales covering July 2004 through June 2005, day performers in television earned a minimum wage of $695, solo dancers earned the same minimum wage, and singers (as solo or duo) earned

$750. Weekly performers earned a minimum daily wage of $2,411, solo dancers a minimum of $2,233, and singers (solo or duo) $2,411.

If a performer is covered by AFTRA, minimum daily wages for the same time period ranged from $200 to $1,875, depending on the length of the program and the type of program (dramatic prime time, serial, nondramatic, or non–prime time). Multiple performances airing in the same calendar week bring even higher minimum wages. For dancers (in a group, not solo), the daily minimums ranged from $235 to $1,206, and for singers (in a group, not solo), parallel minimums ranged from $130 to $575.

Payment for participating in television commercials is even more complicated. A base session fee is paid whether or not a commercial is aired, and a complex formula defines additional payments once it is broadcast and for each subsequent broadcast. A few individuals get work on continuing television series, situation comedies, or soaps, where a featured performer or star can sometimes earn millions of dollars annually. Most performers, however, are fortunate to be employed a few weeks each year.

According to the U.S. Department of Labor's *Occupational Outlook Handbook,* median annual earnings of salaried actors were $23,470 in 2002. The middle 50 percent earned between $15,320 and $53,320 yearly. The lowest 10 percent earned less than $13,330, and the highest 10 percent earned more than $106,360 annually.

Employment Prospects

According to the U.S. Bureau of Labor Statistics, actors, directors, and producers accounted for about 139,000 paying jobs in 2002. Most of these were in the motion picture and video, performing arts, and broadcast industries of television and radio.

Employment in television, both for regular fare and in made-for-television films, is largely centered in New York and especially Hollywood, but cable television services and local television stations around the country also employ performers. However, competition is extremely tough. Performing jobs are always available, but with so many individuals vying for them, employment opportunities are poor. It is difficult to become an employed performer of any kind. Many professional performers rely on agents or managers to find them work, negotiate contracts, and plan their careers. Agents usually earn a percentage of the salary specified in the performer's contract. Other Performing Artists rely solely on attending open auditions for parts and jobs. Trade publications and online sites list the times, dates, and locations of these tryouts. Full-time, yearlong employment is rare, as most commercial television opportunities, other than long-running shows, are limited to one or two performances. Only performers with the most stamina and talent (and luck) will find regular employment in the business.

Performing Artists may occasionally find work outside of television in such non-broadcast areas as business, educational, governmental, or health media operations. Expanding cable and satellite television operations, continued growth and development of interactive media, such as direct-for-Web movies and short-form films, and video games should increase demand for talent. Performers frequently find further work in theater, both in large cities and in small towns, in touring productions and repertory theaters in most major metropolitan areas, in summer festivals, on cruise lines, and at theme parks and resorts.

Advancement Prospects

In most professions, a good worker can expect to be rewarded with a promotion, more responsibility, and a higher salary. Generally, this is not true for Performing Artists, who have to locate their next job on their own. Although agents and managers can be helpful, performers have to be successful at auditions and callbacks. While talent, exposure, solid credits, and good fortune all contribute to a performer's continuing success, advancement opportunities are poor.

Relatively few performers achieve any kind of feature or star status. A few experienced performers with particular talents (and the right look) can become well known and may be cast in supporting roles on a regular basis. However, the large majority of performers, even those with extensive television, film, or stage credits, have to work hard to get their next assignment and frequently find they have to supplement their incomes with jobs unrelated to performing. On the other hand, some experienced and successful actors may be able to become directors or producers.

Education and Training

Acting, singing, or dancing in school or college productions is a start. Getting training in the performing arts from private teachers, schools, workshops, studios, and colleges is helpful in learning and perfecting skills. A broad liberal arts education is recommended, along with courses in television production techniques. Many performers obtain an undergraduate degree in theater arts, and some actors study at one of the more than 50 conservatory-style acting schools. On-the-job training—acting, singing, or dancing in theater, commercials, television, or film—is also helpful.

Even after graduating from a performing arts school or majoring in drama in college, performers frequently continue to work on their techniques by studying with specific teachers or by taking further classes. Actors may also need specialized training for the specific parts for which they are auditioning or for which they are hired. They may also spend time in observing and studying social or environmental settings similar to the ones in which they will play. Sometimes they learn a foreign language or train with a dialect coach to develop various accents to make their characters more realistic. Above all, fine-tuning both their performance techniques and their physical bodies is important throughout their professional career.

Experience, Skills, and Personality Traits

Experience is as important as educational background, and aspiring performers are urged to grab every opportunity to perform in school and college plays and in benefits, community theater, local productions, and workshops. Performers need innate talent, creative ability, and intense training to follow their goals. Performing Artists must be totally committed, ambitious, and imaginative. Being resourceful and having a wide range of related performance skills, such as singing, dancing, juggling, or miming, are useful traits. Experience in horseback riding, fencing, or stage combat can lift some actors above the average and get them noticed by casting agents, producers, and directors. Actors must have presence (even when not on stage), be capable of affecting an audience, and be able to follow direction. For many actors, modeling experience also may be helpful.

An individual looking to work in television must develop knowledge of and an appreciation for the medium's production techniques. To succeed performers have to be versatile and able to adapt to a range of casting needs. Above all, they have to be determined and extremely persistent in seeking employment.

Unions and Associations

There are two major unions covering performers in television (and film). AFTRA is an open union and can be joined by paying an initiation fee. Membership, however, does not guarantee work, and many beginning performers wait until they get their first job before joining. SAG also covers television performers in particular cases, and some performers belong to both unions. Actors must join SAG after getting their first film job in a principal role.

Four other guilds represent television performers. Actors Equity Association (Equity) primarily cover performers in live theater. The American Guild of Musical Artists (AGMA), the American Guild of Variety Artists (AGVA), and the Screen Extras Guild (SEG) cover their respective types of performers.

Tips for Entry

1. Gain as much acting experience as you can in college, amateur, and regional productions, and pursue dramatic training at an acting school before attempting to audition for television programs.
2. Maintain a positive attitude, and follow up on every legitimate audition or acting lead.
3. As there is a lot of luck and timing involved in breaking into acting for television, be prepared for the lulls between jobs and just keep acting wherever you can.
4. Read in hard copy or online the trade publications, such as *Backstage,* the *Hollywood Reporter,* and *Variety* and study the work of television performers who have succeeded for their technique and talent.

STUNT COORDINATOR

CAREER PROFILE

Duties: Responsible for the organization, implementation, and safety of all stunts used as part of a television production

Alternate Title(s): Stunt Director; Fight Choreographer

Salary Range: $695 (Screen Actors Guild daily minimum) to $2,588 (Screen Actors Guild weekly minimum)

Employment Prospects: Good

Advancement Prospects: Good

Prerequisites:

Education and Training—Ability to manage a team of stunt people; master of physical activities, such as high dives, horseback riding, pratfalls, and race car driving

Experience—On-the-job experience as a stuntperson in television productions or films

Special Skills and Personality Traits—Ability to work with entire production team; attention to detail; capable of working under extreme pressure; precision; team player

CAREER LADDER

```
┌─────────────────────────────────┐
│     Second Unit Director;        │
│  Assistant Director; Actor       │
└─────────────────────────────────┘

┌─────────────────────────────────┐
│       Stunt Coordinator          │
└─────────────────────────────────┘

┌─────────────────────────────────┐
│          Stuntperson             │
└─────────────────────────────────┘
```

Position Description

A stunt is described as a dangerous or potentially hazardous act, action, or series of actions performed by an actor or a specially trained stuntperson. The Stunt Coordinator is the individual who takes on the responsibility of assisting the director in the staging and execution of stunts used on a television production. While stunt work has been traditionally confined to theatrical film work, the edges between movie and television projects have blurred, with many television companies making both films and elaborate dramatic series. Stunt work is common to both media. Stunts, fights, driving scenes, and other action scenes, including sequences of mayhem such as explosions and fire, requiring stunt activity have become a common part of a television station's daily output. All Stunt Coordinators and stuntpersons are members of the Screen Actors Guild (SAG).

Stunt Coordinators are the experts who understand and suggest the most effective camera placement during stunt action sequences. They instruct the stuntpersons on the dramatic execution of the action in terms of telling the story as set out by the script. Working closely with the director, one of the Stunt Coordinator's primary concerns is safety. As many stunts are risky to begin with, all necessary precautions have to be taken to ensure that the stuntperson will survive the feat unharmed. Thus, thorough preparation is the key to success, safety, and the avoidance of costly, time-consuming retakes. An experienced Stunt Coordinator will know which stunt activities are possible and which will have to be replaced by computer-generated digital special effects graphics. Most Stunt Coordinators hire the stuntpersons to be a part of their team, and thus they will know which ones are most likely to survive any particular stunt unharmed.

Stunt Coordinators may be employed weekly or daily for a television project, and their usual work day is for a full eight hours, as they often need to be on hand early to plan a shot or sequence of shots. In addition, they are sometimes kept on the set even when stunts are not scheduled. A director may need a Stunt Coordinator to help instruct an actor on how to throw a realistic punch or to provide safety equipment for an actor who is required to do an action scene or who wants to perform the stunts indicated. Stunt Coordinators need to be sure that such actors are capable of doing the stunt(s) or, if not, whether they need specific training. On some larger television entries a Stunt Coordinator may also function as the second unit director and will be given the entire responsibility of executing the stunts without the presence of the primary director, with additional compensation according to union pay scales.

Salaries

According to SAG guidelines, Stunt Coordinators may be hired in two different ways. In the first, they are paid on a flat deal basis for which no overtime, penalties, or premiums (that is, additional compensation) will apply, provided that the coordinator is paid at the same rate, or higher than, those listed by SAG as minimum wage scales. The second type applies to those employed on a non–flat deal basis, and under those circumstances, the Stunt Coordinator has to be paid no less than the minimum wage of a stuntperson. In this case, the producer also has to pay for overtime, penalties, and premiums as they apply.

According to SAG minimums, the rate for Stunt Coordinators hired on a day-by-day basis is $695. For those hired on a weekly basis, the weekly rate is $2,588. For those Stunt Coordinators hired on a flat rate basis, their daily wage is $810, and their weekly wage rate is $3,126. If they are hired for three days for a half-hour or an hour program, their rate is $2,204. If they are contracted for three days for a one-and-a-half-hour or a two-hour show, their rate is $2,465. These are minimum wages as set by union contracts. More experienced coordinators or those in demand for special skills may be paid higher rates by producers.

Employment Prospects

As long as action sequences are part of television productions, Stunt Coordinators will be required on the production team. The only real inroad on the necessity for using Stunt Coordinators is the increased reliance on computer-generated digital special effects graphics to portray difficult (or ultraperilous) action sequences. Nonetheless, prospects for employment remain good for the foreseeable future, and it is a natural career path for stuntpersons no longer interested in or able to do the stunts they have been doing.

Advancement Prospects

Some Stunt Coordinators may be able to make a transition to become a principal actor, a second unit or action director, or even a principal director, particularly with their expanding expertise in television production techniques and methods.

Education and Training

Stunt Coordinators have been stuntpersons previously, so they already have the physical dexterity and the athletic skills required to undertake a variety of challenging and/or dangerous stunts (such as falling without getting hurt). These athletic abilities should include boxing, climbing, gymnastics, horse riding, karate, scuba diving, skiing, and swimming. Training in and careful attention to safety measures is as important as the preparation for the stunts they will supervise.

Experience, Skills, and Personality Traits

Prior experience as a stuntperson is critical for the demanding job of Stunt Coordinator. In addition to all the skills needed by a stuntperson, Stunt Coordinators must have the know-how to manage and lead a team of professionals. They also have to have good interpersonal skills and patience, as they will have to interact harmoniously with directors, producers, talent of all kinds, and writers. A lively imagination as to the possibilities of creating stunts is also helpful.

Unions and Associations

Most stuntpersons and Stunts Coordinators are members of the Screen Actors Guild, though there are some that are nonguild as well. There are two major associations that represent stuntpersons: the Stuntmen's Association of Motion Pictures (http://www.stuntmen.com) and Stunts Unlimited (http://www.stuntsunlimited.com).

Tips for Entry

1. Since moving from the status of a stuntperson to a Stunt Coordinator is a traditional career progression, let it be known when you are performing stunts that you want to take this career step.
2. Network with directors, producers, and writers as well as other stuntpersons about job openings for coordinators.
3. Be aware of any moves of Stunt Coordinators onward to director positions, indicating possible openings for their jobs on particular television programs.

STUNTPERSON

CAREER PROFILE

Duties: Perform the demanding physical stunts or activities that actors cannot or prefer not to do as part of a television production

Alternate Title(s): Stunt Actor; Stunt Double; Stunt Driver; Stunt Pilot; Stunt Rider

Salary Range: $695 (Screen Actors Guild daily minimum) to $2,588 (Screen Actors Guild weekly minimum) or more depending on the length of the television program

Employment Prospects: Good

Advancement Prospects: Fair

Prerequisites:

Education and Training—Background in athletics; safety instruction; stunt training

Experience—On-the-job seasoning within the television industry and/or motion picture industry

Special Skills and Personality Traits—Assertiveness and bravado mixed with caution; willingness to follow stunt coordinator's orders and be a part of a production team

CAREER LADDER

```
┌─────────────────────────────────┐
│   Stunt Coordinator; Actor      │
└─────────────────────────────────┘

┌─────────────────────────────────┐
│        Stuntperson              │
└─────────────────────────────────┘

┌─────────────────────────────────┐
│   Athlete; Daredevil Performer  │
└─────────────────────────────────┘
```

Position Description

A stunt is defined as any act or action performed by an actor or a specially trained individual that is potentially dangerous or potentially hazardous. Stuntpersons are the specially trained individuals who are qualified to perform the physical stunts that actors cannot, will not, or are not permitted to undertake in a television production or a movie. Stuntpersons do every kind of exceptional action, from car chases and horseback riding to karate fighting and jumping off buildings. Stuntpersons may perform many different kinds of exploits but may specialize in certain types of stunts. Others may limit the kind of stunts they will do.

A Stuntperson works for the stunt coordinator. The latter prepares and choreographs each stunt, making sure all safety precautions have been taken. The desired goal is to achieve the illusion that the principal actor is doing the action and that the stunts look creatively and dramatically right for the television project. Stuntpersons standing in for a principal actor are chosen to be similar in height and build to that actor and are referred to as stunt doubles. When, for example, the script has the actor falling off a roof following

a chase or a punch, it is the Stuntperson, costumed and made up to look as much like the actor as possible, who will be the one actually tumbling from the height. With today's computer-generated digital graphics, the actor's face can be digitized over that of a Stuntperson, so that it truly seems as if the actor has done the falling.

It is indicative of how important actors consider stuntpersons to be that many star performers request a particular stunt double as part of their contractual arrangements on a TV project. Some actors, primarily male actors, often prefer to do their own stunts. This is usually allowed only if an insurance policy can be obtained by the producer to cover any losses due to delays in shooting scenes if the actor should be injured on the set.

Stuntpersons use a variety of safety equipment in their work. A stunt mask is a form-fitting covering for the face providing protection from ill effects of heat and flames. Stunt gel is a thick, nonburning liquid applied to a Stuntperson's skin and clothing prior to stunt scenes involving fire. Stunt padding consists of shock-absorbing body attachments worn by a Stuntperson to protect against or to lessen physical injury. Stunt pads (for the knees, elbows, shoulders, back, and other body parts) are similar to those used in professional sports and gymnastics.

Salaries

According to Screen Actors Guild (SAG) minimums, the rate for Stuntpersons hired on a day-by-day basis is $695. For those contracted on a weekly basis, the rate is $2,588. For those Stuntpersons employed for three days of work (on a half-hour or one-hour show), their three-day wage is $1,757. Those hired on a weekly basis for multiple programs have weekly salaries that range from $2,851 to $3,509 depending on the length of the shows in which they participate. These are minimum wages as set by union contracts. More experienced Stuntpersons or those in demand for special skills may be paid higher rates by producers.

Beyond being paid for their expertise, their stunt performances, and their time, stuntpersons are frequently paid an additional fee just for performing the actual staged stunt. This is called a stunt adjustment. The amount is agreed on by the stunt performer and the production manager (who acts for the producer) before the routine is undertaken. This is done so production is not delayed while this compensation is determined. Stuntpersons usually negotiate this fee based on the relative difficulty and danger connected with the stunt. These adjustments to the base wage rate are considered salary, as are overtime and other premiums.

Employment Prospects

While computer-generated (animated) effects are being substituted for some stunts in high-end television productions as well as theatrical film projects, there is still a great deal of action in both areas that require real stunt work. The recent and continuous increase in the number of television and cable productions that incorporate action sequences of one kind or another should help to provide steady opportunities for Stuntpersons.

Advancement Prospects

By mastering the physical skills of stunt work, qualified Stuntpersons have a fair chance for advancement. Because the activity is so very physically demanding (and the resultant cumulative injuries to the Stuntperson's body so nearly inescapable), there are always concerns about how long any individual can, or would want to, continue performing stunt work. Advancing to the positions of stunt coordinator, actor, or second unit director are definite career possibilities.

Education and Training

Stuntpersons need to have extensive athletic training, including learning such skills as boxing, climbing, gymnastics, horseback riding, karate, scuba diving, skiing, and swimming. Training in how to fall without injury is a necessity, as is extensive safety instruction. Special courses and training for stuntpersons are available from such registered and licensed schools as the United Stuntmen's Association (http://www.stuntschool.com). College or graduate school education is not a requirement, but at least a college education might prove beneficial for pursuing other jobs in or out of the television industry.

Experience, Skills, and Personality Traits

A Stuntperson's necessary experience must include a total familiarity and expertise in the required athletic skills for stunts to be performed safely. An overriding concern with safety is critical, as is the ability to work efficiently and harmoniously with the stunt coordinator and other members of the production squad. In many instances, Stuntpersons need to resemble physically already hired actors, for whom they are going to substitute in action scenes.

Unions and Associations

Most Stuntpersons and stunt coordinators are members of the Screen Actors Guild, though there are some who are nonguild as well. There are two major associations that represent stuntpersons: the Stuntmen's Association of Motion Pictures (http://www.stuntmen.com) and Stunts Unlimited (http://www.stuntsunlimited.com).

Tips for Entry

1. Strive to hone and expand your athletic skills. Network with appropriate people at sports contests and events, letting them know that you want to apply your athletic talents to a career as a Stuntperson.
2. Attend workshops for Stuntpersons, networking with other attendees and class leaders.
3. Investigate specific training courses in stunt work given at accredited and registered schools for Stuntpersons.
4. Network with casting directors, directors, producers, and writers, informing them of your availability as a Stuntperson.

PRODUCING

ASSOCIATE PRODUCER

CAREER PROFILE

Duties: Provide administrative and professional assistance to a television producer

Alternate Title(s): Assistant Producer

Salary Range: $10,000 to $67,000

Employment Prospects: Fair

Advancement Prospects: Fair

Prerequisites:

Education and Training—Undergraduate degree in communications or radio/TV broadcasting

Experience—Minimum of two to three years in any one of an array of production positions

Special Skills and Personality Traits—Creativity; interpersonal skills and cooperativeness; leadership qualities; organizational aptitude; writing ability

CAREER LADDER

```
┌─────────────────────────────────┐
│           Producer              │
└─────────────────────────────────┘

┌─────────────────────────────────┐
│       Associate Producer        │
└─────────────────────────────────┘

┌─────────────────────────────────┐
│ Production Assistant; Floor Manager; │
│    Unit Production Manager;      │
│       Assistant Director        │
└─────────────────────────────────┘
```

Position Description

The title of Associate Producer varies from one production to another. Sometimes the title is given to a production manager as an additional credit, or it can be merely an honorary title given to one of the project's financiers or to the person responsible for bringing the project concept to the attention of the producer.

Usually, however, this individual is the producer's second in command. As such, the Associate Producer provides general administrative and professional support to the producer, taking care of time-consuming details. As chief aide, the Associate Producer shares business and creative responsibilities with the producer in conceiving, developing, and producing a television program prerecorded or broadcast live from a studio or remote location. In the producer's absence, the Associate Producer typically assumes full responsibility for the work in progress. Some complex television productions (particularly made-for-TV films) employ several Associate Producers, each of whom is assigned specific functions within the production process. In addition to helping producers execute their concepts, Associate Producers also develop their own original story lines and ideas. In some instances, they are tasked to create prerecorded elements or segments that will be inserted into the completed program.

Generally, Associate Producers help to prepare the budget, arrange the production schedule, and in some cases supervise specific members of the production team. While Associate Producers do not have as much creative responsibility for the whole project as the producer does, they assist the producer in specific ways during the production process. They may evaluate scripts and program proposals, assist in the design of sets and lighting, select music to be used to connect scenes within the production, and even create sections or segments to be taped and to be inserted into the finished show. They may be asked to negotiate rights for film, slide, or tape inserts and performer "step-up" fees (residual payments for any distribution of the program beyond what was negotiated in the original contract). They may interact with the operations manager in scheduling the use of facilities and equipment or participate in research into audience acceptance of the program.

The television and film industries tend to resist standardization in defining production jobs. The process of developing and shooting a single program (let alone a television series or a made-for-television film) is complex and continually changing. Each project has its own challenges and requires wide-ranging techniques and methods in reaching its conclusion. As a result, Associate Producers often find themselves in different roles, depending on the specifics or type of production at hand. On a talk, game, or variety show, an Associate Producer may be in charge of finding and scheduling guests and may even supervise the shooting of the resulting segments in the studio. On a news show, an Associate Producer may aid a producer or reporter in developing a story or a documentary by doing some of the needed research and writing. In addition, an Associate Producer may conduct background interviews and supervise the prerecording of segments that will be incorporated into the finished program. On a network series, the Associate Producer is frequently in charge of postproduction but may also serve as the producer's point person in casting, working with the writers, or managing the budget and schedules.

Associate Producers usually have a certain latitude in helping to develop the production. Generally, they report to a production manager and are assigned to one producer for specific projects or programs. Program responsibilities can vary from news shows to sports, documentaries, talk shows, entertainment specials, series, or made-for-television films. In each case, the emphasis of a particular project is different. In all cases, though, the Associate Producer is primarily a liaison between senior and junior production staff members and between different departments involved in the production.

Salaries

According to a salary survey taken by Broadcast Employment Services, annual salaries for Associate Producers in 2004 ranged from a low of $10,000 for beginners in the smaller-market stations to $67,000 per year for experienced individuals who work on major television programs, series, or films for network broadcast. The mean average yearly salary for an Associate Producer, according to this survey, was $30,657. In a further survey taken of Associate Producers for news programs, it was found that annual incomes ranged from a low of $11,000 to a high of $60,000, with the mean average pay being $28,850. Salaries in public television tended to be similar at the low range but did not rise much above $45,000 per year at the high end, according to industry observers.

Employment Prospects

Although some smaller-market stations (and some producers) often consider the Associate Producer to be a person involved primarily in detail work to lessen the producer's burden, most television productions need individuals who are more experienced. Thus, Associate Producers usually must have a thorough knowledge of television production. They can usually gain this experience while working as a production assistant, floor manager, unit manager, or assistant director.

Many stations and most networks employ more than one Associate Producer, sometimes several for larger and more complex productions. Competition for these positions is usually quite keen. However, there is a lot of upward mobility among Associate Producers, with the result that job opportunities do open up. There are also other avenues for Associate Producers, such as working for production units of advertising agencies or joining the production teams that produce music videos. Thus, the potential for employment as an Associate Producer is fair.

Advancement Prospects

Most Associate Producers are both highly energetic and determined. As they acquire their considerable experience in television production, they seek more responsible positions, usually as producers. The more talented and creative Associate Producers may find such openings at smaller-market stations or become producers of specific types of fare at their own stations, such as news, public affairs, or sports programs. However, the competition for these producing positions is extremely intense, and only the most ambitious and brightest achieve their hopes of advancement.

Some Associate Producers make a career move to such venues as advertising agencies or business, educational, health, or governmental television productions, where they tend to specialize in certain types of programs. Overall, advancement prospects for an aspiring, goal-oriented, and dedicated individual are fair.

Education and Training

Television stations most often require Associate Producers to have an undergraduate degree in broadcasting, communications, or radio/TV. However, a broad liberal arts background is helpful, as is some theater training. Courses in writing are also recommended. Associate Producers who want to work in a specialized area such as news, sports, or music have a better prospect with some educational background in their subject area or discipline.

Experience, Skills, and Personality Traits

Most employers require a minimum of two to three years of varied experience in television production. Potential Associate Producers can gain such seasoning as production assistants, floor managers, or unit managers. Many of them also have been assistant directors, and most of them have had experience operating film and editing equipment.

Employers look for sharp, ambitious people who have good writing and organizational skills. They seek production people who are creative but also demonstrate leadership talents. Associate Producers should be versatile to handle a highly varied set of duties, show persistence, and possess a temperament to work well with a wide variety of people. They should have a good visual sense and understanding of informational graphics as well as a mastery of the technology of television production.

Unions and Associations

There are no unions that represent Associate Producers. However, they may join the Producers Guild of America to network with members of various production teams in film, television, and other media.

Tips for Entry

1. Obtain a solid liberal arts education along with your concentration on communications, journalism, or radio/TV broadcasting.
2. While in college, look for intern programs at local television stations to get an introduction to the production techniques employed in television.
3. Work as a production assistant on any nonunion or student films or television programs to gain production experience.

CASTING DIRECTOR

CAREER PROFILE

Duties: Find, audition, recommend, and negotiate the selection of actors for a television program, series, or film

Alternate Title(s): Casting Agent

Salary Range: $30,000 to $125,000

Employment Prospects: Fair

Advancement Prospects: Fair

Prerequisites:

Education and Training—No educational requirements, although a knowledge of acting and television production is helpful, as is on-the-job training in the casting department of a television station, network, independent production company, or casting agency.

Experience—Several years in lower-level positions, such as administrative assistant, receptionist, or assistant to a Casting Director

Special Skills and Personality Traits—Creative instinct and sense for talent; excellent networking skills; highly organized; knowledgeable about holding auditions and negotiating contracts; team player

CAREER LADDER

```
┌─────────────────────────────────────┐
│   Casting Agency Head; Producer     │
└─────────────────────────────────────┘

┌─────────────────────────────────────┐
│          Casting Director           │
└─────────────────────────────────────┘

┌─────────────────────────────────────┐
│   Assistant to Casting Director;    │
│       Production Assistant          │
└─────────────────────────────────────┘
```

Position Description

The Casting Director's task is to find actors for a particular TV show and audition them. To do this, the Casting Director goes through a personal file or rolodex of actors or contacts agents to search for actors, or puts a casting notice with a breakdown announcement service.

The largest and best known of these industry announcement services is Breakdown Services, Inc., of Los Angeles (http://www.breakdownservices.com). This company prepares a synopsis of the project's story and a descriptive analysis of each character and any other information the producer feels is pertinent. These sheets are then sent to the Casting Director or to the producer if there is no Casting Director assigned to the project for approval and use. The data also may be sent to actors' agents and personal managers who are clients of this service. Another well-known service is Casting Call Pro (http://us.castingcallpro.com).

During the planning stages for a new television production, series, or special program, Casting Directors use either their own breakdown sheets or those of a service to guide them in their search throughout their own extensive files for likely actors to audition. In addition, these breakdowns may be sent to talent agents and personal managers.

It is the job of the Casting Director to find the right face and voice for each part in the production. As there is so much competition and since acting talent is so interchangeable in the roles to be played, the Casting Director must be able to spot winners. Casting Directors usually receive hundreds or, in the case of large productions, thousands of résumé submissions for projects. Weeding through these is a laborious chore. Casting Directors use a combination of intuition and experience to narrow down the choices to the most likely candidates. They then bring in the producers and director (and sometimes scriptwriter) for callback auditions of the candidates. While final decisions on casting rest entirely with producers and the director, most of them find it wise to use a Casting Director whose creative instincts they trust. In some cases, smaller roles (including extras) may be chosen entirely by the Casting Director. Once the director and producer(s) have finalized which actors to hire, the

Casting Director then negotiates money, schedules, and billing with the actors and/or their agents.

All large television studios and networks have casting and talent departments, but some use independent casting agents as well. Most Casting Directors are freelance contractors and have learned their trade through an informal apprenticeship, since there is no school that teaches their particular skills. Independent Casting Directors may be hired for a particular project or segments of a series. Another category of Casting Director is those who work for advertising agencies and find actors for television commercials.

Salaries

As there is no union that represents Casting Directors, salaries vary depending upon the production's budget and whether Casting Directors are freelance independent agents or a salaried member of a station's casting department. Most independent Casting Directors work on a flat rate for the job. This rate will be based on the amount of casting to be done and the complexity of the roles being cast, as well as the Casting Director's reputation and prior relationship with the producer and the production's budget.

For salaried Casting Directors, as members of the production team of a station or network, yearly earnings can range from $30,000 to $125,000, with a mean average salary of $63,400, according to the 2005 salary survey conducted by Broadcast Employment Services. Well-established Casting Directors, independent or connected to the casting department of a television station or network, may earn more than $200,000 or $300,000 a year.

Employment Prospects

Casting is so pivotal to the success of most television productions, series, and special programs that there will always be a need for entry-level workers at studio casting departments and independent casting offices. Most Casting Directors start out as assistants to other Casting Directors and learn the trade from their fellow workers, acquiring knowledge by working from the bottom up and immediately starting to collect details about all different kinds of performers. They do this so they eventually can cast from their burgeoning contacts files and begin building a reputation for success on their own.

Advancement Prospects

Casting is a highly specialized skill that is developed over years of continuous experience, either as an independent Casting Director or as a member of the production team of a station or network. Frequently, producers and directors request a specific Casting Director based on their previous positive experiences working with him or her. Some Casting Directors, by taking a larger view of their career, may successfully move on to become producers themselves.

Education and Training

Studying acting or TV/radio broadcasting and production techniques may be helpful. Being able to recognize acting talent, having the capacity to understand the vision that a director or producer has for a character in the production, and being equipped to find an actor who best fulfills that vision are skills acquired only through on-the-job training. Studying actors in both film and theater and becoming knowledgeable about good acting as well as the skill of available actors are important ongoing activities for Casting Directors.

Experience, Skills, and Personality Traits

Taking on casting activities for school plays, local amateur or professional theater productions, or independent films offers beginning training. The key ability of a Casting Director is being able to pick the right talent for each part, as well as being geared to meet deadlines and work well as a part of the production team. Casting Directors need to spend a lot of time in assessing actors' abilities, and be constantly on the lookout for fresh new talent. They need to have a good idea how much certain actors cost and work at getting indications of the types of roles for which particular actors are looking. They must have a thorough knowledge of the rules and regulations of both the American Federation of Television and Radio Artists (AFTRA) and the Screen Actors Guild (SAG) concerning the hiring of actors and must establish a good working rapport with actors' agents.

Organizational abilities will help the Casting Director manage all data, as well as the résumés and head shots that are submitted from talent. Networking skills will help the Casting Director to know what actor is doing what as well as to obtain introductions to talent agents whose clients may come under consideration for roles.

Unions and Associations

There is no union representing Casting Directors. However, membership in the Casting Society of America (http://www.castingsociety.com) can be very useful for networking, learning about potential jobs, and gaining professional support and resources. The majority of Casting Directors belong to this organization.

Tips for Entry

1. Seek employment as an administrative assistant or a receptionist in a casting agency or the casting department of a television station.
2. Offer your services to cast a cable-access program, a student film, a low-budget independent feature, or a local theater production and alert those individuals that you know in the industry, including Casting Directors, about this hands-on example of your casting skills.
3. Attend TV and film festivals and activities of media associations, and sign up for seminars that include Casting Directors to network for jobs.

EXECUTIVE PRODUCER

CAREER PROFILE

CAREER LADDER

Duties: Envision, develop, finance, and produce a television program, series, or special production

Alternate Title(s): Coproducer

Salary Range: $20,000 to $300,000

Employment Prospects: Fair

Advancement Prospects: Fair

Prerequisites:

Education and Training—Minimum of undergraduate degree in communications, radio/TV broadcasting, or related subject area

Experience—Three to five years as a television producer

Special Skills and Personality Traits—Business and financial talents; interpersonal skills; leadership qualities; organizational aptitude; originality

Production Manager; Program Manager; Executive Producer (production company)

Executive Producer

Producer

Position Description

Executive Producers are the senior managers and business-people responsible for getting a television show made. They often conceive or develop the idea for a television series, program, or special production. Their primary function is to formulate the rationale for the project, determine its format, frame its budget, arrange for its financing, and then oversee the promotion of the project.

Executive Producers work for local television stations, the television networks, and independent production companies that create programming for network or cable broadcast syndication. Some Executive Producers attached to commercial television and syndicated programs are actually owners of production companies. Some are staff members of major market stations in charge of news, documentary, or public affairs entries. Others are employed at networks, where they supervise all creative aspects of programs, developing shows for specific audiences or in targeted subject areas. At local television stations, Executive Producers typically are in charge of news and report to the news director. For those stations that continue to create and produce original fare, the Executive Producer for non-news programming usually reports to the program director and supervises the original productions. In a few cases, the Executive Producer credit may be taken by the person who has arranged for all the financing of the project or is involved in a major or noteworthy way with a production and who may have a significant personal financial stake in it. Sometimes this financial person may not know (or even care) much about the small details of making a television program because, for them, television is a business, not an art.

Most Executive Producers, however, are actively involved in the production process. Their duties may include any or all of the following. They seek and identify concepts that can be creatively developed into television offerings, research these ideas, determine whether they can be realistically manufactured within the available technical resources and facilities, and in many cases write, edit, or approve scripts for the program. The overall budget for the project is established by the Executive Producer, who then vigilantly watches all expenses connected to the project and often locates and persuades sponsors to fund the program or series. Executive Producers are deal makers, often devoting more effort to the development of a project than its actual production.

In addition, Executive Producers usually pick the project's producers, writers, directors, performers, and special technical craft and production staff members (which include costume designers, music directors, and scenic designers). Furthermore, Executive Producers approve scripts, the technical facilities to be used, and the business arrangements of all those involved with the effort. In theory, Executive Producers are more focused on supervision and guidance than actual execution. However, they have the ultimate responsibility for the success or failure of the production as it is seen on the air or in syndication. During the postproduction phase, Executive Producers scrutinize all the promotion and publicity attached to the project and thereafter evaluate audience response to the final production.

Salaries

Due to the talent, versatility, and overarching responsibilities demanded by their job, Executive Producers are usually well paid. The lowest income is at the smaller-market commercial stations, where the annual salaries of full-time Executive Producers ranged from a low of $20,000 to a high of $50,000, according to the 2004 salary study made by Broadcast Employment Services. At major-market stations and networks, Executive Producer yearly salaries ranged from a low of $35,000 to a high of $300,000. According to the study, the overall annual salaries for Executive Producers ranged from $20,000 to $300,000, with a mean average salary of $58,486 and a median salary of $64,000. At the highest level at television networks, Executive Producers of the best-rated shows can make more than $4 million per season. In public television, salaries are somewhat lower but comparable, according to industry sources.

Employment Prospects

Employment opportunities for Executive Producers are generally fair, as only the most shrewd and capable achieve the post, and the competition is extremely intense. While many major-market public and commercial television stations employ two or more Executive Producers, there is much less chance of employment at small-market stations or at television producing departments in education, government, or the health industry, where producers often perform all the tasks of the Executive Producer. Nonetheless, with the expansion of commercial, cable, and satellite television stations and new networks, programming needs are continuously expanding. The call for Executive Producers is ongoing.

Most working Executive Producers are promoted from within a station's ranks. Having produced a variety of successful television programs, a savvy and talented individual may be given the overriding responsibility for high-budget productions. In other instances, entrepreneurs with initiative and exciting ideas (and often solid financial contacts) may be hired from outside the station's ranks to be Executive Producers for particular series or special programming.

Advancement Prospects

The possibilities of advancement from Executive Producer to production manager or program manager are fair. Some of these individuals may obtain these elevated jobs in the smaller-market stations, but their assumption of these basically administrative posts reduces their involvement in creative matters. Still others may scout for these positions within independent production firms. Some Executive Producers may even form their own companies to develop offerings for syndicated sale to stations and networks. Only the especially talented and skilled few can obtain staff positions of Executive Producer or higher at the commercial networks.

Education and Training

Most stations and networks require candidates for the post of Executive Producer to have the minimum of an undergraduate degree in communications or radio/TV broadcasting. Courses in business and finance or direct business experience are a definite plus. Many Executive Producers also have training and specific education in the topic areas for which they develop programs. In addition, a degree in a particular area may be necessary for an Executive Producer specializing in specific kinds of broadcasts, such as political science and journalism for news programs or theater arts for dramatic productions.

Experience, Skills, and Personality Traits

Executive Producers should have three to five years of hands-on experience as television producers. They must have a thorough practical knowledge of all aspects of producing a television program as well as an understanding of state-of-the-art television and film technology.

While many Executive Producers are idea people, able to create and develop concepts or formats into viable television productions, they are primarily businesspeople. They must exhibit leadership qualities and great interpersonal abilities to manage both creative and technical people effectively. As Neil Machlis, a seasoned Executive Producer, has stated, "It's a people business. You have to be able to get along with people. You have to be able to see what makes people tick." Executive Producer Duncan Henderson makes the point that "You have to actually know about and respect the jobs other people do so you understand what their problems are. . . . It's really trying to inspire people to do their very best work."

In addition, Executive Producers must boast well-organized minds and a sound business sense accompanied by financial sharpness. They have to be able to estimate costs accurately and build realistic budgets for their television productions. They must be good communicators and have a knack for setting priorities and allocating resources.

Unions and Associations

Although there are no unions or professional organizations that specifically represent Executive Producers, many belong to the National Academy of Television Arts and Sciences, the National Association of Television Program Executives, or the Producers Guild of America to exchange ideas with their peers, network, and sell programming ideas.

Tips for Entry

1. While earning your degree in communications or broadcasting, take business and finance courses, as these are skills you will need as Executive Producer.

2. Seek a job as a production assistant or intern on a television production and observe what everyone does.

3. As a production assistant, strive to join the Director's Guild so you can function as an assistant director and then make the career leap into producing.

PRODUCER

CAREER PROFILE

Duties: Create and develop television productions

Alternate Title(s): Producer-Director; Writer-Producer

Salary Range: $20,000 to $120,000 or more

Employment Prospects: Fair

Advancement Prospects: Fair

Prerequisites:

Education and Training—Undergraduate degree in broadcasting, communications, radio/TV, or theater

Experience—Minimum of three to four years as a director or an associate producer in television or theater production

Special Skills and Personality Traits—Business insight and financial expertise; creativity; detail-oriented; good communication and interpersonal skills; leadership qualities; organizational abilities; problem-solving skills; thorough understanding of television production and technology

CAREER LADDER

```
┌─────────────────────────────┐
│   Production Manager;        │
│   Executive Producer         │
└─────────────────────────────┘

┌─────────────────────────────┐
│        Producer             │
└─────────────────────────────┘

┌─────────────────────────────┐
│  Director; Associate Producer; │
│   Production Assistant       │
└─────────────────────────────┘
```

Position Description

The Producer of a television program is a highly skilled professional responsible for the creative, logistic, budgetary, and technical aspects of an individual project or series. The individual in this post envisions and develops ideas for a program or series that are consistent with the theme and scheme established by an executive producer or production manager (to whom the Producer reports). Television producers make sure that shows run smoothly in all details and take responsibility for everything, from coordinating writers and performers/correspondents to overseeing the fact-checking of names and titles on the credits. In addition, they ensure that the program meets all the station's or network's objectives and is well-matched to perceived audience interests. Producers work throughout the industry, in cable and home video/DVD firms as well as in business, educational, governmental, and health media organizations.

Producers are usually selected by an executive producer to supervise a single program, an episode of a TV series, or several shows. (Producers in charge of the production of an entire TV series are frequently called supervising producers, while Producers of specific segments within a larger pro-

duction are called segment producers.) They are tasked with the selection of scripts and performers and the planning of sets, costumes, props, lights, sounds, and camera angles. The Producer hires the director and the actors either directly or with the help of supervising and executive producers. Frequently, Producers are staff members of a television station, network, or independent production company that creates programming for stations or networks. Most commercial, public, and cable stations employ several full-time Producers. At network and independent production companies, two or three Producers may be responsible for individual offerings or programs within a series and may have differing responsibilities on a daily or weekly basis, depending on the complexity and size of the projects.

Within the parameters of the creative goals of a show or a series, the Producer has considerable latitude in developing ideas and determining the specific approach and format of each entry. Some Producers are concerned primarily with the creative aspects of the production, while others concentrate on logistics. For a prime-time network series, the Producer may focus almost exclusively on the creative aspects of the production, with other staff members or other Producers coordinating logistics. Many Producers of prime-time programs are also writers who shape the program's characters, story lines, and overall development through close supervision of the other writers as well as being involved in casting decisions. In fact, a prime-time series may have several Producers working at different levels.

In addition to their creative supervision, Producers maintain programs on budget and on schedule. They handle business arrangements and contracts with performers. They expedite needed clearances, order technical facilities and equipment, and schedule rehearsals and performances. They supervise all negotiations with talent as well as the needed production and technical people. They select the performers who will appear in the production, including guest hosts and musicians, and when they will appear. They coordinate all production assignments and supervise directors. In short, they make all critical decisions about the production.

For newscasts and documentaries, Producers often choose the pieces to be aired and the particular events to be covered. They frequently select which issues will be discussed, help pick the individuals to be interviewed, and supervise any needed research. During the postproduction phase, the Producer's role is to make certain the postproduction crew has everything needed to complete its work. Producers must monitor this process as closely as they scrutinize the production phase. Following postproduction, Producers work with the marketing and publicity teams in mounting the promotional campaign for the program.

Salaries

Median annual earnings of salaried producers and directors throughout the performing industry were $46,240 in 2002, according to the Bureau of Labor Statistics' *Occupational Outlook Handbook.* The *Handbook* also indicated that the middle 50 percent earned between $31,990 and $70,910 in 2002. The lowest 10 percent earned less than $23,300 yearly, and the highest 10 percent earned more than $119,760 annually. In radio and television broadcasting, Producers' median annual income was $38,480.

In a salary survey of the television industry conducted by Broadcast Employment Services in 2004, earnings of Producers ranged from a low of $15,000 to a high of $200,000, with a mean average salary of $42,635. According to Leonard Mogel in his 2004 book *This Business of Broadcasting,* it is not unusual for Producers of prime-time shows to make about $400,000 a season and more when they are associated with one of the top 10 most highly rated shows.

Employment Prospects

The position of Producer is highly coveted in television, and the competition at most stations is intense. Most television stations and networks employ from two to 10 or more Producers to work on specific assignments such as game shows, talk shows, or news programs or on special productions during a given season. Some Producers move on to similar positions at independent production companies, advertising agencies, video/DVD production companies, or higher-market stations, so positions become available from time to time. Because of the expertise and amount of training required to handle the complexity of jobs that a Producer does, as well as the competition for this position, employment prospects for this position in television broadcasting are only fair. Nonetheless, the demand for Producers is constant and, per the U.S. Department of Labor, employment is expected to grow about as fast as the average for all occupations through 2012.

Educational, governmental, health, and private industry production operations also employ Producers who often are specialists in particular subject areas. While employment prospects are slightly better than in broadcasting, opportunities are still only fair.

Advancement Prospects

Many Producers consider their job the ultimate step in their career, particularly as competition for the higher positions of executive producer or production manager at major-market stations or networks is extremely tough. Some, however, become executive producers or production managers at smaller-market outlets. Still others seek administrative, production, or program posts at independent production companies or at private educational, health, or governmental media organizations.

Some Producers specialize in news and public affairs, commercials, sports, or entertainment programs. They advance their careers by working on higher-budgeted or more prestigious shows where they can apply their expertise. A few Producers with outstanding talent and ability obtain positions with the networks or with independent production companies that produce programs for network, cable, television, or home video.

Education and Training

Many employers require that a Producer have a degree in communications, journalism, radio/TV, or theater. A broad liberal arts background and/or a business degree can also be helpful. Specific education in the subject area in which the Producer is going to specialize may be compulsory. However, it should be noted that many Producers never attended film school or majored in drama at college. Some even started on the lower rungs on television shows, working their way to the top and gaining the needed experience along the way. Other Producers may have taken extension courses in television production to supplement their regular degree program.

Experience, Skills, and Personality Traits

To be prepared to take on the responsibilities of a full-fledged Producer, an individual should have a minimum of three to five years of experience as an associate producer or a director, having already gained experience and knowledge of the television industry as a production assistant. Producers have to have a thorough practical knowledge of television production. They need to be familiar with budget estimation methods and should have background in all phases of program development, from the original conception to the final tape editing.

Producers need excellent leadership qualities to lead a team of collaborators through the often-laborious production process. They need to be able to coordinate numerous individuals during this process, from performers to technical and production people. Creativity is important, and Producers must be original in their development of fresh formats and techniques for television production. They have to be well organized, highly detail-oriented, and financially astute. They must be decisive at all times and boast solid business and industry judgment.

Unions and Associations

Although a few Producers who also are directors may belong to the Directors Guild of America, there are no unions representing Producers. Membership in the Producers Guild of America may be useful for networking and enhancing skills through educational seminars. The guild attempts to provide a forum for its members, whether they work in film or television.

Tips for Entry

1. Get a solid liberal arts education along with your concentration on communications, journalism, or radio/TV broadcasting.
2. Take additional business and financial courses, as knowledge of business is important in a Producer's job.
3. Start out as a production assistant, secretary, or assistant for an independent production company or Producer to learn the business and make contacts.

PROGRAMMING, PUBLIC RELATIONS, AND MARKETING

COMMUNITY RELATIONS DIRECTOR

CAREER PROFILE

Duties: Determine local public needs and create TV programs and announcements to meet them

Alternate Title(s): Director of Community Affairs; Public Relations Officer; Public Relations Specialist; Public Service Director

Salary Range: $23,000 to $90,000

Employment Prospects: Poor

Advancement Prospects: Fair

Prerequisites:

Education and Training—Undergraduate degree in communications, government, sociology, or urban affairs

Experience—Minimum of two to three years working in civic, community, cultural, or service organizations

Special Skills and Personality Traits—Excellent writing and speaking abilities; exceptional interpersonal skills and sensitivity; good business sense; service orientation

CAREER LADDER

```
┌─────────────────────────────────────┐
│      Producer; Program Manager       │
└─────────────────────────────────────┘

┌─────────────────────────────────────┐
│    Community Relations Director      │
└─────────────────────────────────────┘

┌─────────────────────────────────────┐
│    Director of Civic or Service      │
│   Organization; Publicity/Promotion  │
│             Assistant                │
└─────────────────────────────────────┘
```

Position Description

A Community Relations Director (sometimes known as public relations officer) is tasked with developing a continuing program of station services in response to the needs and interests of the local community. The Community Relations Director is typically the television station's primary contact with both public and private agencies, businesses, and professional organizations within the station's broadcast region. The director is expected to keep a finger on the community's pulse as well as represent the station's point of view to the community. Because of the specialized aspects of this position, the job is more frequently found at commercial television stations.

All commercial and public television stations are licensed by the Federal Communications Commission (FCC) to operate "in the public interest, convenience, and necessity." Stations meet this responsibility by broadcasting local programs, public service announcements (PSAs), and special events coverage that address local interests and concerns. Much of the Community Relations Director's time is allocated to representing the station at public meetings in order to determine these interests and concerns. They establish and nurture the informal and contractual relationships that make viable the involvement of individual organizations and associations in the station's public affairs programming. As the direct link with business associations, civic organizations, social service agencies, and youth organizations, Community Relations Directors are responsible for the effective use of specialized station programming to meet the interests of these groups.

At most stations, Community Relations Directors are in charge of the planning and producing of the public affairs panel programs, interviews, or talk shows that deal with community-oriented issues. Often they serve as television hosts for these offerings. They also supervise the production of all local PSAs (and often write the copy for them) and screen those that are produced elsewhere for quality and appropriateness for broadcasting by the station.

Community Relations Directors have to evaluate requests for on-air promotion from many worthy organizations. As service-oriented professionals, they are concerned with using television to deal effectively with community needs. Because they deal with many special interest groups, Community Relations Directors need to be very familiar with FCC regulations, including the fairness doctrine and equal-time provisions. They have to be able to turn down inappropriate and unfeasible requests for station broadcasting time while at the same time avoiding negative repercussions for the station. In this respect, one of their duties is to administer the ascertainment files of comments by community members about the station's programming, as required by the FCC.

Directors plan and organize public service events with community members to discuss the station's programming as well as coordinate and conduct station tours for local organizations and groups. They arrange for station personnel, frequently news anchors and reporters, to appear at local events and functions. They establish and train a speakers' bureau composed of the station's employees and schedule their appearances at public or organizational meetings. Because Community Relations Directors have such close contact with the community, they often research and help to develop station editorial positions on community issues. The director's position is partly that of a public relations professional and partly that of an overseer, reflecting both the needs of the station and those of the community.

Community Relations Directors are usually employed only at middle- and major-market commercial stations, generally reporting to the program manager. At smaller-market operations, the program manager and/or the general manager share the duties related to community relations. In public television, a station's entire programming operation (and its staff, from general manager to the director of development) is designed to be highly responsive to community needs.

Salaries

According to the U.S. Department of Labor, Bureau of Labor Statistics, the median annual earnings for salaried public relations specialists in 2002 were $41,710. The middle 50 percent earned between $31,300 and $56,180 yearly, the lowest 10 percent earned less than $24,240 annually, and the top 10 percent earned more than $75,100. In contrast, annual earnings during 2004 at commercial stations for Community Relations Directors and public relations officers ranged from $23,000 to $90,000, according to the yearly salary survey made by Broadcast Employment Services. The mean average salary for this position was $39,710.

Employment Prospects

Opportunities for the position of Community Relations Director are poor, as there are few openings in commercial television for this type of position. At many stations the duties of this position are contracted out to a director of a service or civic group specializing in local problems and the organizations designed to deal with them, or to an individual experienced in community relations who is put under contract to the station. Some positions may be available at low-power television (LPTV) stations, but usually most of these stations are too small to support a full-time staff member as a Community Relations Director.

Advancement Prospects

Opportunities for advancement to other broadcast-related posts at a station are fair. Some Community Relations Directors move on to become full-time producers of public affairs or news programs. Some may use their television broadcasting skills and their knowledge of programming to become program managers. Some may choose to move away from the broadcasting industry to apply their knowledge to higher-paid public relations positions at government agencies, nonprofit organizations or other business associations.

Education and Training

Usually, an undergraduate degree in government, sociology, or urban affairs is a requirement for this position. However, a degree in communications or public relations may be preferred in some cases. A broad liberal arts background with courses in government, public affairs, and the social sciences may also be acceptable.

Experience, Skills, and Personality Traits

Most Community Relations Directors must have at least two to four years of previous experience as a director or a public information/relations officer for a community, civic, cultural, or service organization. They should have experience in dealing with a wide range of social concerns and a familiarity with local business, community, and governmental groups. It is helpful also to have some experience in communications, journalism, marketing, or a related field.

Directors have to be attentive and sensitive individuals with a strong impetus to assist in alleviating problems. They should be good listeners and adept as negotiators and mediators. They must have excellent communication skills, both written and verbal, as well as exceptional public speaking abilities. They need to have strong event planning skills and excellent attention to detail, accuracy, and deadlines. They should have a working knowledge of television production and program scheduling. They must have good management talents, be able to work cooperatively with other station staff, and recruit and manage volunteer teams. Above all, a Community Relations Director has to be extremely service oriented and capable of dealing with a large number of varied organizations and people in a courteous, professional, and understanding manner.

Unions and Associations

There are no unions that serve as bargaining agents for Community Relations Directors. Many directors join the National Broadcast Association for Community Affairs, a professional organization, as well as a variety of civic and service organizations in the course of performing their duties. They may also belong to such umbrella organizations as the International Association of Business Communicators or the Public Relations Society of America. Both of these organizations have accreditation programs for public relations specialists.

Tips for Entry

1. Volunteer for local civic, community, and professional organizations to gain an understanding of their concerns and interests.

2. Look for intern programs at local television stations to learn about television production and program scheduling firsthand.

3. Hone your public speaking abilities by participating in debate or drama, and add writing courses to your curriculum.

DIRECTOR OF PUBLICITY AND PROMOTION

CAREER PROFILE

Duties: Conduct all public relations and promotion at a television station or network

Alternate Title(s): Director of Advertising and Promotions; Director of Creative Services; Director of Information; Director of Public Relations; Promotion Director

Salary Range: $14,000 to $126,000

Employment Prospects: Fair

Advancement Prospects: Fair

Prerequisites:

Education and Training—Undergraduate degree in advertising, communications, marketing, or public relations

Experience—Minimum of three to four years in advertising, promotion, public relations, or publicity

Special Skills and Personality Traits—Good writing and editing abilities; imagination and creativity; interpersonal skills; sales talent

CAREER LADDER

```
┌─────────────────────────────────────┐
│ Director of Publicity and Promotion  │
│ or Marketing (large station, network,│
│ cable TV, or nonmedia field)         │
└─────────────────────────────────────┘

┌─────────────────────────────────────┐
│ Director of Publicity and Promotion  │
└─────────────────────────────────────┘

┌─────────────────────────────────────┐
│ Publicity/Promotion Assistant        │
└─────────────────────────────────────┘
```

Position Description

A Director of Publicity and Promotion for a television station or network devises and implements comprehensive public relations campaigns to promote the activities, image, and programming of the station or network. Various approaches are used to help augment the audience for the station's programming and to attract and hold both new and current advertisers.

The main task of a Director of Publicity and Promotion is to promote the station and its programs, on-air personalities, and stars to current and potential audiences through all kinds of imaginative campaigns. Directors use many types of advertising and on-air and print promotional techniques to accomplish their goals. These include printed materials such as press kits, news releases, posters, fliers, fact sheets, and feature articles in publications. Promotion to consumers extends to advertising on billboards, in newspapers, on radio, and advertisements in consumer and trade magazines, as well as the increasing extensive use of Internet resources.

The Director of Publicity and Promotion ensures that program listings are both accurate and creatively written to help entice viewers to watch the production. Both listings and schedule changes must be promptly distributed to the media. To promote upcoming programs, the director oversees the production and scheduling of promotional spot announcements to be aired on the station during broadcast days before the actual event occurs. The director also previews and selects prerecorded excerpts from other sources and chooses actors and announcers to promote the station and its fare.

In addition, the Director of Publicity and Promotion supervises special events, such as parades and other appearances of on-air talent at public functions, and arranges for interviews of the station's talent in other media. Directors arrange for advance screenings and Internet-based previews of special programs and speak on behalf of the station or network at public or community functions. Directors also oversee research on audiences, media analyses, and rating demographics. They work directly with the traffic/continuity department in scheduling spot announcements promoting the station or network.

At commercial stations or networks, Directors of Publicity and Promotion interact closely with general sales managers to increase advertisers' awareness of the station or network, and work with the art department to produce effective print and promotional materials. In the same manner, directors coordinate with public relations directors all public functions involving the station or network and provide printed material and other public relations support at these functions. If the station is affiliated with a network, the Director of Publicity and Promotion works closely with the network's own promotion and publicity department to advertise the station's programs. At a public TV station, the Director of Publicity and Promotion collaborates with the volunteer coordinator, the director of development, and other members of the publicity staff to promote the station and its image as well as interfaces with the equivalent staffs at the Public Broadcasting Service (PBS). In both cases, directors administer the promotion departmental budget.

The Director of Publicity and Promotion typically reports to the program manager or directly to the general manager of the station or network. Because of the magnitude, complexity, and wide range of responsibilities of this job, most stations have at least two to five assistants employed to support the director. Most of these assistants specialize in different media or techniques of promotion and publicity.

Salaries

According to the salary survey conducted by Broadcast Employment Services, annual earnings for Promotion and Publicity Directors during 2004 ranged from a low of $14,000 (for entry-level employees) to $36,000 in the smallest-market stations. For directors at the top 50 major-market stations, yearly income ranged from $21,000 (for entry-level employees) to $108,000 or more for experienced directors with seniority. Overall, the mean average salary for Promotion and Publicity Directors was $39,117.

Employment Prospects

Chances of advancing into the position of Director of Promotion and Publicity are only fair, as this post is the top rung in promotion departments at television stations and networks. Openings at this advanced level occur only occasionally. Nonetheless, it is possible for talented and ambitious promotion and publicity assistants to move up to this position within their own stations or with the parent company's organization, or to move on to a larger-market station or network. It also is not unheard of for qualified people in other types of public relations fields to transfer into the television industry as Directors of Publicity and Promotion. Similar jobs are also available at cable systems, home entertainment companies, and some low-power television (LPTV) stations.

Advancement Prospects

Since the position of Director of Publicity and Promotion at commercial television stations is often the top job in the promotion and publicity department, there are few chances to advance within the station organization. However, some individuals may obtain higher-paid jobs in the same post with larger-market television stations, cable systems, or networks. Other directors may choose to move into other public relations fields or to more responsible promotion and publicity positions in other media-related organizations. In public television, a few Directors of Publicity and Promotion may be able to switch to fund-raising positions, such as director of development, at their own stations or at other operations in either smaller or larger markets.

Education and Training

An undergraduate degree in advertising, communications, or public relations is usually mandatory for this post. Courses in photography, printing, speech, and writing are considered valuable for this job. Art, design, and media research courses may also be helpful, as all of these skills are necessary in the position.

Experience, Skills, and Personality Traits

A minimum of three to four years of experience in all phases of advertising, public relations, publicity, and promotion is considered essential. Expert knowledge in using the computer, the Internet, and print design programs would be useful, as well as some business experience in dealing with outside vendors.

Candidates for this position should possess solid editing and writing skills and have a vivid imagination. They need to be excellent salespersons who are articulate and personable, poised and persuasive, and fully capable of dealing in relatively sophisticated environments. They must be both creative and enthusiastic in their capacity of developing promotional concepts and themes.

Unions and Associations

There are no unions that specifically represent Directors of Publicity and Promotion in commercial or public television. However, many directors belong to the Public Relations Society of America (PRSA) or to ProMax International, Inc., to share mutual concerns with their peers and to network and advance their careers.

Tips for Entry

1. During your college education in advertising, communications, or public relations, include courses in art, design, photography, and printing—necessary background for publicity and promotion activities in television work.

2. Work in any advertising or marketing position in business or advertising firms to gain necessary skills that can be applied to your work in the television industry.

3. Take an internship or an apprenticeship in the advertising or marketing department of an independent film company or production company, as this experience will be directly applicable to your promotion and publicity work at a television station or network.

FILM/TAPE/DIGITAL LIBRARIAN

Duties: Acquire, prescreen, and handle shipping arrangements for commercials, film, tape, and programs at a television station or network

Alternate Title(s): Film/Tape/Digital Specialist; Media Librarian

Salary Range: $20,000 to $65,000 or more

Employment Prospects: Fair

Advancement Prospects: Good

Prerequisites:

Education and Training—High school diploma required; technical or film school training helpful

Experience—Library experience; operation of audiovisual equipment and videotape machines helpful

Special Skills and Personality Traits—Detail oriented; good organizational abilities; record timing accuracy; timing skills

```
┌─────────────────────────────────────┐
│   Traffic/Continuity Supervisor;     │
│      Operations Manager;             │
│      Engineering Technician          │
└─────────────────────────────────────┘

┌─────────────────────────────────────┐
│     Film/Tape/Digital Librarian      │
└─────────────────────────────────────┘

┌─────────────────────────────────────┐
│  High School; Technical or Film School │
└─────────────────────────────────────┘
```

Position Description

The Film/Tape/Digital Librarian at a commercial or public television station classifies, catalogs, and maintains a library of all prerecorded programming and commercials (whether on film, tape, or digital format), and prepares them for broadcast. Librarians order, receive, file, and ship such materials from and to a variety of sources. They are responsible for getting all on-air media to the proper location at the station in time for the planned broadcast or to clients in time for their usage.

At a station or network, the Film/Tape/Digital Librarian is responsible for prescreening all incoming prerecorded materials, classifying them, and evaluating their technical quality prior to broadcast. As television shows and news broadcasts in particular rely on split-second timing in airing their various segments, a program that runs too long or short can interfere with the station's entire operation. In the case of a prerecorded commercial, if it is aired while scratched, dirty, or damaged in any way, the station would most likely have to rerun it at no cost to the client. Thus, the main responsibility of the Film/Tape/Digital Librarian is to ensure that all footage to be used is correctly timed and ready for broadcast.

The use of film at television stations has virtually disappeared. Some stations still use videotapes instead of film, but most have switched to digital tape format (DTF) as the most convenient medium to use. For those television stations still using videotapes, the librarian receives and processes new incoming blank videotapes, assigns control numbers to them, and readies them for technical evaluation by the engineering department. When they have been returned ready for use, the librarian inventories the tape for future use by the production unit. As opposed to the physical storage of videotapes, digital footage is stored within computers. However, it also has to be maintained and controlled by the librarians in a similar manner for its eventual use in broadcast.

The Film/Tape/Digital Librarian works closely with the traffic/continuity supervisor and generally reports to the program manager or to the operations manager. In either case, the librarian reviews the daily advance log provided by the programming department of the programs to be aired during the day. The librarian then determines that all the scheduled prerecorded materials are at the station and ready for broadcast.

In addition, the librarian maintains an accurate and up-to-date inventory of all such materials, with an exact guide to their format, location, disposition, as well as a record of their usage. Librarians also have the responsibility of editing such media to conform to the logged time for their broadcast between commercial breaks. They also edit and insert commercials into prerecorded programs according to the production log, assembling and labeling these commercials for inventory purposes.

In large postproduction facilities and dubbing operations, Film/Tape/Digital Librarians may supervise others in the handling, shipping, or transmission of prerecorded media to clients. In such circumstances, the group operates as a team to ensure the correct and safe delivery of the material.

Salaries

Annual salaries for Film/Tape/Digital Librarians in commercial and public television are generally low. According to a salary survey by Broadcast Employment Services, 2004 earnings for Film/Tape/Digital Librarians ranged from a low of $21,000 to a high of $79,000, with a mean average annual salary being $33,000, and the median yearly salary being $27,000. In another survey of minimum wages of a wide variety of jobs, done in 2003 by the Advanced Integration Group, minimum hourly wages for film-tape librarians ranged from a low of $7.47 per hour (approximately $13,595 in annual wages) to a high of $25.47 (approximately $46,355 in yearly income). However, it is estimated by industry observers that earnings are higher for those librarians working in private industry and at some government agencies and postproduction facilities.

Employment Prospects

Most television stations employ one or two Film/Tape/Digital Librarians. This job is often considered entry level, so openings do occur as people in this position are promoted. Cable TV systems, advertising agencies, and some low-power television (LPTV) stations also employ Film/Tape/Digital Librarians. In contrast, the networks often employ more than 30 people in their videotape-digital library facilities to handle the thousand or more pieces of tape and digital media used each day. Postproduction houses also use Film/Tape/Digital Librarians to keep track of all their tape and digital media, as do videotape dubbing facilities. While the overall opportunities for employment are only fair, the position is still one of the easier entry-level jobs in television to obtain.

Advancement Prospects

Film/Tape/Digital Librarians often can advance to become traffic/continuity supervisors. Those individuals with some

engineering proficiency and talent may obtain licenses from the Federal Communications Commission (FCC) and eventually move to a more responsible post at a television station as an operations manager or an engineering technician. Still others may use this entry-level job to learn all they can about the station or postproduction facility and transfer into openings in production or programming. Opportunities for advancement from the post of librarian are good but greatly depend on the individual's attitude, initiative, interests, and talents.

Education and Training

Most employers require a high school diploma. Some may consider additional training in electronics or film production at a technical school as helpful background. At larger stations and networks, a degree in communications might also be required.

Experience, Skills, and Personality Traits

Most employers consider this job to be an entry-level post and will provide on-the-job training under the supervision of the program or operations manager. Newly hired individuals may find an advantage if they have experience operating audiovisual equipment, including videotape machines, digital Betacams, and associated gear. Computer skills and experience with home videocassette machines are almost a requirement. Some knowledge of common transportation carriers and shipping procedures will also be useful.

A Film/Tape/Digital Librarian has to be extremely careful, organized, and detail oriented. Accurate records must be meticulously maintained on a daily basis, and programs scheduled for use timed precisely. Diligence and patience is a necessity, and the individual must be comfortable being part of a team.

Unions and Associations

There are no unions or professional organizations that represent Film/Tape/Digital Librarians.

Tips for Entry

1. While earning your high school diploma, be sure to include courses in computer technology, as you will need these skills in handling the digital media aspects of your duties as a Film/Tape/Digital Librarian.
2. Look for possible internships at television stations to learn the basics of television production.
3. Take part-time work (during the school year and summer months) at a library to become familiar with classifying and cataloging materials.

PROGRAM MANAGER

CAREER PROFILE

Duties: Pick and schedule all programming for broadcast by a television station

Alternate Title(s): Director of Programming and Production; Program(ming) Coordinator; Program Director; Vice President of Programming

Salary Range: $14,000 to $125,000

Employment Prospects: Fair

Advancement Prospects: Good

Prerequisites:

Education and Training—Undergraduate degree in business, communications, journalism, marketing, or radio/television broadcasting

Experience—Minimum of five to seven years in television production and marketing

Special Skills and Personality Traits—Creativity; good taste; organizational ability; sound judgment; thorough knowledge of television programming and production

CAREER LADDER

```
┌─────────────────────────────────┐
│      General Manager;            │
│  Production Company President    │
└─────────────────────────────────┘

┌─────────────────────────────────┐
│      Program Manager             │
└─────────────────────────────────┘

┌─────────────────────────────────┐
│      Executive Producer;         │
│      Production Manager          │
└─────────────────────────────────┘
```

Position Description

The Program Manager is accountable for all local, network, independent, and syndicated programming broadcast by a television station. Program Managers are the decision makers and overseers of the programming department. Reporting to the general manager of the station, the Program Manager must make certain that all programming complies with all Federal Communications Commission (FCC) regulations. Guided by the general manager, Program Managers define the station's objectives in terms of the kind of fare it will acquire and produce. Program Managers select and schedule all programs on a daily basis, taking into consideration the competitive programming from rival stations. They seek to choose the best shows for each time slot and aim to create a mix that will guarantee the largest possible viewing audience and highest ratings. At commercial stations, Program Managers work closely with the sales department to determine what shows are most marketable to advertisers during the various available times in the broadcast schedule.

During this daily process, Program Managers keep track of the needs of their viewing audience and monitor the quality, type, and profitability of entries broadcast by the station. They use local and national research organizations, reports, and rating services to determine the demographics of the station's viewing audience at various intervals during the broadcast day and to measure viewers' reaction to any given program. Much of this analysis is done with the aid of computers.

At stations owned and operated by one of the big networks (known as O&Os) and at network-affiliated stations, the network supplies most of the programming. However, fare such as news and public service offerings are produced locally at the station. Similarly, independent stations and public television stations acquire portions of their programming from outside sources, such as syndicators (providers of syndicated shows), and they also produce programs in-house. The Program Manager decides which film packages, syndicated shows, reruns of previously aired network programs, and locally produced entries will be selected, produced, or purchased to provide the overall programming balance. In the case of O&Os and affiliated stations, the selection process includes the regular shows programmed by the networks for daily broadcast. Program Managers also supervise the scheduling of spot announcements, commercials, public service messages, and station breaks.

Additionally, they must also create and schedule local public affairs programs to comply with the station's obligation to operate in the "public interest, convenience, and necessity" required by FCC regulations. For this purpose, Program Managers must understand their community's needs and problems to select appropriate material for the station's viewing audiences. They devote a portion of their time to evaluating local program ideas for possible production as well as negotiate with independent producers and program syndicators to purchase product for the station. Finally, they are responsible for the programming budget and allocations of equipment and personnel needed to keep within the station's affordable limits.

Salaries

Regardless of the many demands and responsibilities of this position, Program Managers receive relatively lower salaries than do other personnel within the television industry. Those at independent commercial stations are usually paid more than those at network-affiliated stations due to their increased duties in selecting programs.

According to the 2005 salary survey by Broadcast Employment Services, annual salaries in 2004 ranged from a low of $14,000 (at a smaller-market station) to a high of $178,000 (at one of the top 10 market affiliated stations). The mean average yearly income for the personnel surveyed was $45,075. Program Managers at the smallest-market stations earned annually from $14,000 to $29,000. Salaries for Program Managers in public television are similar to those in commercial broadcasting, even though they may have more responsibilities in selecting programs for broadcast.

Employment Prospects

Although every station has a Program Manager, opportunities for employment are only fair, as there are a limited number of stations in operation. Cable TV and multichannel multipoint distribution service (MMDS) operations offer some other opportunities, as do low-power television (LPTV) stations. Nonetheless, the number of new available posts is not expected to expand significantly, and competition for the job is great.

Advancement Prospects

Most Program Managers at both commercial and noncommercial stations have good opportunities to move on to more responsible positions in broadcasting, usually becoming Program Managers at larger stations with higher salaries. Typically, Program Managers of commercial stations or cable television stations start at a smaller station and then move progressively to larger stations in the same capacity. In public television, Program Managers often move on to the job of general manager of the station. In these cases, they move to smaller stations to assume this top post at a higher salary. In contrast, others may wait for an opening at their own station.

Some Program Managers at commercial stations join network programming staffs, while others become salespersons of syndicated programs. Still others may form their own television production companies.

Education and Training

An undergraduate degree in business administration, communications, journalism, marketing, or radio/TV broadcasting is recommended. Virtually all Program Managers have an undergraduate degree, and many have graduate degrees as well in such fields as mass communications or media arts. Speech, drama, writing, sales, and marketing courses are also recommended.

Experience, Skills, and Personality Traits

Individuals seeking positions as Program Managers should have at least five to seven years of experience in television production. For commercial television stations, experience in sales is considered as important as production experience. Many Program Managers have previously held a position of general sales manager and have had some on-air experience in radio or television. In public television, many Program Managers have been executive producers or production managers before their present post. Some even have been directors, performers, or writers.

Program Managers are expected to have imagination, good taste, and organizational capabilities. They should have an aptitude for show business and possess superior business skills. Above all, Program Managers must have a thorough understanding of television production and programming.

Unions and Associations

There are no unions that represent Program Managers. Most commercial and many public television Program Managers belong to the National Association of Television Program Executives (NATPE) to share mutual concerns, network, and learn about programs that may be available for purchase.

Tips for Entry

1. Combine your educational coursework in communications or radio/TV broadcasting with solid business administration and marketing courses.
2. Learn about television production techniques and programming by interning at local television stations while getting your undergraduate or graduate degree.
3. Study the lineup of network programs throughout the day as to how they mix their offerings and how they compete with each other for their viewer audiences.

PUBLICITY/PROMOTION ASSISTANT

CAREER PROFILE

Duties: Manage details concerning public relations, promotion, and publicity at a television station

Alternate Title(s): Assistant Promotion Director; Assistant Promotion Manager; Promotion Specialist; Public Information Assistant; Public Relations Specialist

Salary Range: $20,000 to $60,000 or more

Employment Prospects: Fair

Advancement Prospects: Good

Prerequisites:

Education and Training—Undergraduate degree in advertising, communications, English, journalism, or public relations

Experience—Some previous work with promotion and public relations recommended

Special Skills and Personality Traits—Familiarity with media and the Internet; good language and television production skills; writing facility

CAREER LADDER

```
┌──────────────────────────────────────────┐
│   Director of Publicity and Promotion     │
└──────────────────────────────────────────┘

┌──────────────────────────────────────────┐
│      Publicity/Promotion Assistant        │
└──────────────────────────────────────────┘

┌──────────────────────────────────────────┐
│  Media or Nonmedia Promotion/Public       │
│  Relations Position; Secretary; College   │
└──────────────────────────────────────────┘
```

Position Description

It is the task of a Publicity/Promotion Assistant to handle all details of the work involved in supplying a television station with public relations, promotion, and publicity services in support of its programs and other activities. Assistants report directly to and assist the Director of Publicity and Promotion of the station in all assigned duties. Similar posts can be found in most of the larger cable TV systems and multichannel multipoint distribution service (MMDS) operations as well as commercial networks.

At smaller commercial stations, there is usually only one Promotion/Publicity Assistant, who will perform a wide range of chores. In middle-market and larger-market commercial and public TV stations, three or more assistants are frequently used. Typically, each has a specified major responsibility, such as on-air promotions, or advertising for the station, or working on public relations and publicity. Nonetheless, most publicity/promotion divisions are small, and the assistant is assigned to many activities related to the general goal of attracting new viewers and advertisers to the station.

At commercial stations, Publicity/Promotion Assistants work closely with the public relations officer (or community relations director) and the traffic and art departments to implement projects involving public relations or promotion of the station's business. At a public television station, the assistant works with the coordinator of volunteers and the director of development to help raise money effectively for the station. In either of these positions, the Publicity/Promotion Assistant is responsible for maintaining a current mailing (and/or e-mail) list of the station's advertisers (if a commercial station), volunteers (if a public station), viewers, and supporters.

Publicity/Promotion Assistants prepare press releases and feature articles about the station and its activities, as well as compile and distribute press kits. They make arrangements for special events and appearances and frequently conduct tours of the station. They also create, develop, and edit on-air promotion spots and media material to publicize the station's upcoming offerings. They work with the videotape/digital engineer or editor to create sophisticated and effective spots for broadcast. Some assistants specialize in generating computer-produced promotional announcements. Most assistants write the program announcements (otherwise known as overcrawls) to be superimposed on the video image during newscasts and other programs.

Publicity/Promotion Assistants maintain daily contact with a wide range of media individuals to publicize and promote station activities, even to the extent of spending a significant portion of the working day outside the station or on the telephone or the Internet when at the station. At times, they may draft speeches for meetings and represent the station at community and business events.

In addition, other responsibilities include writing and designing promotional fliers, brochures, direct mail pieces, and other promotional literature about the station, its programming, and its activities. They respond to viewer comments, complaints, suggestions, and questions about programming. They work closely with the sales staff of the station (or contracted marketing service) to develop meaningful research information for the station's advertising clients. They also are responsible for maintaining all promotion and publicity files, photographs, stories, press releases, and prerecorded promotional spots for the station.

Salaries

According to the U.S. Department of Labor's Bureau of Labor Statistics, median annual earnings during 2002 for salaried public relations specialists were $41,710. The middle 50 percent earned between $31,300 and $56,180 yearly, while the lowest 10 percent earned less than $24,240 a year and the top 10 percent earned more than $75,100 annually. A survey of 2004 salaries of Publicity/Promotion Assistants done by Broadcast Employment Services indicates that salaries ranged from a yearly low of $20,000 to an annual high of $75,000, with a mean/average salary being $38,800.

Employment Prospects

Chances of obtaining a job at a television station as a Publicity/Promotion Assistant remain generally fair. As this position is often entry level, competition among recent college graduates with a degree in advertising, communications, marketing, or public relations remains stiff, with the number of applicants frequently exceeding the number of jobs available.

Employment of all types of public relations specialists is expected to increase faster than the average of all occupations through 2012, according to the Bureau of Labor Statistics. The need for good promotion of a television station in an increasingly competitive business environment will help to guarantee a demand for specialists, even at the entry level.

Advancement Prospects

Opportunities for advancement for intelligent, capable, and successful Publicity/Promotion Assistants are good, particularly those who have displayed imagination and

flair and have acquired specialized skills. Some become directors of publicity and promotion at their own station, while others move to cable TV or to larger-market stations to gain better-paid positions. Still others obtain rewarding and more responsible positions by transitioning into nonbroadcast companies, such as independent production firms. Other areas for potential advancement include MMDS operations and low-power television (LPTV) stations. Some use their television experience to gain responsible positions in public relations or promotion at companies, organizations, associations, or public relations firms outside the media industry.

Education and Training

An undergraduate degree in advertising, communications, English, journalism, or public relations is an absolute requirement for this position. While courses in liberal arts help expand general knowledge, writing courses are obligatory for an applicant for a position as Publicity/Promotion Assistant. It is recommended that applicants also take courses in art and design (including layout and Web design).

Experience, Skills, and Personality Traits

It is expected that an applicant for this post has some experience in promotion and public relations at a media- or non-media-related organization. Even a background in promoting a nonprofit organization is helpful, even if it is only on a part-time basis. Writing experience is also essential.

Assistants have to be both enthusiastic and creative. They must be dependable, versatile, and geared to adapting to many situations and assignments. Their language skills must be exemplary in order to write short articles and press releases. They should be affable with good interpersonal skills. Above all, they must be competent with computer hardware and software.

Unions and Associations

There are no unions that represent Publicity/Promotion Assistants. Many, however, belong to ProMax International, Inc., or to the Public Relations Society of America to improve their skills, network, and advance their careers.

Tips for Entry

1. While in college, investigate internship possibilities at local television stations to gain firsthand experience in the industry.
2. Volunteer to provide publicity and promotion for college or community events to gain practical experience in the field.
3. Be sure you are well versed in computer-aided design and layout techniques, as these are talents you will need as a Publicity/Promotion Assistant.

TECHNICAL PRODUCTION

CAMERA

ASSISTANT CAMERA OPERATOR

CAREER PROFILE

Duties: Assist camera operator on television productions; maintain and assemble all camera equipment

Alternate Title(s): Assistant Cameraman; First Assistant Photographer

Salary Range: $1,300 to $1,600 or more per week

Employment Prospects: Fair to Good

Advancement Prospects: Good

Prerequisites:

Education and Training—High school diploma required; additional coursework in photography helpful

Experience—Some television production work

Special Skills and Personality Traits—Ability to follow instructions; good interpersonal skills; keen eye; knowledge of camera equipment and elements of photography

CAREER LADDER

```
┌─────────────────────────────────┐
│        Camera Operator          │
└─────────────────────────────────┘

┌─────────────────────────────────┐
│    Assistant Camera Operator    │
└─────────────────────────────────┘

┌─────────────────────────────────┐
│      Production Assistant;      │
│     Engineering Technician      │
└─────────────────────────────────┘
```

Position Description

Assistant Camera Operators work directly for the camera operator as part of the camera team. On large-budget productions and many made-for-television films, there may be two Assistant Camera Operators, the First Assistant Camera Operator, and the Second Assistant Camera Operator. Whether there are two designated assistants or only one, the full range of duties of the post of Assistant Camera Operator are the same.

First Assistant Camera Operators are in charge of running the camera department in terms of ordering cameras and equipment needed for specific projects. They log in both cameras and any equipment, assemble equipment needed for the shoot, make sure everything is running properly, thread the camera, and maintain it during the production. They are also responsible for changing the lenses and filters, keeping the gate of the camera clean, and, most important, measuring and following the proper focus of the camera on the main action as decided by the cinematographer (or director of photography). As the focus puller during the shooting, the First Assistant Camera Operator makes sure the proper focus is used during each shot. This is a critical part of the individual's duties, and it is important to work closely with the camera operator to get the focus just right, especially during mobile shots when the camera and the performers are moving in and out of a designated depth of field where a wrong decision could lead to fuzzy imaging on the film. During the appropriate rehearsal moments, measurements and notations have to be made on the proper focus in relation to the camera's position to the performer. Sometimes it requires four people working in conjunction with one another to maintain a sharp focus for a particular shot: the Assistant Camera Operator, the crane operator, the dolly grip, and the camera operator. By also shooting digital video simultaneously, the Assistant Camera Operator can instantly see whether the focus is precise enough for each shoot, rather than waiting until after the film has been developed in the laboratory.

Second Assistant Camera Operators load and unload the film in the camera magazine before it reaches the First Assistant. They maintain accurate information about the shot on a slate, known as a clapboard or clapper, and keep track of the paperwork, including the camera reports for film developing and the postproduction process. Camera reports are critical in noting the exact takes the director wishes printed by the laboratory as well as the amount and use of footage from take to take. These camera reports are then checked for continuity and accuracy before copies are provided to the laboratory and the film editor. Both the First and Second Assistant Camera Operators may be involved with preparing the camera for production, with all appropriate camera tests applied, and wrapping the camera in protective covering at the end of the day's shoot before it is stored or returned to the camera rental house.

Salaries

Salaries for Assistant Camera Operators are set by the International Cinematographers Guild, a unit (Local 600) of the International Alliance of Theatrical Stage Employees (IATSE). The minimum hourly wage set for First Assistants is $34.97, and the minimum hourly wage for Second Assistants is $32.19. Depending on the hourly length of the workweek, weekly minimums range from $1,391.81 to $1,636.55. As these figures are minimum wage guidelines and do not include overtime pay, most Assistants, and especially top-flight ones, can earn much more than these minimums.

Employment Prospects

Large television productions, established television series, and made-for-TV films often have at least one Assistant Camera Operator. Thus, employment opportunities at the larger-market stations and networks are good, but only fair at smaller-market stations. However, the camera requirements of most live news programs help to ensure the need for at least one Assistant Camera Operator.

Advancement Prospects

The obvious career move for most Assistant Camera Operators is to the position of camera operator. However, the competition is extremely stiff. Ambitious Assistant Camera Operators have to develop the right skills, establish a solid and good reputation in their position, and exhibit positive behavior at all times.

Education and Training

A high school degree is essential. While a college degree with a major in film or television production is not essential, it is recommended. Applicants for this position can get on-the-job training by working on student or low-budget nonunion films or through an apprentice training program for television production set up by the IATSE union. In these programs, they learn about the latest technology and master a variety of camera systems.

Experience, Skills, and Personality Traits

Assistant Camera Operators must have a well-rounded knowledge of cameras, lenses, and light-meter readings. They need a strong visual sense, visual creativity, and an intimate knowledge of a variety of camera systems and lenses. They should have good interpersonal skills and be comfortable following orders and being a member of a team. They should have a passion about what they are doing but also be resilient and hard working.

Assistant Camera Operators need to be intensely attuned to the body language of the cinematographer and main camera operator. The camera department has no margin for error, and all its personnel must be completely focused on the job at hand. For example, if negatives are scratched by undiscovered microscopic hairs from the camera gait, if the film is loaded in the magazine incorrectly and clogs the camera, or if microphone books are caught by the camera from inattention by the operator, a day's work may be ruined. Thus, the work that the camera personnel do is critical and can have far-reaching consequences for the production.

Unions and Associations

Membership in the International Cinematographers Guild, a unit (Local 600) of the IATSE is beneficial and essential for work on some productions. The union sets minimum rates for all Assistant Camera Operators as well as guidelines for overtime and other wages. Assistant Camera Operators who become members of that union and are looking to advance their careers to camera operators or cinematographers may find it helpful to be inducted into the American Society of Cinematographers (ASC).

Tips for Entry

1. During your educational years, work on student, low-budget, independent, and nonunion films in a production capacity to learn the business.
2. Take a job at a camera equipment rental house to learn about the equipment and make contact with Assistant Camera Operators.
3. Take a job as a production assistant on any television offering. As veteran first Assistant Camera Operator Anthony Cappello says, "Ninety percent of the people in this business start out as production assistants. . . . All shows have them and all shows need them."

CAMERA OPERATOR

CAREER PROFILE

Duties: Set up and operate television cameras in a studio or on location

Alternate Title(s): None

Salary Range: $12,000 to $80,000 or more

Employment Prospects: Fair

Advancement Prospects: Good

Prerequisites:

Education and Training—High school graduate; training in audiovisual equipment or photography helpful

Experience—Some television production experience, usually as production assistant

Special Skills and Personality Traits—Creativity; fast reflexes; photographic technical knowledge; versatility

CAREER LADDER

Audio/Video Engineer; Floor Manager; Lighting Director

Camera Operator

Engineering Technician; Production Assistant

Position Description

Typical television camera crews consist of a cinematographer (or director of photography), a Camera Operator, and one or more assistant camera operators. A Camera Operator is responsible for operating a television camera during the rehearsals for and the actual production of television programs, television series, news and sporting events, and other television events. Studio Camera Operators work in a broadcast studio and usually videotape or digitally photograph their subjects from a fixed position. News Camera Operators, also called electronic news gathering (ENG) operators, work as part of the reporting team, following newsworthy events as they unfold.

Equipment used by Camera Operators may be a full-size camera mounted on a tripod, dolly, or crane or a smaller minicam, known as an ENG camera, used for on-location shooting. In the field, these cameras frequently have a motion-stabilizing mount that is attached to its user by means of an upper-body vestlike brace and is known as a Steadicam. This device has a counterbalanced arm projecting from the front, which allows for free and steady movement of the camera (no shaking, jerking, or bumping) by the operator as he or she moves on an uneven surface. Increasingly, compact digital cameras are supplanting the older videotape cameras, as they enhance the number of angles and the clarity that a Camera Operator can provide.

Most television operations have a minimum of two full-time Camera Operators on staff. At the larger stations and networks, there may be eight or more employed for various shifts and assignments. For simple productions, only one or two cameras may be used, whereas for more complex programs, five or more cameras are needed to cover the various elements of the program.

Camera Operators sometimes are considered part of the engineering crew and report to the engineering supervisor. At other stations, they are members of the production department and report to the production manager. When Camera Operators are assigned to the news department, they are given specific assignments by the assistant news director and as ENG operators, may operate somewhat more independently as cinematographers as they may need to edit the raw photographic footage on the spot before relaying it to a television affiliate for broadcast.

In most situations, however, the Camera Operator receives directions (via an intercom system and through headphones) from the director or technical director during rehearsal and actual production of a program either in the studio or on location. In news gathering operations, the Camera Operator typically follows the instructions of a reporter when covering an on-location story. However, experienced and smart Camera Operators go into automatic operation at the scene of a news story, needing little instruction from a director or reporter and finding new, interesting, and imaginative angles and shots for use during the news production. As an integral part of a television studio or remote production team, the Camera Operator is vital to the continuing flow and appearance of any show or newscast.

In addition to their regular tasks, Camera Operators assist the audio/visual engineer in the setup, technical checking of, and simple maintenance of the television cameras. They sometimes assist the lighting director in the setup of scenery, lighting equipment, and other accessories to be used prior to the start of a production and in turn help the floor manager or the unit manager in the dismantling of a production.

Salaries

According to the U.S. Bureau of Labor Statistics, in 2002 the median annual earnings for television Camera Operators were $32,720. The middle 50 percent earned between $20,610 and $51,000 per year. The lowest 10 percent earned less than $14,710 yearly, and the highest 10 percent earned more than $65,070. In their 2005 salary surveys of 2004 earnings of Camera Operators (including studio, news, and sports operators), Broadcast Employment Services found that Camera Operators received salaries ranging from a low of $10,000 to a high of $110,000, with a median average annual salary being $35,000. A few individuals working on the national networks earned even more than $110,000 per year.

Some Camera Operators are self-employed and are contracted to television networks to work on individual projects for a predetermined fee, often a daily or weekly rate. If they are members of the International Cinematographers Guild (ICG), their minimum daily rate is set at $385.15, and their weekly rate is either $1,856.95 or $1,903.37 depending on whether they are working on a set program of four consecutive weeks or on a week-by-week basis. If they are members of the International Alliance of Theatrical Stage Employees (IATSE) as video cameramen, their weekly minimum salary per contract is $1,416.

Employment Prospects

While some television stations may consider the position of Camera Operator to be an entry-level job, most stations promote from within their staff, assigning either an experienced production assistant or an engineering technician to the job. The number of openings depends greatly on the amount of production done. Usually, employment chances at stations with a heavy news schedule are good, as their news departments alone may use five to eight news crews, each with at least one Camera Operator. Networks often employ more than 250 Camera Operators on a full-time basis. Cable systems originating productions employ full-time camera people. Camera Operator positions are also available at educational, governmental, and health television studios.

The U.S. Department of Labor's *Occupational Outlook Handbook* states that employment of Camera Operators is expected to grow about as fast as the average for all occupations through 2012. Despite this positive assessment, there is a lot of competition for the position of Camera Operator, and thus employment prospects are considered to be only fair.

Advancement Prospects

Chances of promotion for Camera Operators in television are considered good. Most Camera Operators are looking for a career in production. The customary advancement path for production-oriented operators is to a job as floor manager or lighting director. In stations where a Camera Operator is considered to be a part of the engineering department, the career path usually leads to an audio/video engineer job. In news or documentary units in a television station, Camera Operators often advance to the position of cinematographer, a position that has more judgment and creativity as well as increased independence.

Education and Training

A high school diploma is an absolute requirement. Additionally, most employers suggest some training in photography (still or motion) or audiovisual equipment. Art or film schools can provide good preparation for the job of Camera Operator. Some employers also may want to see some evidence of further study toward a certificate from one of the industry engineering organizations. Others basically seek people who have had some informal training with home video and film cameras. As veteran Camera Operator Daniel Turrett suggests, "Anybody who thinks they want to become a cameraman ought to be very sure of it and focused. It's very, very competitive, so you need to be serious about it. Seize all opportunities to go to seminars and shoot on your own. Get a video camera, an old Super-8, or a camera of any kind, and go out and shoot film."

Experience, Skills, and Personality Traits

Most Camera Operators have some experience in television production, usually as production assistants, before being assigned to this position. Knowledge of cameras and lenses, light-meter readings, staging, lighting, composition, optics, and specials effects is a necessity. Camera Operators need to have a creative sense of composition and an ability to initiate imaginative angles with their television camera. They need to be able to react rapidly to directors during a production and have good communication skills themselves. In addition, a Camera Operator should have physical and mental stamina and be both alert and versatile.

Unions and Associations

Camera Operators at most commercial television stations may be represented by the International Alliance of Theatrical

Stage Employees (IATSE), the International Cinematographers Guild (ICG), the National Association of Broadcast Employees and Technicians, AFL-CIO (NABET), or the International Brotherhood of Electrical Workers (IBEW). In public television, many Camera Operators are not represented by any union.

Tips for Entry

1. Take courses in film history to broaden your background and learn how veteran Camera Operators in the past have created the visual images you see on film.

2. During your education, volunteer to work for free on student films and nonunion productions, music videos, and commercials to gain experience.

3. Consider working for a motion picture camera rental company, where you will have an opportunity to learn about the equipment and meet members of camera crews currently working on productions.

4. Take any job with a television station or production company just to get on a set where you can learn more about cameras and make contacts.

CINEMATOGRAPHER

CAREER PROFILE

Duties: Shoot and edit film, videotape, and digital formats at a television station

Alternate Title(s): Cameraman; Director of Photography (DP); First Cameraman; News Photographer; Videographer

Salary Range: $15,000 to $90,000 or more

Employment Prospects: Fair to Good

Advancement Prospects: Fair

Prerequisites:

Education and Training—Undergraduate degree in media arts or television production

Experience—Minimum of one to three years of camera work and editing

Special Skills and Personality Traits—Creativity; interpersonal skills; originality; passion and tenacity; resourcefulness; technical abilities

CAREER LADDER

```
┌─────────────────────────────────────┐
│   Independent Production Producer;   │
│        Television Producer           │
└─────────────────────────────────────┘

┌─────────────────────────────────────┐
│           Cinematographer            │
└─────────────────────────────────────┘

┌─────────────────────────────────────┐
│   Camera Operator; Assistant Camera  │
│   Operator; Production Assistant;    │
│            Film Editor               │
└─────────────────────────────────────┘
```

Position Description

The Cinematographer (sometimes known as the director of photography, or DP) is the person in charge of the camera crew and provides expert advice to the director regarding the various shots and angles available and the technical requirements for each. In collaboration with the director, this individual controls the lighting, framing, setting up, and composing of camera shots. Cinematographers usually do not actually operate the camera (that is the job of the camera operator and/or the second camera operator) but are the primary creative contributors to the overall look of a television program, telefeature, special program, news show, or commercial.

The Cinematographer's primary responsibility is to produce quality images and interpret the needs of the director, the news director, or the producer in developing visual approaches to a script or news story. The Cinematographer creates and captures the overall photographic impression of a television production. In some cases, the Cinematographer is viewed as a lighting director, or someone who creates the mood, texture, and feeling of the image with light. In other instances, the Cinematographer also works with the dramatics of the shot and the interpretive use of the camera in telling the story. Whichever role the Cinematographer has depends greatly on the working rapport between the director

and the Cinematographer. They have to be in accord about the creative concept of the production and its execution.

During preproduction, the Cinematographer meets with the director to discuss that individual's overall vision for the project and the specific needs of individual scenes. Based on these meetings, the Cinematographer selects the necessary cameras, lenses, equipment, and film, tape, or digital resources appropriate (given the budget) for each shooting assignment and preps the lighting and grip departments for anticipated needs. Throughout the production, Cinematographers determine how each scene is to be lighted; what filters, lenses, film stock, or digital resources will be used; and the position and movement of the cameras for each scene. In postproduction, Cinematographers work closely with processing labs to check that the footage is processed correctly to preserve the colors and moods aimed for during production.

Most commercial and public television stations are now moving away from the use of film and even videotape to use digital cameras with their on-the-spot editing capabilities. Such digital uses have long been added to the portable electronic news gathering (ENG) equipment employed by news departments of stations for their news coverage outside a studio. It is estimated that soon the use of digital camera equipment will be nearly universal throughout the television industry. Nonetheless, many Cinematographers are still responsible for a station's black-and-white and color still photography.

Most commercial and public television stations employ Cinematographers for commercial productions, news coverage, and special programs. At some commercial stations, they are part of special units that provide production services for advertising clients. Usually, Cinematographers are members of either the production or the programming department. In other cases, Cinematographers may be assigned permanently to a station's news department.

Salaries

Income for Cinematographers is relatively moderate. According to a 2005 survey conducted by Broadcast Employment Services, of 2004 annual earnings of Cinematographers/ videographers working in commercial television, salaries ranged from $14,000 to $90,000, with a mean average income being $33,940. Those Cinematographers employed by public television had slightly lower annual salary ranges according to industry studies.

Cinematographers who work on commercials and network television programs are usually members of Local 600, the International Cinematographers Guild, of the International Alliance of Theatrical Stage Employees (IATSE). As such, they have minimum wages set by union contract. If hired on a daily basis, their daily rate (eight hours) is $626.56. If hired on a weekly basis (five days for a total of 43.2 hours), their weekly rate is $3,010.55. If hired for four consecutive weeks (five-day weeks of 48.6 hours each), their weekly rate is $2,802.34. Experienced Cinematographers generally earn well above these minimum rates.

Employment Prospects

Employment opportunities for Cinematographers in television are fair to good. With the increased number of productions from commercial, cable, and public television stations and networks, the need for experienced Cinematographers is constant. Both camera and assistant camera operators in commercial film production or talented and knowledgeable production assistants can sometimes become Cinematographers. However, as there are many aspiring Cinematographers waiting for the chance, competition can be stiff.

Now that most stations (and all networks) are using digital technology instead of film, it is fortunate that the techniques and skills required of Cinematographers are easily transferable to the new methodology. Lighting and the setting up of scenes for shoots remain approximately the same. Some stations even use the term *cine-videographer* for an individual who applies the techniques of film production to the operation of portable video and/or digital camera equipment.

Opportunities are good at major-market stations that have a heavy news schedule. Often, five to nine news crews work for a station, and each crew has at least one Cinematographer or videographer. Openings also occur at public television stations, independent production firms, and advertising agencies. Many of these organizations still use film in the shooting of their productions or commercials. Other opportunities are available for Cinematographers in educational, governmental, and health video production institutions and corporate media centers.

Advancement Prospects

Opportunities for Cinematographers to advance further in production are only fair. Some look to create full feature films or documentary films for theatrical presentation and use their television experience to obtain positions as producers at independent production firms. In larger television stations and networks, Cinematographers can be promoted to director positions supervising other cinematographers or to a position of producer specializing in on-location productions.

Education and Training

An undergraduate degree in communications or film with some additional training in television production is usually a basic requirement. Additional courses in the use of digital technology in television production are helpful. There are hundreds of college and university film programs as well as television and film studio training programs designed to help aspiring Cinematographers learn the necessary technical skills. In addition, the International Cinematographer Guild, Local 600, of the IATSE has a training program that would prove useful.

Experience, Skills, and Personality Traits

The position of Cinematographer is so crucial to the success of a television production that most employers require at least one to two years of experience in shooting and editing motion picture film and tape. Familiarity with and an understanding of all types of cameras and lenses as well as related audio tape recorders is essential. A background in still camera equipment and technique, processing, and film chemistry in addition to film editing techniques is also useful.

Cinematographers must have a good photographic eye and know how to light a scene properly to achieve their vision. As veteran Cinematographer Richard Crudo puts it, "Look at light in your real life, in your house, in your car, on the street at daytime and nighttime; in the bank, in the supermarket, in a restaurant—you have to look at light. You have to see how light creates feelings."

Cinematographers generally are given considerable independence and latitude in shooting for television. They must be imaginative and have a feel for composition and the aesthetics of shooting film, tape, or digital diskette and what can or cannot be accomplished in the editing phase. As television, like film, is a highly collaborative art form, Cinematographers have to have good people skills to assert their own creative ideas in a nonthreatening way. They need to be original and resourceful in dealing with the variety of circumstances that occur during production but also have to be zealous and tenacious in the pursuit of their art.

Unions and Associations

Most Cinematographers in commercial television are represented by Local 600, the International Cinematographers Guild, of the IATSE. The guild acts as their bargaining agent. Others may be represented by the National Association of Broadcast Employees and Technicians, AFL-CIO (NABET). Many Cinematographers also belong to the American Film Institute (AFI), the American Society of Cinematographers (ASC), the Association of Independent Video and Filmmakers (AIVF), or other local, state, and national film councils to share their ideas, network, and advance their careers.

Tips for Entry

1. While studying in school, work on low-budget, independent, nonunion films or student films to become familiar with the process that a Cinematographer must go through.

2. Find a way to shoot as much footage as you possibly can, whether it is film, video, or digital. Purchase a used manual still camera and a cheap light meter and learn how to expose film. In the process you will acquire knowledge about color, composition, and exposure.

3. Start your television career as a production assistant or a member of the camera crew to learn the trade.

4. Make as many personal connections as you can with Cinematographers or camera people who are in the industry. Contact television people whose work you admire and ask their advice. Come to watch them on the set and offer to work for free to see them at their work.

EDITING

ASSISTANT EDITOR POSITIONS

CAREER PROFILE

Duties: Assist the editor in preparing television productions for broadcast

Alternate Title(s): None

Salary Range: $13,000 to $70,000

Employment Prospects: Fair

Advancement Prospects: Fair to Good

Prerequisites:

Education and Training—High school degree required; college degree preferred with courses in television production and all phases of filmmaking

Experience—Some experience in film editing, particularly in video and digital formats

Special Skills and Personality Traits—Detail-oriented; effective communication skills; good organizational abilities; patience; strong creative nature; good sense of story pacing

CAREER LADDER

```
┌─────────────────────────────────────┐
│              Editor                  │
└─────────────────────────────────────┘

┌─────────────────────────────────────┐
│     Assistant Editor Positions       │
└─────────────────────────────────────┘

┌─────────────────────────────────────┐
│   Production Assistant; College      │
└─────────────────────────────────────┘
```

Position Description

Assistant Editor Positions include the primary Assistant Editor known as First Assistant Editor and, when required for major productions, a Second Assistant Editor. Additional assistant jobs include the entry-level position of apprentice editor and the more specialized job of color timer.

First Assistant Editors usually manage the editing department, allowing editors to devote their time and energy to the creative process of editing the material. After the production's footage has been transferred to videotape, it is logged in by the First Assistant Editor. With the aid of the Second Assistant Editor and any editorial apprentices, the First Assistant Editor organizes the footage, listing every shot and where it starts and ends. If the script has been properly marked by the script supervisor, this list making is merely a process of identifying where shots are. The script supervisor has kept track of such details as to what dialogue lines are included in each scene, which takes provide the best angles, which shots have goofs, and so on. Each clip will have been numbered and lettered to indicate the scene, the shot, and the particular take.

Once the shots are assembled, they are digitized into the computer. This is a time-consuming process, as it is accom-plished in real time. Once digitized, the production as shot is ready for the editor to do a nonlinear edit to prepare the digitized program for broadcast.

First Assistant Editors are also responsible for maintaining all department reports and paperwork and interfacing with outside vendors, such as sound transfer facilities and other production services. They take notes during daily showings of shot footage and throughout the editing process. Once the editor decides that the edit is satisfactory, the project is locked. It is then sent to the sound editors for sound effects work and for the insertion of any designated music. The First Assistant Editor oversees the work through postproduction until it is completed for broadcast.

For major productions and many television series, a Second Assistant Editor is frequently hired, primarily to support First Assistant Editors in all their duties. Their delegated assignments vary according to the particular needs of the production but often include keeping track of the footage shot each day and even doing an initial pick of clips to be used, say, for a news show or selecting and editing the music for teaser spots and promotional clips.

Apprentice editor positions are the entry-level jobs within the editorial department. They assist the Assistant

Editors and the editor as instructed, usually handling the cataloging of films and videotapes and acting as messengers between the studio and labs and sound transfer facilities. They help log in footage and load everything into the Avid editing machine.

There is one more specialized position in the editing department, that of the color timer. The position's title comes from the old Hollywood practice of controlling how much color was to be saturated into the film by controlling how much time the film was emersed in the developing baths. Today, the color timer uses a Hazeltine color analyzer to control changes in color balance and density. The Hazeltine reverses the colors on the negative and displays them on a television monitor, allowing the timer to emphasize or deemphasize the primary colors and adjust the final output for color balance.

Salaries

As these positions are entry level or require only a few years of experience, salaries tend to be low. According to a salary survey conducted by Broadcast Employment Services of the position of Assistant Editor, during 2004 annual salaries for this position ranged from a low of $13,000 to a high of $70,000, with a mean average salary being $33,804. Specialist editorial positions, such as color timer, earned salaries much closer to those of editors, while apprentice editors had earnings at the low end of the range.

The Editors Guild of the International Alliance of Theatrical Stage Employees has set minimum wages for their members who are Assistant Editors. Hourly wages range from $27 to $29.40, depending on how long the assistant has worked in that position.

Employment Prospects

Nearly every television show requires an editor to work with the director in fashioning a final cut that the director can approve for broadcast. Every editor needs a staff to handle all the departmental tasks. Therefore, the position of Assistant Editor is a necessity for most productions. Despite the competition for work in the editing department, employment opportunities are fair.

A good way to become an Assistant Editor is to start out as a production assistant, preferably assigned to the editing department. Another avenue to this post is to start work with a postproduction facility or a local television station where there is less competition for jobs than in such major markets as Los Angeles and New York.

Advancement Prospects

Moving on to the position of editor is a natural career step for an assistant but is very dependent on openings, which do not occur often. It is important for Assistant Editors to realize that the career path they have chosen is a long-term one. While some editors may permit their assistants to gain hands-on experience editing a scene, this is not a common occurrence. Experience is acquired usually through long service and the careful nurturing of relationships.

Education and Training

While a high school diploma is usually required, a college degree may not be a prerequisite for being hired as an Assistant Editor, though courses in film and television production would be helpful. On-the-job experience working in a film lab or interning at a postproduction facility is recommended.

Experience, Skills, and Personality Traits

Assistant Editors should obtain whatever experience they can by volunteering to work for free on student and low-budget films, commercials, or music videos. From there it is suggested that they try to find a position as a production assistant assigned to editorial or gain an entry-level post as an apprentice editor.

Assistant Editors need to be good communicators, extremely well organized, and heavily detail oriented. Computer aptitude and a basic understanding of television production and film/video editing are additional assets.

Unions and Associations

Membership in the Motion Picture and Video Tape Editors Guild, Local 700, of the International Alliance of Theatrical Stage Employees may prove to be beneficial.

Tips for Entry

1. During high school or college, get involved in any facet of filmmaking you can, offering to work for free on student or low-budget projects to gain the experience.
2. If you go to film school, network with classmates, editing their school projects so that they know you and your reputation as they go to work on projects in the industry.
3. Go overboard in being helpful by doing extra things, staying late and getting to work early. Being good in your job (say, as a production assistant) does not guarantee career advancement. Networking and telling people what you want to do does.

EDITOR

CAREER PROFILE

Duties: Choose the best shots or takes and assemble them in the most effective way to reflect the director's vision of a television production

Alternate Title(s): Film Editor; Video (or Digital) Film Editor

Salary Range: $13,000 to $146,000

Employment Prospects: Fair to Good

Advancement Prospects: Fair to Good

Prerequisites:

Education and Training—Undergraduate degree required; advanced degree recommended, with courses in television production and all phases of filmmaking

Experience—Editing experience with student films; successful completion of Editors Guild training program

Special Skills and Personality Traits—Creativity; effective communication skills; good vision; sense of story pacing; strong judgment ability

CAREER LADDER

```
┌─────────────────────────────────────┐
│    Director; Cinematographer         │
└─────────────────────────────────────┘

┌─────────────────────────────────────┐
│              Editor                  │
└─────────────────────────────────────┘

┌─────────────────────────────────────┐
│     Assistant Editor Positions       │
└─────────────────────────────────────┘
```

Position Description

Editing is a multilayered creative process. Takes are assembled from dailies (the daily shootings of the production) to create scenes, and scenes are assembled to make a show, all according to the blueprint provided by the script. In consultation with the director, the Editor is responsible for the complex process of assembling and sorting the film, video, or digital footage of a television production into a cohesive sequence to ensure continuity and to execute the director's vision.

Even before the shoot is finished, the Editor is busy assembling the footage into a rough version known as the Editor's cut. In the course of a project, Editors have countless reels of film, videotape, or digital images to review, an impossibly short schedule, and changes to incorporate at every turn. Working with the director, the Editor refines the material through several stages until it is deemed ready to be shown to the producer(s). Once approved, further changes may be necessary before creating the final cut for broadcast.

Feature and made-for-TV movie Editors start work the first day of production and are usually employed until the last day of the mix for the final cut. Some television producers cut their budgets by letting the Editor go when the direc-

tor's cut is locked and keep only the lower-paid assistant editor through the process to the final cut. Editors employed on TV series are usually with the show for the run of the series. Often there are several Editors employed, each working on a different episode, and two or more episodes are often in different stages of completion at the same time.

Editors work at both commercial and public television stations, at production/facilities companies, and at many cable and satellite systems. They are also employed at corporate television centers and at some nonprofit media centers. They are seldom found at multipoint multichannel distribution service (MMDS) stations or low-power television (LPTV) stations. Some of them work as freelancers, hired on a per-project basis, and a few operate their own editing companies.

Today film is seldom used as a medium within the television industry, as videotape has become the preferred medium. Up until the 1980s, the only process of editing videotape was linear (or online) editing. In this process, the videotaped footage is mounted onto the source (video) deck. Then a second, blank tape is mounted on the master deck. They both then are plugged into an editing controller, a device that tells the deck what to do. The Editor chooses and tags the beginning and end of each shot in both decks, and the controller then transfers the picture and sound from the source to the master. Each shot has to be handled separately and in sequence, which made transposing scenes difficult. Transitions, or fades, from one shot to the next were not possible unless a separate process, called off-line editing was set up. The off-line Editor put together the edit of the video without any fancy transitions, and the on-line Editor, using the edit decision list (EDL)—a computer-generated list of which shots would be used in what order—would program multiple-source decks to recreate the whole program with all the required transitions. The entire process was unwieldy and time consuming.

In the early 1980s, nonlinear editing was introduced along with the development of cable television and a new format called a "music video." This exciting and creative medium used an extremely fast manner of editing and soon became the dominant style of television editing. At the same time, a new machine, the Avid editing system, was introduced. It digitized the videotape footage, loading it into a computer. The Editor, sitting at a computer terminal, then could arrange the shots on a time line, accurately trim frames, do quick searches for scenes, shift them around at will, and rapidly create new sequences. The Avid gave Editors (and directors) unlimited ability to change, manipulate, and make their final product more intricate. Under the new procedure, the Editor can add new shots, moving all other shots aside to make room, or let the new shot wipe out part of an older one. The Editor can add effects, split screens, graphics, and color effects as well as all kinds of transitions from one shot to another. One of the great advantages of the off-line system is that the Editor at any point can see how the project is coming together, complete with at least rudimentary dissolves, fades, titles, color correction, and other effects. However, the effects created in this off-line system can be used only as a gauge, as what comes out as dissolves, fades, and other optical effects will be only as good as the information going into the system. Without accurate footage counts to give to the processing lab, these effects will become useless until they fit into the negative properly. The Editor must work closely with lab technicians to ensure the effects are translated properly.

The concept of on- and off-line editing still exists in non-linear editing. Once the EDL is complete on the nonlinear computer, it is sent to an online Editor, who does a high-quality edit using the original video footage at its full resolution, attaching the final soundtrack at the same time.

Another method is sometimes used by low-budget film-makers, borrowing from the news media, by working with digital video (DV) cameras. These DV cameras can be plugged into a desktop or laptop computer and the images downloaded. Then, editing can be done right on the desktop or laptop computer. Thus, today's sophisticated editing hardware, software, and networking capabilities allow for seg-

ments of tape to be digitized, cut, pasted, and manipulated by Editors to create a seamless and imaginative content flow.

Salaries

Wages for Editors at television stations are relatively moderate. According to the U.S. Department of Labor's *Occupational Outlook Handbook,* median annual earnings for film and video editors in 2002 were $38,270. Their yearly salaries ranged from a low of $20,030 to more than $78,070. In surveys of Avid and nonlinear Editors in television during 2004, Broadcast Employment Services found that salaries ranged from an annual low of $16,000 to a high of $146,000, with a mean average income being $41,236. In further surveys of online Editors and offline Editors, it was found that offline Editors had yearly salaries that ranged from $13,000 to $75,000, with a mean average of $32,108. For online Editors, the per-year pay ranges were from $18,000 to $135,000, with a mean average income of $48,301. For those Editors who belong to Local 700 of the International Alliance of Theatrical Stage Employees (IATSE), their hourly minimum wage as set by union contract is $42.20. If they are hired on a weekly basis (total of 48.6 hours), their minimum hourly wage is $38.92, or $1,891.33. If they are put on an "on call" basis, their five-day minimum rate is $2,387.23.

Employment Prospects

As the television industry is a growth industry, particularly in the expansion of cable stations and programming, and since the Editor is a key position in the production process of much programming, employment prospects for Editors are relatively fair to good. Editors who have the needed skills to work with new digitizing processes have the best chances for continued employment. For many Editors, membership in the Editors Guild of the International Alliance of Theatrical Stage Employees (IATSE) can bolster their employment prospects, as they can shift their work between films and television. Job security is further enhanced by how well Editors work with directors (and, in some cases, with star performers and/or producers).

Advancement Prospects

Many Editors stay in their position, as the job itself is so demanding as well as rewarding. A few Editors open their own editing firms. Some may want to become cinematographers, producers, or directors. Their position as Editor is one of the best ways to learn about directing and the production process. Generally, the skills and aesthetics learned as an Editor are applicable to many other higher-level production jobs in both television and film, and the opportunities for those with skill, dedication, and ambition are good. However, the competition is always stiff.

Education and Training

A high school diploma is a basic requirement. Most employees expect prospective Editors to have some college training in film production and editing as well as an undergraduate degree. The Motion Picture and Video Tape Editors Guild has training programs designed to help the aspiring Editor. These programs are designed to train members in the latest editing equipment and software programs. The American Cinema Editors Society also offers an internship program to college graduates who have majored in film.

Experience, Skills, and Personality Traits

Most employers require at least one to two years of experience in editing, usually as an assistant Editor, and knowledge of television production processes. The process of editing is both an art and a craft. Editors need to be visual storytellers and must be able to reorganize visual shots to tell the same or different stories in different ways. They need to be both highly organized and logical in their thinking. They must have strong creative and artistic abilities (both visual and auditory), be able to communicate well, and have good manual dexterity.

Editors have to be able to work well with strong ego-centered individuals. A director or a performer may be counting on them to fix a scene or improve on a performance. Editors must also be good listeners and collaborators and still have the ability to work long hours on a complex task alone. As veteran television editor M. Edward Salier observes, "You can't allow your own ego to get in the way . . . It's not what I want to see, it's what the director wants to see. I really have to be able to sit and listen to him, get a sense of what he wants to accomplish, and deliver that as quickly and effi-

ciently as possible. . . . It's an intense job. It's a long workday. You have to be able to work on your own."

Unions and Associations

Many Editors belong to the International Alliance of Theatrical Stage Employees (IATSE), while some at commercial stations may be members of the National Association of Broadcast Employees and Technicians AFL-CIO (NABET). (Membership in IATSE is obligatory if an Editor wants to work on a studio or union motion picture.) Some Editors may find it beneficial to belong to the Association of Independent Video and Filmmakers (AIVF) for networking purposes.

Tips for Entry

1. During high school and college, get involved in any aspect of filmmaking available to you, such as creating student films with a video or digital camera, and then edit the footage.
2. Be willing to start out in an internship, where you can learn the skills, meet people, and build relationships. These relationships will be critical to your advance in your career. Look for these internships at local television stations, commercial production houses, or post-production facilities.
3. Attend seminars given by Editors to learn how they got started, how they trained, and how they got their first break.
4. Go to film festivals to meet directors, as they usually are the ones who hire Editors. In addition, network with Editors at these functions who may be looking for assistants.

POSTPRODUCTION SUPERVISOR

CAREER PROFILE

Duties: Supervise postproduction work on a television production

Alternate Title(s): Director of Postproduction; Postproduction Facility Manager

Salary Range: $25,000 to $135,000

Employment Prospects: Fair

Advancement Prospects: Poor

Prerequisites:

Education and Training—Undergraduate degree required; advanced degree recommended, with courses in television production and all phases of filmmaking, particularly editing techniques

Experience—Editing experience with student films; successful completion of Editors Guild training program

Special Skills and Personality Traits—Creativity; effective communication skills; supervisory capacity; strong judgment ability

CAREER LADDER

```
┌─────────────────────────────────┐
│      Producer; Owner            │
│   (postproduction facility)     │
└─────────────────────────────────┘

┌─────────────────────────────────┐
│   Postproduction Supervisor     │
└─────────────────────────────────┘

┌─────────────────────────────────┐
│     Editor; Assistant Editor;   │
│      Production Assistant        │
└─────────────────────────────────┘
```

Position Description

Before most television productions are aired, they go through an after-production process known as postproduction. Postproduction includes all the steps necessary to complete a television project for distribution and broadcast. It occurs after all principal and any second-unit filming/videotaping has been completed. It is an umbrella term that covers editing, the addition of special effects, sound mixing, and preparation of the completed master mix in film, videotape, or digital format. There are several phases in the postproduction process, and the complexity of each step is defined by the needs of the project.

This process takes place at a postproduction facility, which may be either a part of the station's or network's organizational structure or a separate company under contract with the station or network for the specific production. The Postproduction Supervisor at this facility or company is in charge of the team that helps to achieve a director's postproduction goals. They are problem solvers, from the initial questions of "How do we do this?" to providing suggestions and explaining what can be achieved with different effects, to creating the master tapes that meet the technical specifi-

cations of the production's director and producer(s). They report to the director or producer of the television production or to the executive in charge of postproduction, who is usually a station or network executive.

The supervisor manages the personnel within the facility, sets up all work schedules, and provides the budget for each job. Postproduction Supervisors are basically assistant directors of the process of postproduction and frequently are the company's senior editors. As such, they may also do hands-on editing of material that the facility produces as well as being hired to edit for outside clients. Postproduction work includes creating optical or computer-generated special effects, mixing sound and music with the visual shots, creating titles, correcting colors, adding voice-overs, and the infusion of any required animation. The processes of cutting both visuals and sound are designed according to the director's established plan and vision.

The postproduction team consists of one or more editors to edit the raw material accrued during production and adding additional material that will be created and used for the show. Though digital technology has made organizing and handling the material far easier than before, most editors have one or more assistant editors to take care of all the organizational details. Titles and credits are usually handled by separate companies that specialize in creating them. Visual effects are handled by a visual effects supervisor. This person locates companies or individuals who will handle matte work, compositing, rotoscoping, and other postproduction special effects. For the audio side, a dialogue editor will repair and replace dialogue, a Foley artist will record sound effects, and a music supervisor/editor will manage the music, including hiring a composer and getting permission to use already-composed music to be used in the production. Once all these elements have been gathered, cleaned up, edited, created, cleared, and placed, a rerecording mixer will mix them and place them into the final show. Then, final release prints or copies are made, and frequently promotional materials are prepared. Overseeing this entire process is the main occupation of the Postproduction Supervisor.

Salaries

Wages for most Postproduction Supervisors are relatively modest. According to the salary survey of 2004 wages conducted by Broadcast Employment Service, annual earnings of postproduction management people ranged from a low of $25,000 to a high of $135,000, with a mean average salary being $48,075.

Employment Prospects

While every postproduction facility needs a supervisor for the team of postproduction personnel, there are a limited number of these jobs available at any one time. Thus, prospects for employment are only fair, and much depends on the experience and reputation of the applicant.

All supervisors have been or are editors. All have started in the television industry as production assistants, grips, or some other entry-level post in the production department. Interest in the production aspects of television can lead to internship at a television station during school years and employment thereafter.

Advancement Prospects

Some supervisors may have ambitions of becoming producers of television programs or owners of their own postproduction facilities. Such career advancements are difficult and rare. Generally, this position is considered to be a culminating point in the career of postproduction personnel.

Education and Training

Most film and TV schools have courses in editing, and training programs are available from other organizations, such as the Motion Picture and Video Tape Editors Guild. In these programs, editors are trained in the latest editing equipment and software programs. Obtaining a position as Postproduction Supervisor takes several years of experience working as an editor within the postproduction process.

Experience, Skills, and Personality Traits

Postproduction Supervisors start out as editors in the postproduction process and may continue editing (as senior editors) as well as supervise the postproduction team. As such, they need to have had several years of experience in editing usually starting as an assistant editor and then moving up to editor. In addition to editing skills and a thorough knowledge of both the filmmaking and television production processes, they must possess a strong work ethic.

As editors, supervisors needed to be visual storytellers, able to reorganize visual shots to tell the same or different stories in different ways. This takes intense concentration, creativity, and a devotion to the work that transcends all other concerns. To become supervisors, editors also need to have management talents as well as excellent interpersonal skills. Postproduction Supervisors must be highly organized, logical in their thinking, and able to communicate well to all under their supervision. Above all, they must have a thorough knowledge of all aspects and techniques of the postproduction process.

Unions and Associations

Most Postproduction Supervisors, as editors, belong to the International Alliance of Theatrical Stage Employees (IATSE). Some supervisors may find it beneficial to belong to the Association of Independent Video and Filmmakers (AIVF) for networking purposes.

Tips for Entry

1. While completing your high school, college, and/or film-TV school education, take courses in management and psychology to prepare for a supervisory position dealing with a wide range of technical and artistic personnel.
2. Get your hands on a video camera and begin editing your own footage on your computer to discover whether you have a talent for editing.
3. Keep abreast of all new applicable technology. Postproduction Supervisors and their teams always have tight deadlines and need every possible advantage to increase their efficiency and workflow.

HAIR, MAKEUP, AND WARDROBE

COSTUME DESIGNER

CAREER PROFILE

Duties: Design or select the costumes used for television productions

Alternate Title(s): Costume Director

Salary Range: $1,900 to $3,300 weekly minimum

Employment Prospects: Fair

Advancement Prospects: Poor

Prerequisites:

Education and Training—Undergraduate degree in fashion or costume design helpful

Experience—Several years of costuming for theater, film, or television productions

Special Skills and Personality Traits—Attention to detail; creative flair; design talent; excellent memory and research skills; fashion sense; good communication and time management skills; knowledge of TV production; sewing ability; team worker

CAREER LADDER

```
┌─────────────────────────────────────┐
│          Costume Designer            │
│  (major theater or film production)  │
└─────────────────────────────────────┘

┌─────────────────────────────────────┐
│          Costume Designer            │
└─────────────────────────────────────┘

┌─────────────────────────────────────┐
│  Costuming Apprentice (theater, film,│
│  television); Costume Sketch Artist  │
└─────────────────────────────────────┘
```

Position Description

The Costume Designer is the creative head of the costume department of a television show and is responsible for creating the designs, or using preexisting clothing for all costumes worn on-camera in a television production. Costume designing is really storytelling, in that the function of an outfit is to help television audiences grasp easily who a specific character is. Thus, Costume Designer works to conceptualize and design garments that capture and define the personality of fictional characters from a script. The Costume Designer strives to create believable characters with the costume with the intent of advancing the story's progress.

When a television production is set in the present time, performers are frequently asked to wear their own clothes during the shooting of the production. In these instances, Costume Designers usually are called on to approve the performers' on-camera wardrobes in light of the script. When a Costume Designer receives a script, the process of developing a visual shorthand for each character begins. Costume Designers often work at drawing boards or on the computer in their own studios, but they also spend considerable time in dressing or fitting rooms and in costume and tailor shops. The time available to conduct this important research is contingent on the nature of the television production and its budget.

As a result of this research, Costume Designers usually compile a scrapbook (or digital images/files) of photos, family albums, yearbooks, hairstyles, makeup, costume sketches, fabric swatches, and color palettes, all to help develop the characters and establish the time period in which the action of the television script takes place. Using this book as a basis, Costume Designers work closely with the production designer, the art department, the cinematographer, and the hair and makeup artists to determine the overall design approach and color palette for the show. Then they must decide how the costumes will blend with the concept they have created. As veteran Costume Designer Jill Ohanneson says, "In costume design you're designing for a character. You don't have to just design pants and a shirt and a tie. You're also designing sadness and droopiness and wiltiness. There are so many emotional ways that we play with color and texture and patterns and the way things hang that contribute to what the character is really about." Sometimes a glamorous entrance may be inappropriate and actually destructive to a scene. Costume Designers must serve first the story and the director.

In most instances, Costume Designers do not actually sew and construct costumes (or redesign already existing ones), but these activities are always under their supervision. Depending on the size of the production, Costume Designers may supervise several workers, including costumers, tailors, and fitters. In many instances, these individuals may be employees of a costume company owned by the Costume Designer. Whether it is a scene with two characters or a thousand extras, Costumer Designers collaborate with their crew: the assistant costume designer, the costume illustrator, the costume supervisor, and the set costumers. Together, they create a costume breakdown (to determine the number of costumes needed), calculate a budget, and arrange to manufacture, rent, purchase, and fit the costumes for the production. For most television projects, Costume Designers report to the director of the production, and they are usually on hand in the studio and control room during the production to handle any last-minute changes or emergencies.

The Costume Designer must consider lighting, makeup, hairstyles, and set design in determining the colors and styles of the costumes. The more specific and articulate a costume is, the more effective it will be with audiences. Minute details also frequently enhance an actor's performance in imperceptible ways. Actors sometimes need sensitive costume design for imperfect bodies. Flattering figures, camouflaging flaws, and enhancing inadequacies are all part of the job of a Costume Designer. In addition, Costume Designers must be capable of designing costumes for a wide variety of assignments, from primitive cavemen to 21st-century businesswomen to futuristic aliens. For variety programs or entertainment specials, they must be capable of creating exciting costumes for the chorus, supporting players, and featured performers that complement and add to the overall production. Costume Designers are also usually in charge of the wardrobe for on-screen talents such as newscasters and hosts.

Salaries

Costume Designers on the West Coast belong to Local 892, the Costume Designers Guild, of the International Alliance of Theatrical Stage Employees (IATSE). By union contract, their minimum daily wage is $457.74. On a weekly basis, that is, five days, their minimum rate is $1,910.34. Costume Designers on the East Coast are represented by the United Scenic Artists, Local 829. Their minimum weekly rates range from $2,314 to $2,515 depending on the type of production and size of budget. If hired as an independent, the weekly rate may go as high as $3,300.

As most Costume Designers do not work steadily throughout the year, their income will depend on the number of months they are employed on television projects. As their reputation grows or their style becomes an established factor in the industry, higher rates can be negotiated. Many Costume Designers also work for theatrical productions,

films, industrial shows, or nightclub acts, where the standard pay is usually the minimum union scale but negotiable based on the type of work and/or the Costume Designer's reputation.

Employment Prospects

Opportunities for work in the television industry are only fair to good. Most Costume Designers work freelance on a project-by-project basis. They often own their own companies and, in turn, employ freelance costume people when they get an assignment, mostly miniseries, made-for TV movies, and television series. Most major-market stations and cable systems do not have the budget or the need for a full-time staff position of Costumer Designer. Nearly all work for television Costumer Designers is to be found in either Hollywood or New York City.

In most cases, one Costume Designer is hired for a program or series. When costuming demands become extensive and complicated, the production may employ one or more costumers who function as assistants to the Costume Designer. Most Costume Designers have been costumers or sketch artists in the early stages of their careers.

Advancement Prospects

Successful Costume Designers who have worked for relatively small-budget productions may move into more lucrative costume design positions in motion pictures or make a transition to the Broadway stage. Many Costume Designers work on both coasts and in a variety of settings to advance their careers. Peer recognition and reputation as well as a distinctive style can lead to more important assignments and higher salaries, but opportunities remain limited.

Education and Training

Style and design abilities are more important than a formal education in getting jobs as Costume Designers on television productions. However, an undergraduate degree in fashion or costume design from an art, design, or fashion institute can be helpful. Studying composition, drawing, illustration, and color theory as well as costume history, television production, and theater art are also useful. Coursework in staging and lighting techniques for television and theatre are additional aids in pursuing a career as a Costume Designer.

Experience, Skills, and Personality Traits

Most Costume Designers have spent considerable time at the start of their careers as informal assistants in the theater or film industry as costumers, dressers, wardrobe assistants, or tailors. They may have gained on-the-job experience through an apprenticeship, internship, or entry-level position as a Costumer Designer for a professional, regional, or amateur theater company or even doing similar costume design work on a feature film, documentary, or music video. A balanced portfolio of costumes in all types of entertainment, from musicals to dramas to nightclub shows or music videos, is an additional asset.

Costume Designers need to be heavily detail oriented, since color and fabric can have as much bearing on whether a costume works as overall design and style. They have to be very creative and have an eye for fashion and design. They must be expert at sewing and possess superior drawing, painting, and graphic art skills. They must have an understanding of the techniques, limitations, and capabilities of television production and have good interpersonal skills, as their work is a collaborative effort.

Unions and Associations

Costume Designers on the East Coast are represented by Local 829, the United Scenic Artists, and those on the West Coast by Local 892, the Costume Designers Guild.

Tips for Entry

1. During your classroom years, look for internship programs at local television stations to gain an understanding and some experience of television production.
2. Work in a paid or apprenticeship capacity for a Costume Designer in a music video, play, television production, or film.
3. Work in all types of entertainment media to gain a varied portfolio of design experience.

COSTUMER

CAREER PROFILE

Duties: Assist the costume designer; supervise the entire wardrobe for a television production

Alternate Title(s): Wardrobe Supervisor; Assistant Costume Designer; Costumer Keyperson

Salary Range: $50,000 to $90,000 or more

Employment Prospects: Good

Advancement Prospects: Fair to Good

Prerequisites:

Education and Training—Undergraduate degree in fashion and design useful, but not required

Experience—Working in the costume department of a film, television, or theatrical production as a fitter or cutter

Special Skills and Personality Traits—Creative; knowledgeable of fashion's past and present; organized; reliable

CAREER LADDER

```
┌─────────────────────────────────────┐
│          Costume Designer            │
└─────────────────────────────────────┘

┌─────────────────────────────────────┐
│              Costumer                │
└─────────────────────────────────────┘

┌─────────────────────────────────────┐
│   Costumer Assistant; Set Costumer   │
└─────────────────────────────────────┘
```

Position Description

Costumers are responsible for the care of costumes on the set during a television production. As such, they frequently are known as wardrobe supervisors. For productions that do not have a costume designer, Costumers act as wardrobe supervisors and are also responsible for acquiring the clothes worn by the cast. (This position is a union category separate from that of a Costumer). On larger productions, a Costumer (or wardrobe supervisor) may oversee the work of one or more assistant Costumers or dressers.

As they are in charge of the wardrobe, Costumers fix any problem pertaining to costumes, assist in setting up and following the production's budget for costumes, and select the costumes the performers will be wearing. Under the direction of the costume designer, Costumers make sure that each costume works, does not clash with or look too much like another performer's, and that the costume makes its planned statement about the character. In low-budget productions, the Costumer may take on the duties of a costume designer.

Costumers both pick the costumes to be used and decide whether to rent it, buy it, or have it made specifically for the production. They also ensure that the costume survives the shoot or the day-to-day usage if for a television series and determine how many identical costumes may be needed for

costumes that are likely to be torn or affected during the production process. It is up to the Costumer to supervise all fittings, and they frequently hire those set costumers who do the actual fittings of the performers and the creation of the final costume. Set costumers frequently act as dressers for the performers during the production. In addition, they take photographs and make notes on the set during filming to maintain continuity, such as making sure that a coat carried in one scene is not worn on a retake of that scene. Set Costumers frequently are also in charge of the wardrobe for such on-screen talents as newscasters, show hosts, and so forth.

As head of the wardrobe department at a television station or network, the Costumer works closely with the costume designer, the production designer, and the cinematographer (or director of photography) to make certain that all the costumes are appropriate for the overall design and look of the production. During this entire process, Costumers must keep track of all costumes for the purposes of continuity and maintenance.

Salaries

As set by union contract (the International Alliance of Theatrical Stage Employees), the minimum hourly salary of a costume department supervisor in Los Angeles, if hired day by day, is $30.97. If hired on a weekly basis (five days, 54 hours), the hourly minimum wage is $29.35, or weekly, $1,790.34. For a Costumer keyperson, the hourly minimum is $29.40, and the weekly is $1,717.32.

Costumers who are known as assistant costume designers are covered by the Costume Designers Guild, Local 892, in California, and by the United Scenic Artists, Local 829, in New York. In California, their minimum weekly (five-day) rate is $1,565.12, whereas in New York their minimum daily rate ranges from $267.59 to $312.26, depending on the type of television production with which they are involved. Costumers in New York who are known as wardrobe supervisors have minimum daily rates that range from $289.92 to $354.69, depending on the type of television production for which they are employed and the fiscal year in which they work. It is likely that fully employed Costumers would have annual incomes ranging from $50,000 to $90,000 or more.

Employment Prospects

With the tremendous expansion of television programming on both commercial, cable, and public television, the need for costume people is continually growing. As most dramatic and comedic television productions and series require performers to wear some sort of costume, employment prospects for Costumers are good.

Advancement Prospects

Costumers have a good chance of advancing to full-fledged costume designers. From that position, it is possible to move on to other art- and design-related positions within a major-market station or as a freelancer. Career advancement also occurs by working on higher-profile, larger-budget television productions or series.

Education and Training

While formal fashion or design training is considered useful, it is seldom a requirement. The best training can be acquired by working at a costume house. Costume houses are businesses that specialize in providing wardrobes for film, television, and theatrical productions.

Experience, Skills, and Personality Traits

Costumers must be visually creative and have an acute sense of fashion and design. They need to have basic sewing skills as well as knowledge of clothing and styles from various historical periods. They must be highly organized, as does their wardrobe collection. They also must have good interpersonal skills, as they will have to be very diplomatic in their dealings with performers, directors, and other technicians.

Unions and Associations

Generally, Costumers are represented by the International Alliance of Theatrical Stage Employees (IATSE) but may belong to different locals depending on where they reside (for example, Local 892, the Costume Designers Guild, in Los Angeles; Local 829, the United Scenic Artists, or Local 764, Wardrobe Attendants, in New York). Membership in other industry associations may be useful for networking.

Tips for Entry

1. Attend the Fashion Institute of Technology or a similar school for your education.
2. Work as a production assistant in a wardrobe department for a film or television production to get your opportunities for advancement from the people for whom you work.
3. Work in a costume house to get your initial training as a Costumer.

HAIRSTYLIST

CAREER PROFILE

Duties: Style and dress the hair of performers in a television production or series; prepare wigs as necessary

Alternate Title(s): Hairdresser

Salary Range: $45,000 to $80,000

Employment Prospects: Fair to Good

Advancement Prospects: Poor

Prerequisites:

Education and Training—High school diploma and special training required; certificate from beauty school preferable; some states may require licenses for Hairstylists working on television or film productions.

Experience—Minimum of two or three years of hairstyling for men and women, either commercially (in a hair salon) or in the performing arts, preferably television or film

Special Skills and Personality Traits—Creativity; good interpersonal skills; knowledge of television lighting and camera techniques; manual dexterity; willingness to work long hours, standing on one's feet extensively

CAREER LADDER

```
┌─────────────────────────────────────┐
│ Hairstylist (major film or theater   │
│ productions); Creator of Hair Product│
│ Line; Owner, Hair Salon              │
└─────────────────────────────────────┘

┌─────────────────────────────────────┐
│ Hair Stylist                         │
└─────────────────────────────────────┘

┌─────────────────────────────────────┐
│ Commercial Hairdresser; Assistant Hair│
│ Stylist; Hair Salon Assistant        │
└─────────────────────────────────────┘
```

Position Description

A Hairstylist is responsible for creating and maintaining the hairstyles of performers in a television production. The job is not a supervisory one, and a Hairstylist usually report to the director of the production. The director provides the Hairstylist with the script and, together, they decide about the style, color, and length of hair for each character, including whether a wig or hairpiece will be needed. During this preproduction period, Hairstylists research hairstyles or periods of style, depending on the script, and then ensure that they have all the necessary supplies for use on the production. While some dramatic productions, musical variety programs, and miniseries may require styles that are elaborate and extreme, most Hairstylists work with those styles that are considered natural, fashionable, and attractive by present standards.

Hairstyling for a television production differs from that used in the theater, as the television camera (especially high-definition broadcasts) reveals more detail than is visible to most of the audience of a stage production. As with much makeup, hairstyles created for television are usually subtle and natural. Hairstylists for this medium also must solve problems caused by the lighting, which generates a considerable amount of heat, often making it difficult to maintain hairdos during the shoot. While Hairstylists begin their work in the dressing room before a live television show or before the beginning of lensing a project, they remain available throughout the entire shoot for any needed touch-ups and adjustments.

In the course of the styling, Hairstylists often shampoo, cut, shape, and trim performers' hair, apply hair coloring agents demanded by the script, create accepted styling techniques with both standard and specialized equipment, and when necessary use wigs, hairpieces, falls, and other accessories to achieve the desired effect. Working in conjunction with costume designers and makeup artists, they complement and enhance the specific facial shapes of performers as well as ensure that the performers feel comfortable with their look. In addition, they create hairstyles that suggest the personality traits of specific characters as laid out in the script and approved by the director.

Hairstylists are employed by large independent production companies and by networks for particular television shows, series, or special productions. In small- and middle-sized production organizations and stations, hairstyling often is done by the same person who serves as the makeup artist. Large-scale television projects that involve a large number of featured and supporting performers may require more than one Hairstylist. Many star performers negotiate their contract to include a personal Hairstylist. Other stars employ their own Hairstylist who works with them on a regular basis. For most other productions, a Hairstylist works alone on a project-by-project basis.

Salaries

Generally, Hairstylists freelance for specific productions. However, a few of them are steadily employed as part of the ongoing production team for a network series, soap opera, or miniseries.

Minimum union wage scales for this position range from an hourly rate of $31 to $38 and a weekly rate ranging from $1,522 to $1,716. If they are required to be on call for work at any time, their weekly rate is $1,892. Most Hairstylists work only irregularly on television throughout the year, and they generally earn a minimum of $45,000 annually. People who work steadily may have an income of $65,000 or more a year from their television work alone. As Hairstylists become established in their trade, fees may be negotiated upward from the union minimum scale. If they work regularly, their annual income may well exceed $80,000.

Employment Prospects

Employment possibilities at the television network level or with independent production companies producing for the networks are generally good. However, relatively few positions exist in the television industry overall, as turnover is extremely low and employment tends to be intermittent and seasonal, which makes work prospects for the industry as a whole only fair. While there is always a need for Hairstylists in any major television production, small- and medium-sized stations seldom hire Hairstylists for their regular programming, and, when they do, they usually serve as both Hairstylist and makeup artist.

Personal contacts and connections are the means for building a career as a Hairstylist. Contacts can be acquired as a result of a previous assignment or through recommendations by influential friends or relatives. Most Hairstylists also work in other show business environments, including theater, film, and nightclubs featuring entertainment shows. Some production facility companies also hire Hairstylists on an occasional basis.

Advancement Prospects

Realistically, advancement can come only by developing a reputation. Television Hairstylists sometimes move on to major motion picture assignments or Broadway theater productions. A very few individuals land positions as personal Hairstylists to star performers.

It usually is very hard to get started in this profession, but as one's credits and reputation grow, so do the important assignments (and the resultant continual employment and higher pay). Nonetheless, advancement prospects for most television Hairstylists remain poor.

Education and Training

The usual minimum educational requirement for this position is a high school diploma with some additional specialized training. A certificate or diploma from an accredited beauty culture school that specializes in hair styling is often an additional requirement. Many vocational schools offer courses that can lead to a specialty in hairstyling and/or hair coloring.

Experience, Skills, and Personality Traits

Virtually all Hairstylists begin their career working on a daily basis in a commercial beauty salon. Employment opportunities for work in television industry depend greatly on the experience that the individual stylist has gained. A minimum of two to three years of previous professional work in theater or film is helpful (and necessary in order to apply for union membership). Experience as a Hairstylist for commercial photography studios or in the modeling industry is also useful. Because of the particular technical requirements of television (particularly in lighting), some experience in staging, lighting, and television production is also helpful.

Like commercial Hairstylists, television Hairstylists need to have artistic flair, a sense of style, and good manual dexterity. They must be organized, efficient, and have good interpersonal skills. Computer graphic arts skills and the ability to research may be helpful for employment on major historical television productions.

Unions and Associations

For bargaining purposes, Hairstylists are represented by Local 706 of the International Alliance of Theatrical Stage Employees (IATSE) in both New York and Hollywood/Los Angeles. While union membership is not a requirement for television industry work, it is highly recommended (particularly when advancing into the feature film field). Some Hairstylists working for individual television stations may belong to the National Association of Broadcast Employees and Technicians AFL-CIO (NABET). In addition, some Hairstylists find it useful to belong to the National Hairdressers and Cosmetologists Association for professional support and networking.

Tips for Entry

1. While in school, volunteer to work in campus or community theater productions as good background training.
2. Work in a salon to gain experience as a Hairstylist to gain the necessary skills for a television position as Hairstylist.
3. Work as a production assistant in a television station to gain an understanding of technical requirements of television production and what effect they have on the look of performers.

MAKEUP ARTIST

CAREER PROFILE

Duties: Design and apply makeup as needed by performers in a television production, newscast, or series

Alternate Title(s): None

Salary Range: $45,000 to $90,000 or more

Employment Prospects: Fair

Advancement Prospects: Poor

Prerequisites:

Education and Training—High school diploma required; undergraduate degree preferable; specialized training in cosmetology and makeup required; some states may require cosmetology licenses for makeup artists working on television or film productions.

Experience—College or amateur theater experience; apprenticeship in legitimate theater, or work with a Makeup Artist or a makeup studio

Special Skills and Personality Traits—Creativity; familiarity with television production techniques; good interpersonal skills; patience; visual imagination

CAREER LADDER

```
┌─────────────────────────────────────┐
│   Special Effects Makeup Producer or │
│       Owner; Makeup Director         │
│        (film, theater, or TV);       │
│        Owner of Makeup Line          │
└─────────────────────────────────────┘

┌─────────────────────────────────────┐
│            Makeup Artist             │
└─────────────────────────────────────┘

┌─────────────────────────────────────┐
│  Theatrical Apprentice; Cosmetologist│
└─────────────────────────────────────┘
```

Position Description

Makeup Artists are tasked with designing and applying cosmetics on performers and with ensuring that their physical appearances are in keeping with the look and requirements of a television program. Makeup Artists consult with the director of the production to determine the proper effects that makeup should achieve for the particular program. They work on all formats of programming, applying makeup on dancers, newscast persons, talk show hosts and guests, singers, actors, and supporting players. Throughout the show, makeup must be maintained to ensure continuity, so Polaroid or digital photographs are taken for reference.

Makeup consists of cream, powder, mascara, eyeliner, and other cosmetic products applied to the face of a performer (and sometimes, as required by the script, to the body as well, usually by a specified body Makeup Artist). The application of makeup in a television production or program usually serves two purposes. The first is to enhance the performer's natural features, counteract the washed-out effects that television lighting can produce, and generally improve the performer's appearance on-camera. The television camera can exaggerate skin blemishes and tone, and most Makeup Artists working in the medium devote most of their time to minimizing these flaws by applying straight (noncharacter) makeup, making the performer appear natural to the television audience.

The second function of television makeup is to alter a performer's appearance so that it conforms to the character being portrayed. Makeup may be used to create an effect (such as old age) or an illusion (such as baldness), cover a blemish or scar (or contrive a blemish, scar, or wound), or transform the performer into a completely different person altogether. Applying character or corrective makeup is a more ambitious and demanding undertaking, sometimes requiring the Makeup Artist to devise and apply artificial features or use prosthetic devices to achieve the desired effect. Such work, however, is usually essential only for more complex dramatic or entertainment productions. Performers may be changed to assume particular racial characteristics or their appearances altered to resemble actual historical figures. For these purposes, Makeup Artists maintain a computer file of facial pictures from all historical periods and nationalities as well as of any unusual or interesting characters. In tandem, they develop and maintain their own collection of cosmetic supplies, application devices, and other related cosmetological equipment.

At times, Makeup Artists must create special effects that simulate the results of excessive violence, such as a bloody face or body wounds, broken noses and other bones, or knife wounds. At other times, they may be called on to transform performers into science fiction creatures or characters in a horror production. Many of these specialized makeup effects can be accomplished only after elaborate testing and experimentation and then a lengthy process of application requiring many hours. Nonetheless, the skillful use of such makeup gives a performer an additional edge in portraying a character.

The position of Makeup Artist is seldom a supervisory one, and the Makeup Artist usually reports to the director of the television production. When no hairstylist has been hired or when, due to budget restrictions (usually at smaller-market television stations), the production team has no hairstylist, the Makeup Artist may also assume those duties.

Salaries

While most Makeup Artists are nonsalaried and work on a freelance basis, all are union members. Union minimum wage scales are typically complex, covering a variety of situations. Generally, the minimum hourly wage is $38.48, making the typical eight-hour-day wage $307.84. If a Makeup Artist is employed based on a five-day, 54-hour week, the minimum hourly wage scale drops to $36.60 (or $1,976.27). There are separate wage scales for body Makeup Artists as well as for overtime and distant location work. It is not unusual for Makeup Artists to work eight to 10 months on television productions in any given year. Dependent on the number of hours worked each week and at what rate, their minimum annual income can range from $45,000 to $90,000 or more.

As Makeup Artists acquire both experience and a reputation and their skills become more highly developed, salaries can be negotiated at higher rates than the union minimum wage scales. Those Makeup Artists concentrating on special effects makeup can command significantly higher rates than the minimum, grossing well in excess of $130,000 a year.

Employment Prospects

Opportunities for employment are generally only fair, as it is difficult to break into this crowded field and maintain a presence there. Many Makeup Artists are freelance, which means that the end of one job is the beginning of the search for another.

Very few television stations employ full-time Makeup Artists. The networks do hire them, but employment is irregular and the competition is extremely tough. Independent television production companies employ them, too,

usually only in Hollywood or New York City. Besides their television chores, most Makeup Artists also work for feature films, industrial shows, stage musicals, or theatrical plays on a project basis. Some stars hire their own Makeup Artists, who follow them from production to production.

Advancement Prospects

Developing a good reputation, making and developing important contacts, and sheer luck all are key elements in advancement and continued employment. As they create their own procedures and techniques, some Makeup Artists develop their own line of makeup products or become producers or owners of special effects makeup companies. Others may advance to positions of makeup directors for major television dramas, theatrical productions, or motion pictures. Competition is extremely heavy, making advancement prospects poor.

Education and Training

Courses in television and stage makeup are vital and can be taken at colleges or universities that have a television or theater arts curriculum. There are also specialized institutes and studio or workshop programs. Veteran special effects Makeup Artist Justin Raleigh recommends also taking art classes: "Take illustration and take sculpting classes. Take color theory. Also, go to a makeup school. Many makeup artists have gone through cosmetology school. If you're going more into special makeup effects, I suggest chemistry." Another experienced Makeup Artist, Suzanne Patterson, adds, "You also need knowledge in makeup principles . . . and that includes skin tones, application techniques, cosmetic chemistry, product knowledge for proper selections, and the right tools to do the job."

Additional courses in staging and lighting, television production, and costume design would be helpful. While a college degree is usually not necessary, studies leading to such a degree can provide good basic training.

Experience, Skills, and Personality Traits

Experience with theatrical makeup is mandatory and may be acquired in college or at many community, regional, summer stock, and dinner theaters. An apprenticeship in the theater is a good way to gain broad expertise in applying makeup theory to actual facial anatomy.

Makeup Artists need to be creative and visually imaginative. They must develop good interpersonal talents and excellent business practices, as many of them will remain freelance, and good public relations become crucial to their career success.

Unions and Associations

Makeup artists are members of Local 706, the Makeup Artists and Hairstylists Guild, of the International Alliance of Theatrical Stage Employees (IATSE) in both Hollywood and New York City. At some major-market stations, they may be represented by the National Association of Broadcast Employees and Technicians AFL-CIO (NABET). They may also belong to the National Hairdressers and Cosmetologists Association to network and share mutual professional concerns.

Tips for Entry

1. During your education, take a stage makeup class to study facial anatomy and work in three-dimensional makeup.

2. Read books by Makeup Artists and study films and television shows, and then begin working with makeup products to apply what you have studied to learn by trial and error.

3. Get on-the-job training doing makeup in any performing arts setting you can find, and start building your portfolio, taking photos of everything you do and replacing them with better shots as your craft gets better.

LIGHTING AND ELECTRICAL

BEST BOY POSITIONS

CAREER PROFILE

Duties: Gaffer Best Boy: Supervise the lighting crew and be responsible for the electronic equipment; Grip Best Boy: Supervise the grip crew and be responsible for all equipment and supplies

Alternate Title(s): Second Electrician, Second Grip

Salary Range: $45,000 to $70,000 or more

Employment Prospects: Good

Advancement Prospects: Good

Prerequisites:

Education and Training—High school diploma; undergraduate degree in radio/TV or theater recommended

Experience—Any work experience in television, film, commercials, or music videos

Special Skills and Personality Traits—Ability to work well with people; able to move heavy equipment; knowledge of lighting, electricity and colors; strong mechanical abilities; working knowledge of equipment used by gaffers and grips

Special Requirements—Certificate as an electrician may be required

CAREER LADDER

```
┌─────────────────────────────────┐
│         Gaffer; Grip            │
└─────────────────────────────────┘

┌─────────────────────────────────┐
│          Best Boy               │
└─────────────────────────────────┘

┌─────────────────────────────────┐
│      Lighting Assistant;        │
│      Production Assistant        │
└─────────────────────────────────┘
```

Position Description

The Best Boy position (so-called regardless of the gender of the person performing the job) is the second in command after either the gaffer or the grip. Gaffers and their Best Boy subordinate are in charge of the lighting and electrical department. Grips, and their Best Boy subordinate are the support staff working with the electrical department.

The actual responsibilities of a Best Boy vary depending on the size of the crew. On smaller shows, there may be no one other than the gaffer, the grip, and the Best Boy. In that cast, the Best Boy simply places and operates the grip and lighting equipment and ensures its continuous and safe operation. On larger shows, Best Boys are more like managers. They are the individuals who hire and supervise the rest of the crew. They take care of equipment, hire extra people as needed, and make sure that equipment and supplies are ordered, arranging their delivery and ensuring that they arrive in the right place at the right time. They are also in charge of dealing with any damaged or malfunctioning

equipment, and they guarantee that the sets are prerigged for the gaffer and the grip.

On the set, the director and the cinematographer (director of photography) will decide how to shoot the scene. Then the cinematographer, gaffer, and head grip (often called key grip to distinguish the individual from other grip positions) will work out how to light it. Once these decisions are made, it is the job of the Best Boys to follow through on these decisions about where to position the lights, scrims (mesh material), and reflectors. Gaffer Best Boys have to know exactly what gaffers want when they ask for a specific light, because different lights provide dissimilar effects. Thus, they need to understand voltage and whether enough power is available for the desired lighting, and they need to be fully aware about diffusion and whether the right types of materials for such are available.

Both gaffer Best Boys and grip Best Boys are involved with a lot of moving of heavy lighting equipment and cable. Both participate in the prerigging of sets, which involves building scaffolds, installing heavy lights and generators, laying cable, and moving camera equipment around (the particular responsibility of grips).

Best Boys also liaise with other members of the production department, such as the assistant director, the special effects director, and the art director. If the production goes on location, they may also interface with the maintenance team or electrician on staff in a particular building being used for the shoot. When the production is large enough to have a full lighting crew, Best Boys are then responsible for checking the lighting team members' time sheets, preparing the weekly invoices that are handed over to production for their respective department teams, and making sure that earned overtime is paid. The work is demanding and the hours long and unpredictable. A six-day week and 12- to 13-hour days are not unusual.

The origin of the term *best boy* is unclear. Some feel it started in the days of hand-cranked silent cameras, when the camera operator would have his most dependable crewmember, or "best boy," help in lighting the shot. As Michael Agger, in an article on the term *best boy* for the *New Yorker,* points out, another possible derivation comes from Victorian England, where many assistants were called boys. According to this theory, the name stuck when an English foreman was hiring theatrical laborers and said, "Give me your best boy!"

Salaries

Salaries vary widely, depending on the number of productions a year on which Best Boys work. Annual earnings may range from $45,000 to $70,000 or more. The International Alliance of Theatrical Stage Employees (IATSE) has set a basic minimum rate for these two positions. For gaffer Best Boys, if hired on a weekly basis, the minimum is $29.81 hourly, or $1,818.54 weekly. If hired on a daily basis, the minimum hourly wage is $30.37. For grip Best Boys, the minimum weekly wage is $1,815.26.

Employment Prospects

Except for smaller or low-budget productions, both gaffers and grips require the services of a Best Boy. Thus, employment prospects are good. If the size of the television production or series requires a lighting crew to handle the equipment, the need for a crew leader (Best Boy) for grips and gaffers becomes a necessity.

Advancement Prospects

Advancement for members of the gaffer or grip lighting crews (with the requisite years of experience) to the position of Best Boy is typically good because turnover is fairly steady. Advancing from Best Boy to becoming either grip or gaffer also is usually likely due to the constant need for these posts to be filled during productions and the increase in television productions from year to year.

Education and Training

Besides a high school education and some college coursework in television and/or film production, training as an electrician, lighting specialist, or technician is essential. The IATSE union offers a training program that teaches Best Boys important health and safety procedures. Most Best Boys are fully qualified and experienced electricians with any necessary certificates for their work.

Special Requirements

In order to obtain employment either as a gaffer Best Boy or a grip Best Boy, it may be necessary for an applicant for either of these positions to be certified as an electrician.

Experience, Skills, and Personality Traits

On-the-job training as a lighting technician provides the best background for advancing to the position of Best Boy. Some start work in a lighting-for-hire company to gain a thorough knowledge of all types of lighting equipment, while some begin their careers working in theater.

Best Boys need to be completely familiar with the electricity and lighting requirements of television production. They must be highly organized, geared to motivate other team members, and able to communicate effectively with other production department persons. They must be strong enough to move heavy equipment and be willing to labor long hours.

Unions and Associations

Membership in the IATSE is often a requirement for employment and is beneficial in guaranteeing wage levels, bargaining, and networking.

Tips for Entry

1. During college, take a course in management or business administration to learn necessary organizational techniques and a psychology course to learn about human interaction.
2. Look for an internship at a television station to learn about television production firsthand.
3. Take any lighting position you can on a television production or on a film so you can get exposure to the technical aspects of lighting on productions.

GAFFER

CAREER PROFILE

Duties: Responsible for all lighting setups on a television production

Alternate Title(s): Lighting Designer; Lighting Director, Chief Lighting Technician; Key Electrician; Chief Electrician; Supervising Lighting Technician

Salary Range: $20,000 to $70,000 or more

Employment Prospects: Fair to Good

Advancement Prospects: Good

Prerequisites:

Education and Training—High school diploma; undergraduate degree in radio/TV or electrical engineering

Experience—Three to four years of experience in lighting department of a television station

Special Skills and Personality Traits—Ability to work with people; comfortable working at heights and for long hours; detail-oriented and organized; excellent communication skills; fast decision maker; imaginative; knowledge of lighting, electricity, and colors; problem-solving skills; self-confident and assertive; strong mechanical abilities

Special Requirements—Certification as an electrician usually required

CAREER LADDER

```
┌─────────────────────────────────────┐
│  Floor Manager; Technical Director   │
└─────────────────────────────────────┘

┌─────────────────────────────────────┐
│               Gaffer                 │
└─────────────────────────────────────┘

┌─────────────────────────────────────┐
│  Grip; Best Boy; Lighting Technician │
└─────────────────────────────────────┘
```

Position Description

The Gaffer (sometimes known in television as the lighting director) designs and executes the lighting for productions, either in the studio or on remote locations. They are employed at both public and commercial stations and also work in full-service production facilities.

As the chief electrician in charge of all lighting setups for television productions, the Gaffer works with the grip (often called the key grip) in the selection and positioning of lights and lighting equipment for a TV project. While the grip focuses on the scaffolding required to rig the lighting hardware, the Gaffer is responsible for installing the lights themselves and the electrical power supplying those lights. Gaffers lead the team of lighting technicians who install and position the lighting equipment and the power supply to create the desired lighting effects as envisioned by the cinematographer (director of photography) and the director. Gaffers maintain and supervise the use of all electrical equipment as well as the loading, transportation, placement, operation, and striking (when done) of all lighting equipment.

Lighting a set can be complicated. By incorporating theatrical lighting techniques to sharpen, balance, and add dimension to the setting that the camera photographs, the Gaffer uses different kinds of lights, such as key lights, fill lights, and backlights as well as floodlights, filters, light meters (to measure the available light), and other equipment. The key light (usually the brightest) illuminates the crucial elements of the action in any given scene. A fill light is used to remove shadows caused by the key light, and backlight is added to provide different visual effects. Each light must be focused and diffused using reflectors, scrims (mesh material), gels, or filters.

To obtain the desired results, the Gaffer works with a floor plan created by the scenic designer and the director and a copy of the script that is annotated to indicate lighting needs for each scene. The Gaffer then designs and lays out a lighting plot for the program—a complex and detailed version of the floor plan showing how and where each piece of lighting equipment will be placed. Much of this design work today is done with the aid of computer software programs. With their crew of part-time or on-assignment technicians, Gaffers ensure that the lighting is properly focused and balanced (as to intensity). They then set up a cue sheet of instructions for their second-in-command (i.e., the best boy) to supervise the actual positioning of the lights. Adjustments are made in rehearsal and, as needed, during the actual shoot.

Another of the Gaffer's responsibilities is health and safety on the set. In order to ensure that working conditions are safe, they conduct risk assessments, reporting their results to the director. In addition, Gaffers must maintain a tight control of the lighting budget. For this reason, they aid the director and production crew in preproduction to select the best lights and equipment, ensuring that they remain within available funds.

Nearly all television stations employ individuals whose primary responsibility is lighting. In a few cases, the technical director will light the studio set, but usually it is the Gaffer. At some smaller stations, Gaffers may have additional responsibilities in staging, engineering, camera work, or other production activities. While some stations consider Gaffers to be part of the engineering staff, others deem the position a production job. Depending on the station, a Gaffer may report to an engineering supervisor or to the production manager. However, during the actual production, Gaffers generally are accountable to the director of the program. On the largest projects, there may be an additional Gaffer known as a rigging Gaffer (or rigging technician). This individual is solely in charge of the rigging team, placing the lighting equipment in the scaffolding that the grip crew has set up for the shoot.

Salaries

Annual salaries vary widely, ranging from $20,000 to $70,000 or more. The International Alliance of Theatrical Stage Employees (IATSE) has set a basic minimum rate for Gaffers. If hired on a weekly basis, the minimum is $33.09 hourly, or $2,018.18 weekly. If hired on a daily basis, the minimum hourly wage is $33.53. For rigging Gaffers (or technicians), the union sets a minimum hourly wage of $29.81, which is a weekly rate of $1,818.54.

Employment Prospects

Gaffers (or lighting directors) are used on every television production. It is *never* an entry-level job at a television station or network, as several years as an electrician on television productions is necessary before being eligible for this position. However, at small public and commercial television facilities, opportunities are more limited, as the lighting duties are sometimes handled by members of the production crew. This situation is also true for many smaller television productions.

Possibilities for employment at middle- and major-market stations or the larger production organizations are greater. Many of the larger stations (and the networks) employ more than one Gaffer for various units or production teams. All full-service production facility companies have Gaffers as members of their staff.

Advancement Prospects

Regardless of the lack of job possibilities at smaller stations and on smaller productions, advancement opportunities for Gaffers are generally good. Professional and alert Gaffers have the opportunity for promotion to floor manager in the production department or to technical director or other middle-management positions in the station's engineering department. Gaffers with a reputation for continued success at middle-market stations often move to larger-market stations, networks, or the larger independent film and television production organizations.

Education and Training

A high school diploma is required, and undergraduate studies in television or film production are recommended, as well as training as an electrician. Most Gaffers are fully qualified electricians and usually rise through the ranks of the lighting department, working for several years in various lighting roles before becoming Gaffers. They also need to have a thorough knowledge of the technical aspects of television production, transmission, and operation. They must attend trade shows to keep up to date about the latest equipment. Many Gaffers work freelance and are self-employed, though most work with specific cinematographers (directors of photography).

If they are members of the IATSE union, Gaffers are required to complete training and safety programs sponsored by the local union groups. These programs teach both safety measures and full knowledge of voltage, amperage, and lighting capacities for use on television productions.

Special Requirements

A certificate as an electrician is usually required of all Gaffers.

Experience, Skills, and Personality Traits

Several years of work as a lighting technician or electrician on television productions provide the necessary experience in actual television production of in-studio and remote programs for the position of Gaffer. As professional Gaffer Russell Caldwell says, "Get in the field and work as an electrician and do some rigging. You have to understand the concept of power and lighting. Find somebody who is willing to teach you. There are a lot of older gaffers who are willing to go for coffee and sit down and talk about their career, what interested them in lighting, and points to remember." In addition, a background in theater staging and lighting can be quite helpful.

Gaffers must be imaginative and have the necessary high level of technical skills, including knowledge of photography and film processing techniques. They must understand the language of filmmaking and television production and pay close attention to details. They need to be problem solvers and be able to communicate well, not only with the director and the cinematographer (director of photography), but also when giving information to their crew. As Caldwell states, "I can't stress how important communication is when you're meeting with the director, production designer, or director of photography. If I don't understand, I ask questions until I do."

Along with communication skills, they need to have team leadership abilities, coupled with self-confidence and assertiveness. Often, fast decision making is an essential part of their job, as well as the ability to justify their decisions. They also need to be patient, tactful, and able to compromise while balancing differing opinions.

Unions and Associations

A few Gaffers at some stations may work as part of the engineering department or the production department and are represented by the National Association of Broadcast Employees and Technicians AFL-CIO (NABET) or by the International Brotherhood of Electrical Workers (IBEW). However, most Gaffers are members of the IATSE.

Tips for Entry

1. While completing your formal education, look for internships at television stations to learn about the television production process.
2. Take any job you can find on a television program and begin networking to work your way into the television community.
3. To understand lighting better, visit an art museum, see how artists controlled the light within their paintings, and work on how you can do as well or better with lighting.

KEY GRIP

Duties: Supervise the grip crews responsible for the positioning of the lights, scrims, and reflectors and for moving walls and set construction

Alternate Title(s): None

Salary Range: $25,000 to $90,000

Employment Prospects: Good

Advancement Prospects: Fair to Good

Prerequisites:

Education and Training—High school diploma required; undergraduate degree in radio/TV or theater not required but preferable

Experience—College or amateur scenic or lighting work in television or theater helpful

Special Skills and Personality Traits—Ability to handle cranes and dollies; carpentry skills; comfortable working at heights and for long hours; familiarity with television production techniques; knowledge of colors, electricity, and lighting; physical strength to lift and carry equipment; strong mechanical abilities; working knowledge of equipment used by grips

```
┌─────────────────────────────────────────┐
│   Assistant Camera Operator; Assistant   │
│    Scenic Designer; Floor Manager;       │
│    Property Master; Unit Manager         │
└─────────────────────────────────────────┘

┌─────────────────────────────────────────┐
│              Key Grip                    │
└─────────────────────────────────────────┘

┌─────────────────────────────────────────┐
│   Grip Best Boy; Lighting Technician;    │
│         Production Assistant             │
└─────────────────────────────────────────┘
```

Position Description

The Key Grip is the head of the grip department. While grips have a wide range of jobs on a television set, their major responsibility is to aid the gaffer and lighting crew in handling and taking care of the camera equipment, lights, and everything associated with the camera operation. In this, they work primarily for the cinematographer (director of photography). They mount, rig, and operate all the machines the cameras go on: the cranes, dollies, and track that the camera rides on. The camera crew, of course, handle cameras themselves, but the grips lay the tracks, set up the cranes, and assemble the dollies.

Grips, under the supervision of the Key Grip, work closely with the head electrician (the gaffer) in the positioning of lights and operate all the equipment not directly attached to the lights—flags, scrims, and reflectors—that shape, filter, and diffuse those lights. Along with the gaffer, the Key Grip has a copy of the shooting script that has been annotated with the camera directions and movements as

well as locations (interior or exterior) and the time (day or night). Working with the gaffer and the cinematographer, the Key Grip supervises any rigging of the lights that needs to be done. On larger productions, there will be grips assigned to each piece of equipment. (The grip assigned to moving the dolly during the shoot is called the dolly grip.) On low-budget or smaller television productions, the Key Grip may have to be this dolly grip, which is why it is desirable for the Key Grip to know how to operate a dolly and a crane. During production, it is up to the Key Grip to oversee the moving, rigging, positioning, operating, and striking (after the shoot is completed) of all the equipment used by the various members of the lighting and camera crews, who report to the cinematographer.

Grips also support other departments as general laborers (in the theater, such crew members are called stagehands). As Key Grip Russell Senato points out, "Basically, we do anything that needs to be done—if a bridge needs to be built across a stream, and it's doable, we'll put a bridge across the stream." If grips are doing construction work, such as putting sets up, hanging pipe for lighting, or rigging backdrops, they are part of what is called a "gang grip." After sets have been constructed or requisitioned and delivered to a television studio, the gang grip crew helps in assembling them according to the plan as set forth by the scenic designer. They aid in the setting up of backdrops, scenery, and any set pieces for both rehearsals and the production itself. They ensure that the furniture and sets are moved or changed as the script indicates. When the production is completed, grips help strike (dismantle) and store them in the scene shop or prepare them for transport to an outside storage area.

Most Key Grips live near Los Angeles or New York, where most of the work originates. Grips work at both public and commercial television stations and at independent television and film production companies. Occasionally, they work on location, where they report to a unit manager prior to production or to a floor manager during production if they are working as general handymen. Many grips work on a freelance basis, and some purchase their own equipment and form their own company.

Salaries

Salaries for the union position of grip are relatively good. Annual salaries vary widely, ranging from $25,000 to $90,000 or more. The International Alliance of Theatrical Stage Employees (IATSE) has set a basic minimum rate for the various grip positions. For Key Grips, their minimum weekly (five-day) rate is $2,018.18, which is an hourly wage of $33.09. For the other grip positions, hourly minimum wages range from $29.03 to $31.45. Overtime work pays more, and on-location minimum rates for Key Grips are higher (i.e., their weekly rate goes up to $2,315.96).

Employment Prospects

Opportunities for employment as a grip are good. All major market commercial and public television stations employ grips, either as members of the lighting crew or as general handymen. While major television productions are usually confined to New York and Hollywood, television and film productions do occur in virtually every state. With the expansion of television programs being produced, the requirement for grips to work on the sets is steady. A job as a production assistant is a good way to get to work on a television set, see what grips do, and make contacts that might lead to a future position with the grip department.

Advancement Prospects

The opportunities for experienced and ambitious grips to become Key Grips are fair. Key Grips who decide to advance their careers may decide on more training to apply for the position of assistant scenic designer. Grips who become proficient at their job may decide to move to a larger production company or a major-market television station for the higher salary and for the opportunity to become involved with more ambitious and complex television productions. Some Key Grips look to become camera operators or propmasters. With their experience in managing people as Key Grips, others may move on to other production management positions, such as floor manager or unit manager.

Education and Training

A high school diploma is a basic requirement. In addition, there are hundreds of college and university film programs of study, as well as studio and union training programs designed to help individuals looking to become grips (and moving up the ladder to become Key Grips). A college degree in radio/TV or theater production, including courses in theatrical staging and lighting techniques, would be helpful background for the position of grip.

Experience, Skills, and Personality Traits

Specific experience in television production is not necessarily a requirement for beginning grips. As a general background, any experience in set construction, lighting, or related scenic responsibilities in college television or theater or in any amateur or community theater production is a distinct advantage. However, several years of experience on television productions as a grip are necessary to obtain the position of Key Grip.

The strength to lift and carry equipment, agility, and being comfortable with heights are important skills for a grip. In addition, carpentry skills, electrical experience, and mechanical aptitude are necessary assets. For a Key Grip, leadership qualities are also important. Above all, grips must like manual labor and be willing to put in long hours of work.

Unions and Associations

Most grips belong to the IATSE. Some at major-market stations may belong, instead, to the National Association of Broadcast Employees and Technicians AFL-CIO (NABET).

Tips for Entry

1. Look at union training programs as the best way to become a grip.
2. Accept a production assistant position to get on a television production to learn and to network. Remember, so often, it's not what you know but who you know.
3. Once you've landed a job as a grip, learn from those working around you. Watch what everyone is doing to see how all the work on the set (not just that of the grip) fits together to achieve a successful television production.

LIGHTING TECHNICIAN

CAREER PROFILE

Duties: Provide the relevant lighting and power supply for a television production

Alternate Title(s): Lighting Operator; Lamp Operator; Lighting Electrician

Salary Range: $25.46 to $31.48 hourly minimum

Employment Prospects: Fair to Good

Advancement Prospects: Good

Prerequisites:

Education and Training—High school diploma required

Experience—Experience as an electrician; some experience in commercials, film, theater, or television recommended

Special Skills and Personality Traits—Ability to accept direction; capable of quick thinking; comfortable working at heights and for long hours; eye for detail; good communication and interpersonal skills; problem-solving abilities; stamina and agility; teamworking skills

Special Requirements—Electrician certification usually required

CAREER LADDER

```
┌─────────────────────────────────┐
│            Best Boy             │
└─────────────────────────────────┘

┌─────────────────────────────────┐
│       Lighting Technician       │
└─────────────────────────────────┘

┌─────────────────────────────────┐
│  Apprentice Lighting Technician; │
│       Production Assistant       │
└─────────────────────────────────┘
```

Position Description

A Lighting Technician's responsibilities vary according to the size of the television production and the number of Lighting Technicians in the lighting crew for the production. He or she is required to keep the lighting equipment clean and maintained in good working condition. Many Lighting Technicians work for production companies, but others freelance once they have established an industry reputation.

Some Lighting Technicians have the task of setting up the lighting equipment before the shooting of the television production starts. They are often referred to as rigging electricians or technicians. They also carry out lighting tests. Other technicians work in the lighting store, usually set up as a temporary store in a corner of a studio. They are in charge of all the light bulbs and other lighting items, such as traces, filters, and scrims that are used to create particular lighting effects. Other Lighting Technicians are responsible for positioning the lights during the production.

An additional specialized type of electrician job is that of the console operator (otherwise known as the dimmer board operator). Console operators handle and run the conventional or fixed lights on a television sound stage. They set up the dimmer board and then wire, program, and operate it to mix the lighting effects during the production as established by the cinematographer and the gaffer. They balance the picture and program the lights to increase or decrease in intensity to maintain the agreed-upon production "look." As many lamps may be connected to one dimmer, this job can be a complex operation.

Shooting on location, there are several other specialty Lighting Technician positions, depending on the size of the television production. Practical Lighting Technicians are responsible for accessing suitable power supplies at out-of-studio locations, ensuring that all the "practical" electrical equipment used is safely installed and maintained and that it conforms to health and safety requirements. There is also the generator operator (or "genny operator"), whose role is to maintain and operate the electricity generators that are taken to and used at locations where a suitable electricity supply is difficult to obtain or is insufficient for the project's requirements. (Generators are also used to supplement the electricity supply when a particular lighting lamp requires more power than can be obtained from the ordinary electricity mains in the studio.)

Finally, there are apprentice Lighting Technicians, trainees hired to learn on-the-job how to become a fully qualified technician. Their work involves testing machines; cleaning, repairing, and maintaining equipment; fixing distribution boards and boxes as well as lights; and wiring dimmers and circuit boards. As health and safety measures are of vital importance when dealing with electricity, apprentices are made aware during their training of the implications of these measures in what they do every day. Apprenticeship can last from one to three years and usually involves both working for a lighting production company and taking college courses.

Salaries

The International Alliance of Theatrical Stage Employees (IATSE) sets minimum wage rates for Lighting Technicians. Hourly rates range from $25.46 for entry-level employees to $31.48 for senior Lighting Technicians. If hired on a weekly basis (five days, 54 hours), senior Lighting Technicians have a minimum hourly wage of $29.812, or a weekly minimum of $1,818.54. For distant location shootings, the minimum hourly wages stay much the same, but the weekly minimum salaries increase to $2,086.85.

Employment Prospects

As Lighting Technicians are needed for every television production at major-market public and commercial stations, cable stations, and networks, employment potentials are good. At smaller-market operations and on low-budget TV projects, all lighting technical work may be accomplished by a gaffer alone or with a best boy as second in command, with no need for further technical assistance.

Many Lighting Technicians work for production firms and are hired for specific productions. As they become established and gain a standing, many of them work freelance.

Advancement Prospects

It takes several years of experience before a Lighting Technician can become a best boy (second in command of the lighting department). Beyond their skills as electricians, they need to be highly organized, be able to motivate other members of the department, and be able to communicate effectively with other production departments. These are skills learned by watching best boys and gaffers (head electricians) at work.

Education and Training

A high school diploma is a basic requirement. Additionally, certificates in electricity and electrotechnical technology are requirements for most Lighting Technician positions. There are union (IATSE) training programs that teach Lighting Technicians important safety procedures. Lighting Technicians must be prepared to undertake additional training throughout their careers to keep up to date on both equipment and safety procedures.

Special Requirements

Certification as an electrician is a usual requirement for Lighting Technicians.

Experience, Skills, and Personality Traits

Working as an apprentice Lighting Technician is the best way to learn how to become a full-fledged Lighting Technician. It is a skilled technical post that is also physically demanding, requiring both stamina and agility. Lighting Technicians have to be comfortable working at heights and be able to work the long and unpredictable hours that the job demands.

They should have good communication and interpersonal skills, as well as have good team-working skills. They must be able to take direction, be able to work quickly and accurately, and have a good eye for detail. In addition, they must be flexible and good problem solvers. If they choose to be generator operators, they need to have knowledge of different types of generators as well a general mechanical awareness of their machines. Above all, Lighting Technicians, whatever their specialties may be, must be aware of health and safety regulations pertaining to their equipment and its use.

Unions and Associations

Generally, Lighting Technicians are represented by the IATSE. While membership in this union may not be obligatory for work in some of the smaller-market television stations, it is a requirement for Lighting Technicians in most television work and a requirement for work on any studio or union motion picture. Some Lighting Technicians may belong to the National Association of Broadcast Employees and Technicians AFL-CIO (NABET).

Tips for Entry

1. Look for an internship at a television station to learn about television production firsthand.
2. Take any lighting position you can on a television production or on a film so you can get exposure to the technical aspects of lighting on productions.
3. Be prepared for several years of hard work gaining the necessary experience of working on an assortment of television productions with their varying lighting needs.

LOCATION AND TRANSPORTATION

LOCATION MANAGER

CAREER PROFILE

Duties: Find appropriate shooting locations outside the studio and arrange for necessary permissions; supervise any assistants (location scouts) used to do needed legwork

Alternate Title(s): Location Scout

Salary Range: $900 to $2,200 weekly minimum

Employment Prospects: Good

Advancement Prospects: Fair

Prerequisites:

Education and Training—High school diploma required; courses on film in college or film school helpful

Experience—Work as a television (or film) production assistant or assistant to a producer or director

Special Skills and Personality Traits—Able to take still photographs of or videotape potential locations; capable of breaking down script into the necessary locations needed outside the studio; detail-oriented; experienced team player; good memory and strong research skills; imagination in determining how a location can be altered to fit script requirements; wide travel experience

CAREER LADDER

```
┌─────────────────────────────┐
│   Production Manager;        │
│   Second Assistant Director  │
└─────────────────────────────┘

┌─────────────────────────────┐
│   Location Manager           │
└─────────────────────────────┘

┌─────────────────────────────┐
│   Production Assistant;      │
│   Assistant to Director      │
└─────────────────────────────┘
```

Position Description

Many medium-to-large television productions require that suitable locations away from the studio sound stage be found as settings for shooting specific scenes. For some productions, it may be too expensive (outside budgetary limitations) to have scenes shot in one potential location, but such shooting may be financially feasible in a completely different locale. Location Managers are the individuals responsible for finding the appropriate potential shooting sites that fit the needs of the script, the director, and—especially—the production's budget.

Location Managers receive a copy of the script from the director and then break down that script into all requisite locations. Because they are well traveled, both within the United States and abroad, and maintain a photographic record of their trips, they can call upon this firsthand and secondary information to choose the right location for scenes that must be shot outside the studio.

On many small productions, the Location Manager does the actual scouting for locations. On medium-sized to large productions, a separate individual, the location scout, is hired to do the legwork of finding and photographing potential sites. In those instances, these scouts report directly to the Location Manager. On some television miniseries, films, or very large productions, multiple Location Managers and scouts may be necessary.

Location Managers negotiate the use of property with the owner(s); obtain all requisite city, county, and state permits, licenses, and variances; and determine what fees must be paid. In their choices, they always must work within the project's budgetary constraints. In addition, they are responsible for smoothing out any potential problems before the shooting begins (e.g., causing an annoyance within a neighborhood by closing off streets for shooting) and then do the logistical planning for transporting performers and crew to the chosen location.

Location Managers may be affiliated with a local or state film commission, or they may be hired by the director as freelancers for specific productions. Networks may have location personnel on staff, but many directors prefer to hire

Location Managers with whom they have worked before or know about by industry reputation.

Salaries

The International Brotherhood of Teamsters has set minimum rates for location personnel who are members. For Location Managers, their weekly minimum rate is $2,236. For assistant Location Managers and scouts, their weekly minimum rate ranges from $911 to $1,336, depending on the number of assistants (and scouts) that are needed for the television production. For their traveling, the union sets a car allowance of $60 a day, with no mileage reimbursement and leaving gasoline reimbursement up to negotiation between the scout or manager and the production company.

Employment Prospects

Many television productions, series, miniseries, and films now require that suitable locations be found to add variety and realism to their scripts. Their budgets reflect this need for settings outside the studio, and the continuous need for Location Managers (or scouts) becomes obvious. For these reasons, employment opportunities for Location Managers, their assistants, and location scouts remain good. The job requires a good deal of research and legwork as well as travel and detail work, making it an interesting job to embark on near the beginning of a television career. As other career paths open for such individuals, they move on, creating openings on a more regular basis than in many other television jobs.

Advancement Prospects

Advancement for Location Managers depends greatly on where they reside as well as the reputation they begin to establish so that television directors or producers begin requesting their services. Many Location Managers find opportunities to move on to become directors, production managers, or producers.

Education and Training

Beyond a high school education, it is recommended to take courses in television history and production techniques as good background as well as to ascertain what a Location Manager really does. In the process, it is important to develop good research skills, be able to network to get leads and contacts, and become adept at photography in order to record potential sites for future location shooting.

Experience, Skills, and Personality Traits

It is important to gain both an understanding of television production and a means to get to know people in the business. That is why such professional production managers as Charlie Baxter, who was once a Location Manager, recommend working as a production assistant as the best way to begin such a career. As he points out, "Start in a position that allows you to see what other people do. . . . You just have to go out and try and hook up with people. . . . If you get along well with people and they like your attitude and your energy, they'll recognize that."

Successful Location Managers are inveterate problem solvers. They need to listen carefully, follow instructions, and be able to negotiate tactfully with people. A sense of humor is an additional asset. Charlie Baxter suggests that Location Managers should "not take it too seriously. Don't let the pressure that the production company and other parties are applying become insurmountable. Focus and let common sense be your guide." As they travel, they need to keep both mental and physical records of particular settings and even restaurants, stores, and locales that could be used in a television production. They need to be able to network with all sorts of individuals to get leads or contacts for potential locations and have the imagination to see how a site could be easily altered to fit the requirements of the scene as set by the script.

Unions and Associations

Location Managers, their assistants, and location scouts in California (and 12 other western states) should find it beneficial to belong to Local 399 of the International Brotherhood of Teamsters for guaranteed minimum wage rates and other wage bargaining. In New York, Location Managers are members of the Directors Guild of America. Nonunion Location Managers and scouts may find work in local television station productions and commercials.

Tips for Entry

1. While in college or film school, look for students who are making their own films or any independent filmmakers in your area and volunteer to scout locations for them.
2. Work on your people skills at every opportunity.
3. Get a position as an administrative assistant or a production assistant and volunteer to accompany the Location Manager or location scout to see how they accomplish their job.
4. Travel and make notes and photographic records of where you've been.

TRANSPORTATION COORDINATOR

CAREER PROFILE

Duties: Transport performers, crew, vehicles, and equipment wherever they must go to shoot the television production

Alternate Title(s): Transportation Captain

Salary Range: $40,000 to $70,000

Employment Prospects: Fair to Good

Advancement Prospects: Fair

Prerequisites:

Education and Training—High school diploma recommended

Experience—Driving a wide variety of vehicles, from tractor-trailers to trucks, recreational vehicles, buses, and vans

Special Skills and Personality Traits—Clean driver's record; conscientious and punctual; courteous; excellent driving skills; good sense of direction; knowledge of fundamental maintenance and repair of vehicles

Special Requirements—Special driver licenses usually required

CAREER LADDER

```
┌─────────────────────────────────┐
│      Production Manager          │
└─────────────────────────────────┘

┌─────────────────────────────────┐
│   Transportation Coordinator     │
└─────────────────────────────────┘

┌─────────────────────────────────┐
│     Transportation Driver        │
└─────────────────────────────────┘
```

Position Description

The Transportation Coordinator is the head of the transportation department, which is responsible for getting people and equipment where they need to be for the shoot. The primary function of the Transportation Coordinator is to ensure that everything moves smoothly and that everyone and everything arrive on time and in good shape. Most Transportation Coordinators are experienced drivers of all types of vehicles as well. Reporting to the production manager, the Transportation Coordinator hires assistants as needed (usually called transportation captains), office coordinators if needed (to handle accounting paperwork, purchase orders, and timecards), and drivers. The coordinator also assigns the drivers to the vehicles.

During preproduction, the Transportation Coordinator breaks down the script to determine what type and age of "picture cars" (the vehicles that will be used on-camera) will be needed, what cars are required for any stunt work, and what cars will be used by the principal performers. Once all this is resolved, then a budget and a schedule are worked out with the production manager to decide on the most cost-efficient method of acquiring the requisite vehicles. This budget should include allowances for any special equipment that may be required as well as fuel and any maintenance anticipated for the vehicles during production.

The vehicles needed for moving the production team and equipment will depend on how many on-location shootings there will be or whether the production will be shot entirely on a television set in a studio. At this point, Transportation Coordinators decide on how many drivers will be needed. They then choose, obtain (or rent), and maintain all vehicles that will be associated with the television production. These are mainly used for on-location shootings as determined by the script, and they include big trucks and trailers for makeup, hair, lighting, camera, prop, and wardrobe departments. (The trailer for the makeup and hair personnel must have hot and cold running water, lights, mirrors, counters, hair dryers, and its own generator. The lighting, camera, prop, and wardrobe trailers need to carry the gear necessary for each function, and most of them should have lift gates attached to the truck.) There are also a production van (which hauls the lights, rigging, and generators); trailers with toilet facilities (known as "honeywagons") for the performers; personal trailers for the director, performers, and others (such as producers); the picture cars to be used on-camera; and all rental cars needed for cast and crew on location.

Transportation Coordinators need to scout the various locations to be sure there will be no conflict with what is planned in the script (such as bridges or tunnels that do not provide enough clearance for the trucks or whether there are sufficient parking spaces for all the trucks). Before any of the rental vehicles are assigned, coordinators ensure that a purchase order has been processed for each and that each is insured. They also have to take note of specific trailer requirements for individual cast members, some of which are predetermined by contractual obligation.

Throughout production, Transportation Coordinators oversee the department, ensuring that all equipment and drivers are where they should be and on time. They are like military strategists in that they are given the responsibility of moving large companies of people and equipment. As veteran Transportation Coordinator Bob Fosters states, "Being a driver, you're the first one on set and generally the last to leave. . . . We have to be there . . . to get the trailer set up. If it's cold outside, we have to get it warm inside, so that everybody is comfortable when they come in. We make sure all the lights are working and the generators are up and running. At the end of the day we have to take it down, move it, and get ready for the next day."

Salaries

Obviously, annual salaries vary according to the size and time needed for the shooting of the television production and whether the shooting involves going on location. The Teamster's Union sets minimum wage rates. Hourly rates range from $17 to $31.67 depending on what type of driving is being done. Since union Transportation Coordinators are not required to drive vehicles, their salaries are generally negotiable, but they may not be paid less than the lowest paid full-time driver employed for the production, and usually a lot more. They may earn an average of $40,000 to $70,000 a year.

Employment Prospects

Employment opportunities on television productions depend on the need for vehicles to be used during the shoot. Most major productions, series, miniseries, and made-for-television films demand a Transportation Coordinator. Thus, chances for employment range from fair to good.

Advancement Prospects

Competition for the job of Transportation Coordinator is tough and tends to be very political and even personal. There are many drivers but few coordinators in comparison. Some coordinators move on to other production jobs, among which the most sought after job is that of the production manager. Again, competition for such a career move is extremely stiff.

Education and Training

A high school diploma is recommended. In addition, training in driving trucks, trailers, and recreational vehicles is a requirement. Drivers need a commercial driver license, and it is suggested that they enroll at a reputable trucking company or driving school to gain the needed experience. Drivers who want to be generator operators should work with a vending company that specializes in production equipment and learn the trade.

Special Requirements

A commercial driver license to drive trucks, trailers, vans, and recreational vehicles is a usual requirement for this post.

Experience, Skills, and Personality Traits

The Transportation Coordinator and all drivers must have a commercial driver license as well as experience driving big trucks, vans, and trailers. Union television productions require both the coordinator and drivers to be members of the Teamster's Union.

Transportation Coordinators must be safe, careful drivers themselves and be able to work long hours. They need to be conscientious, courteous, punctual, and reliable and have good people skills. They also must be able to make minor repairs and properly maintain the vehicles under their supervision.

Unions and Associations

Being a member of the Teamster's Union is a requirement in such television production markets as Los Angeles and New York. Not all states, however, have this requirement for drivers who work on television productions. Nonetheless, membership in the union helps to guarantee earnings and overtime wages.

Tips for Entry

1. Contact car and truck rental companies and volunteer to intern so you can be trained and learn the range of equipment.
2. Get a position as a production assistant in the transportation department of a television production company or as an intern to understand what is done and to start to work your way up the career ladder within the department.
3. Work on your people skills, as your position as Transportation Coordinator will depend on them as well as your organizational skills.

MANAGEMENT (TECHNICAL)

FLOOR MANAGER

CAREER PROFILE

Duties: Coordinate the director's instructions with all studio and remote location television production activities

Alternate Title(s): Crew Chief; Floor Director; Television Stage Manager

Salary Range: $16,000 to $55,000 or more

Employment Prospects: Fair

Advancement Prospects: Fair

Prerequisites:

Education and Training—High school diploma required; college degree recommended

Experience—Minimum of one to three years of television production experience

Special Skills and Personality Traits—Cooperative; even-tempered; organizational abilities; versatile; strong attention to detail

CAREER LADDER

```
┌─────────────────────────────┐
│     Assistant Director;      │
│  Unit Production Manager     │
└─────────────────────────────┘

┌─────────────────────────────┐
│        Floor Manager         │
└─────────────────────────────┘

┌─────────────────────────────┐
│     Production Assistant      │
└─────────────────────────────┘
```

Position Description

Floor Managers are the director's link to the cast involved in a television production. They are responsible for coordinating the director's instructions with the production crew and the performers in the studio or on remote location both during rehearsals and during the actual production. During rehearsal and production, they follow the script and cue performers. This specific task is a crucial one during actual production. While Floor Managers are typically assigned to a particular show, series, or production, they report to the director during both rehearsals and the shooting of the production.

Like stage managers—their counterparts in the theater—Floor Managers are in charge of scenery moves and prop changes as well as the performer cues and directions given to the performers by the director. Prior to the actual production, the Floor Manager supervises all staging activities, including the setup of scenery and all production-related equipment and devices. Floor Managers work closely with the art director and set designer for any needed on-the-spot construction, painting, or modifications to sets already completed. They also confirm that all props and costumes are accounted for and ready at hand for the wardrobe personnel. In small studio talk shows, the Floor Manager may be responsible for the application of simple makeup on guests and the proper placement of microphones on both the host and interviewees.

During the actual production, the Floor Manager places props, gives timing signals and other cues to performers, and may be in charge of positioning easels and graphics as well as operating the TelePrompTer equipment. During production, Floor Managers are usually connected to the director (who may be in the control room) by way of a two-way radio communication link. They relay instructions from the director to the production crew and performers by using hand signals and cue cards.

Floor Managers are ultimately responsible for all studio activity before and during production. They may make some independent immediate decision regarding the solution of any production problems that occur during rehearsal or even the actual production. As the director's on-site representative, the Floor Manager must remain calm and efficient, thus diffusing any tensions that may arise during the production.

In addition, Floor Managers frequently assist the lighting director in the transport, setup, and placement of lights and their accessories, both in the studio and on location. They may position the video monitors during rehearsal and production, and they supervise the dismantling and storage of set pieces and production equipment at the completion of a shoot.

Salaries

Floor Managers are moderately well paid in both commercial and public television. In a study of 2004 annual salaries of Floor Managers, Broadcast Employment Services found that the salaries ranged from a beginning low of $16,000 to a high of $55,000 or more. The average yearly pay for this position was $35,450.

Floor Managers who are members of the Directors Guild of America have compensation minimums set by contract. For prime-time dramatic programs, Floor Managers (called stage managers) have weekly salaries of $2,812. For productions other than prime-time, their minimum weekly pay is $2,016. The guild also sets overtime minimums and production fees for Floor Managers.

Employment Prospects

Chances of employment as a Floor Manager are only fair. It is not an entry-level post in either commercial or public television. Most employers want Floor Managers to have had two or three years of experience in the production crew, usually as production assistants. In many stations, it is only the most experienced production crew members who have a chance at the position of Floor Manager.

Some major-market stations may use one or more Floor Managers to handle various programs or shifts, but most small stations have only one individual in this position. Floor Managers may also work on the station's news programs or in the production of commercials. Public television stations do local productions, but a large number of their programs are already scheduled productions and therefore have no need for a Floor Manager. Floor Managers may also find work in corporate television productions and in educational, health, and governmental television units where significant amounts of productions are scheduled.

Advancement Prospects

Opportunities for advancement for experienced and competent Floor Managers are fair. The position of Floor Manager is frequently a stepping-stone for more ambitious and talented individuals. Potential advancement paths include moving up to an assistant director at their station or switching to a larger- or major-market station (or an independent production company) in the more responsible position of unit production manager. However, the competition is heavy for any of these moves. Most Floor Managers hope to become directors some day.

Education and Training

A high school diploma is an absolute necessity. In addition, some college training in theater or radio/television production is often a requirement. An undergraduate degree in mass communications or television-film production is particularly useful in obtaining a job in the production department of the larger television stations. In addition, courses in theater arts (staging and lighting) and cinematography are helpful.

Experience, Skills, and Personality Traits

A minimum of two to three years of experience as a member of a television station's production squad is usually required before moving on to the position of Floor Manager. Floor Managers need to comprehend all aspects of television production, from lighting to camerawork, staging, and makeup.

Floor Managers must be highly organized, as they will have to arrange many elements of a show into a smoothly running operation. They need to be resourceful and imaginative and be able to take initiative in managing the complex aspects of television production, either in the studio or on location. Above all, they must appear to be calm at all times and always confident in the midst of the usual hectic atmosphere of television production.

Unions and Associations

While many Floor Managers in commercial and public television may be considered members of the production team and thus not eligible for the usual union representation, they may be members of the Directors Guild of America (DGA) in their capacity as, essentially, director's assistants. In some cases, they may be represented instead by the National Association of Broadcast Employees and Technicians AFL-CIO (NABET).

Tips for Entry

1. While in high school or college, get involved in any aspect of filmmaking available to you, such as creating student films with a video or digital camera, to become familiar with the process.
2. While in college, take a business course to learn methods of organizing material and a psychology course to aid you in understanding people and developing effective people skills.
3. Get any position you can with a television production department to learn firsthand the process and to observe individuals and their work in the department with regard to what they do and how they do it.

OPERATIONS MANAGER

CAREER PROFILE

Duties: Schedule and coordinate all technical and production resources at a television station

Alternate Title(s): Director of Operations; Operations Supervisor

Salary Range: $24,000 to $130,000 or more

Employment Prospects: Fair

Advancement Prospects: Fair

Prerequisites:

Education and Training—High school diploma required; technical school or college training also required; college degree in broadcasting or communications preferred

Experience—Minimum of two to four years in various television station positions

Special Skills and Personality Traits—Cooperative; detail oriented; leadership capabilities; logical mind and good organizational abilities; scheduling talent

CAREER LADDER

```
┌─────────────────────────────┐
│   Director of Broadcasting;  │
│     Production Manager       │
└─────────────────────────────┘

┌─────────────────────────────┐
│      Operations Manager      │
└─────────────────────────────┘

┌─────────────────────────────────┐
│ Floor Manager; Engineering Supervisor; │
│    Unit Production Manager       │
└─────────────────────────────────┘
```

Position Description

The Operations Manager is responsible for allocating all resources and facilities at a television station to effect and maintain its smooth and professional operation. This individual schedules all production, engineering, and technical facilities from sign-on to sign-off and coordinates all the facility's on-air activities. The Operations Manager oversees all programming and the feeding of programs to and from networks and other locations.

The Operations Manager's primary duty is to schedule the use of production studios, control rooms, videotape and digital machines, and other technical equipment used during the station's daily broadcasting. In some cases, this post may also be responsible for the operating staff. Operations Managers frequently also synchronize the activities of the traffic/continuity, programming, production, and engineering departments. Due to the wide extent of responsibilities, an Operations Manager needs to be a skilled generalist, familiar with the functions of every department of the station.

In addition, Operations Managers acquire, process, and distribute all program data, including the station transmitter operating logs and any video or digital tapes used for station breaks. As an extension of this duty, they usually also supervise the station's library of video or digital tapes, films, and

records as well as oversee any cataloging procedures needed. In their daily overseeing of the station, they also establish the procedures for the timely procurement, scheduling, and delivery of commercials for broadcast and the recording of programs or program elements from networks and other sources.

The specific duties of an Operations Manager may differ from one station to another. At some, the job may be incorporated into the post of director of broadcasting. In some small facilities, the Operations Manager may be mainly a traffic coordinator whose main obligation is the delivery of films, tapes, or other material to be used on the broadcasts and the delivery of commercials for breaks between the scheduled programming. In most middle- and major-market stations with their usual heavy production and programming schedules, this position has considerable accountability. At some stations, Operations Managers report to the program manager or production manager. At others, they may report instead to the assistant chief engineer, depending on the scope of their actual duties.

Salaries

Depending on the scope of their responsibilities, Operations Managers generally are paid well. According to a survey of

2004 annual salaries of Operations Managers conducted by Broadcast Employment Services in 2005, salaries ranged from $27,000 to $139,000, with a mean average salary of $55,570.

Employment Prospects

The chances of obtaining a post as Operations Manager are only fair. This position is held by an experienced individual who must have a broad understanding of station operations and a full knowledge of the specific duties of each department. Talented floor managers or unit managers already on staff may have a chance at being elevated to the position of Operations Manager when an opening occurs. At small stations, a program manager may find career advancement by moving to a larger-market station as Operations Manager before jumping into the higher position as program manager.

While many of the larger cable operations have operations as complex as those at commercial stations, some of the smaller cable companies as well a multichannel multipoint distribution service (MMDS) and other production organizations may not. As a result, opportunities for employment as an Operations Manager in these settings are extremely limited. Most of the smaller educational, health, governmental, and corporate media centers do not employ Operations Managers but combine their duties with other management positions. While some production facilities may have Operations Managers, their duties are more involved in scheduling rather than operational work.

Advancement Prospects

Possibilities for advancement are fair. Efficient and experienced Operations Managers with a record of achievement may be able to move to the position of production manager. Operations Managers at smaller market stations can obtain similar posts at larger stations with more responsibility and higher salaries. Some Operations Managers at middle market operations may be able to advance by going to smaller market stations in positions of higher responsibility, such as director of broadcasting. Since each station operates in a slightly different manner, skills acquired at one station will not automatically be applicable to a similar position at another station. Unlike some other positions in the television industry, Operations Managers tend not to move from one station to another, but look for advancement within their own station.

Education and Training

A high school diploma is always required. Some employers call for technical school training, and many require an appli-

cant to have a college degree in radio/TV broadcasting or mass communications.

Experience, Skills, and Personality Traits

Most employers require a minimum of two years of seasoning in the engineering, production, or programming departments of a television station when promoting an individual to Operations Manager. Many Operations Managers have gained the necessary experience as floor managers, or unit production managers, while others may obtain that experience while working in the traffic/continuity department. A few may have been engineering supervisors, acquiring know-how in scheduling and supervising operations and technical people. Individuals applying for this position must be well-acquainted with the operation of every department in the station, as well as have knowledge of the production, engineering, and technical equipment used at the station. They must be very well organized and have strong analytical and problem-solving skills. They need to be logical and able to set up and manage a detailed schedule of people and equipment. They must be cooperative, exhibit strong leadership abilities, have strong interpersonal communication skills, and be able to deal with the expected day-to-day pressure situations.

Unions and Associations

Most Operations Managers are considered to be part of the management team, either in the programming or production departments, and hence are not represented by a union or a professional organization. Some Operations Managers who are part of the engineering department at major-market stations may be members of the National Association of Broadcast Employees and Technicians AFL-CIO (NABET) or of the International Brotherhood of Electrical Workers (IBEW).

Tips for Entry

1. While in school, look for intern programs at local television stations to become familiar with television operations.
2. Accept any beginning positions at a television station and observe what other people in your department and the other areas do and how they do it.
3. Take additional technical education courses to gain necessary technical background in equipment used in television production and broadcasting.

PRODUCTION ASSISTANT

CAREER PROFILE

Duties: Assist in the production of studio and on-location television programs

Alternate Title(s): Floor Assistant; Floor Person; Staging Assistant

Salary Range: $10,000 to $55,000

Employment Prospects: Good

Advancement Prospects: Good

Prerequisites:

Education and Training—High school diploma required; college degree in broadcasting or mass communications preferable

Experience—Some film, photography, theater, or work-related experience at film school recommended

Special Skills and Personality Traits—Ability to take orders and follow directions; cooperative; dependable; initiative; organizational abilities; resourceful; willing to put in long hours; word-processing skills

CAREER LADDER

```
┌─────────────────────────────────────────┐
│  Camera Operator; Floor Manager;         │
│  Associate Producer; Assistant Director; │
│  Production Supervisor                   │
└─────────────────────────────────────────┘

┌─────────────────────────────────────────┐
│           Production Assistant           │
└─────────────────────────────────────────┘

┌─────────────────────────────────────────┐
│        High School / College;            │
│        Production Secretary              │
└─────────────────────────────────────────┘
```

Position Description

Commonly known as a PA, the Production Assistant is the entry-level member of the production crew of a local, network, or independent television production. The key duty of this post is to assist the production team in nonengineering matters by providing helpful and timely support in all phases of a production. At most stations, Production Assistants serve as apprentices, filling in wherever needed. They act as the chief message and communications liaison between staff members. As such they work with the producer, director, production manager, production coordinator, camera operator(s), assistant director, associate producer, and floor manager. They run errands, carry equipment, post signs, and perform any other chores that need to be undertaken.

As an apprentice laboring in all aspects of television production, the Production Assistant has the chance to gain experience in a wide mixture of television programming, from news to documentaries, talk shows, and entertainment specials. Often, Production Assistants are assigned to specific program projects by the production manager and work with that assignment until its completion. During the actual production process, however, they usually report to the assistant director, floor manager, or production unit manager.

While Production Assistants typically work on assignment in the studio or on location, they may also assist in the planning, scheduling, coordination, and daily operation of the production department or on-location production unit. Their duties can embrace preparing and distributing the daily shooting schedules and notifying the crew of all script changes and production arrangements. They may also be directed to record all production shot sheets, detailing the timing of various program segments to be used by the continuity staff during postproduction. In addition, they may assist in the setting up of lighting equipment and may help in the striking (dismantling) of the set. They may help out in the research, development, coordination, and finalization of program scripts and then collect the files and records upon completion of a production. These files include visual materials, photos, personnel worksheets, on-air performer releases, and other related production material.

Production Assistants are crucial for a production to maintain its methodical flow to completion. They may do research or copywriting, assist in casting or scheduling guests, and work on sets, costumes, or makeup. Their tasks may include helping in the control room or studio by holding cue cards and slate cards, placing monitors on stands, and performing in any other production duties that are required. Thus, the PA position provides a valuable learning experience for the beginner and is a vital element in the production team.

Salaries

Wages for Production Assistants tend to be low. In its 2005 survey of 2004 salaries, Broadcast Employment Services found that annual earnings ranged from $10,000 to $55,000 for general Production Assistants, and from $12,000 to $42,000 for Production Assistants assigned to news productions. The mean average yearly salary for general Production Assistants was $22,940, and $24,573 for news Production Assistants.

Employment Prospects

The chances of obtaining employment as a Production Assistant for a television station are good. The position is invariably an entry-level one in commercial, cable, and public television. The need for general assistants (or gofers) in the television production process is an ongoing one. Production secretaries are sometimes promoted from within the station to Production Assistant. As is often the case, opportunities for employment depend on being in the right spot at the optimum time.

Most stations employ from three to 15 PAs, depending on the size of the market they serve and on the amount of production work done by the facility. In addition to the favorable opportunities at television stations, all independent TV production companies employ Production Assistants, and some corporate, educational, governmental, and health centers that produce television programs offer employment for beginners as Production Assistants.

Advancement Prospects

The opportunity for advancement from the post of Production Assistant to other production and programming positions is good. The position offers individuals the chance to determine what line of television work they would like to pursue. Station management scrutinizes Production Assistants carefully to spot future candidates for various production positions, from camera operators (in nonunion shops only) to floor managers, associate producers, and assistant directors. Enthusiasm and resourcefulness on the part of a Production Assistant often lead to promotion. Competition for more responsible production positions is stiff, but a reputation for reliability coupled with experience helps. At some local stations, Production Assistants are very often promoted directly to news, production, and other technical jobs. Some assistants at the larger stations may move to smaller-market stations to gain a position of more responsibility and higher salary.

Education and Training

A high school diploma is a minimum requirement. Many larger-market commercial, cable, and public television stations prefer a candidate to have a college degree as well, usually in mass communications, radio/TV, or theater.

Experience, Skills, and Personality Traits

As the position of Production Assistant is a beginner's job, most employers do not demand extensive experience in television production. While this is a learner's position, some background in theater staging and lighting, photography, or film work is helpful.

Production Assistants must be bright, cheerful, organized, and resourceful. They need to be able to think intuitively and effectively. While many of their duties will be boring and menial, their work enables them to experience and learn every phase of television production. They must be able to function under pressure with a wide assortment of people in both a cooperative and creative manner and get each assigned task completed effectively. Some word processing knowledge is also helpful. Above all, a Production Assistant must be eager and willing to operate within a teamwork atmosphere.

Unions and Associations

There are no unions that represent Production Assistants, as they are usually considered part of the production department at most stations. In a few major-market stations, however, because of their assigned duties they may be represented by the National Association of Broadcast Employees and Technicians AFL-CIO (NABET). In California, there is an organization called the Production Assistants Association, which may be beneficial for networking.

Tips for Entry

1. During high school or college, investigate a potential internship at a local television station to gain firsthand knowledge of production processes. You may find you will be functioning as a Production Assistant.
2. During high school or college, volunteer to work on theater productions or at campus television stations in production jobs of any kind.
3. Work as a PA on any nonunion or student film.
4. Use contacts gained during high school and college to get a salaried Production Assistant job.

PRODUCTION COORDINATOR AND PRODUCTION SECRETARY

CAREER PROFILE

Duties: Provide coordination and clerical support for a television production department

Alternate Title(s): Production Office Coordinator

Salary Range: $11,000 to $44,000

Employment Prospects: Good

Advancement Prospects: Good

Prerequisites:

Education and Training—High school diploma required; one to two years of business school recommended; some college may be required

Experience—Minimum of one to two years of experience as a secretary running an office; some experience with cable or television companies a bonus

Special Skills and Personality Traits—Ability to get along with a wide variety of personalities; detail-oriented; good communication skills, especially on the telephone and online; familiarity with office equipment; filing and paper management skills; shorthand or speed writing; strong organizational abilities; time-management skills; word-processing proficiency

CAREER LADDER

```
┌─────────────────────────────────┐
│   Unit Production Manager;       │
│   Production Assistant           │
└─────────────────────────────────┘

┌─────────────────────────────────┐
│   Production Coordinator and     │
│   Production Secretary           │
└─────────────────────────────────┘

┌─────────────────────────────────┐
│ Receptionist / Office Clerk; High School / │
│ Business School / College        │
└─────────────────────────────────┘
```

Position Description

Production Coordinators, sometimes called Production Secretaries, are the individuals responsible for the office support of the production department at a television station, network, or independent production company. They coordinate much of the work within the department and provide general clerical assistance. They prepare, organize, file, receive, and transmit forms, correspondence, and other paperwork necessary for a television production. Their general secretarial assistance may include word processing, transcribing, taking dictation, and other general office work.

As the office coordinator, they schedule appointments, provide information to callers, fill out forms, route mail, answer telephones, respond to e-mail, compile and maintain reports, and prepare correspondence. They may assist production personnel in obtaining clearances for location work, schedule performers and guests that will appear on television shows, monitor the production schedule, and maintain the production files that contain scripts, program information data, contracts, business records, talent sheets, and other production records. In some cases, Production Coordinators may be requested to research and develop the basic material and information necessary for the development of a show script. This development would include preparing and organizing the script from draft through final form, then duplicating, collating, and distributing it to the production staff.

Generally, the Production Coordinator (or Production Secretary) reports directly to the production manager and in the smaller- and middle-market stations may also provide general support for producers, directors, and other production personnel. It is usual for Production Coordinators and Production Secretaries to serve more than one person. Besides the usual office skills, they must also be knowledgeable about current practices, terms, and nomenclature used in the TV industry and must be resourceful and organized in their dealings with staff, performers, guests, and others involved in the production.

On large productions, there may be several assistant Production Coordinators to handle all the paperwork. On such projects, the Production Coordinator runs the production office, and there may be beginner trainees as Production Secretaries assigned strictly to secretarial duties.

Salaries

Production Coordinators and Production Secretaries are usually considered support personnel and, as such, have relatively low salaries compared to most other television positions. Their salaries are comparable to those of most production assistants, or lower. Annual earnings may range from a low of $11,000 to a high of $44,000, with a mean average income of about $21,000.

Employment Prospects

The opportunities for employment are generally good. The position of Production Secretary usually is considered to be an entry-level post. Smaller-market stations will sometimes employ such beginners and provide on-the-job training. At some of the larger-market stations, various program units within the production department will employ Production Secretaries.

Individuals with more experience in television production or secretaries who gain that experience are usually hired for the vital position of Production Coordinator. Coordinators are needed for every television production, and thus employment possibilities are good. In addition, all independent production companies and many corporate, educational, governmental, and health television operations that are engaged in production need Production Coordinators to handle all the production paperwork and scheduling.

Advancement Prospects

The prospects for advancement for bright, resourceful people are good. The responsibilities of this position require that the individual learn all aspects of television production. Many Production Secretaries become production assistants to further their experience in television production. Production Coordinators (or secretaries who have been promoted to that position) may advance to become unit production managers or even in some cases assistant directors or associate producers, usually within the television station or unit of the station. Some may use their experience to obtain more responsible posts at other production organizations, major-market stations, or networks.

Education and Training

The minimum educational requirement for the position of Production Coordinator or Production Secretary is a high school diploma. Most employers, if hiring the individual as a Production Secretary, prefer at least one to two years of training in a business school or an associate degree in business. For Production Coordinators, many employers require some education in mass communications, or even a college degree in radio/TV or theater. Knowledge of word processing techniques is an important asset.

Experience, Skills, and Personality Traits

In hiring individuals as Production Secretaries, employers in middle- and major-market television stations often require one to two years of experience as a receptionist or office clerk, preferably in a television station, advertising agency, or media center. In many cases, an undergraduate degree in radio/TV is an acceptable alternative. At many smaller-market stations, the position is considered to be an entry-level job, requiring little experience other than good secretarial skills.

Both Production Coordinators and Production Secretaries must be knowledgeable of both standard office equipment and word processing technology. They must be proficient in spelling, punctuation, and grammar, have a good command of the English language, and have an aptitude for numbers. They need to have strong organizational skills and the ability to retain as many details as possible. The job entails a lot of details and stress. Paperwork can become overwhelming, and other production staff members can be vociferous in their demand for action or information. Coordinators need to stay calm and handle whatever crisis occurs. In addition, they need to have solid time management skills and be able to prioritize among often conflicting assignments in the hectic environment of television production.

Unions and Associations

There are no unions or professional organizations that represent Production Secretaries or Production Coordinators. However, for Production Coordinators who have gained experience in their job, membership in the International Alliance of Theatrical Stage Employees (IATSE) may provide networking opportunities and other benefits.

Tips for Entry

1. Polish your word processing skills while in school, and consider taking business courses along with your communications or radio/TV work.
2. Take any paid or unpaid job or internship at a local television station.
3. Gain office work experience in part-time jobs while finishing your education.

UNIT PRODUCTION MANAGER AND LINE PRODUCER

CAREER PROFILE

Duties: Oversee the logistics, budget control, and administration of a television production or series in the studio or on location

Alternate Title(s): Remote Supervisor; Studio Supervisor; Unit Manager; Unit Supervisor

Salary Range: $3,841 to $5,341 weekly minimum

Employment Prospects: Fair to Good

Advancement Prospects: Fair

Prerequisites:

Education and Training—High school diploma; college degree in communications, radio/TV, or film preferred; advanced degree optional

Experience—Minimum of two to three years of TV-film production in as many positions as possible

Special Skills and Personality Traits—Financial management capability; flexible but decisive in decision making process; good interpersonal skills and mediation abilities; organizational and administrative skills; technical aptitude

CAREER LADDER

```
┌─────────────────────────────────────────┐
│ Associate Producer; Producer; Director   │
└─────────────────────────────────────────┘

┌─────────────────────────────────────────┐
│       Unit Production Manager;           │
│           Line Producer                  │
└─────────────────────────────────────────┘

┌─────────────────────────────────────────┐
│      Floor Manager; Production           │
│ Coordinator; Production Assistant        │
└─────────────────────────────────────────┘
```

Position Description

The Unit Production Manager (frequently called the UPM) is the primary logistics organizer of all elements of a television production or series and is the individual immediately in charge of all budget expenditures. He or she ensures that all production costs are kept within the budget limitations. Unit Production Managers report to either an associate producer, a producer (who may have hired them for the production), or in some cases to an assistant director.

On large productions, there may be another post as well, that of the Line Producer, directly senior to the Unit Production Manager. In these cases, the Unit Production Manager reports to this individual, and they both, in turn, are responsible to the producer. On other productions, these job titles may be interchangeable, with the Unit Production Manager being known as a Line Producer instead, who again is directly responsible to the producer. Both positions have much the same responsibilities (with the Line Producer hav-

ing the ultimate accountability when overseeing a Unit Production Manager): preparing and supervising budgets, administering the production, allocating resources, and supervising the production on a day-to-day basis to make sure production goals are met.

Unit Production Managers and Line Producers are employed both at commercial and public television stations as well as the networks. They are also employed at production companies that prepare made-for-TV products. They may work in both the studio and on location as needed.

Unit Production Managers and Line Producers are primarily tasked with coordinating and supervising all administrative, financial, and technical details of the television production or series and oversee the activities of the entire crew. During preproduction they prepare a budget for the project by breaking down the script, prepare the shooting scheduling, and negotiate, approve, and arrange for the setup of all equipment (including cameras, lights, audio equipment, monitors, sets and scenery, easels, props, and any other necessary items) as well as the maintenance and operation of all facilities and equipment both in the studio and on location shoots. They hire and organize staging and lighting personnel, camera operators, production assistants, and other production personnel in the preparation of rehearsals and in other preproduction activities. They also negotiate and complete the contracts with performers (other than stars, who negotiate with and contract to the producer), location owners, and, crew and equipment (with union paperwork where applicable). During this period, they work primarily in the production office or meeting with vendors and suppliers, and they usually report to an assistant director or an associate producer.

During production, Unit Production Managers and Line Producers divide their time between the office and the set (or exterior location), monitoring the production in progress and ensuring that if the production begins to go over budget or over schedule steps are taken immediately to rectify the problems before they multiply. They approve all expenses from other departments and oversee the orderly flow of paperwork from the set to the production office. For on-location shooting, they oversee the preliminary searches for suitable locations and survey and coordinate arrangements for the transportation and housing (if necessary) of cast, crew, and staff. At the end of location shooting, they organize the strike (dismantling) of the remote production and the return of all equipment and personnel. Additionally, throughout this process, they supervise the completion of status reports on each day's work as well as reports on the production's overall status.

Salaries

The Directors Guild of America (DGA) has established minimums for Unit Production Managers (UPMs) who work on a union production. The studio weekly minimum salary is $3,814, and the location weekly minimum salary is $5,341. On nonunion television productions, UPM salaries depend on the budget for the production and whatever the UPM is able to negotiate with the producer or the financial department of the station or network. Generally, annual salaries for Unit Production Managers range from a low of $24,000 to a high of $80,000 or more, depending on the number of productions in any given year (and their budgets) on which they are employed.

Similarly, salaries for Line Producers depend on the television production's budget. They earn nearly as much as Unit Production Managers and frequently more, estimated at between $4,500 and $5,000 a week, or $18,000 to $85,000 or more annually.

Employment Prospects

The positions of Unit Production Manager and Line Producer are not entry-level jobs, and opportunities are fair to good for diligent and ambitious production employees at a station. Unit Production Managers and Line Producers are often assigned by producers to specific productions, ongoing series, or specific remote location shoots. Because of this, there are opportunities for UPMs and Line Producers to be assigned periodically to various projects during a year. In addition, some major-market stations maintain standing production units for ongoing series. Opportunities exist for experienced and practiced floor managers or production assistants to be promoted to Unit Production Managers or Line Producers on a permanent basis. Commercial networks employ more than 100 UPMs on a regular basis, but the competition for these coveted (and financially remunerative) positions is stiff, as it is at most independent production companies.

Advancement Prospects

Most Unit Production Managers and Line Producers are naturally aggressive and well organized. In large stations and networks, the opportunities for advancement by successful UPMs or Line Producers to associate producers or to other responsible production posts are fair. In some cases, Unit Production Managers may advance to the position of a Line Producer for the station's or network's larger productions. On smaller-budget productions, in most cases the UPM acts as the Line Producer. In turn, many Line Producers become producers themselves.

Education and Training

A high school diploma and confirmation of technical training in television or film production is necessary for employment as or promotion to either a Unit Production Manager or a Line Producer. Most major-market stations and all networks prefer or require an undergraduate degree in mass communications, radio/TV, or theater. While courses in theater staging and lighting are helpful, training in television production is even more key.

Experience, Skills, and Personality Traits

Both Unit Production Managers and Line Producers are expected to have had at least two to three years of experience in assorted television production positions. They both need to have a thorough knowledge of television equipment and facilities. They must be able to work well with a wide variety of people, both personally and collectively, and be able to mediate differences amiably and effectively. They both must understand budgets, have sound financial management capabilities, be detail-oriented, and have good organizational and administrative skills. In addition, they both need to be flexible but decisive in their decision making, capable of making quick creative and financial choices.

Unions and Associations

Many Unit Production Managers, especially those working on television films for network release, are members of and are represented by the Directors Guild of America. If the television program, series, or film is a union production, the UPM has to be a member of the guild. Some UPMs at local commercial and public television stations, however, may not belong to a union.

While there is no specific union for Line Producers, many of them belong to the Directors Guild of America as Union Production Managers or are members of the Producers Guild of America.

Tips for Entry

1. While in school or college, take business courses, as you will need business and financial skills in your job as a Unit Production Manager or Line Producer.

2. Be ready to work on a project-by-project basis, with potentially long periods of time between projects. You will need to budget your finances accordingly.

3. Take any entry-level job at a television station to gain experience. One good place to start if you hope to become a Unit Production Manager or a Line Producer, is in the budget or financial department.

MUSIC

COMPOSER AND SONGWRITER

CAREER PROFILE

Duties: Compose music to be used as background for a television production; write songs and/or lyrics to songs used in a television project

Alternate Title(s): Lyricist

Salary Range: $10,000 to $60,000 or more

Employment Prospects: Poor to Fair

Advancement Prospects: Fair

Prerequisites:

Education and Training—College degree in music recommended, but not required

Experience—Work as a Composer, or a Songwriter

Special Skills and Personality Traits—Able to express emotions and ambiance musically or in song; a background in classical music training or in songwriting for film, music videos, or theater

CAREER LADDER

```
┌─────────────────────────────────────┐
│   Music Director or Supervisor       │
└─────────────────────────────────────┘

┌─────────────────────────────────────┐
│     Composer and Songwriter          │
└─────────────────────────────────────┘

┌─────────────────────────────────────┐
│  Orchestra Conductor or Arranger;    │
│     Songwriter; Musician             │
└─────────────────────────────────────┘
```

Position Description

The primary job of the Composer or Songwriter is to create a musical score, and in some cases one or more songs, that add an emotional layer to the television production. This includes the dramatic underscoring of the action (of the television film, production, or series episode) and a musical theme (possibly used as the theme for the show) and/or songs to be used in the production. Some Composers write their own songs, or individual Songwriters may be hired to create numbers for a production.

As composer Steve Dorff explains, "Writing a score is a different skill than songwriting, where you come up with a melody and you either write a lyric yourself or you collaborate with another person to write a song. Writing a score for a film is an integral part of the postproduction process, where you're musicalizing every moment of the movie with orchestral or some kind of music—generally without lyrics—that underscores the action. . . . The creative process is the same with television as it is with film. The only difference being, there is a much smaller budget for television than for film."

While most Composers do not begin their chores until the production is in its final postproduction editing stages, they may have already begun composing themes or songs for the production. However, it is not until the final cut is ready that the Composer will begin actually creating the dramatic underscore of music that will be used to heighten the drama, suspense, action, comedy, or flavor of a particular scene. The main reason for waiting as long as possible is mainly economic: to avoid creating music for footage that may not be incorporated into the final production.

To compose a score for a television production (as in a film), Composers first study a rough cut of the production to gain a creative perspective of what variety of musical themes will be needed as well as ideas for possible theme songs for the project. Next, they work with the director during a screening of the production to determine where music should emerge in a scene, when it should fade out, and which sequences should have background music. When the director feels the postproduction editing is complete, the Composer, with the production playing on a screen, begins creating the music that will accompany every scene for which it has been decided that music is needed. The score will contain beats and measures to match fully the action.

Today, many scores are created first on a computer using a language known as the Musical Instrument Digital Interface (MIDI), which allows a computer (PC) to control all kinds of musical electronics, including keyboards, synthesizers, and drum machines. With this computerized orchestra, a Composer and a director can make changes at will, quickly and easily cutting, pasting, and shifting music around until if fits the director's overall concept of the production.

In some cases, an orchestrator or arranger is brought in to orchestrate the various voices and instruments of the Composer's composition or adapt the Composer's music to the timing constraints of the musical score. In other cases, Composers may adapt, with permission, an already existing score, thus producing additional, similar-sounding music (e.g., for use in a sequel to the original production).

Once the score is completed and written out, musicians are brought in to a scoring session to work with the Composer, orchestrator, music editor, and conductor to perform the music on a scoring stage, which consists of a mixing console and a screen to show the production. After the score is recorded, the music editor, Composer, and orchestrator mix the music and then turn it over to a final mixing stage to be mixed onto the final soundtrack. For some television shows, this process is streamlined, with the computerized orchestra score going directly to the final picture edit rather than through the intermediate step of a live orchestra or band.

While this process is as true for television as it is for film, a good deal of the music heard on television is prerecorded by companies that specialize in creating and producing such canned music. News program music, show themes, music for promos and commercials—all are customized music types. These production companies have Composers on their staffs to create the specialized music for television producers.

Salaries

Salaries vary widely and depend greatly on the television production's budget. Composers and Songwriters are not covered by the American Federation of Musicians (AFM) and are customarily paid a flat fee for the composition or through a package deal that may include the union scale due for any union-covered services they perform beyond the composing (such as conducting, orchestrating, or arranging). Orchestrators and arrangers, depending on the situation, may be paid by the hour or by a page rate as established by the union. Television Composers and Songwriters may have annual earnings from $10,000 to $60,000 or more. In some cases, beginning Composers and Songwriters may receive a deferred salary and use the opportunity to showcase their talents in order to get additional paid work with the station or music production company.

Employment Prospects

While the competition is tough, television productions, like films, need music. Established Composers and Songwriters may take the lion's share of television work, but opportunities do exist for newcomers in the field. Many Composers and Songwriters work both in films and in television.

Advancement Prospects

There are very few advancement prospects for Composers or Songwriters, as it is a top position for most such individuals. In some cases, they may become the music director (or supervisor) for the station or network. They frequently hire Composers or Songwriters for a television production. If they work for a music production company, there may be openings in the higher management of these companies.

Education and Training

It is helpful to have musical training in the classics or even opera. Taking courses in composing for films and the art of orchestrating also is useful. Most Composers and many Songwriters are adept at playing piano as well as other instruments. They may also be accomplished with a sequencer or a synthesizer and have the ability to produce the music they write.

Experience, Skills, and Personality Traits

Successful Composers and Songwriters need the ability to compose memorable melodies and lyrics. They must be musically oriented and be able to create music that will form an emotional undertone and background for a visual moment. Composing itself is a very solitary art, as Composers work alone and within their own time frames. However, in writing music for television, they must be patient in the process of editing (with directors) and be able to produce results under tight deadlines. They should also have good computer skills.

Unions and Associations

Unlike orchestrators and arrangers, Composers and Songwriters are not represented by the main music union, the American Federation of Musicians (AFM). Many Composers are members of such performing rights organizations as the American Society of Composers, Authors and Publishers (ASCAP), Broadcast Music, Inc. (BMI), or SESAC, Inc., which greatly aids their guarantees of fair earnings on their compositions. Other associations, such as the National Academy of Recording Arts and Sciences and Screen Composers of America, may be helpful for networking.

Tips for Entry

1. Contact film schools and volunteer to write music for a student or low-budget film to gain actual experience in writing music to fit visual scenes.
2. Prepare a sample CD recording or audiotape of your work to aid in your search for a composing job.
3. Work as a musician in a studio score orchestra to network with other musicians, Composers, and Songwriters

MUSIC DIRECTOR

CAREER PROFILE

Duties: Evaluate, select, and supervise music for a television production; hire composers and songwriters

Alternate Title(s): Music Supervisor; Music Coordinator

Salary Range: $48,000 to $120,000 or more

Employment Prospects: Poor

Advancement Prospects: Poor

Prerequisites:

Education and Training—College degree with a major in music recommended; extensive training in music

Experience—Minimum of five to six years in television, radio, or film music

Special Skills and Personality Traits—Creativity; good taste; love of and talent for music; synthesizer literacy; working knowledge of licensing and the music industry

CAREER LADDER

```
┌─────────────────────────────────────────┐
│  Music Director (of major film production │
│  or independent production company);      │
│  Producer                                 │
└─────────────────────────────────────────┘

┌─────────────────────────────────────────┐
│           Music Director                  │
└─────────────────────────────────────────┘

┌─────────────────────────────────────────┐
│   Composer; Music Editor; Musician        │
└─────────────────────────────────────────┘
```

Position Description

A Music Director (frequently called music supervisor) is responsible for evaluating, selecting, and supervising all the music used for a television production, program, series, or film. Music Directors are most often employed in major television film productions, situation comedies, dramatic series and miniseries, and variety shows. They may also work on documentary programs and are sometimes hired for large-budget corporate, educational, or governmental television projects.

Music Directors are typically hired early in the production process so they can gain a grasp for what kinds of music would be most appropriate for the production. Diverse types and styles of music are used in television productions to augment and accentuate the visual images. Working closely with the director, Music Directors establish when and if music should be employed for specific scenes to capture the audience's attention, complement the action, or create a special mood. They analyze each scene and then audition, preview, and select musical pieces appropriate for the production's visual aspect. After all the music has been recorded, they add the music to the visual, voice, and non-musical sound effects material of the master tape or film.

For major television productions or films, the Music Director often commissions original compositions from composers or original songs from songwriters, both of whom usually work specifically within the film and television industries. In the analysis of each scene (called music spotting), Music Directors develop a map and a set of instructions for the composer to follow in the creation of the score. The Music Director acts as a liaison between the director and the composer and ensures that the director's vision of the production is communicated to the composer in terms of the type of musical palette the composer will use as well as all the technical details of this process. Once the score is finished and with the approval of the director and/or producer, the Music Director supervises the arrangement of the music, chooses the size of the orchestra or band to perform it, and oversees the recording of the music. In some cases, the Musical Director will be the conductor of the orchestra and may, in some instances, also compose, orchestrate, or arrange the music. As a composer, the Music Director may find it necessary to complete a score for a TV movie or miniseries. Some Music Directors specialize in creating and supervising music for commercials.

As coordinators of music for television productions, Music Directors must maintain a file of existing music and music sources for future possible use as well as keep a contact list of composers, music researchers, musicians, and other potential resources. If prerecorded music is used in the television production, Music Directors are responsible for seeing that the proper licensing fees are paid and all musical rights are respected. Whether such musical material is used will depend on the production's budget, as licensing fees can be expensive.

At times, Music Directors find they need to use existing musical selections as bridges, cues, themes, or other types of short sections. For this, they frequently use music production companies that specialize in such music and select specific portions of music tapes maintained by the music libraries of these companies. They then supervise the insertion of this musical material into the soundtrack of the television production.

Music Directors typically work in recording studios but may also be found in the control room and in the tape and film editing rooms of major production firms or television studios. Usually, the Music Director supervises sound editors, audio engineers, and recording engineers. In turn, Music Directors usually report to the producer or the director of the television production.

Salaries

Music Directors are usually hired on a project-by-project basis. Their salaries vary considerably, based on the scope and extent of the music to be used in the production (very much dependent on the production's budget). Some Music Directors with established names and impressive credentials may command salaries exceeding $100,000 for the complete scoring of a major television production, film, or series. More often, however, Music Directors work on simpler productions, usually using prerecorded music (from a music production company), and are paid from $12,000 to $35,000 or more for their effort. They will most likely work on three or four such projects in a year. Those who compose (or arrange) music for commercials charge between $15,000 and $30,000 for each job. Generally, the total yearly income for a Music Director ranges from $50,000 for those who have some reputation in the industry to well over $120,000 for those directors who have an established standings with impressive credits.

Employment Prospects

Opportunities for employment in commercial, public, and cable television are generally poor. Most talk shows, newscasts, and other such programming seldom use music. While many other television programs do include music, the duties of a Music Director in most lower-budget projects are usually taken up by the producer, the director, or the sound or music editor. Major-market commercial, cable, and public television stations use Music Directors, but competition for positions is extremely stiff. Music Directors are usually hired for a specific job on a program-by-program or series-by-series basis, much like freelancers. Employment usually depends on contacts within the industry. With the proper training and experience, some musicians may become Music Directors.

Advancement Prospects

Opportunities for advancement are poor, and the competition is heavy. Advancement possibilities depend greatly on the talent and ongoing industry reputation of the individual. With success and peer recognition, along with critical acclaim and a growing list of television credits, new opportunities for more projects and larger fees become possible.

Some television Music Directors increase their earnings by working on major film projects or become employed on long-lasting television series. Some are also staff Music Directors of independent production companies. A few Music Directors may go on to become producers in their own right in either film, television, or the theater.

Education and Training

Most Music Directors are well trained and exceedingly talented musicians. They have an extensive music education background, including studies in music theory, harmony, arranging, and history. Almost all have an undergraduate degree in music, and many have graduate degrees.

Experience, Skills, and Personality Traits

At least five or six years of experience in the use of music in television (or film) are necessary. A thorough knowledge of television production techniques is also required. A Music Director has to be familiar with audio recording processes and have extensive experience in working with short, precisely timed music segments.

Music Directors are talented, creative persons who have a wide knowledge of musical styles and an innate, finely honed musical taste. They are proficient at manipulating timbres of recorded music, changing rhythms, and developing small motifs or musical themes that will create memorable musical imagery. A complete understanding of synthesizers and other computer-generated electronic musical gear is essential. Above all, they have to be keenly sensitive to what is happening in a scene in a television production, how the characters feel, what is happening to their lives in the production, and what music could enhance all these feelings.

Unions and Associations

There are no unions that represent or bargain specifically for Music Directors. However, as musicians, they usually belong to the American Federation of Musicians (AFM). In addition, membership in industry associations such as the National Academy of Recording Arts and Sciences may be helpful for networking.

Tips for Entry

1. Get experience working for a record company or a music publishing firm that caters to the television or film industry.
2. Become familiar with all types and styles of music and what music has sounded like in the past.
3. Network with songwriters to keep abreast of what is happening in the musical culture.
4. Volunteer to work as an assistant to a Music Director.

PROPS AND SET MAINTENANCE

PROPERTY ASSISTANTS

CAREER PROFILE

Duties: Place, maintain, and remove props for a television production

Alternate Title(s): Leadperson; Prop Handler; Prop Person; Property Person; Set Dresser; Swing Gang Member

Salary Range: $27.75 to $34 hourly minimum

Employment Prospects: Fair

Advancement Prospects: Poor to Fair

Prerequisites:

Education and Training—College degree preferred; additional training in television or theater production recommended

Experience—At least one year as a production assistant in the art department

Special Skills and Personality Traits—Ability to take orders; artistic flair; detail-oriented; good communication skills; imaginative; well organized

CAREER LADDER

```
┌─────────────────────────────────────┐
│   Property Master; Set Decorator     │
└─────────────────────────────────────┘

┌─────────────────────────────────────┐
│        Property Assistants           │
└─────────────────────────────────────┘

┌─────────────────────────────────────┐
│   Production Assistant; College      │
└─────────────────────────────────────┘
```

Position Description

There are a variety of Property Assistants who may be hired for larger television productions, series and miniseries, made-for-television films, commercials, and music videos. These jobs include that of the property assistant, leadperson (or gang boss), prop maker (when required props are difficult to find and need to be made from scratch to meet the shooting schedule), set dresser, and various property individuals handling specific tasks, such as furniture handling, flower props, upholstering/draperies and sewing tasks, hand props, and electrical props. All such persons report directly to the property master or, in some cases, either the art director or the set decorator.

On large television productions, particularly those requiring many props for assorted scene settings, the property master will have a property assistant, who is in charge of all the props used throughout the production. Some projects may even designate an outside props assistant to purchase (or rent) props, and an inside props assistant to oversee their placement, use, and maintenance on the sets. The job is stressful, as there are so many details to be kept constantly in mind while ensuring that the set is correct in every detail. As veteran prop person, Jason Ivey, says, "You

have to stay true to what the person [on the set] would really use and make sure the environment matches the script. If a glass is half full or a light wasn't on, you have to make sure it is the same [if and] when they reshoot the scene."

Another position that may be needed in the property department on large productions is the leadperson (or lead man). This individual is responsible for overseeing the moving on and off the set of all furniture, accessories, pictures, larger props, and other set decorations. The leadperson ensures that the set is ready when the rest of the production crew arrives to shoot scenes. Once the shooting begins, all responsibilities for the set lie in the hands of the property master. However, when the shooting is finished, this responsibility then falls back into the hands of the leadperson. Leadpersons may have a crew of individuals to do this work, usually known as a swing gang. It is these people who physically decorate (dress) and take down (strike) the set. While leadpersons frequently report to the property master, others may instead report to the set decorator.

The set dresser is the individual tasked with placing and removing diverse objects, such as furniture, paintings, lamps, and other smaller objects used as props, on the production prior to the start of shooting of each scene. Their additional responsibility is to maintain the integrity of the set during a television production. All props used on a set, as finalized by the property master and the set decorator, have to be noted as to their exact position on the set by the set dresser. If a cup is moved or a piece of furniture is rearranged, the set dresser is responsible for getting them back in their original places before any reshooting of the scene is done, so as to maintain the continuity of the shot. Frequently, set dressers take Polaroid photos or digital pictures of the set to aid them in this meticulous process. On smaller television productions and some commercials, the functions of the leadperson and set dresser may be combined into that of the Property Assistant or Property master.

Salaries

Most Property Assistants are members of the International Association of Theatrical Stage Employees (IATSE). The union sets minimum wages for its members. For assistant property masters, the minimum hourly wage (minimum eight-hour day) is $29.66, or, if hired on a weekly basis (five days with a cumulative 54 hours), a minimum weekly wage of $1,782.83. For leadpersons, the minimum hourly wage is $29.66, or a weekly minimum wage of $1,745.64. Set dressers have a minimum hourly wage of $27.75. Other specialty Property Assistant positions (including that of prop makers) have hourly minimum wages that range from $27.75 to $34.01, depending on the complexity of the work and whether they supervise a crew.

Employment Prospects

On most major television productions, the property master has at least one Property Assistant. Depending on the budget and complexity of the project, there may also be the need for a leadperson to supervise the swing crew handling the props as well as a set dresser. For the most elaborate of productions, other Property Assistants (prop makers and other property persons) may also be hired. However, on most smaller television productions, such jobs will be handled by the property master along with production assistants. For these reasons, chances for employment range from poor to fair.

Advancement Prospects

The next step in advancement for a property person is the post of property master. As openings for this more prestigious and responsible position do not occur often, advancement prospects are rather poor. Leadpersons and Property Assistants may be promoted to set decorators, though infrequently. Property Assistants who have accumulated several years of experience may find that advancement to a more responsible position within either the property or art department becomes more likely.

Education and Training

A high school degree is an absolute requirement for all positions, except possibly for members of the swing gang. For most Property Assistants, additional training in television or theater production is beneficial, both for being hired and for working on television production sets. For some, such as set dressers, additional education in design and period furnishings is helpful. On-the-job training as production assistants also is recommended.

Experience, Skills, and Personality Traits

Property Assistants (and particularly swing gang members, set dressers, and assistant property masters) must be physically fit to lift and carry furniture and other heavy objects. They need to be willing to take direction and must have the ability to get along with people of varied personalities and temperaments. As they are supervisors, leadpersons and assistant property masters need to exhibit leadership qualities.

Set dressers should have the ability to understand the characters in the script. To dress a set, they need to interpret the character; ascertain what the individual in the script wants, like, or dislikes; decide whether they are neat persons or messy; and decide whether they are a collector and, if so, of what. Both set dressers and assistant property masters must be extremely detail-oriented and well organized, as they must be able to remember all the details of the set environment. They also need strong people skills.

Unions and Associations

Membership in the IATSE may be obligatory on most major television productions and is beneficial in guaranteeing at least minimum wage levels for the various Property Assistant positions. For some assistants membership in such industry associations as the Set Decorators Society of America may be helpful for networking.

Tips for Entry

1. Take courses in television production as well as in such subject areas as furniture/furnishings and design.
2. Seek a production assistant job in the art department at a television station or production company as a means of learning about television production design and decorating as well as making contacts.
3. Be willing to do any task, learn how professional property people do their work, and meet as many people in the business as you can, staying friendly and in touch with them, as the television industry (and the film industry) is all about "who you know."

PROPERTY MASTER

CAREER PROFILE

Duties: Select, obtain, maintain, store, and place all props in a television production

Alternate Title(s): Propmaster; Prop Person; Director of Props

Salary Range: $33.35 hourly minimum, $2,018.18 weekly minimum

Employment Prospects: Fair to Poor

Advancement Prospects: Poor

Prerequisites:

Education and Training—College degree preferred; additional training in television or theater production recommended

Experience—Minimum of one to two years as a set dresser, a grip, or a stagehand

Special Skills and Personality Traits—Artistic flair; detail oriented; good communication skills; imaginative; knowledge of television and/or theater carpentry and production; precision; research skills; well organized

CAREER LADDER

```
┌─────────────────────────────────────┐
│ Head of Property Department; Property│
│ Master (theater or film production)  │
└─────────────────────────────────────┘

┌─────────────────────────────────────┐
│          Property Master             │
└─────────────────────────────────────┘

┌─────────────────────────────────────┐
│     Set Dresser; Grip; Stagehand     │
└─────────────────────────────────────┘
```

Position Description

The Property Master is responsible for the acquisition, maintenance, storage, use, and placement of properties (props) required for a television production, series, film, or program. A prop is a portable object that enhances the set or is handled by a performer on the set as a part of the production. These objects can include such items as lamps, pictures, books, dishes, vases, a desktop computer, and other decorative or functional pieces. The Property Master also supplies hand articles essential to performers, hosts, guests, or the plot of a drama, such as magazines, canes, drinks, guns and knives, and other belongings.

Property Masters determine what props will be needed for a production by studying the script during the preproduction phase and consulting with the art director, set decorator (or set designer), director, performers, and in some cases even the producer. Sometimes a prop is referenced in the script, but the art director or the set designer may add a prop that is not mentioned because they determine it is required.

Property Masters then determine how much each prop will cost and develop a prop budget. They are responsible for purchasing or renting props and obtaining them from storage, or, if unobtainable (because of special requirements or budgetary restrictions), they supervise their construction. They maintain a list of all props used in a production and ensure that they are in place, in usable condition, and available and positioned properly for use in each scene. They also oversee that the props are stored afterward for possible reuse in a reshot of the scene or in a different scene. They pack and unpack props when accompanying the production on location, and they arrange for the shipping and transportation of props when they have been removed from the set after production, returning any rented or borrowed items and arranging storage as appropriate.

When choosing props for a period or historical program, the Property Master must study the era or the geographic locale of the script to ensure the authenticity of the props selected for use. For contemporary settings, props must complement the presentation and the style of the production as set by the director. In addition, the Property Master must instruct the performers on the proper and safe method of handling a prop, especially a weapon. In particular, the Property Master is responsible for maintaining a safe and secure environment when firearms or explosives are involved.

Property Masters are used on most major dramatic television programs, series, and films. They are employed at networks, independent production companies, and film sound stages, and, occasionally, they work on location. At many small- and medium-sized television stations, the duties of the Property Master may be handled by floor managers or production assistants under the guidance of the director or set designer.

On many major television productions, Property Masters may supervise an entire department of assistants, including set dressers, prop makers (if props have to be constructed, and who work with the scenic design crew), property buyers (who purchase the necessary items), weapons masters (who handle the weaponry used in the production), model makers, and any necessary stagehands. If a major television production has special requirements, it is up to the Property Master to provide technical advisers for these needs, such as animal handlers, food specialists, computer technicians, law enforcement and military advisers, medical technicians, and special mechanics. On many smaller productions, the Property Master is expected to carry out all necessary duties related to props. Generally, Property Masters report to a set designer or the director of the production.

Salaries

Basic minimum wages for Property Masters are set by the union that represents them, the International Alliance of Theatrical Stage Employees (IATSE). The minimum hourly rate is $33.53. If they are hired on a weekly basis (five days and 54 hours), the hourly rate is $33.09, or a weekly rate of $2,018.18. On location, the minimum pay scale is the same. These rates, of course, are usually negotiated upward by an experienced Property Master with a solid reputation for efficiency and capability. For seasoned Property Masters, annual income ranges from a low of $50,000 to a high of $85,000 or more.

Employment Prospects

Opportunities for employment are poor to fair. Property Master positions require experience gained from working in television, films, or commercials and therefore are not open to individuals seeking entry-level jobs in television. All major television productions (entertainment programs, series, films, talk shows, and so forth) must have an individual handling the props to be used. However, competition is tough, and employment depends heavily on contacts and relationships that the individual has built in the industry. Promotion from within the art department usually comes for set dressers, who function as assistants to the Property Master, or grips or stagehands.

Most Property Masters work freelance on a project-by-project basis. The seasonal nature of much television production tends to contribute to the probable lengthy periods of unemployment. For these reasons, many Property Masters also work in other entertainment fields (films, commercials, and theater) to augment their annual income from television.

Advancement Prospects

Prospects for advancement for a Property Master are very limited. Usually, this position is considered the top rung of a career ladder that may have begun at one of the entry-level jobs (such as production assistant) in television, film, or theater. Some Property Masters seek to become heads of property departments at film studios or theater companies. Again, competition is stiff, and these jobs usually go to people who have had many years of experience and have gained many contacts in the respective industries.

Education and Training

A high school diploma is a must. Some post–high school training in television or theatrical production at the college level or special theatrical or film workshops is recommended. Further studies in art, theater and film history, and scenic design and construction are also helpful. There are apprenticeship programs as well as safety-training programs available at appropriate branches of the IATSE.

Experience, Skills, and Personality Traits

At least one to two years of experience as a set dresser or a grip (or stagehand) is usually obligatory before an individual may expect to be promoted to Property Master. The best experience is gained by working in the art department, as Property Masters have to know all the things that the department handles. As veteran Property Master Rick Toone states, "Once the camera rolls, the set is yours. If they've hung the drapes a certain way, you've got to understand the various ways of doing that, because invariably the director wants to lower them three inches or pull them back. You've got to solve the problem without rerigging the whole thing."

Property Masters need to have a general knowledge of where to go to obtain any type of prop possible. They must have the contacts, abilities, and skills to find items from stores, theatrical supply houses, thrift shops, museums, art galleries, and even the homes of friends and relatives. They need to be both precise and extremely detail-oriented, be able to supervise others, and have good communication skills.

Artistic flair and good organizational skills are absolute necessities, as is a basic knowledge of theatrical and television carpentry and construction as well as television production techniques. In addition, the creative ability to make a prop that is unavailable through other means and the knowledge of how colors will photograph and how different camera lenses will affect an image are important components of the job of Property Master. Finally, a general decorating sense of color, style and texture, good communication abilities, and excellent research skills are additional qualities of a successful Property Master.

Unions and Associations

Property Masters are represented by local units of the IATSE in New York City and Los Angeles for negotiating and bargaining purposes. Some Property Masters who work at television stations may be represented by the National Association of Broadcast Employees and Technicians AFL-CIO (NABET).

Tips for Entry

1. Be willing to take any job you can get in the art department of a television station as your entry point into the handling of props.
2. Pay attention at all times to everything that is happening around you on the set. Details matter.
3. Consider getting any job related to props for commercials or music videos, as you will learn more about what every department does and how they affect your control of the props.

SOUND

ADR (AUTOMATED DIALOGUE REPLACEMENT) SUPERVISOR

CAREER PROFILE

Duties: Replace recorded dialogue for a television production

Alternate Title(s): ADR Editor; Dialogue Mixer

Salary Range: $20,000 to $90,000 or more

Employment Prospects: Good

Advancement Prospects: Fair to Poor

Prerequisites:

Education and Training—High school diploma required; formal training in sound technology usually necessary

Experience—Work as a sound recordist or for a sound equipment rental company

Special Skills and Personality Traits—Able to work well with personalities for long hours; detail-oriented; knowledge about sound; sense of timing; thorough knowledge of television production

CAREER LADDER

```
┌─────────────────────────────────┐
│     Production Sound Mixer       │
└─────────────────────────────────┘

┌─────────────────────────────────┐
│         ADR Supervisor           │
└─────────────────────────────────┘

┌─────────────────────────────────┐
│  Sound Technician; Sound Engineer;│
│           Recordist              │
└─────────────────────────────────┘
```

Position Description

The ADR (Automated Dialogue Replacement) Supervisor is responsible for the replacement of dialogue recorded during the production (known as set dialogue) that is unusable due to poor sound quality, script changes, or any other reason. It's tricky to record dialogue, especially if the set is on location or outdoors rather than in the sound stage studio. A performer's voice may be obscured by the distracting noise of an airplane flying overhead, or the framing of the shot may prevent the boom operator from getting sufficiently close to the performer without being seen on camera. Even in the sound stage, dialogue is not always recorded perfectly. The performer may turn away at the wrong moment, he or she or may speak too softly for the microphone to pick up clearly, or a background noise can cover a word or two.

Thus, in situations where the dialogue is not clean enough to use, a postproduction crew will replace it using an ADR system. In the past, a dialogue editor would make a film loop of the portion of the scene containing the unusable dialogue and play it during the ADR session (thus the well-known nickname of "looping"). Today, the ADR machine plays the line on videotape and then rewinds it automatically.

The ADR Supervisor studies the recorded production with the sound editor, the director, and the film editor to spot the sections of the dialogue that need to be replaced. Then the ADR Supervisor goes through the entire recorded production, listing the starts and ends of the footage that needs replacement, along with time codes for each section or line. Once all the material to be replaced has been noted and then broken down for each individual performer, the production office is informed of which performers are needed for looping and for how long. The performer stands in a soundproof room, called a dubbing stage, watching himself or herself on a monitor showing the original production, and then attempts to recreate his or her performance. ADR Supervisors (or a dialogue editor under their direction) will have added some beeps into the scene in order to cue the performer when to speak the replacement dialogue. As the scene loops over and over again, the performer repeats the line until the performance matches the movement of the lips on-screen. Once recorded, the next line is brought up for dubbing.

Through ADR, the intonation and performance of the dialogue can be altered. The words may be the same as originally recorded, but the subtext of the performance can be changed. Occasional words can be altered if the movement of the mouth matches the new word (commonly used to replace foul language for the public broadcast of the production). Sometimes new dialogue may be required to clarify the storyline. The ADR stage is also used for any type of voices needed to be added to the recorded production, such as narration, public address announcements, the sounds of television shows playing in the background in a scene, a couple fighting or talking in the apartment above or outside the scene that was recorded, and so on. Background sound for crowd scenes can be created in the ADR sessions where a small group of people, known as the loop group, will stand on the ADR stage and mumble, talk, and laugh among themselves, thus creating a whole room of talking and laughing people without actually saying anything intelligible.

Most ADR studios use video playback to accomplish their work. It is cheaper and quicker than film. Once the dubbing sessions are completed, ADR Supervisors prepare the various rerecorded sessions for the mixer, along with their notes as to which new takes are good and what alternates the director wishes to use. The ADR mixer follows these guidelines and prepares the tracks for the final mix of the production. The mixer needs to be experienced in the use and placement of microphones and must know how to listen to the production track to match seamlessly the colorization and timbre of the ADR recording with that track. The ADR Supervisor has the final say on what is rerecorded (always in consultation with the director) and supervises both editors and mixers throughout the sessions.

Salaries

ADR Supervisors may earn a minimum hourly wage of $53.66 (or daily wage of $482.94), as set by their union, Local 700 of the International Alliance of Theatrical Stage Employees. According to the U.S. Bureau of Labor's *Occupational Employment Statistics,* mean annual earnings of sound engineering technicians generally in 2004 were $46,180. The middle 50 percent earned yearly between $26,620 and $56,740. The lowest 10 percent grossed less than $19,460 per year, and the highest 10 percent earned more than $87,610. In the radio and television broadcasting industry, the 2004 annual mean average wage earnings of sound engineering technicians was $42,740.

Employment Prospects

ADR is a necessary component of the completion of the sound mix of a television production in preparation for broadcast. ADR work is usually needed for every recorded television program, and thus employment opportunities for ADR Supervisors are good.

Advancement Prospects

Advancement opportunities, usually to the overall supervisory position of production sound mixer, are only fair. The position of ADR Supervisor is the highest rung in the ADR postproduction crew, and the competition for higher positions in the area of sound production is very strong; positions do not open up frequently. Thus, advancement prospects are average at best and usually poor.

Education and Training

A high school diploma is an absolute requirement, and additional formal training in sound equipment and technology is usually necessary. A well-rounded background in television production is an additional asset.

Experience, Skills, and Personality Traits

Experience as a sound technician is an important asset for the jobs of ADR Supervisors. They must be very detail oriented and exhibit patience at all times, as the ADR process is both lengthy and tedious. They need good supervisory skills and must be able to work well with a wide range of personalities over long periods of time. Their technical proficiency in sound technology must be exemplary.

Unions and Associations

Like most postproduction sound personnel, ADR Supervisors generally belong to Local 700 of the International Alliance of Theatrical Stage Employees (IATSE) for salary and job security. Other industry associations, such as the International Association of Audio/Video Communicators, may also be beneficial for networking purposes.

Tips for Entry

1. Take any general production assistant position in the television industry to gain background in production.
2. Find an ADR Supervisor or equipment rental house that will allow you to apprentice to learn the ADR gear and understand the basics of ADR work.
3. Be willing to do other jobs, such as film editing or sound editing, to maintain consistent employment.

BOOM OPERATOR

CAREER PROFILE

Duties: Handle and place the overhead boom microphone and conceal the wireless microphones for a television production

Alternate Title(s): Microphone Operator

Salary Range: $1,500 to $1,721 weekly minimum

Employment Prospects: Fair to Good

Advancement Prospects: Fair

Prerequisites:

Education and Training—High school diploma minimum requirement; some education in television production helpful

Experience—Work as a sound assistant, technician, or cabler for student or nonunion productions

Special Skills and Personality Traits—Ability to get along well with a variety of personalities; able to follow directions; physically fit to carry and hold heavy equipment for long periods of time; patient; possess working knowledge of television production, dynamics of sound, lighting, and camera lenses and composition; reliable

CAREER LADDER

```
┌─────────────────────────────────┐
│     Production Sound Mixer      │
└─────────────────────────────────┘

┌─────────────────────────────────┐
│         Boom Operator           │
└─────────────────────────────────┘

┌─────────────────────────────────┐
│      Sound Assistant; Cabler    │
└─────────────────────────────────┘
```

Position Description

The Boom Operator is responsible for placing all microphones on a television set and handling the boom microphone during the production. The boom is a pole or a beam, handheld (called a fishpole boom) or an overhead pole, attached to and operated from a mobile platform or truck on which a microphone (or a camera or other device) is attached. Using this equipment, the Boom Operator's job is to get the best quality sound possible and be sure that none of the microphones (or the boom) are visible during the shooting of the production.

Boom Operators work with the production sound mixer (who is in charge of the production sound crew) and are present on the set at all times. They have to follow the director closely as the scene is set up for a shot in order to know where best to place microphones and how best to keep the boom microphone out of the frame of the shot. As the shots progress, the Boom Operator and the production sound mixer communicate closely, usually through the headset that the Boom Operator wears so he or she can hear what is being recorded.

Boom Operators have to carry heavy equipment and hold the boom microphone steadily in place over extended periods of time. They also need to be agile enough to move between lights and other production equipment without knocking them over or casting their shadows on the set. They must be aware of lighting procedures so as to determine whether a mike will cast a shadow. Usually, the sound mixer selects the types of microphones to be used (such as an omnidirectional mike, which can pick up sound from a wide area, or a "shotgun" mike—with its narrow field—which can capture dialogue from a distance). The Boom Operator needs to know all the different types of mikes that are used and how they perform.

One of the main problems with boom microphones is that they tend to dip and may become visible in the frame of the shot. Camera operators usually see this beginning to happen and they alert Boom Operators to move their mikes, but sometimes they don't. As Kevin Sorrenson, a veteran Boom Operator, says, "Your rookie year as a boom operator is really tough, because it's when you make all your mistakes. You dip the microphone into the picture because you don't quite understand framing yet, how a camera operator is going to compose the picture. You have to start learning lens sizes. For instance, 14mm lenses are very wide, so you can't get very close to the actor. You have to learn telephoto lenses; things you can't really learn out of a book."

Salaries

Boom Operators are usually members of Local 695 of the International Alliance of Theatrical Stage Employees (IATSE) and are covered by their wage negotiations. The union has set an hourly minimum wage for an experienced operator at $36.36, and an hourly minimum for an entry-level operator at $31.72. If they are paid on a weekly basis (five days, 48.6 hours), experienced Boom Operators have a weekly minimum of $1,720.75, and an entry-level individual has a weekly minimum of $1,504.68.

Employment Prospects

As every television production requires certain sound personnel, including Boom Operators, employment opportunities are fair to good. However, often television industry jobs (like the film business) last only as long as the production takes to complete its shoot. Boom Operators are hired for each production (or series, or film), not by the station. So job security consists of constantly looking for the next assignment.

Advancement Prospects

The next step up the advancement ladder for most Boom Operators is to become a production sound mixer. Prospects for such advancement are only fair, as the competition is very stiff and the job openings not frequent. However, once such advancement is accomplished, Boom Operators can look to become eventually a sound effects coordinator or a sound editor.

Education and Training

A high school diploma is a requirement. A college degree in film or television production or a diploma from a film school is recommended but not required. However, some training in sound technology is a necessity, and a college degree in sound engineering may be helpful.

Experience, Skills, and Personality Traits

Boom operating is a physically demanding job. Individuals have to be in good shape to move heavy equipment and be able to hold a boom with a microphone for extended periods of time. They have to be extremely alert and able to memorize dialogue quickly. They must remain calm under pressure and be able to get along with a wide variety of individuals. They need strong audio skills and a detailed and clear understanding of the dynamics of sound.

Many Boom Operators start out in the sound department as cablers, setting up the sound equipment, running the cable from the mikes to the sound recording hardware, and assisting in the placing of mikes on performers. At times, experienced cablers may be called on to handle a second boom and with that experience fill in for a Boom Operator who needs to leave the set.

Unions and Associations

Membership in the production sound local of the IATSE will help guarantee wages and otherwise be beneficial to Boom Operators. Other industry associations, such as the International Association of Audio/Video Communicators, may be helpful for networking.

Tips for Entry

1. Work for a sound equipment rental house to learn about sound gear and meet production sound mixers and their crew.
2. Look for nonunion, low-budget productions where you can work for free to gain experience using sound equipment.
3. Practice moving a boom by using a fishing pole in your home, moving through doorways and around furniture and chandeliers. When working as part of a sound crew, practice moving a boom during lunch periods.

FOLEY ARTIST

CAREER PROFILE

Duties: Create natural background sounds to be synchronized with recorded dialogue for a television production

Alternate Title(s): None

Salary Range: $1,575 to $2,025 weekly minimum

Employment Prospects: Good

Advancement Prospects: Fair

Prerequisites:

Education and Training—High school diploma required; formal training in sound technology helpful, but not required

Experience—Work as a television or film sound assistant or for a sound equipment rental company

Special Skills and Personality Traits—All-encompassing knowledge and sensibility about sound; creativity; detail oriented; good hand-eye coordination; imaginative; keen ear for sounds and how to create them; sense of timing

CAREER LADDER

```
┌─────────────────────────────────────┐
│ Foley Editor; Production Sound Mixer;│
│      Sound Effects Coordinator       │
└─────────────────────────────────────┘

┌─────────────────────────────────────┐
│            Foley Artist              │
└─────────────────────────────────────┘

┌─────────────────────────────────────┐
│           Sound Assistant            │
└─────────────────────────────────────┘
```

Position Description

A foley is defined as any sound created by the body movement of a human performer, which is recreated as a sound effect and recorded in a studio (while the already shot television production runs). This recorded sound is then synchronized into the completed soundtrack during the postproduction phase of a television production. These specific types of sound effects are named after the late Jack Foley, the inventor of this process of custom-designing sound effects in a specially equipped sound studio, known as a foley studio.

A Foley Artist is the individual who specializes in creating these ordinary sound effects, such as footsteps, the swishing noise of a person slamming a door, clothes rustling, glasses clinking, and so forth. The Foley Artist recreates these human sounds to match the action on the recorded television project. For example, for a chase scene on foot, a Foley Artist will watch the scene and recreate, with believable sounds such as footsteps and panting, the actions of the performers on screen. This is done because during taping of the production, much of the background sound is not recorded loudly enough, since the boom mikes

and other microphones are aimed at capturing the clearest dialogue from the performers. This re-creation is done in a soundproofed foley studio on what is called a foley stage, which is equipped with assorted types of sound effects producing materials, gizmos, and a screen for watching the sections of the production requiring additional sounds.

The person in charge of the Foley Artist team is called the foley editor. This individual screens the recorded production and then directs members of the team to act out physically the sounds. A large portion of the floor of a foley stage is divided into a number of different surfaces (called pits)—concrete, gravel, dirt, and so forth—to allow the Foley Artists to do all types of footsteps using different kinds of shoes as seen in the recorded production. Surrounding the stage are hundreds of objects that Foley Artists employ to create every sound imaginable, from the jingling of keys to a bone-crunching punch to a romantic kiss to a body falling down a flight of stairs. The process of simulating these sounds is called "walking the foley." Understandably, Foley Artist crew members who make the sounds are called "walkers," since many of the sounds they make replicate sounds of feet walking on a variety of surfaces. For a musical, the sound of taps in a dancing number will be recreated by dancers on the stage as they watch the dancers move on the screen.

While much of the world of sound effects now has been computerized, foley is still one area where the sounds are produced by real people. It is still faster and cheaper for Foley Artists to watch performers on the screen and follow their motions on the foley stage, recreating the necessary background sounds. For another thing, human movements are irregular and hard to program. The best way to imitate a person's movements is to use another human being.

Salaries

A good Foley Artist can earn from $35 to $45 an hour ($315 to $405 daily), and up to $70,000 or more in a good year of steady work. Income depends on experience, frequency of employment, reputation, and, of course, the budget restrictions of the television production on which the Foley Artist works.

Employment Prospects

Foley Artists are an essential part of the postproduction process for most major television productions, series (and miniseries), made-for-TV films, and other large productions. Thus, prospects for employment are good.

Advancement Prospects

The chance of advancement for a Foley Artist to become head of the foley team as foley editor is only fair, as the competition is quite strong. Likewise, further advancement to higher positions of greater responsibility in the sound department, such as production sound mixer or sound effects coordinator, is also difficult due to the competition and the fact that openings do not occur often.

Education and Training

A high school diploma is an expected requirement, and some formal study of television production techniques and sound technology can be beneficial. Musical training may also prove useful as well as some hands-on experience with sound equipment. However, most training for this post occurs on the job.

Experience, Skills, and Personality Traits

Any experience gained by working on a sound stage in any capacity or assisting senior members of the sound department is valuable background. Foley Artists need to study the way people move in order to create a real-life auditory experience for the audience. They have to be able to create natural or unusual sounds from everyday objects. The talent of Foley Artists is the ability to distinguish between what something looks like and what it sounds like and to use this knowledge to recreate the required sound. They also have to be able to follow directions quickly, and their audio skills must be sharply tuned.

Unions and Associations

Membership in the Sound Technicians (Postproduction) Local 700 of the International Alliance of Theatrical Stage Employees (IATSE) will help guarantee wages and may prove beneficial for job protection and networking.

Tips for Entry

1. While in school, work as an intern on a sound stage or get part-time work at a sound equipment rental house.
2. Become conscious of the way you sound as you move, how your clothes rustle, and how your footsteps sound and imagine how (and with what objects) you would re-create these sounds.
3. Start as a "walker" (a person who makes the sound of walking) on a postproduction sound crew.

MUSIC EDITOR

CAREER PROFILE

Duties: With the composer, prepare the dramatic underscore for a television production; edit and assist in the final synchronization of all music elements prior to the final mix of the soundtrack

Alternate Title(s): Music Mixer

Salary Range: $1,700 to $1,900 weekly minimum

Employment Prospects: Fair to good

Advancement Prospects: Fair

Prerequisites:

Education and Training—High school degree required; music education courses recommended; college degree in music not required, but a bonus

Experience—Work as a composer or a songwriter; post-production editing experience

Special Skills and Personality Traits—Background in classical music; familiarity with music-editing equipment; good people skills; self-motivated and able to work on a very tight schedule

CAREER LADDER

```
┌─────────────────────────────────────────┐
│ Production Sound Mixer; Sound Editor;    │
│        Composer/Songwriter               │
└─────────────────────────────────────────┘

┌─────────────────────────────────────────┐
│              Music Editor                │
└─────────────────────────────────────────┘

┌─────────────────────────────────────────┐
│               Musician                   │
└─────────────────────────────────────────┘
```

Position Description

The Music Editor works with the composer in the preparation of the score used for a television production. This score is the background music used to underscore the action of the production. In addition, there may be "source" music indicated as part of the story, such as music that may come from a radio, a record or CD player, or a live performance by musicians during the production. There may also be songs used as source material in the script, as part of the background score, or for the underscoring of opening and end titles.

Music Editors coordinate the technical aspects of the scoring between the production company and the composer. Usually working with the music director or supervisor, they provide the composer with the timings of the various sections of the production where source music will be needed to punctuate the narrative. These timings (or timecode positions) are made during a spotting session (similar to that used for spotting sounds that need to be added to the final production) of the entire filmed production. During these sessions, the director indicates where music will be needed to underscore the action. Music Editors take extensive notes

during these sessions and then work as the composer's aide to ensure that all the music that he or she writes will work perfectly with the cues indicated by the director.

In this process, the Music Editor, working with the composer, prepares the music timing notes, makes sure correct copies of the production are made for the composer and for the music recording, and assists in all preparations of the recording. Music Editors attend and assist in all the recording sessions and finally edit the recorded music cues for the final mix of the soundtrack of the television production.

During these recording sessions, the Music Editor must keep extensive notes on each selected take and keep timings for each cue as well as a record of how much material has been covered in each session and a record of anything that will need to be overdubbed (such as a vocal track or a solo). During the following music premix session, the Music Editor and the sound engineer mix the score. Then the Music Editor goes to the rerecording stage and supervises the process of fitting the music to each scene. The editor may ask for certain instruments to be mixed or dropped in a specific section of the soundtrack (for example, if speech audibility becomes a problem over the use of French horns in the orchestration). During this premix of just the music part of the soundtrack, the Music Editor has to lay up the music against the correct timecode positions of the production and may have to recut the music for any subsequent changes in the filmed production in order to preserve the composer's original intentions. Depending on the size and length of the television production, this rerecording process can take from three days to three or four weeks. From there, the music soundtrack goes to the final mixing process.

In the final sound mixing, the separate audio elements (the ADR, foley, music, and special sound effects) are brought together into a combined format. It is a creative step that combines the separate sound and music processes and is guided by the production's story, characters, and concept. During this final mix, the Music Editor usually joins the sound editor/mixer (sometimes known as the headmixer) and the special effects coordinator/mixer. The Music Editor is present to correct or improve on any technical musical issues that may arise there and to raise or lower the music elements wherever the head mixer, who has the final say, wants modifications made on the balance and dynamics of the sound. Another responsibility of the Music Editor is to organize and edit source music tracks that are not written by the composer and assist in obtaining legal clearances for the use of this music by preparing music cue sheets, which are then given to the production company to pass on to personnel who handle performing rights.

It should be noted that there are various software programs that aim to automate music editing completely, as well as some that seek to do the organizational tasks related to the cueing and timing parameters of a live recording session. In addition, there are plug-in programs that enable the Music Editor to adjust the pitch and tempo of a piece of music or to perform noise reduction tasks automatically.

Salaries

Minimum salary rates for Music Editors are set by the International Alliance of Theatrical Stage Employees (IATSE) and average from $36.25 to $43.57 per hour (or from $290.03 to $348.58 for a day). If hired on a weekly basis (five days, or 48.6 hours), the union minimum wage for Music Editors is $1,744.17. Veteran Music Editors, of course, earn considerably more than the minimum rate.

Employment Prospects

Employment opportunities are fair to good. While Music Editors are used on most medium- to large-scale television projects (and most film productions), some smaller productions may have the sound editor or the supervising sound coordinator fill in as Music Editor. In any case, competition for the position of Music Editor remains strong. For musical individuals wanting to become Music Editors, the best way

to start is to work on low-budget and no-budget TV offerings (or films) to gain editing skills and network.

In addition, a Music Editor has to make an investment in material. As veteran Music Editor Jim Charbonneau states, "You have to essentially own a mini recording studio in order to be viable in the present film economy. No one wants to rent equipment for you, they want you to come fully equipped with state-of-the-art equipment and know how to operate it effectively."

Advancement Prospects

Music Editors who want to advance their careers in sound production look to become sound mixers or sound editors, thus broadening their experience and skills. Other Music Editors may want to emphasize their musical talents by becoming full-time (or part-time) composers and/or songwriters.

Education and Training

A musical background is critical for this position. Musical abilities as a practicing musician, accompanied by courses in music theory, history, and so forth, are vital. A college degree in music is a plus. In addition, some training in television, most likely as a production assistant, is beneficial. Working as an apprentice to an established Music Editor provides editing experience and establishes that expertise.

Experience, Skills, and Personality Traits

The position of Music Editor is not entry level. Music Editors must have musicality, skill in using music editing equipment, and knowledge of state-of-the-art computer editing programs. They have to be highly self-motivated and be able to work within tight production timeframes. They need to be diplomatic and be willing to listen carefully to coworkers. They need to be efficient, punctual, and well organized and be equipped to fulfill the task as laid out for them by the director and the composer.

Unions and Associations

Music Editors, like most postproduction sound personnel, generally belong to Local 700 of the IATSE for salary and job security.

Tips for Entry

1. Take educational courses in music to add to your skills as a musician.
2. Be willing to work on low-budget productions (or become an apprentice to an established Music Editor) to become familiar with music editing equipment and gain necessary music editing skills.
3. Become acquainted with software programs that may aid you in your music editing.

PRODUCTION SOUND MIXER

CAREER PROFILE

Duties: Supervise the on-set sound department; record and mix sounds captured during a television production

Alternate Title(s): Floor Mixer; Recording Supervisor; Sound Mixer

Salary Range: $26,000 to $90,000

Employment Prospects: Fair to Good

Advancement Prospects: Poor

Prerequisites:

Education and Training—A broad liberal arts, music, and television (or film) background recommended; formal training with sound and recording equipment

Experience—Work in a variety of electronics and sound areas, including mixing, recording, and editing

Special Skills and Personality Traits—Able to work as a team member; all-inclusive knowledge about sound and how sound affects emotions; creativity; excellent people skills; musical; patient; strong electronics background

CAREER LADDER

| Sound Editor |

| Production Sound Mixer |

| Boom Operator; Sound Engineer |

Position Description

As chief sound engineer on a television set, the Production Sound Mixer is the head of the on-set sound department and hires and supervises the production sound crew. This squad will include one or more boom operators, cable personnel (to run the cable to the mikes and place mikes on performers), a soundman or recordist (who operates the recording equipment on the set), and occasionally a playback operator (when music or dancing is involved in the shot). Production Sound Mixers are also responsible for obtaining and maintaining all sound recording and mixing equipment employed in the production.

The other chief duty of Production Sound Mixers is to monitor the recording of dialogue and ambient sound during the production. They must guarantee the best quality of all sound recorded during the production and a correct mix of the diverse sounds into the production's overall soundtrack. Recording clean production sound is the top priority of the production sound department.

Production Sound Mixers are usually hired by the director and start their work in preproduction. After reading the script of the television project, they determine what microphones, sound, and recording equipment will be required to best capture the sound for each part of the production. They often meet with postproduction staff to get technical sound information for the mixing phase, which may impact how the sound should be recorded originally on the set. Production Sound Mixers maintain microphone levels throughout the production to ensure that the performers' dialogue is even and clearly heard. If a voice is too soft, muffled, or mushy, the mixer alerts the director, who then decides whether a retake of the scene is necessary. The Production Sound Mixer oversees the setting up of all sound equipment, microphones, booms, and cables. Next, this individual cues tape in the recording gear to capture speech and intended background noise in the best way possible. Working with the director, the mixer passes along any instructions that pertain to sound, such as asking performers to speak louder or softer or to change the angle of a microphone to improve clarity. During breaks, the Production Sound Mixer records something called "room tone," which is the natural way a room or location sounds when no one is talking and there are no background noises. Even in such silence, different places have different sounds, so these sounds are captured to obtain a standard in case any dialogue must be recorded (or "looped") afterwards. In addition, at the end of a shot (or at the end of the day), the mixer may request "wild lines," which are dialogue lines recorded without rolling the camera. They are to ensure, in case a line is lost during a scene, that there is a replacement on tape.

Throughout this process, the mixer directs and monitors the boom operator and makes sure that the boom mike and any other recording devices are not caught on camera. As the boom mike usually has to be as close to the performers as possible, this task is not an easy one. There are factors other than just sound, as well, such as how the shot is being set up, where the sound equipment will cast shadows on the set, and whether it is a close-up or a farther-distanced establishing shot, which requires the boom to be farther back. In addition, Production Sound Mixers adjust sound levels and keep track of the sound recorded on each take so that it can be synchronized to the footage. Also during the production, they monitor the activities of the cable crew and the placement of cables and wires.

Salaries

Minimum salary rates for Production Sound Mixers are set by the International Alliance of Theatrical Stage Employees (IATSE) and average $53.66 per hour (or $482.94 a day). Veteran Production Sound Mixers earn considerably more than the minimum, averaging from a low of $26,000 annually to a high of $90,000 or more.

Employment Prospects

Employment opportunities are fair to good. While a Production Sound Mixer is needed on every television production, the competition for jobs is heavy. For individuals wanting to get into the sound field, the best way to start is to offer to work for free for an established mixer. Then move on to work for another mixer and look for assistant posts. As veteran Production Sound Mixer Tim Cooney points out, "You have to do a few nonpaying jobs first in order to get some kind of credit, some validity. Eventually somebody is going to give you a break. Once you get enough hours, you can join the union."

Advancement Prospects

Advancement prospects are somewhat poor, as the position of Production Sound Mixer is both a technical job and a supervisory one. Some Sound Mixers may look to become sound editors. However, the need for high-quality sound is crucial to television productions, and experienced sound

mixers may further their careers by moving to major television productions or to films.

Education and Training

A college education in the liberal arts and television is recommended. Formal training in sound technology is important. A background in electronics will aid in becoming proficient in all aspects of the recording equipment used for television productions.

Experience, Skills, and Personality Traits

Gaining experience as a boom operator apprentice and/or cabler is a good way to acquire the necessary knowledge about recording equipment. Most Production Sound Mixers start as boom operators, considered one of the hardest jobs during production. Boom operators have to be aware of much more than just the sound. How the lighting is set, what type of shot is being taken, and how it is being set up are all key factors that a boom operator must take into account, which makes excellent training for a sound mixer.

Production Sound Mixers must have strong audio skills and an all-encompassing understanding of the dynamics of sound, very similar to the proficiency of a musician. Production Sound Mixers must be ready to follow the director's lead and work within and around the particular circumstances of each shot. They need to be both patient and creative and must have excellent people skills.

Unions and Associations

Membership in the Production Sound Technicians, Local 695, of the IATSE helps to guarantee wages and provides other job support. Other industry associations, such as the International Association of Audio/Video Communicators, may also be beneficial for networking purposes.

Tips for Entry

1. Be willing to work for free for any Production Sound Mixer to gain experience and make contacts.
2. Work as an apprentice to a cabler or a boom operator to get some credit and begin to build hours toward your application to join the union.
3. Make contact with everyone on the set with whom you work (not just the sound personnel) and remember their names and on which production you both worked, as it is personal contacts that aid advancement.

SOUND EDITOR

CAREER PROFILE

Duties: Assemble and synchronize ordinary and special sound effects during postproduction and assist in creating the finished soundtrack of a television production

Alternate Title(s): Sound Mixer; Sound Effects Mixer

Salary Range: $1,200 to $1,850 weekly minimum

Employment Prospects: Good

Advancement Prospects: Fair

Prerequisites:

Education and Training—High school diploma necessary; computer literacy essential; film school recommended, but not required

Experience—Work as an apprentice sound editor and/or a television production assistant

Special Skills and Personality Traits—Basic understanding of rhythm and pitch of speech and sounds; creativity; familiarity with digital audio workstations (DAWS) and mixing consoles; strong audio sense for sounds and dialogue; working knowledge of how sounds function as part of an overall scene

CAREER LADDER

```
┌─────────────────────────────────┐
│   Postproduction Supervisor;    │
│    Supervising Sound Editor     │
└─────────────────────────────────┘

┌─────────────────────────────────┐
│          Sound Editor           │
└─────────────────────────────────┘

┌─────────────────────────────────┐
│    Apprentice Sound Editor;     │
│      Production Assistant       │
└─────────────────────────────────┘
```

Position Description

Before Sound Editors start to work on the sound editing of a television (or film) production, a "spotting session" is held with the director. Depending on the size and complexity of the production, this can be anything from a brief chat about the general style of the production to a lengthy and detailed discussion of all aspects of the soundtrack. On most larger projects, Sound Editors specifically designated to handle dialogue or sound effects (fx editors) are asked to attend the session so they can be briefed on a scene-by-scene basis regarding the director's requirements and offer their own suggestions. Detailed notes are taken in this session with timecode references on all sounds that will be required (such as fx and foley sounds, required ADR for revoicing or any change in performance on the filmed track, voice-over requirements, crowd noises, and where music must predominate the soundtrack).

On most medium-sized and large television projects, one Sound Editor is assigned to supervise a team of Sound Editors specializing in particular areas, such as a dialogue editor, an editor in charge of automatic dialogue replacement, a foley editor, and a special sound effects editor. Besides overseeing the work of these editors, the supervising Sound Editor also superintends any needed looping sessions (where actors or special voice-over artists, while watching footage, respeak or re sing words or lyrics that need to be improved or changed) and any other audio special effects needed. It is this supervising Sound Editor who coordinates with the music editor in joining the sounds with the music for the final mixing.

The primary aim in preparing the soundtrack for final mixing is to edit the sound in such a way that any particular scene is perceived by the future audience to be the full-spectrum audio they would hear in reality. Sound Editors must use audio editing techniques to make each filmed shot transition inaudible to the ear, covering over the fact that each scene actually includes various discontinuous audio sources.

Previous to the introduction of computer technology, the traditional method of placing recorded sounds in sync with filmed pictures was by cutting a recording on perforated magnetic stock and placing it with sticky tape onto a roll of perforated spacing the same length as the picture material. When the sound and picture rolls were locked and run together, the sound would be played back at the exact frame on which it was placed in alignment with the picture. This was known as linear editing. It is still used in a limited way in low-budget television work as well as corporate video, TV promos, and some televised news operations, where a fast turnaround can be achieved by editing tapes straight from the camera.

However, today most sound editing is almost entirely digital. All sound source material is logged and then digitized into a digital audio workstation (DAW). This is essentially a computer-controlled system that can record, edit, process, and play back audio in sync with the picture. Most DAWs now offer fully automated on-board sound mixing, enabling the digital editing (in a single computer environment) of an entire project. Needless to say, this new technology has changed the requirements and specifics of sound editing.

Audio postproduction is completed with the mixing of separate soundtracks that have been prepared on the DAW. Some of these tracks may have already been mixed by an editor, depending on how much time was allotted to the production and the expertise of the Sound Editor in charge of the track. Some productions may employ sound mixers separate from Sound Editors, but that distinction is blurring as the mixing equipment becomes more versatile by incorporating edit functions. The separate soundtracks are combined into a single soundtrack.

Technically, the most important part of audio postproduction is to produce as fine as possible a match of the sound to the visuals, so that the sound appears to come from the pictures. Creatively, audio postproduction is concerned with mixing the various soundtracks together to produce a cohesive, pleasing whole that complements the visual images of the production and satisfies the director's wishes.

Salaries

Minimum salary rates for the various Sound Editors are set by the International Alliance of Theatrical Stage Employees (IATSE). For special effects editors, salaries range from a beginning weekly salary of $1,288.52 to $1,419.34 for experienced editors with a year of work behind them. For Sound Editors generally, the minimum weekly salary ranges from $1,512.29 to $1,744.17. For supervising Sound Editors, the minimum weekly salary is $1,850.35

Employment Prospects

Every television production, small, medium, or large, needs sound technicians, both during production and postproduction. For this reason, job prospects for sound technicians of

all sorts, including Sound Editors, are good, especially with the tremendous growth in the television industry as seen over the last several years.

Advancement Prospects

Advancement to a supervisory position in postproduction may be difficult, as there are many Sound Editors but few supervisory positions, either in the area of sound editing or in the overall management of postproduction. Competition, therefore, is stiff.

Education and Training

While only a high school diploma is required, training in a film program at college or obtaining a degree from a good cinema/TV school is extremely helpful. Knowledge of various sound editing systems and the new digital technology used in postproduction are valuable in gaining a position with an audio team.

Experience, Skills, and Personality Traits

A thorough knowledge of computers, audio mixing consoles, digital audio workstations, audio recording techniques, theory of sound, and concepts of analog and digital audio technology are all important skills for Sound Editors. A familiarity with film history, a musical background, and a working knowledge of the television industry and techniques used in shooting television productions are also helpful.

Sound Editors have to be good listeners, well organized, and creative, but a team player, as they have to follow what the director wants for the television production. As a supervising Sound Editor, they have to be firm in their leadership and be very detail oriented. It is an intense job, and Sound Editors have to be willing to put in the time required to complete their work for each production.

Unions and Associations

Membership in the Sound Technicians Local, Local 700, of the IATSE is a basic requirement to gain work on most television productions. Other industry associations related to television production may be helpful for networking.

Tips for Entry

1. While in school or college, work for a local television station as a production assistant to gain industry experience.
2. Consider working in a music or sound studio to acquire experience in the techniques of sound recording.
3. Take any job you can find on a postproduction sound crew to learn about sound editing and establish relationships with experienced crew members.

SOUND EFFECTS COORDINATOR

CAREER PROFILE

Duties: Provide and edit sound effects for a television production

Alternate Title(s): Sound Effects Designer; Sound Effects Editor; Sound Effects Mixer

Salary Range: $1,288 to $1,744 weekly minimum

Employment Prospects: Good

Advancement Prospects: Fair to Good

Prerequisites:

Education and Training—High school diploma required; some formal training in sound technology and television production recommended

Experience—Work as a sound assistant or for a sound equipment rental company

Special Skills and Personality Traits—Creativity; detail-oriented; good people skills; patience; thorough knowledge of sound technology and equipment

CAREER LADDER

```
┌─────────────────────────────────────────┐
│  Production Sound Mixer; Sound Editor    │
└─────────────────────────────────────────┘

┌─────────────────────────────────────────┐
│       Sound Effects Coordinator          │
└─────────────────────────────────────────┘

┌─────────────────────────────────────────┐
│  Production Assistant; Sound Technician   │
└─────────────────────────────────────────┘
```

Position Description

Most people watching television programs do not realize that virtually every background sound they hear on the show was added *after* the scene was shot. Sound effects provide the sense of reality that an audience expects. Good sound effects can entice, forewarn, lead, or shock viewers. They give the sensibilities of audio reality that give dimension to the flat image seen on the television set. Sounds can bring viewers into the action rather than letting them watch it at a safe distance. They are an essential part of the storytelling.

Basically, sound effects are divided into two different kinds: foley effects and regular (or not so regular) sound effects. Foley is any sound created by the movement of a performer (rustle of clothing, footsteps, and so forth). These sounds are created and mixed by foley artists and editors. Other sounds (such as airplane engines, wind in the trees, car tires screeching, and so forth) are added to a soundtrack by the Sound Effects Coordinator (also called a sound effects designer or sound effects editor) during the postproduction phase of the television production.

Most Sound Effects Coordinators work for postproduction sound companies (often called post houses). These firms have vast storehouses of recorded sounds used to

enhance the sound effects tracks for both film and television. Some of the larger companies ("houses") have computer networks that link several sound studios to a central server loaded with thousands or even hundreds of thousands of distinct sounds. In addition to this digital creation of sounds, some sound effects can be originally recorded and then altered digitally if desired. Many Sound Effects Coordinators have their own unique specialties. While one might be particularly creative with mechanical sounds, another may specialize in explosions.

Sound Effects Coordinators view the television production—along with the director, sound editor, and, sometimes, the film editor and the ADR supervisor—to gain an overview of what will be needed for the soundtrack This process is called a "spotting session" because this team spots where all sound (excluding music) will eventually go in the final sound mix for the production. Sound Effects Coordinators' expertise allows them to hear variations of sounds and subtleties of texture that will heighten the feel and concept of the production. Their creativity is the foundation for good sound.

The soundtrack for television projects is different from a soundtrack for theatrical films. It is usually smaller in scope, has to be created with a smaller budget, and usually does not require hundreds of postproduction sound specialists. Nonetheless, modern television productions still may have thousands of discrete sound effects that need to be provided, especially now that computers in sound studios make these tasks so much easier. The industry standard is a software program called Pro Tools, made by Digidesign. Pro Tools allows a Sound Effects Coordinator to capture sound digitally and then move the elements around as easily as a writer uses a word processor. All Sound Effects Coordinators need to know how to sync up the sound and edit cues into scenes, but the more experienced of them can elevate the cue and give it and the scene a special spark. Sound Effects Coordinators also have to take the room tone (the level at which the room reflects sound) in which the scene was recorded and then add that to the effects track to balance out the dialogue and provide a credible presence for the sound.

Sound Effects Coordinators are generally hired by either the director or the production sound mixer. They may come attached to a contract that the director or producer has made with specific postproduction sound houses.

Salaries
Minimum earnings for Sound Effects Coordinators (usually styled as editors) are set by Local 700 of the International Alliance of Theatrical Stage Employees (IATSE) and are based on an escalating scale dependent on how long the individual has worked as a sound effects editor. For beginners (during the first six months), the daily minimum is $28.74, and the weekly (five days, 43.2 hours) minimum is $1,288.52. For experienced sound effects editors, the daily hourly minimum can reach as high as $35.90, and the weekly minimum up to $1,744.17. It is not unusual for experienced Sound Effects Coordinators to earn yearly salaries from $60,000 to $100,000 or more.

Employment Prospects
Sound effects are a vital component of all television productions except live productions. Even in live productions some sound editing processes may be required. Thus, the need for Sound Effects Coordinators is always present, making employment prospects for experienced individuals very good.

Advancement Prospects
The production of sound effects is a very specialized field. Many Sound Effects Coordinators may feel they have reached the apex of their career with their full-time position with a sound effects company. Some, however, may want to become sound editors for television productions who, generally, are in charge of the postproduction of a television program's sound. Another career advancement may be made to that of a production sound mixer, in charge of the specific mixing of sounds for the soundtrack of television productions.

Education and Training
A high school diploma is an expected requirement, as well as some formal study of television production techniques and sound technology. As this job is a highly specialized sound position, experience with sound recording techniques and sound equipment is an absolute requirement. A position as a sound assistant in a sound effects company may be the best training for this job. In addition, a thorough familiarity with the latest computer technology and software is an important asset for this position.

Experience, Skills, and Personality Traits
Any experience gained by working on a sound stage, assisting senior members of the sound department, or working as a sound assistant in a sound effects company is valuable background. Special Effects Coordinators have to be able to create natural or unusual sounds from all kinds of everyday objects. They need to be able to distinguish what something looks like and what it sounds like. They must gain an expertise that allows them to hear variations of sounds and subtleties of texture that can be translated into sounds to be used in a soundtrack. Their creativity in this respect is the basis of good sound.

The audio skills of Special Effects Coordinators have to be highly trained, and they need to be (or become) familiar with computerized digital methods of creating sounds. They need to be extremely patient and also able to work under considerable amounts of pressure. Sound is the last thing added to a television production, and extra time in the schedule has usually been eaten up by other steps of the production processes. It is not unusual for sound effects studios to have only a few weeks to complete their work.

Unions and Associations
Sound Effects Coordinators, like most postproduction sound personnel, generally belong to Local 700 of the IATSE for salary and job security. Other industry associations, such as the International Association of Audio/Video Communicators, may also be beneficial for networking purposes.

Tips for Entry
1. While in high school (or during your additional television production education), look for internships at local television stations to gain firsthand experience in the production process.
2. Work on your computer skills, as they will be necessary for a job in sound effects.
3. Be willing to accept any low-paid (or nonsalaried) position at a sound effects company to gain necessary experience, knowledge, and contacts.

SOUND RECORDIST

CAREER PROFILE

Duties: Operate the sound recording equipment on a television production

Alternate Title(s): Production Sound Mixer; Production Soundperson; Recordist; Sound Technician; Soundperson

Salary Range: $285 to $327 daily minimum

Employment Prospects: Fair to Good

Advancement Prospects: Fair

Prerequisites:

Education and Training—High school diploma; formal training in sound equipment and technology usually required

Experience—Work as a television production assistant or for a sound equipment rental company

Special Skills and Personality Traits—Able to work well as a team member of the sound crew; familiarity with sound equipment and technology; thorough knowledge of television production

CAREER LADDER

```
┌─────────────────────────────────────────┐
│ Production Sound Mixer; Sound Editor;    │
│ Sound Effects Coordinator                │
└─────────────────────────────────────────┘

┌─────────────────────────────────────────┐
│            Sound Recordist               │
└─────────────────────────────────────────┘

┌─────────────────────────────────────────┐
│ Production Assistant; Sound Technician   │
└─────────────────────────────────────────┘
```

Position Description

A Sound Recordist operates the recording equipment during the shoot of a television production. In some instances, particularly for smaller-budget programs, the production sound mixer operates the recording equipment instead of a Sound Recordist. The Sound Recordist works during the recording of the show and should not be confused with the individual, sometimes called a postproduction soundperson, who works in postproduction and mixes all the soundtracks when the program is edited.

Good sound on the set is important, and high-quality sound is one of the real achievements of modern television and film production. Most television shows are broadcast in stereo and/or digital sound, and in general the viewing public has become quite sophisticated in its understanding and appreciation of high-quality sound.

However, many television (and film) production people view sound as something that can be added, changed, and fooled around with in the postproduction process, after the initial shooting is done. While this is true, the process takes both time and capital. The procedures of putting a television production soundtrack together in postproduction can be made much easier by giving the Sound Recordist on the production the chance to record dialogue clearly on the set.

The sound crew in general and the Sound Recordist in particular have one basic mission: record the dialogue as faithfully as possible. The more dialogue that is recorded cleanly, the less time and money will be spent recreating the soundtrack in postproduction. In capturing the dialogue, Sound Recordists use a variety of microphones to pick up as much of the dialogue as possible and as cleanly as possible. These microphones are positioned by the Sound Recordist or boom operator on the set under the direction of the production sound mixer. The Sound Recordist also has to ensure that the right type of low-impedance cables are employed in the recording process to eliminate unwanted extraneous electronic noise.

In some situations, directors prefer to use wireless microphones, giving them creative mobility to stage the performers. However, all Sound Recordists need to be aware of the effects of using such mics on some clothing, as some material, such as taffeta and leather, creates a lot of extraneous noise, which will be picked up by the wireless microphone. In today's sound world in both television and film, digital recording has become the standard, replacing analog recording. Besides its greater speed in the recording process, digital recording is less susceptible to interference noise.

Sound Recordists, along with other members of the sound crew, are generally hired by the production sound mixer. On smaller television productions (or lower-budget projects), the actual recording may be done by the production sound mixer instead.

Salaries

Hourly and daily minimum wages for Sound Recordists (frequently called under the generic title of utility sound technicians or service recorder engineers) are set by Local 695 of the International Alliance of Theatrical Stage Employees (IATSE). For entry-level positions, the hourly pay is $31.72, and the daily wage is $285.48. For practiced sound technicians (journeypersons), the hourly pay is $36.36, and the daily wage is $327.24. Union minimum wage standards also cover overtime situations and on-location shooting.

Employment Prospects

As every television production needs certain sound personnel, including Sound Recordists, employment opportunities are fair to good. However, television industry jobs last only as long as the time needed to complete the production. Sound Recordists are hired for each individual project or series, not as regular staff at the station or network. Thus, job security for most members of the sound crew (including Sound Recordists) consists of constantly looking for the next job.

Advancement Prospects

Sound Recordists can look for advancement to the position of production sound mixer. Prospects for such career progress are only fair, as the competition is strong and job openings infrequent. However, once accomplished, this post can lead to that of a sound editor or a sound effects coordinator and even eventually a director, if that is their inclination. As with so much else in television, meeting and working with people and following up with them can bring both new jobs and potential advancement.

Education and Training

A high school diploma is a basic requirement. A college degree in film or television production or a diploma from a film school might be helpful. However, some formal training in sound technology is an absolute necessity, and a college degree in sound engineering might also be useful.

Experience, Skills, and Personality Traits

Sound recording is a painstaking and demanding job. Individuals have to be extremely patient and be prepared to move heavy equipment. They have to be very alert, able to take directions, and remain calm under pressure. They must be able to get along with a wide variety of individuals. Above all, they need strong audio skills and a detailed and clear understanding of the dynamics of sound.

Many Sound Recordists start out as production assistants or, in the sound department, as cablers, setting up the sound equipment, running the cable from the mikes to the sound recording equipment, and assisting in the placing of mics on performers. Experience can lead cablers to the more responsible (and higher-paid) position of Sound Recordist.

Unions and Associations

Membership in the production sound Local 695 of the IATSE helps guarantee at least minimum wages and can otherwise be beneficial to Sound Recordists. Other industry associations, such as the International Association of Audio/Video Communicators, may be helpful for networking.

Tips for Entry

1. Work in a sound equipment rental house to learn about sound recording devices, in particular DAT (digital) recording gear, and meet professional sound crew members.
2. Look for nonunion, low-budget productions where you can work for free to gain experience using sound equipment.
3. Be willing to work for free at first, as the name of the game is meeting people, letting them see how hard you can work, and using your connection with them to get hired.

SPECIAL EFFECTS AND VISUAL EFFECTS

SPECIAL EFFECTS SUPERVISOR

CAREER PROFILE

Duties: Oversee the creation and use of special physical effects on the set of a television production

Alternate Title(s): Special Effects Coordinator; FX Supervisor; Special Effects Unit Director; Special Effects Producer

Salary Range: $1,815 weekly minimum to $3,000 per week or more

Employment Prospects: Fair to Good

Advancement Prospects: Fair to Good

Prerequisites:

Education and Training—College degree with a major in film, graphic arts, photography, or television is recommended

Experience—Work as an apprentice in a special effects company, or work as a member of a special effects team for various television or film productions

Special Skills and Personality Traits—Able to visualize how to create special effects physically on a set; artistic sense; creativity; good communication skills; management skills

CAREER LADDER

```
┌─────────────────────────────────────┐
│  Visual Effects Supervisor; Unit    │
│  Production Manager; Producer        │
└─────────────────────────────────────┘

┌─────────────────────────────────────┐
│     Special Effects Supervisor      │
└─────────────────────────────────────┘

┌─────────────────────────────────────┐
│     Special Effects Assistant;      │
│     Physical Effects Designer       │
└─────────────────────────────────────┘
```

Position Description

When the script for a television production calls for action sequences too dangerous to allow an actor to perform, a creature that does not really exist, or physical activity of a specialized nature, the special effects team is called in. Such things as runaway vehicles, shootings and bullet strikes, and explosions are examples of physical effects—special effects that are staged during the shoot without the use of photographic tricks or computer manipulations (such as the addition of snow drifts to a scene already filmed). As veteran physical effects coordinator Jim Gill says, "We come in and build or fabricate custom equipment for the shoot. A physical effects person also deals with elemental effects such as wind and rain, and other offshoots like pyrotechnics—where we blow things up and create fire and things like that." Special physical effects also include the application of special makeup to satisfy the requirements of the script and the use of stunt persons to perform physical activity involved in special effects (such as crashing cars, explosions, and floods).

A typical special effects team is composed of designers and technicians who actually create and execute the special physical effects; special effects makeup artists who design and create the complex makeup; pyrotechnicians who are responsible for special effects involving fire or explosives; weapons specialists who provide, maintain, and oversee the use of real weaponry; and a Special Effects Supervisor who organizes, coordinates, and oversees the on-set physical effects.

The Special Effects Supervisor, along with the visual effects supervisor (who oversees the special visual illusions usually created during postproduction), are usually hired during the preproduction phase or before. The two effects supervisors work closely with the production's director and producer to decide what special effects and visual images will be needed. They do a script breakdown to estimate how much the required special effects will cost and also determine the methods to be employed to create the effects. The project's budget usually determines which methods are used to create the needed effects. If the budget is stretched too far by the cost of the effects, scenes may have to be eliminated or rewritten to avoid the need for the special effects.

During preproduction, the special effects team works with storyboards to decide how to create the requested visual images. (Some of these might lend themselves to miniature models, whereas others may have to be created by the visual effects team using computers during postproduction.) During the actual production, the Special Effects Supervisor and his or her team are on the set whenever the shooting of scenes requires a special effect, such as rain, snow, or an explosion.

As the television and film industries move more and more toward computer-generated visual effects, the demand for actual physical effects on the set also will change. In some ways, the use of computers and computer graphics has made the job of the on-set special effects team easier. For example, as Jim Gill, a professional special effects designer, notes, "We don't have to take a lot of pain to fly somebody with thin wires. We can slap a couple of big cables on them and fly across the room and let the wires be removed in post [via computer]." However, the increased reliance on computer graphics to supply required special effects will also lessen the number of jobs available for on-set special effects technicians.

Salaries

Salaries vary according to the production's special effects budget. Nonetheless, the average minimum weekly salary, as set by the Property Local 44 of the International Alliance of Theatrical Stage Employees (IATSE), is $1,815.26. Depending on the reputation and efficiency of the Special Effects Supervisor as well as the technicians under his or her supervision, yearly salaries can extend well into the six figures.

Employment Prospects

As special effects are used constantly in both dramatic and comedic television productions as well as made-for-television films, job prospects for special effects technicians and Special Effects Supervisors are relatively good. However, with the increased reliance on visual postproduction computerized and digitized effects, potential job offerings may lessen in the coming years.

Advancement Prospects

As the use of postproduction visual effects and computer-generated imagery (CGI) photography increases, some Special Effects Supervisors may want to add to their specialized knowledge such digital wizardry tricks and advance into a supervisory capacity within the postproduction process. Others may prefer to advance into the management areas of production or move on to become producers or directors in their own right.

Education and Training

An educational background provided by a film school is helpful but is seldom required. However, work in a special effects lab is necessary to provide practical experience in the creation of special effects. Some background and work in photography and a color darkroom also are helpful.

Experience, Skills, and Personality Traits

Special Effects Supervisors and their technicians need to be visually imaginative and technically astute in the development of the equipment and methods to be used in creating special effects on the set of television productions. They need to be good team players and be able to follow instructions from the director. They also need to be comfortable with working long hours and under considerable pressure.

Unions and Associations

Most special effects technicians and supervisors are members of Local 44, Affiliated Property Craftsmen, of the IATSE. Other industry associations may be helpful for networking.

Tips for Entry

1. Consider taking courses in photography and electronics and hydraulics engineering to prepare you to devise special physical effects.
2. Take a job with a special effects firm for hands-on experience.
3. Learn a variety of effects talents, primarily computer graphics skills, to expand your techniques into postproduction processes.

VISUAL EFFECTS SUPERVISOR

CAREER PROFILE

Duties: Supervise the creation of special visual illusions and effects used in a television production

Alternate Title(s): Visual Effects Producer; Visual Effects Coordinator

Salary Range: $1,900 to $2,500 weekly minimum

Employment Prospects: Good

Advancement Prospects: Fair to Good

Prerequisites:

Education and Training—College degree with a major in film, graphic arts, photography, or television recommended but not required

Experience—Apprentice work in a special effects company with emphasis on computer-generated imagery (CGI), photography, matte painting, and blue screen; training as a visual effects researcher

Special Skills and Personality Traits—Artistic; capable of visualizing things that may not be real and then creating them; knowledgeable about photography; well-organized

CAREER LADDER

Producer Positions

Visual Effects Supervisor

Visual Effects Editor; Visual Effects Researcher

Position Description

With the advances made in technology, particularly computerized and digital processes, the way major television projects are made has changed greatly. There is now a greater reliance on creating images on the computer that once either had to be filmed in a costly and untimely manner or could not even be done. Today nearly anything can be created through computer-generated imagery, or CGI, technology. Thus, frequently there is a distinction made between special effects as physical effects done on the set and special effects as visual effects added afterward during the postproduction phase or done in conjunction with physical effects accomplished on the set.

A visual effects team usually consists of a Visual Effects Supervisor, a visual effects producer (who oversees both the budget and the production schedule), a visual effects art director or designer (who designs the visual effects), a visual effects editor (who coordinates with the supervisor and the film editor of the project), and, if needed, an effects animator (who digitally enhances already shot special effects). The Visual Effects Supervisor is responsible for the design and implementation of those visual special effects that cannot be produced on a set due to practical, budgetary, or safety reasons. For example, if a script calls for two cars to avoid narrowly a head-on collision, it is both safer and less costly to shoot the two cars separately and then combine the footage using computer-generated effects to get the most action value per the script. Visual effects technicians are also responsible for correcting or adding to scenes already shot, such as removing unwanted guy wires (used to aid actors in leaping through the air) or telephone lines or adding more snow to a scene. Their motivation is the story and its characters, and their challenge is to make the visual effects invisible to the production's audience.

Visual Effects Supervisors along with special effects supervisors are generally present during the preproduction phase. They read the script and make notes about possible special effects and then meet with the director and/or the producer to discuss the director's vision for various effects. After deciding what effects will be needed (and whether they can be done more cost effectively on the set or must be added during postproduction), they work with the art director, cinematographer, production designer, stunt coordinator, makeup specialists, and film editor to discuss who will handle the various aspects of each special effect. As veteran Visual Effects Supervisor Al Magliochetti enumerates, "If it's a transformation, makeup effects can handle the altering of the person's body structure up to a certain point. After that, a digital effect might take over to blend, or morph, to the next stage of the makeup. In the case of stunts, the stunt people will outline what they can safely do. Let's say they are going to perform a high fall off a building, but need to be tethered by some type of safety wire. We will discuss the best angle to shoot from and what it will cost to remove the wire using visual effects."

Another example of visual imagery effects used in both film and television is called the bluescreen process. This consists of filming actors or model miniatures against a uniform, nonglossy, bright blue background and then replacing the blue background with a new background, such as an outdoor scene or outer space, by means of a special effects process involving color separation filters, mattes, and an optical printer. Parts of an actor's body can also be covered, or masked, with a blue-colored fabric and then replaced with another costume or to create the effect of an invisible person. Support structures can also be painted or covered if they are not supposed to be visible in the finished shot, such as a pole holding up a miniature spaceship. In television (most often in TV news and weather reports), this electronic process, called a chroma key process as opposed to the bluescreen process prevalent in films, has a person or object placed in front of or within a uniform, nonglossy blue or green background. Then, this background is eliminated electronically and replaced with a new still or moving image background. (Blue or green is used because neither color is found in any significant quantity in human skin tones and thus will not interfere with the depiction of natural skin tones on the television screen.)

When the decisions are made concerning special visual effects to be used, the Visual Effects Supervisor submits a budget that outlines the costs involved in each effect. In some cases, several special effects companies or individuals may bid on work, and it will be up to the supervisor and either the director or the producer to decide what is the most cost-effective way to go. Frequently, Visual Effects Supervisors work with storyboards to decide how to create a particular visual image. Once the production starts filming, Visual Effects Supervisors usually are on the set, assisting the director in shooting the elements for the visual effects. Being on the set, supervisors are able to correct any potential problems or continuity errors. At the same time, they take photographs, measurements, and notes to use when the effect is put together later. While prep work can be done at this stage, generally Visual Effects Supervisors have to wait until the filming of the production is locked down and a cut of the footage is available before the visual effects can be created.

An original negative of the filmed production is pulled and scanned to the specific lengths required to complete each shot of every scene that needs a special effect. Once the footage is scanned, it is loaded into a computer as a series of sequential files, each individual frame loaded as a separate photograph. Temporary shots are completed first to help ensure that the visual effect is proceeding in the manner that the director and/or producer envision. Any changes can be made more easily at this stage. When the temps have been approved, the computer completes the shot, the sequential files are then transferred to a data tape, and a new negative of the film is made, essentially a duplicate negative of the originally shot production with the newly created visual effects now in place.

Salaries

Salaries vary according to the visual effects used or budgeted. An average weekly salary for a Visual Effects Supervisor ranges from $1,900 to $2,100 or more. Most Visual Effects Supervisors work in both television and film and earn more working on big studio films, major television productions, or, more important, if they are well known and in demand. Some established supervisors might earn more than six figures on an annual basis.

Employment Prospects

Although many television series do not have the budget for extensive visual effects, their use is on the rise in the TV industry. Therefore, job opportunities for visual effects persons are relatively plentiful. Individuals with several years of experience in visual special effects have good chances of becoming a supervisor of a visual effects team.

Advancement Prospects

Advancing to the position of Visual Effects Supervisor is a natural step for many members of visual effects teams, but the competition is stiff. Experienced Visual Effects Supervisors might want to move into management positions, such as unit production manager or producer. Again, competition is stiff.

Education and Training

Being a film major in college is good background for special or visual effects, but any work in a special effects lab or company is extremely helpful. It is important to have training in the use of the latest computer-generated imagery technology. Training in animation and illustration are also helpful.

Experience, Skills, and Personality Traits

Visual Effects Supervisors need to know not only the latest computer technology but also the entire process of filmmaking and television production. Working in television is a very collaborative occupation, and visual effects people must be aware of other people's jobs. Additionally, knowing about the chemical structure of film—how it works and how it reacts to light—will aid them in making the effects look like they were shot on film. The work of a visual effects technician is to integrate the digital effect into the film seamlessly.

Visual Effects Supervisors need to be visually creative and technologically astute to be able to tell the stories that the script has ordained with images created from illusions. They need to be team players, ready to follow the instructions of the director, and they must be comfortable with working very long hours.

Unions and Associations

Most Visual Effects Supervisors as well as their fellow members of the team are affiliated with the International Alliance of Theatrical Stage Employees (IATSE). In addition, membership in such industry associations as the Academy of Science Fiction, Fantasy and Horror Films and Women in Film may be helpful for networking.

Tips for Entry

1. Become completely computer literate and attend film school, making and maintaining contacts.
2. Take a drawing class because such study will make you look at real life and see how a shadow falls and the effects of light on a curved surface or reflected light, skills needed to create visual illusions.
3. Learn filmmaking because it will tell you what you need to know about doing a visual effects supervising job.
4. Join a visual effects company (preferably a small one where the opportunities to learn are usually the greatest) as an apprentice to learn the trade.
5. Accept any position possible on a television production and try various jobs to learn the process of putting together a television project.

WRITING

SCRIPT SUPERVISOR

CAREER PROFILE

Duties: Maintain all details and continuity relating to the creative and technical elements of a television production

Alternate Title(s): Continuity Editor; Continuity Coordinator

Salary Range: $1,505 to $1,674 weekly minimum

Employment Prospects: Good

Advancement Prospects: Poor

Prerequisites:

Education and Training—High school diploma required; undergraduate degree in film or theatre arts helpful

Experience—One to two years of work as a production or technical assistant in television or film production. To join the union, you must work 30 days on a set and complete an introductory script supervisor course.

Special Skills and Personality Traits—Detail-oriented; highly organized; personable and able to work harmoniously with others; union membership often required

CAREER LADDER

```
┌─────────────────────────────────────┐
│   Production Manager; Director        │
└─────────────────────────────────────┘

┌─────────────────────────────────────┐
│         Script Supervisor             │
└─────────────────────────────────────┘

┌─────────────────────────────────────┐
│        Production Assistant;          │
│         Technical Assistant           │
└─────────────────────────────────────┘
```

Position Description

The Script Supervisor is a critical position in both the preproduction process and the actual shoot. The post is an extremely challenging one that requires working alongside the director and his or her key people.

The Script Supervisor has two main functions during preproduction. First, the supervisor "breaks down" the script to match scenes with each other for continuity purposes. The number of breakdowns will depend on how complicated the script story is. For most TV movies (and many series), there will always be an analysis to gain an accurate count of the number of days (and/or nights) that the script spans. Second, the Script Supervisor pretimes the sequences of the script to approximate how long each scene will run to ensure that the full running time of the show will not go beyond its allowed length. Both of these functions are accomplished in conjunction with the director before production begins.

During production, the Script Supervisor maintains a written "continuity log," which contains all the details relating to the consistency of the creative and technical elements that occur during the filming. This log is critical to the entire process and is given to the film editor after production. It reflects, through specific markings on the script, all the details that took place on each take of a shot. The Script Supervisor also notes the type of camera shot, the lens size, whether filters were used, the camera and sound roll numbers, and any comments that the director might have made regarding the shot (concerning whether the take was good or bad, noting any problems that occurred). A smart Script Supervisor also details any of the director's reactions to a shot, writing the comment in the margin of the log. These written comments are used during postproduction to remind the director of any creative comments made at the time of the shoot. As Script Supervisors are basically the "secretaries" of the production company, at the end of each day of shooting they need to gather information from various production departments and correlate it with the notations in the continuity log. All of this is extremely valuable to the postproduction phase.

This continuity log is filled also with notes on wardrobe used, hair and makeup, props, lighting, camera angles, and even what lines individual actors are speaking. In this way, the Script Supervisor keeps track of every element of every shot to ensure that nothing has been missed.

The most important aspect of script supervising is to preserve continuity, making the story line correlate from scene to scene, whether it concerns matching the words that are said, the temperament of the scene, or the actual actions taken during the scene. The director relies heavily on the Script Supervisor to maintain accuracy in the dialogue of the script, as well as the visual matching of movements and actor eye lines from shot to shot. If, for example, on various takes of the same scene, an actor turns to look over her left shoulder rather than her right, all sorts of problems may occur. All of these moves for each take have to be noted so that the film editor will know how to cut the scene and put it together properly. In addition, Script Supervisors may be required to keep a list of pickup shots (additional footage to be inserted into the scene) and any sounds or dialogue that will need to be added in postproduction. In addition to the log, and because it is almost impossible for Script Supervisors to write down everything that occurred during the shoot, they usually rely on still photographs taken during each scene with either a digital or Polaroid camera.

Salaries

If a Script Supervisor belongs to the Local 871 of the International Alliance of Theatrical Stage Employees (IATSE), the minimum rates set by contract depend on the number of years employed in the position. For a Script Supervisor during the first year of employment, the hourly rate is $25.12 or, for a five-day week (54 hours), the rate is $1,504.79. During the second year of employment, the hourly rate changes to $26.77, and the weekly rate to $1,583.26. For the third year in the industry and thereafter, the hourly rate becomes $28.35, and the weekly rate moves to $1,673.55. There are also separate rate provisions for preparation pay and wrap-up time. According to a 2005 salary survey of Script Supervisors taken by Broadcast Employment Services, annual salaries in 2004 ranged from $18,000 to $35,000.

Employment Prospects

Since the role of Script Supervisor is so critical to the production process, prospects for employment are at least fair. Every TV film production and series needs a Script Supervisor to ensure its continuity and credibility. Most live television productions also use Script Supervisors in preproduction steps and to aid continuity between tapings of shows from week to week.

Advancement Prospects

Chances of advancement from production or technical assistant (or assistant script supervisor for larger and more expensive productions) to Script Supervisor are relatively good. It is not as easy for Script Supervisors to advance to the positions of production manager or director. In particular, this is because separate unions and their different requirements are involved. Script Supervisors belong to the IATSE, whereas production managers and directors belong to the Directors Guild.

Education and Training

A high school diploma is a requirement for this position, as well as being articulate in spoken and written English and having strong verbal skills. Further background in theatrical or film production is an additional advantage.

Experience, Skills, and Personality Traits

The union IATSE has a training program for Script Supervisors. In some cases, this course program is necessary before membership and employment. Some Script Supervisors may take on individuals to mentor on a one-on-one basis.

Script Supervisors should exhibit extreme attention to detail. They need to be highly observant, have strong communication skills, and be thick-skinned in dealing with their fellow workers in the production. A working knowledge of camera angles and lenses, film production, photography, and shorthand is almost a requirement. Above all, they have to be very well organized.

Unions and Associations

For union productions (most network films and series), membership in IATSE is required, and for nonunion productions, such membership is helpful.

Tips for Entry

1. The IATSE training program is an excellent starting place for aspiring Script Supervisors, whether in film or television production. Classes elsewhere may be found at schools that have film/television programs.
2. Learn all you can about film and television production while in school. Look for any internships available and volunteer to work on any student film production.
3. Look for any type of administrative assistant jobs at a film company or a television station, as such jobs may lead to a Script Supervisor position. As an alternative, try to get hired as a Script Supervisor's intern or assistant.

SCRIPTWRITER

CAREER PROFILE

Duties: Write scripts for television programs, productions, series, and films

Alternate Title(s): Screenwriter

Salary Range: $17,000 to $100,000 or more

Employment Prospects: Poor

Advancement Prospects: Poor

Prerequisites:

Education and Training—Undergraduate degree in communications, English, or theater

Experience—Writing for any medium; some television or film production writing helpful

Special Skills and Personality Traits—Creativity; television production knowledge; writing talent

CAREER LADDER

```
┌─────────────────────────────────┐
│      Producer; Director         │
└─────────────────────────────────┘

┌─────────────────────────────────┐
│         Scriptwriter            │
└─────────────────────────────────┘

┌─────────────────────────────────┐
│    Writer (other media);        │
│    TV Production Position        │
└─────────────────────────────────┘
```

Position Description

A television Scriptwriter creates a visually oriented story for a commercial or public television drama, documentary, series episode(s), situation comedy, talk show, variety show, or other television production (such as a station fund-raiser). Scriptwriters may also develop and produce scripts for television programs produced by educational, health, or governmental agencies or departments. Scriptwriters are either station staff or contracted for a certain program or series, usually by the director or producer. In creating and writing a potential prime-time show, the Scriptwriter originates and builds on the concept and pitches it to a production company or network. If a pilot episode is ordered, the Scriptwriter writes it (sometimes in collaboration with others at the company or network). If this pilot episode is accepted and placed on a network's schedule, the Scriptwriter is charged with maintaining the show's vision and perspective. Sometimes the Scriptwriter becomes the show's executive producer in charge of all the writing and, in some cases, of many other aspects of the production.

Scriptwriters must appreciate the particular characteristics of television as a medium. They have to think visually and sense the way the camera will "see" the characters and action. They need to know what prerequisites a sitcom character must have that a serious drama figure does not. Scriptwriters have to be well versed in handling dialogue, as

characters usually say much more on television than they do in film. Scriptwriters also need to be aware of the specific conventions that writing for television demands.

The television script is really a blueprint for production. The complete script must be keyed in two columns, with "audio" indications on the right and "video" ones on the left. The audio column—that is, the content portion—contains the dialogue or the narration as well as instructions for any musical or other sound effects. The video side contains, typically, visual instructions, such as camera shots and generalized key production notes as to timing, descriptions of the sets, and directions to the actors. The director will fill in the specific details. Efficient television scripts make sense only when the two columns are read in conjunction with each other.

Writing for television is quite demanding. The structure of a script is tight, and the style must be more concentrated, imaginative, and powerful than that found in ordinary life and speech. The Scriptwriter needs to be both talented and entertaining and, when working on series, soaps, or comedies, must have an attention-grabbing story to tell. First, Scriptwriters must determine what is to be the subject matter for the genre piece they are writing and think out the entry's purpose and the intended audience for the program. After doing the necessary research, they must organize the material and develop it in a manner that the intended audience will both understand and enjoy, while keeping within the confines of the format (or series) for which they are preparing a new work.

For original scripts, Scriptwriters decide on characters to inhabit the plot, their past, their future, and what they say; for comedies, they have to devise funny situations (both visual and verbal); and for soap operas and thrillers, they need to devise episode cliffhangers. On short series, the Scriptwriter invents characters and sees them through to the end of the story. On soaps and longer series, the Scriptwriter may be but one of several Scriptwriters and will have to handle characters initiated by other writers. In documentaries, the Scriptwriter creates a narrative based on known (or generally accepted) facts. This narrative is often spoken by one or more performers in a voice-over form, guided by a series of still pictures or film footage and, perhaps, interviews. With documentaries, the Scriptwriter is sometimes also the producer or the director.

Television dramas thrive on exciting scripts packed with dynamic and entertaining characters who are forced to make the best of difficult situations in which they find themselves. Scriptwriters are responsible for these scenarios and the characters who live through them. Some nonfiction television programs, however, are shot before they are actually written. Scriptwriters then have to match their prose to the existent visual images.

Writing television scripts for educational organizations, governmental groups, health care businesses, or private industry requires melding an entertaining presentation to information that educates, enlightens, or trains. Considerable research and strict attention to accuracy and detail are needed, and the script is often reviewed by content experts and thus open to editing. Generally, Scriptwriters do not write for news programs, as these shows have their own news writers.

During the scriptwriting process, television Scriptwriters need to develop a sequence-by-sequence narrative describing the events in their proper continuity. This is called a treatment. In addition, Scriptwriters are expected to attend story conferences and planning sessions to change, delete, or add to their treatment and be available for production meetings and rehearsals in order to follow up with script additions, deletions, or rewrites.

Salaries

For most Scriptwriters, the Writers Guild of America (WGA) has set minimum wages for writing for television. There are a variety of minimums dependent on the type of writing, the length of the script, and a host of other factors.

As an example, concerning writing for network prime-time shows, minimums are set for stories, for teleplays (making the story into a television script), and for doing both. Furthermore, the rates are dependent on the length of broadcast time (15 minutes up to 120 minutes). The mini-

mums for a story range from $3,566 to $22,401, for a teleplay from $8,658 to $38,267, and for providing both a story and a teleplay from $10,712 to $58,340. Writing for basic cable pays significantly less and is also dependent on whether it is a low- or high-budget production. The WGA also sets differing minimums for writing segments of programs or dramatic TV series, writing plot outlines, writing narration, writing for comedy shows, writing for quiz and variety shows, writing for serials, writing for children's shows, writing for documentaries, and writing for single news programs. According to a salary survey conducted by Broadcast Employment Services in 2005, annual salaries for television writers in 2004 ranged from a low of $17,000 to a high of $98,000, with a mean average salary being $44,100.

Employment Prospects

The chances of obtaining a full-time position as a Scriptwriter for a television station or network are relatively poor. Staff Scriptwriters or script editors/supervisors are employed at some middle- and large-market commercial and public television stations, but there is generally scant turnover in these posts.

A television Scriptwriter has several options for kick-starting a career. A Scriptwriter may come from a related entertainment medium, such as film or theater. Having gained a reputation in these fields, the possibility of part- or full-time scriptwriting for television is greatly enhanced. Some Scriptwriters start cold by developing the concept of their program or series-to-be and then pitching and selling it to a production company or a network.

In other cases, television production workers who have demonstrated that they have writing skills may be asked to handle a writing assignment in addition to their regular chores. In business, education, government, or health care, some individuals become Scriptwriters because they have already exhibited their writing abilities (as copywriters, journalists, or publicists) or because their special insight into their areas of expertise make them best suited to write the appropriate scripts meant to education, inform, and train.

A small number of Scriptwriters are continuously employed by television personalities, by network shows, or by shows packaged by independent production firms. Most Scriptwriters, however, freelance their writing while pursuing full-time (or part-time) careers in another field sometimes completely unrelated to television.

Advancement Prospects

Excellent credits, personal connections, and an industry standing for reliability and solid scripts are the ways to ensure continuing writing assignments. In this process, a small number of well-established Scriptwriters may become head writers for commercial television series. Some Scriptwriters become producers or directors, particularly if they have had success at being an executive producer of a program or series that they pitched and sold. Most dedicated scriptwriters, however, continue to do some writing for their own or for other shows. In noncommercial arenas, some Scriptwriters may become directors or producers of informational and instructional programs. Nevertheless, advancement opportunities in general are poor unless a Scriptwriter opts to assume broader creative or managerial responsibilities.

Education and Training

An undergraduate degree, usually in English, is absolutely crucial, even when it is not actually required by the television station or network. Many Scriptwriters have an undergraduate or graduate degree in theater, radio and television, or writing. Some colleges even offer short courses in scriptwriting. Specific courses in composition, playwriting, and writing as well as in film and television production are helpful. Most writers have a basic and broad-based liberal arts education.

Experience, Skills, and Personality Traits

Most Scriptwriters begin practicing their craft in one form or another generally at an early age and continue to do so throughout their lives. Part- or full-time employment at a television station is useful for them to master the special techniques, opportunities, and specifics of writing for the medium.

The main ingredients that Scriptwriters have to show are that they can write and that they have ideas. Thus, creativity and imagination are important as well as a mastery of the language and knowledge of basic writing construction. Successful television Scriptwriters are well organized and disciplined, have an endless inquisitiveness about topics and people, and display an intense appreciation of the English language.

Unions and Associations

Full-time or freelance professional Scriptwriters in the entertainment field often are members of the Writers Guild of America, which is the paramount association for writers. Union membership is required of Scriptwriters who submit scripts for network television productions. Scriptwriters in educational or training environments seldom are represented by a union for bargaining purposes. The Screenwriters Guild of America (SGA) and the Authors Guild (AG) also represent Scriptwriters. They may also hold memberships in the National Writers Club as well as in many specific content area professional associations for purposes of professional growth and support.

Tips for Entry

1. Get as much structured writing experience as you can during your high school, undergraduate, and graduate years by writing for school publications, by preparing a play, or by creating student films with a video or digital camera.
2. Consider a beginning career in journalism or in writing advertising copy, radio programs, or Internet video programming to gain seasoning as a professional writer.
3. Attend seminars that have successful screenwriters or Scriptwriters on panels and listen to how they got started, what books they may have read, and how they trained.
4. Discipline yourself to write and keep writing until you have a finished script (or have completed a collaboration on a script with one or more fellow writers) to show to a producer, director, production company, or network.

APPENDIXES

APPENDIX I
EDUCATIONAL INSTITUTIONS

For those entering the television industry, especially in behind-the-camera posts, a college degree (whether from a two- or four-year program) is generally preferred and often a must. Many institutions offer degrees in acting, communications, and other specialties such as radio and television, broadcast journalism, broadcasting, cinematography and film/video production, communications technology, dance, film/video arts, media studies, playwriting/screenwriting, telecommunications technology, and so forth. The following is a list of many of the United States' four-year colleges/universities and two-year institutions that offer undergraduate degrees in various areas of the television industry. Many of these establishments also offer master's and other higher degrees that are *not* detailed herein. For the undergraduate schools included in this appendix, the listings below provide addresses, telephone numbers, fax numbers, e-mail addresses, and Web sites. Also provided (in alphabetical order) are each school's majors and specialties allied to the television industry. For further information about courses offered, admission requirements, and such topics as scholarships, campus housing, and academic calendar, contact the institution(s) of choice. Since the e-mail addresses of college admissions offices frequently change, it is advised to check the institution's Web site. (Increasingly, colleges now provide a link or form on their Web sites for directly contacting school departments.)

An asterisk (*) denotes institutions whose programs have satisfied the standards established by the Accrediting Council on Education in Journalism and Mass Communications (ACE-JMC). Note that the ACEJMC does not always accredit all the listed degree programs for an asterisked school. (Thus, while the ACEJMC may have accredited only communications at a particular institution, the school may offer—and have listed in this volume—other related majors within the television industry. The ACEJMC Web site [http://www.ku.edu/~~acejmc] provides information on which programs it has accredited at each institution and the most recent year of accreditation. Typically, the ACEJMC makes accreditation evaluations every six years.)

A *double asterisk (**)* denotes institutions offering two-year programs.

Information about these and the other colleges and universities offering courses in radio/TV and film can be acquired from:

Broadcast Education Association (BEA)
1771 N Street NW
Washington, DC 20036
Phone: (888) 380-7222
E-mail: beainfo@beaweb.org
http://www.beaweb.org

National Communication Association (NCA)
1765 N Street NW
Washington, DC 20036
Phone: (202) 464-4622
Fax: (202) 464-4600
E-mail: at Web site
http://www.natcom.org

ALABAMA

Alabama A&M University
P.O. Box 908
Normal, AL 35762
Phone: (256) 851-5245
Fax: (256) 851-5249
E-mail: aboyle@asnaam.aamu.edu
http://www.aamu.edu
Communications, communications technology.

Alabama State University
915 South Jackson Street
Montgomery, AL 36104
Phone: (334) 229-4291
Fax: (334) 229-4984
E-mail: dlamar@asunet.alasu.edu
http://www.alasu.edu
Communications.

Auburn University—Auburn*
202 Mary Martin Hall
Auburn, AL 36849
Phone: (334) 844-4080
Fax: (334) 844-6179
E-mail: admissions@auburn.edu
http://www.auburn.edu
Broadcast journalism, communications.

Auburn University—Montgomery
P.O. Box 244023
Montgomery, AL 36124
Phone: (334) 244-3611
Fax: (334) 244-3795
E-mail: mmoore@mail.aum.edu
http://www.aum.edu
Communications.

Birmingham-Southern College
900 Arkadelphia Road
Birmingham, AL 35254
Phone: (205) 226-4696
Fax: (205) 226-3074
E-mail: admission@bsc.edu
http://www.bsc.edu
Dance.

Calhoun Community College**
6250 Highway 31 North
Tanner, AL 35671
Phone: (800) 626-3628, ext. 2594
Fax: (256) 306-2941
E-mail: pml@calhoun.ccc.al.us
http://www.calhoun.cc.al.us
Photographic/film/video technology.

**Enterprise-Ozark Community
    College****
P.O. Box 1300
Enterprise, AL 36331
Phone: (334) 347-2623, ext. 2273
E-mail: sbaum@eocc.edu
http://www.eocc.edu
Communications.

Gadsden State Community College**
P.O. Box 227
Gadsden, AL 35902
Phone: (800) 226-5563
Fax: (256)-549-8205
E-mail: info@gadsenstate.edu
http://www.gadsdenst.cc.al.us
Communications, communications
    technology, telecommunications
    technology.

Huntingdon College
1500 East Fairview Avenue
Montgomery, AL 36106
Phone: (334) 833-4497
Fax: (334) 833-4347
E-mail: admiss@huntingdon.edu
http://www.huntingdon.edu
Communications.

Jacksonville State University
700 Pelham Road North
Jacksonville, AL 36265
Phone: (256) 782-5268
Fax: (256) 782-5953
E-mail: info@jsucc.jsu.edu
http://www.jsu.edu
Communications, radio and television.

Jefferson State Community College**
2601 Carson Road
Birmingham, AL 35215
Phone: (800) 239-5900
Fax: (205) 856-6070
E-mail: help@jeffstateonline.com
http://www.jscc.cc.al.us
Radio/television broadcasting.

Lawson State Community College**
3060 Wilson Road SW
Birmingham, AL 35221
Phone: (205) 929-6361

Fax: (205) 923-7106
E-mail: At Web site
http://www.ls.cc.al.us
Radio and television.

Miles College
5500 Myron Massey Boulevard
Attn.: Admissions
Fairfield, AL 35064
Phone: (205) 929-1656
Fax: (205) 929-1656
E-mail: admissions@miles.edu
http://www.miles.edu
Communications.

Samford University
800 Lakeshore Drive
Birmingham, AL 35229
Phone: (205) 726-3676
Fax: (205) 726-2171
E-mail: admissions@samford.edu
http://www.samford.edu
Communications.

Spring Hill College
4000 Dauphin Street
Mobile, AL 36608
Phone: (251) 380-3030
Fax: (251) 460-2186
E-mail: admit@shc.edu
http://www.shc.edu
Communications, radio and television.

Trenholm State Technical College
1125 Air Base Boulevard
Montgomery, AL 36108
Phone: (334) 420-4200
Fax: (334) 834-9136
E-mail: At Web site
http://www.trenholmtech.cc.al.us
Broadcast journalism.

Troy State University
111 Adams Administration
Troy, AL 36082
Phone: (334) 670-3179
Fax: (334) 670-3733
E-mail: admit@trojan.trost.edu
http://www.troyst.edu
Communications, radio and television.

University of Alabama—Birmingham
HUC 260
1530 3rd Avenue South
Birmingham, AL 35294
Phone: (205) 934-8221
Fax: (205) 975-7114
E-mail: undergradadmit@uab.edu
http://www.uab.edu
Communications, dance.

University of Alabama—Tuscaloosa
P.O. Box 879132
Tuscaloosa, AL 35487
Phone: (205) 348-5666
Fax: (205) 348-9046
E-mail: admissions@ua.edu
http://www.ua.edu
Film/video arts, radio and television.

University of Montevallo
Station 6030
Montevallo, AL 35115
Phone: (205) 665-6030
Fax: (205) 665-6042
E-mail: admissions@montevallo.edu
http://www.montevallo.edu
Radio and television.

University of South Alabama
182 Administration Building
Mobile, AL 36688
Phone: (334) 460-6141
Fax: (334) 460-7023
E-mail: admiss@jaguari.usouthal.edu
http://www.usouthal.edu
Communications.

ALASKA

University of Alaska—Anchorage*
3211 Providence Drive
Anchorage, AK 99508
Phone: (907) 786-1480
Fax: (907) 786-4888
E-mail: At Web site
http://www.uaa.alaska.edu
Communications.

University of Alaska—Fairbanks*
P.O. Box 757480
Fairbanks, AK 99775
Phone: (907) 474-7500
Fax: (907) 474-5379
E-mail: fyapply@uaf.edu
http://www.uaf.edu
Communications.

University of Alaska—Southeast
11120 Glacier Highway
Juneau, AK 99801
Phone: (907) 465-6462
Fax: (907) 465-6365
E-mail: jingaw@acad1.alaska.edu
http://www.jun.alaska.edu
Communications.

ARIZONA

Arizona State University East*
P.O. Box 870112

Tempe, AZ 85387
Phone: (480) 965-7788
Fax: (480) 727-1008
E-mail: Stacie.dana@asu.edu
http://www.east.asu.edu
Communications, dance, media studies, radio and television.

Arizona State University West
4701 West Thunderbird Road
Phoenix, AZ 85306-4908
Phone: (602) 543-813
Fax: (602) 543-8312
E-mail: west-admissions@asu.edu
http://www.west.asu.edu
Communications, dance, media studies.

Arizona Western College
2020 South Avenue 8 East
Yuma, AZ 85366
Phone: (888) 293-0392
Fax: (928) 344-7543
E-mail: At Web site
http://www.azwestern.edu
Broadcast journalism.

Art Institute of Phoenix**
2233 West Dunlap Avenue
Phoenix, AZ 85021
Phone:(800) 474-2479
Fax: NA
E-mail: aipadm@aii.edu
http://www.aipx.edu
Cinematography, film/video production.

Cochise College**
Douglas Campus
4190 West State Highway 80
Douglas, AZ 85607
Phone: (800) 966-7946
Fax: (520) 364-0236
E-mail: At Web site
http://www.cochise.edu
Communications.

Glendale Community College**
6000 West Olive Avenue
Glendale, AZ 85302
Phone: (623) 845-3000
Fax: (623) 845-3303
E-mail: info@gc.maricopa.edu
http://www.gc.maricopa.edu
Radio/television broadcasting.

Grand Canyon University
P.O. Box 11097
3300 West Camelback Road
Phoenix, AZ 85061
Phone: (602) 589-2855

Fax: (602) 589-2580
E-mail: admissions@grand-canyon.edu
http://www.grand-canyon.edu
Broadcast journalism, communications.

Northern Arizona University
P.O. Box 4080
Flagstaff, AZ 86011
Phone: (926) 523-5511
Fax: (928) 523-0226
E-mail: undergraduate.admissions@nau.
edu
http://www.nau.edu
Broadcast journalism, communications.

Northland Pioneer College**
P.O. Box 610
Holbrook, AZ 86025
Phone: (800) 266-7845
Fax: (928) 536-6211
E-mail: At Web site
http://www.npc.edu
Communications technology.

Phoenix College**
1202 West Thomas Road
Phoenix, AZ 85013
Phone: (602) 285-7500
Fax: (602) 285-7813
E-mail: dl-pc-info@pcmail.maricopa.edu
http://www.pc.maricopa.edu
Communications.

Pima Community College**
4905 East Broadway Boulevard
Tucson, AZ 85709
Phone: (800) 860-PIMA2
Fax: (520)-206-4790
E-mail: infocenter@pima.edu
http://www.pima.edu
Broadcast journalism.

Prescott College
220 Grove Avenue
Prescott, AZ 86301
Phone: (928) 776-5180
Fax: (928) 776-5252
E-mail: admissions@prescott.edu
http://www.prescott.edu
Communications.

Scottsdale Community College**
9000 East Chaparral Road
Scottsdale, AZ 85256
Phone: (602) 423-6128
Fax: (602) 423-6200
E-mail: At Web site
http://www.sc.maricopa.edu
Cinematography, film/video production.

University of Arizona*
P.O. Box 210040
Tucson, AZ 85721
Phone: (520) 621-3237
Fax: (520) 621-9799
E-mail: appinfo@arizona.edu
http://www.arizona.edu
Broadcast journalism, communications, dance, media studies.

ARKANSAS

Arkansas State University*
P.O. Box 1630
State University, AR 72467
Phone: (870) 972-3024
Fax: (870) 910-8094
E-mail: admissions@astate.edu
http://www.astate.edu
Communications technology, radio and television.

Harding University
P.O. Box 12255
Searcy, AR 72149
Phone: (501) 279-4407
Fax: (501) 279-4865
E-mail: admissions@harding.edu
http://www.harding.edu
Broadcast journalism, communications.

Henderson State University
1100 Henderson Street
HSU P.O. Box 7560
Arkadelphia, AR 71999
Phone: (870) 230-5028
Fax: (870) 230-5066
E-mail: hardwrv@hsus.edu
http://www.hsu.edu
Communications.

Ouachita Baptist University
410 Ouachita Street
Arkadelphia, AR 71988
Phone: (870) 235-5110
Fax: (870) 235-5500
Media studies.

Southern Arkansas University
P.O. Box 9382
Magnolia, AR 71754
Phone: (870) 235-4040
Fax: (870) 235-5072
E-mail: muleriders@saumag.edu
http://www.saumag.edu
Communications.

University of Arkansas—Fayetteville*
232 Silas Hunt Hall
Fayetteville, AR 72701
Phone: (479) 575-5346
Fax: (479) 575-7515
E-mail: uofa@uark.edu
http://www.uark.edu
Communications.

University of Arkansas—Little Rock
2801 South University Avenue
Little Rock, AR 72204
Phone: (501) 569-3127
Fax: (501) 569-8915
E-mail: admissions@ualr.edu
http://www.ualr.edu
Communications, communications
    technology.

University of Arkansas—Pine Bluff
1200 North University Drive
Mail Slot 4981
Pine Bluff, AR 71601
Phone: (870) 575-8000
Fax: (870) 543-8014
E-mail: fulton_E@uapb.edu
http://www.uapb.edu
Communications.

University of Central Arkansas
201 Donaghey Avenue
Conway, AR 72035
Phone: (501) 450-3128
Fax: (501) 450-5228
E-mail: admissions@mail.uca.edu
http://www.uca.edu
Broadcast journalism, communications.

University of the Ozarks
415 College Avenue
Clarksville, AR 72830
Phone: (479) 979-1227
Fax: (4798) 979-1355
E-mail: jdecker@ozarks.edu
http://www.ozarks.edu
Communications.

CALIFORNIA

Allan Hancock College**
800 South College Drive
Santa Maria, CA 93454
Phone: (805) 922-6966, ext. 3272
Fax: (805) 922-3477
E-mail: At Web site
http://www.hancock.cc.ca.us
Film/video arts.

**American Academy for Dramatic
    Arts—West****
1336 North LaBrea Avenue
Hollywood, CA 90028
Phone: (800) 222-2867
Fax: (626) 229-9977
E-mail: admissions-ca@aada.org
http://www.aada.org
Acting.

Academy of Art University
79 New Montgomery Street
San Francisco, CA 94105
Phone: (415) 274-2222
Fax: (415) 263-4130
E-mail: info@academyart.edu
http://www.academyart.edu
Cinematography, film/video production,
    photographic/film/video technology.

Antelope Valley College**
3041 West Avenue K
Lancaster, CA 93536,
Phone: (661) 722-6300
Fax: NA
E-mail: info@avc.edu
http://www.avc.edu
Cinematography, film/video production.

Art Center College of Design
1700 Lida Street
Pasadena, CA 91103
Phone: (626) 396-2373
Fax: (626) 795-0578
E-mail: admissions@artcenter.edu
http://www.artcenter.edu
Cinematography, film/video production.

Azusa Pacific University
901 East Alosta Avenue
Azusa, CA 91702
Phone: (626) 812-3016
Fax: (626) 812-3096
E-mail: admissions@apu.edu
http://www.apu.edu
Broadcast journalism, communications.

Bakersfield College
1801 Panorama Drive
Bakersfield, CA 93305
Phone: (661) 395-4011
Fax: (661) 395-4500
E-mail: bcadmission@bc.cc.ca.us
http://www.bc.cc.ca.us
Broadcast journalism.

Barstow College**
2700 Barstow Road
Barstow, CA 92311

Phone: (760) 252-2411
Fax: (760) 252-1875
E-mail: At Web site
http://www.barstow.edu
Communications.

Biola University
13800 Biola Avenue
La Mirada, CA 90639
Phone: (562) 903-4752
Fax: (562) 903-4709
E-mail: admission@biola.edu
http://www.biola.edu
Broadcast journalism, communications.

Brooks Institute of Photography
801 Alston Road
Santa Barbara, CA 93108
Phone: (805) 966-3888
Fax: (805) 564-1475
E-mail: admissions@brooks.edu
http://www.brooks.edu
Cinematography, film/video
    production.

Butte College
3536 Butte Campus Drive
Oroville, CA 95965
Phone: (530) 895-2511.
E-mail: At Web site
http://www.butte.edu
Broadcast journalism, cinematography,
    film/video production,
    communications technology.

California Baptist University
8432 Magnolia Avenue
Riverside, CA 92504
Phone: (909) 343-4212
Fax: (909) 343-4525
E-mail: admissions@calbaptist.edu
http://www.calbaptist.edu
Communications.

California College of the Arts
1111 Eighth Street
San Francisco, CA 94107
Phone: (415) 703-9523
Fax: (415) 703-9539
E-mail: enroll@cca.edu
http://www.cca.edu
Cinematography, film/video
    production.

California Institute of the Arts
24700 McBean Parkway
Valencia, CA 91355
Phone: (661) 255-1050
Fax: (661) 255-7710

E-mail: admiss@calarts.edu
http://www.calarts.edu
Acting, cinematography, film/video
    production, dance, film/video arts.

California Lutheran University
60 West Olsen Road, 1350
Thousand Oaks, CA 91300
Phone: (805) 493-3135
Fax: (805) 493-3114
E-mail: cluadm@clunet.edu
http://www.clunet.edu
Broadcast journalism, communications.

**California State Polytechnic
    University—Pomona**
3801 West Temple Avenue
Pomona, CA 91768
Phone: (909) 468-5020
Fax: (909) 869-5020
E-mail: cppadmit@csupomona.edu
http://www.csu.pomona.edu
Communications, dance.

**California State University—
    Bakersfield**
9001 Stockdale Highway
Bakersfield, CA 93311
Phone: (661) 664-3036
Fax: (661) 664-3389
E-mail: swatkin@csub.edu
http://www.csub.edu
Broadcast journalism, communications.

California State University—Chico*
400 West First Street
Chico, CA 95929
Phone: (530) 898-4428
Fax: (530) 898-6456
E-mail: info@csuchico.edu
http://www.csuchico.edu
Communications, radio and television.

**California State University—
    Dominguez Hills**
100 East Victoria Street
Carson, CA 90747
Phone: (310) 243-3600
Fax: (310) 516-3609
E-mail: 1wise@csudh.edu
http://www.csudh.edu
Communications.

California State University—Fresno
5150 North Maple Avenue M/S JA 57
Fresno, CA 93740
Phone: (559) 278-2261
Fax: (559) 278-4812
E-mail: vivian_franco@csufresno.edu

http://www.csufresno.edu
Communications, dance.

California State University—Fullerton*
800 North State College Boulevard
Fullerton, CA 92834
Phone: (714) 773-2370
Fax: (714) 278-2356
E-mail: admissions@fullerton.edu
http://www.fullerton.edu
Acting, communications, dance, radio
    and television.

California State University—Hayward
25800 Carlos Bee Boulevard
Hayward, CA 94542
Phone: (510) 885-2624
Fax: (510) 885-4059
E-mail: adminfo@csuhayward.edu
http://www.csuhayward.edu
Broadcast journalism, communications,
    dance.

**California State University—Long
    Beach**
1250 Bellflower Boulevard
Long Beach, CA 90840
Phone: (562) 985-5471
Fax: (562) 985-4973
E-mail: eslb@csulb.edu
http://www.csulb.edu
Broadcast journalism, cinematography,
    film/video production, communications,
    film/video arts, dance.

**California State University—Los
    Angeles**
5151 State University Drive
Los Angeles, CA 90032
Phone: (323) 343-3901
Fax: (323) 343-6306
E-mail: admission@calstatela.edu
http://www.calstatela.edu
Communications, communications
    technology, radio and television.

**California State University—Monterey
    Bay**
100 Campus Center
Seaside, CA 93955
Phone: (831) 582-3000
E-mail: onestop@csumb.edu
http://www.csumb.edu
Communications.

**California State University—
    Northridge***
P.O. Box 1286
Northridge, CA 91328
Phone: (818) 677-3773

Fax: (818) 677-4665
E-mail: lorraine.newlon@csun.edu
http://www.csun.edu
Broadcast journalism, communications,
    communications technology, dance.

**California State University—
    Sacramento**
6000 J Street
Lassen Hall
Sacramento, CA 95819
Phone: (916) 278-3901
Fax: (916) 279-5603
E-mail: admissions@csus.edu
http://www.admissions@csus.edu
Communications, dance.

**California State University—San
    Bernardino**
5500 University Parkway
San Bernardino, CA 92407
Phone: (909) 880-5188
Fax: (909) 880-7034
E-mail: moreinfo@mail.csusb.edu
http://www.csusb.edu
Communications, radio and television.

**California State University—San
    Marcos**
333 South Twin Oaks Valley Road
San Marcos, CA 92096
Phone: (760) 750-4848
Fax: (760) 750-3248
E-mail: apply@csusm.edu
http://www.csusm.edu
Communications.

**California State University—
    Stanislaus**
801 West Monte Vista Avenue
Turlock, CA 95382
Phone: (209) 667-3070
Fax: (209) 667-3788
E-mail: outreach_help_desk@stan.
    csustan.edu
http://www.csustan.edu
Communications.

Chabot College**
25555 Hesperian Boulevard
Hayward, CA 94545
Phone: (510) 723-6700
Fax: (510) 723-7510
E-mail: At Web site
http://www.chabotcollege.edu
Broadcast journalism, communications
    technology, dance.

Chaffey Community College**
5885 Haven Avenue
Rancho Cucamonga, CA 91737
Phone: (909) 941-2631
E-mail: At Web site
http://www.chaffey.edu
Broadcast journalism, communications, dance.

Chapman University
One University Drive
Orange, CA 92866
Phone: (714) 997-6711
Fax: (714) 997-6713
E-mail: admit@chapman.edu
http://www.chapman.edu
Broadcast journalism, cinematography, film/video production, communications, dance, playwriting/screenwriting.

Christian Heritage College
2100 Greenfield Drive
El Cajon, CA 92019
Phone: (619) 588-7747
Fax: (619) 440-0209
E-mail: chcadm@adm.christianheritage.edu
http://www.christianheritage.edu
Communications.

City College of San Francisco**
800 Mission Street
San Francisco, CA 94112
Phone: (415) 239-3291
Fax: (415) 239-3936
E-mail: At Web site
http://www.ccsf.edu
Broadcast journalism, communications technology.

Claremont McKenna College
890 Columbia Avenue
Claremont, CA 91711
Phone: (909) 621-8088
Fax: (909) 621-8516
E-mail: admissions@claremontmckenna.edu
http://www.claremontmckenna.edu
Media studies.

College of Marin**
835 College Avenue
Kentfield, CA 94904
Phone: (415) 457-8811, ext. 8822
E-mail: At Web site
http://www.marin.cc.ca.us
Broadcast journalism, communications.

College of the Desert**
43-500 Monterey Avenue
Palm Desert, CA 92260
Phone: (760) 773-2516
E-mail: At Web site
http://www.collegeofthedesert.edu
Communications.

College of San Mateo**
1700 West Hillsdale Boulevard
San Mateo, CA 94402
Phone: (650) 574-6594
E-mail: csmadmission@smccd.net
http://collegeofsanmateo.edu
Broadcast journalism.

College of the Canyons**
26455 Rockwell Canyon Road
Santa Clarita, CA 91355
Phone: (888) 206-7827
Fax: (661) 254-7996
E-mail: pio@canyons.edu
http://www.canyons.edu
Broadcast journalism, communications technology.

Columbia College—Hollywood
18618 Oxnard Street
Tarzana, CA 91356
Phone: (818) 345-8414
Fax: (818) 345-9053
E-mail: cchadfin@columbiacollege.edu
http://www.columbiacollege.edu
Broadcast journalism, cinematography, film/video production, communications technology, film/video arts.

Concordia University—Irvine
1530 Concordia West
Irvine, CA 92612
Phone: (949) 854-8002
Fax: (949) 854-6894
E-mail: admission@cui.edu
http://www.cui.edu
Communications.

Cosumnes River College**
8401 Center Parkway
Sacramento, CA 95823
Phone: (916) 691-7423
Fax: (916) 688-7467
E-mail: crc_pio@crc.losrios.edu
http://www.crc.losrios.edu
Broadcast journalism, communications technology.

Cuesta College**
Highway 1
San Luis Obispo, CA 93403

Phone: (805) 546-3140
Fax: (805) 546-3975
E-mail: admit@cuesta.edu
http://www.cuesta.edu
Broadcast journalism, communications.

Foothill College**
12345 El Monte Road
Los Altos Hills, CA 94022
Phone: (650)-949-7326
Fax: (650) 949-7375
E-mail: At Web site
http://www.foothill.fhda.edu
Broadcast journalism, communications, media studies.

Golden West College**
15744 Golden West Street
Huntington Beach, CA 92647
Phone: (714) 892-7711, ext. 58196
Fax: (714) 895-8231
E-mail: At Web site
http://www.gwc.info
Broadcast journalism.

Glendale Community College**
1500 North Verdugo Road
Glendale, CA 91208
Phone: (818) 551-5115
Fax: (818) 551-5255
E-mail: info@glendale.edu
http://www.glendale.edu
Broadcast journalism, dance.

Grossmont Community College**
8800 Grossmont College Drive
El Cajon, CA 92020
Phone: (619) 644-7170
Fax: (619) 644-7922
E-mail: At Web site
http://www.grossmont.edu
Broadcast journalism, dance.

Humboldt State University
1 Harpst Street
Arcata, CA 95521
Phone: (707) 826-4402
Fax: (707) 826-6194
E-mail: hsuinfo@humboldt.edu
http://www.humboldt.edu
Communications.

Laney College**
900 Fallon Street
Oakland, CA 94607
Phone: (510) 466-7369

E-mail: At Web site
http://www.peralta.cc.ca.us/laney
Broadcast journalism, communications
  technology, dance.

La Sierra University
4700 Pierce Street
Riverside, CA 92515
Phone: (909) 785-2176
Fax: (909) 785-2447
E-mail: ivy@lasierra.edu
http://www.lasierra.edu
Communications.

Long Beach City College**
44901 East Carson Street
Long Beach, CA 90808
Phone: (562) 938-4130
Fax: (562) 938-4858
E-mail: lluuga@lbcc.edu
http://www.lbcc.cc.ca.us
Broadcast journalism, communications
  technology, dance, film/video arts.

Los Angeles City College**
855 North Vermont Avenue
Los Angeles, CA 90029
Phone: (323) 953-4000
Fax: (323) 953-4013
E-mail: webmaster@lacitycollege.edu
http://www.lacitycollege.edu
Broadcast journalism, communications
  technology, film/video arts.

Los Angeles Valley College**
5800 Fulton Avenue
Valley Glen, CA 91401
Phone: (818) 947-2353
Fax: (818) 947-2501
E-mail: At Web site
http://www.lavc.edu
Cinematography, film/video production.

Loyola Marymount University
One LMU Drive, Suite 100
Los Angeles, CA 90045
Phone: (310) 338-2750
Fax: (310) 338-2797
E-mail: admissions@lmu.edu
http://www.lmu.edu
Cinematography, film/video production,
  communications, communications
  technology, dance.

Master's College and Seminary
21726 Placenta Canyon Road
Santa Clara, CA 91321
Phone: (661) 259-3540

Fax: (661) 288-1037
E-mail: enrollment@masters.edu
http://www.masters.edu
Media studies, radio and television.

Menlo College
1000 El Camino Real
Atherton, CA 94027
Phone: (650) 543-3753
Fax: (650) 543-4496
E-mail: admissions@menlo.edu
http://www.menlo.edu
Communications, media studies.

Mills College
5000 MacArthur Boulevard
Oakland, CA 94613
Phone: (510) 430-2135
Fax: (510) 430-3314
E-mail: admission@mills.edu
http://www.mills.edu
Communications, dance.

Modesto Junior College**
435 College Avenue
Modesto, CA 9535470
Fax: (209) 575-6859
E-mail: mjcadmissions@yosemite.cc.ca.
  us
http://www.mjc.yosemite.cc.ca.us
Broadcast journalism.

Monterey Peninsula College**
Admissions and Records Office
980 Fremont Street
Monterey, CA 93940
Phone: (831) 645-1372
Fax: (831) 646-4015
E-mail: vcoleman@mpc.edu
http://www.mpc.edu
Acting, communications, dance.

Moorpark College**
7075 Campus Road
Moorpark, CA 93021
Phone: (805) 378-1415
Fax: (805) 378-1583
E-mail: At Web site
http://www.moorpark.cc.ca.us
Broadcast journalism, communications,
  communications technology.

Mount Saint Antonio College**
1100 North Grand Avenue
Walnut, CA 91789
Phone: (800) 672-2463, ext. 4115
Fax: NA
E-mail: admissions@mtsac.edu

http://www.mtsac.edu
Broadcast journalism, communications
  technology.

Ohlone College**
43600 Mission Boulevard
P.O. Box 3909
Fremont, CA 94539
Phone: (510) 659-6108
E-mail: At Web site
http://www.ohlone.cc.ca.us
Broadcast journalism.

Orange Coast College**
2701 Fairview Road
Costa Mesa, CA 92626
Phone: (714) 432-5788
Fax: (714) 432-5072
E-mail: At Web site
http://www.orangecoastcollege.edu
Broadcast journalism, dance, film/video
  arts.

Pacific Union College
Enrollment Services
One Angwin Avenue
Angwin, CA 94508
Phone: (800) 862-7080
Fax: (707) 965-6432
E-mail: enroll@puc.edu
http://www.puc.edu
Cinematography, film/video production,
  communications.

Palomar College**
1140 West Mission Road
San Marcos, CA 92069
Phone: (760) 744-1150, ext. 2171
Fax: (760) 744-2932
E-mail: admissions@palomar.edu
http://www.palomar.edu
Film/video arts.

Pasadena City College**
1570 East Colorado Boulevard
Pasadena, CA 91106
Phone: (626) 585-7397
Fax: (626) 585-7915
E-mail: cjkaser@pasadena.edu
http://www.pasadena.edu
Broadcast journalism, communications,
  communications technology.

Pepperdine University
24255 Pacific Coast Highway
Malibu, CA 90263
Phone: (310) 456-4861
Fax: (310) 506-4861

E-mail: admission-seaver@pepperdine.edu
http://www.pepperdine.edu
Broadcast journalism, communications.

Pitzer College
1050 North Mills Avenue
Claremont, CA 91711
Phone: (909) 621-8129
Fax: (909) 621-8770
E-mail: admissions@pitzer.edu
http://www.pitzer.edu
Cinematography, film/video production, dance, film/video arts.

Point Loma Nazarene University
3900 Lomaland Drive
San Diego, CA 92106
Phone: (619) 849-2273
Fax: (619) 849-2601
E-mail: admissions@ptloma.edu
http://www.ptloma.edu
Communications.

Pomona College
333 North College Way
Claremont, CA 91711
Phone: (909) 621-8134
Fax: (909) 621-8952
E-mail: admissions@pomona.edu
http://www.pomona.edu
Media studies.

Saddleback College**
28000 Marguerite Parkway
Mission Viejo, CA 92692
Phone: (949) 582-4555
Fax: NA
E-mail: scadmissions@saddleback.edu
http://www.saddleback.cc.ca.us
Broadcast journalism, dance.

Saint Mary's College of California
P.O. Box 4800
Moraga, CA 94575-4800
Phone: (925) 631-4224
Fax: (925) 376-7193
E-mail: smcadmit@stmarys-ca.edu
http://www.stmarys-ca.edu
Communications, dance.

San Diego City College**
1313 Park Boulevard
San Diego, CA 92101
Phone: (619) 388-3400
Fax: NA
E-mail: admissions@sdcity.edu
http://www.sdcity.edu

Broadcast journalism, communications technology.

San Diego State University
5500 Campanile Drive
San Diego, CA 92182
Phone: (619) 594-7800
Fax: (619) 594-1250
E-mail: At Web site
http://www.sdu.edu
Broadcast journalism, communications, dance.

San Francisco Art Institute
800 Chestnut Street
San Francisco, CA 94133
Phone: (415) 749-4500
Fax: (415) 749-4592
E-mail: admissions@sfai.edu
http://www.sfai.edu
Film/video arts.

San Francisco State University*
1600 Holloway Avenue
San Francisco, CA 94132
Phone: (415) 338-6486
Fax: (415) 338-7196
E-mail: ugadmit@sfsu.edu
http://www.sfsu.edu
Broadcast journalism, dance, film/video arts.

San Joaquin Delta College**
5151 Pacific Avenue
Stockton, CA 95207
Phone: (209) 954-5635
Fax: (209) 954-5769
E-mail: sjdchelp@deltacollege.edu
http://www.sjdccd.cc.ca.us
Broadcast journalism.

San Jose State University*
1 Washington Square
San Jose, CA 95112
Phone: (408) 283-7500
Fax: (408) 924-2050
E-mail: contact@sjsu.edu
http://www.sjsu.edu
Dance, film/video arts.

Santa Ana College**
Admissions & Records, S-101
1530 West 17th Street
Santa Ana, CA 92706
Phone: (714) 564-6053
Fax: (714) 564-4379
E-mail: Adm_Records@rsccd.org

http://www.sac.edu
Broadcast journalism, communications, dance.

Santa Barbara City College**
721 Cliff Drive
Santa Barbara, CA 93109
Phone: (805) 965-0581, ext. 7222
Fax: (805) 962-0497
http://www.sbcc.edu
Film/video arts.

Santa Clara University
500 El Camino Real
Santa Clara, CA 95053
Phone: (408) 554-4700
Fax: (408) 554-5255
http://www.scu.edu
Communications.

Santa Monica College**
1900 Pico Boulevard
Santa Monica, CA 90405
Phone: (310) 434-4880, ext. 4774
E-mail: At Web site
http://www.smc.edu
Communications technology, dance.

Santiago Canyon College**
8045 East Chapman Avenue
Orange, CA 92869
Phone: (714) 628-4900
Fax: (714) 564-4379
E-mail: At Web site
http://www.sccollege.edu
Photographic/film/video technology.

Sierra College**
5000 Rocklin Road
Rocklin, CA 95677
Phone: (800) 242-4004
E-mail: At Web site
http://www.sierracollege.edu
Communications.

Simpson College
2211 College View Drive
Redding, CA 96003
Phone: (530) 226-4606
Fax: (530) 226-4861
E-mail: admissions@simpsonca.edu
http://www.simpson.ca.edu
Communications.

Sonoma State University
1801 East Cotati Avenue
Rohnert Park, CA 94928
Phone: (707) 664-2778
Fax: (707) 664-2060

E-mail: admitme@sonoma.edu
http://www.sonoma.edu
Communications.

Southwestern College**
900 Otay Lakes Road
Chula Vista, CA 91910
Phone: (619) 482-6550
E-mail: admissions@swc.cc.ca.us
http://www.swc.cc.ca.us
Broadcast journalism, communications
    technology, telecommunications
    technology.

Stanford University
Undergraduate Admission
Old Union 232
Stanford, CA 94305
Phone: (650) 723-2091
Fax: (650) 723-6050
E-mail: admissions@stanford.edu
http://www.stanford.edu
Communications.

University of California—Berkeley*
110 Sproul Hall
Berkeley, CA 94720
Phone: (510) 642-3175
Fax: (510) 642-7333
E-mail: ouars@uclink.berkeley.edu
http://www.berkeley.edu
Communications, film/video arts, dance.

University of California—Irvine
204 Administration Building
Irvine, CA 92697
Phone: (949) 824-6703
Fax: (949) 824-2711
E-mail: admissions@uci.edu
http://www.uci.edu
Dance, film/video arts.

University of California—Los Angeles
405 Hilgard Avenue
P.O. Box 951436
Los Angeles, CA 90095
Phone: (310) 825-3101
Fax: (310) 206-1206
E-mail: ugadm@saonet.ucla.edu
http://www.ucla.edu
Communications, film/video arts.

University of California—Riverside
1138 Hinderaker Hall
Riverside, CA 92521
Phone: (909) 787-3411
Fax: (909) 787-6344
E-mail: ugadmiss@pop.ucr.edu

http://www.ucr.edu
Dance, film/video arts.

University of California—San Diego
9500 Gilman Drive, 0021
La Jolla, CA 92093
Phone: (858) 534-4831
Fax: (858) 534-5723
E-mail: admissionsinfo@ucsd.edu
http://www.ucsd.edu
Communications,

**University of California—Santa
    Barbara**
Office of Admissions
1210 Cheadle Hall
Santa Barbara, CA 93106
Phone: (805) 893-2881
Fax: (805) 893-2676
E-mail: appinfo@sa.ucsb.edu
http://www.ucsb.edu
Communications, dance, film/video arts.

University of California—Santa Cruz
Office of Admissions, Cook House
1156 High Street
Santa Cruz, CA 95064
Phone: (831) 459-4008
Fax: (831) 459-4452
E-mail: admissions@ucsc.edu
http://www.admissions.ucsc.edu
Dance, film/video arts.

University of La Verne
1950 Third Street
La Verne, CA 91750
Phone: (909) 392-2800
Fax: (909) 392-2714
E-mail: admissions@ulv.edu
http://www.ulv.edu
Communications, radio and television.

University of San Francisco
2130 Fulton Street
San Francisco, CA 94117
Phone: (415) 422-6563
Fax: (415) 422-2217
E-mail: admission@usfca.edu
http://www.usfca.edu
Communications, media studies.

University of Southern California*
700 Childs Way
Los Angeles, CA 90089
Phone: (213) 740-1111
Fax: (213) 740-6364)
E-mail: admitusc@usc.edu
http://www.usc.edu

Acting, broadcast journalism,
    communications, film/video arts,
    playwriting/screenwriting, radio and
    television.

University of the Pacific
3601 Pacific Avenue
Stockton, CA 95211
Phone: (209) 946-2211
Fax: (209) 946-2413
E-mail: admissions@pacific.edu
http://www.pacific.edu
Communications.

**Vanguard University of Southern
    California**
55 Fair Drive
Costa Mesa, CA 92626
Phone: (714) 556-3601
Fax: (714) 966-5471
E-mail: admissions@vanguard.edu
http://www.vanguard.edu
Communications.

Westmont College
955 La Paz Road
Santa Barbara, CA 93108
Phone: (805) 565-6200
Fax: (805) 565-6234
E-mail: admissions@westmont.edu
http://www.westmont.edu
Broadcast journalism, communications,
    dance, media studies.

Yuba Community College District**
2088 North Beale Road
Marysville, CA 95901
Phone: (530) 741-6720
E-mail: At Web site
http://www.yccd.edu
Media studies.

COLORADO

Adams State College
Office of Admissions
1 Adams State College
Alamosa, CO 81102
Phone: (719) 587-7712
Fax: (719) 587-7522
E-mail: ascadmit@adams.edu
http://www.adams.edu
Communications.

Art Institute of Colorado
1200 Lincoln Street
Denver, CO 80203
Phone: (800) 275-2420

E-mail: aicadm@aii.edu
http://www.aic.artinstitutes.edu
Broadcast journalism, cinematography,
    film/video production,
    communications, communications
    technology.

Colorado Christian University
180 South Garrison Street
Lakewood, CO 80226
Phone: (303) 963-3200
Fax: (3030) 963-3201
E-mail: admission@ccu.edu
http://www.ccu.edu
Communications.

Colorado College**
14 East Cache La Poudre Street
Colorado Springs, CO 80903
Phone: (719) 389-6000
E-mail: At Web site
http://www.coloradocollege.edu
Film/video arts.

Colorado Mountain College—
    Timberline Campus
Admissions Office
901 South Highway 24
Leadville, CO 80461
Phone: (800) 621-8559
Fax: (719) 947-8324
E-mail: joinus@coloradomtn.edu
http://www.coloradomtn.edu
Photographic/film/video technology.

Colorado State University—Pueblo
Office of Admissions and Records
2200 Bonforte Boulevard
Pueblo, CO 81001
Phone: (719) 549-2461
Fax: (719) 549-24
E-mail: info@colostate-pueblo.edu
http://www.colostate-pueblo.edu
Broadcast journalism, communications,
    dance.

Jones International University
9697 East Mineral Avenue
Englewood, CO 80112
Phone: (800) 811-5663
Fax: (303) 799-0966
E-mail: admissions@international.edu
http://www.jonesinternational.edu
Communications, communications
    technology.

Mesa State University
P.O. Box 2647
Grand Junction, CO 81502

Phone: (970) 248-1875
Fax: (970) 248-1973
E-mail: admissions@mesastate.edu
http://www.mesastate.edu
Communications.

Metropolitan State College of Denver
Campus Box 16
P.O. Box 173362
Denver, CO 80217
Phone: (303) 556-3058
Fax: (303) 556-6345
E-mail: askmetro@mscd.edu
http://www.mscd.edu
Communications.

Northeastern Junior College**
100 College Avenue
Sterling, CO 80751
Phone: (800) 626-4637
Fax: (970) 521-6801
E-mail: At Web site
http://www.njc.edu
Broadcast journalism, communications,
    communications technology.

Red Rock Community College**
13300 West Sixth Avenue
Lakewood, CO 80228
Phone: (303) 914-6600
Fax: NA
E-mail: college.relations@rrcc.edu
http://www.rrcc.edu
Cinematography, film/video production,
    communications.

Regis University
3333 Regis Boulevard
Denver, CO 80221
Phone: (303) 458-4900
Fax: (303) 964-5534
E-mail: regisadm@regis.edu
http://www.regis.edu
Communications.

University of Colorado—Boulder*
Campus Box 30
Boulder, CO 90309
Phone: (303) 492-6301
Fax: (303) 492-7115
E-mail: apply@colorado.edu
http://www.colorado.edu
Communications, film/video arts,
    telecommunications technology.

University of Colorado—Colorado
    Springs
Admissions Office
P.O. Box 7150

Colorado Springs, CO 80933
Phone: (719) 262-3383
Fax: (719) 262-3116
E-mail: admrec@mail.uccs.edu
http://www.uccs.edu
Communications.

University of Colorado—Denver
P.O. Box 173304
Campus Box 167
Denver, CO 80217
Phone: (303) 556-3287
Fax: (303) 556-4838
E-mail: admissions@carbon.cudenver.edu
http://www.cudenver.edu
Communications.

University of Denver
University Hall, Room 110
2197 South University Boulevard
Denver, CO 80208
Phone: (303) 871-2036
Fax: (303) 871-3301
E-mail: admission@du.edu
http://www.du.edu
Communications.

University of Northern Colorado
UNC Admissions Office
Greenley, CO 80639
Phone: (970) 351-2881
Fax: (970) 351-2984
E-mail: unc@mail.unco.edu
http://www.unco.edu
Communications.

University of Southern Colorado
Admissions
2200 Bonforte Boulevard
Pueblo, CO 81001
Phone: (719) 549-2461
Fax: (719) 549-2419
E-mail: info@uscolo.edu
http://www.uscolo.edu
Communications.

Western State College of Colorado
600 North Adams Street
Gunnison, CO 91231
Phone: (970) 943-2119
Fax: (970) 943-2212
E-mail: discover@western.edu
http://www.western.edu
Communications.

Westwood College of Technology
7350 North Broadway
Denver, CO 80221
Phone: (303) 426-7000

Fax: (303) 426-1832
E-mail: bsimms@westwood.edu
http://www.westwood.edu
Communications.

CONNECTICUT

Albertus Magnus College
700 Prospect Street
New Haven, CT 06551
Phone: (203) 773-851
Fax: (203) 773-5248
E-mail: admissions@albertus.edu
http://www.albertus.edu
Communications.

Briarwood College**
2279 Mount Vernon Road
Southington, CT 06489
Phone: (800) 952-2444
Fax: (860) 628-6444
E-mail: admis@briarwood.edu
http://www.briarwood.edu
Broadcast journalism.

Central Connecticut State College
1615 Stanley Street
New Britain, CT 06050
Phone: (860) 832-2278
Fax: (860) 832-2295
E-mail: admissions@ccsu.edu
http://www.ccsu.edu
Communications.

Connecticut College
270 Mohegan Avenue
New London, CT 06320
Phone: (860) 439-2200
Fax: (860) 439-4301
E-mail: admission@conncoll.edu
http://www.conncoll.edu
Dance.

Eastern Connecticut State University
83 Windham Street
Willimantic, CT 06226
Phone: (860) 465-5286
Fax: (860) 465-5544
E-mail: admissions@easternct.edu
http://www.easternct.edu
Communications.

Fairfield University
1073 North Benson Road
Fairfield, CT 06824
Phone: (203) 254-4100
Fax: (203) 254-4199
E-mail: admis@mail.fairfield.edu
http://www.fairfield.edu
Communications.

Manchester Community College**
P.O. Box 1046, MS #12
Manchester, CT 06045
Phone: (860) 512-3210
Fax: (860) 512-3221
E-mail: At Web site
http://www.mcc.commnet.edu
Communications technology.

Middlesex Community College**
100 Training Hill Road
Middletown, CT 06457
Phone: (860) 343-5897
Fax: (860) 344-7488
E-mail: At Web site
http://www.commnet.edu
Broadcast journalism, communications.

Naugatuck Valley Community College**
760 Chase Parkway
Waterbury, CT 06708
Phone: (203) 575-8016
Fax: (203) 596-8766
E-mail: nv_admissions@commnet.edu
http://www.nvctc.commnet.edu
Communications technology.

Quinnipiac University
275 Mount Carmel Avenue
Hamden, CT 06518
Phone: (800) 462-1944
E-mail: admissions@quinnipiac.edu
http://www.quinnipiac.edu
Broadcast journalism, communications.

Sacred Heart University
5151 Park Avenue
Fairfield, CT 06432
Phone: (203) 371-7880
Fax: (203) 365-7607
E-mail: enroll@sacredheart.edu
http://www.sacredheart.edu
Communications.

Southern Connecticut State University
131 Farnham Avenue
New Haven, CT 06515
Phone: (203) 392-5656
Fax: (203) 392-5727
E-mail: adminfo@scsu.ctstateu.edu
http://www.southernct.edu
Communications.

Trinity College
300 Summit Street
Hartford, CT 06016
Phone: (860) 297-2180
Fax: (860) 297-2287

E-mail: admissions.office@trincoll.edu
http://www.trincoll.edu
Film/video arts.

University of Bridgeport
380 University Avenue
Bridgeport, CT 06601
Phone: (203) 576-4552
Fax: (203) 576-4941
E-mail: admit@bridgeport.edu
http://www.bridgeport.edu
Communications, media studies.

University of Connecticut*
2131 Hillside Road, Unit 3088
Storrs, CT 06286
Phone: (860) 486-3137
Fax: (860) 486-1476
E-mail: beahusky@uconn.edu
http://www.uconn.edu
Acting, cinematography, film/video
    production, communications.

University of Hartford
200 Bloomfield Avenue
West Hartford, CT 06117
Phone: (860) 768-4296
Fax: (860) 768-4961
E-mail: admissions@mail.hartford.edu
http://www.hartford.edu
Communications, dance, film/video arts.

University of New Haven
300 Orange Avenue
West Haven, CT 06516
Phone: (203) 932-7319
Fax: (203) 931-6093
E-mail: adminfo@newhaven.edu
http://www.newhaven.edu
Communications.

Wesleyan University
The Stewart M. Reid House
70 Wyllys Avenue
Middleton, CT 06459
Phone: (860) 685-3000
Fax: (860) 685-3001
E-mail: admiss@wesleyan.edu
http://www.wesleyan.edu
Dance, film/video arts.

Western Connecticut State University
Undergraduate Admissions Office
181 White Street
Danbury, CT 06810
Phone: (203) 837-9000
E-mail: At Web site
http://www.wcsu.edu
Communications.

Yale University
P.O. Box 208234
New Haven, CT 06520
Phone: (203) 432-9316
Fax: (203) 432-9392
E-mail: undergraduate_admissions@
    yale.edu
http://www.yale.edu
Film/video arts.

DELAWARE

Delaware State University
1200 North DuPont Highway
Dover, DE 19901
Phone: (302) 857-6361
Fax: (302) 857-6362
E-mail: admissions@desu.edu
http://www.desu.edu
Broadcast journalism, communications.

University of Delaware
Admissions Office
116 Hullihen Hall
Newark, DE 19716
Phone: (302) 831-8123
Fax: (302) 931-6095
E-mail: admissions@udel.edu
http://www.udel.edu
Communications.

Wesley College
120 North State Street
Dover, DE 19901
Phone: (302) 736-2400
Fax: (302) 736-2301
E-mail: admissions@wesley.edu
http://www.wesley.edu
Communications.

Wilmington College
320 Dupont Highway
New Castle, DE 18720
Phone: (302) 328-9401
Fax: (302) 328-5902
E-mail: mlee@wilmcoll.edu
http://www.wilmcoll.edu
Communications, communications
    technology.

DISTRICT OF COLUMBIA

American University*
4400 Massachusetts Avenue NW
Washington, DC 20016
Phone: (202) 885-6000
Fax: (202) 885-1025
E-mail: afa@american.edu
http://www.american.edu

Cinematography, film/video production,
    communications, film/video arts,
    media studies, radio and television.

Catholic University of America
Office of Enrollment Services
Washington, DC 20064
Phone: (202) 319-6305
Fax: (202) 319-6533
E-mail: cua-admissions@cua.edu
http://www.cua.edu
Communications.

Gallaudet University
800 Florida Avenue NE
Washington, DC 20002
Phone: (202) 651-5750
Fax: (202) 651-5744
E-mail: admissions@gallaudet.edu
http://www.gallaudet.edu
Broadcast journalism, communications.

George Washington University
2121 I Street NW, Suite 201
Washington, DC 20052
Phone: (202) 994-6040
Fax: (202) 994-0325
E-mail: gwadm@gwu.edu
http://www.gwu.edu
Communications, dance.

Howard University*
2400 Sixth Street NW
Washington, DC 20059
Phone: (202) 806-2700
Fax: (202) 806-4462
E-mail: admission@howard.edu
http://www.howard.edu
Broadcast journalism, communications,
    dance, film/video arts, radio and
    television.

Trinity College
125 Michigan Avenue NE
Washington, DC 20017
Phone: (202) 884-9400
Fax: (202) 884-9403
E-mail: admissions@trinitydc.edu
http://www.trinitydc.edu
Communications.

FLORIDA

Art Institute of Fort Lauderdale*
1799 SE 17th Street.
Fort Lauderdale, Fl 33316
Phone: (800) 275-7603
E-mail: At Web site

http://www.aifl.edu
Cinematography, film/video production.

Barry University
11300 NE Second Avenue
Miami Shores, FL 33161
Phone: (305) 899-3100
Fax: (305) 899-2971
E-mail: Des-forms@mail.barry.edu
http://www.barry.edu
Communications, radio and television.

Brevard Community College*
1519 Clearlake Road
Cocoa, FL 32922
Phone: (321) 632-1111
E-mail: At Web site
http://www.brevard.cc.fl.us
Broadcast journalism.

Broward Community College*
111 East Las Olas Boulevard
Fort Lauderdale, FL 33301
Phone: (954) 761-7465
Fax: (954) 201-6966
E-mail: success@broward.cc.fl.us
http://www.broward.edu
Broadcast journalism

Chipola Junior College*
3094 Indian Circle
Marianna, FL 32446
Phone: (850) 526-2761, ext. 2292
Fax: (850) 718-2287
E-mail: RobertsJ@chipola.edu
http://www.chipola.edu
Communications.

Clearwater Christian College
3400 Gulf-to-Bay Boulevard
Clearwater, FL 33759
Phone: (727) 726-1153
Fax: (727) 726-8597
E-mail: admissions@clearwater.edu
http://www.clearwater.edu
Communications.

Eckerd College
4200 54th Avenue South
St. Petersburg, FL 33711
Phone: (727) 864-8331
Fax: (727) 866-2304
E-mail: admissions@eckerd.edu
http://www.eckerd.edu
Communications.

**Embry Riddle Aeronautical
    University**
600 South Clyde Morris Boulevard
Daytona Beach, FL 32114

Phone: (386) 226-6100
Fax: (386) 226-7070
E-mail: dbadmit@erau.edu
http://www.embryriddle.edu
Communications.

Flagler College
74 King Street
P.O. Box 1027
St. Augustine, FL 32085
Phone: (800) 304-4208
Fax: (904) 826-0094
E-mail: admiss@flagler.edu
http://www.flagler.edu
Communications.

Florida A&M University*
Suite G-9, Foote-Hilyer Administration
    Center
Tallahassee, FL 32307
Phone: (850) 599-3796
E-mail: adm@famu.edu
http://www.famu.edu
Broadcast journalism.

Florida International University*
University Park, PC 140
Miami, FL 33119
Phone: (305) 348-2363
Fax: (305) 348-3648
E-mail: admiss@flu.edu
http://www.flu.edu
Communications, dance.

Florida Southern College
111 Lake Hollingsworth Drive
Lakeland, FL 33801
Phone: (863) 680-4131
Fax: (863) 680-4120
E-mail: fscadm@flsouthern.edu
http://www.flsouthern.edu
Communications.

Florida State University
2500 University Center
Tallahassee, FL 32306
Phone: (850) 644-6200
Fax: (850) 644-0197
E-mail: admissions@admin.fsu.edu
http://www.fsu.edu
Acting, cinematography, film/video
    production, communications, dance,
    media studies.

Gulf Coast Community College**
Gulf/Franklin Center
3800 Garrison Avenue
Port St. Joe, FL 32456
Phone: (800) 311-3685

Fax: (850) 913-3308
E-mail: At Web site
http://www.gc.cc.fl.us
Communications.

Hillsborough Community College**
Brandon Campus
10414 East Columbus Drive
Tampa, Florida 33619
Phone: (813) 253-7802
Fax: NA
E-mail: At Web site
http://www.hccfl.edu
Broadcast journalism, dance, radio and
    television.

Jacksonville University
700 Pelham Road North
Jacksonville, FL 36252
Phone: (904) 256-7000
Fax: (904) 256-7012
E-mail: admissions@ju.edu
http://www.jacksonville.edu
Communications, dance.

Lynn University
3601 North Military Trail
Boca Raton, FL 33431
Phone: (561) 237-7900
Fax: (561) 237-7100
E-mail: admission@lynn.edu
http://www.lynn.edu
Communications.

Manatee Community College**
5840 26th Street West
Bradenton, FL 34207
Phone: (941) 752-5422, ext. 65422
Fax: (941) 727-6380
E-mail: admissions@mccfl.edu
http://www.mccfl.edu
Broadcast journalism, communications,
    media studies, radio and television,
    radio/television broadcasting.

Miami Dade College**
MDC Kendall Campus
11011 SW 104th Street
Miami, FL 33176
Phone: (305) 237-0633
Fax: (305) 237-2964
E-mail: At Web site
http://www.mdc.edu/kendall
Broadcast journalism, communications
    technology, dance.

Palm Beach Atlantic University
P.O. Box 24708
901 South Flagler Drive

West Palm Beach, FL 33416
Phone: (561) 803-2100
Fax: (561) 803-2115
E-mail: admit@pba.edu
http://www.pba.edu
Acting, broadcast journalism,
    communications,
    playwriting/screenwriting, radio and
    television.

Palm Beach Community College**
4200 Congress Avenue
Lake Worth, FL 33461
Phone: (866) 576-7222
Fax: (561) 868-3584
E-mail: At Web site
http://www.pbcc.cc.fl.us
Cinematography, film/video production,
    dance, telecommunications
    technology.

Polk Community College**
999 Avenue H NE
Winter Haven, FL 33881
Phone: (863) 297-1000, ext. 5016
Fax: (863) 297-1010
E-mail: Student Services@polk.edu
http://www.polk.edu
Broadcast journalism, communications.

Rollins College
Campus Box 2720
Winter Park, FL 32789
Phone: (407) 646-2161
Fax: (407) 646-1502
E-mail: admission@rollins.edu
http://www.rollins.edu
Communications.

St. Petersburg College**
P.O. Box 13489
St. Petersburg, FL 33733
Phone: (727) 712-5892
Fax: (727) 712-5872
E-mail: information@spcollege.edu
http://www.spjc.edu
Telecommunications technology.

South Florida Community College**
600 West College Drive
Avon Park, FL 33825
Phone: (863) 453-6661, ext. 7401
E-mail: info@sfcc.edu
http://www.southflorida.edu
Broadcast journalism, communications.

**Southeastern College of the Assemblies
    of God**
1000 Longfellow Boulevard

Lakeland, FL 33801
Phone: (863) 667-5081
Fax: (863) 667-5200
E-mail: admission@secolleg.edu
http://www.secolleg.edu
Communications.

Stetson University
421 North Woodland Boulevard, Unit 8378
DeLand, FL 32723
Phone: (386) 822-7100
Fax: (386) 822-7112
E-mail: admissions@stetson.edu
http://www.stetson.edu
Communications.

Tallahassee Community College**
444 Appleyard Drive
Tallahassee, FL 32304
Phone: (850) 201-8555
Fax: (850) 201-8474
E-mail: enroll@tcc.fl.edu
http://www.tcc.fl.edu
Film/video arts.

University of Central Florida
P.O. Box 160111
Orlando, FL 32816
Phone: (407) 823-3000
Fax: (407) 823-5625
E-mail: admission@mail.ucf.edu
http://www.ucf.edu
Cinematography, film/video production,
    media studies, radio and television.

University of Florida*
201 Criser Hall, P.O. Box 11400
Gainesville, FL 32611-4000
Phone: (352) 392-1365
Fax: (352) 392-3987
E-mail: At Web site
http://www.ufl.edu
Dance.

University of Miami*
P.O. Box 248025
Coral Gables, FL 33124
Phone: (305) 284-4323
Fax: (305) 284-2507
E-mail: admission@miami.edu
http://www.miami.edu/admissions
Broadcast journalism, cinematography,
    film/video production,
    communications, dance, film/video
    arts.

University of North Florida
4567 St. Johns Bluff Road, South
Jacksonville, FL 32224

Phone: (904) 620-2624
Fax: (904) 620-2414
E-mail: osprey@unf.edu
http://www.unf.edu
Communications, media studies.

**University of South Florida—St.
    Petersburg***
140 Seventh Avenue South
St. Petersburg, FL 33701
Phone: (727) 553-4USF
Fax: (727) 553-974-2592
E-mail: admissions@stpt.usf.edu
http://www.http.usf.edu
Communications, dance.

University of South Florida—Tampa*
4202 East Fowler Avenue SVC-1036
Tampa, FL 33620-9951
Phone: (813) 874-3350
Fax: (813) 974-9689
E-mail: jglassma@admin.usf.edu
http://www.usf.edu
Communications, dance.

University of West Florida
11000 University Parkway
Pensacola, FL 32514
Phone: (850) 474-2230
Fax: (850) 474-3360
E-mail: admissions@uwf.edu
http://uwf.edu
Acting, broadcast journalism,
    communications.

Warner South College
13995 Highway 27
Lake Wales, FL 33859
Phone: (863) 63807212
Fax: (863) 638-7290
E-mail: admissions@warner.edu
http://www.warner.edu
Communications.

GEORGIA

Art Institute of Atlanta**
6600 Peachtree Dunwoody Road
100 Embassy Row
Atlanta, GA 30328
Phone: (800) 275-4242
E-mail: aiaadm@aii.edu
http://www.aia.aii.edu
Cinematography, film/video production.

Atlanta College of Art
1280 Peachtree Street NE
Atlanta, GA 30309

Phone: (404) 733-5100
Fax: (404) 733-5107
E-mail: acinfo@woodruffcenter.org
http://www.aca.edu
Cinematography, film/video production.

Augusta State University
2500 Walton Way
Augusta, GA 3094
Phone: (706) 737-1632
Fax: (706) 667-4355
E-mail: admission@aug.edu
http://www.aug.edu
Communications.

Berry College
P.O. Box 490159
Mount Berry, GA 30149
Phone: (706) 236-2215
Fax: (706) 236-2248
E-mail: admissions@berry.edu
http://www.berry.edu
Communications.

Brenau University Women's College
1 Centennial Circle
Gainesville, GA 30501
Phone: (770) 534-6100
Fax: (770) 538-4306
E-mail: wcadmissions@lib.brenau.edu
http://www.brenau.edu
Communications, dance, media studies.

Brewton-Parker College
P.O. Box 2011
Mt. Vernon, GA 30445
Phone: (912) 583-3265
Fax: (912) 583-3598
E-mail: admissions@bpc.edu
http://www.bpc.edu
Communications.

Clark Atlanta University
223 James P. Brawley Drive
Atlanta, GA 30314
Phone: (404) 880-8000
Fax: (404) 880-6174
E-mail: admissions@panthernet.cau.edu
http://www.cau.edu
Broadcast journalism, communications,
    communications technology, media
    studies.

Emory University
Boisfeuillet Jones Center
201 Dowman Drive NE
Atlanta, GA 30322
Phone: (404) 727-6036
Fax: (404) 727-4303

E-mail: admiss@emory.edu
http://www.emory.edu
Dance, film/video arts.

Floyd College**
3175 Highway 27 South
P.O. Box 1864
Rome, GA 30162
Phone: (800) 332-2406, ext. 6339
Fax: (706) 295-6610
E-mail: At Web site
http://www.floyd.edu
Communications.

Georgia Southern University
P.O. Box 8024
Statesboro, GA 30460
Phone: (912) 681-5391
Fax: (912) 486-7240
E-mail: admissions@georgiasouthern.edu
http://www.georgiasouthern.edu
Communications.

Georgia State University
P.O. Box 4009
Atlanta, GA 30302
Phone: (404) 651-2365
Fax: (404) 651-4811
E-mail: admissions@gsu.edu
http://www.gsu.edu
Communications, film/video arts, media
    studies.

Kennesaw State University
1000 Chastain Road, Campus Box 0115
Kennesaw, GA 30144
Phone: (770) 423-6000
Fax: (770) 423-6541
E-mail: ksuadmit@kennesaw.edu
http://www.kennesaw.edu
Communications.

Macon State College
100 College Station Drive
Macon, GA 31206
Phone: (800) 272-7619
E-mail: mscinfo@mail.maconstate.edu
http://www.maconstate.edu
Communications.

Mercer University—Macon
Admissions Office
1400 Coleman Avenue
Macon, GA 31207
Phone: (478) 301-2650
Fax: (478) 301-2828
E-mail: admissions@mercer.edu
http://www.mercer.edu
Media studies.

Oglethorpe University
4484 Peachtree Road NE
Atlanta, GA 30319
Phone: (404) 364-8307
Fax: (404) 364-8491
E-mail: admission@oglethorpe.edu
http://www.oglethorpe.edu
Communications.

Reinhardt College
7399 Reinhardt College Circle
Waleska, GA 30183
Phone: (770) 720-5526
Fax: (770) 720-5899
E-mail: admissions@reinhardt.edu
http://www.reinhardt.edu
Communications.

Piedmont College
P.O. Box 10
Demorest, GA 30535
Phone: (706) 776-0103
Fax: (706) 776-6635
E-mail: ugrad@piedmont.edu
http://www.piedmont.edu
Media studies.

Savannah College of Art and Design
P.O. Box 3146
Savannah, GA 31402
Phone: (912) 525-5100
Fax: (912) 525-5986
E-mail: admission@scad.edu
http://www.scad.edu
Cinematography, film/video production.

Savannah State University
College Station, P.O. Box 20209
Savannah, GA 31404
Phone: (912) 356-2181
Fax: (912) 356-2256
E-mail: SSUAdmission@savstate.edu
http://www.savstate.edu
Communications.

Shorter College
315 Shorter Avenue, P.O. Box 1
Rome, GA 30165
Phone: (706) 233-7319
Fax: (706) 233-7224
E-mail: admissions@shorter.edu
http://www.shorter.edu
Communications.

Southern Polytechnic State University
1100 South Marietta Parkway
Marietta, GA 30060
Phone: (678) 915-4188
Fax: (678) 915-7292

E-mail: admissions@spsu.edu
http://www.spsu.edu
Telecommunications technology.

Toccoa Falls College
Toccoa Falls, GA 30598
Phone: (888) 785-5624
Fax: NA
E-mail: admissions@tfc.edu
http://www.tfc.edu
Broadcast journalism.

University of Georgia*
Terrell Hall
Athens, GA 30602
Phone: (706) 542-8776
Fax: (706) 542-1466
E-mail: undergrad@admissions.uga.edu
http://www.uga.edu
Communications, communications
    technology, film/video arts.

Valdosta State University
1500 North Patterson Street
Valdosta, GA 31698
Phone: (229) 333-5791
Fax: (229) 333-5482
E-mail: admissions@valdosta.edu
http://www.valdosta.edu
Communications.

Wesleyan College
4760 Forsyth Road
Macon, GA 31210
Phone: (912) 757-5206
Fax: (912) 757-4030
E-mail: admissions@wesleyancollege.edu
http://www.wesleyancollege.edu
Communications.

HAWAII

Brigham Young University—Hawaii
55-220 Kulanui Street
Laie, HI 96762
Phone: (808) 293-3738
Fax: (808) 293-3457
E-mail: At Web site
http://www.byuh.edu
Communications.

Chaminade University of Honolulu
3140 Waialae Avenue
Honolulu, HI 96816
Phone: (808) 735-4735
Fax: (808) 739-4647
E-mail: admissions@chaminade.edu
http://www.chaminade.edu

Broadcast journalism, communications, media studies.

Hawaii Pacific University
1164 Bishop Street
Honolulu, HI 96813
Phone: (808) 544-0238
Fax: (808) 544-1136
E-mail: admissions@hpu.edu
http://www.hpu.edu
Communications, media studies.

Leeward Community College**
96-045 Ala Ike
Pearl City, HI 96782
Phone: (808) 455-0217
E-mail: leeward@hawaii.edu
http://www.lcc.hawaii.edu
Broadcast journalism.

University of Hawaii—Hilo
200 West Kawili Street
Hilo, HI 96720
Phone: (808) 974-7414
Fax: (808) 933-0861
E-mail: uhhadm@hawaii.edu
http://www.hawaii.edu
Communications.

University of Hawaii—Manoa
2600 Campus Road, QLCSS Room 001
Honolulu, HI 96822
Phone: (808) 956-8975
Fax: (808) 956-4148
E-mail: ar-info@hawaii.edu
http://www.uhm.hawaii.edu
Communications, dance.

IDAHO

Boise State University
1910 University Drive
Boise, ID 83725
Phone: (208) 426-1156
Fax: (208) 426-3765
E-mail: bsuinfo@boisestate.edu
http://www.boisestate.edu
Broadcast journalism, communications.

Brigham Young University
Admissions Office
KIM 120
Rexburg, ID 83460
Phone: (208) 496-1020
Fax: (208) 496-1220
E-mail: admissioins@byui.edu
http://www.byui.edu
Broadcast journalism, communications.

Idaho State University
Admissions Office
Campus P.O. Box 8270
Pocatello, ID 93208
Phone: (208) 282-2475
Fax: (208) 282-4231
E-mail: info@isu.edu
http://www.isu.edu
Communications, media studies.

North Idaho College**
1000 West Garden Avenue
Coeur d'Alene, ID 83814
Phone: (877) 404-4536
Fax: NA
E-mail: At Web site
http://www.nidc.edu
Communications.

University of Idaho
UI Admissions Office
P.O. Box 44264
Moscow, ID 83844
Phone: (308) 885-6326
Fax: (308) 885-9119
E-mail: admappl@uidaho.edu
http://www.uidaho.edu
Communications, dance.

ILLINOIS

Augustana College
639 38th Street
Rock Island, IL 61201
Phone: (309) 794-7341
Fax: (309) 794-7422
E-mail: admissions@augustina.edu
http://www.augustina.edu
Communications.

Aurora University
347 South Gladstone Avenue
Aurora, IL 60506
Phone: (630) 844-5533
Fax: (630) 844-5535
E-mail: admission@aurora.edu
http://www.aurora.edu
Communications.

Benedictine University
5700 College Road
Lisle, IL 60532
Phone: (630) 829-6300
Fax: (630) 829-6301
E-mail: admissions@ben.edu
http://www.ben.edu
Communications.

Blackburn College
700 College Avenue
Carlinville, IL 62026
Phone: (217) 854-3231
Fax: (217) 854-3713
E-mail: jmali@mail.blackburn.edu
http://www.blackburn.edu
Communications.

Bradley University
1501 West Bradley Avenue
Peoria, IL 61625
Phone: (309) 677-1000
Fax: (309) 677-2797
E-mail: admissions@bradley.edu
http://www.bradley.edu
Broadcast journalism, communications, radio and television.

Chicago State University
9501 South King Drive, ADM-200
Chicago, IL 60628
Phone: (773) 995-2513
Fax: (773) 995-3820
E-mail: ug-Admissions@csu.edu
http://www.csu.edu
Broadcast journalism

College of DuPage**
425 Fawell Boulevard
Glen Ellyn, IL 60137
Phone: (630) 942-2442
Fax: (630) 790-2686
E-mail: At Web site
http://www.cod.edu
Communications technology.

Columbia College—Chicago
600 South Michigan Avenue
Chicago, IL 60605
Phone: (312) 344-7130
Fax: (312) 344-8024
E-mail: admissions@colum.edu
http://www.colum.edu
Cinematography, film/video production, communications technology, dance, film/video arts, playwriting/ screenwriting.

Concordia University—River Forest
7400 Augusta Street
River Forest, IL 60305
Phone: (708) 209-3100
Fax: (708) 209-3473
E-mail: crfadmis@curf.edu
http://www.curf.edu
Communications.

DePaul University
1 East Jackson Boulevard
Chicago, IL 60604
Phone: (312) 362-8300
Fax: (312) 362-5749
E-mail: admitdpu@depaul.edu
http://www.depaul.edu
Communications, playwriting/
　screenwriting.

Eastern Illinois University*
600 Lincoln Avenue
Charleston, IL 61920
Phone: (217) 581-2223
Fax: (217) 581-7060
E-mail: cdadmit@www.eiu.edu
http://www.eiu.edu
Communications.

Elmhurst College
190 Prospect Avenue
Elmhurst, IL 60126
Phone: (630) 617-3400
Fax: (630) 617-5501
E-mail: admit@elmhurst.edu
http://www.elmhurst.edu
Communications.

Eureka College
300 East College Avenue
Eureka, IL 61530
Phone: (309) 467-6350
Fax: (309) 467-4574
E-mail: admissions@eureka.edu
http://www.eureka.edu
Communications.

Governors State University
1 University Parkway
University Park, IL 60456
Phone: (708) 534-4490
Fax: (708) 534-1640
E-mail: gsunow@govst.edu
http://www.govst.edu
Communications.

Greenville College
315 East College Avenue
Greenville, IL 62246
Phone: (618) 664-7100
Fax: (618) 664-9841
E-mail: admissions@greenville.edu
http://www.greenville.edu
Media studies.

Kennedy-King College**
6800 South Wentworth Avenue
Chicago, IL 60621

Phone: (773) 602-5000
E-mail: At Web site
http://kennedyking.ccc.edu
Broadcast journalism.

Illinois Central College**
1 College Drive
East Peoria, IL 61635
Phone: (800) 422-2293
Fax: (309) 694-5450
E-mail: At Web site
http://www.icc.edu
Broadcast journalism, dance.

Illinois State University
Admissions Office
Campus P.O. Box 2200
Normal, IL 61790
Phone: (309) 438-2181
Fax: (309) 438-3932
E-mail: ugradadm@ilstu.edu
http://www.ilstu.edu
Communications.

Lake Forest College
555 North Sheridan Road
Lake Forest, IL 60045
Phone: (847) 735-5000
Fax: (847) 735-6291
E-mail: admissions@lakeforest.edu.
http://www.lakeforest.edu
Communications.

Lake Land College**
5001 Lake Land Boulevard
Mattoon, IL 61938
Phone: (800) 252-4121
Fax: (217) 234-5390
E-mail: admissions@lakeland.cc.il.us
http://www.lakeland.cc.il.us
Broadcast journalism.

Lewis and Clark Community College**
5800 Godfrey Road
Godfrey, IL 62035
Phone: (800) 500-LCCC
Fax: (618) 467-2310
E-mail: twebb@lc.edu
http://www.lc.edu
Radio and television.

Lewis University
One University Parkway
P.O. Box 297
Romeoville, IL 60446
Phone: (815) 836-5250
Fax: (815) 836-5002
E-mail: admissions@lewisu.edu

http://www.lewisu.edu
Broadcast journalism, communications,
　communications technology.

Loyola University of Chicago
Admissions Office
820 North Michigan Avenue
Chicago, IL 60611
Phone: (312) 915-6500
Fax: (312) 915-7216
E-mail: admission@luc.edu
http://www.luc.edu
Communications.

Moraine Valley Community College**
10900 South 88th Avenue
Palos Hills, IL 60465
Phone: (708) 974-5357
Fax: (708) 974-0681
E-mail: At Web site
http://www.morainevalley.edu
Telecommunications technology.

McKendree College
701 College Road
Lebanon, IL 62254
Phone: (618) 537-6831
Fax: (618) 637-6496
E-mail: inquiry@mckendree.edu
http://www.mckendree.edu
Communications.

Millikin University
1184 West Main Street
Decatur, IL 62522
Phone: (217) 424-6210
Fax: (217) 425-4669
E-mail: admis@mail.millikin.edu
http://www.millikin.edu
Communications.

Monmouth College
700 East Broadway
Monmouth. IL 61462
Phone: (309) 457-2131
Fax: (309) 457-2141
E-mail: admit@monm.edu
http://www.monm.edu
Communications.

North Central College
30 North Brainard Street
P.O. Box 3063
Naperville, IL 60506
Phone: (630) 637-5800
Fax: (630) 637-5819
E-mail: ncadm@noctrl.edu
http://www.northcentralcollege.edu

Broadcast journalism, communications, radio/television broadcasting.

North Park University
3225 West Foster Avenue
Chicago, IL 60625
Phone: (773) 244-5500
Fax: (773) 244-4953
E-mail: admission@northpark.edu
http://www.northpark.edu
Communications.

Northern Illinois University
Office of Admissions
Williston Hall 101, NIU
DeKalb, IL 60115
Phone: (815) 753-0446
Fax: (815) 753-1783
E-mail: admissions-info@niu.edu
http://www.reg.niu.edu
Communications.

Northwestern University*
P.O. Box 3060
1801 Hinman Avenue
Evanston, IL 60208
Phone: (847) 491-7271
Fax: (847) 491-5565
E-mail: ug-admission@northwestern.edu
http://www.northwestern.edu
Broadcast journalism, communications, communications technology, dance, radio and television.

Olivet Nazarene University
One University Avenue
Bourbonnais, IL 60914
Phone: (815) 939-5203
Fax: (815) 935-4998
E-mail: admissions@olivet.edu
http://www.olivet.edu
Communications.

Parkland College**
Admission Representative
2400 West Bradley Avenue
Champaign, IL 61821
Phone: (800) 346-8089
Fax: (217) 351-7640
E-mail: At Web site
http://www.parkland.edu
Radio/television broadcasting.

Quincy University
1800 College Avenue
Quincy, IL 62301
Phone: (217) 228-5215

Fax: (217) 228-5479
E-mail: admissions@quincy.edu
http://www.quincy.edu
Radio and television.

Roosevelt University
430 South Michigan Avenue
Chicago, IL 60605
Phone: (312) 341-3515
Fax: (312) 341-3523
E-mail: applyRU@roosevelt.edu
http://www.roosevelt.edu
Communications.

St. Xavier University
3700 West 103rd Street
Chicago, IL 60655
Phone: (773) 298-3050
Fax: (773) 298-3076
E-mail: admissions@sxu.edu
http://www.sxu.edu
Communications.

School of the Art Institute of Chicago
37 South Wabash Avenue
Chicago, IL 60603
Phone: (312) 899-5219
Fax: (312) 899-1840
E-mail: admiss@artic.edu
http://www.artic.edu
Cinematography, film/video production.

South Suburban College of Cook Country**
15800 South State Street
South Holland, IL 60473
Phone: (708) 596-2000, ext. 2314
Fax: (708) 225-5806
E-mail: admissionsquestions@ southsuburbancollege.edu
http://www.southsuburbancollege.edu
Broadcast journalism.

Southern Illinois University— Carbondale*
Admissions & Records, MC 4710
Carbondale, IL 62901
Phone: (618) 453-4405
Fax: (618) 453-3250
E-mail: joinsiuc@siuc.edu
http://www.siuc.edu
Cinematography, film/video production, media studies, radio and television.

Southern Illinois University— Edwardsville*
P.O. Box 1600
Edwardsville, IL 62026
Phone: (618) 650-3705

Fax: (618) 650-5013
E-mail: admis@siue.edu
http://www.siue.edu
Communications, dance, media studies.

Southwestern Illinois College**
2500 Carlyle Avenue
Belleville, IL 62221
Phone: (800) 222-5131
Fax: (618) 277-0631
E-mail: At Web site
http://www.southwestern.cc.il.us
Communications, communications technology.

Trinity Christian College
6601 West College Drive
Palos Heights, IL 60453
Phone: (708) 239-4708
Fax: (708) 239-4826
E-mail: admissions@trnty.edu
http://www.trnty.edu
Communications.

University of Illinois—Springfield
P.O. Box 19243
Springfield, IL 62794
Phone: (217) 206-6626
Fax: (217) 206-786-6620
E-mail: admissions@uis.edu
http://www.uis.edu
Communications.

University of Illinois—Urbana-Champaign*
901 West Illinois Street
Urbana, IL 61801
Phone: (217) 333-0302
Fax: (217) 333-9758
E-mail: admissions@oar.uiuc.edu
http://www.uiuc.edu
Broadcast journalism, communications, dance, media studies.

University of Saint Francis
500 Wilcox Street
Joliet, IL 60435
Phone: (815) 740-5037
Fax: (815) 740-5032
E-mail: admissions@stfrancis.edu
http://www.stfrancis@edu
Broadcast journalism, communications, media studies, radio and television.

Wabash Valley College**
2200 College Drive
Mt. Carmel, IL 62863

Phone: (866) 982-4322
Fax: NA
E-mail: wvcadmissions@iecc.edu
http://www.iecc.cc.il.us
Broadcast journalism.

Western Illinois University
1 University Circle
115 Sherman Hall
Macomb, IL 61455
Phone: (309) 298-3157
Fax: (309) 298-3111
E-mail: wiuadm@wiu.edu
http://www.wiu.edu
Communications, radio and television.

Wheaton College
501 College Avenue
Wheaton, IL 60187
Phone: (630) 752-5005
Fax: (630) 752-5285
E-mail: admissions@wheaton.edu
http://www.wheaton.edu
Communications.

INDIANA

Ancilla College**
Donaldson, IN 46513
Phone: (864) 262-4552, ext. 350
Fax: (574) 935-1773
E-mail: admissions@ancilla.edu
http://www.ancilla.edu
Media studies.

Anderson University
1100 East Fifth Street
Anderson, IN 46012
Phone: (765) 641-4080
Fax: (765) 641-4091
E-mail: info@anderson.edu
http://www.anderson.edu
Communications.

Ball State University*
Office of Admissions
2000 West University Avenue
Muncie, IN 47306
Phone: (765) 285-8300
Fax: (765) 285-1632
E-mail: askus@bsu.edu
http://www.bsu.edu
Broadcast journalism, communications,
    communications technology, film/
    video arts.

Bethel College
1001 West McKinley Avenue
Mishawaka, IN 46545

Phone: (574) 257-3339
Fax: (574) 257-3335
E-mail: admissions@bethelcollege.edu
http://www.bethel.college.edu
Communications.

Butler University
4600 Sunset Avenue
Indianapolis, IN 46208
Phone: (317) 940-8100
Fax: (317) 940-8150
E-mail: admission@butler.edu
http://www.butler.edu
Broadcast journalism, communications.

Calumet College of Saint Joseph
2400 New York Avenue
Whiting, IN 46394
Phone: (219) 473-4215
Fax: (219) 473-4259
E-mail: admissions@ccsj.edu
http://www.ccsj.edu
Communications, media studies.

DePauw University
101 East Seminary
Greencastle, IN 46135
Phone: (765) 658-4006
Fax: (765) 658-4007
E-mail: admission@depauw.edu
http://www.depauw.edu
Communications, media studies.

Goshen College
1700 South Main Street
Goshen, IN 46526
Phone: (574) 535-7535
Fax: (574) 535-7609
E-mail: admissions@goshen.edu
http://www.goshen.edu
Communications.

Grace College and Seminary
200 Seminary Drive
Winona Lake, IN 46590
Phone: (800) 544-7223
Fax: (574) 372-5114
E-mail: enroll@grace.edu
http://www.grace.edu
Communications.

Hanover College
P.O. Box 108
Hanover, IN 47243
Phone: (812) 866-7021
Fax: (812) 866-7098
E-mail: admission@hanover.edu
http://www.hanover.edu
Communications.

Huntington College
2303 College Avenue
Huntington, IN 46750
Phone: (260) 359-4000
Fax: (260) 358-3699
E-mail: admissions@huntington.edu
http://www.huntington.edu
Broadcast journalism, communications,
    media studies.

Indiana State University
Office of Admissions
Trey Hall 134
Terra Haute, IN 47809
Phone: (812) 237-2121
Fax: (812) 237-8023
E-mail: admissions@indstate.edu
http://www.indstate.edu
Communications, film/video arts, radio
    and television.

Indiana University—Bloomington*
300 North Jordan Avenue
Bloomington, IN 47405
Phone: (812) 855-0661
Fax: (812) 855-5102
E-mail: iuadmit@indiana.edu
http://www.indiana.edu
Communications, media studies.

Indiana University East
2325 Chester Boulevard, WZ 116
Richmond, IN 47374
Phone: (765) 973-8208
Fax: (765) 973-8288
E-mail: eaadmit@indiana.edu
http://www.iu.edu
Communications.

Indiana University Northwest
3400 Broadway
Hawthorn 100
Gary, IN 46408
Phone: (219) 980-6991
Fax: (219) 981-4219
E-mail: admit@iun.edu
http://www.iun.edu
Communications.

**Indiana University—Purdue University
    Fort Wayne**
2101 East Coliseum Boulevard
Fort Wayne, IN 46805
Phone: (260) 481-6812
Fax: (260) 481-6880
E-mail: ipfwadms@ipfw.edu
http://www.ipfw.edu
Communications.

Indiana University—Purdue University Indianapolis
425 North University Boulevard
Cavanaugh Hall, Room 129
Indianapolis, IN 46202
Phone: (317) 274-4591
Fax: (317) 278-1862
E-mail: apply@iupui.edu
http://www.iu.edu
Communications, communications technology, media studies.

Indiana University South Bend
1700 Mishawaka Avenue
P.O. Box 7111, A169
South Bend, IN 46634
Phone: (574) 237-4840
Fax: (219) 237-4834
E-mail: admission@iusb.edu
http://www.iusb.edu
Media studies.

Indiana University Southeast
4201 Grant Line Road, ULC-100
New Albany, IN 47150
Phone: (812) 941-2212
Fax: (812) 941-2595
E-mail: admissions@ius.edu
http://www.ius.edu
Communications.

Manchester College
604 College Avenue, North
Manchester, IN 46962
Phone: (260) 982-5055
Fax: (260) 982-5239
E-mail: admitinfo@manchester.edu
http://www.manchester.edu
Broadcast journalism, communications.

Marian College
3200 Cold Spring Road
Indianapolis, IN 46222
Phone: (317) 955-6300
Fax: (317) 955-6401
E-mail: admit@marian.edu
http://www.marian.edu
Communications.

Purdue University—Calumet
Office of Admissions
2200 169th Street
Hammond, IN 46323
Phone: (219) 989-2213
Fax: (219) 989-2775
E-mail: adms@calumet.purdue.edu
http://www.calumet.purdue.edu
Broadcast journalism, communications.

Purdue University—North Central Campus
1401 South U.S. Highway 421
Westville, IN 46391
Phone: (219) 785-5458
Fax: (219) 785-5538
E-mail: admissions@pnc.edu
http://www.pnc.edu
Communications.

Purdue University—West Lafayette
1080 Schleman Hall
West Lafayette, IN 47907
Phone: (765) 494-1776
Fax: (765) 494-0544
E-mail: admissions@purdue.edu
http://www.purdue.edu
Communications, film/video arts.

Saint Joseph's College
P.O. Box 890
Rensselaer, IN 47978
Phone: (219) 866-6170
Fax: (219) 866-6122
E-mail: admissions@saintjoe.edu
http://www.saintjoe.edu
Communications, media studies.

Saint Mary's College
Admission Office
Notre Dame, IN 46556
Phone: (219) 284-4587
Fax: (219) 284-4841
E-mail: admission@saintmarys.edu
http://www.saintmarys.edu
Communications.

Saint Mary-of-the-Woods College
Office of Admissions
Guerin Hall
Saint Mary-of-the-Woods, IN 47876
Phone: (812) 535-5106
Fax: (812) 535-4900
E-mail: smwcadms@smwc.edu
http://www.smwc.edu
Communications technology, media studies.

Taylor University—Fort Wayne Campus
1025 West Rudisill Boulevard
Fort Wayne, IN 46807
Phone: (800) 233.3922
Fax: (260) 744-8660
E-mail: admissions_f@tayloru.edu
http://www.tayloru.edu/fw
Broadcast journalism, communications.

Taylor University—Upland
236 West Reade Avenue
Upland, IN 46989
Phone: (765) 998-5134
Fax: (765) 998-4925
E-mail: admissions_U@tayloru.edu
http://www.tayloru.edu
Broadcast journalism, communications.

University of Evansville
1800 Lincoln Avenue
Evansville, IN 47722
Phone: (812) 479-2468
Fax: (812) 474-4076
E-mail: admission@evansville.edu
http://www.evansville.edu
Communications.

University of Indianapolis
1400 East Hanna Avenue
Indianapolis, IN 46227
Phone: (317) 788-3216
Fax: (317) 788-3300
E-mail: admissions@uindy.edu
http://www.uindy.edu
Broadcast journalism, communications.

University of Southern Indiana*
8600 University Boulevard
Evansville, IN 47712
Phone: (812) 464-1765
Fax: (812) 465-7154
E-mail: enroll@usi.edu
http://www.usi.edu
Communications technology, media studies, radio and television.

Valparaiso University
Office of Admissions, Kretzman Hall
1700 Chapel Drive
Valparaiso, IN 46383-4520
Phone: (219) 464-5011
Fax: (219) 464-6898
E-mail: undergrad.admissions@valpo.edu
http://www.valpo.edu
Communications, media studies.

Vincennes University**
Admissions Office, GVH 72
1002 North First Street
Vincennes, IN 47591
Phone: (800) 742-9198
Fax: (812) 888-5707
E-mail: yourfuture@vinu.edu
http://www.vinu.edu
Broadcast journalism, communications, media studies, radio/television broadcasting.

IOWA

Briar Cliff University
Admissions Office
P.O. Box 100
Sioux City, IA 51104
Phone: (712) 279-5200
Fax: (712) 279-1632
E-mail: admissions@briarcliff.edu
http://www.briarcliff.edu
Media studies.

Buena Vista University
610 West Fourth Street
Storm Lake, IA 50588
Phone: (712) 749-2235
Fax: (712) 749-1459
E-mail: admissions@bvu.edu
http://www.bvu.edu
Communications, media studies.

Central College
812 University Street
Pella, IA 50219
Phone: (877) 462-3687
Fax: (641) 628-5316
E-mail: admission@central.edu
http://www.central.edu
Communications.

Clarke College
1550 Clarke Drive
Dubuque, IA 52001
Phone: (563) 588-6316
Fax: (563) 588-6789
E-mail: admissions@clarke.edu
http://www.clarke.edu
Communications.

Coe College
1220 First Avenue NE
Cedar Rapids, IA 52402
Phone: (319) 399-8500
Fax: (319) 399-8816
E-mail: admission@coe.edu
http://coe.edu
Acting.

Dordt College
498 4th Avenue Northeast
Sioux Center, IA 51250
Phone: (712) 722-6080
Fax: (712) 722-1987
E-mail: admissions@dordt.edu
http://www.dordt.edu
Broadcast journalism, communications.

Drake University*
2507 University Avenue
Des Moines, IA 50311
Phone: (515) 271-3181
Fax: (515) 271-2831
E-mail: admission@drake.edu
http://www.choose.drake.edu
Acting, broadcast journalism,
    communications, media studies.

Ellsworth Community College**
1100 College Avenue
Iowa Falls, IA 50126
Phone: (800)-322-9235
Fax: (641) 648-3128
E-mail: eccinfo@iavalley.cc.ia.us
http://www.iavalley.cc.ia.us/ecc
Communications.

The Franciscan University
400 North Bluff Boulevard
P.O. Box 2967
Clinton, IA 52793
Phone: (563) 242-4153
Fax: (563) 243-6102
E-mail: admissns@tfu.edu
http://www.ffu.edu
Communications.

Grand View College
1200 Grandview Avenue
Des Moines, IA 50316
Phone: (515) 263-2810
Fax: (515) 263-2974
E-mail: admiss@gvc.edu
http://www.gvc.edu
Broadcast journalism, communications.

Iowa Central Community College**
330 Avenue M
Fort Dodge, IA 50501
Phone: (800) 362-2793
Fax: (515) 576-7724
E-mail: At Web site
http://www.iccc.cc.ia.us
Broadcast journalism, communications
    technology.

Iowa State University*
100 Alumni Hall
Ames, IA 50011
Phone: (515) 294-5836
Fax: (515) 294-2592
E-mail: admissions@iastate.edu
http://www.iastate.edu
Communications.

Iowa Wesleyan College
601 North Main Street

Mt. Pleasant, IA 52641
Phone: (319) 385-6231
Fax: (319) 385-6296
E-mail: admitrwl@iwc.edu
http://www.iwc.edu
Broadcast journalism, communications.

Loras College
1450 Alta Vista Street
Dubuque, IA 52003
Phone: (800) 245-6727
Fax: (563) 588-7119
E-mail: admissions@loras.edu
http://www.loras.edu
Media studies.

Luther College
700 College Drive
Decorah, IA 52101
Phone: (563) 387-1287
Fax: (563) 387-2159
E-mail: admissions@luther.edu
http://www.luther.edu
Media studies.

Mount Mercy College
1330 Elmhurst Drive Northeast
Cedar Rapids, IA 52402
Phone: (319) 368-6460
Fax: (319) 363-5270
E-mail: admission@mtmercy.edu
http://www.mtmercy.edu
Communications.

Northwestern College
101 7th Street SW
Orange City, IA 51041
Phone: (712) 707-7130
Fax: (712) 707-7164
E-mail: admissions@nwciowa.edu
http://www.nwciowa.edu
Communications.

Saint Ambrose University
518 West Locust Street
Davenport, IA 52803
Phone: (563) 444-6300
Fax: (563) 333-6297
E-mail: admit@sau.edu
http://www.sau.edu
Communications, media studies.

Simpson College
701 North C Street
Indianola, IA 50125
Phone: (515) 961-1624
Fax: (515) 961-1870

E-mail: admiss@simpson.edu
http://www.simpson.edu
Communications.

University of Dubuque
2000 University Avenue
Dubuque, IA 52001
Phone: (319) 589-3200
Fax: (319) 589-3690
E-mail: admssns@dbq.edu
http://www.dbq.edu
Communications.

University of Iowa*
107 Calvin Hall
Iowa City, IA 52242
Phone: (319) 335-3847
Fax: (319) 335-1535
E-mail: admissions@uiowa.edu
http://www.uiowa.edu
Acting, broadcast journalism.
  cinematography, film/video
  production, communications, dance,
  film/video arts, media studies, radio/
  television broadcasting.

University of Northern Iowa
1227 West 27th Street
Cedar Falls, IA 50614
Phone: (319) 273-2281
Fax: (319) 273-2885
E-mail: admissions@uni.edu
http://www.uni.edu
Acting, communications.

Waldorf College
106 South 6th Street
Forest City, IA 50436
Phone: (641) 585-8112
Fax: (641) 585-8125
E-mail: admissions@waldorf.edu
http://www.waldorf.edu
Broadcast journalism, communications
  technology, media studies.

Wartburg College
100 Wartburg Boulevard
Waverly, IA 50677
Phone: (800) 772-2085
Fax: (319) 352-8579
E-mail: admissions@wartburg.edu
http://www.wartburg.edu
Broadcast journalism, communications.

William Penn University
201 Trueblood Avenue
Oklahoma, IA 52577

Phone: (641) 673-1012
Fax: (614) 673-2113
E-mail: admissions@wmpenn.edu
http://www.wmpenn.edu
Communications.

KANSAS

Baker University
Eighth and Grove
Baldwin City, KS 66006
Phone: (785) 594-8307
Fax: (785) 594-8372
E-mail: admission@bakeru.edu
http://www.bakeru.edu
Communications.

Bethany College
421 North First Street
Lindsborg, KS 67456
Phone: (785) 227-3311
Fax: (785) 227-8993
E-mail: admiossions@bethanylb.edu
http://www.bethanylb.edu
Communications.

Central Christian College of Kansas
1200 South Main Street
McPherson, KS 67460
Phone: (800) 835-0078
Fax: (620) 241-6032
E-mail: admissions@centralchristian.edu
http://www.centralcollege.edu
Acting, broadcast journalism,
  communications, communications
  technology, media studies,
  photographic/film/video technology,
  playwriting/screenwriting, radio and
  television, radio/television
  broadcasting.

Coffeyville Community College**
400 West 11th Street
Coffeyville, KS 67337
Phone: (800) 782-4732
Fax: (620) 252-7098
E-mail: kellib@coffeyville.edu
http://www.coffeyville.edu
Broadcast journalism, communications.

Colby Community College**
CCC Admissions
1255 South Range Avenue
Colby, KS 67701
Phone: (888) 634-9350, ext. 690
Fax: (785) 462-4691

E-mail: bobbi@colbycc.edu
http://www.colbycc.edu
Broadcast journalism

Dodge City Community College**
2501 North 14th Avenue
Dodge City, KS 67801
Phone: (800) FOR-DCCC
Fax: (316) 225-0918
E-mail: At Web site
http://www.dccc.cc.ks.us
Broadcast journalism.

Emporia State University
1200 Commercial Street
Emporia, KS 66801
Phone: (620) 341-5465
Fax: (620) 341-5599
E-mail: goto@emporia.edu
http://www.emporia.edu
Communications.

Fort Hays State University
600 Park Street
Hays, KS 67601
Phone: (785) 628-5666
Fax: (785) 628-4187
E-mail: tigers@fhsu.edu
http://www.fhsu.edu
Communications.

Hutchinson Community College**
1300 North Plum Street
Hutchinson, KS 67501
Phone: (800) 289-3501
Fax: (620) 665-3310
E-mail: info@hutchcc.edu
http://www.hutchcc.edu
Communications technology.

Independence Community College**
College Avenue and Brookside Drive
Independence, KS 67301
Phone: (800)842-6063
Fax: (620) 331-5344
E-mail: admissions@indycc.edu
http://www.indycc.edu
Broadcast journalism, communications.

Kansas State University*
119 Anderson Hall
Manhattan, KS 66506
Phone: (785) 532-6250
Fax: (785) 532-6393
E-mail: kstate@ksu.edu
http://www.consider.k-state.edu
Communications.

McPherson College
P.O. Box 1402
1600 East Euclid Avenue

McPherson, KS 67460
Phone: (316) 241-0731
Fax: (316) 241-8443
E-mail: admiss@mcpherson.edu
http://www.mcpherson.edu
Communications.

Kansas Wesleyan University
100 East Claflin Avenue
Salina, KS 67401
Phone: (785) 827-5541
Fax: (785) 827-0927
E-mail: admissions@kwu.edu
http://www.kwu.edu
Communications.

MidAmerica Nazarene University
2030 College Way
Olathe, KS 66062
Phone: (913) 791-3380
Fax: (913) 791-3481
E-mail: admission@mnu.edu
http://www.mnu.edu
Communications, media studies.

Newman University
3100 McCormick Avenue
Wichita, KS 67213
Phone: (316) 942-4291
Fax: (316) 942-4483
E-mail: admissions@newman.edu
http://www.newman.edu
Media studies.

Ottawa University
1001 South Cedar Street
Ottawa, KS 66067
Phone: (785) 242-5200
Fax: (785) 229-1008
E-mail: admiss@ottawa.edu
http://www.ottawa.edu
Communications.

Pittsburg State University
1701 South Broadway
Pittsburg, KS 66762
Phone: (620) 235-4251
Fax: (620) 235-6003
E-mail: psuadmit@pittstate.edu
http://www.pittstate.edu
Acting, broadcast journalism,
    communications, film/video arts, radio
    and television.

Southwestern College
100 College Street
Winfield, KS 67156
Phone: (620) 229-6236
Fax: (620) 229-6344

E-mail: scadmit@sckans.edu
http://www.sckans.edu
Communications.

Sterling College
P.O. Box 98
Sterling, KS 67579
Phone: (620) 278-4275
Fax: (620) 278-4416
E-mail: admissions@sterling.edu
http://www.sterling.edu
Communications.

Tabor College
400 South Jefferson Street
Hillsboro, KS 67063
Phone: (620) 947-3121
Fax: (620) 947-6276
E-mail: admissions@tabor.edu
http://www.tabor.edu
Communications.

University of Kansas*
Office of Admissions and Scholarships
1502 Iowa Street
Lawrence, KS 66045-7575
Phone: (785) 864-3911
Fax: (785) 864-5017
E-mail: adm@ku.edu
http://www.ku.edu
Broadcast journalism, dance.

Washburn University
1700 SW College Avenue
Topeka, KS 66621
Phone: (785) 231-1030
Fax: (785) 296-7933
E-mail: zzdpadm@washburn.edu
http://www.washburn.edu
Communications, media studies.

Wichita State University
1845 Fairmount Street
Wichita, KS 67260
Phone: (316) 978-3085
Fax: (316) 978-3174
E-mail: admissions@wichita.edu
http://www.wichita.edu
Communications.

KENTUCKY

Asbury College
1 Macklem Drive
Wilmore, KY 403390
Phone: (859) 858-3511
Fax: (859) 858-3921
E-mail: admissions@asbury.edu
http://www.asbury.edu
Communications technology.

Bellarmine University
2001 Newburg Road
Louisville, KY 40205
Phone: (502) 452-8131
Fax: (502) 452-8002
E-mail: admissions@bellarmine.edu
http://www.bellarmine.edu
Communications.

Campbellville University
1 University Drive
Campbellville, KY 42718
Phone: (270) 789-5220
Fax: (270) 789-5071
E-mail: admissions@campbellville.edu
http://www.campbellville.edu
Broadcast journalism, communications.

Cumberland College
6178 College Station Drive
Williamsburg, KY 40769
Phone: (606) 539-4241
Fax: (606) 539-4303
E-mail: admiss@cumberlandcollege.edu
http://www.cumberlandcollege.edu
Communications.

Eastern Kentucky University
Student Services 112, SSB CPO 54
521 Lancaster Avenue
Richmond, KY 40475
Phone: (859) 622-2106
Fax: (606) 622-8024
E-mail: stephen.byn@eku.edu
http://www.eku.edu
Broadcast journalism, communications.

Henderson Community College*
660 South Green Street
Henderson, KY 42420
Phone: (800) 696-9958
E-mail: At Web site
http://www.henderson.kctcs.edu
Communications.

Kentucky Wesleyan College
3000 Frederica Street
P.O. Box 1039
Owensboro, KY 42302
Phone: (270) 852-3120
Fax: (270) 852-3133
E-mail: admitme@kwc.edu
http://www.kwc.edu
Communications, media studies.

Lindsey Wilson College
210 Lindsey Wilson Street
Columbia, KY 42728
Phone: (800) 264-0138

Fax: (270) 384-8591
E-mail: admissions@lindsey.edu
http://www.lindsey.edu
Communications.

Morehead State University
100 Admission Center
Morehead, KY 40351
Phone: (606) 783-2000
Fax: (606) 783-5038
E-mail: admissions@moreheadstate.edu
http://www.moreheadstate.edu
Communications.

Murray State University*
P.O. Box 9
Murray, KY 42071
Phone: (270) 762-3741
Fax: (270) 762-3780
E-mail: admissions@murraystate.edu
http://www.murraystate.edu
Communications, media studies, radio
    and television.

Northern Kentucky University
Administrative Center 400
Nunn Drive
Highland Heights, KY 41099
Phone: (859) 572-5220
Fax: (859) 572-6665
E-mail: admitnku@nku.edu
http://www.nku.edu
Broadcast journalism, communications,
    communications technology.

Pikeville College
Admissions Office
147 Sycamore Street
Pikeville, KY 41501
Phone: (606) 218-5251
Fax: (606) 218-5255
E-mail: wewantyou@pc.edu
http://www.pc.edu
Communications.

Spalding University
851 South Fourth Street
Louisville, KY 40203
Phone: (502) 585-7111
Fax: (502) 992-2418
E-mail: admission@spalding.edu
http://www.spalding.edu
Communications.

Thomas More College
333 Thomas More Parkway
Crestview Hill, KY 40107
Phone: (859) 344-3332
Fax: (859) 344-3444

E-mail: admissions@thomasmore.edu
http://www.thomasmore.edu
Communications.

Union College
310 College Street, Box 5
Barbourville, KY 40906
Phone: (606) 546-1657
Fax: (606) 546-1667
E-mail: enroll@unionky.edu
http://www.unionky.edu
Communications.

University of Kentucky*
100 Funkhuser Building
Lexington, KY 40506
Phone: (859) 257-2000
Fax: (859) 257-2000
E-mail: admission@uky.edu
http://www.uky.edu
Communications.

**West Kentucky Community and
    Technical College****
4810 Alben Barkley Drive
P.O. Box 7380
Paducah, KY 42002
Phone: (270) 554-9200
E-mail: WKAdmissions@westkentucky.
    kctcs.edu
http://www.westkentucky.kctcs.edu
Communications.

Western Kentucky University*
Potter Hall 117
1 Big Red Way
Bowling Green, KY 42101
Phone: (270) 745-2551
Fax: (270) 745-6133
E-mail: admission@wku.edu
http://www.wku.edu
Broadcast journalism, communications.

LOUISIANA

Bossier Parish Community College**
6220 East Texas Street
Bossier City, LA 71111
Phone: (318) 746-9851, ext. 215
Fax: (318) 742-8664
E-mail: At Web site
http://www.bpcc.edu
Radio and television.

Centenary College of Louisiana
P.O. Box 41188
Shreveport, LA 71134
Phone: (318) 869-5131
Fax: (318) 869-5005

E-mail: admissions@centenary.edu
http://www.centenary.edu
Cinematography, film/video production,
    communications, dance, media
    studies.

Dillard University
2601 Gentilly Boulevard
New Orleans, LA 70122
Phone: (504) 816-4670
Fax: (504) 816-4895
E-mail: admissions@dillard.edu
http://www.dillard.edu
Communications.

Grambling State University*
P.O. Box 864
Grambling, LA 71245
Phone: (318) 274-6423
Fax: (318) 274-3292
E-mail: taylorn@gram.edu
http://www.gram.edu
Communications.

Louisiana College
1140 College Drive
P.O. Box 560
Pineville, LA 71359
Phone: (318) 487-7259
Fax: (318) 487-7550
E-mail: admissions@lacollege.edu
http://www.lacollege.edu
Broadcast journalism, communications.

**Louisiana State University—Baton
    Rouge***
110 Thomas Boyd Hall
Baton Rouge, LA 70803
Phone: (225) 578-1175
Fax: (225) 578-4433
E-mail: admissions@lsu.edu
http://www.lsu.edu
Communications, media studies.

Loyola University—New Orleans
6363 St. Charles Avenue, P.O. Box 18
New Orleans, LA 70811
Phone: (504) 865-3240
Fax: (504) 865-3383
E-mail: admit@loyno.edu
http://www.loyno.edu
Communications, communications
    technology.

McNeese State University
P.O. Box 92495
Lake Charles, LA 90609
Phone: (318) 475-5146
Fax: (318) 475-5189

E-mail: info@mail.mcneese.edu
http://www.mcneese.edu
Communications.

Nicholls State University*
P.O. Box 2004
Thibodaux, LA 70310
Phone: (985) 448-4507
Fax: (985) 448-4929
E-mail: nicholls@nicholls.edu
http://www.nicholls.edu
Communications.

Southeastern Louisiana University
SLU 10752
Hammond, LA 70402
Phone: (985) 549-2066
Fax: (985) 549-5632
E-mail: admissions@selu.edu
http://www.selu.edu
Communications.

**Southern University and A&M
    College***
P.O. Box 9901
Baton Rouge, LA 70813
Phone: (225) 771-2430
Fax: (225) 771-2500
E-mail: admit@subr.edu
http://www.subr.edu
Communications, media studies.

Tulane University
6823 St. Charles Avenue
New Orleans, LA 70118
Phone: (504) 865-5731
Fax: (504) 862-8715
E-mail: undergrad.admission@tulane.
    edu
http://www.tulane.edu
Media studies.

University of Louisiana—Lafayette*
P.O. Drawer 41210
Lafayette, LA 70504
Phone: (337) 482-6457
Fax: (337) 482-6195
E-mail: admissions@louisiana.edu
http://www.louisiana.edu
Communications, media studies,
    telecommunications technology.

University of Louisiana—Monroe*
700 University Avenue
Monroe, LA 71209
Phone: (318) 342-5252
Fax: (318) 342-5274
E-mail: rehood@ulm.edu
http://www.ulm.edu

Broadcast journalism, communications,
    communications technology, film/
    video arts.

University of New Orleans
Office of Admissions
103 Administration Building
New Orleans, LA 70148
Phone: (504) 280-6595
Fax: (504) 280-5522
E-mail: admissions@uno.edu
http://www.uno.edu
Communications.

Xavier University of Louisiana
One Drexel Drive
Attn: Admissions Office
New Orleans, LA 70125
Phone: (504) 483-7388
Fax: (504) 485-7941
E-mail: apply@xula.edu
http://www.xula.edu
Communications.

MAINE

**New England School of
    Communications**
1 College Circle
Bangor, ME 04401
Phone: (888) 877-1876
Fax: NA
E-mail: GrantL@nescom.edu
http://www.nescom.edu
Broadcast journalism, cinematography,
    film/video production,
    communications, communications
    technology, photographic/film/video
    technology, radio and television,
    radio/television broadcasting.

Thomas College
180 West River Road
Waterville, ME 04901
Phone: (207) 859-1101
Fax: (207) 859-1114
E-mail: admiss@thomas.edu
http://www.thomas.edu
Communications.

University of Maine—Augusta
46 University Drive
Augusta, ME 04330
Phone: (207) 621-3185
Fax: (207) 621-3116
E-mail: umaar@maine.edu
http://www.uma.maine.edu
Communications.

University of Maine—Orono
5713 Chadbourne Hall
Orono, ME 04469
Phone: (207) 581-1561
Fax: (207) 581-1213
E-mail: um-admit@maine.edu
http://www.maine.edu
Communications.

Southern Maine Community College**
2 Fort Road
South Portland, ME 04106
Phone: (877) 282-2182
Fax: (207) 741-5671
E-mail: MEnrollmentservices@smccme.
    edu
http://www.smccme.edu
Cinematography, film/video production.

University of Southern Maine
37 College Avenue
Gorham, ME 04038
Phone: (207) 780-5670
Fax: (207) 780-5640
E-mail: usmadm@usm.maine.edu
http://usm.maine.edu
Acting, broadcast journalism,
    cinematography, film/video
    production, communications, media
    studies.

MARYLAND

Allegany College**
12401 Willowbrook Road SE
Cumberland, MD 21502
Phone: (301) 784-5000, ext. 5202
Fax: (301) 784-5220
E-mail: At Web site
http://www.ac.cc.md.us
Communications technology.

Bowie State University
14000 Jericho Park Road
Henry Administration Building
Bowie, MD 20715
Phone: (301) 860-3415
Fax: (301) 860-3438
E-mail: schanaiwa@bowiestate.edu
http://www.bowiestate.edu
Communications, communications
    technology.

College of Notre Dame of Maryland
4701 North Charles Street
Baltimore, MD 21210
Phone: (410) 532-5330
Fax: (410) 532-6287
E-mail: admiss@ndm.edu

http://www.ndm.edu
Communications.

Columbia Union College
7600 Flower Avenue
Takoma Park, MD 20912
Phone: (301) 891-4080
Fax: (301) 891-4230
E-mail: enroll@cuc.edu
http://www.cuc.edu
Broadcast journalism, communications.

Community College of Baltimore County**
Catonsville Campus
800 South Rolling Road
Baltimore, MD 21228
Phone: (410) 455-4392
E-mail: At Web site
http://www.ccbcmd.edu
Telecommunications technology.

Coppin State College
2500 West North Avenue
Baltimore, MD 21216
Phone: (410) 951-3600
Fax: (410) 523-7351
E-mail: admissions@coppin.edu
http://www.coppin.edu
Media studies.

Frederick Community College**
7932 Opossumtown Pike
Frederick, MD 21702
Phone: (301) 846-2432
Fax: (301) 624-2799
E-mail: admissions@frederick.edu
http://www.frederick.edu
Broadcast journalism, communications,
    photographic/film/video technology.

Frostburg State University
FSU, 101 Braddock Road
Frostburg, MD 21532
Phone: (301) 687-4201
Fax: (301) 687-7074
E-mail: fsuadmissions@frostburg.edu
http://www.frostburg.edu
Communications, dance.

Goucher College
1021 Dulaney Valley Road
Baltimore, MD 21204
Phone: (410) 337-6100
Fax: (410) 337-6354
E-mail: admissions@goucher.edu
http://www.goucher.edu
Media studies.

Hood College
401 Rosemont Avenue
Frederick, MD 21701
Phone: (301) 696-3400
Fax: (301) 696-3819
E-mail: admissions@hood.edu
http://www.hood.edu
Communications.

Howard Community College**
10901 Little Patuxent Parkway
Columbia, MD 21044
Phone: (410) 772-4856
Fax: (410) 772-4589
E-mail: adm-adv@howardcc.edu
http://www.howardcc.edu
Cinematography, film/video production,
    dance, telecommunications
    technology.

Johns Hopkins University
3400 North Charles Street
140 Garland Hall
Baltimore, MD 21218
Phone: (410) 516-8171
Fax: (410) 516-6025
E-mail: gotojhu@jhu.edu
http://www.jhu.edu
Film/video arts.

Loyola College in Maryland
4501 North Charles Street
Baltimore, MD 21210
Phone: (800) 221-9107
Fax: (410) 617-2176
E-mail: admissions@loyola.edu
http://www.loyola.edu
Communications.

McDaniel College
2 College Hill
Westminster, MD 21157
Phone: (410) 857-2230
Fax: (410) 857-2757
E-mail: admissions@mcdaniel.edu
http://www.mcdaniel.edu
Communications.

Montgomery College**
Takoma Park/Silver Spring Campus
7600 Takoma Avenue
Takoma Park, MD 20912
Phone: (301) 650-1300
E-mail: At Web site
http://www.montgomerycollege.edu
Broadcast journalism, dance.

Morgan State University
1700 East Cold Spring Lane

Baltimore, MD 21251
Phone: (800) 332-6674
Fax: (410) 319-3684
E-mail: tjenness@moac.morgan.edu
http://www.morgan.edu
Broadcast journalism.

Salisbury University
Admissions Office
1101 Camden Avenue
Salisbury, MD 21801
Phone: (410) 453-6161
Fax: (410) 546-6016
E-mail: admissions@salisbury.edu
http://www.salisbury.edu
Communications.

Towson University
8000 York Road
Towson, MD 21252
Phone: (410) 704-2113
Fax: (410) 704-3030
E-mail: admissions@towson.edu
http://www.towson.edu
Communications, dance.

University of Maryland—Baltimore County
1000 Hilltop Circle
Baltimore, MD 21250
Phone: (410) 455-2291
Fax: (410) 455-1094
E-mail: admissions@umbc.edu
http://www.umbc.edu
Acting, cinematography, film/video
    production, dance.

University of Maryland—College Park*
Mitchell Building
College Park, MD 20742
Phone: (301) 314-8385
Fax: (301) 314-9693
E-mail: um-admit@uga.umd.edu
http://www.umd.edu
Communications.

University of Maryland—Eastern Shore
Office of Admissions
Backbone Road
Princess Anne, MD 21853
Phone: (410) 651-6410
Fax: (410) 651-7922
E-mail: ccmills@mail.umes.edu
http://www.umes.edu
Communications, dance.

University of Maryland—University College
3501 University Boulevard, East
Adelphi, MD 20783
Phone: (301) 985-7000
Fax: (301) 985-7364
E-mail: umucinfo@nova.umuc.edu
http://www.umuc.edu
Communications.

Villa Julia College
1525 Greenspring Valley Road
Stevenson, MD 21153
Phone: (410) 486-7001
Fax: (410) 602-6600
E-mail: admissions@vjc.edu
http://www.vjc.edu
Cinematography, film/video production, communications, communications technology.

MASSACHUSETTS

Ai The New England Institute of Art and Design**
Office of Admissions
10 Brookline Place West
Brookline, MA 02445
Phone: (800) 903-4425
Fax: (617) 582-4500
E-mail: neiaadm@aii.edu
http://www.neia.aii.edu
Broadcast journalism, communications technology, photographic/film/video technology, radio and television, radio/television broadcasting.

American International College
1000 State Street
Springfield, MA 01109
Phone: (413) 205-3201
Fax: (413) 205-3051
E-mail: inquiry@www.aic.edu
http://www.aic.edu
Communications.

Boston College
140 Commonwealth Avenue
Devlin Hall 208
Chestnut Hill, MA 02467
Phone: (617) 552-3100
Fax: (617) 552-0798
E-mail: ugadmis@bc.edu
http://www.bc.edu
Communications, film/video arts.

Boston University
121 Bay State Road
Boston, MA 02215
Phone: (617) 353-2300
Fax: (617) 353-9695
E-mail: admissions@bu.edu
http://www.bu.edu
Acting, broadcast journalism, cinematography, film/video production, communications, film/video arts.

Bridgewater State College
Gates House
Bridgewater, MA 02325
Phone: (508) 531-1237
Fax: (508) 531-1746
E-mail: admission@bridgew.edu
http://www.bridgew.edu
Communications.

Bunker Hill Community College**
250 New Rutherford Avenue
Boston, MA 02129
Phone: (617) 228-BHCC
Fax: (617) 228-2082
E-mail: enrollment@bhcc.mass.edu
http://www.bhcc.mass.edu
Communications, media studies.

Cape Cod Community College**
2240 Iyanough Road
West Barnstable, MA 02668
Phone: (877) 846-3672
Fax: (508) 375-4089
E-mail: info@capecod.edu
http://www.capecod.mass.edu
Communications, dance, media studies.

Clark University
950 Main Street
Worcester, MA 01610
Phone: (508) 793-7431
Fax: (508) 793-8821
E-mail: admissions@clarku.edu
http://www.clarku.edu
Communications, film/video arts.

College of the Holy Cross
Admissions Office
1 College Street
Worcester, MA 01610
Phone: (313) 664-7425
Fax: (313) 872-2739
E-mail: admissions@ccscad.edu
http://www.ccscad.edu
Cinematography, film/video production.

Curry College
1071 Blue Hill Avenue
Milton, MA 02186
Phone: (617) 333-2210
Fax: (617) 333-2114
E-mail: curryadm@curry.edu
http://www.curry.edu
Broadcast journalism, communications.

Dean College**
99 Main Street
Franklin Station, MA 02308
Phone: (877) TRY-DEAN
Fax: (508) 541-8726
E-mail: admission@dean.edu
http://www.dean.edu
Broadcast journalism, communications, dance,

Eastern Nazarene College
23 East Elm Avenue
Quincy, MA 02170
Phone: (617) 745-3000
Fax: (617) 745-3490
E-mail: admissions@enc.edu
http://www.enc.edu
Communications.

Emerson College
120 Boylston Street
Boston, MA 02116
Phone: (617) 824-8600
Fax: (617) 824-8609
E-mail: admission@emerson.edu
http://www.emerson.edu
Acting, broadcast journalism, cinematography, film/video production, communications, communications technology, film/video arts, media studies, playwriting/screenwriting.

Emmanuel College
400 The Fenway
Boston, MA 02115
Phone: (617) 735-9715
Fax: (617) 735-9801
E-mail: enroll@emmanuel.edu
http://www.emmanuel.edu
Communications.

Endicott College
376 Hale Street
Beverly, MA 01915
Phone: (978) 921-1000
Fax: (978) 232-2520
E-mail: admissio@endicott.edu
http://www.endicott.edu
Communications.

Fitchburg State College
160 Pearl Street
Fitchburg, MA 01420

Phone: (978) 665-3144
Fax: (978) 665-4540
E-mail: admissions@fsc.edu
http://www.fsc.edu
Cinematography, film/video production,
   communications.

Framingham State College
P.O. Box 9101
Framingham, MA 01701
Phone: (508) 626-4500
Fax: (508) 626-4017
E-mail: admiss@fc.mass.edu
http://www.framingham.edu
Communications.

Gordon College
255 Grapevine Road
Wenham, MA 01984
Phone: (978) 927-2300
Fax: (978) 867-4657
E-mail: admissions@hope.gordon.edu
http://www.gordon.edu
Communications.

Hampshire College
Admissions Office
893 West Street
Amherst, MA 01002
Phone: (413) 559-5471
Fax: (413) 559-5631
E-mail: admissions@hampshire.edu
http://www.hampshire.edu
Broadcast journalism, cinematography,
   film/video production,
   communications, dance, film/video
   arts, playwriting/screenwriting.

Harvard College
Byerly Hall
8 Garden Street
Cambridge, MA 02138
Phone: (617) 495-1551
Fax: (617) 495-8821
E-mail: college@fas.harvard.edu
http://www.fas.harvard.edu
Cinematography, film/video production,
   film/video arts.

Lasell College
Office of Admissions
1844 Commonwealth Avenue
Newton, MA 02406
Phone: (617) 243-2225
Fax: (617) 243-2380
E-mail: info@lasell.edu
http://www.lasell.edu
Communications.

Massachusetts College of Art
621 Huntington Avenue
Boston, MA 02115
Phone: (617) 879-7222
Fax: (617) 879-7250
E-mail: admissions@massart.edu
http://www.massart.edu
Cinematography, film/video production,
   film/video arts.

**Massachusetts Institute of
   Technology**
MIT Admissions Office Room 3108
77 Massachusetts Avenue
Cambridge, MA 02139
Phone: (617) 253-4791
Fax: (617) 258-8304
E-mail: admissions@mit.edu
http://www.mit.edu
Media studies.

Massasoit Community College**
One Massasoit Boulevard
Brockton, MA 02302
Phone: (800) 227-3377, ext. 1411
E-mail: At Web site
http://www.massasoit.mass.edu
Telecommunications technology.

Merrimack College
Office of Admission
Austin Hall
North Andover, MA 01845
Phone: (978) 837-5100
Fax: (978) 837-5133
E-mail: admission@merrimack.edu
http://www.merrimack.edu
Communications.

Mount Ida College
777 Dedham Street
Newton, MA 02459
Phone: (617) 928.4500
E-mail: admissions@mountida.edu
http://www.mountida.edu
Communications.

**Mount Wachusett Community
   College****
444 Green Street
Gardner, MA 01440
Phone: (978) 632-9110
Fax: (978) 630-9554
E-mail: admissions@mwcc.mass.edu
http://www.mwcc.mass.edu
Broadcast journalism, communications
   technology.

Newbury College**
161 Granite Avenue, Suite 10
Dorchester Center, MA 02124
Phone: (617) 730-7007
Fax: NA
E-mail: info@newbury.edu
http://www.newbury.edu
Broadcast journalism, communications
   technology, radio and television,
   radio/television broadcasting.

Northeastern University
260 Huntington Avenue
150 Richards Hall
Boston, MA 02115
Phone: (617) 373-2200
Fax: (617) 373-8780
E-mail: admissions@neu.edu
http://www.neu.edu
Communications.

Regis College
235 Wellesley Street
Weston, MA 02493
Phone: (781) 768-7100
Fax: (781) 768-7071
E-mail: admission@regiscollege.edu
http://www.regiscollege.edu
Broadcast journalism, communications.

Roxbury Community College**
1234 Columbus Avenue
Roxbury Crossing, MA 02120
Phone: (617) 541-5310
Fax: (617) 427-5316
E-mail: At Web site
http://www.rcc.mass.edu
Radio/television broadcasting.

Salem State College
352 Lafayette Street
Salem, MA 019780
Phone: (978) 542-6200
Fax: (978) 542-6893
E-mail: admissions@salemstate.edu
http://www.salemstate.edu
Communications.

School of the Museum of Fine Arts
230 The Fenway
Boston, MA 02115
Phone: (617) 369-3626
Fax: (617) 369-4264
E-mail: admissions@smfa.edu
http://www.smfa.edu
Cinematography, film/video production.

Simmons College
300 The Fenway
Boston, MA 02115

Phone: (617) 521-2051
Fax: (617) 521-3190
E-mail: ugadm@simmons.edu
http://www.simmons.edu
Communications.

Simon's Rock College of Bard
84 Alford Road
Great Barrington, MA 01230
Phone: (413) 528-7312
Fax: (413) 528-7334
E-mail: admit@simons-rock.edu
http://www.simons-rock.edu
Acting, cinematography, film/video
    production, dance, film/video arts,
    photographic/film/video technology,
    playwriting/screenwriting.

**Springfield Technical Community
    College****
One Armory Square
P.O. Box 9000, Suite 1
Springfield, MA 01102
Phone: (413) 781-7822, ext. 4380
Fax: NA
E-mail: admissions@stccadm.stcc.mass.
    edu
http://www.stcc.edu
Radio/television broadcasting,
    telecommunications technology.

Stonehill College
320 Washington Street
Easton, MA 02357
Phone: (508) 565-1373
Fax: (508) 565-1545
E-mail: admissions@stonehill.edu
http://www.stonehill.edu
Communications.

Suffolk University
8 Ashburton Place
Boston, MA 02108
Phone: (617) 573-8460
Fax: (617) 742-4291
E-mail: admission@suffolk.edu
http://www.suffolk.edu
Acting, broadcast journalism,
    communications, communications
    technology, film/video arts, media
    studies, radio/television broadcasting.

University of Massachusetts—Amherst
University Admissions Center
Amherst, MA 01003
Phone: (413) 545-0222
Fax: (413) 545-4312
E-mail: mail@admissions.umass.edu
http://www.umass.edu
Communications, dance.

Wentworth Institute of Technology
555 Huntington Avenue
Boston, MA 02115
Phone: (800) 556-0610
Fax: (617) 989-4591
E-mail: admissions@wit.edu
http://www.wit.edu
Telecommunications technology.

Westfield State College
Westfield State
Westfield, MA 01086
Phone: (413) 572-5218
Fax: (413) 572-0520
E-mail: admission@wsc.ma.edu
http://www.wsc.ma.edu
Broadcast journalism, communications.

MICHIGAN

Adrian College
110 South Madison Street
Adrian, MI 49221
Phone: (517) 265-5161
Fax: (517) 264-3331
E-mail: admissions@adrian.edu
http://www.adrian.edu
Communications.

Albion College
611 East Porter Street
Albion, MI 49224
Phone: (517) 629-0321
Fax: (517) 629-0569
E-mail: admissions@albion.edu
http://www.albion.edu
Communications.

Alma College
614 West Superior Street
Alma, MI 48801
Phone: (989) 463-7139
Fax: (989) 463-7057
E-mail: admissions@alma.edu
http://www.alma.edu
Media studies.

Andrews University
Office of Admissions
Berien Springs, MI 49104
Phone: (800) 253-2874
Fax: (616) 471-3228
E-mail: enroll@andrews.edu
http://www.andrews.edu
Communications, communications
    technology.

Aquinas College
1607 Robinson Road SE

Grand Rapids, MI 49506
Phone: (616) 732-4460
Fax: (616) 732-4469
E-mail: admissions@aquinas.edu
http://www.aquinas.edu
Communications.

Bay de Noc Community College**
2001 North Lincoln Road
Escanaba, MI 49829
Phone: (800) 221-2001
E-mail: At Web site
http://www.baydenoc.cc.mi.us
Broadcast journalism, communications.

Calvin College
3201 Burton Street Southeast
Grand Rapids, MI 49546
Phone: (616) 526-6106
Fax: (616) 526-6777
E-mail: admissions@calvin.edu
http://www.calvin.edu
Communications, film/video arts, media
    studies.

Central Michigan University*
205 Warriner Hall
Mount Pleasant, MI 48859
Phone: (989) 774-3076
Fax: (989) 774-7267
E-mail: cmuadmit@cmich.edu
http://www.cmich.edu
Broadcast journalism, communications.

College for Creative Studies
201 East Kirby
Detroit, MI 48202
Phone: (313) 664-7425
Fax: (313) 872-2739
E-mail: admissions@ccscad.edu
http://www.ccscad.edu
Cinematography, film/video production.

Eastern Michigan University
400 Pierce Hall
Ypsilanti, MI 48197
Phone: (734) 487-3060
Fax: (734) 487-1484
E-mail: admissions@emich.edu
http://www.emich.edu
Communications, communications
    technology, film/video arts,
    radio/television broadcasting.

Ferris State University
1201 South State Street
Center for Student Services
Big Rapids, MI 49307

Phone: (231) 591-2100
Fax: (231) 591-3944
E-mail: admissions@ferris.edu
http://www.ferris.edu
Communications, communications
 technology.

Grand Valley State University
1 Campus Drive
Allendale, MI 49401
Phone: (616) 331-5000
Fax: (616) 331-2000
E-mail: go@gvsu@gvsu.edu
http://www.gvsu.edu
Broadcast journalism, communications.

Hillsdale College
35 East College Street
Hillsdale, MI 49242
Phone: (517) 607-2377
Fax: (517) 607-2223
E-mail: admissions@hillsdale.edu
http://www.hillsdale.edu
Communications.

Lansing Community College**
419 North Capitol Avenue
Lansing, MI 48901
Phone: (800) 644-4LCC
Fax: (517) 483-9668
E-mail: At Web site
http://www.lcc.edu
Cinematography, film/video production,
 communications, communications
 technology, dance.

Macomb Community College**
Center Campus, G Building
44575 Garfield Road
Clinton Township, MI 48038
Phone: (866) 622-6624
Fax: (586).445-7140
E-mail: answer@macomb.edu
http://www.macomb.edu
Broadcast journalism.

Madonna University
36600 Schoolcraft Road
Livonia, MI 48150
Phone: (734) 432-5339
Fax: (734) 432-5393
E-mail: muinfo@smtp.munet.edu
http://www.munet.edu
Communications, media studies.

Michigan State University*
250 Administration Building
East Lansing, MI 48824-1046
Phone: (517) 355-8332

Fax: (517) 353-1647
E-mail: adis@msu.edu
http://www.msu.edu
Communications, media studies, radio
 and television.

Michigan Technological University
1400 Townsend Drive
Houghton, MI 49931
Phone: (906) 487-2335
Fax: (906) 487-2125
E-mail: mtu4u@mtu.edu
http://www.mtu.edu
Communications.

Northern Michigan University
1401 Presque Isle Avenue
304 Cohodas
Marquette, MI 49855
Phone: (906) 227-2650
Fax: (906) 227-1747
E-mail: admiss@nmu.edu
http://www.nmu.edu
Broadcast journalism, cinematography,
 film/video production,
 communications, media studies, radio
 and television.

Oakland Community College**
2480 Opdyke Road
Bloomfield Hills, MI 48304
Phone: (248) 341-2186
E-mail: At Web site
http://www.oaklandcc.edu
Radio/television broadcasting.

Oakland University
Office of Admissions
101 North Foundation Hall
Rochester, MI 48309
Phone: (248) 370-3360
Fax: (248) 370-4462
E-mail: ouinfo@oakland.edu
http://www.oakland.edu
Communications, dance.

Olivet College
320 South Main Street
Olivet, MI 49076
Phone: (269) 749-7635
Fax: (269) 749-3821
E-mail: admissions@olivetcollege.edu
http://www.olivetcollege.edu
Communications, media studies.

Sagniaw Valley State University
7400 Bay Road
University Center, MI 48710
Phone: (989) 964-4200

Fax: (989) 790-0180
E-mail: admissions@svsu.edu
http://www.svsu.edu
Communications, communications
 technology.

Siena Heights University
1247 East Siena Heights Drive
Adrian, MI 49221
Phone: (517) 263-0731
Fax: (517) 264-7704
E-mail: admissions@alpha.sienahts.edu
http://www.sienahts.edu
Communications.

Spring Arbor University
106 East Main Street
Spring Arbor, MI 49283
Phone: (517) 750-6458
Fax: (517) 750-6620
E-mail: admissions@admin.arbor.edu
http://www.arbor.edu
Communications, film/video arts.

University of Detroit—Mercy
P.O. Box 19900
Detroit, MI 48219
Phone: (313) 993-1245
Fax: (313) 993-3326
E-mail: admissions@udmercy.edu
http://www.udmercy.edu
Broadcast journalism, communications.

University of Michigan—Ann Arbor
1220 Student Activities Building
Ann Arbor, MI 48109
Phone: (734) 764-7433
Fax: (734) 936-0740
E-mail: ugadmiss@umich.edu
http://www.umich.edu
Broadcast journalism, communications,
 dance, film/video arts, media studies,
 playwriting/screenwriting.

University of Michigan—Dearborn
4901 Evergreen Road
Dearborn, MI 48128
Phone: (313) 593-5100
Fax: (313) 436-9167
E-mail: admissions@umd.umich.edu
http://www.umd.umich.edu
Communications.

University of Michigan—Flint
University Pavilion, Suite 245
Flint, MI 48502
Phone: (810) 762-3300
Fax: (810) 762-3272
E-mail: admissions@umflint.edu

http://www.flint.umich.edu
Communications.

Wayne County Community College**
Downtown Campus
1001 West Fort Street
Detroit, MI 48226
Phone: (313) 496-2600
Fax: (313) 961-2791
E-mail: At Web site
http://www.wcccd.edu
Telecommunications technology.

Wayne State University
656 West Kirby Street
Detroit, MI 48202
Phone: (313) 577-3577
Fax: (313) 577-7536
E-mail: admissions@wayne.edu
http://www.wayne.edu
Broadcast journalism, communications,
    film/video arts, dance.

Western Michigan University
1903 West Michigan Avenue
Kalamazoo, MI 49008
Phone: (269) 387-2000
Fax: (269) 387-2096
E-mail: ask-wmu@wmich.edu
http://www.wmich.edu
Communications, radio and television.

MINNESOTA

Alexandria Technical College**
1601 Jefferson Street
Alexandria, MN 56308
Phone: (888) 234-1222
Fax: (320) 762-4501
E-mail: joanj@alx.tec.mn.us
http://www.alextech.edu
Telecommunications technology.

Augsburg College
2211 Riverside Avenue South
Minneapolis, MN 55454
Phone: (612) 330-1001
Fax: (612) 330-1590
E-mail: admissions@augsburg.edu
http://www.augsburg.edu
Communications.

Bemidji State University
1500 Birchmont Drive NE
Deputy Hall
Bemidji, MN 56601
Phone: (218) 755-2040
Fax: (218) 755-2074
E-mail: admissions@bemidjistate.edu

http://www.bemidjistate.edu
Communications.

Bethel College
3900 Bethel Drive
Saint Paul, MN 55112
Phone: (651) 638-6242
Fax: (651) 635-1490
E-mail: bcol.admit@bethel.edu
http://www.bethel.edu
Communications, media studies.

Central Lakes College**
501 West College Drive
Brainerd, MN 56401
Phone: (800) 933-0346, ext. 2586
E-mail: At Web site
http://www.clc.mnscu.edu
Photographic/film/video technology.

College of St. Catherine
2004 Randolph Avenue
Saint Paul, MN 55105
Phone: (651) 690-8850
Fax: (651) 690-8824
E-mail: admissions@stkate.edu
http://www.stkate.edu
Communications.

The College of Saint Scholastica
1200 Kenwood Avenue
Duluth, MN 55811
Phone: (217) 723-6046
Fax: (217) 723-5991
E-mail: admissions@css.edu
http://www.css.edu
Communications.

Concordia College—Moorhead
901 Eighth Street South
Moorhead, MN 56562
Phone: (218) 299-3004
Fax: (218) 299-4720
E-mail: admissions@cord.edu
http://www.goconcordia.com
Broadcast journalism, communications,
    media studies.

Gustavus Adolphus College
800 West College Avenue
Saint Peter, MN 56082
Phone: (507) 933-7676
Fax: (507) 933-7474
E-mail: admissions@gustavus.edu
http://www.gustavus.edu
Communications, dance.

Hamline University
1536 Hewitt Avenue, MS-C1930

Saint Paul, MN 05104
Phone: (651) 523-2207
Fax: (651) 523-2458
E-mail: CLA-admis@hamline.edu
http://www.hamline.edu
Communications.

Hennepin Technical College**
Eden Prairie Campus
13100 College View Drive
Eden Prairie, MN 55347
Phone: (800) 345-4655
Fax: (952) 995-1399
E-mail: info@hennepintech.edu
http://www.hennepintech.edu
Communications technology,
    photographic/film/video technology.

Lake Superior College**
2101 Trinity Road
Duluth, MN 55811
Phone: (800) 432-2884
Fax: (218) 733-5945
E-mail: At Web site
http://www.lsc.edu
Communications.

Macalester College
1600 Grand Avenue
Saint Paul, MN 55105
Phone: (651) 696-6357
Fax: (651) 696-6724
E-mail: admissions@macalester.edu
http://www.macalester.edu
Communications.

**Minneapolis Community and Technical
College****
Downtown Campus
1501 Hennepin Avenue
Minneapolis, MN 55403
Phone: (800) 247-0911
Fax: (612) 659-1357
E-mail: At Web site
http://www.mctc.mnscu.edu
Playwriting/screenwriting.

Minnesota College of Art and Design
2501 Stevens Avenue
Minneapolis, MN 55404
Phone: (612) 874-3760
Fax: (612) 874-3701
E-mail: admissions@mcad.edu
http://www.mcad.edu
Cinematography, film/video production.

Minnesota State University—Mankato
Office of Admissions
122 Taylor Center

Mankato, MN 56001
Phone: (507) 389-1822
Fax: (507) 389-1511
E-mail: admissions@mnsu.edu
http://www.mnsu.edu
Communications, media studies.

**Minnesota State University—
  Moorhead**
Owens Hall
Moorhead, MN 56563
Phone: (218) 236-2161
Fax: (218) 291-4374
http://www.mnstate.edu
Communications, media studies.

**Northland Community & Technical
  College****
2022 Central Avenue NE
East Grand Forks, MN 56721
Phone: (800) 451-3441
Fax: (218) 773-4502
E-mail: At Web site
http://www.northland.cc.mn.us
Broadcast journalism, communications.

Northwestern College
3003 Snelling Avenue North
Saint Paul, MN 55113
Phone: (651) 631-5111
Fax: (651) 631-5680
E-mail: admissions@nwc.edu
http://www.nwc.edu
Communications, film/video arts, radio
  and television.

Saint Cloud State University*
720 South 4th Avenue
Saint Cloud, MN 56301
Phone: (320) 308-2244
Fax: (320) 308-2243
E-mail: scsu4u@stcloudstate.edu
http://www.stcloudstate.edu
Acting, broadcast journalism,
  communications, media studies, radio
  and television.

Saint Mary's University of Minnesota
700 Terrace Heights #2
Winona, MN 55987
Phone: (507) 457-1600
Fax: (507) 457-1722
E-mail: admissions@smumn.edu
http://www.smumn.edu
Communications technology.

Southwest Minnesota State University
Admission Office
1501 State Street

Marshall, MN 46258
Phone: (800) 642-0684
Fax: (507) 537-7154
E-mail: shearerr@southwest.msus.edu
http://www.southwest.msus.edu
Broadcast journalism.

University of Minnesota—Duluth
23 Solon Campus Center
1117 University Drive
Duluth, MN 55812
Phone: (218) 726-7171
Fax: (218) 726-7040
E-mail: undadmis@d.umn.edu
http://www.d.umn.edu
Communications.

University of Minnesota—Morris
600 East 4th Street
Morris, MN 56267
Phone: (320) 589-6035
Fax: (320) 589-1673
E-mail: admisfa@mrs.umn.edu
http://www.mrs.umn.edu
Communications.

University of Minnesota—Twin Cities*
240 Williamson Hall
231 Pillsbury Drive SE
Minneapolis, MN 55455
Phone: (612) 625-2008
Fax: (612) 626-1693
E-mail: admissions@tc.umn.edu
http://www1.umn.edu/twincities
Dance, film/video arts.

University of Saint Thomas
2115 Summit Avenue, Mail #32-F1
Saint Paul, MN 55105
Phone: (651) 962-6150
Fax: (651) 962-6160
E-mail: admissions@stthomas.edu
http://www.stthomas.edu
Communications.

Winona State University
Office of Admissions
P.O. Box 5838
Winona, MN 55987
Phone: (507) 457-5100
Fax: (507) 457-5620
E-mail: admissions@winona.edu
http://www.winona.edu
Broadcast journalism, communications,
  communications technology, dance,
  media studies.

MISSISSIPPI

Alcorn State University
1000 ASU Drive #300
Alcorn State, MS 39096
Phone: (601) 877-6147
Fax: (601) 877-6347
E-mail: ebarnes@lorman.alcorn.redu
http://www.alcorn.edu
Media studies.

Belhaven College
1500 Peachtree Street
Jackson, MS 39202
Phone: (601) 968-59040
Fax: (601) 968-8946
E-mail: admissions@belhaven.edu
http://www.belhaven.edu
Communications, dance.

Coahoma Community College**
3240 Friars Point Road
Clarksdale, MS 38614
Phone: (800) 844-1222
E-mail: At Web site
http://www.ccc.cc.ms.us
Broadcast journalism

Jackson State University*
1400 Lynch Street
P.O. Box 17330
Jackson, MS 39217
Phone: (601) 979-2100
Fax: (601) 979-3445
E-mail: schatman@ccaix.jsums.edu
http://www.jsums.edu
Broadcast journalism, communications,
  communications technology.

Meridian Community College**
910 Highway 19 North
Meridian, MS 39307
Phone: (800) 622-8731
Fax: (601) 484-8635
E-mail: qcarlisl@mcc.cc.ms.us
http://www.mcc.cc.ms.us
Communications, communications
  technology.

Mississippi College
P.O. Box 4026
Clinton, MS 39058
Phone: (601) 925-3800
Fax: (601) 925-3950
E-mail: enrollment-services@mc.edu
http://www.mc.edu
Communications.

Mississippi Gulf Coast Community College**
Jefferson Davis Campus
2226 Switzer Road
Gulfport, MS 39507
Phone: (228) 896-2500
E-mail: At Web site
http://www.mgccc.edu
Communications.

Mississippi State University
P.O. Box 6305
Mississippi State, MS 39762
Phone: (662) 325-2224
Fax: (662) 325-7360
E-mail: admit@admissions.msstate.edu
http://www.msstate.edu
Communications.

Mississippi University for Women
West Box 1613
Columbus, MS 39701
Phone: (662) 329-7106
Fax: (662) 241-7481
E-mail: admissions@muw.edu
http://www.muw.edu
Broadcast journalism, communications.

Mississippi Valley State University
14000 Highway 82 West
Itta Bena, MS 38941
Phone: (662) 254-3344
Fax: (662) 254-3655
E-mail: leewilson@msvu.edu
http://www.msvu.edu
Communications.

Northwest Mississippi Community College**
Office of Admissions, P.O. Box 7047
4975 Highway 51 North
Senatobia, MS 38668
Phone: (800) 555-2154
E-mail: admissions@northwestms.edu
http://www.northwestms.edu
Broadcast journalism, communications technology.

Rust College
150 Rust Avenue
Holly Springs, MS 38635
Phone: (662) 252-8000
Fax: (662) 252-8895
E-mail: jbmcdonald@rustcollege.edu
http://www.rustcollege.edu
Communications.

University of Mississippi*
145 Martindale
University, MS 38677
Phone: (662) 915-7226
Fax: (662) 915-5869
E-mail: admissions@olemiss.edu
http://www.olemiss.edu
Broadcast journalism, communications technology.

University of Southern Mississippi*
P.O. Box 5166
Southern Station
Hattiesburg, MS 38406
Phone: (601) 266-5000
Fax: (601) 266-5148
E-mail: admissions@usm.edu
http://www.usm.edu
Broadcast journalism, communications, dance.

William Carey College
498 Tuscan Avenue
Hattiesburg, MS 39401
Phone: (601) 318-6103
Fax: (601) 318-6765
E-mail: admissions@wmcarey.edu
http://www.wmcarey.edu
Communications.

MISSOURI

Avila University
11901 Wornall Road
Kansas City, MO 64145
Phone: (816) 942-8400
Fax: (816) 942-3362
E-mail: admissions@mail.avila.edu
http://www.avila.edu
Communications.

Calvary Bible College and Theological Seminary
15800 Calvary Road
Kansas City, MO 64147
Phone: (816) 322-3960
Fax: (816) 331-4474
E-mail: admissions@calvary.edu
http://www.calvary.edu
Broadcast journalism, media studies.

Central Missouri State University
Office of Admissions
WDE 1401
Warrensburg, MO 64093
Phone: (660) 543-4290
Fax: (660) 543-8517
E-mail: admit@cmsuvmb.cmsu.edu
http://www.cmsu.edu

Broadcast journalism, communications, film/video arts.

College of the Ozarks
Office of Admissions
Point Lookout, MO 65726
Phone: (417) 334-6441
E-mail: admiss4@cofo.edu
http://www.cofo.edu
Broadcast journalism, communications.

Culver-Stockton College
One College Hillanton
Canton, MO 63435
Phone: (217) 231-6331
Fax: (217) 231-6618
E-mail: enrollment@culver.edu
http://www.culver.edu
Communications.

Drury University
900 North Benton Avenue
Springfield, MO 65802
Phone: (417) 873-7205
Fax: (417) 866-3873
E-mail: druryad@drury.edu
http://www.drury.edu
Broadcast journalism, communications.

Evangel University
1111 North Glenstone Avenue
Springfield, MO 65802
Phone: (417) 865-2811
Fax: (417) 520-0545
E-mail: admissions@evangel.edu
http://www.evangel.edu
Broadcast journalism, communications, communications technology.

Fontbonne University
6800 Wydown Boulevard
St. Louis, MO 63105
Phone: (314) 889-1478
Fax: (314) 889-1451
E-mail: fcadmis@fontbonne.edu
http://www.fontbonne.edu
Communications, media studies.

Hannibal-LaGrange College
2800 Palmyra Road
Hannibal, MO 63401
Phone: (573) 221-3113
Fax: (573) 221-6594
E-mail: admissio@hlg.edu
http://www.hlg.edu
Communications.

Kansas City Art Institute
44415 Warwick Boulevard
Kansas City, MO 64111
Phone: (816) 474-5225
Fax: (816) 802-3309
E-mail: admiss@kcai.edu
http://www.kcai.edu
Cinematography, film/video
    production.

Lindenwood University
309 South Kingshighway
St. Charles, MO 63301
Phone: (314) 949-4949
Fax: (314) 949-4989
E-mail: admissions@lindenwood.edu
http://www.lindenwood.edu
Broadcast journalism, communications,
    dance, media studies, radio and
    television.

Maryville University of Saint Louis
13550 Conway Road
St. Louis, MO 63141
Phone: (314) 529-9350
Fax: (314) 529-9927
E-mail: admissions@maryville.edu
http://www.maryville.edu
Media studies.

Mineral Area College**
5270 Flat River Road
P.O. Box 1000
Park Hills, MO 63601
Phone: (573) 431-4593
E-mail: At Web site
http://www.mac.cc.mo.us
Communications.

Missouri Baptist College
One College Park Drive
St. Louis, MO 63141
Phone: (314) 434-1115
Fax: (314) 434-7596
E-mail: admissions@mobap.edu
http://www.mobap.edu
Communications.

Missouri Southern State University
3950 East Newman Road
Joplin, MO 64801
Phone: (417) 625-9378
Fax: (417) 659-4429
E-mail: admissions@mssu.edu
http://www.mssu.edu
Communications.

Missouri Valley College
500 East College Street

Marshall, MO 65340
Phone: (660) 831-4114
Fax: (660) 831-4233
E-mail: admissions@moval.edu
http://www.moval.edu
Media studies.

Missouri Western State College
4525 Downs Drive
St. Joseph, MO 64507
Phone: (816) 271-4266
Fax: (816) 271-5833
E-mail: admissn@mwsc.edu
http://www.mwsc.edu
Communications.

Northwest Missouri State University
800 University Drive
Maryville, MO 64468
Phone: (800) 633-1175
Fax: (660) 562-1121
E-mail: admissions@mail.nwmissouri.
    edu
http://www.nwmissouri.edu
Communications.

Park University
8700 River Park Drive, Campus Box 1
Parkville, MO 64152
Phone: (816) 741-2000
Fax: (816) 741-4462
E-mail: admissions@mail.park.edu
http://www.park.edu
Communications.

Penn Valley Community College**
Main Campus
3201 Southwest Trafficway
Kansas City, MO 64111
Phone: (816) 759-4101
Fax: (816) 759-4478
E-mail: At Web site
http://www.kcmetro.edu
Communications technology.

Rockhurst University
1100 Rockhurst Road
Kansas City, MO 64110
Phone: (816) 501-4100
Fax: (816) 501-4241
E-mail: admission@rockhurst.edu
http://www.rockhurst.edu
Communications.

Southeast Missouri State University*
One University Plaza
Mail Stop 3550
Cape Giradeau, MO 63701
Phone: (573) 651-2590

Fax: (573) 651-5936
E-mail: admissions@semo.edu
http://www.semo.edu
Communications, communications
    technology.

Southwest Baptist University
1600 University Avenue
Bolivar, MO 65613
Phone: (417) 328-1810
Fax: (417) 328-1808
E-mail: admitme@sbuniv.edu
http://www.sbuniv.edu
Communications.

Southwest Missouri State University
901 South National
Springfield, MO 65804
Phone: (417) 836-5517
Fax: (417) 836-6334
E-mail: smsuinfo@smsu.edu
http://www.smsu.edu
Broadcast journalism, communications,
    dance.

Stephens College
1200 East Broadway
P.O. Box 2121
Columbia, MO 65215
Phone: (573) 876-7207
Fax: (573) 876-7237
E-mail: apply@wc.stephens.edu
http://www.stephens.edu
Broadcast journalism, communications,
    dance.

University of Missouri—Columbia*
230 Jesse Hall
Columbia, MO 65211
Phone: (573) 882-786
Fax: (573) 882-7887
E-mail: admissions@missouri.edu
http://www.missouri.edu
Broadcast journalism, communications,
    radio and television.

University of Missouri—Kansas City
5100 Rockhill Road, 101 AC
Kansas City, MO 64114
Phone: (816) 235-1111
Fax: (816) 235-5544
E-mail: admit@umkc.edu
http://www.umkc.edu
Communications, dance.

University of Missouri—Saint Louis
351 Millennium Student Center
9001 Natural Bridge Road
St. Louis, MO 63121

Phone: (314) 516-8675
Fax: (314) 516-5310
E-mail: admissions@umsl.edu
http://www.umsl.edu
Communications.

Washington University in St. Louis
Campus Box 1089
One Brookings Drive
St. Louis, MO 63130
Phone: (314) 935-6000
Fax: (314) 935-4290
E-mail: admissions@wustl.edu
http://www.wustl.edu
Film/video arts.

Webster University
470 East Lockwood Avenue
St. Louis, MO 63119
Phone: (314) 968-6991
Fax: (314) 968-7115
E-mail: admit@webster.edu
http://www.webster.edu
Acting, broadcast journalism,
   cinematography, film/video production,
   communications, dance, film/video arts,
   media studies.

William Jewell College
500 College Hill
Liberty, MO 64068
Phone: (816) 781-7700
Fax: (816) 415-5040
E-mail: admission@william.jewell.edu
http://www.jewell.edu
Broadcast journalism, radio and
   television.

William Woods University
Office of Enrollment Services
One University Avenue
Fulton, MO 65251
Phone: (573) 592-4221
Fax: (573) 592-1146
E-mail: admissions@williamwoods.
   edu
http://www.williamwoods.edu
Broadcast journalism.

MONTANA

Carroll College
1601 North Benton Avenue
Helena, MT 59625
Phone: (406) 447-4384
Fax: (406) 447-4533
E-mail: enroll@carroll.edu
http://www.carroll.edu
Communications.

Montana State University—Billings
1500 University Drive
Billings, MT 59101
Phone: (406) 657-2158
Fax: (406) 657-2051
E-mail: keverett@msubillings.edu
http://www.msubillings.edu
Communications.

Montana State University—Bozeman
New Student Services
P.O. Box 172190
Bozeman, MT 59717
Phone: (406) 994-2452
Fax: (406) 994-1923
E-mail: admissions@montana.edu
http://www.montana.edu
Cinematography, film/video production.

Montana State University—Northern
P.O. Box 7751
Havre, MT 59501
Phone: (406) 265-3704
Fax: (406) 265-3777
E-mail: msuadmit@msun.edu
http://www.msun.edu
Communications.

**Montana Tech of the University of
   Montana**
1300 West Park Street
Butte, MT 59701
Phone: (406) 496-4178
Fax: (406) 496-4710
E-mail: admissions@mtech.edu
http://www.mtech.edu
Communications, communications
   technology.

University of Montana—Missoula*
103 Lodge Building
Missoula, MT 59812
Phone: (406) 243-62667
Fax: (406) 243-5711
E-mail: admiss@selway.umt.edu
http://www.umt.edu
Broadcast journalism, communications,
   dance.

NEBRASKA

Bellevue University
1000 Galvin Road South
Bellevue, NE 68005
Phone: (402) 293-2000
Fax: (402) 293-3730
E-mail: info@bellevue.edu
http://www.bellevue.edu
Communications.

Central Community College**
P.O. Box 1027
Columbus, NE 68602
Phone: (877) 222-0780
Fax: NA
E-mail: admissions@cccneb.edu
http://www.cccneb.edu
Broadcast journalism.

Concordia University—Nebraska
800 North Seward Street
Seward, NE 68434
Phone: (800) 535-5494
Fax: (402) 643-4073
E-mail: admiss@seward.cune.edu
http://www.cune.edu
Communications.

Creighton University
2500 California Plaza
Omaha, NE 68178
Phone: (402) 280-2703
Fax: (402) 280-2685
E-mail: admissions@creighton.edu
http://www.creighton.edu
Communications.

Doane College
1014 Boswell Avenue
Crete, NE 68333
Phone: (402) 826-8222
Fax: (402) 826-8600
E-mail: admissions@doane.edu
http://www.doane.edu
Communications, media studies.

Grace University
1311 South 9th Street
Omaha, NE 68108
Phone: (402) 449-2831
Fax: (402) 341-9587
E-mail: admissions@graceu.com
http://www.graceuniversity.com
Broadcast journalism.

Hastings College
800 Turner Avenue
Hastings, NE 68901
Phone: (800) 532-7642
Fax: (402) 461-7490
E-mail: mmollicon@hastings.edu
http://www.hastings.edu
Broadcast journalism, communications,
   communications technology, media
   studies, radio and television.

Midland Lutheran College
900 North Clarkson Street
Fremont, NE 68025

Phone: (402) 721-5487
Fax: (402) 721-0250
E-mail: admissions@admin.mlc.edu
http://www.mlc.edu
Communications.

Northeast Community College**
801 East Benjamin Avenue
P.O. Box 469
Norfolk, NE 68702
Phone: (800) 348-9033, ext. 7260
Fax: (402) 844-7400
E-mail: admissions@northeastcollege.com
http://www.northeastcollege.com
Broadcast journalism, media studies, radio and television.

University of Nebraska—Kearney
905 West 25th Street
Kearney, NE 68849
Phone: (800) 532-7639
Fax: (308) 865-8987
E-mail: admissionsug@unk.edu
http://www.unk.edu
Broadcast journalism, communications.

University of Nebraska—Lincoln*
313 North 13th Street
Van Brunt Visitors Center
Lincoln, NE 68588
Phone: (402) 472-2023
Fax: (402) 472-0670
E-mail: nuhusker@unl.edu
http://www.unl.edu
Broadcast journalism, communications, film/video arts, telecommunications technology.

University of Nebraska—Omaha
Office of Admissions
6001 Dodge Street, EAB Room 103
Omaha, NE 68182
Phone: (402) 554-2393
Fax: (402) 554-3472
E-mail: unoadm@unomaha.edu
http://www.unomaha.edu
Broadcast journalism, communications.

Wayne State College
1111 Main Street
Wayne, NE 68787
Phone: (402) 375-7234
Fax: (402) 375-7204
E-mail: admit1@wsc.edu
http://www.wsc.edu
Communications, media studies.

York College
1125 East 8th Street

York, NE 68467
Phone: (800) 950-9675
E-mail: At Web site
http://www.york.edu
Communications.

NEVADA

Community College of Southern Nevada**
6375 West Charleston Boulevard
Las Vegas, NV 89030
Phone: (702) 651-5610
Fax: At Web site
E-mail: admrec@ccsn.nevada.edu
http://www.ccsn.nevada.edu
Communications.

University of Nevada—Las Vegas
4505 Maryland Parkway
P.O. Box 451021
Las Vegas, NV 89154
Phone: (702) 774-8658
Fax: (702) 774-8008
E-mail: undergraduate.recruitment@ccmail.nevada.edu
http://www.unlv.edu
Communications, dance, film/video arts.

University of Nevada—Reno*
1664 North Virginia Street
Reno, NV 89557
Phone: (775) 784-4700
Fax: (775) 784-4283
E-mail: asknevada@unr.edu
http://www.unr.edu
Communications.

NEW HAMPSHIRE

Dartmouth College
6016 McNutt Hall
Hanover, NH 03755
Phone: (603) 646-2875
Fax: (603) 646-1216
E-mail: admissions.office@dartmouth.edu
http://www.darmouth.edu
Film/video arts.

Franklin Pierce College
Admissions Office
P.O. Box 60
20 College Road
Rindge, NH 03461
Phone: (603) 899-4050
Fax: (603) 889-4394
E-mail: admissions@fpc.edu

http://www.fpc.edu
Acting, broadcast journalism, communications, dance, media studies, radio and television.

Keene State College
229 Main Street
Keene, NH 03435
Phone: (603) 358-2276
Fax: (603) 358-2767
E-mail: admissions@keene.edu
http://www.keene.edu
Communications, dance, film/video arts.

New Hampshire Technical Institute**
31 College Drive
Concord, NH 03301
Phone: (800) 247-0179
Fax: (603) 271-7139
E-mail: info@nhti.edu
http://www.nhti.edu
Communications technology.

Plymouth State University
17 High Street, MSC 52
Plymouth, NH 03264
Phone: (603) 535-2237
Fax: (603) 535-2714
E-mail: plymouthadmit@plymouth.edu
http://www.plymouth.edu
Communications.

Rivier College
420 Main Street
Nashua, NH 03060
Phone: (603) 897-8507
Fax: (603) 891-1799
E-mail: rivadmit@rivier.edu
http://www.rivier.edu
Broadcast journalism, communications.

Southern New Hampshire University
2500 North River Road
Manchester, NH 03108
Phone: (603) 645-9611
Fax: (603) 645-9693
E-mail: admission@snhu.edu
http://www.snhu.edu
Communications.

University of New Hampshire—Durham
4 Garrison Avenue
Durham, NH 03024
Phone: (603) 862-1360
Fax: (603) 862-0077
E-mail: admissions@unh.edu
http://www.unh.edu
Communications, media studies.

**University of New Hampshire—
Manchester**
400 Commercial Street
Manchester, NH 03101
Phone: (603) 629-4150
Fax: (603) 629-2745
E-mail: unhm-admissions@unh.edu
http://www.unh.edu/unhm
Communications, media studies.

NEW JERSEY

Bergen Community College**
400 Paramus Road
Paramus, NJ 07652
Phone: (201) 612-5482
Fax: (201) 444-7036
E-mail: regoffice@bergen.edu
http://www.bergen.cc.nj.us
Acting, broadcast journalism,
    communications, communications
    technology, dance.

Centenary College
400 Jefferson Street
Hackettstown, NJ 07840
Phone: (800) 236-8679
Fax: (908) 852-3454
E-mail: admissions@centenarycollege.
    edu
http://www.centenarycollege.edu
Communications.

The College of New Jersey
P.O. Box 7718
Ewing, NJ 08628
Phone: (609) 771-2131
Fax: (609) 637-5174
E-mail: admiss@vm.tcnj.edu
http://www.tcnj.edu
Communications.

College of Saint Elizabeth
Admissions Office
2 Convent Road
Morristown, NJ 07960
Phone: (973) 290-4700
Fax: (973) 290-4710
E-mail: apply@cse.edu
http://www.cse.edu
Communications.

Cumberland County College**
P.O. Box 1500, College Drive
Vineland, NJ 08362
Phone: (856) 691-8600, ext. 228
E-mail: At Web site
http://www.cccnj.net
Cinematography, film/video production,
    radio and television.

Essex County College**
303 University Avenue
Newark, NJ 07102
Phone: (973) 877-3119
Fax: (973) 623-6449
E-mail: At Web site
http://www.essex.edu
Media studies.

**Farleigh Dickinson University, College
    at Florham**
285 Madison Avenue
Madison, NJ 07940
Phone: (800) 338-8803
Fax: (973) 443-8088
E-mail: globaleducation@fdu.edu
http://www.fdu.edu
Cinematography, film/video production,
    communications.

**Farleigh Dickinson University,
    Metropolitan Campus**
1000 River Road
Teaneck, NJ 07666
Phone: (201) 692-2553
Fax: (201) 692-7319
E-mail: globaleducation@fdu.edu
http://www.fdu.edu
Communications.

Felician College
262 South Main Street
Lodi, NJ 07644
Phone: (201) 559-6131
Fax: (201) 559-6138
E-mail: admissions@inet.felician.edu
http://www.felician.edu
Broadcast journalism.

Kean University
P.O. Box 411
Union, NJ 07083
Phone: (908) 737-7100
Fax: (908) 737-7105
E-mail: admitme@kean.edu
http://www.kean.edu
Communications.

Monmouth University
Admission
400 Cedar Avenue
West Long Branch, NJ 07764
Phone: (732) 571-3456
Fax: (732) 263-5166
E-mail: admission@monmouth.edu
http://www.monmouth.edu
Communications.

New Jersey City University
2039 Kennedy Boulevard
Jersey City, NJ 07305
Phone: (201) 200-3234
Fax: (201) 200-2044
E-mail: admissions@njcu.edu
http://www.njcu.edu
Communications.

Montclair State University
One Normal Avenue
Upper Montclair, NJ 07043
Phone: (973) 655-5116
Fax: (973) 655-7700
E-mail: undergraduate.admissions@
    montclair.edu
http://www.montclair.edu
Broadcast journalism.

Ocean County College**
College Drive
P.O. Box 2001
Toms River, NJ 08754
Phone: (732) 255-0304, ext. 2016
E-mail: At Web site
http://www.ocean.edu
Communications technology.

Ramapo College of New Jersey
505 Ramapo Valley Road
Mahwah, NJ 07430
Phone: (201) 684-7300
Fax: (201) 684-7964
E-mail: admissions@ramapo.edu
http://www.ramapo.edu
Communications.

**Richard Stockton College of New
    Jersey**
Jim Leeds Road
P.O. Box 195
Pomona, NJ 08240
Phone: (609) 652-4261
Fax: (609) 748-5541
E-mail: admissions@stockton.edu
http://www.stockton.edu
Communications.

Rider University
2083 Lawrenceville Road
Lawrenceville, NJ 08648
Phone: (609) 896-5042
Fax: (609) 895-6645
E-mail: admissions@rider.edu
http://www.rider.edu
Communications.

Rowan University
201 Mullica Hill Road
Glassboro, NJ 08028

Phone: (856) 256-4200
Fax: (856) 256-4430
E-mail: admissions@rowan.edu
http://www.rowan.edu
Broadcast journalism, communications, communications technology, dance, film/video arts.

Rutgers, The State University of New Jersey—University College at New Brunswick
65 Davidson Road
Piscataway, NJ 08854
Phone: (732) 932-4636
Fax: (732) 445-0237
E-mail: admissions@ugadm.rutgers.edu
http://www.rutgers.edu
Communications, dance.

Seton Hall University
Enrollment Services
400 South Orange Avenue
South Orange, NJ 07079
Phone: (973) 761-9332
Fax: (973) 275-2040
E-mail: thehall@shu.edu
http://www.shu.edu
Communications.

Thomas Edison State College
101 West State Street
Trenton, NJ 08608
Phone: (609) 984-1150
Fax: (609) 984-8447
E-mail: info@tesc.edu
http://www.tesc.edu
Communications.

Union County College**
1033 Springfield Avenue
Cranford, NJ 07016
Phone: (908) 709-7000
E-mail: At Web site
http://www.ucc.edu
Communications.

William Patterson University
Admissions Hall
300 Pompton Road
Wayne, NJ 07470
Phone: (973) 720-2125
Fax: (973) 720-2910
E-mail: admissions@wpunj.edu
http://www.wpunj.edu
Communications, media studies.

NEW MEXICO

College of Santa Fe
1600 St. Michaels Drive

Santa Fe, NM 87505
Phone: (505) 473-6133
Fax: (505) 473-6129
E-mail: admissions@csf.edu
http://www.csf.edu
Acting, film/video arts.

Eastern New Mexico University
Station #7, ENMU
1500 South Avenue K
Portales, NM 88130
Phone: (505) 562-2178
Fax: (505) 562-2118
E-mail: admissions@enmu.edu
http://www.enmu.edu
Broadcast journalism, communications.

New Mexico Highlands University
NMHU Office of Student Recruitment
P.O. Box 900
Las Vegas, NM 87701
Phone: (505) 454-3593
Fax: (505) 454-3511
E-mail: recruitment@nmhu.edu
http://www.nmhu.edu
Communications.

New Mexico Junior College**
5317 Lovington Highway
Hobbs, NM 88240
Phone: (800) 657-6260
Fax: (505) 392-5092
E-mail: At Web site
http://www.nmjc.edu
Communications.

New Mexico State University*
P.O. Box 30001, MSC 3A
Las Cruces, NM 88003
Phone: (505) 646-3121
Fax: (505) 646-6330
E-mail: admissions@nmsu.edu
http://www.nmsu.edu
Communications, dance, photographic/film/video technology.

San Juan College*
4601 College Boulevard
Farmington, NM 87402
Phone: (505) 566-3318
Fax: (505) 566-3500
E-mail: At Web site
http://www.sjc.cc.nm.us
Communications technology.

University of New Mexico
Office of Admissions
Student Services Center 150
Albuquerque, NM 87131

Phone: (505) 277-2446
Fax: (505) 277-6686
E-mail: apply@unm.edu
http://www.unm.edu
Communications, dance, film/video arts, media studies.

NEW YORK

Adelphia University
Levermore Hall 114
South Avenue
Garden City, NY 11530
Phone: (516) 877-3050
Fax: (516) 877-339
E-mail: admissions@adelphi.edu
http://www.adelphi.edu
Communications, dance.

Alfred University
Alumni Hall
1 Saxon Drive
Alfred, NY 14802
Phone: (607) 871-2115
Fax: (607) 871-2198
E-mail: admwww@alfred.edu
http://www.alfred.edu
Communications.

Bard College
Office of Admissions
Annandale-on-Hudson, NY 12504
Phone: (845) 758-7472
Fax: (845) 758-5208
E-mail: admissions@bard.edu
http://www.bard.edu
Acting, cinematography, film/video production, dance, film/video arts, playwriting/screenwriting.

Barnard College
3090 Broadway
New York, NY 10027
Phone: (212) 854-2014
Fax: (212) 854-6220
E-mail: admissions@barnard.edu
http://www.barnard.edu
Film/video arts.

Canisius College
2001 Main Street
Buffalo, NY 14208
Phone: (716) 888-2200
Fax: (716) 888-3230
E-mail: inquiry@canisius.edu
http://www.canisius.edu
Communications.

Cayuga County Community College**
Auburn Campus
197 Franklin Street
Auburn, NY 13021
Phone: (315) 255-1743
Fax: (315) 255-2117
E-mail: admissions@cayuga-cc.edu
http://www.cayuga-cc.edu
Photographic/film/video technology,
    radio and television,
    telecommunications technology.

**City University of New York—Baruch
College**
Undergraduate Admissions
1 Bernard Baruch Way
P.O. Box H-0720
New York, NY 10010
Phone: (646) 312-1400
Fax: (646) 312-1361
E-mail: admissions@baruch.cuny.edu
http://www.baruch.cuny.edu
Communications.

**City University of New York—
Brooklyn College**
3000 Bedford Avenue
Brooklyn, NY 11210
Phone: (718) 951-5001
Fax: (718) 951-4506
E-mail: adminqry@brooklyn.cuny.edu
http://www.brooklyn.cuny.edu
Acting, broadcast journalism,
    cinematography, film/video
    production, communications,
    film/video arts, playwriting/
    screenwriting, radio and television,
    radio/television broadcasting.

**City University of New York—City
College**
Convent Avenue at 138th Street
New York, NY 100031
Phone: (212) 650-6977
Fax: (212) 650-6417
E-mail: admissions@ccny.cuny.edu
http://www.ccny.cuny.edu
Cinematography, film/video production,
    communications, film/video arts.

**City University of New York—College
of Staten Island**
2800 Victory Boulevard, Bldg 2A,
    Room 104
Staten Island, NY 10314
Phone: (718) 982-2010
Fax: (718) 982-2500
E-mail: recruitment@postbox.csi.cuny.
    edu

http://www.csi.cuny.edu
Cinematography, film/video production,
    communications.

**City University of New York—Hunter
College**
695 Park Avenue
New York, NY 10021
Phone: (212) 772-4490
Fax: (212) 650-3336
E-mail: admissions@hunter.cuny.edu
http://www.hunter.cuny.edu
Cinematography, film/video production,
    communications, dance, film/video
    arts, media studies.

**City University of New York—
Kingsborough Community
College****
Admissions Information Center
2001 Oriental Boulevard
Brooklyn, NY 11235
Phone: (718) 368-4600
Fax: NA
E-mail: info@kingsborough.edu
http://www.kingsborough.edu
Broadcast journalism.

**City University of New York—Lehman
College**
350 Bedford Park Boulevard West
Bronx, NY 10468
Phone: (718) 960-8000
Fax: (718) 960-8712
E-mail: wilkes@alpha.lehman.cuny.edu
http://www.lehman.cuny.edu
Communications, dance, media studies.

**City College of New York—Queens
College**
65-30 Kissena Boulevard
Flushing, NY 11367
Phone: (718) 997-5000
Fax: (718) 997-5617
E-mail: admissions@qc.cuny.edu
http://www.qc.cuny.edu
Communications, dance, film/video arts.

Clarkson University
P.O. Box 5605
Potsdam, NY 13699
Phone: (315) 268-6479
Fax: (315) 268-7647
E-mail: admission@clarkson.edu
http://www.clarkson.edu
Communications.

College of Mount Saint Vincent
6301 Riverdale Avenue

Riverdale, NY 10471
Phone: (718) 405-3267
Fax: (718) 549-7945
E-mail: admissions@mountsaintvincent.
    edu
http://www.mountsaintvincent.edu
Communications.

Columbia University*
212 Hamilton Hall MC 2807
1130 Amsterdam Avenue
New York, NY 10027
Phone: (212) 854-2521
Fax: (212) 894-1209
E-mail: At Web site
http://www.college.columbia.edu
Communications, film/video arts.

Cornell University
Undergraduate Admissions
410 Thurston Avenue
Ithaca, NY 14850
Phone: (607) 255-5241
Fax: (607) 255-0659
E-mail: admissions@cornell.edu
http://www.cornell.edu
Acting, communications, dance, film/
    video arts.

Dutchess Community College**
Office of Admissions
53 Pendell Road
Poughkeepsie, NY 12601
Phone: (800) 763-3933
E-mail: At Web site
http://www.sunydutchess.edu
Communications.

Excelsior College
7 Columbia Circle
Albany, NY 12203
Phone: (518) 464-8500
Fax: (518) 464-8777
E-mail: admissions@excelsior.edu
http://www.excelsior.edu
Communications.

Five Towns College
305 North Service Road
Dix Hills, NY 11746
Phone: (631) 424-7000
Fax: (631) 424-7008
E-mail: admissions@ftc.edu
http://www.fivetowns.edu
Acting, broadcast journalism,
    cinematography, film/video
    production, communications,
    communications technology,
    film/video arts, media studies.

Fordham University
441 East Fordham Road
Thebaud Hall
Bronx, NY 10458
Phone: (718) 817-4000
Fax: (718) 367-9404
E-mail: enroll@fordham.edu
http://www.fordham.edu
Communications, dance, film/video arts.

Genesee Community College**
One College Road
Batavia, NY 14020
Phone: (800) CALL-GCC
Fax: (585) 345-6892
E-mail: At Web site
http://www.genesee.edu
Communications, radio/television
    broadcasting.

Hamilton College
198 College Hill Road
Clinton, NY 13323
Phone: (315) 859-4421
Fax: (315) 859-4457
E-mail: admission@hamilton.edu
http://www.hamilton.edu
Communications, dance.

Hobart and William Smith College
629 South Main Street
Geneva, NY 14456
Phone: (315) 781-3472
Fax: (315) 781-3471
E-mail: admissions@hws.edu
http://www.hws.edu
Media studies.

Hofstra University*
Admission Center
Bernon Hall
1000 Fulton Avenue
Hempstead, NY 11549
Phone: (516) 463-6700
Fax: (516) 463-5100
E-mail: admitme@hofstra.edu
http://www.hofstra.edu
Broadcast journalism, cinematography,
    film/video production,
    communications, dance, film/video
    arts, media studies, radio and
    television, radio/television
    broadcasting.

Houghton College
P.O. Box 128
Houghton, NY 14744
Phone: (800) 777-2556
Fax: (716) 567-9522

E-mail: admissions@houghton.edu
http://www.houghton.edu
Communications.

Iona College*
715 North Avenue
New Rochelle, NY 10801
Phone: (914) 633-2502
Fax: (914) 633-2642
E-mail: icad@iona.edu
http://www.iona.edu
Communications, film/video arts, media
    studies, radio/television broadcasting.

Ithaca College
100 Job Hall
Ithaca, NY 14850
Phone: (607) 274-3124
Fax: (607) 274-1900
E-mail: admission@ithaca.edu
http://www.ithaca.edu
Acting, broadcast journalism,
    cinematography, film/video
    production, communications, dance,
    film/video arts, media studies, radio
    and television.

Keuka College
Office of Admissions
Keuka Park, NY 14478
Phone: (315) 279-5254
Fax: (315) 536-5386
E-mail: admissions@mail.keuka.edu
http://www.keuka.edu
Communications.

Le Moyne College
1419 Salt Springs Road
Syracuse, NY 13214
Phone: (315) 445-4300
Fax: (315) 445-4711
E-mail: admission@lemoyne.edu
http://www.lemoyne.edu
Communications.

Long Island University—Brooklyn
One University Plaza
Brooklyn, NY 11201
Phone: (800) 548-7526
Fax: (718) 797-2399
E-mail:admissions@brooklyn.liu.edu
http://www.brooklyn.liu.edu
Communications, dance.

**Long Island University—C.W. Post
    Campus**
720 Northern Boulevard
Brookville, NY 11548
Phone: (516) 299-2900

Fax: (516) 299-2137
E-mail: enroll@cwpost.liu.edu
http://www.liu.edu
Cinematography, film/video production,
    communications, dance,
    radio/television broadcasting.

Manhattan College
Manhattan College Parkway
Riverdale, NY 10471
Phone: (718) 862-7200
Fax: (718) 862-8019
E-mail: admit@manhattan.edu
http://www.manhattan.edu
Broadcast journalism, communications.

Marist College
3399 North Road
Poughkeepsie, NY 12601
Phone: (845) 575-3226
Fax: (845) 575-3215
E-mail: admissions@marist.edu
http://www.marist.edu
Broadcast journalism, communications,
    film/video arts, media studies, radio
    and television.

**Marymount College of Fordham
    University**
100 Marymount Avenue
Tarrytown, NY 10591
Phone: (914) 323-8295
Fax: (914) 332-7442
E-mail: admiss@mmc.marymt.edu
http://www.marymt.edu
Communications.

Marymount Manhattan College
221 East 71st Street
New York, NY 10021
Phone: (212) 517-0430
Fax: (212) 517-0465
E-mail: admissions@mmm.edu
http://www.marymount.mmm.edu
Communications, dance.

Metropolitan College
75 Varick Street
New York, NY 100013
Phone: (212) 343-1234
Fax: (212) 343-8470
E-mail: admissions@metropolitan.edu
http://www.metropolitan.edu
Communications.

Mohawk Valley College**
Utica Campus
1101 Sherman Drive
Utica, NY 13501

Phone: (315) 792-5354
E-mail: At Web site
http://www.mvcc.edu
Photographic/film/video technology.

Molloy College
1000 Hempstead Avenue
Rockville Center, NY 11570
Phone: (516) 678-5000
Fax: (516) 255-2247
E-mail: admissions@molloy.edu
http://www.molloy.edu
Communications.

Monroe Community College**
1000 East Henrietta Road
Rochester, NY 14623
Phone: (585) 292-2000, ext. 2221
Fax: (585) 292-3860
E-mail: admissions@monroecc.edu
http://www.monroecc.edu
Communications technology.

Mount Saint Mary College
330 Powell Avenue
Newburgh, NY 12550
Phone: (845) 569-3248
Fax: (845) 562-6762
E-mail: mtstmary@msmc.edu
http://www.msmc.edu
Communications.

Nassau Community College**
One Education Drive
Garden City, NY 11530
Phone: (516) 572-7501
E-mail: At Web site
http://www.sunynassau.edu
Broadcast journalism, communications
   technology.

New York Institute of Technology
P.O. Box 8000
Northern Boulevard
Old Westbury, NY 11568
Phone: (516) 686-7520
Fax: (516) 686-7613
E-mail: admissions@nyit.edu
http://www.nyit.edu
Broadcast journalism, communications,
   communications technology, radio and
   television.

New York University
22 Washington Square North
New York, NY 10011
Phone: (212) 998-4500
Fax: (212) 995-4902
E-mail: admissions@nyu.edu

http://www.nyu.edu
Acting, communications,
   cinematography, film/video
   production, communications
   technology, dance, film/video arts,
   media studies,
   playwriting/screenwriting, radio and
   television.

Niagara University
Bailo Hall
P.O. Box 2011
Niagara Falls, NY 14109
Phone: (716) 286-8700
Fax: (716) 286-8710
E-mail: admissions@niagara.edu
http://www.niagara.edu
Communications.

Nyack College
1 South Boulevard
Nyack, NY 10960
Phone: (845) 358-1710
Fax: (845) 358-3047
E-mail: enroll@nyack.edu
http://www.nyack.edu
Communications.

Pace University
1 Pace Plaza
New York, NY 10038
Phone: (212) 346-1323
Fax: (212) 346-1040
E-mail: infoctr@pace.edu
http://www.pace.edu
Communications.

Pace University—
   Pleasantville/Briarcliff
861 Bedford Road
Pleasantville, NY 10570
Phone: (914) 773-3746
Fax: (914) 773-3851
E-mail: infotr@pace.edu
http://www.pace.edu
Communications.

Pratt Institute
200 Willoughby Avenue
Brooklyn, NY 11205
Phone: (718) 636-3660
Fax: (718) 636-3670
E-mail: admissions@pratt.edu
http://www.pratt.edu
Cinematography, film/video production.

Rensselaer Polytechnic Institute
110 Eighth Street
Troy, NY 12180

Phone: (518) 276-6216
Fax: (518) 276-4072
E-mail: At Web site
http://www.rpi.edu
Communications.

Roberts Wesleyan College
2301 Westside Drive
Rochester, NY 14624
Phone: (585) 594-6400
Fax: (585) 594-6371
E-mail: admissions@roberts.edu
http://www.roberts.edu
Communications.

Rochester Institute of Technology
60 Lomb Memorial Drive
Rochester, NY 14623
Phone: (585) 475-6631
Fax: (585) 475-7424
E-mail: admissions@rit.edu
http://www.rit.edu
Cinematography, film/video production,
   media studies, telecommunications
   technology.

Saint Bonaventure University
P.O. Box D
Bonaventure, NY 14778
Phone: (716) 375-2400
Fax: (716) 375-4005
E-mail: admissions@sbu.edu
http://www.sbu.edu
Media studies.

Saint Francis College
180 Remsen Street
Brooklyn, NY 11201
Phone: (718) 489-5200
Fax: (718) 802-0453
E-mail: admissions@stfranciscollege.edu
http://www.stfranciscollege.edu
Communications.

Saint John Fisher College
3690 East Avenue
Rochester, NY 14618
Phone: (585) 385-8064
Fax: (585) 385-8386
E-mail: admissions@sjfc.edu
http://www.sjfc.edu
Broadcast journalism, communications.

Saint John's University
8000 Utopia Parkway
Jamaica, NY 11439
Phone: (718) 990-2000
Fax: (718) 990-5728
E-mail: admissions@stjohns.edu

http://www.stjohns.edu
Cinematography, film/video production,
    communications, communications
    technology, film/video arts.

Saint Thomas Aquinas College
125 Route 340
Sparkill, NY 109976
Phone: (845) 398-4100
Fax: (845) 398-4224
E-mail: admissions@stac.edu
http://www.stac.edu
Communications.

Sarah Lawrence College
One Mead Way
Bronxville, NY 10708
Phone: (914) 395-2510
Fax: (914) 395-2676
E-mail: slcadmit@slc.edu
http://www.slc.edu
Cinematography, film/video production,
    dance, film/video arts,
    playwriting/screenwriting.

Schenectady County Community
College*
Office of Admissions
78 Washington Avenue
Schenectady, NY 12305
Phone: (518) 381-1200
E-mail: At Web site
http://www.sunysccc.edu
Telecommunications technology.

School of Visual Arts
209 East 23rd Street
New York, NY 100010
Phone: (212) 592-2100
Fax: (212) 592-2116
E-mail: admissions@sva.edu
http://www.sva.edu
Cinematography, film/video production,
    film/video arts.

State University of New York at Albany
Office of Undergraduate Admissions
1400 Washington Avenue
Albany, NY 12222
Phone: (518) 442-5435
Fax: (518) 442-5383
E-mail: ugadmissions@albany.edu
http://www.albany.edu
Communications.

State University of New York at
Binghamton
P.O. Box 6001
Binghamton, NY 13902

Phone: (607) 777-2171
Fax: (607) 777-4445
E-mail: admit@binghamton.edu
http://www.binghamton.edu
Film/video arts.

State University of New York College at
Brockport
350 New Campus Drive
Brockport, NY 14420
Phone: (585) 395-2751
Fax: (585) 395-5452
E-mail: admit@brockport.edu
http://www.brockport.edu
Broadcast journalism, communications,
    media studies.

State University of New York College at
Buffalo
1300 Elmwood Avenue
Buffalo, NY 14222
Phone: (716) 878-4017
Fax: (716) 878-6100
E-mail: admissions@buffalostate.edu
http://www.buffalostate.edu
Communications, dance, film/video arts,
    media studies.

State University of New York College at
Cortland
P.O. Box 2000
Cortland, NY 13045
Phone: (607) 753-4712
Fax: (607) 753-5998
E-mail: admissions@cortland.edu
http://www.cortland.edu
Broadcast journalism.

State University of New York College at
Fredonia
178 Central Avenue
Fredonia, NY 14063
Phone: (716) 673-3251
Fax: (716) 673-3249
E-mail: admissions.office@fredonia.edu
http://www.fredonia.edu
Broadcast journalism, communications.

State University of New York College at
Geneseo
1 College Circle
Geneseo, NY 14454
Phone: (716) 245-5671
Fax: (716) 245-5550
E-mail: admissions@geneseo.edu
http://www.geneseo.edu
Communications.

State University of New York College at
New Paltz
75 South Manheim Boulevard, Suite 1
New Paltz, NY 12561
Phone: (845) 257-3200
Fax: (914) 257-3209
E-mail: admissions@newpaltz.edu
http://www.newpaltz.edu
Broadcast journalism, communications.

State University of New York College at
Old Westbury
P.O. Box 307
Old Westbury, NY 11568
Phone: (516) 876-3073
Fax: (516) 876-3307
E-mail: enroll@oldwestbury.edu
http://www.oldwestbury.edu
Communications.

State University of New York College at
Oneonta
Alumni Hall 116
State University College
Oneonta, NY 13820
Phone: (607) 436-2524
Fax: (607) 436-3074
E-mail: admissions@oneonta.edu
http://www.oneonta.edu
Communications, media studies.

State University of New York College at
Oswego
211 Culkin Hall
Oswego, NY 13126
Phone: (315) 312-2250
Fax: (315) 312-3260
E-mail: admiss@oswego.edu
http://www.oswego.edu
Broadcast journalism, communications.

State University of New York College at
Plattsburgh
1001 Kehoe Building
Plattsburgh, NY 12091
Phone: (518) 564-2040
Fax: (518) 564-2045
E-mail: admissions@plattsburgh.edu
http://www.plattsburgh.edu
Communications, communications
    technology.

State University of New York College at
Purchase
Admissions Office
735 Anderson Hill Road
Purchase, NY 10577
Phone: (914) 251-6300
Fax: (914) 251-6314

E-mail: admissn@purchase.edu
http://www.purchase.edu
Cinematography, film/video production,
    communications, dance,
    playwriting/screenwriting.

Syracuse University*
201 Tolley
Administration Building
Syracuse, NY 13244
Phone: (315) 443-3611
Fax: (315) 443-4226
E-mail: orange@syr.edu
http://www.syracuse.edu
Acting, broadcast journalism,
    cinematography, film/video
    production, communications,
    film/video arts, media studies, radio
    and television.

Touro College
1602 Avenue J
Brooklyn, NY 11230
Phone: (718) 252-7800
Fax: (718) 253-6479
E-mail: lasadmit@touro.edu
http://www.touro.edu
Communications.

University of Rochester
300 Wilson Boulevard
P.O. Box 270251
Rochester, NY 14627
Phone: (585) 275-3221
Fax: (585) 461-4595
E-mail: admit@admissions.rochester.edu
http://www.rochester.edu
Film/video arts.

Utica College of Syracuse University
1600 Burnstone Road
Utica, NY 13502
Phone: (315) 792-3006
Fax: (315) 792-3003
E-mail: admiss@utica.ucsu.edu
http://www.utica.edu
Communications.

Vassar College
124 Raymond Avenue
Poughkeepsie, NY 12604
Phone: (845) 437-7300
Fax: (845) 437-7063
E-mail: admissions@vassar.edu
http://www.vassar.edu
Film/video arts.

Westchester Community College**
75 Grasslands Road

Valhalla, NY, 10595
Phone: (914) 606-6600
E-mail: admissions@sunywcc.edu
http://www.sunywcc.edu
Communications.

NORTH CAROLINA

Appalachian State University
Office of Admissions
P.O. Box 32004
Boone, NC 28608
Phone: (828) 262-2120
Fax: (828) 262-3296
E-mail: admissions@appstate.edu
http://www.appstate.edu
Broadcast journalism, communications.

Campbell University
P.O. Box 546
Buies Creek, NC 27506
Phone: (910) 893-1320
Fax: (910) 893-1288
E-mail: adm@mailcenter.campbell.edu
http://www.campbell.edu
Broadcast journalism, radio and television.

Cape Fear Community College**
411 North Front Street
Wilmington, NC 28401
Phone: (910) 362-7000
Fax: NA
E-mail: admissions@cfcc.edu
http://www.cfcc.edu
Cinematography, film/video production.

Carteret Community College**
505 Arendell Street
Morehead City, NC 28557
Phone: (252) 222-6153, ext. 4218
Fax: (252) 222-6265
E-mail: At Web site
http://www.gofish.carteret.cc.nc.us
Makeup artist, photographic/film/video
    technology.

Catawba College
2300 West Innes Street
Salisbury, NC 28144
Phone: (704) 637-4402
Fax: (704) 637-4222
E-mail: admission@catawba.edu
http://www.catawba.edu
Communications.

Central Carolina Community College**
1105 Kelly Drive
Sanford, NC 27330

Phone: (800) 682-8353, ext. 7300
Fax: (919) 718-7380
E-mail: tgraves.@cccc.edu
http://www.cccc.edu
Broadcast journalism.

Cleveland Community College**
137 South Post Road
Shelby, NC 28152
Phone: (704) 484-4073
Fax: (704) 484-5305
E-mail: At Web site
http://www.cleveland.cc.nc.us
Communications technology.

East Carolina University
Office of Undergraduate Admissions
100 Whichard Building
Greenville, NC 27858
Phone: (252) 328-6640
Fax: (252) 328-6945
E-mail: admis@mail.ecu.edu
http://www.ecu.edu
Broadcast journalism, communications,
    dance.

ECPI Technical College**
North Carolina Campus
4800 Airport Center Parkway
Charlotte, NC 28208
Phone: (704) 399-1010
E-mail: At Web site
http://www.ecpi.edu
Telecommunications technology

Elon University
2700 Campus Box
Elon, NC 27244
Phone: (336) 278-3566
Fax: (336) 278-7699
E-mail: admissions@elon.edu
http://www.elon.edu
Broadcast journalism, communications,
    dance.

Fayetteville Technical College**
P.O. Box 35236
Fayetteville, NC 28303
Phone: (910) 678-8274
Fax: (910) 678-8407
E-mail: At Web site
http://www.faytech.cc.nc.us
Telecommunications technology.

Gardner-Webb University
P.O. Box 817
Boiling Springs, NC 28017
Phone: (704) 406-4498

Fax: (704) 406-4488
E-mail: admissions@gardner-webb.edu
http://www.gardner-webb.edu
Broadcast journalism, communications.

Gaston College**
201 Highway 321 South
Dallas, NC 28034
Phone: (704) 922-6214
E-mail: At Web site
http://www.gaston.cc.nc.us
Broadcast journalism.

Greensboro College
815 West Market Street
Greensboro, NC 27401
Phone: (800) 346-8226
Fax: (336) 378-0154
E-mail: admissions@gborocollege.edu
http://www.gborocollege.edu
Communications.

Isothermal Community College**
Polk Campus
1255 West Mills Street
Columbus, NC 28722
Phone: (828) 894-3092
E-mail: At Web site
http://www.isothermal.cc.nc.us
Radio/television broadcasting.

Johnson C. Smith University
100 Beatties Ford Road
Charlotte, NC 28216
Phone: (704) 378-1011
E-mail: admissions@jcsu.edu
http://www.jcsu.edu
Communications, media studies.

Louisburg College**
501 North Main Street
Louisburg, NC 27549
Phone: (919) 496-2521
E-mail: admissions@louisburg.edu
http://www.louisburg.edu
Communications, dance.

Mars Hill College
P.O. Box 370
Mars Hills, NC 28754
Phone: (828) 689-1201
Fax: (828) 689-1473
E-mail: admissions@mhc.edu
http://www.mhc.edu
Communications.

Martin Community College**
1161 Kehukee Park Road
Williamston, NC 27892

Phone: (252) 792-1521, ext. 243
Fax: (252) 792-0826
E-mail: lmurdock@martin.cc.nc.us
http://www.martin.cc.nc.us
Makeup artist.

Meredith College
3800 Hillsborough Street
Raleigh, NC 27607
Phone: (919) 760-8581
Fax: (919) 760-2348
E-mail: admissions@meredith.edu
http://www.meredith.edu
Communications, dance.

Methodist College
5400 Ramsey Street
Fayetteville, NC 28311
Phone: (910) 630-7027
Fax: (910) 630-7285
E-mail: rlowe@methodist.edu
http://www.methodist.edu
Communications.

Mount Olive College
634 Henderson Street
Mount Olive, NC 29365
Phone: (919) 658-7164
Fax: (919) 658-7180
E-mail: admissions@moc.edu
http://www.moc.edu
Communications.

North Carolina A&T University*
1601 East Market Street
Greensboro, NC 27411
Phone: (336) 334-7946
Fax: (336) 334-7478
E-mail: uadmit@ncat.edu
http://www.ncat.edu
Broadcast journalism, communications.

North Carolina School of the Arts
1433 South Main Street
P.O. Box 12189
Winston-Salem, NC 27127
Phone: (336) 770-3290
Fax: (336) 770-3370
E-mail: admissions@ncarts.edu
http://wwwncarts.edu
Cinematography, film/video production,
  dance.

North Carolina State University
P.O. Box 7103
Raleigh, NC 27695
Phone: (919) 515-2434
Fax: (919) 515-5039

E-mail: undergrad_admissions@ncsu.
  edu
http://www.ncsu.edu
Broadcast journalism, media studies.

Saint Augustine's College
1315 Oakwood Avenue
Raleigh, NC 27610
Phone: (919) 516-4016
Fax: (919) 516-5805
E-mail: admissions@st-aug.edu
http://www.st-aug.edu
Cinematography, film/video production,
  communications.

Shaw University
118 East South Street
Raleigh, NC 27601
Phone: (919) 546-8275
Fax: (919) 546-8271
E-mail: admissions@shawu.edu
http://www.shawu.edu
Media studies.

**University of North Carolina—
  Asheville**
CPO #2210
117 Lipinsky Hall
Asheville, NC 28804
Phone: (828) 251-6481
Fax: (828) 251-6482
E-mail: admissions@unca.edu
http://www.unca.edu
Communications.

**University of North Carolina—Chapel
  Hill***
Office of Undergraduate Admissions
Jackson Hall 153A
Campus P.O. Box 2220
Chapel Hill, NC 27599
Phone: (919) 966-3621
Fax: (919) 962-3045
E-mail: uadm@email.unc.edu
http://www.unc.edu
Communications, media studies.

**University of North Carolina—
  Charlotte**
9201 University City Boulevard
Charlotte, NC 28223
Phone: (704) 687-2213
Fax: (704) 687-6483
E-mail: uncadm@email.uncc.edu
http://www.uncc.edu
Communications, dance.

**University of North Carolina—
  Greensboro**
123 Mossman Building

Greensboro, NC 27402
Phone: (336) 334-5243
Fax: (336) 334-4180
E-mail:
    undergrad_admissions@uncg.edu
http://www.uncg.edu
Broadcast journalism, cinematography,
    film/video production, dance,
    film/video arts.

**University of North Carolina—
    Pembroke**
One University Drive
P.O. Box 1510
Pembroke, NC 28372
Phone: (910) 521-6262
Fax: (910) 521-6407
E-mail: admissions@papa.uncp.edu
http://www.uncp.edu
Media studies.

**University of North Carolina—
    Wilmington**
601 South College Road
Wilmington, NC 28403
Phone: (910) 962-3243
Fax: (910) 962-3038
E-mail: admissions@uncwil.edu
http://www.uncwil.edu
Film/video arts.

Wake Forest University
P.O. Box 7305, Reynolds Station
Winston-Salem, NC 27109
Phone: (336) 758-5201
Fax: (336) 758-4324
E-mail: admissions@wfu.edu
http://www.wfu.edu
Communications.

Western Carolina University
232 HFR Administration
Cullowhee, NC 28723
Phone: (828) 227-7317
Fax: (828) 227-7319
E-mail: cauley@emai.wcu.edu
http://www.wcu.edu
Communications.

Wilkes Community College**
P.O. Box 120
1328 Collegiate Drive
Wilkesboro, NC 28697
Phone: (336) 838-6100
Fax: (336) 838-6277
E-mail: At Web site
http://www.wilkes.cc.nc.us
Radio/television broadcasting.

Wingate University
Campus Box 3059
Wingate, NC 28174
Phone: (704) 223-8200
Fax: (704) 233-8130
E-mail: admit@wingate.edu
http://www.wingate.edu
Communications.

Winston-Salem State University
601 MLK Jr. Drive
Winston-Salem, NC 27110
Phone: (336) 750-2070
Fax: (336) 750-2079
E-mail: admissions@wssu1.adp.wssu.
    edu
http://www.wssu.edu
Communications, media studies.

NORTH DAKOTA

Bismarck State College**
1500 Edwards Avenue
P.O. Box 5587
Bismarck, ND 58506
Phone: (800) 445-5073
Fax: (701) 224-5643
E-mail: At Web site
http://www.bismarckstate.edu
Media studies.

Dickinson State University
Office of Student Recruitment
P.O. Box 173
Dickinson, ND 58601
Phone: (701) 483-2331
Fax: (701) 483-2409
E-mail: dsu.hawks.dus.nodak.edu
http://www.dickinsonstate.com
Communications.

Jamestown College
6081 College Lane
Jamestown, ND 58405
Phone: (701) 252-3467
Fax: (701) 253-4318
E-mail: admissions@jc.edu
http://www.jc.edu
Communications.

Minot State University—Minot
500 University Avenue
West Minot, ND 58707
Phone: (701) 858-3350
Fax: (701) 858-3386
E-mail: msu@minotstateu.edu
http://www.minotstateu.edu
Broadcast journalism, communications
    technology, radio and television.

North Dakota State University
P.O. Box 5454
Fargo, ND 58105
Phone: (701) 231-8643
Fax: (701) 231-8802
E-mail: ndsu.admission@ndsu.nodak.edu
http://www.ndsu.edu
Communications, media studies.

University of North Dakota
Enrollment Services
Twamley Hall Room 312
P.O. Box 8135
Grand Forks, ND 58202
Phone: (701) 777-4463
Fax: (701) 777-2696
E-mail: enrolser@sase.und.nodak.edu
http://www.und.edu
Communications.

OHIO

Antioch College
795 Livermore Street
Yellow Springs, OH 45387
Phone: (937) 769-1100
Fax: (937) 769-1111
E-mail: admissions@antioch-college.edu
http://www.antioch-college.edu
Cinematography, film/video production,
    communications, dance.

Ashland University
401 College Avenue
Ashland, OH 44805
Phone: (419) 289-5052
Fax: (419) 289-5999
E-mail: auadmsn@ashland.edu
http://www.ashland.edu
Communications, radio and television.

Baldwin-Wallace College
275 Eastland Road
Berea, OH 44017
Phone: (440) 826-2222
Fax: (440) 826-3830
E-mail: admission@bw.edu
http://www.bw.edu
Communications, dance, media studies,
    radio and television.

Bowling Green State University*
110 McFall Center
Bowling Green, OH 43403
Phone: (419) 372-2478
Fax: (419) 372-6955
E-mail: admissions@bgnet.bgsu.edu
http://www.bgsu.edu

Broadcast journalism, communications, dance, film/video arts.

Capital University
2199 East Main Street
Columbus, OH 43209
Phone: (614) 236-6101
Fax: (614) 236-6926
E-mail: admissions@capital.edu
http://www.capital.edu
Broadcast journalism, communications.

Cedarville University
251 North Main Street
Cedarville, OH 45314
Phone: (937) 766-7700
Fax: (937) 766-7575
E-mail: admissions@cedarville.edu
http://www.cedarville.edu
Broadcast journalism, communications, communications technology.

Central State University
P.O. Box 1004
Wilberforce, OH 45384
Phone: (937) 376-6384
Fax: (937) 376-6648
E-mail: admissions@csu.ces.edu
http://www.centralstate.edu
Broadcast journalism.

Cleveland State University
East 24th and Euclid Avenue
Cleveland, OH 44114
Phone: (216) 687-2100
Fax: (216) 687-9210
E-mail: admissions@csuohio.edu
http://www.csuohio.edu
Communications.

College of Mount Saint Joseph
5701 Delhi Road
Cincinnati, OH 45233
Phone: (513) 244-4531
Fax: (513) 244-4629
E-mail: peggy_minnich@mail.msj.edu
http://www.msj.edu
Communications.

The College of Wooster
847 College Avenue
Wooster, OH 44691
Phone: (330) 263-2322
Fax: (330) 263-2621
E-mail: admissions@wooster.edu
http://www.wooster.edu
Communications, dance.

Cuyahoga Community College**
Metro Campus
2900 Community College Avenue
Cleveland, OH 44115
Phone: (800) 954-8742
Fax: (216) 696-2567
E-mail: At Web site
http://www.tri-c.edu
Communications technology.

Denison University
P.O. Box H
Granville, OH 43023
Phone: (740) 587-6276
Fax: (740) 587-6306
E-mail: admissions@denison.edu
http://www.denison.edu
Communications, dance, film/video arts.

Franciscan University of Steubenville
1235 University Boulevard
Steubenville, OH 43952
Phone: (740) 283-6226
Fax: (740) 284-5456
E-mail: admissions@franciscan.edu
http://www.franciscan.edu
Communications.

Heidelberg College
310 East Market Street
Tiffin, OH 44883
Phone: (419) 448-2330
Fax: (419) 448-2334
E-mail: adminfo@heidelberg.edu
http://www.heidelberg.edu
Communications.

John Carroll University
20700 North Park Boulevard
University Heights, OH 44118
Phone: (216) 397-4294
Fax: (216) 397-3098
E-mail: admission@jcu.edu
http://www.jcu.edu
Communications.

Kent State University*
161 Michael Schwartz
Kent, OH 44242
Phone: (330) 672-2444
Fax: (330) 672-2499
E-mail: kentadm@admissions.kent.edu
http://www.kent.edu
Broadcast journalism, communications, dance, film/video arts.

Lakeland Community College**
7700 Clocktower Drive
Kirtland, OH 44094

Phone: (800) 589-8520
E-mail: At Web site
http://www.lakeland.cc.oh.us
Media studies.

Malone College
515 25th Street NW
Canton, OH 44709
Phone: (330) 471-8145
Fax: (330) 471-8149
E-mail: admissions@malone.edu
http://www.malone.edu
Communications, radio and television,

Marietta College
215 Fifth Street
Marietta, OH 45750
Phone: (740) 376-4643
Fax: (740) 376-8888
E-mail: admit@marietta.edu
http://www.marietta.edu
Broadcast journalism, communications, radio and television.

Miami University
301 South Campus Avenue
Oxford, OH 45056
Phone: (513) 529-2531
Fax: (513) 529-1550
E-mail: admission@muohio.edu
http://www.muohio.edu
Communications.

Mount Union College
1972 Clark Avenue
Alliance, OH 44601
Phone: (800) 334-6682
Fax: (330) 823-3457
E-mail: admissn@muc.edu
http://www.muc.edu
Communications, media studies.

Mount Vernon Nazarene University
800 Martinsburg Road
Mount Vernon, OH 43050
Phone: (740) 392-6868
Fax: (740) 393-0511
E-mail: admissions@mvnu.edu
http://www.mvnu.edu
Broadcast journalism, communications.

Oberlin College
101 North Professor Street
Oberlin College
Oberlin, OH 44074
Phone: (440) 775-8411
Fax: (440) 775-6905
E-mail: college.admissions@oberlin.edu
http://www.oberlin.edu
Film/video arts.

Ohio Dominican University
1216 Sunbury Road
Columbus, OH 42319
Phone: (614) 251-4500
Fax: (614) 251-0156
E-mail: admissions@ohiodominican.edu
http://www.ohiodominican.edu
Communications.

Ohio Northern University
525 South Main Street
Ada, OH 45810
Phone: (419) 772-2260
Fax: (419) 772-2313
E-mail: admissions-ug@onu.edu
http://www.onu.edu
Broadcast journalism, communications.

Ohio State University—Columbus
Third Floor Lincoln Tower
1800 Cannon Drive
Columbus, OH 43210
Phone: (614) 292-3980
Fax: (614) 292-4818
E-mail: askabuckeye@osu.edu
http://www.osu.edu
Communications.

Ohio University—Athens*
120 Chubb Hall
Athens, OH 45701
Phone: (740) 593-4100
Fax: (740) 593-0560
E-mail: admissions.freshmen@ohiou.edu
http://www.ohiou.edu
Cinematography, film/video production,
    communications, film/video arts,
    media studies, radio/television
    broadcasting.

Ohio University—Southern
Office of Enrollment Services
1804 Liberty Avenue
Ironton, OH 45638
Phone: (740) 533-4600
Fax: (740) 533-4632
E-mail: askousc.@mail_southern.ohiou.
    edu
http://www.southern.ohiou.edu
Communications.

Ohio Wesleyan University
Admissions Office
61 South Sandusky Street
Delaware, OH 43015
Phone: (740) 368-3020
Fax: (740) 368-3314
E-mail: owuadmit@owu.edu
http://www.owu.edu
Broadcast journalism, dance.

Otterbein College
Office of Admission
One Otterbein College
Westerville, OH 43081
Phone: (614) 823-1500
Fax: (614) 823-1200
E-mail: uotterb@otterbein.edu
http://www.otterbein.edu
Broadcast journalism, communications.

Owens Community College—
    Toledo**
P.O. Box 10000
Toledo, OH 43699-1947
Phone: (800) GO-OWENS
E-mail: At Web site
http://www.owens.edu
Dance.

Shawnee State University
940 Second Street
Portsmouth, OH 45662
Phone: (740) 351-4SSU
Fax: (740) 351-3111
E-mail: to_ssu@shawnee.edu
http://www.shawnee.edu
Communications.

Sinclair Community College**
Office of Admissions, Building 10,
    Room 10112
444 West Third Street
Dayton, OH 45402
Phone: (800) 315-3000
Fax: (937) 512-2393
E-mail: At Web site
http://www.sinclair.edu
Photographic/film/video technology.

University of Akron
381 Butchel Common
Akron, OH 44325
Phone: (330) 972-7100
Fax: (330) 972-7022
E-mail: admissions@uakron.edu
http://www.uakron.edu
Acting, communications, dance, media
    studies.

University of Cincinnati
P.O. Box 210091
Cincinnati, OH 45221
Phone: (513) 556-1100
Fax: (513) 556-1105
E-mail: admissions@uc.edu
http://www.uc.edu
Communications, media studies.

University of Dayton
300 College Park
Dayton, OH 45469
Phone: (937) 229-4411
Fax: (937) 229-4729
E-mail: admission@udayton.edu
http://www.udayton.edu
Communications, media studies.

University of Findlay
1000 North Main Street
Findlay, OH 45840
Phone: (419) 424-4732
Fax: (419) 434-4898
E-mail: admissions@findlay.edu
http://www.findlay.edu
Broadcast journalism, cinematography,
    film/video production, communications,
    communications technology.

University of Rio Grande
218 North College Avenue, Admissions
Rio Grande, OH 45774
Phone: (740) 245-7206
Fax: (740) 245-7260
http://www.rio.edu
Communications.

University of Toledo
2801 West Bancroft Street
Toledo, OH 43606
Phone: (419) 530-8700
Fax: (419) 530-5713
E-mail: enroll@utnet.utoledo.edu
http://www.utoledo.edu
Communications, film/video arts.

Urbana University
579 College Way
Urbana, OH 4378
Phone: (937) 484-1356
Fax: (937) 484-1389
E-mail: admiss@urbana.edu
http://www.urbana.edu
Communications.

Walsh University
2020 East Maple Street
North Canton, OH 44720
Phone: (800) 362-9846
Fax: (330) 490-7165
E-mail: admissions@walsh.edu
http://www.walsh.edu
Communications.

Washington State Community
    College**
710 Colegate Drive
Marietta, OH 45750

Phone: (740) 374-8716
Fax: (740) 376-0257
E-mail: admissions@wscc.edu
http://www.wscc.edu
Broadcast journalism.

Wilmington College
Pyle Center, Box 1325
251 Ludovic Street
Wilmington, OH 45117
Phone: (937) 382-6661
Fax: (937) 382-7077
E-mail: admission@wilmington.edu
http://www.wilmington.edu
Communications.

Wittenberg University
P.O. Box 720
Springfield, OH 45501
Phone: (800) 677-7558
Fax: (937) 327-6379
E-mail: admission@wittenberg.edu
http://www.wittenberg.edu
Communications.

Wright State University
3640 Colonel Glenn Highway
Dayton, OH 54435
Phone: (937) 775-5700
Fax: (937) 775-5795
E-mail: admissions@wright.edu
http://www.wright.edu
Film/video arts, media studies.

Xavier University
3800 Victory Parkway
Cincinnati, OH 45207
Phone: (513) 745-3301
Fax: (513) 745-4319
E-mail: xuadmit@xavier.edu
http://www.xavier.edu
Radio and television.

Youngstown State University
One University Plaza
Youngstown, OH 44555
Phone: (330) 941-2000
Fax: (330) 941-3674
E-mail: enroll@ysu.edu
http://www.ysu.edu
Radio and television.

OKLAHOMA

Cameron University
2800 West Gore Boulevard
Lawton, OK 73505
Phone: (580) 581-2230
Fax: (580) 581-5514

E-mail: admiss@cua.cameron.edu
http://www.cameron.edu
Broadcast journalism, communications.

Connors State College**
Route 1, P.O. Box 1000
Warner, OK 74469
Phone: (918) 463-2931, ext. 6241
Fax: NA
E-mail: dary@connorsstate.edu
http://www.connors.cc.ok.us
Communications.

East Central University
Office of Admissions & Records
1100 E 14 PMB J8
Ada, OK 74820
Phone: (580) 332-8000
Fax: (580) 436-5495
E-mail: pdenny@mailclerk.ecok.edu
http://www.ecok.edu
Broadcast journalism, communications,
    media studies.

Langston University
P.O. Box 728
Langston, OK 73050
Phone: (405) 466-2231
Fax: (405) 466-3381
E-mail: admissions@speedy.lunet.edu
http://www.lunet.edu
Broadcast journalism, communications,
    communications technology.

**Northeastern Oklahoma A&M
    College****
200 I Street NE
Miami, OK 74354
Phone: (888) 464-6636
Fax: (918) 540-0946
E-mail: neoadmission@neoam.edu
http://www.neoam.cc.ok.us
Communications, media studies, radio
    and television.

Northeastern State University
Office of Admissions and Records
600 North Grand Avenue
Tahlequah, OK 74464
Phone: (918) 456-5511
Fax: (918) 458-2342
E-mail: nsuadmis@cherkoee.nsuok.edu
http://www.nsuok.edu
Communications.

**Northwestern Oklahoma State
    University**
709 Oklahoma Boulevard
Alva, OK 73717

Phone: (580) 327-8545
Fax: (580) 327-1881
E-mail: krschroc@ranger1.nwalva.edu
http://www.nwalva.edu
Broadcast journalism.

Oklahoma Baptist University
500 West University
Shawnee, OK 74804
Phone: (405) 275-2850
http://www.okbu.edu
Broadcast journalism, communications.

Oklahoma Christian University
P.O. Box 11000
Oklahoma City, OK 73136
Phone: (405) 425-5050
Fax: (405) 425-5269
E-mail: ifo@oc.edu
http://www.oc.edu
Broadcast journalism, communications.

Oklahoma City Community College**
7777 South May Avenue
Oklahoma City, OK 73159
Phone: (405) 682-7515
Fax: NA
E-mail: bmorgan@okccc.edu
http://www.okccc.edu
Broadcast journalism.

Oklahoma City University
2501 North Blackwelder Avenue
Oklahoma City, OK 73106
Phone: (405) 521-5050
Fax: (405) 521-5264
E-mail: uadmission@okcu.edu
http://www.okcu.edu
Broadcast journalism, cinematography,
    film/video production,
    communications, dance, media
    studies, radio and television.

Oklahoma State University*
323 Student Union
Stillwater, OK 74078
Phone: (405) 744-6858
Fax: (405) 744-5285
E-mail: admit@okstate.edu
http://www.okstate.edu
Broadcast journalism, communications,
    media studies.

Oral Roberts University
7777 South Lewis Avenue
Tulsa, OK 74171
Phone: (918) 495-0518
Fax: (918) 495-6222
E-mail: admissions@oru.edu

http://www.oru.edu
Communications.

Rogers State University
1701 West Will Rogers Boulevard
Claremore, OK 74017
Phone: (800) 256-7511
Fax: (918) 343-7550
E-mail: At Web site
http://www.rsuonline.edu
Broadcast journalism, communications
    technology.

Rose State College**
6420 SE 15th Street
Midwest City, OK 73110
Phone: (405) 733-7673
Fax: (405) 736-0309
E-mail: At Web site
http://www.rose.edu
Telecommunications technology.

**Southeastern Oklahoma State
    University**
1405 North 4th Avenue, PMB 4225
Durant, OK 74701
Phone: (580) 745-2060
Fax: (580) 745-7502
E-mail: admissions@sosu.edu
http://www.sosu.edu
Broadcast journalism, communications.

**Southwestern Oklahoma State
    University**
100 Campus Drive
Weatherford, OK 73096
Phone: (580) 772-6611
Fax: (580) 774-3795
E-mail: admissions@swosu.edu
http://www.swosu.edu
Communications.

Tulsa Community College**
909 South Boston Avenue
Tulsa, OK 74119
Phone: (918) 595-7811
E-mail: At Web site
http://www.tulsacc.edu
Communications technology.

University of Central Oklahoma
100 North University Drive
Edmond, OK 73034
Phone: (405) 974-2338
Fax: (405) 341-4964
E-mail: admituco@ucok.edu
http://www.ucok.edu
Broadcast journalism, communications.

University of Oklahoma*
1000 Asp Avenue
Norman, OK 73019
Phone: (405) 325-2252
Fax: (405) 325-7124
E-mail: admrec@ou.edu
http://www.ou.edu
Broadcast journalism, cinematography,
    film/video production, communications,
    dance, film/video arts.

**University or Science and Arts of
    Oklahoma**
1727 West Alabama Avenue
Chickasha, OK 73018
Phone: (405) 574-1204
Fax: (405) 574-1220
E-mail: jwevans@usao.edu
http://www.usao.edu
Communications.

University of Tulsa
500 South College Avenue
Tulsa, OK 741045
Phone: (918) 631-2307
Fax: (918) 631-5003
E-mail: admission@utulsa.edu
http://www.utulsa.edu
Communications, film/video arts.

OREGON

Central Oregon Community College**
2600 NW College Way
Bend, OR 9770
Phone: (541) 383-7500
Fax: (541) 383-7506
E-mail: welcome@cocc.edu
http://www.cocc.edu
Communications.

George Fox University
414 North Meridian Street
Newberg, OR 97132
Phone: (503) 554-2240
Fax: (503) 554-3110
E-mail: admissions@georgefox.edu
http://www.georgefox.edu
Communications, radio and television.

Lewis & Clark College
0615 SW Palatine Hill Road
Portland, OR 97219
Phone: (503) 768-7040
Fax: (503) 768-7055
E-mail: admissions@lclark.edu
http://www.lclark.edu
Communications.

Linfield College
900 South East Baker Street
McMinnville, OR 97128
Phone: (503) 883-2213
Fax: (503) 883-2472
E-mail: admission@linfield.edu
http://www.linfield.edu
Media studies.

Mount Hood Community College**
26000 SE Stark Street
Gresham, OR 97030
Phone: (503) 491-7265
E-mail: At Web site
http://www.mhcc.edu
Broadcast journalism

Oregon Institute of Technology
3201 Campus Drive
Klamath Falls, OR 97601
Phone: (541) 885-1150
Fax: (541) 885-1115
E-mail: oit@oit.edu
http://www.oit.edu
Communications.

Pacific University
2043 College Way
Forest Grove, OR 9116
Phone: (503) 352-2218
Fax: (503) 352-2975
E-mail: admissions@pacificu.edu
http://www.pacificu.edu
Communications.

Portland Community College**
Sylvania Campus
12000 SW 49th Avenue
Portland, OR 97219
Phone: (866) 922-1010
E-mail: At Web site
http://www.pcc.edu
Cinematography, film/video production,
    communications, communications
    technology.

Southern Oregon University
Office of Admissions
1250 Siskiyou Boulevard
Ashland, OR 97520
Phone: (541) 552-6411
Fax: (541) 552-6614
E-mail: admissions@sou.edu
http://www.sou.edu
Communications.

University of Oregon*
1217 University of Oregon
Eugene, OR 97403
Phone: (541) 346-3201
Fax: (541) 346-5815
E-mail: uoadmit@oregon.uoregon.edu
http://www.uoregon.edu
Broadcast journalism, dance.

University of Portland
5000 North Willamette Boulevard
Portland, OR 97203
Phone: (503) 943-7147
Fax: (503) 283-7315
E-mail: admission@up.edu
http://www.up.edu
Communications.

PENNSYLVANIA

Albright College
P.O. Box 15234
13th and Bern Streets
Reading, PA 19612
Phone: (610) 921-7512
Fax: (610) 921-7294
E-mail: admissions@albright.edu
http://www.albright.edu
Communications.

Allegheny College
Office of Admissions
Meadville, PA 16335
Phone: (814) 332-4351
Fax: (814) 337-0431
E-mail: admissions@allegheny.edu
http://www.allegheny.edu
Communications, media studies.

Alvernia College
400 St. Bernardine Street
Reading, PA 19607
Phone: (610) 798-8220
Fax: (610) 796-8336
E-mail: admissions@alvernia.edu
http://www.alvernia.edu
Communications.

Arcadia University
450 South Easton Road
Glenside, PA 19038
Phone: (215) 572-2910
Fax: (215) 572-4049
E-mail: admiss@arcadia.edu
http://www.arcadia.edu
Acting, communications.

The Art Institute of Philadelphia
1622 Chestnut Street

Philadelphia, PA 19103
Phone: (800) 275-2474
Fax: (215) 405-6399
E-mail: At Web site
http://www.aiph.artinstitutes.edu
Cinematography, film/video production,

The Art Institute of Pittsburgh
420 Boulevard of the Allies
Pittsburgh, PA 15219
Phone: (412) 263-6600
Fax: (412) 263-6667
E-mail: aip_admissions@ail.edu
http://www.aip.ail.edu
Cinematography, film/video production.

Bloomsburg University of Pennsylvania
104 Student Services Center
400 East Second Street
Bloomsburg, PA 17815
Phone: (570) 389-4316
Fax: (570) 389-4741
E-mail: buadmiss@bloomu.edu
http://www.bloomu.edu
Communications, media studies.

Bucks County Community College**
275 Swamp Road
Newtown, PA 18940
Phone: (215) 968-8119, ext. 8119
Fax: (215) 968-8110
E-mail: admissions@bucks.edu
http://www.bucks.edu
Broadcast journalism, cinematography,
    film/video production,
    communications.

California University of Pennsylvania
250 University Avenue
California, PA 15419
Phone: (724) 938-4404
Fax: (724) 938-4564
E-mail: inquiry@cup.edu
http://www.cup.edu
Broadcast journalism, communications
    technology.

Cabrini College
610 King of Prussia Road
Radnor, PA 19087
Phone: (610) 902-8552
Fax: (610) 902-8508
E-mail: admit@cabrini.edu
http://www.cabrini.edu
Communications.

Carlow College
3333 Fifth Avenue
Pittsburgh, PA 15213

Phone: (412) 578-6059
Fax: (412) 578-6668
E-mail: admissions@carlow.edu
http://www.carlow.edu
Communications.

Cedar Crest College
100 College Drive
Allentown, PA 18104
Phone: (610) 740-3780
Fax: (610) 606-4647
E-mail: ccadmis@cedarcrest.edu
http://www.cedarcrest.edu
Communications, film/video arts.

Chatham College
Woodland Road
Pittsburgh, PA 15232
Phone: (412) 365-1290
Fax: (412) 365-1609
E-mail: admissions@chatham.edu
http://www.chatham.edu
Broadcast journalism, communications.

Cheyney University of Pennsylvania
Cheyney and Creek Roads
Cheyney, PA 19319
Phone: (610) 399-2275
Fax: (610) 399-2099
E-mail: jbrowne@cheyney.edu
http://www.cheyney.edu
Communications, communications
    technology.

Clarion University of Pennsylvania
Admissions Office
840 Wood Street
Clarion, PA 16214
Phone: (814) 393-2306
Fax: (814) 393-2030
E-mail: admissions@clarion.edu
http://www.clarion.edu
Communications.

College Misericordia
301 Lake Street
Dallas, PA 18612
Phone: (570) 674-6264
Fax: (570) 675-2441
E-mail: admiss@misericordia.edu
http://www.misericordia.edu
Communications.

Delaware Community College**
Main Campus
Room 3545, Founders Hall
901 South Media Line Road
Media, PA 19063
Phone: (610) 359-5333

Fax: (610) 359-5343
E-mail: admiss@dccc.edu
http://www.dccc.edu
Communications, communications
 technology.

DeSales University
2755 Station Avenue
Center Valley, PA 18034
Phone: (610) 282-4443
Fax: (610) 282-0131
E-mail: admiss@desales.edu
http://www.desales.edu
Communications, dance, film/video arts.

Drexel University
3141 Chestnut Street
Philadelphia, PA 19104
Phone: (215) 895-2400
Fax: (215) 895-5939
E-mail: enroll@drexel.edu
http://www.drexel.edu
Cinematography, film/video production,
 communications,
 playwriting/screenwriting.

Duquesne University
600 Forbes Avenue
Pittsburgh, PA 15282
Phone: (412) 396-5000
Fax: (412) 396-5644
E-mail: admissions@duq.edu
http://www.duq.edu
Communications, media studies.

**East Stroudsburg University of
 Pennsylvania**
200 Prospect Street
East Stroudsburg, PA 18301
Phone: (570) 422-3542
Fax: (570) 422-3933
E-mail: undergrads@po-box.esu.edu
http://www.esu.edu
Communications, communications
 technology.

Eastern University
1300 Eagle Road
St. Davids, PA 19087
Phone: (610) 341-5967
Fax: (610) 341-1723
E-mail: ugadm@eastern.edu
http://www.eastern.edu
Communications.

Edinboro University of Pennsylvania
Biggers House
Edinboro, PA 16444
Phone: (814) 732-2761

Fax: (814) 732-2420
E-mail: eup_admissions@edinboro.edu
http://www.edinboro.edu
Broadcast journalism, communications.

Elizabethtown College
Leffler House
One Alpha Drive
Elizabethtown, PA 17022
Phone: (717) 361-1400
Fax: (717) 361-1365
E-mail: admissions@etown.edu
http://www.etown.edu
Communications.

Gannon University
University Square
Erie, PA 16541
Phone: (814) 871-7240
Fax: (814) 871-5803
E-mail: admissions@gannon.edu
http://www.gannon.edu
Communications, communications
 technology.

Geneva College
3200 College Avenue
Beaver Falls, PA 15010
Phone: (724) 847-6500
Fax: (724) 847-6776
E-mail: admissions@geneva.edu
http://www.geneva.edu
Communications.

Gettysburg College
300 North Washington Street
Gettysburg, PA 17325
Phone: (717) 337-6100
Fax: (717) 337-6145
E-mail: admiss@gettysburg.edu
http://www.gettysburg.edu
Communications.

Grove City College
100 Campus Drive
Grove City, PA 16127
Phone: (724) 458-2100
Fax: (724) 458-3395
E-mail: admissions@gcc.edu
http://www.gcc.edu
Communications.

Holy Family University
Grant and Frankford Avenue
Philadelphia, PA 19114
Phone: (215) 637-3050
Fax: (215) 281-1022
E-mail: undergrad@hfu.edu
http://www.holyfamily.edu
Communications.

Immaculata University
1145 King Road
P.O. Box 642
Immaculata, PA 19345
Phone: (610) 647-4400
Fax: (610) 647-0836
E-mail: admiss@immaculata.edu
http://www.immaculata.edu
Communications, communications
 technology.

Indiana University of Pennsylvania
216 Pratt Hall
Indiana, PA 15075
Phone: (724) 357-2230
Fax: (724) 357-6281
E-mail: admissions-inquiry@iup.edu
http://www.iup.edu
Communications, media studies.

Juniata College
1700 Moore Street
Huntington, PA 16652
Phone: (814) 641-3420
Fax: (814) 641-3100
E-mail: info@juniata.edu
http://www.juniata.edu
Communications.

Keystone College**
One College Green
La Plume, PA 18440
Phone: (877)-4COLLEGE
Fax: NA
E-mail: admissions@keystone.edu
http://www.keystone.edu
Radio and television.

Kutztown University of Pennsylvania
Admission Office
P.O. Box 730
Kutztown, PA 19530
Phone: (610) 683-4060
Fax: (610) 683-1375
E-mail: admission@kutztown.edu
http://www.kutztown.edu
Communications.

La Roche College
9000 Babcock Boulevard
Pittsburgh, PA 15237
Phone: (412) 536-1271
Fax: (412) 536-1048
E-mail: admissions@laroche.edu
http://www.laroche.edu
Communications, dance.

La Salle University
1900 West Olney Avenue
Philadelphia, PA 19141

Phone: (215) 951-1500
Fax: (215) 951-1656
E-mail: admiss@lasalle.edu
http://www.lasalle.edu
Broadcast journalism, cinematography, film/video production, communications, film/video arts, media studies, radio and television, radio/television broadcasting.

Lackawana College**
501 Vine Street
Scranton, PA 18509
Phone: (877) 346-3552
Fax: (570) 961-7853
E-mail: adminfo@lackawanna.edu
http://www.lackawanna.edu
Media studies.

Lebanon Valley College
101 North College Avenue
Annville, PA 17003
Phone: (717) 867-6181
Fax: (717) 867-6026
E-mail: admissioin@lvc.edu
http://www.lvc.edu
Communications, communications technology, radio/television broadcasting.

Lehigh Carbon Community College**
4525 Education Park Drive
Schnecksville, PA 1807
Phone: (610) 799-1575
Fax: (610) 799-1527
E-mail: tellme@lccc.edu
http://www.lccc.edu
Communications.

Lehigh University
27 Memorial Drive West
Bethlehem, PA 18015
Phone: (610) 758-3000
Fax: (610) 758-4361
E-mail: admissions@lehigh.edu
http://www.lehigh.edu
Communications.

Lincoln University
1570 Baltimore Pike
Lincoln Hall, Third Floor
Lincoln University, PA 19352
Phone: (610) 932-8300
Fax: (610) 932-1209
E-mail: admiss@lu.lincoln.edu
http://www.lincoln.edu
Communications.

Lycoming College
700 College Place

Williamsport, PA 17701
Phone: (570) 321-4026
Fax: (570) 321-4317
E-mail: admissions@lycoming.edu
http://www.lycoming.edu
Communications.

Marywood University
2300 Adams Avenue
Scranton, PA 18509
Phone: (570) 348-6234
Fax: (570) 961-4763
E-mail: ugadm@ac.marywood.edu
http://www.marywood.edu
Broadcast journalism, media studies, radio/television broadcasting.

Mercyhurst College
Admissions
501 East 38th Street
Erie, PA 16546
Phone: (800) 825-1926
Fax: (814) 824-2071
E-mail: admug@mercyhurst.edu
http://www.mercyhurst.edu
Broadcast journalism, communications, dance.

Messiah College
One College Avenue
P.O. Box 3005
Grantham, PA 17027
Phone: (717) 691-6000
Fax: (717) 796-5374
E-mail: admiss@messiah.edu
http://www.messiah.edu
Communications, radio and television.

Millersville University of Pennsylvania
P.O. Box 102
Millersville, PA 19551
Phone: (717) 872-3371
Fax: (717) 871-2147
E-mail: admissions@millersville.edu
http://www.millersville.edu
Communications.

Muhlenberg College
2400 West Chew Street
Allentown, PA 18104
Phone: (484) 664-3200
Fax: (484) 664-3234
E-mail: admission@muhlenberg.edu
http://www.muhlenberg.edu
Communications, dance.

Neumann College
One Neumann Drive
Aston, PA 19014

Phone: (610) 558-5616
Fax: (610) 558-5652
E-mail: neumann@neumann.edu
http://www.neumann.edu
Communications.

Northampton County Area Community College**
3835 Green Pond Road
Bethlehem, PA 18020
Phone: (610) 861-5506
Fax: (610) 861-5551
E-mail: adminfo@northampton.edu.
http://www.northampton.edu
Acting, radio/television broadcasting.

Pennsylvania College of Technology**
One College Avenue
Williamsport, PA 17701
Phone: (800) 367-9222
Fax: (570) 321-5551
E-mail: admissions@pct.edu
http://www.pct.edu
Broadcast journalism, media studies.

Pennsylvania State University— Abington
106 Sutherland
Abington, PA 19001
Phone: (215) 881-7600
Fax: (215) 881-7317
E-mail: abingtonadmissions@psu.edu
http://www.abington.psu.edu
Acting, cinematography, film/video production, media studies, telecommunications technology.

Pennsylvania State University— Altoona
E108 Raymond Smith Building
Altoona, PA 16601
Phone: (814) 949-5466
Fax: (814) 949-5564
E-mail: aaadmit@psu.edu
http://www.aa.psu.edu
Acting, cinematography, film/video production, media studies, telecommunications technology.

Pennsylvania State University—Beaver
100 University Drive
Monaca, PA 15061
Phone: (724) 773-3800
Fax: (724) 773-3658
E-mail: br-admissions@psu.edu
http://www.br.psu-edu
Acting, cinematography, film/video production, media studies, telecommunications technology.

Pennsylvania State University—Berks
14 Perkins Student Center
Reading, PA 19610
Phone: (610) 396-6060
Fax: (610) 396-6077
E-mail: admissions@psu.edu
http://www.bk.psu.edu
Acting, cinematography, film/video
  production, media studies,
  telecommunications technology.

**Pennsylvania State University—
  Delaware County**
25 Yearsley Mill Road
Media, PA 19083
Phone: (610) 892-1200
Fax: (610) 892-1357
E-mail: admissions-delco@psu.edu
http://www.de.psu.edu
Acting, media studies,
  telecommunications technology.

Pennsylvania State University—Dubois
108 Hiller
Dubois, PA 15801
Phone: (814) 375-4720
Fax: (814) 375-4784
E-mail: ds-Admissions@psu.edu
http://www.ds.psu.edu
Acting, cinematography, film/video
  production, media studies,
  telecommunications technology.

**Pennsylvania State University—Erie,
  The Behrend College**
5091 Station Road
Erie, PA 16563
Phone: (814) 898-6100
Fax: (814) 898-6044
E-mail: behrend.admissions@psu.edu
http://www.pserie.psu.edu
Communications, media studies,
  telecommunications technology.

Pennsylvania State University—Fayette
P.O. Box 519
Route 119 North
108 Williams Building
Uniontown, PA 15041
Phone: (724) 430-4130
Fax: (724) 430-4175
E-mail: feadm@psu.edu
http://www.fe.psu.edu
Acting, cinematography, film/video
  production, media studies,
  telecommunications technology.

**Pennsylvania State University—
  Harrisburg**
Swatapa Build

777 West Harrisburg Pike
Middletown, PA 17057
Phone: (717) 948-6250
Fax: (717) 948-6325
E-mail: hbgadmit@psu.edu
http://www.hbg.psu.edu
Communications, media studies,
  telecommunications technology.

**Pennsylvania State University—
  Hazelton**
110 Administrative Building
76 University Drive
Hazelton, PA 18202
Phone: (570) 450-3142
Fax: (570) 450-3182
E-mail: admissions-hn@psu.edu
http://www.hn.psu.edu
Acting, cinematography, film/video
  production, telecommunications
  technology.

**Pennsylvania State University—Lehigh
  Valley**
8380 Mohr Lane
Academic Building
Fogelsville, PA 19051
Phone: (610) 285-5035
Fax: (610) 285-5220
E-mail: admission-lv@psu.edu
http://www.an.psu.edu
Acting, cinematography, film/video
  production, media studies,
  telecommunications technology.

**Pennsylvania State University—
  McKeesport**
100 Frable Building
4000 University Drive
McKeesport, PA 15132
Phone: (412) 675-9010
Fax: (412) 675-9056
E-mail: psumk@psu.edu
http://www.mk.psu.edu
Acting, cinematography, film/video
  production, telecommunications
  technology.

**Pennsylvania State University—Mont
  Alto**
1 Campus Drive
Mont Alto, Pennsylvania 17237
Phone: (717) 749-6130
Fax: (717) 749-6132
E-mail: psuma@psu.edu
http://www.ma.psu.edu
Acting, cinematography, film/video
  production, media studies,
  telecommunications technology.

**Pennsylvania State University—New
  Kensington**
3550 7th Street Road
Upper Barrell, PA 15068
Phone: (724) 334-5466
Fax: (724) 334-6111
E-mail: nkadmissions@psu.edu
http://www.nk.psu.edu
Acting, cinematography, film/video
  production, media studies,
  telecommunications technology.

**Pennsylvania State University—
  Schuylkill**
200 University Drive
A102 Administrative Building
Schuylkill Haven, PA 17072
Phone: (570) 385-6252
Fax: (570) 385-6272
E-mail: sl-admissions@psu.edu
http://www.sl.psu.edu
Acting, cinematography, film/video
  production, film/video arts, media
  studies, telecommunications
  technology.

**Pennsylvania State University-
  University Park***
201 Shields Building
P.O. Box 3000
University Park, PA 16802
Phone: (814) 865-5471
Fax: (814) 863-7590
E-mail: admissions@psu.edu
http://www.psu.edu
Communications, film/video arts, media
  studies, media studies,
  telecommunications technology.

**Pennsylvania State University—
  Wilkes-Barre**
P.O. Box PSU
Lehman, PA 18627
Phone: (570) 675-9238
Fax: (570) 675-9113
E-mail: wbadmissions@psu.edu
http://www.psu.edu.
Cinematography, film/video production,
  media studies, telecommunications
  technology.

**Pennsylvania State University—
  Worthington Scranton**
120 Ridge View Drive
Dunmore, PA 18512
Phone: (570) 963-2500
Fax: (570) 963-2524
E-mail: wsadmissions@psu.edu
http://www.sn.psu.edu

Cinematography, film/video production, media studies, telecommunications technology.

Pennsylvania State University—York
1031 Edgecomb Avenue
York, PA 17403
Phone: (717) 771-4040
Fax: (717) 771-4005
E-mail: ykadmisson@psu.edu
http://www.yk.psu.edu
Acting, cinematography, film/video production, telecommunications technology.

Point Park College
201 Wood Street
Pittsburgh, PA 15222
Phone: (412) 392-3430
Fax: (412) 391-1980
E-mail: enroll@ppc.edu
http://www.ppc.edu
Broadcast journalism, cinematography, film/video production, communications, dance, film/video arts.

Robert Morris University
6001 University Boulevard
Moon Township, PA 15108
Phone: (412) 262-8206
Fax: (412) 299-2425
E-mail: enrollmentoffice@rmu.edu
http://www.rmu.edu
Communications.

Saint Francis University
P.O. Box 600
Loretto, PA 15940
Phone: (814) 472-3000
Fax: (814) 472-3335
E-mail: admissions@francis.edu
http://www.francis.edu
Communications.

Saint Joseph's University
5600 City Avenue
Philadelphia, PA 19131
Phone: (610) 660-1300
Fax: (610) 660-1314
E-mail: admit@sju.edu
http://www.sju.edu
Communications.

Saint Vincent College
3000 Fraser Purchase Road
Latrobe, PA 10650
Phone: (724) 537-4540
Fax: (724) 532-5069
E-mail: admission@stvincent.edu
http://www.stvincent.edu

Communications, communications technology.

Seton Hill University
1 Seton Hill Drive
Greensburg, PA 15061
Phone: (724) 838-4255
Fax: (724) 830-1294
E-mail: admit@setonhill.edu
http://www.setonhill.edu
Communications.

Shippensburg University of Pennsylvania
Old Main 105
1871 Old Main Drive
Shippensburg, PA 17257
Phone: (717) 477-1231
Fax: (717) 477-4016
E-mail: admiss@ship.edu
http://www.ship.edu
Communications, media studies.

Slippery Rock University of Pennsylvania
Office of Admissions
146 North Hall Welcome Center
Slippery Rock, PA 16057
Phone: (724) 738-2015
Fax: (724) 738-2913
E-mail: apply@sru.edu
http://www.sru.edu
Communications, dance.

Susquehanna University
514 University Avenue
Susquehanna, PA 17870
Phone: (570) 372-4260
Fax: (570) 372-2722
E-mail: suadmiss@susque.edu
http://www.susque.edu
Broadcast journalism, communications, media studies.

Temple University*
1801 North Broad Street
Philadelphia, PA 19122
Phone: (215) 204-7200
Fax: (215) 204-5694
E-mail: tuadm@mail.temple.edu
http://www.temple.edu
Acting, communications, dance, film/video arts, media studies, radio and television.

Thiel College
75 College Avenue
Greenville, PA 16125
Phone: (724) 589-2345
Fax: (724) 589-2013

E-mail: admission@thiel.edu
http://www.thiel.edu
Communications.

University of Pennsylvania
1 College Hall
Philadelphia, PA 19104
Phone: (215) 898-7507
Fax: (215) 898-9670
E-mail: info@admissions.ugao.upenn.edu
http://www.upenn.edu
Communications.

University of Pittsburgh—Greensburg
1150 Mount Pleasant Road
Greensburg, PA 15601
Phone: (724) 836-9880
Fax: (724) 836-7160
E-mail: upgadmit@pitt.edu
http://www.pitt.edu/~upg
Communications, media studies.

University of Pittsburgh—Johnstown
157 Blackington Hall
450 Schoolhouse Road
Johnstown, PA 15904
Phone: (814) 269-7050
Fax: (814) 269-7044
E-mail: upjadmit@pitt.edu
http://www.upj.pitt.edu
Communications, media studies.

University of Pittsburgh—Pittsburgh
4227 Fifth Avenue
First Floor Alumni Hall
Pittsburgh, PA 15260
Phone: (412) 624-7488
Fax: (412) 648-8815
E-mail: oafa@pitt.edu
http://www.pitt.edu
Communications, film/video arts, media studies.

University of Scranton
800 Linden Street
Scranton, PA 18501
Phone: (570) 941-7540
Fax: (570) 941-5928
E-mail: admissions@scranton.edu
http://www.scranton.edu
Communications.

Ursinus College
Ursinus College Admissions Office
Collegeville, PA 19426
Phone: (619) 409-3200
Fax: (619) 409-3662
E-mail: admissions@ursinus.edu
http://www.ursinus.edu
Communications.

Villanova University
800 Lancaster Avenue
Villanova, PA 19085
Phone: (610) 519-4000
Fax: (610) 519-6450
E-mail: gotovu@villanova.edu
http://www.villanova.edu
Communications.

Waynesburg College
51 West College Street
Waynesburg, PA 15370
Phone: (724) 852-3248
Fax: (724) 627-8124
E-mail: admissions@waynesburg.edu
http://www.waynesburg.edu
Broadcast journalism, communications.

West Chester University of
Pennsylvania
Messikomer Hall
100 West Rosedale Avenue
West Chester, PA 19363
Phone: (610) 436-3411
Fax: (610) 436-2907
E-mail: ugadmiss@wcupa.edu
http://www.wcupa.edu
Communications.

Westmoreland County Community
College*
400 Armbrust Road
Youngwood, PA 15697
Phone: (800) 262-2103
Fax: (724) 925-1150
E-mail: admissions2@wccc.pa.edu
http://www.wccc-pa.edu
Communications technology.

Widener University
One University Place
Chester, PA 19013
Phone: (610) 499-4126
Fax: (610) 499-4676
E-mail: admissions.office@widener.edu
http://www.widener.edu
Communications.

York College of Pennsylvania
Country Club Road
York, PA 17405
Phone: (717) 849-1600
Fax: (717) 849-1607
E-mail: admissions@ycp.edu
http://www.ycp.edu
Communications.

RHODE ISLAND

Bryant College
50 Douglas Pike

Smithfield, RI 02917
Phone: (401) 232-6100
Fax: (401) 232-6741
E-mail: admission@bryant.edu
http://www.bryant.edu
Communications.

Johnson & Wales University—
Providence
8 Abbott Park Place
Providence, RI 02903
Phone: (401) 598-2310
Fax: (401) 598-2948
E-mail: admissions@jwu.edu
http://www.jwu.edu
Communications.

New England Institute of Technology*
2500 Post Road
Warwick, RI 02886
Phone: (800) 736-7744
E-mail: At Web site
http://www.neit.edu
Broadcast journalism, cinematography,
    film/video production.

Rhode Island College
Office of Undergraduate Admissions
600 Mt. Pleasant Avenue
Providence, RI 02908
Phone: (401) 456-8234
Fax: (401) 456-8817
E-mail: admissions@ric.edu
http://www.ric.edu
Communications, film/video arts.

Rhode Island School of Design
2 College Street
Providence, RI 02903
Phone: (401) 454-6300
Fax: (401) 454-6309
E-mail: admissions@risd.edu
http://www.risd.edu
Cinematography, film/video production.

Roger Williams University
One Old Ferry Road
Bristol, RI 02809
Phone: (401) 254-3500
Fax: (401) 254-3557
E-mail: admit@rwu.edu
http://www.rwu.edu
Communications, dance.

Salve Regina University
100 Ochre Point Avenue
Newport, RI 02840
Phone: (401) 341-2908
Fax: (401) 848-2823
E-mail: sruadmis@salve.edu

http://www.salve.edu
Communications technology, media
    studies.

University of Rhode Island
Undergraduate Admissions Office
14 Upper College Road
Kingston, RI 02881
Phone: (401) 874-7100
Fax: (401) 874-5523
E-mail: uriadmit@etal.uri.edu
http://www.uri.edu
Communications.

SOUTH CAROLINA

Anderson College
316 Boulevard Anderson
Anderson, SC 29621
Phone: (864) 231-5607
Fax: (864) 231-2033
E-mail: admissions@ac.edu
http://www.ac.edu
Communications.

Claflin University
400 Magnolia Street
Orangeburg, SC 29115
Phone: (803) 535-5339
Fax: (803) 535-5387
E-mail: kboyd@clafl.claflin.edu
http://www.claflin.edu
Media studies.

Clemson University
106 Sikes Hall, Box 345124
Clemson, SC 219634
Phone: (864) 656-2987
Fax: (864) 656-2464
E-mail: cuadmissions@clemson.edu
http://www.clemson.edu
Communications.

Coker College
300 East College Avenue
Hartsville, SC 29550
Phone: (843) 383-8050
Fax: (843) 383-8056
E-mail: admissions@coker.edu
http://www.coker.edu
Acting, communications, dance.

College of Charleston
66 George Street
Charleston, SC 29424
Phone: (843) 953-5670
Fax: (843) 953-6322
E-mail: admissions@cofc.edu
http://www.cofc.edu
Communications.

Francis Marion University
Office of Admissions
P.O. Box 100547
Florence, SC 29501
Phone: (843) 661-1231
Fax: (843) 661-4635
E-mail: admissions@marion.edu
http://www.marion.edu
Media studies.

Furman University
3300 Poinsett Highway
Greenville, SC 29613
Phone: (864) 294-2034
Fax: (864) 294-3127
E-mail: admissions@furman.edu
http://www.furman.edu
Communications.

Morris College
100 West College Street
Sumter, SC 29150
Phone: (803) 934-3225
Fax: (803) 773-8241
E-mail: gscriven@morris.edu
http://www.morris.edu
Broadcast journalism.

North Greenville College
P.O. Box 1892
Tigerville, SC 29688
Phone: (864) 977-7001
Fax: (864) 977-7177
E-mail: admissions@ngc.edu
http://www.ngc.edu
Broadcast journalism.

Tri-County Technical College**
P.O. Box 587
7900 Highway 76E
Pendleton, SC 29670
Phone: (866) 269-5677
E-mail: At Web site
http://www.tctc.edu
Broadcast journalism.

Trident Community College**
7000 Rivers Avenue
North Charleston, SC 29406
Phone: (877) 349-7184
E-mail: At Web site
http://www.tridenttech.edu
Cinematography, film/video production,
    communications technology.

University of South Carolina—Aiken
471 University Parkway
Aiken, SC 29801
Phone: (803) 641-3366
Fax: (803) 641-3727

E-mail: admit@sc.edu
http://www.usca.edu
Communications, film/video arts.

University of South Carolina—
    Columbia*
Office of Undergraduate Admissions
Columbia, SC 29208
Phone: (803) 777-7000
Fax: (803) 777-0101
E-mail: admissions-ugrad@sc.edu
http://www.sc.edu
Film/video arts, media studies.

University of South Carolina—
    Spartanburg
800 University Way
Spartanburg, SC 29303
Phone: (864) 503-5246
Fax: (864) 503-5727
E-mail: dstewart@uscs.edu
http://www.uscs.edu
Communications, film/video arts.

Winthrop University*
233 Drinkins
Rock Hill, SC 29733
Phone: (803) 323-2395
Fax: (803) 323-2137
E-mail: admissions@winthrop.edu
http://www.winthrop.edu
Communications, dance.

York Technical College**
452 South Anderson Road
Rock Hill, SC 29730
Phone: (800) 922-8324
Fax: (803) 981-7237
E-mail: At Web site
http://www.yorktech.com
Radio/television broadcasting,
    telecommunications technology.

SOUTH DAKOTA

Augustana College
2001 South Summit Avenue
Sioux Falls, SD 57197
Phone: (605) 274-5516
Fax: (605) 274-5518
E-mail: info@augie.edu
http://www.augie.edu
Communications.

Black Hills State University
1200 University Avenue, USB 9502
Spearfish, SD 57799
Phone: (605) 642-6343
Fax: (605) 642-6022
E-mail: admissions@bhsu.edu

http://www.bhsu.edu
Communications, media studies.

South Dakota State University*
P.O. Box 2201
Brookings, SD 57007
Phone: (605) 688-4121
Fax: (605) 688-6891
E-mail: admissions@sdstate.edu
http://www.sdstate.edu
Communications.

University of South Dakota*
414 East Clark Street
Vermillion, SD 57069
Phone: (605) 677-5434
Fax: (605) 677-6753
E-mail: admiss@usd.edu
http://www.usd.edu
Communications, media studies.

TENNESSEE

Belmont University
1900 Belmont Boulevard
Nashville, TN 37212
Phone: (615) 460-6785
Fax: (615) 460-5434
E-mail: buadmission@mail_belmont.edu
http://www.belmont.edu
Broadcast journalism, communications,
    media studies.

Carson-Newman College
1646 Russell Avenue
Jefferson City, TN 37760
Phone: (865) 471-3223
Fax: (865) 471-3502
E-mail: sgray@cn.edu
http://www.cn.edu
Communications.

Columbia State Community College**
P.O. Box 1315
Columbia, TN 38402-1315
Phone: (931) 540-2540
Fax: (931) 540-2830
E-mail: At Web site
http://www.coscc.cc.tn.us
Dance.

East Tennessee State University*
ETSU P.O. Box 70731
Johnson City, TN 37614
Phone: (423) 439-4213
Fax: (423) 439-4630
E-mail: go2etsu@etsu.edu
http://www.etsu.edu
Communications, media studies.

Freed-Hardeman University
158 East Main Street
Henderson, TN 38340
Phone: (731) 989-6651
Fax: (731) 989-6047
E-mail: admissions@fhu.edu
http://www.fhu.edu
Communications.

Jackson State Community College**
2046 North Parkway
Jackson, TN 38301
Phone: (800) 355-5722
Fax: (731) 425-9559
E-mail: At Web site
http://www.jscc.edu
Communications.

Lee University
P.O. Box 3450
Cleveland, TN 37320
Phone: (423) 614-8500
Fax: (423) 614-8533
E-mail: admissions@leeuniversity.edu
http://www.leeuniversity.edu
Communications.

Lipscomb University
3901 Granny White Pike
Nashville, TN 37204
Phone: (615) 269-1776
Fax: (615) 269-1804
E-mail: admissions@lipscomb.edu
http://www.lipscomb.edu
Communications.

Middle Tennessee State University*
Office of Admissions
1301 East Main Street
Murfreesboro, TN 37132
Phone: (800) 433-6878
Fax: (615) 898-5478
E-mail: admissions@mtsu.edu
http://www.mtsu.edu
Communications, media studies.

Nashville State Community College*
20 White Bridge Road
Nashville, TN 37209
Phone: (800) 272-7363
E-mail: At Web site
http://www.nscc.edu
Communications technology.

**Pellissippi State Technical Community
    College****
10915 Hardin Valley Road
Knoxville, TN 37933
Phone: (865) 694-6681

Fax: (865) 539-7217
E-mail: At Web site
http://www.pstcc.edu
Cinematography, film/video production.

Southern Adventist University
P.O. Box 370
Collegedale, TN 37315
Phone: (423)-238-2844
Fax: (423) 238-3005
E-mail: admissions@southern.edu
http://www.southern.edu
Broadcast journalism, cinematography,
    film/video production,
    communications technology, media
    studies.

Tennessee Technological University
P.O. Box 5006
Cookeville, TN 38505
Phone: (931) 372-3888
Fax: (931) 372-6250
E-mail: admissions@tntech.edu
http://www.tntech.edu
Communications, communications
    technology.

Trevecca Nazarene University
333 Murfreesboro Road
Nashville, TN 37210
Phone: (888) 210-4868
E-mail: At Web site
http://www.trevecca.edu
Broadcast journalism, communications,
    communications technology.

Union University
1050 Union University Drive
Jackson, TN 38305
Phone: (731) 661-5000
Fax: (731) 661-5017
E-mail: cgriffin@uu.edu
http://www.uu.edu
Broadcast journalism, communications.

University of Memphis*
229 Administration Building
Memphis, TN 38152
Phone: (901) 678-2111
Fax: (901) 678-3053
E-mail: recruitment@memphis.edu
http://www.memphis.edu
Media studies.

**University of Tennessee—
    Chattanooga***
615 McCallie Avenue
131 Hooper Hall
Chattanooga, TN 37403

Phone: (423) 425-4662
Fax: (423) 425-4157
E-mail: yancy-freeman@utc.edu
http://www.utc.edu
Communications, film/video arts.

University of Tennessee—Knoxville*
320 Science Building
Circle Park Drive
Knoxville, TN 37996
Phone: (865) 974-2184
Fax: (865) 974-6341
E-mail: admissions@tennessee.edu
http://www.utk.edu
Broadcast journalism, communications,
    film/video arts.

University of Tennessee—Martin*
200 Hall-Moody
Administrative Building
Martin, TN 38238
Phone: (731) 587-7020
Fax: (731) 587-7029
E-mail: admitme@utm.edu
http://www.utm.edu
Communications.

Vanderbilt University
2305 West End Avenue
Nashville, TN 37203
Phone: (615) 322-2561
Fax: (615) 343-7765
E-mail: admissions@vanderbilt.edu
http://www.vanderbilt.edu
Communications.

TEXAS

Abilene Christian University*
ACU P.O. Box 29000
Abilene, TX 79699
Phone: (325) 674-2650
Fax: (325) 674-2130
E-mail: info@admissions.acu.edu
http://www.acu.edu
Communications.

Alvin Community College**
3110 Mustang Road
Alvin, TX 77511
Phone: (281) 756-3531
Fax: (281) 756-3531
E-mail: admiss@alvincollege.edu
http://www.alvin.cc.tx.us
Radio and television.

Angelina College**
P.O. Box 1768
Lufkin, TX 75902
Phone: (936) 633-1301, ext. 213

Fax: (936) 639-4299
E-mail: gfarley@angelina.edu
http://www.angelina.edu
Communications.

Angelo State University
2601 West Avenue North
San Angelo, TX 76909
Phone: (325) 942-2041
Fax: (325) 942-2078
E-mail: admissions@angelo.edu
http://www.angelo.edu
Communications.

Austin College
90 North Grand Avenue, Suite 6N
Sherman, TX 75090
Phone: (903) 813-3000
Fax: (903) 813-3198
E-mail: admissions@austincollege.edu
http://www.austincollege.edu
Communications.

Austin Community College**
5930 Middle Fiskville Road
Austin, TX 78752
Phone: (512) 223-7765
Fax: (512) 223-7665
E-mail: At Web site
http://www.austincc.edu
Broadcast journalism, dance.

Baylor University*
P.O. Box 97056
Waco, TX 76798
Phone: (254) 710-3435
Fax: (254) 710-3436
E-mail:
    admissions_serv_office@baylor.edu
http://www.baylor.edu
Acting, broadcast journalism,
    communications.

Coastal Bend College**
3800 Charco Road
Beeville, TX 78102
Phone: (361) 354-2251
Fax: (361) 354-2254
E-mail: At Web site
http://www.vct.coastalbend.edu
Communications technology.

Dallas Baptist University
3000 Mountain Creek Parkway
Dallas, TX 75211
Phone: (214) 333-5360
Fax: (214) 333-5447
E-mail: admiss@dbu.edu
http://www.dbu.edu
Communications.

El Paso Community College**
P. O. Box 20500
El Paso, TX 79998
Phone: (915) 831-2580
E-mail: At Web site
http://www.epcc.edu
Cinematography, film/video production,
    communications, communications
    technology.

Hardin-Simmons University
2200 Hickory Street
Abilene, TX 79698
Phone: (915) 670-1206
Fax: (915) 670-1527
E-mail: enroll@hsutx.edu
http://www.hsutx.edu
Broadcast journalism, communications,
    radio and television.

Houston Baptist University
7502 Fondren Road
Houston, TX 77074
Phone: (281) 649-3211
Fax: (281) 649-3217
E-mail: unadm@hbu.edu
http://www.hbu.edu
Communications, media studies.

Houston Community College**
1300 Holman Street
Houston, TX, 77004.
Phone: (713) 718-8500
Fax: (713) 718-2111
E-mail: central.website@hccs.edu
http://www.hccs.cc.tx.us
Radio/television broadcasting.

Howard Payne University
Howard Payne Station
Brownwood, TX 76801
Phone: (325) 649-8027
Fax: (325) 649-8901
E-mail: enroll@hputx.edu
http://www.hputx.edu
Communications.

Lamar University
P.O. Box 10009
Beaumont, TX 77710
Phone: (409) 880-8888
Fax: (409) 880-8463
E-mail: admissions@hal.lamar.edu
http://www.lamar.edu
Communications, dance.

Lubbock Christian University
5601 19th Street
Lubbock, TX 79407

Phone: (806) 720-7151
Fax: (806) 720-7162
E-mail: admissions@lcu.edu
http://www.lcu.edu
Communications.

Laredo Community College**
West End Washington Street
Laredo, TX 78040
Phone: (956) 721-5177
Fax: (956) 721-5493
E-mail: admissions@laredo.edu
http://www.laredo.edu
Broadcast journalism.

McMurray University
South 14th and Sayles Boulevard
Abilene, TX 79697
Phone: (915) 793-4700
Fax: (915) 793-4718
E-mail: admissions@mcm.edu
http://www.mcm.edu
Communications.

Midwestern State University
3410 Taft Building
Wichita Falls, TX 76308
Phone: (940) 397-4334
Fax: (940) 397-4672
E-mail: admissions@mwsu.edu
http://www.mwsu.edu
Communications, media studies.

Northwest Vista College**
3535 North Ellison Drive
San Antonio, TX 78251
Phone: (210) 348-2016
E-mail: nvcinfo.accd.edu
http://www.accd.edu/nvc
Media studies.

Odessa College**
Admissions Office
201 West University, SUB 205
Odessa, TX 79764
Phone: (432)-335-6432
Fax: (432) 335-6824
E-mail: ngarcia@odessa.edu
http://www.odessa.edu
Radio and television.

Prairie View A&M University
P.O. Box 3089
University Drive
Prairie View, TX 77446
Phone: (936) 857-2626
Fax: (936) 857-2699
E-mail: admissions@pvamu.edu
http://www.pvamu.edu
Communications.

Saint Mary's University
One Camino Santa Maria
San Antonio, TX 78228
Phone: (210) 436-3126
Fax: (210) 431-6742
E-mail: uadm@stmarytx.edu
http://www.stmarytx.edu
Communications.

Sam Houston State University
P.O. Box 2418, SHSU
Huntsville, TX 77341
Phone (936) 294-1828
Fax: (936) 294-3758
E-mail: admissions@shsu.edu
http://www.shsu.edu
Dance, radio and television.

San Antonio College**
1300 San Pedro Avenue
San Antonio, TX 78212
Phone: (210) 733-2582
E-mail: At Web site
http://www.accd.edu/sac/sacmain/sac.htm
Telecommunications technology.

South Plains College**
1401 South College Avenue
Levelland, TX, 79336
Phone (806) 894-9611, ext. 2370
Fax: (806) 897-3167
E-mail: info@southplainscollege.edu
http://www.southplainscollege.edu
Cinematography, film/video production,
    communications.

Southern Methodist University
P.O. Box 750296
Dallas, TX 75275
Phone (214) 768-2058
Fax: (214) 768-2507
E-mail: enroll_serv@mail.smu.edu
http://www.smu.edu
Broadcast journalism, communications,
    dance, film/video arts, media studies.

Southwestern Adventist University
P.O. Box 567
Keene, TX 76059
Phone (800) 433-2240
Fax: (817) 645-3921
E-mail: illingworth@swac.edu
http://www.swac.edu
Broadcast journalism.

Southwestern University
Admissions Office
P.O. Box 770
Georgetown, TX 78627

Phone (512) 863-1200
Fax: (512) 863-9601
E-mail: admission@southwestern.edu
http://www.southwestern.edu
Communications.

Stephen F. Austin State University
P.O. Box 13051, SFA Station
Nacogdoches, TX 75962
Phone (936) 468-2504
Fax: (936) 468-3849
E-mail: admissions@sfasu.edu
http://www.sfasu.edu
Communications, dance, radio and
    television.

Sul Ross State University
P.O. Box C-2
Alpine, TX 79832
Phone (915) 837-8050
Fax: (915) 837-8431
E-mail: admissions@sulross.edu
http://www.sulross.edu
Communications.

Tarleton State University
P.O. Box T-0030
Tarleton Station
Stephenville, TX 76402
Phone (254) 968-9125
Fax: (254) 968-9951
E-mail: uadm@tarleton.edu
http://www.tarleton.edu
Communications.

Texas A&M University—Commerce
P.O. Box 3011
Commerce, TX 75429
Phone (903) 886-5106
Fax: (903) 886-5888
E-mail: admissions@tamu-
    commerce.edu
http://www.tamu-commerce.edu
Broadcast journalism, communications.

**Texas A&M University—Corpus
    Christie**
6300 Ocean Drive
Corpus Christi, TX 78412
Phone (361) 825-2624
Fax: (361) 825-5887
E-mail: judith.perales@mail.tamucc.edu
http://www.tamucc.edu
Communications.

Texas A&M University—Kingsville
700 University Boulevard, MSC 128
Kingsville, TX 78363
Phone (361) 593-2315

Fax: (361) 593-2195
E-mail: ksossrx@tamuk.edu
http://www.tamuk.edu
Communications.

Texas Christian University*
Office of Admissions
TCU, P.O. Box 297013
Fort Worth, TX 76129
Phone (817) 257-7490
Fax: (817) 257-7268
E-mail: frogmail@tcu.edu
http://www.tcu.edu
Broadcast journalism, communications,
    film/video arts, media studies,
    telecommunications technology.

Texas Lutheran University
10000 West Court Street
Seguin, TX 78155
Phone (800) 771-8521
Fax: (830) 372-8096
E-mail: admissions@tlu.edu
http://www.tlu.edu
Communications.

Texas Southern University
3100 Cleburne Street
Houston, TX 77004
Phone (713) 313-7420
Fax: (713) 313-4317
E-mail: admissions@tsu.edu
http://www.tsu.edu
Broadcast journalism, communications.

Texas State Technical College**
Admissions Office
2400 East End Boulevard South
Marshall, TX 75672
Phone (800) 592-8784
Fax: (915) 235-7416
E-mail: At Web site
http://www.tstc.edu
Communications technology,
    telecommunications technology.

Texas State University—San Marcos*
429 North Guadalupe Street
San Marcos, TX 78666
Phone (512) 245-2364
Fax: (512) 245-9020
E-mail: admissions@txstate.edu
http://www.txstate.edu
Communications, dance, media studies,
    radio and television.

Texas Tech University*
P.O. Box 45005

Lubbock, TX 79409
Phone (806) 742-1480
Fax: (806) 742-0062
E-mail: admissions@ttu.edu
http://www.ttu.edu
Dance, radio and television,
    telecommunications technology.

Texas Wesleyan University
1201 Wesleyan
Fort Worth, TX 76105
Phone (817) 531-4422
Fax: (817) 531-7515
E-mail: info@txwesleyan.edu
http://www.txwesleyan.edu
Communications, radio and television.

Texas Woman's University
P.O. Box 425589
Denton, TX 76204
Phone (940) 898-3188
Fax: (940) 898-3081
E-mail: admissions@twu.edu
http://www.twu.edu
Communications, dance, media studies.

Trinity University
One Trinity Place
San Antonio, TX 78212
Phone (210) 999-7207
Fax: (210) 999-8164
E-mail: admissions@trinity.edu
http://www.trinity.edu
Communications.

University of Houston—Clear Lake
2700 Bay Area Boulevard
Houston, TX 77058
Phone (281) 283-7600
Fax: (281) 283-2530
E-mail: admissions@cl.uh.edu
http://www.uhcl.edu
Communications.

University of Houston—Houston
Office of Admissions
122 East Cullen Building
Houston, TX 77204
Phone: (713) 743-1010
Fax: (713) 743-9633
E-mail: admissions@uh.edu
http://www.uh.edu
Broadcast journalism, communications,
    communications technology, media
    studies.

University of Houston—Victoria
    Campus
Enrollment Management Office, UHV

Victoria, TX 77901
Phone: (361) 788-6222
Fax: (361) 572-9377
E-mail: urbanom@jade.vic.uh.edu
http://www.vic.uh.edu
Communications.

University of Mary Hardin-Baylor
UMHB Box 8004
900 College Street
Belton, TX 76513
Phone: (254) 295-4520
Fax: (254) 295-5049
E-mail: admission@umhb.edu
http://www.umhb.edu
Communications.

University of North Texas*
P.O. Box 311277
Denton, TX 76203
Phone: (940) 565-2681
Fax: (940) 565-2408
E-mail: undergrad@unt.edu
http://www.unt.edu
Broadcast journalism, communications,
    communications technology, dance,
    film/video arts.

University of St. Thomas
2800 Montrose Boulevard
Houston, TX 77006
Phone: (713) 525-3500
Fax: (713) 525-3558
E-mail: admissions@stthom.edu
http://www.stthom.edu
Communications.

University of Texas—Arlington
Office of Admissions
P.O. Box 19111
Arlington, TX 76019
Phone: (817) 272-6287
Fax: (817) 272-3435
E-mail: admissions@uta.edu
http://www.uta.edu
Broadcast journalism, communications.

University of Texas—Austin*
P.O. Box 8058
Austin, TX 78713
Phone: (512) 475-7440
Fax: (512) 475-7475
E-mail: frmn@uts.cc.utexas.edu
http://www.utexas.edu
Communications, dance, film/video arts,
    radio and television.

University of Texas—El Paso
500 West University Avenue

El Paso, TX 79968
Phone: (915) 747-5576
Fax: (915) 747-8893
E-mail: admission@utep.edu
http://www.utep.edu
Communications, dance, media studies.

University of Texas—Pan American
Office of Admissions and Records
1201 West University Drive
Edinburgh, TX 78541
Phone: (956) 381-2201
Fax: (956) 381-2212
E-mail: admissions@panam.edu
http://www.panam.edu
Communications, dance.

University of Texas—San Antonio
6900 North Loop 1604 West
San Antonio, TX 78249
Phone: (210) 458-4530
Fax: (210) 458-7716
E-mail: prospects@utsa.edu
http://www.utsa.edu
Media studies.

West Texas A&M University
P.O. Box 60907
Canyon, TX 79016
Phone: (806) 651-2020
Fax: (806) 651-5268
E-mail: lvars@mail.wtamu.edu
http://www.wtamu.edu
Broadcast journalism communications.

UTAH

Brigham Young University*
A-153 ASB
Provo, UT 84602
Phone: (801) 422-2507
Fax: (801) 422-0005
E-mail: admissions@byu.edu
http://www.byu.edu
Acting, broadcast journalism,
    cinematography, film/video
    production, communications, dance,
    film/video arts, media studies,
    playwriting/screenwriting.

Southern Utah University
Admissions Office
351 West Center
Cedar City, UT 84720
Phone: (435) 865-7740
Fax: (435) 865-8223
E-mail: Adminfo@suu.edu
http://www.suu.edu
Communications, dance.

University of Utah*
210 South 1460 East, Room 250 South
Salt Lake City, UT 84112
Phone: (801) 581-7281
Fax: (801) 585-7864
E-mail: admiss@sa.utah.edu
http://www.utah.edu
Communications, dance, film/video arts,
    media studies.

Utah State University
0160 Old Main Hill
Logan, UT 84322
Phone: (435) 797-1079
Fax: (435) 797-3708
E-mail: admit@cc.usu.edu
http://www.usu.edu
Dance.

Utah Valley State College**
800 West University Parkway
Mail Code 106
Orem, UT 84058
Phone: (801) 863-8466
E-mail: At Web site
http://www.uvsc.edu
Communications, dance,
    telecommunications technology.

Weber State University
1137 University Circle
Ogden, UT 84408
Phone: (801) 626-6744
Fax: (801) 626-6747
E-mail: admissions@weber.edu
http://www.weber.edu
Broadcast journalism, communications,
    dance.

Westminster College
1840 South 1300 East
Salt Lake City, UT 84105
Phone: (801) 832-2200
Fax: (801) 484-3252
E-mail: admispub@westminstercollege.
    edu
http://www.westminstercollege.edu
Communications.

VERMONT

Bennington College
Office of Admissions and Financial Aid
Bennington, VT 05201
Phone: (802) 440-4312
Fax: (802) 440-4320
E-mail: admissions@bennington.edu
http://www.bennington.edu

Cinematography, film/video production,
    communications, dance, film/video
    arts, playwriting/screenwriting.

Burlington College
95 North Avenue
Burlington, VT 05401
Phone: (802) 862-9616
Fax: (802) 660-4331
E-mail: admissions@burcol.edu
http://www.burlingtoncollege.edu
Cinematography, film/video production,
    film/video arts, photographic/film/
    video technology.

Castleton State College
Office of Admissions
Castleton, VT 05735
Phone: (802) 468-1213
Fax: (802) 468-1476
E-mail: info@castleton.edu
http://www.castleton.edu
Broadcast journalism, media studies.

Champlain College
163 South Willard Street
P.O. Box 670
Burlington, VT 05402
Phone: (802) 860-2727
Fax: (802) 860-2767
E-mail: admission@champlain.edu
http://www.champlain.edu
Cinematography, film/video production,
    media studies.

Lyndon State College**
1000 College Road
P.O. Box 919
Lyndonville, VT 05851
Phone: (802) 626-6200
E-mail: At Web site
http://www.lsc.vsc.edu
Communications, communications
    technology, radio and television.

Marlboro College
P.O. Box A, South Road
Marlboro, VT 05344
Phone: (802) 258-9236
Fax: (802) 451-7555
E-mail: admissions@marlboro.edu
http://www.marlboro.edu
Cinematography, film/video production,
    dance, film/video arts,
    playwriting/screenwriting.

Middlebury College
Emma Willard House

Middlebury, VT 05763
Phone: (802) 443-3000
Fax: (802) 443-2056
E-mail: admissions@middlebury.edu
http://www.middlebury.edu
Cinematography, film/video production,
    dance, film/video arts.

Norwich University
Admissions Office
158 Harmon Drive
Northfield, VT 05663
Phone: (802) 485-2001
Fax: (802) 485-2032
E-mail: nuadm@norwich.edu
http://www.norwich.edu
Communications.

VIRGINIA

Bridgewater College
402 East College Street
Bridgewater, VA 22812
Phone: (540) 828-5375
Fax: (540) 828-5481
E-mail: admissions@bridgewater.edu
http://www.bridgewater.edu
Media studies.

Christopher Newport University
1 University Place
Newport News, VA 23608
Phone: (757) 594-7015
Fax: (757) 594-7333
E-mail: admit@cnu.edu
http://www.cnu.edu
Communications.

ECPI College of Technology**
Virginia Beach Campus
5555 Greenwich Road, Suite 100
Virginia Beach, VA 23462
Phone: (800) 986-1200
E-mail: At Web site
http://www.ecpi.edu/campus/vab
Telecommunications technology.

ECPI Technical College—Roanoke**
5234 Airport Road
Roanoke, VA 24012
Phone: (800) 986-1200
E-mail: At Web site
http://www.ecpitech.edu
Telecommunications technology.

Emory & Henry College
P.O. Box 947
Emory, VA 24327

Phone: (800) 848-5493
Fax: (276) 944-6935
E-mail: ehadmiss@ehc.edu
http://www.ehc.edu
Communications.

Hampton University*
Office of Admissions
Hampton, VA 23668
Phone: (757) 727-5328
Fax: (757) 727-5095
E-mail: admissions@hamptonu.edu
http://www.hamptonu.edu
Broadcast journalism, communications, media studies.

James Madison University
Sonner Hall, MSC 0101
Harrisonburg, VA 22807
Phone: (540) 568-5681
Fax: (540) 568-3332
E-mail: gotojmu@jmu.edu
http://www.jmu.edu
Communications, media studies.

J. Sergeant Reynolds Community College**
P.O. Box 85622
Richmond, VA 23285
Phone: (804) 371-3029
Fax: (804) 371-3650
E-mail: At Web site
http://www.jsr.vccs.edu
Cinematography, film/video production, communications technology.

Liberty University
1971 University Boulevard
Lynchburg, VA 24502
Phone: (434) 582-5985
Fax: (800) 542-2311
E-mail: admissions@liberty.edu
http://www.liberty.edu
Communications, radio/television broadcasting.

Longwood University
Admissions Office
201 High Street
Farmville, VA 23909
Phone: (434) 395-2060
Fax: (434) 395-2332
E-mail: admit@longwood.edu
http://www.longwood.edu
Communications.

Lord Fairfax Community College**
Middletown Campus
173 Skirmisher Lane

Middletown, VA 22645
Phone: (800) 906-5322, ext. 7107
Fax: (540) 868-7005
E-mail: At Web site
http://www.lf.cc.va.us
Communications.

Lynchburg College
1501 Lakeside Drive
Lynchburg, VA 24501
Phone: (804) 544-8300
Fax: (804) 544-8653
E-mail: admissions@lynchburg.edu
http://www.lynchburg.edu
Communications.

Mary Baldwin College
P.O. Box 1500
Staunton, VA 24402
Phone: (540) 887-7019
Fax: (540) 887-7279
E-mail: admit@mbc.edu
http://www.mbc.edu
Communications.

Marymount University
2807 North Glebe Road
Arlington, VA 22207
Phone: (703) 284-1500
Fax: (703) 522-0349
E-mail: admissions@marymount.edu
http://www.marymount.edu
Communications.

Norfolk State University*
700 Park Avenue
Norfolk, VA 23504
Phone: (757) 823-8396
Fax: (757) 823-2078
E-mail: admissions@nsu.edu
http://www.nsu.edu
Broadcast journalism, communications, media studies.

Old Dominion University
108 Rollins Hall
5215 Hampton Boulevard
Norfolk, VA 23529
Phone: (757) 683-3685
Fax: (757) 683-3255
E-mail: admit@odu.edu
http://www.odu.edu
Acting, communications, dance.

Radford University
P.O. Box 6903
RU Station
Radford, VA 24142

Phone: (540) 831-5371
Fax: (540) 831-5038
E-mail: ruadmiss@radford.edu
http://www.radford.edu
Communications.

Shenandoah University
1460 University Drive
Winchester, VA 22601
Phone: (540) 665-4581
Fax: (540) 665-4627
E-mail: admit@su.edu
http://www.su.edu
Communications, dance.

University of Virginia's College at Wise
1 College Avenue
Wise, VA 24293
Phone: (276) 328-0102
Fax: (276) 328-0251
E-mail: admissions@uvawise.edu
http://www.uvawise.edu
Communications.

Virginia Commonwealth University
821 West Franklin Street
P.O. Box 842526
Richmond, VA 23284
Phone: (804) 828-1222
Fax: (804) 828-1899
E-mail: vcuinfo@vcu.edu
http://www.vcu.edu
Communications, dance, media studies.

Virginia Polytechnic Institute and State University
7054 Haycock Road
Blacksburg, VA 24061
Phone: (540) 231-6267
Fax: (540) 231-3242
E-mail: admissions@vt.edu
http://www.vt.edu
Communications.

Virginia State University
One Hayden Street
P.O. Box 9018
Petersburg, VA 23806
Phone: (804) 524-5902
Fax: (804) 524-5056
E-mail: admiss@vsu.edu
http://www.vsu.edu
Media studies.

Virginia Wesleyan College
1584 Wesleyan Drive
Norfolk/Virginia Beach, VA 23502
Phone: (757) 455-3208
Fax: (757) 455-3208

E-mail: admissions@vwc.edu
http://www.vwc.edu
Communications.

**Virginia Western Community
   College****
P.O. Box 14007
Roanoke, VA 24038
Phone: (540) 857-7231
Fax: (540) 857-6102
E-mail: infocenter@vw.vccs.edu
http://www.vw.vccs.edu
Broadcast journalism.

WASHINGTON

Art Institute of Seattle**
2323 Elliott Avenue
Seattle, WA 98121
Phone: (800) 275-2471
Fax: (206) 269-0275
E-mail: aisadm@ais.edu
http://www.ais.edu
Cinematography, film/video production.

Central Washington University
Admissions Office
400 East 8th Avenue
Ellensburg, WA 98926
Phone: (509) 963-1211
Fax: (509) 963-3022
E-mail: cwuadmis@cwu.edu
http://www.cwu.edu
Communications.

Centralia College**
Centralia, WA, 98531
Phone: (360) 736-9391, ext. 682
Fax: (360) 330-7503
E-mail: admissions@centralia.ctc.edu
http://www.centralia.ctc.edu
Broadcast journalism, radio and
   television, radio/television
   broadcasting.

Clark College**
1800 East McLoughlin Boulevard
Vancouver, WA 98663
Phone: (360) 992-2107
Fax: (360) 992-2867
http://www.clark.edu
Telecommunications technology.

Clover Park Technical College*
4500 Steilacoom Boulevard SW
Lakewood, WA 98499
Phone: (253) 589-5570
Fax: (253) 589-5852
E-mail: admissions@cptc.edu

http://www.cptc.edu
Radio/television broadcasting.

Cornish College of the Arts
710 East Roy Street
Seattle, WA 98102
Phone: (800) 726-5016
Fax: (206) 720-1011
E-mail: admissions@cornish.edu
http://www.cornish.edu
Acting, cinematography, film/video
   production, dance,
   playwriting/screenwriting.

Eastern Washington University
526 Fifth Street
Cheney, WA 99004
Phone: (509) 359-2397
Fax: (509) 359-6692
E-mail: admissions@mail.ewu.edu
http://www.ewu.edu
Broadcast journalism, communications,
   communications technology.

Evergreen State College
2700 Evergreen Parkway NW
Office of Admissions
Olympia, WA 98505
Phone: (360) 867-6170
Fax: (360) 867-6576
E-mail: admissions@evergreen.edu
http://www.evergreen.edu
Cinematography, film/video production.

Gonzaga University
502 East Boone Avenue
Spokane, WA 99258
Phone: (509) 323-6572
Fax: (509) 324-5780
E-mail: admissions@gonzaga.edu
http://www.gonzaga.edu
Broadcast journalism.

Green River Community College**
12401 SE 320th Street
Auburn, WA, 98092
Phone: (253) 833-9111, ext. 2513
Fax: (253) 288-3454
E-mail: admissions@greenriver.edu
http://www.greenriver.edu
Broadcast journalism.

Olympic College**
1600 Chester Avenue
Bremerton, WA 98337
Phone: (800) 259-6718
Fax: (360) 475-7020
E-mail: At Web site
http://www.olympic.edu

Cinematography, film/video production,
   photographic/film/video technology.

Pacific Lutheran University
Office of Admissions
12180 Park Street South
Tacoma, WA 98447
Phone: (253) 535-7151
Fax: (253) 536-5136
E-mail: admissions@plu.edu
http://www.plu.edu
Communications.

Seattle Central Community College**
1701 Broadway
Seattle, WA 98122
Phone: (206) 587-5450
Fax: NA
E-mail: At Web site
http://www.seattlecentral.org
Photographic/film/video technology.

Seattle Pacific University
3307 3rd Avenue West
Seattle, WA 98119
Phone: (206) 281-2021
Fax: (206) 281-2669
E-mail: admissions@spu.edu
http://www.spu.edu
Communications.

Seattle University
Admissions Office
900 Broadway
Seattle, WA 98122
Phone: (206) 296-2000
Fax: (206) 296-5656
E-mail: admissions@seattleu.edu
http://www.seattleu.edu
Communications.

Skagit Valley College**
Mount Vernon Campus
2405 East College Way
Mount Vernon, WA 98273
Phone: (877) 385-5360
Fax: (360) 416-7890
E-mail: At Web site
http://www.skagit.edu
Communications.

University of Puget Sound
1500 North Warner Street
Tacoma, WA 98416
Phone: (253) 879-3211
Fax: (253) 879-3993
E-mail: admissions@ups.edu
http://www.ups.edu
Communications.

University of Washington*
1410 NE Campus Parkway
320 Schmitz, P.O. Box 355840
Seattle, WA 98195
Phone: (206) 543-9686
Fax: (206) 685-3655
E-mail: askuwadm@u.washington.edu
http://www.washington.edu
Communications, dance.

Walla Walla College
Office of Admissions
204 South College Avenue
College Place, WA 99324
Phone: (509) 527-2327
Fax: (509) 527-2397
E-mail: info@wwc.edu
http://www.wwc.edu
Communications, media studies.

Washington State University
370 Lighty Student Services
Pullman, WA 99164
Phone: (509) 335-5586
Fax: (509) 335-4902
E-mail: admiss2@wsu.edu
http://www.wsu.edu
Broadcast journalism, communications.

Western Washington University
Mail Stop 9009
Bellingham, WA 98225
Phone: (360) 650-3440
Fax: (360) 650-7369
E-mail: admit@cc.wwu.edu
http://www.wwu.edu
Broadcast journalism, communications,
    media studies.

Whitman College
345 Boyer Avenue
Walla Walla, WA 99362
Phone: (509) 527-5176
Fax: (509) 527-4967
E-mail: admissions@whitman.edu
http://www.whitman.edu
Film/video arts.

Whitworth College
300 West Hawthorne Road
Spokane, WA 99251
Phone: (509) 777-4786
Fax: (509) 777-3758
E-mail: admission@whitworth.edu
http://www.whitworth.edu
Communications.

Yakima Valley Community College**
P.O. Box 22520

Yakima, WA 98907-2520
Phone: (509) 574-4713
Fax: (509) 574-6860
E-mail: At Web site
http://www.yvcc.edu
Communications technology.

WEST VIRGINIA

Alderson-Broddus College
P.O. Box 2003
Philippi, WV 26416
Phone: (800) 263-1549
Fax: (304) 457-6239
E-mail: admissions@ab.edu
http://www.ab.edu
Broadcast journalism, communications.

Bethany College
Office of Admissions
Bethany, WV 26032
Phone: (304) 829-7611
Fax: (304) 829-7142
E-mail: admission@bethanywv.edu
http://www.bethanywv.edu
Broadcast journalism, communications,
    radio and television.

Concord College—Athens
1000 Vermillion Street
P.O. Box 1000
Athens, WV 24712
Phone: (304) 384-5248
Fax: (304) 384-9044
E-mail: admissions@concord.edu
http://www.concord.edu
Broadcast journalism, communications.

Fairmont State College
1201 Locust Avenue
Fairmont, WV 26554
Phone: (304) 367-4141
Fax: (304) 367-4789
E-mail: admit@mail.fscwv.edu
http://www.fscwv.edu
Communications.

Marshall University*
One John Marshall Drive
Huntington, WV 25755
Phone: (304) 696-3160
Fax: (304) 696-3135
E-mail: admissions@marshall.edu
http://www.marshall.edu
Communications.

Mountain State University
609 South Kanawha Street
Beckley, WV 25801

Phone: (304) 929-1433
Fax: (304) 253-3463
E-mail: gomsu@mountainstate.edu
http://www.mountainstate.edu
Broadcast journalism.

Shepherd College
Office of Admissions
P.O. Box 3210
Shepherdstown, WV 25443
Phone: (304) 876-5212
Fax: (304) 876-5165
E-mail: admoff@shepherd.edu
http://www.shepherd.edu
Communications, communications
    technology.

West Liberty State College
P.O. Box 295
West Liberty, WV 26074
Phone: (304) 336-8076
Fax: (304) 336-8403
E-mail: wladmsn1@wlsc.edu
http://www.wlsc.edu
Communications.

West Virginia University*
Admissions Office
P.O. Box 6009
Morgantown. WV 26506
Phone: (304) 293-2121
Fax: (304) 293-3080
E-mail: wvuadmissions@arc.wvu.edu
http://www.wvu.edu
Broadcast journalism, communications.

West Virginia Wesleyan College
59 College Avenue
Buckhannon, WV 26201
Phone: (304) 473-8510
Fax: (304) 473-8108
E-mail: admission@wvwc.edu
http://www.wvwc.edu
Communications.

WISCONSIN

Alvernia College
3400 South 43rd Street
P.O. Box 343922
Milwaukee, WI 19607
Phone: (610) 796-8220
Fax: (610) 796-8336
E-mail: admissions@alvernia.edu
http://www.alvernia.edu
Communications.

Carroll College
100 North East Avenue

Waukesha, WI 53186
Phone: (262) 524-7220
Fax: (262) 951-3037
E-mail: ccinfo@ccadmin.cc.edu
http://www.cc.edu
Communications.

Carthage College
2001 Alford Park Drive
Kenosha, WI 53140
Phone: (262) 551-6000
Fax: (262) 551-5762
E-mail: admissions@carthage.edu
http://www.carthage.edu
Communications.

Concordia University—Wisconsin
12800 North Lakeshore Drive
Cequon, WI 53097
Phone: (262) 243-5700
Fax: (262) 243-4545
E-mail: admission@cuw.edu
http://www.cuw.edu
Broadcast journalism, communications.

Edgewood College
1000 Edgewood College Drive
Madison, WI 53711
Phone: (608) 663-2294
Fax: (608) 663-3291
E-mail: admissions@edgewood.edu
http://www.edgewood.edu
Media studies.

Gateway Technical College**
3520 30th Avenue
Kenosha, WI 53144
Phone: (262) 564-2301
Fax: (262) 564-2301
E-mail: At Web site
http://www.gtc.edu
Communications technology.

Marian College of Fond Du Lac
45 South National Avenue
Fond du Lac, WI 54935
Phone: (920) 923-7650
Fax: (920) 923-8755
E-mail: admissions@mariancollege.edu
http://www.mariancollege.edu
Communications.

Marquette University*
P.O. Box 1881
Milwaukee, WI 53201
Phone: (414) 288-7302
Fax: (414) 288-3764
E-mail: admissions@marquette.edu
http://www.marquette.edu

Broadcast journalism, communications,
media studies, radio and television.

Milwaukee Area Technical College**
700 West State Street
Milwaukee, WI 53233
Phone: (414)-297-6274
Fax: (414) 297-6371
E-mail: apply@matc.edu
http://www.matc.edu
Cinematography, film/video production,
communications technology,
photographic/film/video technology,
radio/television broadcasting.

Milwaukee School of Engineering
1025 North Broadway
Milwaukee, WI 53202
Phone: (414) 277-6763
Fax: (414) 277-7475
E-mail: explore@msoe.edu
http://www.msoe.edu
Communications.

Moraine Park Technical College**
235 North National Avenue
Fond du Lac, WI 54936
Phone: (800) 472-4554
Fax: (920) 924-3421
E-mail: At Web site
http://www.morainepark.edu
Communications.

St. Norbert College
100 Grant Street
De Pere, WI 54115
Phone: (920) 403-3005
Fax: (920) 403-4072
E-mail: admit@snc.edu
http://www.snc.edu
Communications.

University of Wisconsin—Eau Claire*
105 Garfield Avenue
Eau Claire, WI 54701
Phone: (715) 836-5415
Fax: (715) 836-2409
E-mail: admissions@uwec.edu
http://www.uwec.edu
Communications, media studies.

University of Wisconsin—Green Bay
2420 Nicolet Drive
Green Bay, WI 53411-7001
Phone: (920) 465-2111
Fax: (920) 465-5754
E-mail: admissions@uwgb.edu
http://www.uwgb.edu
Communications.

University of Wisconsin—LaCrosse
1725 State Street
LaCrosse, WI 54601
Phone: (608) 785-8939
Fax: (608) 785-8940
E-mail: admissions@uwlax.edu
http://www.uwlax.edu
Communications.

University of Wisconsin—Madison
Red Gym and Armory
716 Langdon Street
Madison, WI 53706
Phone: (608) 262-3961
Fax: (608) 262-7706
E-mail: onwisconsin@admissions.wisc.
edu
http://www.wisc.edu
Broadcast journalism, cinematography,
film/video production,
communications, dance, film/video
arts.

University of Wisconsin—Milwaukee
P.O. Box 749
Milwaukee. WI 53201
Phone: (414) 229-3800
Fax: (414) 229-6940
E-mail: uwmlook@uwm.edu
http://www.uwm.edu
Communications, dance, film/video arts.

University of Wisconsin—Oshkosh*
Dempsey Hall 135
800 Algoma Boulevard
Oshkosh, WI 54901
Phone: (920) 424-0202
Fax: (920) 424-1098
E-mail: oshadmuw@uwosh.edu
http://www.uwosh.edu
Broadcast journalism, cinematography,
film/video production, film/video arts,
communications.

University of Wisconsin—Parkside
P.O. Box 2000
Kenosha, WI 53141
Phone: (262) 595-2355
Fax: (262) 595-2008
E-mail: matthew.jensen@uwp.edu
http://www.uwp.edu
Communications.

University of Wisconsin—Platteville
1 University Plaza
Platteville, WI 53818
Phone: (608) 342-1125
Fax: (608) 342-1122
E-mail: schumacr@uwplatt.edu

http://www.uwplatt.edu
Communications.

University of Wisconsin—River Falls*
410 South Third Street
112 South Hall
River Falls, WI 54022
Phone: (715) 425-3500
Fax: (715) 425-0676
E-mail: admit@uwrf.edu
http://www.uwrf.edu
Communications.

University of Wisconsin—Stevens Point
Student Services Center
Stevens Point, WI 54481
Phone: (715) 346-2441
Fax: (715) 346-3957
E-mail: admiss@uwsp.edu
http://www.uwsp.edu
Communications, dance.

University of Wisconsin—Superior
Belknap and Catlin
P.O. Box 2000
Superior, WI 54880
Phone: (715) 394-8230
Fax: (715) 394-8107
E-mail: admissions@uwsuper.edu
http://www.uwsuper.edu
Broadcast journalism, communications,
    communications technology, media
    studies.

University of Wisconsin—Whitewater
800 West Main Street
Baker Hall
Whitewater, WI 53190

Phone: (414) 472-1234
Fax: (414) 472-1515
E-mail: uwwadmit@uww.edu
http://www.uww.edu
Broadcast journalism, communications,
    dance.

**Western Wisconsin Technical
    College***
LaCrosse Campus
304 Sixth Street North
P. O. Box C-0908
La Crosse, WI 54602
Phone: (608) 785-9158
Fax: (608) 785-9094
E-mail: At Web site
http://www.western.tec.wi.us
Media studies.

WYOMING

Casper College*
125 College Drive
Casper, WY 82601
Phone: (800) 442-2963
E-mail: At Web site
http://www.cc.whecn.ed
Dance.

Central Wyoming College*
2660 Peck Avenue.
Riverton, WY 82501
Phone: (307) 855-2000
E-mail: At Web site
http://www.cwc.cc.wy.us
Radio/television broadcasting.

Eastern Wyoming College*
3200 West C Street
Torrington, WY 82240
Phone: (866) 327-8996
Fax: (307) 532-8222
E-mail: At Web site
http://www.ewc.wy.edu
Communications.

**Laramie County Community
    College***
Cheyenne Main Campus
1400 East College Drive
Cheyenne, WY 82007
Phone: (800) 522-299
E-mail: learnmore@lccc.wy.edu
http://www.lccc.cc.wy.us
Media studies.

Northwest College*
231 West 6th Street
Powell, WY 82435
Phone: (800) 560-4692
Fax: (307) 754-6249
E-mail: Brad.Hammond@
    northwestcollege.edu
http://www.northwestcollege.edu
Communications.

University of Wyoming
Admissions Office
P.O. Box 3435
Laramie, WY 82071
Phone: (307) 766-5160
Fax: (307) 766-4042
E-mail: why-wyo@uwyo.edu
http://www.uwyo.edu
Communications.

APPENDIX II
MAJOR TRADE PERIODICALS, NEWSLETTERS, AND OTHER PUBLICATIONS

PERIODICALS AND NEWSLETTERS

Acme Resource
10153½ Riverside Drive, Suite 476
Toluca Lake, CA 91602
Phone: (818) 559-2263
Fax: (818) 559-2264
E-mail: NA
http://www.theacme.com

Advertising Age
Crain Communications, Inc.
711 Third Avenue
New York, NY 10017
Phone: (212) 210-0100
Fax: (212) 210-0200
E-mail: editor@adage.com
http://www.adage.com

Adweek
BPI Communications, Inc.
770 Broadway
New York, NY 10003
Phone: (646) 654-5421
Fax: (646) 654-5365
E-mail: editor@adweek.com
http://www.adweek.com

American Cinematographer
P.O. Box 2230
Hollywood, CA 90078
Phone: (800) 448-0415
Fax: (323) 876-4973
E-mail: editor@theasc.com
http://www.theasc.com/magazine

Animation Magazine
30941 West Agoura Road, Suite 102
Westlake Village, CA 91361
Phone: (818) 991-2884
Fax: (818) 991-3773
E-mail: info@animationmagazine.net
http://www.animationmagazine.net

Back Stage East
770 Broadway, 4th floor

New York, NY 10003
Phone: (646) 654-5700
Fax: (646) 654-5743
E-mail: info@backstage.com
http://www.backstage.com

Back Stage West
5055 Wilshire Boulevard
Los Angeles, CA 90036
Phone: (323) 525-2356
Fax: NA
E-mail: info@backstage.com
http://www.backstage.com

Billboard
VNU eMedia, Inc.
1515 Broadway, 14th floor
New York, NY 10036
Phone: (212) 536-5230
Fax: (212) 536-5358
E-mail: info@billboard.com
http://www.billboard.com

Broadcasting and Cable
Reed Business Information Publications
360 Park Avenue South
New York, NY 10014
Phone: (646) 746-6400
Fax: NA
E-mail: max.robins@reedbusiness.com
http://www.broadcastingcable.com

Broadcast Engineering
9800 Metcalf Avenue
Overland Park, KS 66212
Phone: (913) 967-1737
Fax: (913) 967-1905
E-mail: BDick@primediabusiness.com
http://www.broadcastengineering.com

Cable World Magazine
Access Intelligence, LLC
4 Choke Cherry Road, 2nd floor
Rockville, MD 20850
Phone: (301) 354-2000
Fax: (301) 738-8453

E-mail: ddeker@accessintel.com
http://www.accessintel.com

CableFAX Magazine
Access Intelligence, LLC
4 Choke Cherry Road, 2nd floor
Rockville, MD 20850
Phone: (301) 354-2000
Fax: (301) 738-8453
E-mail: ddeker@accessintel.com
http://www.accessintel.com

Cinefex
P.O. Box 20027
Riverside, CA 92516
Phone: (951) 781-1917
Fax: (951) 788-1793
E-mail: info@cinefex.com
http://www.cinefex.com

Communications Daily
Warren Communications News, Inc.
2115 Ward Court NW
Washington, DC 20037
Phone: (800) 771-9202
Fax: (202) 318-8350
E-mail: NA
http://www.warren-news.com

Communications Technology
Access Intelligence, LLC
4 Choke Cherry Road, 2nd floor
Rockville, MD 20850
Phone: (301) 354-1785
Fax: (301) 738-8453
E-mail: jgunderson@accessintel.com
http://www.ct-magazine.com

Creative Screenwriting
404 Hollywood Boulevard, Suite 415
Los Angeles, CA 90028
Phone: (323) 957-1405
Fax: (323) 957-1406
E-mail: info@creativescreenwriting.com
http://www.creativescreenwriting.com

Current Newspaper
6930 Carroll Avenue, Suite 350
Takoma Park, MD 20912
Phone: (301) 270-7240, ext. 36
Fax: NA
E-mail: info@current.org
http://www.current.org

DGA (Directors Guild of America)
Monthly
7920 Sunset Boulevard, 5th floor
Los Angeles CA 90046
Phone: (310) 289-5333
Fax: NA
E-mail: dgamonthly@dga.org
http://www.dga.org

Digital Cinematography
creativePLANETCommunities
865 South Figueroa Street, Suite 2330
Los Angeles, CA 90017
Phone: (213) 228-0381
Fax: NA
E-mail: newsinfo@creativeplanet.com
http://www.dcinematography.com

Emmy Magazine
c/o Academy of Television Arts and
Sciences
5220 Lankershim Boulevard
North Hollywood, CA 91601
Phone: (818) 754-2860
Fax: (818) 761-2827
E-mail: emmymag@emmys.org
http://www.emmys.org

Entertainment Employment Journal
5632 Van Nuys Boulevard, Suite 320
Van Nuys, CA 91401
Phone: (818) 776-2800
Fax: NA
E-mail: NA
http://www.eej.com

Entertainment Weekly
1675 Broadway, 30th floor
New York, NY 10019
Phone: (212) 522-5600
Fax: (212) 522-5600
E-mail: letters@ew.com
http://www.ew.com

Fade In
2289 South Robertson Boulevard,
Suite 465
Beverly Hills, CA 90211
Phone: (800) 646-3896
Fax: N/A
E-mail: inquiries@fadeinonline.com
http://www.fadeinmag.com

Film & Video
110 William Street, 11th floor
New York, NY 10038
Phone: (212) 621-4900
Fax: (212) 621-4635
E-mail: FNV@omeda.com
http://www.studiodaily.com/filmandvideo/
contact.html

Filmmaker Magazine
501 Fifth Avenue, Suite 1714
New York, NY 10017
Phone: (212) 983-3150
Fax: (212) 973-0318
E-mail: NA
http://www.filmmakermagazine.com

Film Music Magazine
1146 North Central Avenue, Suite 103
Glendale, CA 91202
Phone: (888) 456-5020
Fax: NA
E-mail: info@filmmusicmag.com
http://www.filmmusicmag.com

Film Quarterly
University of California Press
Journals Division
2000 Center Street, Suite 303
Berkeley, CA 94704
Phone: (510) 643-7154
Fax: (510) 642-9917
E-mail: journals@ucpress.edu
http://www.ucpress.edu/journals/fq

The Hollywood Reporter
VNU Business Publications
5055 Wilshire Boulevard, 6th floor
Los Angeles, CA 90036
Phone: (323) 525-2000
Fax: (323) 525-2377
E-mail: info@hollywoodreporter.com
http://www.hollywoodreporter.com

Hollywood Scriptwriter
P.O. Box 10277
Burbank, CA 91510
Phone: (818) 845-5525
Fax: N/A
E-mail: info@hollywoodscriptwriter.com
http://www.hollywoodscriptwriter.com

IATSE Official Bulletin
c/o International Alliance of Theatrical
Stage Employees, Moving Picture
Machine Operators of the United
States and Canada
1430 Broadway, 20th floor
New York, NY 10018

Phone: (212) 730-1770
Fax: (212) 921-7699
E-mail: NA
http://www.iatse-intl.org

iCOM Magazine
300 Cloverdale Street
Hillsboro, TX 76645
Phone: (254) 582-3540
Fax: NA
E-mail: jerry@icommag.com
http://www.icommag.com

Journal of Broadcasting and Electronic
Media
Broadcast Education Association
1771 N Street NW
Washington, DC 20036
Phone: ((888) 380-7222
Fax: N/A
E-mail: Don.Godfrey@asu.edu
http://www.beaweb.org/publications.html

Make-Up Artist Magazine
4018 NE 112th Avenue, Suite D-8
Vancouver, WA 98682
Phone: (360) 882-3488
Fax: (360) 885-1836
E-mail: NA
http://www.makeupmag.com

Markee Magazine
HJK Publications, Inc.
366 East Graves Avenue, Suite D
Orange City, FL 32763
Phone: (386) 774-8881
Fax: (386) 774-8908
E-mail: markee@markeemag.com
http://www.markeemag.com

Medialine Magazine
United Entertainment Media
460 Park Avenue South, 9th floor
New York, NY 10016
Phone: (212) 378-0400
Fax: (212) 378-2160
E-mail: ljaffe@cmpinformation.com
http://www.cmpinformation.com

The Mercury Production Report
P.O. Box 461474
West Hollywood, CA 90046
Phone: (323) 816-3642
Fax: NA
E-mail: info@mercuryworld.com
http://www.mercuryprods.com

Millimeter Magazine
Primedia Business Magazines

9800 Metcalf Avenue
Overland Park, KS 66212
Phone: (913) 341-1300
Fax: (913) 967-1898
E-mail: cwisehart@millimeter.com
http://www.millimeter.com

Movieline Magazine
10537 Santa Monica Boulevard,
    Suite 250
Los Angeles, CA 90025
Phone: (310) 234-9501
Fax: NA
E-mail: info@movieline.com
http://www.movieline.com

MovieMaker Magazine
121 Fulton Street, 5th floor
New York, NY 10038
Phone: (212) 766-4100
Fax: (212) 766-4102
E-mail: NA
http://www.moviemaker.com

Multichannel News
Reed Business Information Publications
360 Park Avenue
New York, NY 10010
Phone: (646) 746-6581
Fax: (646) 746-7028.
E-mail: tom.steinerthrelkeld@
    reedbusiness.com
http://www.multichannel.com

MY Entertainment WORLD
P.O. Box 523
Melbourne, FL 32902
Phone: (321) 773-3615
Fax: NA
E-mail: mew@myentertainmentworld.com
http://www.myentertainmentworld.com

Premiere Magazine
Hachette Filipacchi Magazines, Inc.
1633 Broadway
New York, NY 10019
Phone: (212) 767-5400
Fax: (212) 767-5450
E-mail: NA
http://www.premieremag.com

Production Weekly
9669 Santa Monica Boulevard,
    Suite 1177
Beverly Hills, CA 90210
Phone: (800) 284-2230
Fax: (310) 868-2594
E-mail: info@productionweekly.com
http://www.productionweekly.com

P3—Production Update Magazine
7021 Hayvenhurst Avenue, Suite 205
Van Nuys, CA 91406
Phone: (818) 785-6362
Fax: (818) 785-8092
E-mail: NA
http://www.p3update.com

Scenario Magazine
104 Fifth Avenue, 19th floor
New York, NY 10011
Phone: (212) 463-0600
Fax: NA
E-mail: info@scenariomag.com
http://www.scenariomag.com

Screen Magazine
222 West Ontario Street, Suite 500
Chicago, IL 60610
Phone: (312) 640-0800
Fax: (312) 640-1928
E-mail: NA
http://www.screenmag.tv

Screenwriter
655 Fulton Street, Suite 276
Brooklyn, NY 11217
Phone: (800) 418-5637
Fax: (323) 372-3898
E-mail: info@screenwritermag.com
http://www.screenwritermag.com

Scr(i)pt
5638 Sweet Air Road
Baldwin, MD 21013
Phone: (888) 245-2228
Fax: (410) 592-8062
E-mail: editor@scriptmag.com
http://www.scriptmag.com

Sound & Vision
Hachette Filipacchi Magazines, Inc.
1633 Broadway
New York, NY 10019
Phone: (212) 767-6000
Fax: (212) 767-5615
E-mail: soundandvision@hfmus.com
http://www.soundandvisionmag.com

Television Broadcast
Entertainment Technology Network CMP
    Information, Inc.
460 Park Avenue South, 9th floor
New York, NY 10016
Phone: (212) 378-0400
Fax: (212) 378-2160
E-mail: televisionbroadcast@
    cmpinformation.com
http://www.cmpi-us.com

Television Week
6500 Wilshire Boulevard, Suite 7300
Los Angeles, CA 90048
Phone: (323) 370-2400
Fax: (323) 653-4425
E-mail: info@tvweek.com
http://www.tvweek.com

The TV Rundown
P.O. Box 335
Ardmore, PA 19003
Phone: NA
Fax: (610) 519-9221
E-mail: tv@tvrundown.com
http://www.tvrundown.com

TV Technology
IMAS Publishing, Inc.
P.O. Box 1214
Falls Church, VA, 22041
Phone: (703) 998-7600
Fax: (703) 998-2966
E-mail: JButts@imaspub.com
http://www.tvtechnology.com

TV Today
National Association of Broadcasters
1771 N Street NW
Washington, DC 20036
Phone: (202) 429-5300
Fax: (202) 429-4199
E-mail: info@www.nab.org
http://www.nab.org

Variety (Daily)
Reed Business Information, Inc.
5700 Wilshire Boulevard, Suite 120
Los Angeles, CA 90036
Phone: (323) 857-6600
Fax: (323) 857-0494
E-mail: news@reedbusiness.com
http://www.variety.com

Variety (Weekly)
Reed Business Information, Inc.
475 Park Avenue South
New York, NY 10016
Phone: (800) 552-3632
Fax: (310) 978-6901
E-mail: info@variety.com
http://www.variety.com

Videography Magazine
Entertainment Technology Network CMP
    Information, Inc.
460 Park Avenue South, 9th floor
New York, NY 10016
Phone: (212) 378-0400
Fax: (212) 378-2160

E-mail: videography@cmpinformation.com
http://www.cmpi-us.com

Videomaker Magazine
P.O. Box 4591
Chico, CA 95927
Phone: (530) 891-8410
Fax: (530) 891-8443
E-mail: At Web site
http://www.videomaker.com

Video Systems Magazine
Primedia Business Magazine
9800 Metcalf Avenue
Overland Park, KS 66212
Phone: (913) 341-1300
Fax: (913) 967-1898
E-mail: cwisehart@videosystems.com
http://www.videosystems.com

Written By
7000 West 3rd Street
Los Angeles, CA 90048
Phone: (323) 782-4522
Fax: (323) 782-4802
E-mail: info@wga.org
http://www.wga.org

DIRECTORIES AND YEARBOOKS

The ACME Resource Network for Film & Television's Designing Arts
The ACME Resource Network, 2005
http://www.theacme.com

The Alternative Pick
Storm Music Entertainment, 2005
http://www.altpick.com

ASCAP Resource Guide
American Society of Composers, Authors, and Publishers (ASCAP), 2005
http://www.ascap.com

Below-The-Line Talent, 9th Edition
Hollywood Creative Directory, 2004
http://www.hcdonline.com

Blu-Book Production Directory
edited by the staff of Hollywood Creative Directory

The Hollywood Reporter and Hollywood Creative Directory, 2005
http://www.hcdonline.com

Broadcasting and Cable Yearbook 2005
R. R. Bowker, 2004
http://www.bowker.com

Debbies Book: Resources for Professionals in Entertainment Industries
Debbies Book, 2005
http://www.debbiesbook.com

DGA Membership Directory
Directors Guild of America, 2005
http://www.dga.org

Entertainment Partners' Paymaster Book, 2005–2006
Entertainment Partners
https://webstore.entertainmentpartners.com

Film Actors, 6th Edition
Hollywood Creative Directory, 2005
http://www.hcdonline.com

Film Directors, 16th Edition
Hollywood Creative Directory, 2005
http://www.hcdonline.com

Film Writers, 10th Edition
Hollywood Creative Directory, 2005
http://www.hcdonline.com

Gale Directory of Publications and Broadcast Media
Thomson Gale, 2005
http://www.gale.com

High Def 411, Volume 4
411 Publishing Company, 2005
http://www.la411.com

Hollywood Creative Directory, 55th Edition
Hollywood Creative Directory, 2005
http://www.hcdonline.com

Hollywood Distributors Directory, 16th Edition
Hollywood Creative Directory, 2005
http://www.hcdonline.com

Hollywood Music Industry Directory, 2nd Edition
Hollywood Creative Directory, 2005
http://www.hcdonline.com

Hollywood Representation Directory, 30th Edition
Hollywood Creative Directory, 2005
http://www.hcdonline.com

LA 411, 2005 Edition
411 Publishing Company, 2005
http://www.la411.com

Mandy's International Film and Television Production Directory
Lighthouse Internet. Ltd.
http://www.mandy.com

Motion Picture, TV and Theatre Directory
by Herbert R. Pilzer.
Motion Picture Enterprises Publications, Inc., 2005

New York Production Guide
New York Production Guide, Ltd., 2005
http://www.nypg.com

NY 411, 2005–2006 Edition
411 Publishing Company, 2005
http://www.la411.com

Pacific Coast Studio Directory
Visualnet, 2005
http://pacificcoaststudiodirectory.visualnet.com

Plunkett's Entertainment & Media Industry Almanac 2005
Plunkett Research, Ltd.
http://www.plunkettresearch.com

Producer's Masterguide.
Producer's Masterguide, 2005
http://www.producers.masterguide.com

Showbiz Labor Guide, 10th Edition (2004–2005)
Entertainment Publishers, Inc., 2005
http://www.laborguide.com

U.S. Directory of Entertainment Employers, 2005–2006
Studiolot Publishing
http://www.entertainmentemployers.com

APPENDIX III
PROFESSIONAL, INDUSTRY, AND TRADE ASSOCIATIONS, GUILDS, AND UNIONS

Since many of these organizations operate on limited budgets, be sure to enclose a self-addressed, stamped envelope when querying any of them for data not available online. Not all of these groups maintain full-time offices, so some cannot be reached via phone, fax, or e-mail. In addition, contact information for some of these organizations may change when a new president or director is selected.

When an organization has several branch offices listed but only a general e-mail and/or Web site, the latter data is placed flush left *after* the various branch listings.

A. GUILDS AND UNIONS

Actors Equity Association (AEA)
165 West 46th Street
New York, NY 10036
Phone: (212) 869-8530
Fax: (212) 719-9815
E-mail: info@actorsequity.org
http://www.actorsequity.org

Affiliated Property Craftpersons
Local 44 of IATSE
12021 Riverside Drive
North Hollywood, CA 91607
Phone: (818) 769-2500
Fax: (818) 769-1739
E-mail: info@local44.org
http://www.local44.org

American Federation of Musicians (AFM)
Local 802 of AFL-CIO
New York Headquarters
1501 Broadway, Suite 600
New York, NY 10036
Phone: (212) 869-1330
Fax: (212) 764-6134
West Coast Office
3550 Wilshire Boulevard, Suite 1900
Los Angeles, CA 90010
Phone: (213) 251-4510
Fax: (213) 251-4520
E-mail: info@afm.org
http://www.afm.org

American Federation of State, County and Municipal Employees (AFSCEME)
1625 L Street NW

Washington, DC 20036
Phone: (202) 429-1000
Fax: (202) 429-1293
E-mail: info@afscme.org
http://www.afscme.org

American Federation of Television and Radio Artists (AFTRA) New York
National Office
260 Madison Avenue
New York, NY 10016
Phone: (212) 532-0800
Fax: (212) 532-2242
Los Angeles National Office
5757 Wilshire Boulevard, 9th floor
Los Angeles, CA 90036
Phone: (323) 634-8100
Fax: (323) 634-8194
E-mail: info@aftra.org
http://www.aftra.org

The Animation Guild and Affiliated Optical Electronic and Graphic Arts
Local 839 of IATSE
4729 Lankershim Boulevard
North Hollywood, CA 91602
Phone: (818) 766-7151
Fax: (818) 506-4805
E-mail: mpsc839@mindspring.com
http://www.mpsc839.org

Art Directors Guild and Scenic, Title and Graphic Artists
Local 800 of IATSE
11969 Ventura Boulevard, Suite 200
Studio City, CA 91604
Phone: (818) 762-9995
Fax: (818) 762-9997

E-mail: Karen@ialocal800.org [Art Directors Guild]
Lydia@ialocal800.org [Scenic, Title & Graphic Artists]
http://www.ialocal800.org

Communications Workers of America (CWA)
501 Third Street NW
Washington, DC 20001
Phone: (202) 434-1100
Fax: (202) 434-1279
E-mail: cwaweb@cwa-union.org
http://www.cwa-union.org

Costume Designers Guild (CDG)
Local 892 of IATSE
4730 Woodman Avenue, Suite 430
Sherman Oaks, CA 91423
Phone: (818) 905-1557
Fax: (818) 905-1560
E-mail: cdgia@earthlink.net
http://www.costumedesignersguild.com

Directors Guild of America (DGA)
Los Angeles Headquarters
7920 Sunset Boulevard
Los Angeles, CA 90046
Phone: (310) 289-2000
Fax: (310) 289-2029
New York Headquarters
110 West 57th Street
New York, NY 10019
Phone: (212) 581-0370
Fax: (212) 581-1441
E-mail: info@dga.org
http://www.dga.org

Illustrators and Matte Artists
Local 790 of IATSE
13245 Riverside Drive, Suite 300
Sherman Oaks, CA 91423
Phone: (818) 784-6555
Fax: (818) 784-2004
E-mail: NA
http://www.790.org

**International Alliance of Theatrical
Stage Employees, Moving Picture
Machine Operators of the United
States and Canada (IATSE)**
General Office
1430 Broadway, 20th floor
New York, NY 10018
Phone: (212) 730-1770
Fax: (212) 921-7699
West Coast Office
10045 Riverside Drive
Toluca Lake, CA 91602
Phone: 818-980-3499
Fax: 818-980-3496
E-mail: NA
http://www.iatse-intl.org

**International Brotherhood of Electrical
Workers**
National Headquarters
900 Seventh Street NW
Washington, DC 20001
Phone: (202) 833-7000
Fax: (202) 728-7676
Local 40
5643 Vineland Avenue
North Hollywood, CA 91601
Phone: (818) 762-4239
Fax: (818) 762-4379
E-mail: info@ibew.org
http://www.ibew.org

**International Cinematographers
Guild**
Local 600 of IATSE
National Office/Western Region
7755 Sunset Boulevard
Hollywood, CA 90046
Phone: (323) 876-0160
Fax: (323) 876-6383
Eastern Region Office
80 Eighth Avenue, 14th floor
New York, NY 10011
Phone: (212) 647-7300
Fax: (212) 647-7317
E-mail: admin@cameraguild.com
http://www.cameraguild.com

**International Production Sound
Technicians, Television Engineers,
and Video Assist Technicians**
Local 695 of IATSE
5439 Cahuenga Boulevard
North Hollywood, CA 91601
Phone: (818) 985-9204
Fax: (818) 760-4681
E-mail: info@695.com
http://www.695.com

Makeup Artists and Hairstylists
Local 706 of IATSE
828 North Hollywood Way
Burbank, CA 91505
Phone: (818) 295-3933
Fax: (818) 295-3930
E-mail: NA
http://www.local706.org

Motion Picture Editors Guild
Local 700 of IATSE
7715 Sunset Boulevard, Suite 200
Los Angeles, CA 90046
Phone: (323) 876-4770
Fax: (323) 876-0861
E-mail: aherrmann@editorsguild.com
http://www.editorsguild.com

**Motion Picture Set Painters and Sign
Writers**
Local 729 of IATSE
1811 West Burbank Boulevard
Burbank, CA 91506
Phone: (818) 842-7729
Fax: (818) 846-3729
E-mail: ialocal729@earthlink.net
http://www.ialocal729.com

Motion Picture Studio Grips
Local 80 of IATSE
2520 West Olive Avenue
Burbank, CA 91505
Phone: (818) 526-0700
Fax: (818) 526-0719
E-mail: info@iatselocal80.org
http://www.iatselocal80.org

**National Association of Broadcast
Employees and Technicians AFL-
CIO (NABET)**
501 Third Street NW, 8th floor
Washington, DC 20001
Phone: (202) 434-1254
Fax: (202) 434-1426
E-mail: nabet@cwa-union.org
http://www.nabetcwa.org

Producers Guild of America (PGA)
8530 Wilshire Boulevard, Suite 450

Beverly Hills, CA 90211
Phone: (310) 358-9020
Fax: (310) 358-9520
E-mail: info@producersguild.org
http://www.producersguild.org

Screen Actors Guild (SAG)
Los Angeles Office
5757 Wilshire Boulevard, Suite 1900
Los Angeles, CA 90036
Phone: (323) 954-1600
Fax: (323) 549-6603
New York Office
360 Madison Avenue, 12th floor
New York, NY 10017
Phone: (212) 944-1030
Fax: (212) 944-6774
E-mail: saginfo@sag.org
http://www.sag.org

**Script Supervisors/Continuity and
Allied Production Specialists**
Local 871 of IATSE
11519 Chandler Boulevard
North Hollywood, CA 91601
Phone: (818) 509-7871
Fax: NA
E-mail: ialocal871office@aol.com
http://www.ialocal871.org

Set Designers and Model Makers
Local 847 of IATSE
13245 Riverside Drive, Suite 300
Sherman Oaks, CA 91423
Phone: (818) 784-6555
Fax: (818) 784-2004
E-mail: local847@earthlink.net
http://www.local847.org

Songwriters Guild of America (SGA)
Administrative Office
1500 Harbor Boulevard
Weehawken, NJ 070806
Phone: (201) 867-7603
Fax: (201) 867-7535
E-mail: nj@songwritersguild.com
West Coast Office
6430 Sunset Boulevard, Suite 705
Hollywood, CA 90028
Phone: (323) 462-1108
Fax: (323) 462-5430
E-mail: la@songwritersguild.com
Central (Nashville) Office
1222 16th Avenue South, Suite 25
Nashville, TN 37212
Phone: (615) 329-1782
Fax: (615) 329-2623
E-mail: nash@songwritersguild.com

East Coast Office
1560 Broadway, Suite 1306
New York, NY 10036
Phone: (212) 768-7902
Fax: (212) 768-9048
E-mail: ny@songwritersguild.com
http://www.songwritersguild.com

Studio Electrical Lighting Technicians
Local 728 of IATSE
14629 Nordoff Street
Panorama City, CA 91402
Phone: (818) 891-0728
Fax: (818) 891-5288
E-mail: info@728.org
http://www.728.org

Theatrical and Television Stage
  Employees
Local 33 of IATSE
1720 West Magnolia Boulevard
Burbank, CA 91506
Phone: (818) 841-9233
Fax: (818) 567-1138
E-mail: info@ia33.org
http://www.ia33.org

United Scenic Artists
Local 829 of IATSE
New York Office
29 West 38th Street
New York, NY 10018
Phone: (212) 581-0300
Fax: (212) 977-2011
Los Angeles Office
5225 Wilshire Boulevard, Suite 506
Los Angeles, CA 90036
Phone: (323) 965-0957
Fax: (323) 965-0958
E-mail: info@usa829.org
http://www.usa829.org

Writers Guild of America, East
  (WGAE)
555 West 57th Street
New York, NY 10019
Phone: (212) 767-7800
Fax: (212) 582-1909
E-mail: info@wgaeaStreet.org
http://www.wgaeaStreet.org

Writers Guild of America, West
  (WGA)
7000 West Third Street
Los Angeles, CA 90048
Phone: (323) 951-4000
Fax: (323) 782-4800
E-mail: website@wga.org
http://www.wga.org

B. ASSOCIATIONS

Academy of Motion Picture Arts and
  Sciences (AMPAS)
8949 Wilshire Boulevard
Beverly Hills, CA 90211
Phone: (310) 247-3000
Fax: (310) 859-9351
E-mail: ampas@oscars.org
http://www.oscars.org

Academy of Science Fiction, Fantasy
  and Horror
334 West 54th Street
Los Angeles, CA 90037
Phone: (323) 752-8811
Fax: NA
E-mail: scifiacademy@comcaStreetnet
http://www.saturnawards.org

Academy of Television Arts and
  Sciences
5220 Lankershim Boulevard
North Hollywood, CA 91601
Phone: (818) 754-2800
Fax: (818) 761-2827
E-mail: bryce@emmys.org
http://www.emmys.org

Advertising Research Foundation
  (ARF)
641 Lexington Avenue
New York, NY 10022
Phone: (212) 751-5656
Fax: (212) 319-5265
E-mail: info@thearf.org
http://www.arfsite.org

Alliance of Motion Picture and
  Television Producers (AMPTP)
15503 Ventura Boulevard
Encino, CA 91436
Phone: (818) 995-3600
Fax: (818) 382-1793
E-mail: info@amptp.org
http://www.amptp.org

American Academy of Arts & Letters
633 West 155th Street
New York, NY 10032
Phone: (212) 368-5900
Fax: NA
E-mail: NA
http://www.nyc-arts.org

American Advertising Federation
  (AAF)
1101 Vermont Avenue, Suite 500
Washington, DC 2005

Phone: (202) 898-0089
Fax: (202) 898-0159
E-mail: aaf@aaf.org
http://www.aaf.org

American Cinema Editors, Inc. (ACE)
100 Universal City Plaza, Building 2352,
  Room 202
Universal City, CA 91608
Phone: (818) 777-2900
Fax: (818) 733-5023
E-mail: info@ace-filmeditors.org
http://www.ace-filmeditors.org

American Dance Guild (ADG)
P.O. Box 2006
Lenox Hill Station
New York, NY 10021
Phone: (212) 932-2789
Fax: NA
E-mail: info@americandanceguild.com
http://www.americandanceguild.com

American Federation of Television and
  Radio Artists (AFTRA)
260 Madison Avenue
New York, NY 10016
Phone: (212) 532-0800
Fax: (212) 532-2242
E-mail: info@aftra.com
http://www.aftra.org

American Film Institute (AFI)
2021 North Western Avenue
Los Angeles, CA 90027
Phone: (323) 856-7600
Fax: (323) 467-4578
E-mail: info@afi.com
http://www.afi.com

American Institute of Graphic Arts
  (AIGA)
164 Fifth Avenue
New York, NY 10010
Phone: (212) 807-1990
Fax: (212) 807-1799
E-mail: comments@aiga.org
http://www.aiga.org

American Marketing Association
  (AMA)
250 South Wacker Drive, Suite 200
Chicago, IL 60606
Phone: (312) 542-9000
Fax: (312) 542-9001
E-mail: info@ama.org
http://www.marketingpower.com

American Society of Cinematographers (ASC)
1782 North Orange Drive
Hollywood, CA 90028
Phone: (323) 969-4333
Fax: (323) 876-4973
E-mail: info@theasc.com
http://www.theasc.com

American Society of Composers, Authors, and Publishers (ASCAP)
1 Lincoln Plaza
New York, NY 10023
Phone: (212) 621-6000
Fax: (212) 724-9064
E-mail: info@ascap.com
http://www.ascap.com

American Society of Journalists and Authors (ASJA)
1501 Broadway, Suite 302
New York, NY 10036
Phone: (212) 997-0947
Fax: (212) 768-7414
E-mail: staff@asja.org
http://www.asja.org

American Society of Media Photographers (ASMP)
14 Washington Road, Suite 502
Princeton Junction, NJ 08550
Phone: (609) 799-8300
Fax: (609) 799-2232
E-mail: info@asmp.org
http://www.asmp.org

American Society of TV Cameramen
2520 Lotus Hill Drive
Las Vegas, NV 89134
Phone: (702) 228-6704
Fax: (702) 228-6701
E-mail: NA
Web site: NA

American Sportscaster Association (ASA)
225 Broadway, Suite 2020
New York, NY 10007
Phone: (212) 227-8080
Fax: (212) 571-0556
E-mail: NA
http://www.americansportscasters.com

American Women in Radio and Television (AWRT)
8405 Greensboro Drive, Suite 800
McLean, VA 22102
Phone: (703) 506-3290
Fax: (703) 506-3266
E-mail: info@awrt.org
http://www.awrt.com

Associated Press (AP)
450 West 33rd Street
New York, NY 10001
Phone: (212) 621-1500
Fax: NA
Email: info@aps.org
http://www.ap.org

Associated Press Television News
Association Press Broadcast News Center
1825 K Street NW, Suite 800
Washington, DC 20006
Phone: (202) 736-9500
Fax: NA
E-mail: bkalbfeld@ap.org
http://www.ap.org

Association for Educational Communications and Technology (AECT)
1800 North Stonelake Drive, Suite 2
Bloomington, IN 47401
Phone: (812) 335-7675
Fax: (812) 335-7678
E-mail: aect@aect.org
http:www.aect.org

Association for Maximum Service Television, Inc. (MSTV)
4100 Wisconsin Avenue NW
Washington, DC 20016
Phone: (202) 966-1956
Fax: (202) 966-9617
E-mail: sbaurenfeind@mstv.org
http://www.mstv.org

Association for Women in Communications (AWC)
1255 Ritchie Highway, Suite 6
Arnold, MD 21012
Phone: (410) 544-7442
Fax: (410) 544-4640
E-mail: pat@womcom.org
http://www.womcom.org

Association for Women Journalists (AWJ)
P.O. Box 2199
Fort Worth, TX 76113
Phone: (214) 740-9251
Fax: NA
E-mail: ssprague@kera.org
http://www.awjdfw.org

Association of America's Public Television Stations (APTS)
666 11th Street NW
Washington, DC 20001
Phone: (202) 654-4200

Fax: (202) 654-4236
E-mail: kwilson@apts.org
http://www.apts.org

Association of Cinema and Video Laboratories (ACVL)
1000 Hopor Boulevard
Pittsburgh, PA 15205
Phone: (412) 937-7700
Fax: (412) 922-2418
E-mail: kim@webworkscreative.com
http://www.acvl.org

Association of Graphic Communications (AGC)
330 Seventh Avenue, 9th floor
New York, NY 10001
Phone: (212) 279-2100
Fax: (212) 279-5381
E-mail: info@agcomm.org
http://www.agcomm.org

Association of Independent Commercial Producers (AICP)
National Headquarters
3 West 18th Street, 5th floor
New York, NY 10011
Phone: (212) 929-3000
Fax: (212) 929-3359
E-mail: mattm@aicp.com
Los Angeles Office
650 North Bronson Avenue, Suite 223B
Los Angeles, CA 90004
Phone: (323) 960-4763
Fax: (323) 960-4766
E-mail: stevec@aicp.com
http://www.aicp.com

Association of Independent Video and Filmmakers (AIVF)
304 Hudson Street, 6th floor
New York, NY 10013
Phone: (212) 807-1400
Fax: (212) 463-8519
E-mail: info@aivf.org
http:www.aivf.org

Association of Local Television Stations (ALTV)
1320 19th Street NW, Suite 300
Washington, DC 20036
Phone: (202) 887-1970
Fax: (202) 887-0950
E-mail: altv@erols.com or altv@aol.com
http:www.altv.com

Association of Moving Image Archivists (AMIA)
1313 North Vine Street
Hollywood, CA 90028

Phone: (323) 463-1500
Fax: (323) 463-1506
E-mail: AMIA@amianet.org
http://www.amaianet.org

Audio Engineering Society, Inc.
60 East 42nd Street, Room 2520
New York, NY 10165
Phone: (212) 661-8528
Fax: (212) 682-0477
E-mail: at Web site
http://www.aes.org

Authors Guild
31 East 28th Street
New York, NY 10016
Phone: (212) 563-5904
Fax: (212) 564-5363
E-mail: staff@authorsguild.com
http://www.authorsguild.org

Authors League of America
31 East 28th Street, 10th floor
New York, NY 10016
Phone: (212) 564-8350
Fax: (212) 564-8363
E-mail: staff@authorsguild.org
http://www.authorsguild.org

Black Writer's Alliance
c/o Tia Shabazz
P.O. Box 700065
Dallas, TX 75370
Phone: NA
Fax: NA
E-mail: tiashabazz@blackwriters.org
http://www.blackwriters.org

British Broadcasting Corporation (BBC)
BBC Worldwide Americas
747 Third Avenue
New York, NY 10017
Phone: (212) 705-9300
Fax: (212) 888-0576
E-mail: NA
http:www.bbc.co.uk

Broadcast Cable Financial Management Association (BCFMA)
550 West Frontage Road, Suite 3600
Northfield, IL 60093
Phone: (847) 716-7000
Fax: (847) 716-7004
E-mail: NA
http://www.bcfm.com

Broadcast Designers Association International (BDA)
2029 Century Park East, Suite 555
Los Angeles, CA 90067

Phone: (310) 712-0040
Fax: (310) 712-0039
E-mail: BDAnet@aol.com
http:www.bdaonline.org

Broadcast Education Association (BEA)
1771 N Street NW
Washington, DC 20036
Phone: (202) 429-5354
Fax: (202) 429-5343
E-mail: bea@nab.org
http:www.beaweb.org

Broadcast Music, Inc. (BMI)
320 West 57th Street
New York, NY 10019
Phone: (212) 586-2000
Fax: (212) 245-8986
E-mail: info@bmi.com
http://www.bmi.com

Broadcast Technological Society
See **Institute of Electrical and Electronics Engineers, Inc. (IEEE)**

Broadcasting Training Program
P.O. Box 67132
Century City, CA 90067
Phone: (323) 571-0766
Fax: (310) 388-1383
E-mail: EmailUs@theBroadcaster.com
http://www.theBroadcaster.com

Cable and Telecommunications Association for Marketing (CTAM)
201 North Union Street, Suite 440
Alexandria, VA 23314
Phone: (703) 549-2000
Fax: (703) 684-1167
E-mail: info@ctam.com
http://www.ctam.com

Cable Television Advertising Bureau (CAB)
830 Third Avenue, 2nd floor
New York, NY 10022
Phone: (212) 508-1200
Fax: (212) 832-3268
E-mail: info@onetvworld.org
http://www.onetvworld.org

Cable Television Laboratories, Inc. (CableLabs)
858 Coal Creek Circle
Louisville, CO 80027
Phone: (303) 661-9100
Fax: (303) 661-9199
E-mail: m.schwartz@cablelabs.com
http://www.cablelabs.com

Cable Television Public Affairs Association (CTPAA)
P.O. Box 33697
Washington, DC 20033
Phone: (202) 775-1081
Fax: NA
E-mail: at Web site
http://www.ctpaa.org

Casting Society of America (CSA)
606 North Larchmont Boulevard, Suite 4-B
Los Angeles, CA 90004
Phone: (323) 463-1925
Fax: NA
E-mail: info@castingsociety.com
http://www.castingsociety.com

Caucus for Television Producers, Writers and Directors
P.O. Box 11236
Burbank, CA 91510
Phone: (818) 843-7572
Fax: (818) 846-2159
E-mail: caucuspwd@aol.com
http://caucus.org

Center for Communication
561 Broadway, Suite 12-B
New York, NY 10012
Phone: (212) 686-5005
Fax: (212) 504-2632
E-mail: info@cencom.org
http://www.cencom.org

Citizens for Independent Public Broadcasting (CIPB)
901 Old Hickory Road
Pittsburgh, PA 15243
Phone: (412) 341-1967
Fax: (412) 341-6533
E-mail: jmstarr@adelphia.net
http://www.cipbonline.org

Corporation for Public Broadcasting (CPB)
401 Ninth Street NW
Washington, DC 20004
Phone: (202) 879-9600
Fax: (202) 879-9700
E-mail: info@cpb.org
http://www.cpb.org

The Dramatists Guild of America, Inc.
1501 Broadway, Suite 701
New York, NY 10036
Phone: (212) 398-9366
Fax: (212) 944-0420

E-mail: info@dramatistsguild.com
http://www.dramaguild.com

**Entertainment Resources and
  Marketing Association (ERMA)**
5155 Rosecrans Avenue, Suite 217
Los Angeles, CA 90750
Phone: (562) 694-3793
Fax: (562) 697-1397
E-mail: info@emainc.org
http://emainc.org

**Federal Communications Commission
  (FCC)**
445 12th Street SW
Washington, DC 20554
Phone: (888) 225-5322
Fax: (202) 418-0232
E-mail: fccinfo@fcc.gov
http://www.fcc.gov

**Graphic Communications Association
  (GCA)**
100 Dangerfield Road
Alexandria, VA 22314
Phone: (703) 519-8160
Fax: (703) 548-2867
E-mail: info@gca.org
http://www.gca.org

**Great Plains National Instructional
  Television Library (GPN)**
P.O. Box 80669
Lincoln, NE 68501
Phone: (800) 228-4630
Fax: (800) 306-2330
E-mail: gpn@unl.edu
http://gpn.unl.edu

**The Hollywood Foreign Press
  Association (HFPA)**
646 North Robertson Boulevard
West Hollywood, CA 90069
Phone: (310) 657-1731
Fax: (310) 657-5576
E-mail: info@hfpa.org
http://www.hfpa.org

Hollywood Post Alliance
225 East 9th Street, Suite 299
Los Angeles, CA 90025
Phone: (213) 614-0860
Fax: (213) 614-0890
E-mail: ekramer@hpaonline.org
http://www.hpaonline.org

**Hollywood Radio and Television
  Society (HRTS)**
13701 Riverside Drive, Suite 205
Sherman Oaks, CA 91423

Phone: (818) 789-1182
Fax: (818) 789-1210
E-mail: info@hrts.com
http://www.hrts.com

**Independent Film and Television
  Alliance (IFTA)**
(formerly **American Film Marketing
  Association**)
10850 Wilshire Boulevard, 9th floor
Los Angeles, CA 90024
Phone: (310) 446-1000
Fax: (310) 446-1600
E-mail: iffo@ifta-online.org
http://www.ifta-online.org

Independent Television Service (ITVS)
501 York Street
San Francisco, CA 94110
Phone: (415) 356-8383
Fax: (415) 356-8391
E-mail: itvs@itvs.org
http://www.itvs.org

**Institute of Electrical and Electronics
  Engineers, Inc. (IEEE)**
Corporate Office
3 Park Avenue, 17th floor
New York, NY 10016
Phone: (212) 419-7900
Fax: (212) 752-4929
Broadcast Technological Society
445 Hoes Lane
Piscataway, NJ 08854
Phone: (732) 562-3846
Fax: (732) 981-1769
E-mail: a.monroe@ieee.org
http://www.ieee.org/organizations/society
  /bt/online_exhibit.html
Computer Society Headquarters
1730 Massachusetts Avenue NW
Washington, DC 20036
Phone: (202) 371-0101
Fax: (202) 728-9614
Operations Center
445 Hoes Lane
Piscataway, NJ 08854
Phone: (732) 981-0060
Fax: (732) 981-1721
Publications Office
10662 Los Vaqueros Circle
P.O. Box 3014
Los Alamitos, CA 90720
Phone: (714) 821-8380
Fax: (714) 821-4010
E-mail: info@ieee.org
http://www.ieee.org

**International Academy of Television
  Arts and Sciences Foundation**
142 West 57th Street, 16th floor
New York, NY 10019
Phone: (212) 489-6969
Fax: NA
E-mail: info@iemmys.tv
http://www.iemmys.tv

**International Radio and Television
  Society—Alpha Epsilon Rho**
Millersville University, Department of
  Communications and Theatre
Millersville, PA 17551
Phone: (717) 871-03233
Fax: (717) 871-2051
E-mail: At Web site
http://muweb.millersville.edu/~~theatre

**International Radio and Television
  Society Foundation, Inc. (IRTS)**
420 Lexington Avenue, Suite 1601
New York, NY 10170
Phone: (212) 867-6650
Fax: (212) 867-6653
E-mail: info@irts.org
http://www.irts.org

**International Society of Certified
  Electronics Technicians (ISCET)**
3608 Pershing Avenue
Fort Worth, TX 76107
Phone: (817) 921-9101
E-mail: info@iscet.org
http://www.iscet.org

**International Teleproduction Society
  (ITS)**
527 Maple Avenue East, Suite 204
Vienna, VA 22180
Phone: (703) 319-0800
Fax: (703) 319-1120
E-mail: NA
http://www.its.org

Kidsnet
6856 Eastern Avenue NW, Suite 208
Washington, DC 20012
Phone: (202) 291-1400
Fax: (202) 882-7315
E-mail: kidsnet@aol.com
http:///www.kidsnet.org

**Latino Public Broadcasting Project
  (LPBP)**
6777 Hollywood Boulevard, Suite 500
Los Angeles, CA 90028

Phone: (323) 466-7110
Fax: (323) 466-7521
E-mail: lpb@lpbp.org
http://www.lpbp.org

**Media Communications Association—
   International (MCA)**
(formerly **International Television
   Association [ITVA]**)
7600 Terrace Avenue, Suite 203
Middleton, WI 53562
Phone: (608) 927-5034
Fax: NA
E-mail: execdir@mca-i.org
http://www.mca-i.org

Media Networks, Inc. (MNI)
P. O. Box 10096
One Station Place
Stamford, CT 06904
Phone: (203) 967-3100
Fax: (203) 967-6472
E-mail: info@mni.com
http://www.mni.com

**Motion Picture Association of America
   (MPAA)**
15503 Ventura Boulevard
Encino, California 91436
Phone: (818) 995-6600
Fax: NA
E-mail: info@mpaa.org
http://www.mpaa.org

Motion Picture Sound Editors (MPSE)
10061 Riverside Drive
PMB Box 751
Toluca Lake, CA 91602
Phone: (818) 506-7731
Fax: (818) 506-7732
E-mail: mail@mpse.org
http://www.mpse.org

**National Academy of Recording Arts
   and Sciences (NARAS)**
3402 Pico Boulevard
Santa Monica, CA 90405
Phone: (310) 392-3777
Fax: (310) 392-9262
E-mail: losangeles@grammy.com
http://www.grammy.com

**National Academy of Television Arts
   and Sciences (NATAS)**
111 West 57th Street, Suite 1050
New York, NY 10019
Phone: (212) 586-8424
Fax: (212) 246-8129

E-mail: natashq@aol.com
http://www.emmyonline.com

**National Academy of Television
   Journalists (NATJ)**
P.O. Box 31
Salisbury, MD 21803
Phone: (410) 548-5343
Fax: (410) 543-0658
E-mail: nbayne@shore.intercom.net
http://www.GoldenViddyAwards.com

**National Alliance of Media Arts and
   Culture (NAMAC)**
4441 19th Street
San Francisco, CA 94114
Phone: (415) 552-9360
Fax: (415) 276-1873
E-mail: info@mission-minded.com
http://www.mission-minded.com

**National Asian American
   Telecommunications Association
   (NAATA)**
145 Ninth Street, Suite 350
San Francisco, CA 94103
Phone: (415) 863-0814
Fax: (415) 863-7428
E-mail: naata@naatanet.org
http://www.naatanet.org

**National Association for Multi-
   Ethnicity in Communications, Inc.
   (NAMIC)**
336 West 37th Street, Suite 302
New York, NY 10018
Phone: (212) 594-5985
Fax: (212) 594-8391
Email: info@namic.com
http://www.namic.com

**National Association of Broadcasters
   (NAB)**
1771 N Street NW
Washington, DC 20036
Phone: (202) 429-5300
Fax: (202) 775-3520
E-mail: ssiroky@nab.org
http://www.nab.org

**National Association of Farm
   Broadcasters (NAFB)**
P.O. Box 500
Platte City, MO 64079
Phone: (816) 431-4032
Fax: (816) 431-4087
E-mail: info@nafb.com
http://www.nafb.com

**National Association of Recording
   Merchandisers (NARM)**
9 Eves Drive
Marlton, NJ 08053
Phone: (856) 596-2221
Fax: (856) 596-3268
E-mail: info@narm.org
http://www.narm.org

**National Association of
   Telecommunications Officers and
   Advisors (NATOA)**
1800 Diagonal Road, Suite 495
Alexandria, VA 22314
Phone: (703) 519-8035
Fax: (703) 519-8036
E-mail: info@natoa.org
http://www.natoa.org

**National Association of Television
   Program Executives (NATPE)**
2425 Olympic Boulevard, Suite 600E
Santa Monica, CA 90404
Phone: (310) 453-4440
Fax: (310) 453-5258
E-mail: NA
http://www.natpe.org

**National Black Programming
   Consortium (NBPC)**
68 East 131st Street, 7th floor
New York, NY 10037
Phone: (212) 234-8200
Fax: (212) 234-7032
E-mail: info@nbpc.tv
http://www.nbpc.tv

**National Broadcast Association for
   Community Affairs (NBACA)**
1200 19th Street NW, Suite 300
Washington, DC 20036
Phone: (202) 857-1155
Fax: (202) 223-4579
E-mail: nbaca@yourlink.net
http://www.nbaca.com

**National Cable Television Association
   (NCTA)**
1724 Massachusetts Avenue NW
Washington, DC 20036
Phone: (202) 775-3669
Fax: (202) 775-3695
E-mail: webmaster@ncta.com
http://www.ncta.com

National Cable Television Center
2000 Buchtel Boulevard
Denver, CO 80210
Phone: (303) 871-4885

Fax: (303) 971-4514
E-mail: at Web site
http://www.cablecenter.org

National Cable Television Cooperative (NCTC)
11200 Corporate Avenue
Lenexa, KS 66219
Phone: (913) 599-5900
Fax: (913) 599-5903
E-mail: At Web site
http://www.cabletvcoop.org

National Cable Television Institute (NCTI)
8022 Southpark Circle, Suite 100
Littleton, CO 80120
Phone: (303) 797-9393
Fax: (303) 797-9394
E-mail: At Web site
http://www.ncti.org

National Communications Association (NCA)
1765 N Street NW
Washington, DC 20036
Phone: (202) 464-4622
Fax: (202) 464 4600
E-mail: dwallick@natcom.org
http://www.natcom.org

National Educational Telecommunications Association (NETA)
939 Stadium Road
Columbia, SC 29201
Phone: (803) 799-5517
Fax: (803) 771-4831
E-mail: At Web site
http://www.netaonline.org

National Endowment for the Arts (NEA)
1100 Pennsylvania Avenue NW
Washington, DC 20506
Phone: (202) 682-5400
Fax: (202) 682-5666
E-mail: webmgr@arts.endow.gov
http://arts.endow.gov

National Friends of Public Broadcasting (NFPB)
c/o WNET Friends of Thirteen
450 West 33rd Street
New York, NY 10001
Phone: (212) 560-2800
Fax: (212) 560-2091
E-mail: nfpb@thirteen.org
http://www.nfpb.com

National Instructional Television Fixed Service Association (NITFS)
77 West Canfield Street
Detroit, MI 48201
Phone: (305) 949-0175
Fax: (305) 949-1373
E-mail: donmacc@aol.com
http://www.itfs.org

National Religious Broadcasters (NRB)
9510 Technology Drive
Manassas, VA 20110
Phone: (703) 330-7000
Fax: (703) 330-7100
E-mail: info@nrb.org
http://www.nrb.org

National Sportscasters and Sportswriters Association (NSSA)
322 East Innes Street
Salisbury, NC 28144
Phone: (704) 633-4275
Fax: (704) 633-2027
E-mail: NA
http://www.nssahalloffame.com

Native American Public Telecommunications (NAPT)
1800 North 33rd Street
Lincoln, NE 68583
Phone: (402) 472-3522
Fax: (402) 472-8675
E-mail: native@unl.edu
http://www.nativetelecom.org

Network for Instructional TV, Inc. (NITV)
11490 Commerce Park Drive, Suite 110
Reston, Virginia 20191
Phone: (703) 860-9200
Fax: (703) 860-9237
E-mail: info@nitv.org
http://www.nitv.org

New York Women in Film & Television (NYWIFT)
6 East 39th Street, Suite 1200
New York, NY 10016
Phone: (212) 679-0870
Fax: NA
E-mail: info@nywift.org
http://www.nywift.org

Organization of Black Screenwriters (OBS)
1968 West Adams Boulevard
Los Angeles, CA 90018
Phone: (323) 882-4166
Fax: NA

E-mail: At Web site
http://www.obswriter.com

PEN American Center
568 Broadway
New York, NY 10012
Phone: (212) 334-1660
Fax: (212) 334-2181
E-mail: pen@pen.org
http://www.pen.org

PEN Center U.S.A. West
672 South Lafayette Park Place, Suite 42
Los Angeles, CA 90057
Phone: (213) 365-8500
Fax: (213) 365-9616
E-mail: pen@penusa.org
http://www.pen-usa-we/St.org

Promax International
9000 West Sunset Boulevard, Suite 900
Los Angeles, CA 90069
Phone: (310) 788-7600
Fax: (310) 788-7616
E-mail: info@promax.tv
http://www.promax.org

ProMax Systems, Inc.
16 Technology Drive, Suite 106
Irvine, CA 92618
Phone: (949) 727-3977
Fax: (949) 727-3546
E-mail: sales@promax.com
http://www.promax.com

Public Broadcasting Service (PBS)
1320 Braddock Place
Alexandria, VA 22314
Phone: (703) 739-5000
Fax: (703) 739-0775
E-mail: info@pbs.org
http://www.pbs.org

Public Relations Society of America (PRSA)
33 Irving Place, 3rd floor
New York, NY 10003
Phone: (212) 995-2230
Fax: 212-995-0757
E-mail: hq@prsa.org
http://www.prsa.org

Public Television Programmers Association
c/o Trac Media Services
P.O. Box 65120
Tucson, AZ 85728
Phone: (520) 299-1866
Fax: NA

E-mail: info@tracmedia.com
http://www.tracmedia.com

**Radio-Television News Directors
  Association (RTNDA)**
1600 K Street NW, Suite 700
Washington, DC 20036
Phone: (202) 659-6510
Fax: (202) 223-4007
E-mail: rtnda@rtnda.org
http://www.rtnda.org

**Satellite Broadcasting and
  Communications Association
  (SBCA)**
225 Reinekers Lane, Suite 600
Alexandria, VA 22314
Phone: (703) 549-6990
Fax: (703) 549-7640
E-mail: info@sbca.org
http://www.sbca.com

**Science Fiction and Fantasy Writers of
  America (SFWA)**
P.O. Box 877
Chestertown, MD 21620
Phone: (410) 778-3052
Fax: NA
E-mail: execdir@sfwa.org
http://www.sfwa.org

Screenwriters Federation of America
4337 Marina City Drive, Suite 1141
Marina del Rey, CA 90292
Phone: NA
Fax: NA
E-mail: info@screenwritersFederation.
  org
http://www.screenwritersFederation.org

SESAC, Inc.
Headquarters Office
55 Music Square East
Nashville, TN 37203
Phone: (615) 320-0055
Fax: (615) 329-9627
New York Office
152 West 57th Street
New York, NY 10019
Phone: (212) 586-3450
Fax: (212) 489-5699
Los Angeles Office
501 Santa Monica Boulevard, Suite 450
Santa Monica, CA 90401
Phone: (310) 393-9671
Fax: (310) 393-6497
E-mail: info@sesac.com
http://www.sesac.com

**Set Decorators Society of America
  (SDSA)**
1646 North Cherokee Avenue
Hollywood, CA 90028
Phone: (323) 462-3060
Fax: (323) 462-3099
E-mail: contact@setdecorators.org
http://www.setdecorators.org

Small Station Association (SSA)
c/o WTVP
1501 West Bradley Avenue
Peoria, IL 61625
Phone: (309) 677-2789
Fax: NA
E-mail: chet_tomczyk@wtvp.pbs.org
Web site: NA

**Society for Technical Communication
  (STC)**
901 North Stuart Street, Suite 904
Arlington, VA 22203
Phone: (703) 522-4114
Fax: (703) 522-2075
E-mail: stc@stc.org
http://www.stc.org

Society of Broadcast Engineers (SBE)
9247 North Meridian Street, Suite 305
Indianapolis, IN 46260
Phone: (317) 846-9000
Fax: (317) 846-9120
E-mail: info@sbe.org
http://www.sbe.org

**Society of Cable Telecommunications
  Engineers (SCTE)**
140 Philips Road
Exton, PA 19341
Phone: (610) 363-6888
Fax: (610) 363-5898
E-mail: scte@scte.org
http://www.scte.org

Society of Camera Operators
P.O. Box 2006
Toluca Lake, CA 91610
Phone: (818) 382-7020
Fax: NA
E-mail: info@soc.org
http://www.soc.org

**Society of Motion Picture & Television
  Engineers (SMPTE)**
595 West Hartsdale Avenue
White Plains, NY 10607
Phone: (914) 761-1100
Fax: (914) 761-3115
E-mail: smpte@smpte.org
http://www.smpte.org

**Society of Professional Journalists
  (SPJ)**
3909 North Meridan Street
Indianapolis, IN 46208
Phone: (31) 927-8000
Fax: (317) 920-4789
E-mail: questions@spj.org
http://www.spj.org

**Stuntmen's Association of Motion
  Pictures**
10660 Riverside Drive, 2nd Floor, Suite E
Toluca Lake, CA 91602
Phone: (818) 766-4334
Fax: (818) 766-5943
E-mail: info@stuntmen.com
http://www.stuntmen.com

**Television Bureau of Advertising
  (TBA)**
3 East 54th Street, 10th floor
New York, NY 10022
Phone: (212) 486-1111
Fax: (212) 935-5631
E-mail: info@tvb.org
http://www.tvb.org

TRAC Media Services
P.O. Box 65120
Tucson, AZ 85728
Phone: (520) 299-1866
Fax: (520) 577-6077
E-mail: info@tracmedia.com
http://www.tracmedia.com

**Women in Cable and
  Telecommunications (WICT)**
14555 Avion Parkway, Suite 250
Chantilly, Virginia 20151
Phone: (703) 234-9810
Fax: (703) 817-1595
E-mail: aiverson@wict.org
http://www.wict.org

Women in Film (WIF)
8857 West Olympic Boulevard, Suite 201
Beverly Hills, CA 90211
Phone: (310) 657-5144
Fax: NA
E-mail: NA
http://www.wif.org

Women in Film and Video (WIFV)
1400 K Street NW, 10th floor
Washington, DC 20005
Phone: (202) 408-1476
Fax: (202) 408-1479
E-mail: wifv@hers.com
http://www.wifv.org

APPENDIX IV
USEFUL WEB SITES FOR THE
TELEVISION INDUSTRY

For anyone involved in any aspect of the television industry as a vocation, the Internet has become an increasingly valuable resource in today's high-tech electronic age. The following are a selection of useful Web sites to help in your industry research, such as job searching, trade news gathering, and networking. (Web sites that do *not* have self-explanatory names are annotated with an explanation between the site name and its URL.)

These URLs may well be ones you wish to bookmark and/or save in your favorites folder. In addition, by using one or more of the search engines listed below—or using one of your own preferred search engines—you can fairly easily lay the foundation for researching almost any organization, individual, or television-based project. Naturally, the information offered on any Web site is only as good as the source itself and needs to be constantly reevaluated for its track record of providing consistently reliable data. As has

always been true, the Internet is in a constant state of flux. As such, even well-established Web sites often change their URLs. Typically, if you click on a link that has recently changed its URL, you will be switched automatically to its new Web address (which you can then bookmark and/or save in your favorites). If your link proves to be cold or dead, use a search engine to provide hits for the Web site in question. Usually this step will lead you to the new home page of the desired site. (As always, when using a search engine, if your query is more than one word, place the term in quotes to narrow and target the search.)

While the Internet and E-mail are great tools to employ in your career, do not ignore traditional person-to-person contact with colleagues, mentors, family, friends, and others within your support network. They are equally vital in keeping you on track in your work and life.

SEARCH ENGINES
How to Use Search Engines

Bare Bones 101
http://www.sc.edu/beaufort/library/pages/
   bones/bones.shtml

Search.com
http://www.search.com

SearchEngineWatch
http://searchenginewatch.com

Spider's Apprentice
http://www.monash.com/spidap4.html

WebRef
http://webreference.com/content/search

Search Engines (By Country)
http://www.philb.com/countryse.htm

Search Engines (General)

Alltheweb
http://alltheweb.com

Alta Vista
http://www.altavista.com

A9
http://a9.com

AOL
http://www.aol.com

Ask Jeeves
http://www.ask.com

AT1
http://www.at1.com

Blog Search Engines
An increasingly important venue for
   industry news and trends; note that
   many general search engines now
   provide a subcategory targeted for
   locating blogs by subject matter

Blogflux
http://dir.blogflux.com

Bloggernity
http://www.bloggernity.com

Bloogz: World Wide Blog
http://www.bloogz.com

Daypop
http://www.daypop.com

Icecrocket.com
http://blogs.icerocket.com

LS Blog
http://www.lsblogs.com

QuackTrack
http://quacktrack.com

Clusty
http://clusty.com

Copernic
Free and paid versions of special download
    software available at site; generally
    does not work with Macintosh system
http://copernic.com

Ditto
http://www.ditto.com

Dogpile
http://www.dogpile.com

Excite
http://www.excite.com

Findspot
http://www.findspot.com

Galaxy
http://www.galaxy.com

Gigablast
http://www.gigablast.com

GoFish
http://www.gofish.com

Gimpsy
http://www.gimpsy.com

Google
http://www.google.com

Google Scholar
http://scholar.google.com

HotBot
http://www.hotbot.com

HotSheet
http://www.hotsheet.com

Itool
http://www.itools.com

Kartoo
http://www.kartoo.com

LookSmart
http://search.looksmart.com

Lycos
http://www.lycos.com

Metacrawler
http://metacrawler.com

Mr. Sapo
http://mrsapo.com

MSN
http://www.msn.com

Nokodo
http://www.nokodo.com

Seeq
http://www.seeq.com

Singingfish
http://www.singingfish.com

Soople
http://www.soople.com

Starting Page
http://www.startingpage.com

Starting Point
http://www.stpt.com

Teoma
http://www.directhit.com

Topic Hunter
http://www.topichunter.com/index.php

WebCrawler
http://webcrawler.com

Wikipedia
http://en.wikipedia.org

WiseNut
http://www.wisenut.com

Yahoo
http://www.yahoo.com

JOB SEARCH/SALARY SURVEY WEB SITES

Some of these Web sites require a
    subscription fee for their use.

Acting Up
http://www.acting-up.net

CareerPage
http://www.careerpage.org

Careers: Wall Street Journal
http://www.careers.wsj/com

Center for Mobility Resources
http://www.homefair.com/homefair/cmr/s
    alcalc.html

Creative Hot List
http://www.creativehotlist.com

Employnow
http://www.employnow.com

Entertainment Employment Journal
http://www.eej.com

Entertainmentcareers.net
http://www.entertainmentcareers.net

Entertainment Jobs Now.com
http://www.entertainmentjobsnow.com

Film & TV Connection
http://www.film-connection.com

Filmtracker
http://www.filmtracker.com

Hot Jobs
http://www.hotjobs.com

Job Profiles
http://www.jobprofiles.org

Job Search
http://jobsearch.monster.com

Jobsearchtech.about
http://jobsearchtech.about.com/od/salary6
    /index.htm

JobSmart Salary Info
http://jobsmart.org/tools/salary/
    sal-prof.htm

JobStar Central
http://www.jobstar.org/tools/salary/
    sal-prof.cfm#PR

Journalism Jobs
http://www.journalismjobs.com

Media Internship Book
http://www.internships-usa.com

Media Recruiter
http://www.mediarecruiter.com

MediaLine (Journalism Jobs)
http://www.medialine.com

MediaStar
http://www.medialandjobs.com

Production Assistant Association
http://www.productionassistant
    association.com

The Real Rate Survey
http://www.realrates.com/survey.htm

Salary.com
http://www.salary.com

Salary Wizard
http://swz-hoovers.salary.com

Script Shark
http://www.scriptshark.com

Shoots.com
http://www.shoots.com

Showbizjobs.com
http://www.showbizjob.com

TopUSAjobs.com
http://topusajobs.com

TVandRadioJobs.com
http://www.tvandradiojobs.com

TV Jobs
http://www.tvjobs.com

TVSpy.com Job Bank
http://www.tvspy.com/jobbank.cfm

Wageweb Salary Survey Data Online
http://www.wageweb.com/index.htlm

Yahoo
http://careers.yahoo.com/employment/
    carrer_resources/salaries_and_benefits

TELEVISION/CABLE/FILM RESOURCES

Academy of Television Arts and Sciences
Emmy Awards database
http://www.emmys.tv

Current Online
A Web service that reports on public TV
    and public radio
http://www.current.org

Directors World
Online community providing daily news
    and information on the art,
    technology, and business of directing
    for film and video professionals
http://www.directorsworld.com

Directory of International Film & Video Festivals
http://www.britfilms.com/festivals

Done Deal
Resources for script sales in Hollywood,
    along with interviews, advice, and
    contact information for agencies and
    production companies
http://www.scriptsales.com

E! Entertainment Online
An archive of biographies, interviews,
    and news of celebrities
http://www.eonline.com

E-mail newsletters
Some are free, others are subscription-
    based. Sign-up is at the publication's
    Web site.

   Broadcasting and Cable
   https://www.broadcastingcable.com/
       subscribe.asp?screen=ai1

   Cynthia Turner's Cynopsis
   http://www.cynopsis.com

   (Daily) Variety
   http://www.variety.com

   Hollywood Reporter
   http://www.hollywoodreporter.com

   Inside TV Daily
   http://www.webscoutlists.com/cgi-bin/
       subscribe.pl?addlist=1544922

   Laurel's TV Picks
   http://www.tvpicks.net

   Mediabistro
   http://www.mediabistro.com

   Mediaweek
   http://www.mediaweek.com/mw/
       newsletters/email.jsp

   Romanesko
   http://www.poynter.org/column.asp?
       id=45

   TV Newser
   http://www.mediabistro.com/tvnewser

Entertainment Publicists Professional Society
Supplies publicity and marketing
    education, sponsoring media
    workshops on publicity trends and
    protocols in pitching weekly and daily
    entertainment, and provides seminars
    highlighting industry resources and
    networking opportunities
http://www.eppsonline.org

Film Industry Network
A networking organization for the film
    industry providing a means for
    members of the film and television
    industry to communicate in meetings
    and a network of topical e-mails
http://www.filmindustrynetwork.com

Futon Critic
An expansive television industry resource
http://www.thefutoncritic.com/cgi/home.
    cgi

Hollywood Web
A leading resource for entertainment
    industry talent: actors, writers,
    directors, models, technicians, etc.
http://www.hollywoodweb.com

Internet Movie Database (free version)
A film and television database
http://www.imdb.com

Internet Movie Database (paid subscription version)
Subscription database of film and
    television with additional statistics,
    news, and searches available
http://www.pro.imdb.com

I Want Media
Media news and resources
http://www.iwantmedia.com/news/index.
    html

Library of American Broadcasting
The library is located on the campus of
    the University of Maryland.
http://www.lib.umd.edu/UMCP/LAB

Mandy.com
An international film and TV resource
http://www.mandy.com

Musicals101.com
An encyclopedia of musical theater, both
    TV and film
http://www.musicals101.com

NewsLab
A nonprofit television news laboratory
    affiliated with the Columbia
    University Graduate School of
    Journalism and the Project for
    Excellence in Journalism
http://www.NewsLab.org

Nielsen Media Research
http://www.nielsenmedia.com

ProductionHub.com

This leading online resource and industry directory for film, television, video, and digital media production was developed as a tool for people to locate production products, services, and professionals.

http://www.productionhub.com

ProductionLeads.com

Preproduction leads for products or services to film and television production companies

http://www.productionleads.com

Radio & Television News Association of Southern California

http://www.rtna.org

Reality TV News Digest

http://www.realityblurred.com/realitytv

The Rundown

Links to available television jobs and TV career information and advice

http://www.tvrundown.com/resource.html

ShowBiz Data

A subscription source for show business information

http://www.showbizdata.com

Singingfish

A search engine for a variety of audio and video topics

http://www.singingfish.com

Television Week

Online version of the weekly newspaper of broadcast, cable, and interactive media

http://www.emonline.com

TVnewz.com

A webzine for TV news professionals

http://www.tvnewz.com

TV-Now

Much data, trivia, and links on television genres, personalities, and trends

http://www.tv-now.com/index.html

TVSpy.com

The insider resource for TV industry professionals, with a free daily insider newsletter, links to top job listings, and connections with fellow television industry professionals

http://www.tyspy.com

TVTattle

A weblog of TV news and criticism

http://www.tvtattle.com

GLOSSARY

Above-the-line or **above-the-line expenses/costs**   Expenses incurred before production starts, including costs associated with writing (or acquisition of writing), directing, producing, and performing, and listed in the top section of a budget.

Acquisition   The purchase of the distribution rights to a packaged or finished product by a PRODUCTION COMPANY, studio, or distributor; also the purchase of written material as the basis of the SCRIPT for a production; also a TV show or documentary created by one firm or in joint production with several companies that is bought by a network or a combination of companies that become the distributor.

Action   The command given usually by the director to begin shooting a TAKE also, the movement and business going on within the camera's view.

AD   Commonly used abbreviation for an assistant director.

Adaptation (or Adapt)   The process of rewriting a story from one medium (a novel or play, for example) to another (such as a film or television production); also, the right to change (or adapt) a musical composition.

Ad-lib   To perform without any preparation; to improvise dialogue and sometimes action that is not in the script.

ADR   See AUTOMATIC DIALOGUE REPLACEMENT.

Aerial shot   Scene filmed from a helicopter, hot-air balloon, plane, or some other flying device using a special camera mount.

Affiliates   Local television stations that are associated with a particular network, such as CBS, and are operating under an agreement to show a certain amount of that network's programming.

Agent   A person or firm that represents the interests of others, promoting, soliciting work, and negotiating contracts for an ABOVE-THE-LINE or BELOW-THE-LINE talent or property. A "talent agent" represents actors; a "literary agent" represents writers.

Ambient sounds/effects   Normal sounds recorded as part of the dialogue soundtrack during production.

Analog   A signal or a device that is continuously varying in strength or quantity, such as voltage, audio, or video. Also, the video output of nondigital cameras and tape decks that convert or store light rays to electrical signals rather than the 1's and 0's of a DIGITAL process.

Anamorphic lens   A camera lens that compresses the image horizontally while leaving it unchanged vertically, making a wider image fit on a narrower piece of film.

Anchor debrief   The question-and-answer phase in a newscast between an anchor and the on-set reporter immediately after the reporter's story has aired.

Ancillary right   A supplement to the main transaction in an agreement, such as the rights to sell a game, toy, calendar, or poster of the television product. Sometimes called a merchandising tie-in.

Animation   The process of creating cartoon characters, but also the creation of silhouettes, props, and other objects. An animator determines the amount of change needed in each cel or individual frame of film to create the illusion of movement.

Aperture   An adjustable IRIS within the camera lens that can be regulated to control the amount of light entering the camera.

Apple box   A box, usually wooden, used to raise the height of an actor, a piece of furniture, a light, or a prop during a SHOT. It is so known because it resembles the actual apple boxes that were used in the early days of filmmaking.

Arc shot   A camera shot in which the camera moves in a circular path around a subject.

ASA (ISO)   How light sensitivity is rated for film stock. The higher the ASA (American Standards Association) or ISO (International Standards Organization) number, the more sensitive (or "faster") the film is.

Aspect ratio   The ratio of the width of a film or television image to its height. The standard U.S. television aspect ratio is four units wide to three units high. Some films are shot at higher ratios, and if these alternate ratios are preserved in the film-to-tape (or digital) transfer (for transmission on television), there is an option to put a solid black bar at the top and the bottom of the TV screen. Some companies shoot at a higher ratio in the event the material is used for high-definition TV transmission, ensuring a usable negative for the wider aspect ratio.

Assembly   The initial stage of editing a filmed production, when the assorted shots are joined together in a rough order to produce a ROUGH CUT.

Attenuate   To reduce the amplitude or intensity of a sound.

Audiotape   Flexible plastic tape coated with an iron-oxide composition on which sound can be recorded by magnetically reorganizing its sensitive particles. By electronically reading the ANALOG or DIGITAL pattern of the particles formed by this reorganization, sound is played back. VIDEOTAPE recording and playback work in the same manner except that on videotape the audio and visual signals are recorded on separate places on the tape and by separate electromagnetic heads.

Auto assembly (or **Conforming**)   The automatic combining of edits of footage conforming to a prepared EDIT DECISION LIST (EDL), typically using a computerized edit controller with little or no human involvement.

Autofocus   The control on a video camera that scans the image being photographed and automatically moves the camera lens to bring that image into proper FOCUS

Automatic Dialogue Replacement (ADR)   The rerecording of dialogue by performers in a sound studio during POSTPRODUCTION, usually performed against a playback of the edited production to match lip movements on screen. ADR is frequently used to replace production soundtracks of poor quality (such as too much background noise interfering with the dialogue or to change the delivery or inflection of a given line of dialogue). ADR can also be used to insert fresh lines of dialogue, which are conceived during EDITING, although such lines have to come from a performer facing away from the camera. Also known as looping.

Avid   The brand name of the firm that developed the computer-based nonlinear digital film editing system, now used widely in both film and television.

Back lot   An out-of-the-way area of studio property where permanent outdoor settings (often "streets") are erected, each depicting a different geographic location or time and whose look can be altered as necessary.

Background music   Musical soundtrack elements that do not contain any vocals.

Background vocal   Musical sound track elements that contain vocal elements, with the singer(s) not seen on-screen.

Backlight   A light placed opposite the key light illuminating a subject on set and shining down on the subject from behind.

Backstory   Background information about a character in the SCRIPT that explicates that character. The details in a character's backstory may or may not come out in the story.

Barn doors   The hinged (so they can swing), solid metal black doors that fit on the front of lights used on the set so as to control or block the light during filming.

Bel   A relative measure of sound intensity or volume, expressing the ratio of one sound to another.

Below-the-line or **Below-the-line expenses/costs**   Budgeted expenses listed in the lower section of a budget that are assigned to the crew, physical production, POST-PRODUCTION, and any fees not associated with ABOVE-THE-LINE expenses.

Betacam (SP)   A Sony trademark; an analog professional video format often used to create worktapes used in POST-PRODUCTION. SP stands for Superior Performance.

Bias   A high-frequency alternating current fed into an analog magnetic recording circuit to assist the recording process.

Bible   The compendium of all necessary information pertaining to story lines and locations, and the complete history of each character of a television production. Used as a reference guide to ensure CONTINUITY and consistency from one episode to the next during the production.

Billing   The ranking of performers' names in credits, advertising, and so on.

Bin   In NONLINEAR EDITING, the holding place for the master clips and sequences of the filmed production that are currently being edited. Bins allow for a smooth, organized EDITING style.

Binary   Counting using only two digits, rather than the usual 10.

Bit   BINARY digit. Digital and PCM (pulse code modulation) audio systems convert audio into on-or-off pulses known as bits.

Bit depth   The number of bits of information that are used to describe a color. More bits means a more precise color. Commonly used to describe video images.

Bit part   A small, unimportant role for a performer, usually lasting only one SCENE.

Bit rate   The number of pieces of information that a digital audio deck records per second. More bits means better sound.

Blocking   The process of planning movement or position of performers and cameras for a SHOT. "Marks" are taped to the floor or "chalked" on the floor to ensure accuracy and consistency in the process.

Blue eye   A live television news report that consists only of a reporter talking on camera from a remote location, without any supporting video or prerecorded interviews.

Blue screen   A blue backdrop against which a performer is filmed, which will be replaced digitally with background footage during POSTPRODUCTION. If it is done by electronic means for television, it is also called the CHROMA-KEY process.

Boom   A long pole, often on wheels, that holds the microphone above the performers' heads and out of the SHOT, so the sound technician can record their dialogue.

Boom shadow   The shadow cast by the boom operator moving the BOOM over the set and under the lights. If captured on film, it must be removed in POSTPRODUCTION.

Boundary-level mic   A type of microphone that is mounted on a hard surface (such as a floor or a wall) and uses the sound reflections off that floor or wall to increase the volume of the sound.

Box rig   Safety setup for STUNTS consisting of a predetermined number of cardboard boxes and mattresses, used by a stuntperson as a landing target for certain types of falls and as a less-expensive alternative to an air bag.

Breakaway prop   A PROP designed and constructed, usually with a thin line or hairline crack, so it will break, collapse, crumble, or shatter easily, with little or no danger to the performers who come into contact with it.

Break down   The process of analyzing a SCRIPT to gather critical data needed by each department involved in a television production. For example, a description of the action, SHOT by shot, for the cinematographer; specific PROPS called for in the SCRIPT for the prop department; costume changes for each character for the wardrobe department; and VISUAL EFFECTS to be created for on-set SPECIAL EFFECTS personnel and POSTPRODUCTION visual effects work.

Breakout box (or "**Bob**")   An interpreting unit attached to a NONLINEAR video EDITING system that allows both video and audio to be transferred from the videotape deck to a computer hard drive and back.

Broadband   A method of carrying a digital transmission.

Broadcast quality   A term that originally meant the quality of the broadcast signal of television shows as seen on television sets. It has now come to mean the image quality of a show made for the medium.

B-roll   Secondary background filmed footage that will be cut into the television production's primary story line to help establish atmosphere, locations, and so on.

Buzz track   AMBIENT SOUNDS recorded to match the background of an already photographed SCENE, such as the background sounds of voices in a restaurant scene.

Byte   A set of eight bits, used as a measurement of the capacity of digital systems.

Cable   A long piece of rubberized wire that carries power. It is generally used to describe a wire carrying a large amount of power, as opposed to a ZIP CORD or a STINGER.

Callback   Any additional interview(s) or reading(s) with a performer after the initial audition.

Call sheet   Daily schedule of times for performers and crew to report to the set.

Camcorder   A camera that also has a recording deck.

Cameo   A BIT PART played by a famous performer who would ordinarily not take such a small role.

Camera car   Vehicle specially outfitted to carry one or more film or video cameras, sound and lighting equipment, and one or more operators for the purpose of filming another moving vehicle or individual.

Camera package   All equipment related to the camera used on a shoot.

Camera report   Detailed account prepared each day by the assistant cameraman listing scenes shot, number of takes for each shot, amount of film exposed, and instructions as to the disposition of each take (for example, "print" or "no good").

Camera speed   The rate at which film is pulled past the lens, normally 24 frames per second.

Cam-Lok plug   A large plug used to connect large feeder cables to distribution boxes. It is distinguished by its single pin and push-in-and-twist installation.

Canned applause   Prerecorded applause stored on an applause track, that can be served up on cue.

Canned laughter   Prerecorded laughter, as opposed to laughter recorded live from a studio audience. Sometimes called a LAUGH TRACK.

Capsule gun   A special effects rifle using compressed air or nitrogen gas to shoot break-apart capsules (containing powder or other material) or metal balls (to break windows, lamps, or other objects). Thus, during a gunfight scene, an off-camera capsule gun operator aims the gun and shoots the capsules or balls at designated targets to simulate bullet hits.

Caterer   A person or company who provides the main meals for cast and crew either on set or on LOCATION.

Catwalk   Suspended overhead structure or walkway on a sound stage that allows lighting and sound equipment to be hung high above the floor.

CCD   See CHARGE-COUPLED DEVICE.

CD   See COMPACT DISC.

CG   See CHARACTER GENERATOR.

CGI   See CHARACTER GENERATED IMAGERY.

Change page   A script page containing one or more revisions. It replaces another page in the script and is always in a different color.

Character actor   A performer who specializes in playing a particular style of character, often stereotypical, offbeat, or humorous.

Character arc   A term used to describe the growth and development of a character throughout the course of the story for a television production.

Character generator (CG)   A computer devise that electronically produces words to be superimposed over a live or videotaped image.

Character generated imagery (CGI)   This superimposition of words created during POSTPRODUCTION.

Charge-coupled device (CCD)   A light-sensitive computer chip that is at the heart of all video cameras.

Chroma key   A process in television POSTPRODUCTION of superimposing or combining two video images to create one composite visual effect. One of the video sources must be a saturated color (usually either blue or green because neither color is found in any significant quantity in human skin tones). Similar to the BLUE SCREEN process employed in films.

Chryon   A company that manufactures special effects and titling equipment used in ONLINE EDITING of productions. Also used as a common name for this type of equipment.

Clapperboard (**Clapper,** or **Clapboard**)   See MARKER SLATE.

Click track   An audible clicking sound used during recording sessions so the conductor and musicians can hear the proper tempo of the SCENE to which the music is being fitted.

Clip   A short excerpt of a television production's footage used for promotional purposes.

Closed-captioning Television signal that contains text information incorporated into the video images that can be viewed by the use of a decoder.

Closed circuit television (CCTV) System in which the television signal is transmitted over metal or fiber-optic cable and received by one or more connected television sets. It is a "closed circuit" because the TV signal is being transmitted and received directly from the source and is not being broadcast in every direction over the airwaves.

Close-up (CU) Normally a SHOT of the head and shoulders of a person, but can refer to any focusing on some small part of a SCENE, for example, a hand or a phone. The purpose of the shot is to draw the audience's attention to that particular element to create a dramatic effect.

Clothing moves The sounds created by FOLEY artists to imitate the sound of a performer's clothing as he or she moves.

Color correction The process of altering the colors in a photographed image to conform to the artistic intentions of the director and cinematographer. Also, the process of correcting the color of a light source to match the color of other light sources on the set.

Colorist The person who operates the DA VINCI COLOR correction system during the TELECINE process of transferring the film image to video and who controls the color balance of the video output.

Color timer The person in charge of the color balance when prints are made from the original negatives of the photographed television production.

Conforming See AUTO ASSEMBLY.

Console Colloquial term for audio or video mixing devices. Also known as the console board.

Continuity The necessity for consistency of details in a SCENE (dialogue, physical movement, clothing, hairstyles, makeup, furniture, props, and other elements) to be the same in all shots of that scene or related scenes.

Continuity error When props, costumes, gestures, or other elements do not match from SHOT to shot.

Continuity report A detailed list of the events that occurred during the filming of a SCENE. Typically documented are production and crew identification, camera settings, environmental conditions, the status of each TAKE, and exact details of the action that occurs. By detailing all the possible sources for variation in the scene, the report helps cut down CONTINUITY ERRORS between shots or in any reshooting of the scene.

Coverage The filming of a SCENE in a production from multiple camera angles or multiple cameras to provide sufficient choice of footage for the later EDITING process.

Craft service A service responsible for maintaining a table of snacks between meal periods; sometimes they feed the crew or extras.

Crane A piece of heavy equipment with a mobile arm on which the camera is mounted, allowing for sweeping camera movements and high-angle shots.

Credits The names and titles of cast and crew involved with a television production. On film, credits are created optically, whereas on videotape, they are created electronically.

Cross-cutting An EDITING technique that involves intercutting quickly back and forth between two or more scenes (or stories) so that the fragments of each SCENE will be presented alternately to the audience; also cutting between different points of view on one subject.

Cue A command to do something (usually from the director or the cinematographer), such as say a line or change the lighting. Also, a piece of music that goes with a particular SCENE or moment in the production.

Cue sheets A spreadsheet, or road map, of audio cues so sound recordists can locate particular tracks.

Cut Sometimes used to refer to a single edit of a SCENE or of the entire production, such as a straight edit (or cuts-only edit) without fades or crossfades from scene to scene. Also employed to describe the various edited versions of a project (such as ROUGH CUT and FINE CUT).

Cutaway A brief shot that momentarily takes the viewer out of a SCENE, often used to bridge cuts within a scene or between scenes.

Cutting print See WORKPRINT.

Dailies The video or film prints made immediately after a day's shoot from the original negatives so that they can be examined before the next day's shoot begins. Also called rushes.

DAT (digital audio tape) A high-quality tape that uses a two-channel digital format and computerized numbers to record sound.

Da Vinci color corrector A computer used during the process of transferring the film image to videotape (or TELECINE process) that can adjust the colors of the original image.

DAW Digital audio workstation.

Decibel (dB) A unit of measurement showing ratios of currents, voltages, or power used to represent audio transmission levels, gains, and losses. A decibel is the smallest percentage of change in audio level.

Deep focus A FOCUS in which every object in a SHOT, from close-up to infinity, is sharp and clear.

Depth of field The amount of space in front and/or behind the point of FOCUS where the performer (or object) will still be in focus.

Development The initial planning stage of a television project or film. A project is said to be "in development" when the rights to the materia l are being optioned or purchased, a writer is hired, performers are sought to become tentatively and conditionally attached to the project, and the SCRIPT is in one of various writing stages (being written, read, revised, broken down, or budgeted).

Digital The conversion of an ANALOG signal into a BINARY form with regular strength, rather than the varying strength of an analog signal.

Digital editing EDITING a portion of a production by digitizing one or more frames and altering them electronically or combining them with other digitized images and then printing the modified frame.

Digital imaging Process of converting picture information into thousands (or millions) of PIXELS, each one represented numerically with information describing its position and color. Once digitized, an image can be copied exactly without it degrading from one generation of copying to the next.

Digital retouching Alteration of a photographic or video image via a computer. Facial retouching is done to remove wrinkles, moles, scars, acne, and the like; it is also done to repair or restore damaged or old photographs.

Digital still camera Handheld camera using electronic, digital imaging technology instead of light-sensitized film to record color still pictures on an internal memory or removable memory disk. These photos can then be downloaded onto a computer for viewing and manipulation (such as enlarging or reducing).

Digital television Any system of recording, converting, or transmitting television pictures and sound via digital processing of the information.

Digital video camera Consumer or professional grade CAMCORDER or studio camera using digital technology to process still or moving images and sound. Depending on the type, it may use videotape, an optical videodisc, or a memory chip as its recording medium.

Digital zoom Enlarging an image area electronically rather than optically by selecting an area of pixel information and converting it to a greater screen size. Optical zooming is done mechanically or electromechanically using a glass lens system.

Digitize Process of loading video and audio tracks into an OFFLINE EDITING system, which transfers them from tape to disk as DIGITAL data.

Director's cut Rough cut of the finished production by the director once the EDITOR'S CUT is completed. This is usually followed by the PRODUCER'S CUT and the final PICTURE LOCK.

Dissolve An EDITING technique whereby the images of one SHOT are gradually replaced by the images of another.

DME Dialogue, music, and effects—the three categories of sound in both the television and film world.

Dolby A family of audio system/noise reduction technologies. The two most commonly known are Dolby Digital a multichannel surround format of full-bandwidth channels (including left, right, center, left surround, right surround) and the ".1" channel, which is the LFE channel (carrying low-frequency effects only), and Dolby Stereo, an encoding of four channels of audio (left, center, right, surround) into a stereo-compatible two-track format that is fully decoded on playback.

Dolly A rolling platform set on a track on which a camera is mounted, with a place for a cameraperson to sit, and is moved smoothly either toward the subject being photographed or away from it. The dolly is pushed by one of the grip personnel, known as a dolly grip.

Dolly tracks A set of tracks on which a camera can be moved.

Dope sheet A list of scenes from the SCRIPT that have already been filmed, or a listing of the contents of an exposed reel of film stock. An accurate dope sheet is the responsibility of the assistant cameraman.

Drag rig Protective safety harness and attached rigging worn by a STUNT performer who is to be dragged on the ground at the back of a horse or a vehicle.

Dress a set To place props on a set. The opposite is to strike a set.

Drop in A piece of music or recorded speech "dropped in" to a program, such as a tune or jingle that identifies the station.

DTV Digital television, which can be broadcast through land-based, cable, or SATELLITE systems.

Dubbing (Audio) The combining (also known as MIXING) of all soundtracks (dialogue, music, and effects) onto a single master source during POSTPRODUCTION.

Edge code A number printed on the edge of the film allowing frames to be easily identified in an EDIT DECISION list to keep the film and sound track in sync when combined in the EDITING process. Also known as edge numbers, or keycode.

Edit decision list (EDL) The list of shots completed by the EDITING software showing the final order and length of all the shots in the production.

Editing Assembling a production by combining sound and images from various master sources, either film or tape.

Editing controller The electronic device that controls video decks in the linear EDITING process.

Editor's cut The first version of the production completed by the editor before the director becomes involved in the editing process.

Effects See SOUND EFFECTS; SPECIAL EFFECTS; VISUAL EFFECTS.

Electronic press kit (EPK) Videotaped cast and crew interviews and behind the scenes footage used to generate free publicity for the media.

Ellipsoidal spot Spotlight with a fixed or variable lens providing a sharp beam of light; used to illuminate precisely areas or objects on a set.

ENG (electronic news gathering) The process of shooting news footage in the field

Episodic A television show with multiple episodes. Sometimes used in referring to one-hour shows, such as series, but more technically (and commonly) applied only to half-hour programs, such as talk shows and SITCOMS.

Equalization (EQ) The process of controlling how much of each frequency (low, middle, or high) will be heard in the audio track of a production.

Establishing shot   Used to introduce the production's audience to the story's locale or to the story itself.

Event number   A number assigned by an editor to each edit in an EDIT DECISION LIST.

Exposure index   The number showing how sensitive a piece of film is to light.

Exposure latitude   The number reflecting the range of light levels a film can record.

Exposure meter   Handheld or in-camera electronic photocell device that measures the intensity of directed or reflected light so the correct APERTURE size and shutter speed can be selected prior to shooting.

Extra   An individual who appears in a production where a nonspecific, nonspeaking character is required, usually as part of a crowd or in the background of a SCENE.

Extreme close-up (ECU)   A SHOT that, being quite close to the subject, shows only a very small area, such as a portion of a performer's face.

Eyeline   In the EDITING process, it is the direction that the performer appears to be looking out of frame. On the set, it is the direction that the performer is actually looking toward.

Fades   A technique for gradually bringing an image up from black or another color to the full image (a fade-in) or gradually making the image disappear to a black or another color screen (a fade-out). Also applies to audio sounds.

Fair use   A provision of the copyright law that authorizes limited use of copyrighted material.

Fast action   Action filmed at slower than normal speed that, when projected at normal speed, appears faster. Also known as SKIP FRAME.

Field   One-half of a video frame, made up of either the odd or the even scanning lines of a picture on the videotape.

Filmmakers   A collective term used to refer to people who have a significant degree of control over the creation of a television production or film, such as directors, producers, writers, and editors.

Film speed   A measure of a film's sensitivity to light. Films that are very sensitive are called "fast," while "slow" films are less sensitive and require more light.

Film stock   Raw film that has not yet been exposed.

Filter   A plate of glass, plastic, or gelatin put over a lens to change the look and feel of the image being photographed.

Final cut   The final edited version of a production.

Final mix   Sound editing process during POSTPRODUCTION in which all the various soundtracks (dialogue, music, sound effects, and so forth) are combined or blended together completely.

Fine cut   An edit of the film (or production) in which small changes are made and small details are altered, as opposed to the initial ROUGH CUT.

Flag   A rectangular piece of fabric placed in front of a light to block, diffuse, or reduce light or to make shadows.

Flashback   A SCENE that breaks the chronological continuity of the main narrative by depicting events that happened in the past.

Flashforward   A SCENE that breaks the chronological continuity of the main narrative by depicting events that will happen in the future.

Flatbed   See MOVIOLA.

Floating camera   A camera mounted on a wearable harness that reduces shakes and wobbles when filming.

Flutter   Rapid fluctuations in the pitch of recorded sound. Also called "wow."

Foamcore   A white, flexible board used to redirect and diffuse light.

Foam latex   Type of dense foam rubber made by heating latex with other chemical ingredients. Used in the creation of special makeup effects, such as face-altering makeup applications, stop-motion animation creatures, or other types of miniature and life-sized puppets and full-body alien and monster costumes.

Focal length   The designation of a camera lens and its angle of view as determined by measuring the distance from the optical center of the lens to the front surface of the target being photographed.

Focus   The sharpness of an image or the adjustments made on a camera necessary to achieve this.

Focus puller   The person who monitors and changes the FOCUS of a camera.

Foley   The POSTPRODUCTION process of adding SOUND EFFECTS that imitate the sounds caused by the movements of the performers on-screen, such as footsteps, door closings, and breathing.

Frame   A complete video image made up of two or three video fields.

Frame rate (or **Frames-per-second,** or **FPS**)   Films and filmed television productions are created by taking a rapid sequence of pictures (frames) of action. By displaying these frames at the same rate at which they were recorded, the illusion of motion can be created. This rate is the number of frames captured or projected per second.

Freeze frame   An optical printing effect whereby a single FRAME is repeated to give the illusion that all action has stopped.

F-stop   A number (expressed as a fraction) that describes the size of the iris opening in (and thus the amount of light allowed through) the lens of a camera.

Fx   Abbreviation for SOUND EFFECTS.

Gate   A processor used to increase the dynamic range of sounds by removing part of the signal when it drops below a specified threshold—often used to clean up dialogue that has a noisy background. In addition, the opening of a camera that allows light to hit the film.

Geared head   A type of tripod head that uses gears to turn the tripod on which the camera sits, thus creating smooth movement as the tripod is moved following subjects being photographed.

Gel   Abbreviation for gelatin. A diffuser that softens the light of a studio lamp or a colored transparency used to change the color of a light source.

Generation   In film or video, when there is a loss of quality of an image as a result of transferring from one format to another or copying (e.g., second-generation tape).

Gigabyte   One billion bytes.

Gimbal mount   A camera tripod mount that keeps the camera upright even when the floor beneath the tripod is moving.

Glitch   A momentary break in sound due to data errors.

Gofer   The lowest level of production assistant, sometimes unpaid, who performs menial tasks and errands. Literally, the terms means "go for."

Greenlight   The term used when a production studio puts a film or a television production it has been developing into actual production.

Ground glass   A precision-built piece of glass that reflects the image from the lens into the viewfinder of a camera.

Guide track   A soundtrack recording that is likely to be replaced rather than used in the final mix and that may be used as a guide in sound POSTPRODUCTION.

Hazeltine Color Analyzer   A computerized system that alters color when making a print from a negative so as to color-correct the print.

Head-on shot   Describes when the action in the shot is moving directly toward the camera.

Heads   A grip's word for lighting instruments.

Hiatus   A gap in a television series production. It is the time of year (usually sometime between May and July) when a television series is not in production, giving performers in the series the opportunity to work on other projects.

High-angle shot   A SHOT taken with the camera high and looking down at the subject.

High-definition television (HDTV)   A video format (TV signal) with extra lines and bandwidths in which television images are recorded by a special camera for transmission or playback on home television sets with a wide screen, resulting in much greater resolution of sound and image than standard TV formats.

High-pass filter   An audio filter that diminishes the low frequencies, where most wind and some equipment noises originate.

Honey wagon   Large, mobile location unit (often housed in a trailer) containing toilet facilities and frequently dressing rooms that is brought to a LOCATION shoot.

Hot points   A safety warning telling everyone that a piece of equipment is being carried to or from the set.

Hot set   A set on which a SCENE is in the process of being shot. It is labeled such to indicate that it should not be changed or disturbed.

Image enhancement   Improving video signals through electronic correction (by increasing edge sharpness and noise reduction) using a video processor.

Image stabilizer   An electronic feature in some video cameras that stabilizes the image and removes some of the "jitters" of carrying a camera while shooting.

Impedance   The amount of resistance to a signal in a piece of sound equipment. Used to match up cables, microphones, speakers, and other sound equipment.

Incident meter   A light meter that measures the general level of light coming from the lights on a set.

Infomercial   Television advertising presented in a format that resembles regular television programming.

Ingesting   A term that is beginning to be used to describe the importing of sound files into a DIGITAL EDITING system (as opposed to "recording" or "digitizing" in real time).

Insert car   A car specially equipped to carry a camera and crew to accomplish shots while the vehicle is being driven.

Insert shots   Additional footage often shot during POSTPRODUCTION to create an effect, to do a cutaway shot, or to add information.

Instructional television (ITV)   Television programming used for teaching purposes, usually transmitted by a closed-circuit television system into a classroom environment.

Interactive TV   Television programs that enable viewers to participate in a program or to select desired video material.

Intercut   The film EDITING technique of cutting together shots of two separate individuals who are in different places, such as two characters talking on the phone.

Interlace method   The electronic method of creating a picture on a television set by filling in all odd lines from top to bottom and then going back and filling in all the even lines. This process is repeated about every 1/30th of a second.

Internegative (IN)   A duplicating film stock that becomes a negative when printed from a positive print of the filmed production. Internegative prints are used to make opticals and titles and are the source for making interpositive prints of the original film.

Interpositive (IP)   A positive print of a filmed production made from an INTERNEGATIVE on special film stock, allowing a new negative to be created and thus protecting the original negative of the filmed production.

In the can   A production that has finished shooting but has not yet been edited for release.

In turnaround   Term describing a project that has been turned down by a television studio or PRODUCTION COMPANY and the rights of which have reverted back to the author for a period of time stipulated in the original option agreement. If the author cannot place the project with another studio or company within that period of time, the rights go back to the studio (or company) holding the original option.

I/O Inputs/outputs, which may be ANALOG or DIGITAL and which allow a system to receive and send signals.

Iris An adjustable aperture inside a camera lens that can be regulated to control the amount of light entering the camera.

Jenny Nickname for the generator used for power on location or for back-up power in a studio.

Jitter A momentary loss of synchronization of a video signal, which can affect an individual line in a picture or the whole picture.

Journeyman A person who has served as an apprentice at a trade and is now certified to work at that trade under the supervision of another person.

Keycode See EDGE CODE.

Keykode reader The device that reads the EDGE CODE (bar code) along the edge of the film. Keykode is a trademark of the Kodak company.

Key light The most powerful light in any SCENE being filmed. It is where the light is supposedly "coming from" as seen by the viewer of the filmed scene.

Latex Type of rubber used to create special makeup effects, such as aging skin or fake wounds.

Laugh tracks Sound tracks of audience reactions, usually laughter. They are added or enhanced during the DUBBING stage in POSTPRODUCTION and are primarily used for situation comedies.

Laydown The process of recording sound from an audio source or a video element to another audio element. During this process TIMECODES can be added or altered, channel configurations rearranged, or audio levels compressed.

Lead The first shot in a news segment whose purpose is to telegraph the story to come for viewers.

Leader Opaque or clear film attached to the head and tail of film rolls.

Lead-in The anchor news copy in television newscasts that introduces and reveals the news story and sets up the video package of the story to follow.

Letterbox When a widescreen image is projected onto a standard television screen (and does not fill the entire screen), a space is left at the top and the bottom of the screen, which is usually filled in with black bars.

License The proof of legal permission to use copyrighted material in a film or video, usually in the form of a contract.

Light meter An electronic device that measures the amount of light on the set.

Limpet mount A rubber mount that allows cameras to be attached to metal surfaces (such as the outsides of cars) using a vacuum effect.

Linear editing The process by which images are recorded, one after another, on videotape. No change in length is possible in this process without re-editing everything following the change.

Lined script A copy of the SHOOTING SCRIPT which is prepared by the script supervisor during production to indicate, via notations and vertical lines drawn directly onto the SCRIPT pages, exactly what has been shot. A given vertical line indicates, via the line's start and end point, what script material is covered in a particular SHOT, and whether given dialogue or action is on-screen or off-screen in the shot, indicated by the line changing between straight and wavy, respectively. Different colored lines usually represent certain types of shots. The lined script also frequently incorporates the SCRIPT NOTES on the facing pages for a given SCENE. The lined script is used by the film editor as a reference to what coverage was shot and to changes made to the script during production.

Lipsync A term used to describe any on-camera speech and its sync relative to the picture depicting the action of that speech.

Location The setting where a SCENE is filmed, which is usually a preexisting setting away from the studio or soundstage.

Locked cut or locked picture The final version of a television production after all changes have been incorporated.

Longitudinal timecode (LTC) TIMECODE information that is recorded on a videotape, audiotape, or address-track channel. Can be thought of as video sprocket holes.

Long shot (LS) A SHOT that gives the television viewer the context of the setting by showing it from a greater distance and including at least the full figure of a subject.

Loop group A group of voice actors who provide background voices to footage during the postproduction process.

Looping See AUTOMATIC DIALOGUE REPLACEMENT.

Low-angle shot A SHOT taken with the camera low and looking up at the subject.

Lowboy A camera mount that allows the camera to be put at ground level.

Low-power television stations (LPTV) A television station operating at a greatly reduced power and serving a very narrow geographic area, typically 20 to 40 square miles. Most LPTV stations feed low-cost satellite networks to subscribers, and programs usually consist of religious shows, home shopping, music, and Spanish-language services.

Luminance The brightness or contrast of a video signal.

M & E (music and effects) A soundtrack of a movie or a television production that contains only music and effects, from which all dialogue elements have been eliminated. Such a track is used for foreign sales when the dialogue will be dubbed into a non-English language.

Magazine The container that fits into a movie camera that does not admit light and feeds and takes up the film.

Mag stock Magnetic sound recording stock that has edge perforations that match those perforations on the picture stock, thereby allowing it to be pulled along with the picture at the same speed and relative position.

Mark   The place on the floor of a set the performer must move to or stay in during a SCENE in order to say within the frame of the camera shot.

Marker slate   The slate held in front of the camera lens before every SHOT, showing the shot number, TAKE number, and other useful information. Usually, the slate also contains the clapper, the board on top that is slapped down onto the slate to synchronize the audio take of the shot.

Mask   A covering of some type placed in front of the camera lens to block off part of the image to be photographed.

Master   An original recording, video or audio, such as master edit, master music track, and so forth

Matching cut   A cut in which two separate shots are edited together and linked logically and visually, usually by action or movement within the shots. Also known as overlapping action in that the action of one SHOT also is present in the next shot to which it will be joined so that the action flows smoothly and without interruption between the two shots.

Matrix   An encoding device that can mix four sound channels into two stereo channels, which will then be restored to four channels on playback. The four channels are left, center, right, and MONO surround.

Matte   The black bars found at the top and bottom of a picture when a widescreen format is projected onto a television set. Can also mean the blocking out or cutting around an image in VISUAL EFFECTS and graphics.

Matte painting   A painted background inserted into the filmed footage during POSTPRODUCTION.

Maximum depth of field   The maximum or deepest range of depth of field, or what appears to be in FOCUS in a SCENE, available in a given camera SHOT at a particular focus setting, FOCAL LENGTH, and APERTURE setting.

Media file   The actual file containing audio or video that has been converted from tape to DIGITAL information. It is the "raw" track footage within the AVID editing system. Media files are stored on hard drives external to the computer. Master clips serve as the road maps for finding media files and playing them back in an orderly manner during the film editing process.

Medium shot   A camera SHOT that provides approximately a knee to head view of a subject, isolating it from the overall environment. Medium shots are further broken down into medium long shots and medium close-ups.

Megabyte   A million bytes.

Method acting   A style of acting that focuses on reaching the emotional truth of a character by using such internal methods as relaxation and sense memory exercises.

Mic   Abbreviation for a microphone. Also mike.

Microphone boom   Handheld, telescopic pole, beam, or a more elaborate multijointed moveable arm at the end of which a microphone is attached and controlled. In the studio, a microphone may hang from an overhead BOOM attached to a DOLLY and be raised, lowered and/or angled by an off-camera operator. Outdoors it may be attached to the end of a hand-held pole (known as a "fishpole") with a changeable length.

Mitchell mount   A means of mounting a camera to a tripod. It is considered to be the strongest and most stable mount.

Mixing   The combining of all soundtracks (dialogue, music, and effects) onto a single master source. Also known as audio DUBBING.

Mixing stage   A soundstage specifically designed to allow sound designers to mix the final soundtrack for a television production or a film.

Montage   A stylized form of EDITING showing a rapid sequence of filmed images together to provide a lot of information in a short period of time or to suggest visually the passage of time.

Morphing   Computer animation effect in which one image is smoothly transformed into another by means of a steady and continuous manipulation of the onscreen PIXEL information. For example, a human face morphing into a different human face.

Motion control   A camera set-up that records the motion of a camera during a SHOT so that VISUAL EFFECTS can be easily synchronized with the photographed SCENE.

Moving shot   When the camera swivels on a tripod or other fixed base to follow the action in the SCENE being photographed. It is different from a pan because the photographer's motivation is to follow the action rather than to show a static object in panorama.

Moviola   A film editing machine that allows the editor to screen several reels of film at the same time, choosing shots from each one. Also used extensively in the editing process of building soundtracks.

Multi-camera shooting   Using many cameras to cover a SCENE, all shooting at the same time.

Multichannel multipoint distribution services (MMDS)   A television broadcast service that resembles a cross between low-power television (LPTV) and cellular phones. Midrange and local television transmissions of programming are received by a special converter that feeds them to the television set on an otherwise unused normal broadcast channel.

Multiple system operator (MSO)   A large company that controls dozens (or even hundreds) of cable systems. Examples of MSOs are TCI (Tele-Communications Inc.), Comcast Corporation, and Time Warner. They exert some control over the development of the programming services available on the channels they own.

Musical instrument digital interface (MIDI)   A technology (and computer language) that allows electronic instruments to interface with each other and to be controlled by a computer. Originally conceived for the music industry.

National Television Standards Committee (NTSC)   The committee that established the color transmission system used in the United States, Canada, Mexico, and Japan.

Natural sounds (Nats)   Natural sounds from the environment of a SCENE being photographed that communicate a sense of the experience of the scene and serve to heighten the viewers' sense of realism.

Negative film   Film that, when exposed, creates a negative image that must be printed to be viewed.

Nets   Loosely woven fabric pieces or panels that are used to diffuse light or subdue particular areas of illumination within a SCENE being photographed.

News agencies   Companies the collate news to sell to media outlets.

News sources   People or organizations who supply news to broadcasters

Noise   Interference in audio or video signals. Audio noise might be a hum or hiss, while video noise might be snow or streaks in the picture.

Noise contour (NC)   A set of criteria used to assess the quietness of a room.

Nonlinear editing   A computerized EDITING process that allows video and audio sequences of a production (that have been stored as digital images and sounds) to be moved about, shortened, or lengthened independently of one another, similar in manner to that of a word processor with pictures. Anytime an element is added or deleted, the system automatically reconfigures everything before and after the change so as to maintain SYNCHRONIZATION.

Nonspeaking role   See SPEAKING ROLE.

Octave   A musical interval spanning eight full notes. Human hearing spans 10 octaves.

Offline editing   EDITING of a production prior to the ONLINE EDITING in order to create an EDIT DECISION LIST to be used in the final assembly of the program. The process applies only to video and can be done electronically or manually.

Omni microphone   A microphone that picks up sound equally in all directions.

Online editing   The process of EDITING at high resolution and at full broadcast quality the videotapes with all added opticals and SPECIAL EFFECTS. It is the final step before the distribution of the product.

On location   Filming that takes place away from the studio or soundstage.

Open-ended silk   A piece of silk fabric mounted on a three-sided frame used to diffuse light without showing any visible edge.

Optical   An operation done in the film laboratory that creates an effect, such as a FADE or a DISSOLVE.

Optical printer   A camera that rephotographs images to make OPTICAL effects.

Option   The exclusive right, obtained by a deposit fee against an agreed-upon purchase price, to sell a SCRIPT, book, or life story rights within a specified period of time.

Out-take   A TAKE of a SCENE not used in a television production. Sometimes, these out-takes are shown with the closing credits.

Overhead or aerial shot   A SHOT of a SCENE from above, usually made from an airplane, a helicopter, or a crane.

Over-the-shoulder (OTS)   A style of SHOT whereby the camera peeks over a performer's shoulder in order to shoot the face of a second performer or action taking place in front of the main performer.

Pacing   The rhythm, tempo, or rate of movement of the shots (scenes) in a production.

Package   A presentation of a proposed production that includes the SCRIPT and the elements attached to the script, such as the producer, director, and the cast for the leading roles.

Paintbox   The name of the digital graphics generator made by Quantel, in which paint, pen, and airbrush are available electronically to a graphic artist.

Pan   Describes when the camera swivels on a tripod to show an overall SCENE in a single SHOT, or when a handheld camera is moved in a similar fashion. The pan is the most common camera movement.

Parabolic mic   A microphone with a parabolic reflector attached, used to pick up sounds from a long distance away.

Parallel action   A device of story construction in which the development of two pieces of action are presented simultaneously. Also known as parallel cutting.

Per diem   The amount of spending money given to a crew member for daily living expenses.

Persistence of vision   The physiological tendency of the human eye to retain an image for a short moment after the image has disappeared from the field of vision is why film action and motion appears continuous.

Personal mic   A miniaturized microphone that can be clipped to or concealed within clothing.

Photojournalist   An individual who uses or relies on the camera not merely to take pictures but also to tell stories.

Picked up   A television project or series or a film that is purchased, approved for production, or renewed is said to have been "picked up."

Pickup pattern   The area around a microphone where sound can be detected by the microphone.

Pickup shot   A camera shot in which the action in a scene resumes at a specific point in the action, usually with the camera shooting from a different angle or distance. Typically done to provide additional footage to insert into a scene later or to film action or dialogue in a different way, or to repair a problem with continuity.

Picture lock   When the visual part of an edited production is considered complete.

Pitch   The verbal presentation of an idea or story line to those individuals responsible for purchasing it for potential production.

Pixel   The acronym for "picture element," the smallest unit (a dot) from which a picture can be built up.

Plot point   An event or turning point in a story that spins the action in another direction.

Point-of-view (POV) shot   A SHOT that shows a SCENE from the point of view of an individual character.

Port   A digital input/output (I/O) connection through which DIGITAL data can be imported or exported. A serial port sends or receives data bits in series (one after another). A parallel port can send or receive data bits simultaneously.

Postproduction   The production work done on a taped or filmed production after principal photography is completed. The work usually consists of EDITING, DUBBING, and the addition of audio and video SPECIAL EFFECTS.

Postsynchronization   Recording dialogue or sound in a proper acoustical environment; used when sound has not been recorded satisfactorily at the time of shooting or when it was impossible to record the sounds/dialogue concurrently while shooting. Also used to translate the dialogue from one language to another.

Predub   Mixing several sound tracks together prior to the final mix.

Premise   The theme, thesis, central idea, or motivating force of a production or film. A premise is also a thumbnail synopsis of the story.

Preproduction   The process of readying a project for production that occurs between the development and filming phases. During preproduction, financing will be found; the cast will be chosen; the SCRIPT will be purchased, written, or rewritten; the film crew will be hired; and the LOCATION or locations where the production will be SHOT will be scouted.

Preroll   In video EDITING, it is the amount the videotape machine rolls back so that it will be running at the proper speed when it reaches the edit point. In TELECINE, it is the amount the telecine, videotape machines, and audio playback machines roll back so they will all be running at the proper speed when the record point is reached.

Press kit   A publicity package of photographs, cast and crew biographies, production synopsis, and so forth sent out to print media either in hard copy or dispatched via electronic copy.

Principal photography   The period of time allotted to complete the filming of a production.

Producer's cut   Often the final cut prior to PICTURE LOCK.

Production board   Used to organize visually a production into the actual sequence of scenes that will be shot, this board has moveable colored strips that show the schedule for every day of a shoot and the list of performers, locations, and elements needed for each day. Traditionally put together manually, production boards also can be created and assembled through computer programs.

Production company   A firm that develops and produces television or film projects.

Production report   A daily accounting of hours worked, footage shot, and other production information used to monitor budgets and schedules.

Production sound   Dialogue and ambient sound recorded during PRINCIPLE PHOTOGRAPHY on set or on LOCATION.

Promo   Filmed or recorded promotional advertisement or announcement for an upcoming program on a television station or network. Also called a promotional spot, plug, or preview clip.

Prop   Any physical object that is used or handled by a performer or is otherwise needed in a SCENE, such as chairs, books, paintings, lights, and so forth.

Protagonist   The main hero or heroine in a SCRIPT whose actions drive the plot.

Pro Tools   A computer program used to edit sound.

PSA   A public service announcement.

Public domain   Material that was never copyrighted or for which the copyright has lapsed.

Pull focus   An artistic shot in which an object in the foreground is out of focus while an object in the background is in focus (or vice versa); then the focus is slowly switched.

Pulling focus   The process of adjusting the camera lens to compensate for the movement of the camera, usually the job of the assistant camera operator.

Quality control (QC)   The act of inspecting audio, video, or film elements for technical specifications compliance and for any visual or audio defects.

Random access memory (RAM)   Temporary storage on a computer measured in megabytes or gigabytes

Random access editing   In nonlinear video editing, each camera SHOT recorded to the hard drive of the computer is displayed as "raw" (unedited) material that resides on the hard drive. The first frame of every shot is visible, allowing editors to drag and drop or randomly screen any shot on the hard drive.

Rating   A number that rates how well a television show has done by estimating the number of viewers. Most television ratings are through the Nielsen Television Index.

Raw stock   Unexposed film or audio stock.

Reaction shot   A SHOT that shows a subject's reaction to an action in the previous shot.

Real time   The process of creating a special effect in actual clock time, which means the computer needs no additional time to create the effect. Opposite of rendering.

Reenactments   Scenes acted out by performers that recreate either factual or hypothetical situations in a nonfiction production.

Reestablishing shot   A SHOT similar to the original establishing shot of an overall SCENE. It is used to reintroduce locale or to allow the introduction of new action in the original scene.

Reflected light   Illumination bounced off the subject being photographed.

Regen (or **Regenerating**)   The creation of a new TIME-CODE by use of a TIMECODE GENERATOR on an audio or video element.

Remote focus unit   A remote control unit that allows the camera to be focused from some distance away.

Render   The process of building a program within the computer to play back a specific audio or video effect. Rendered effects slow down the EDITING process, and some effects can be accomplished in REAL TIME instead.

Reprise shot   A SHOT, such as an action shot or one of a character speaking dialogue, that is repeated at a later point in the SCRIPT, usually to indicate a character remembering.

Residuals   Additional compensation (equivalent to an author's ROYALTY) paid to performers, directors, and such according to their union contracts. Not all union members receive residuals.

Resolution   The sharpness of a picture, usually measured in lines. The greater the number of lines, the sharper the image. Also, the final scenes of a story in which the complications of the plot are resolved and the growth or change of the main character is made evident.

Reversal film   Film that produces a positive image when exposed, like slide film in still cameras.

Reverse action   The process of printing the last frame first to show the movement in a shot in reverse.

Reverse-angle shot   A shot from the opposite side of a subject. Two-party dialogue scenes are often constructed using alternating reverse-angle shots.

Room tone   Strictly speaking, it is the "sound" of a particular room caused by echoes and background noises within the room. This ambient sound on the set or LOCATION site is generally recorded during production and is used to replace any silences on dialogue or effects tracks. Also known as a BUZZ TRACK.

Rough cut   Usually the first assembly of a filmed production that the editor prepares from selected takes, in SCRIPT order, before any timing or EDITING has been done or any video or audio effects (or music) have been added.

Royalty   Calculated payment to the creator (author, composer, lyricist, inventor) or owner of a property each time that creation (book, musical composition, invention) is sold or licensed.

Runner   Sometimes called a production assistant, the runner's primary function is to run errands for the production crew, such as picking up and delivering packages, videotapes, scripts, contracts, lunch, and so forth. Also known as a GOFER.

Rushes   See DAILIES.

Safety copy   A copy of a master to be used only if the master is damaged.

Sampling   Using a computer to record something electronically, thereby turning it into digital data that can be manipulated.

Satellite   Device outside the Earth's atmosphere used in broadcasting as a transmitter of radio and television signals back to Earth.

Scene   A series of shots in a television production or film constituting a unit of continuous related action in the story or narration, usually taking place in a single LOCATION or focused on a specific character or group of characters, that ends with the movement to another location.

Scene-by-scene transfer   The best and most expensive quality of color correction used during the process of transferring film images to video.

Score   The musical soundtrack, usually original, of a television production or film.

Scoring   The session in which live music is performed and recorded to match an existing production or film.

Scoring stage   A sound stage specifically designed for the performance and recording of a production's musical score.

Scrim   A lightweight fabric used to diffuse light. In addition, a large drop cloth made out of this fabric used to partially hide a person or scenery.

Script   The written story line that the director and performers work from. It contains plot development, characters, dialogue, and action situations.

Script notes   A copy of the SHOOTING SCRIPT prepared by the script supervisor noting camera angles, what script lines were recorded by which camera, the shooting order of scenes, shot lengths, and number and kind of takes. Sometimes these notes are added to the LINED SCRIPT.

Scrubbing   During the EDITING process, the action of repeatedly moving sound or picture over a point or playhead to find a particular CUE.

Second unit   A small subordinate film crew responsible for capturing SHOTS of less importance, such as inserts, crowd scenes, outdoor scenery, and so forth.

Segue   To move from one scene to the next, usually accompanied by a short piece of music known as a "bridge."

Sequence   A series of related shots of an activity in which continuing action flows smoothly from one SHOT to the next to create the illusion of an uninterrupted event. Also, in a NONLINEAR EDITING system, the term that refers to a computerized list of instructions or blueprints of an edited story as it will be aired. These instructions indicate to the computer which media files should play back when and where.

Set   The immediate area where filmed action takes place, usually constructed on a soundstage.

Set-up   The positioning of the camera, lights, sound equipment, performers, and so forth for a particular SCENE or any given SHOT.

Shallow depth of field   When only a narrow area of depth within the SCENE appears to be in FOCUS, such as when a foreground object is reproduced in razor-crisp focus but the background is blurred.

Shallow focus   A situation whereby a performer cannot move toward or away from the lens of the camera without being out of FOCUS.

Shield law A law that protects journalists from having to disclose the identities of confidential sources, which can be overridden in special circumstances, such as national security.

Shoot The act of filming with a camera. Also, the LOCATION where filming is taking place.

Shooting ratio The ratio of footage photographed in the field to that used in the final version of the production.

Shooting schedule A detailed listing of filming days and times, cast and crew members required, LOCATION changes, and transportation needs.

Shooting script The version of the SCRIPT that has been approved for production.

Shop To present or pitch a project to those individuals capable of financing it.

Shot The basic unit of film; a continuously exposed, unedited piece of film of any length, usually devoted to a single cinematic view or TAKE.

Shot list A director's list of every SHOT that will be needed in the production.

Signal-to-noise ratio (S/N ratio) A term used to measure the background noise of a system.

Silent bit Performer with no lines to deliver but who contributes to the action of a scene, such as a waiter who spills hot soup on the primary performer (whereas the other waiters in the scene who are waiting on the tables are considered EXTRAS).

Silks White cloths used for modifying the amount and quality of light during filming, often used to "bounce" light in a particular direction.

Sitcom (Situation Comedy) Colloquial slang that describes a half-hour television comedy.

Skip frame See FAST ACTION.

Slow motion Action filmed at a speed faster than normal that, when projected at normal speed, appears slower on the screen than in reality. This effect can be achieved by using an OPTICAL effect that slows down the action by printing every frame more than once, but the effect will appear jerkier than slow motion achieved by running the camera at a high frame rate.

Soft focus A SCENE or an area within a scene that appears to be out of FOCUS.

Softlight Any of a range of lighting instruments that bounce light off an internal, reflective surface, thereby diffusing and softening it.

Software Any list of instructions written for a computer that allows it to perform specific tasks.

Sound bite A short excerpt from an interview, public statement, or spontaneous comment that normally is aired as part of a broadcast news package.

Sound effects Any sound that must be added to a SCENE after the fact (usually in POSTPRODUCTION), but usually used to describe sounds not made by a human being. (Those are known as FOLEY.)

Sound mix The process of mixing all the sounds that will go into the final form of a production or film.

Soundstage A hangarlike building where filming takes place under controlled conditions on specially constructed sets.

Soundtrack The audio portion of a production, divided into three or four separate tracks or channels: dialogue, music, effects, and spillover track for additional sounds. Also refers to the recorded version of the production's musical score, usually available for purchase.

Source deck In a linear video editing system, this is the tape deck that holds the raw, unedited footage of the production.

Source music Any music that appears to be created or happening on screen, such as the music from a band playing in a SCENE of the production.

Speaking role A role in which the character speaks scripted dialogue. A nonspeaking role is a character specifically mentioned in the SCRIPT but who does not have any lines of dialogue. Speaking roles typically pay much more than nonspeaking roles. While extras may or may not be heard to speak in a production, they are not included as either speaking or nonspeaking roles.

Special effects (FX or SFX) In filmmaking and television production, this is a broad term for a range of shots and processes, including model shots, matte SHOTS, rear projection, and other effects that are artificially created for the camera.

Spec script A completed SCRIPT that has not been contracted from a writer but is being offered for sale literally on speculation.

Splice Joining of two films or audio pieces. Usually done with splicing tape, but can also be "hot waxed."

Split-screen image Two or more separate images that do not overlap within the frame.

Spot effects Spot sounds that are not continuous and are designed to go with a specific action.

Spot meter A light meter that measures light reflecting off a specific spot on the set or on a performer.

Spot news Hard news events, such as fires, explosions, airline crashes, hurricanes, tornados, and earthquakes, that break suddenly and without warning.

Spotting The process of going through the final picture edit of a production and deciding where to place sound effects and music. Music is usually handled in a separate session between the director and the composer to decide the length, location, and style of the musical cues.

Sprocket The driving wheel or synchronizing wheel of a film apparatus provided with teeth to engage the perforations of the film.

Squib A small explosive device that will simulate, when detonated, the effect of a bullet or a small explosion. When worn by performers, they typically include a container of blood that bursts on detonation.

Staging area   An area near a set where crew members can set up and store equipment and supplies.

Stand-in   A person who substitutes for a performer during the long process of blocking and lighting, sitting or standing where the performer will be and allowing the director to envision the SCENE and the lighting crew to adjust the lighting without having to keep the performer on the set.

Steadicam   A movie camera that is mounted to the body of its operator and maneuvered by its operator. It is a special gyroscopically controlled camera that smoothes out the visual effect of bumps and other visual disturbances created by the movements of its operator.

Steinbeck   The brand name of a film editing machine.

Stinger   An extension cord that runs a single light on the set.

Stock footage   Archival materials from film libraries that are recycled from other films or television productions and are available for a fee.

Storyboard   A sequence of drawings that depict the story line of the production as a guide for filming. Similar to cartoon panels, storyboards can be hand drawn, computer generated, or reproduced as photographs from still slides or film.

Stunt   In filmmaking and television production, an action that appears different and more incredible than the actual action filmed.

Sweetener   A sound effect designed to be used in conjunction with other sound effects to add texture and bass elements and never designed to be used by itself

Sweetening   In videotape and digital editing, the process of building up tracks and mixing sound and all audio postproduction sound work.

Swing gang   Part of the set dressing crew, this group moves the furniture and other parts of a set.

Switcher   The control panel for a multicamera video shoot, usually used by the director to select which camera SHOT actually will be seen in the final production.

Sync (Synchronization)   The exact matching of sound to the filmed action.

Syndication   Term for the licensing of television programming for reruns after its original network contract has expired.

Take   An individual piece of film with no cuts, or one SHOT (filmed version) of a particular SCENE. A shot may be filmed several times until a satisfactory TAKE is achieved.

Telecine   The process of converting a film image into a video image. Also describes the equipment used in the process, a movie projector and TV camera combination.

Teleplay   The SCRIPT for a television program, as opposed to a screenplay for a film.

Television movie   A feature-length movie funded by a TV network and intended to be premiered on television.

Television special   A television production of a singular event (such as an awards show) as opposed to a regularly scheduled series.

Telewriter   A writer who either adapts an existing work for production on television or creates a new TELEPLAY.

Temp dub   Temporary music and effects added to a rough cut version of a project for screening by network executives.

Temp track   A set of temporary musical cues assembled by the director to give the composer an idea of what the director wants.

Tilt shot   The vertical equivalent of a PAN shot in which the camera tilts up or down to reveal new action or subject matter.

Timecode   The sequential reference code attached to each frame of film that aids the editor in cutting the footage together. This numbering system, adopted by the Society of Motion Picture and Television Engineers (SMPTE), assigns a number to each video frame indicating hours, minutes, seconds, and frames.

Timecode generator   An electronic device that outputs timecodes.

Timeline   The graphic representation of the story being edited on a system. Using the timeline, changes can be made to the package during its construction or to the completed package. Shots can be deleted and others substituted, or deleted and the others slid together. Shots can be added, lengths can be changed, and natural sound can be spliced in at will. This splicing on the timeline is the foundation of NONLINEAR EDITING.

Track   A single component or channel of a soundtrack.

Tracking shot   The action of moving a camera along a path parallel to the path of the object being photographed.

Trades   The film and television industry trade papers, *Daily Variety* and the *Hollywood Reporter.*

Trailer   A compilation of film clips taken from a soon-to-be broadcast television production and used for promotional purposes.

Transitional shot   A SHOT, such as a cutaway, that bridges two scenes, shots, or camera angles within a SCENE.

Treatment   An initial written narrative of a story that a writer or a PRODUCTION COMPANY hopes to develop into a SCRIPT.

Trucking shot   When a camera moves through space past fixed objects.

T/stop   A camera lens aperture setting somewhat equivalent to an F/STOP but that takes into account the various light-absorbing properties of the lens.

Tyler mount   Device used to attach a camera to a helicopter or camera plane; it is equipped with a gyroscope to eliminate unwanted vibration.

Umbrella lighting   A soft, indirect form of light created by shining artificial light into a metallic-colored, heat-resistant umbrella.

Unidirectional   A microphone pickup pattern in which only sound in front of the mic is picked up.

Union scale   The minimum pay rate approved by a union for its members.

User bits   Areas in the vertical interval where various information, such as keycode and various timecodes, can be recorded. User bits have eight digits.

Vertical interval   The area in a video signal where non-video information, such as TIMECODE or captioning, are stored. This information cannot be seen without the signal being run through a decoder. For example, most closed-captioning information is placed on a specific line but cannot be seen on a TV set without the signal running through a box that decodes that information and puts it in a window on the television screen. Likewise, such information as the linear timecode, audio timecode, KEYCODE, foot and frame numbers, cameral roll, SCENE, and TAKE information can be encoded into this area.

Video   Electronic image-making system recorded on magnetic tape; typically used in television, commercials, music videos, and the home.

Video editing   Process of selecting and electronically assembling VIDEO-recorded material onto a master tape or master disc.

Video mixer   Electronic device used to combine VIDEO SHOTS from two or more sources. Some mixers can also be used to add a variety of transitional and special effects, such as CHROMA KEY, DISSOLVES, FADES, FREEZE FRAMES, WIPES, and ZOOMS.

Videotape   Flexible plastic tape containing a coating of minute iron-oxide particles designed for recording and playing back color images and sound through magnetic alignment and reading of the coating's sensitive particles.

Viewfinder   The part of the camera into which a photographer looks.

Visual effects   Alterations made to a production's images during POSTPRODUCTION.

Visual vocal   Describes a singer who is singing on screen as opposed to a BACKGROUND VOCAL.

Voice over (VO)   Ancillary dialogue, explanatory speech, or narration, separate from the dialogue soundtrack, that is recorded separately on a soundstage. It is added to the footage and superimposed over sound effects and music during POSTPRODUCTION.

Walk-on   Small nonspeaking acting part in which the performer walks onto the set.

Walla   A wash of background voices where no one voice or words can be identified.

Webcasting   Broadcasting specifically on the Web.

Wild lines   Dialogue recorded without reference to the picture.

Wild sound   Audio recorded without a SYNC relationship to a specific picture.

Wild track   A sound recording of dialogue or other sounds that has been made independently of the camera and without synchronizing with the picture.

Wipes   An optical EDITING process whereby one image appears to shove off the screen the preceding image.

Wire services   International news agencies that sell stories from around the world to broadcast stations and other news services via various delivery methods.

Workprint   The positive print used in editing that is printed directly from the original camera negative. Also called a CUTTING PRINT.

Wrap   A shot, shoot, or production that is completed is said to be "wrapped."

Zip cord   A small electrical cable used for very-low-wattage electrical devices.

Zone shot   Camera shot that records a specific section of a production set. It is usually done to process a composited-image visual effect, such as a SPLIT-SCREEN or one involving a MATTE. A performer in a zone shot has to stay in the designated performing area in order to be seen in the final SHOT.

Zoom   A camera SHOT produced from a fixed location with a continuously variable focal length lens. When the lens is said to "zoom in," the subject appears to grow larger and move closer to the screen. When the lens is said to "zoom out," the subject appears to grow smaller and move away from the screen.

Zoom lens   A camera lens that provides for continuously variable focal length settings from wide angle to telephoto.

BIBLIOGRAPHY

Abbott, Langer & Associates, Inc. "Salary Survey Summaries" and "Salary & Benefits Surveys," 2005. Available online at http://www.abbott-langer.com.

Adams, Sally. *Interviewing for Journalists.* New York: Routledge, 2001.

Adler, Stella. *The Art of Acting.* New York: Applause Books, 2000.

Anderson, Bonnie. *News Flash: Journalism, Infotainment and the Bottom-Line Business of Broadcast News.* Indianapolis: Jossey-Bass, 2004.

Anson, Chris M., and Robert A. Schwegler. *The Longman Handbook for Writers and Readers.* New York: Addison Wesley Longman, 2000.

Argentini, Paul. *Elements of Style for Screenwriters: The Essential Manual for Writers of Screenplays.* Los Angeles: Lone Eagle, 1998.

Arya, Bob. *Thirty Seconds to Air: A Field Reporter's Guide to Live Television Reporting.* Ames: Iowa State University Press, 1999.

Ascher, Steven, and Edward Pincus. *The Filmmaker's Handbook: A Comprehensive Guide to the Digital Age.* Rev. ed. New York: Plume, 1999.

Atchity, Kenneth, and Chi-Li Wong. *Writing Treatments That Sell: How to Create and Market Your Story Ideas to the Motion Picture and TV Industry.* New York: Henry Holt, 1997.

Barron's Educational Series Editors. *Barron's Profiles of American Colleges.* 26th ed. Hauppauge, N.Y.: Barron's, 2005.

Barr, Tony. *Acting for the Camera.* Rev. ed. New York: Harper, 1997.

Bayes, Steve. *The Avid Handbook: Intermediate Techniques, Strategies, and Survival Information for Avid Editing Systems.* 4th ed. Burlington, Mass.: Focal Press, 2003.

Berman, Robert A. *Fade In: The Screenwriting Process.* 2nd ed. Studio City, Calif.: Michael Wiese Productions, 1997.

Bernard, Ian. *Film and Television Acting: From Stage to Screen.* 2nd ed. Burlington, Mass.: Focal Press, 1997.

Birn, Jeremy. *Digital Lighting & Rendering.* Berkeley, Calif.: New Riders Press, 2000.

Bizony, Piers. *Digital Domain: The Leading Edge of Visual Effects.* New York: Billboard Books, 2001.

Bliss, Edward, Jr. *Now the News: The Story of Broadcast Journalism.* New York: Columbia University Press, 1991.

Bliss, Edward Jr., and James L. Hoyt. *Writing News for Broadcast.* New York: Columbia University Press, 1994.

Block, Bruce. *The Visual Story: Seeing the Structure of Film, TV and New Media.* Burlington, Mass.: Focal Press, 2001.

Block, Mervin. *Broadcast Newswriting: The RTNDA Reference Guide.* Chicago: Bonus Books, 1994.

———. *Writing Broadcast News—Shorter, Sharper, Stronger.* Rev. ed. Chicago: Bonus Books, 1997.

Block, Mervin, and Joe Durso, Jr. *Writing News for TV and Radio.* Chicago: Bonus Books, 1999.

Blum, Richard A. *Television and Screen Writing: From Concept to Contract.* New York: Hastings House, 1995.

Blumenthal, Howard J., and Oliver R. Goodenough. *This Business of Television.* 2nd ed. New York: Billboard Books, 1998.

Boorstin, Jon. *Making Movies Work: Thinking Like a Filmmaker.* Los Angeles: Silman-James Press, 1995.

Box, Harry C. *Set Lighting Technician's Handbook.* 2nd ed. Burlington, Mass.: Focal Press, 1997.

Boyd, Andrew. *Broadcast Journalism: Techniques of Radio and TV News.* 5th ed. Burlington, Mass.: Focal Press, 2001.

Brinkman, Ron. *The Art and Science of Digital Compositing.* San Francisco: Morgan Kaufmann, 1999.

Broadcast Employment Services. *Salaries.TVJobs.com* (comparative TV jobs salaries). Available by subscription at http://www.tvjobs.com

Brody, Larry. *Television Writing from the Inside Out: Your Channel to Success.* New York: Applause Books, 2003.

Brooks, Brian S., George Kennedy, Daryl R. Moen, and Don Ranly. *Telling the Story: Writing for Print, Broadcast and Online Media.* New York: Bedford/St. Martin's, 2003.

Brooks, Tim, and Earle Marsh. *The Complete Directory to Prime Time Network and Cable TV Shows, 1946–Present.* 8th ed. New York: Ballantine, 2003.

Brown, Blain. *Motion Picture and Video Lighting.* Burlington, Mass.: Focal Press, 1996.

Brown, James, and Quaal Ward. *Radio-Television-Cable Management.* New York: McGraw-Hill, 1998.

Bureau of Labor Statistics, U.S. Department of Labor. *Federal Government General Schedule Pay Rates, 2003.* Compiled by the U.S. Office of Personnel Management. Available online at http://www.bls.gov.

———. *Occupational Employment and Wages, November, 2004.* Sound Engineering Technicians Report. Available online at http://www.bls.gov/oes/current/oes274014.htm.

———. *Occupational Outlook Handbook and Career Guide to Industries, 2004–05 Edition.* Advertising and

Public Relations Services Report. Available online at http://www/bis/gov/oco/cg/cgs030.htm.

———. *Occupational Outlook Handbook and Career Guide to Industries, 2004-05 Edition.* Announcers Report. Available online at http://stats.bls.gov/oco/ocos087.htm.

———. *Occupational Outlook Handbook and Career Guide to Industries, 2004–05 Edition.* Broadcasters Report. Available online at http://www.bls.gov/oco/cg/cgs017.htm.

———. *Occupational Outlook Handbook and Career Guide to Industries, 2004–05 Edition.* Designers Report. Available online at http://www.bls.gov/oco/cg/cgs017.htm.

———. *Occupational Outlook Handbook and Career Guide to Industries, 2004–05 Edition.* Musicians, Singers, and Related Workers Report. Available online at http://www.bls.gov/oco/ocos087.htm.

———. *Occupational Outlook Handbook and Career Guide to Industries, 2004–05 Edition.* News Analysts, Reporters, and Correspondents Report. Available online at http://www.bls.gov/oco/ocos088.htm.

———. *Occupational Outlook Handbook and Career Guide to Industries, 2004–05 Edition.* Secretaries and Administrative Assistants Report. Available online at http://www.bls.gov/oco/cg/cgs017.htm.

———. *Occupational Outlook Handbook and Career Guide to Industries, 2004–05 Edition.* Television, Video, and Motion Picture Camera Operators and Editors Report. Available online at http://www.bls.gov/oco/ocos091.htm.

———. *Occupational Outlook Handbook and Career Guide to Industries, 2004–05 Edition.* Top Executives Report. Available online at http://www.bls.gov/oco/ocos012.htm.

Burton, Graeme. *Talking Television: An Introduction to the Study of Television.* New York: Oxford University Press, 2000.

Button, Bryce. *Nonlinear Editing: Storytelling, Aesthetics & Craft.* Gilroy, Calif.: CMP Books, 2002.

Caine, Michael. *Michael Caine — Acting in Film: An Actor's Take on Movie Making.* New York: Applause Books, 2000.

Campbell, Drew. *Technical Film and TV for Nontechnical People.* New York: Allworth Press, 2002.

Carr, Forrest, Suzanne Huffman, and C. A. Tuggle. *Broadcast News Handbook.* New York: McGraw-Hill, 2001.

Ciciora, Walter, James Farmer, David Large, and Michael Adams. *Modern Cable Television Technology.* 2nd ed. San Francisco: Morgan Kaufmann, 2003.

Clark, Barbara, and Susan J. Spohr. *Guide to Postproduction for TV and Film: Managing the Process.* 2nd ed. Burlington, Mass.: Focal Press, 2002.

Clements, Steve. *Show Runner: Producing Variety & Talk Shots for Television.* Los Angeles: Silman-James Press, 2004.

College Board Editors. *The College Board Book of Majors.* Plano, Tex.: College Board Publications, 2004.

Connect2jobs.org. "Job Descriptions and Information." Available online at http://www./connect2jobs.org.

Covington, William G., Jr. *Creativity in TV & Cable Managing & Producing.* Lanham, Md.: University Press of America, 1999.

Cowgill, Linda J. *Secrets of Screenplay Structure.* Los Angeles: Lone Eagle, 1999.

Crisp, Mike. *The Practical Director.* Burlington, Mass.: Focal Press, 1998.

Crouch, Tanja L. *100 Careers in Film and Television.* Hauppauge, N.Y.: Barron's, 2003

Cury, Ivan. *Directing & Producing for Television: A Format Approach.* 2nd ed. Burlington, Mass.: Focal Press, 2001.

Dancyger, Ken. *The Technique of Film and Video Editing: History, Theory, and Practice.* 3rd ed. Burlington, Mass.: Focal Press, 2002.

Daniels, Bill, David Leedy, and Steven D. Sills. *Movie Money: Understanding Hollywood's (Creative) Accounting Practices.* Los Angeles: Silman-James Press, 1998.

De Abreu, Carlos, and Howard Jay Smith. *Opening the Doors to Hollywood: How to Sell Your Idea, Story, Book, Screenplay, Manuscript.* New York: Three Rivers Press, 1995.

Decina, Rob. *The Art of Auditioning: Techniques for Television.* New York: Allworth Press, 2004.

Demers, Owen. *Digital Texturing & Painting.* Berkeley, Calif.: New Riders Press, 2001.

Dobbert, Tim. *Matchmoving: The Invisible Art of Camera Tracking.* San Francisco: Sybex, 2005.

Dominick, Joseph R., Barry L. Sherman, and Fritz Messere. *Broadcasting, Cable, the Internet and Beyond.* 4th ed. New York: McGraw-Hill, 1999,

Donald, Ralph, and Thomas Spann. *Fundamentals of Television Production.* Ames: Iowa State University Press, 2000.

Donaldson, Michael C. *Clearance and Copyright.* 2nd ed. Los Angeles: Silman-James Press, 2003.

Dotson, Bob, and Matt Lauer. *Make It Memorable: Writing and Packaging TV News with Style.* Chicago: Bonus Books, 2000.

Duignan, Patricia Rose. *Industry Light & Magic: Into the Digital Realm.* New York: Del Rey, 1996.

Elkins, David E. *The Camera Assistant's Manual.* 4th ed. Burlington, Mass.: Focal Press, 2005.

Ellis, Elmo Israel. *Opportunities in Broadcasting Careers.* New York: McGraw Hill/Contemporary Books, 1998.

Engel, Joel. *Screenwriters on Screenwriting: The Best in the Business Discuss Their Craft.* New York: Hyperion, 1995.

Entertainment Partners. *Entertainment Partner's Budgeting, New Version 6.* Burbank, Calif.: Entertainment Partners, 2005. Available online at http//www.entertainmentpartners.com.

———. *Entertainment Partner's Paymaster Book 2005–2006.* Burbank, Calif.: Entertainment Partners, 2005. Available online at http//www.entertainmentpartners.com.

———. *Entertainment Partner's Scheduling, New Version 4.* Burbank, Calif.: Entertainment Partners, 2005. Available online at http//www.entertainmentpartners.com

FastWeb. "Broadcast Journalism: Career Overview." 2004. Available online at http://fastweb.monster.com/fastweb/content/career_db/broadcast_journalism.

Field, Syd. *The Screenwriter's Problem Solver: How to Recognize, Identify, and Define Screenwriting.* New York: Dell, 1998.

Fitzsimmons, April. *Breaking & Entering: A Career Guide About Landing Your First Job in Film Production . . . and Living to Tell About It!* Los Angeles: Lone Eagle Publishing, 1997.

Fraioli, James O. *Storyboarding 101: A Crash Course in Professional Storyboarding.* Studio City, Calif.: Michael Wiese Productions, 2000.

Freedman, Wayne. *It Takes More Than Good Looks to Succeed at TV News Reporting.* Chicago: Bonus Books, 2002.

Gates, Richard. *Production Management for Film and Video.* Burlington, Mass.: Focal Press, 1995.

Gibbons, Sheila. "Top Jobs Elude Women in Broadcast News." *Women's eNews,* November 16, 2004. Available online at http://www./womensenews.org/article.cfm/dyn/aid/1051/context/uncoveringgender.

Gitlin, Todd. *Media Unlimited: How the Torrent of Images and Sounds Overwhelms Our Lives.* New York: Owl Books, 2003.

Gloman, Chuck. *303 Digital Filmmaking Solutions: Solve Any Video Shoot or Edit Problem in Ten Minutes or Less, for Ten Dollars or Less.* New York: McGraw-Hill, 2003.

Gold, Donald L., and Paul Mason. *Producing for Hollywood: A Guide for the Independent Producer.* New York: Allworth Press, 2000.

Goldberg, Lee, and William Rabkin. *Successful Television Writing.* Hoboken, N.J.: Wiley, 2003

Gondek, Mike, and Archie Cocke. *Photoshop for Digital Video: Creative Solutions for Professional Results.* Burlington, Mass.: Focal Press, 2004.

Goodell, Gregory. *Independent Feature Film Production: A Complete Guide from Concept Through Distribution.* Rev. ed. New York: St. Martin's/Griffin, 1998.

Goodman, Robert M., and Patrick McGrath. *Editing Digital Video: The Complete Creative and Technical Guide.* New York: McGraw-Hill, 2002.

Gordon, Sandra. *Action!: Establishing Your Career in Film and Television Production.* New York: Applause Books, 2002.

Gottlieb-Walker, Kim, ed. *Setiquette.* Los Angeles: International Photographers Guild, 1997.

Goulekas, Karen. *Visual Effects in a Digital World: A Comprehensive Glossary of Over 7000 Visual Effects Terms.* San Francisco: Morgan Kaufmann, 2001.

Greene, David. *Motion Graphics: How Did They Do That?* Gloucester, Mass.: Rockport Publishers, 2003.

Griffiths, Alan. *Digital Television Strategies: Business Challenges and Opportunities.* New York: Palgrave Macmillan, 2003.

Griffiths, Richard. *Videojournalism: The Definitive Guide to Multi-Skilled Television Production.* Burlington, Mass.: Butterworth-Heinemann, 1998.

Grotticelli, Michael. *American Cinematographer Video Manual.* 3rd ed. Los Angeles: American Society of Cinematography, 2001.

Harmon, Renee. *Film Directing: Killer Style & Cutting Edge Technique.* Los Angeles: Lone Eagle Publishing, 1997.

Harrington, Richard, Glen Stephens, and Chris Vadnais. *Broadcast Graphics On the Spot: Timesaving Techniques Using Photostop and After Effects for Broadcast and Post Production.* Gilroy, Calif.: CMP Books, 2005.

Head, Sydney W., Thomas Spann, and Michael A. McGregor. *Broadcasting in America: A Survey of Electronic Media.* 9th ed. Boston: Houghton Mifflin, 2001

Henry, Mari Lyn, and Lynne Rogers. *How to Be a Working Actor: The Insider's Guide to Finding Jobs in Theater, Film, and Television.* 4th ed. New York: Watson-Guptill, 2000.

Hilliard, Robert L. *Writing for Television, Radio, and the New Media.* 7th ed. Belmont, Calif.: Wadsworth Publishing, 1999.

Hollingsworth, Mike, and Kimberley Stewart-Mole. *How to Get into Television, Radio and New Media.* New York: Continuum, 2004.

Holman, Tomlinson. *Sound for Film and Television.* 2nd ed. Burlington, Mass.: Focal Press, 2002.

Honthaner, Eve Light. *The Complete Film Production Handbook.* Los Angeles: Lone Eagle Publishing, 1996.

Horton, Andrew. *Writing the Character-Centered Screenplay.* Berkeley; University of California Press, 1999.

Houghton, Buck. *What a Producer Does: The Art of Moviemaking (Not the Business).* Los Angeles: Silman-James Press, 1992.

Hullfish, Steve, and Jaime Fowler. *Color Correction for Digital Video: Using Desktop Tools to Perfect Your Image.* Gilroy, Calif.: CMP Books, 2002.

Hummel, Rob. *American Cinematographer Manual.* 8th ed. Los Angeles: American Society of Cinematography, 2002.

Hynes, Angela. *Fabjob Guide to Become a Screenwriter.* An e-book. Available online at http://www.fabjob.com/Screenwriter.asp.

Jackman, John. *Lighting for Digital Video & Television.* Gilroy, Calif.: CMP Books, 2002.

Job Report. "Radio and Television Announcers and Newscasters." Available online at http://shelomi.com/job_report_radio_and_television.htm.

JobStar: Profession Specific Salary Surveys. *The Wall Street Journal: CareerJournal.com.* Available online at http://www.jobstar.org/tools/salary/sal-prof.cfm#PR.

JobStar: Salary Information Index. *The Wall Street Journal: CareerJournal.com.* Available online at http://jobstar.org/tools/salary/index.cfm.

Jones, Graham. *A Broadcast Engineering Tutorial for Non-Engineers.* 3rd ed. Burlington, Mass.: Focal Press, 2005

Kalbfeld, Brad. *The Associated Press Broadcast News Handbook.* New York: McGraw-Hill, 2000.

Katahn, Terri, and T. A. Katahn. *Reading for a Living: How to Be a Professional Story Analyst for Film and Television.* Pacific Palisades, Calif.: Blue Arrow Books, 1990.

Katz, Steven. *Film Directing Cinematic Motion: A Workshop for Staging Scenes.* Studio City, Calif.: Michael Wiese Productions, 1992.

———. *Film Directing, Shot by Shot.* Studio City, Calif.: Michael Wiese Productions, 1991.

Kaurrmann, Sam. *Avid Editing: A Guide for Beginning and Intermediate Users.* 2nd ed. Burlington, Mass.: Focal Press, 2003.

Kehoe, Vincent. *The Technique of the Professional Make-Up Artist.* Rev. ed. Burlington, Mass.: Focal Press, 1995.

Kelly, Doug. *Digital Compositing in Depth: The Only Guide to Post Production for Visual Effects in Film.* Albany, N.Y.: Coriolis Group Books, 2000.

Kenny, Tom, ed. *Sound for Picture.* New York: Mix Books, 2000.

Kondazian, Karen, and Eddie Shapiro. *The Actor's Encyclopedia of Casting Directors: Conversations with Over 100 Casting Directors and How to Get the Job.* Los Angeles: Lone Eagle Publishing, 2000.

Kosareff, Steve. *Window to the Future: The Golden Age of Television Marketing and Advertising.* San Francisco: Chronicle Books, 2005.

Kouguell, Susan. *The Savvy Screenwriter: How to Sell Your Screenplay (And Yourself) Without Selling Out!* Exeter, N.H.: TL Hoell Books, 2000.

Lampen, Stephen H. *Audio/Video Cable Installer's Pocket Guide.* New York: McGraw-Hill, 2002.

Lee, John L., and Rob Holt. *The Producer's Business Handbook.* 2nd ed. Burlington, Mass.: Focal Press, 2005.

Lent, Michael. *Breakfast with Sharks: A Screenwriter's Guide to Getting the Meeting, Nailing the Pitch, Signing the Deal, and Navigating the Murky Waters of Hollywood.* New York: Three Rivers Press, 2004.

Lerch, Jennifer. *500 Ways to Beat the Hollywood Script Reader: Writing the Screenplay the Reader Will Recommend.* New York: Simon & Schuster, 1999.

Levy, Frederick. *Hollywood 101: The Film Industry.* Los Angeles: Renaissance Books, 2000.

Lindenmuth, Kevin J. *The Independent Film Experience: Interviews with Directors and Producers.* Jefferson, N.C.: McFarland, 2001.

Litwak, Mark. *Contracts for the Film and Television Industry.* Los Angeles: Silman-James Press, 1999.

———. *Dealmaking in the Film and Television Industry From Negotiations Through Final Contracts.* 2nd ed. Los Angeles: Silman-James Press, 2002.

Maisel, Eric. *Coaching the Artist Within: Advice for Writers, Actors, Visual Artists, and Musicians from America's Foremost Creativity Coach.* Novato, Calif.: New World Library, 2005.

Malkiewicz, Kris. *Cinematography.* New York: Simon & Schuster, 1989.

———. *Film Lighting: Talks with Hollywood's Cinematographers and Gaffers.* New York: Simon & Schuster, 1992.

McAlister, Michael J. *The Language of Visual Effects.* Los Angeles: Lone Eagle Publishing, 1993.

McCarthy, Robert. *Secrets of Hollywood Special Effects.* Burlington, Mass.: Focal Press, 1992.

McCoy, Michelle, and Ann S. Utterback. *Sound and Look Professional on Television and the Internet: How to Improve Your On-Camera Presence.* Chicago: Bonus Books, 2000.

McKee, Robert. *Story: Substance, Structure, Style, and the Principles of Screenwriting.* New York: HarperCollins, 1997.

Meisner, Sanford. *Meisner on Acting.* New York: Vintage, 1987.

Merritt, Greg. *Film Production: The Complete Uncensored Guide to Filmmaking.* Los Angeles: Lone Eagle Publishing, 1998.

Meyer, Trish, and Chris Meyer. *After Effects in Production.* Gilroy, Calif.: CMP Books, 2001.

———. *Creating Motion Graphics with After Effects, Volume 1: The Essentials.* 2nd ed. Gilroy, Calif.: CMP Books, 2002.

———. *Creating Motion Graphics with After Effects, Volume 2: Advanced Techniques.* 2nd ed. Gilroy, Calif.: CMP Books, 2003.

Miller, Pat P. *Script Supervising and Film Continuity.* Burlington, Mass.: Focal Press, 1999.

Mitchell, Mitch. *Visual Effects for Film and Television.* Burlington, Mass.: Focal Press, 2004.

Mogel, Leonard. *This Business of Broadcasting: A Practical Guide to Jobs & Job Opportunities in the Broadcasting Industry.* New York: Billboard Books/Watson-Guptil, 2004.

Monahan, Kevin. *Motion Graphics and Effects in Final Cut Pro.* Berkeley, Calif.: Peachpit Press, 2003.

Morawetz, Thomas. *Making Faces, Playing God: Identity and the Art of Transformational Makeup.* Austin: University of Texas Press, 2001.

Mulpuru, Sucharita. *Vault Career Guide to Media & Entertainment.* 2nd ed. New York: Vault.com, 2003.

Murch, Walter. *In the Blink of an Eye.* Los Angeles: Silman-James Press, 1996.

Newcomb, Horace, ed. *Encyclopedia of Television.* 2nd ed. Chicago: Fitzroy Dearborn Publishers, 2004.

Nicholas, Michael S. *An Actor's Guide: Your First Year in Hollywood.* New York: Allworth Press, 2000.

Ohanian, Thomas A. *Digital Nonlinear Editing: Editing Film and Video on the Desktop.* Burlington, Mass.: Focal Press, 1998.

Oldham, Gabriella. *First Cut: Conversations with Film Editors.* Berkeley: University of California Press, 1995.

Oldman, Mark, and Samer Hamadeh. *The Best 109 Internships.* 9th ed. Lawrenceville, N.J.: Princeton Review, 2003.

———. *The Internship Bible, 2005.* 10th ed. Lawrenceville, N.J.: Princeton Review, 2005.

Oram, Fern A., ed. *Peterson's Two-Year Colleges 2006.* Princeton, N.J.: Peterson's Guides, 2005.

Owsinski, Bobby. *The Mixing Engineer's Handbook.* Boston: Artistpro, 1999.

Papper, Robert A. *Broadcast News Writing Stylebook.* Boston: Allyn & Bacon, 2002.

———. "Radio and Television News Salaries, 2004 Data: Salaries Soar." The Radio-Television News Directors Association & Foundation: *Communicator,* June 2004. Available online on a subscription basis at http://www.rtnda.org/communicator/showarticle.asp?id=102.

———. "Women and Minorities in Radio and Television News, 2004 Data: Recovering Lost Ground." The Radio-Television News Directors Association & Foundation: *Communicator,* July/August, 2004. Available online at http://www.rtnda.org/research/research.shtml.

Papper, Robert A., and Michael Gerhard. "2002 Radio and Television Salary Survey." The Radio-Television News Directors Association & Foundation. Available online at http://www.rtnda.org/research/salaries02.shtml.

Parrent, Joanne. *The Complete Idiot's Guide to Filmmaking.* Indianapolis: Alpha Books, 2002.

Penney, Edmund F. *The Facts On File Dictionary of Film and Broadcast Terms.* New York: Facts On File, 1992.

Plunkett, Jack W., ed. *Plunkett's Entertainment & Media Industry Almanac 2004.* Houston: Plunkett Research, 2004.

Pohlmann, Ken C. *Principles of Digital Audio.* 4th ed. New York: McGraw-Hill, 2000.

Press, Skip. *The Complete Idiot's Guide to Screenwriting.* New York: Alpha Books, 2001.

———. *Writer's Guide to Hollywood Producers, Directors, and Screenwriter's Agents, 2002–2003.* New York: Prima Publishing, 2001.

Princeton Review Staff. *Complete Book of Colleges.* New York: Princeton Review, 2005.

Rabiger, Michael. *Directing: Film Techniques and Aesthetics.* 2nd ed. Burlington, Mass.: Focal Press, 1997.

Rannow, Jerry. *Writing Television Comedy.* New York: Allworth Press, 2000.

Reisz, Karel, and Gavin Millar. *The Technique of Film Editing.* Burlington, Mass.: Focal Press, 1995.

Resnik, Gail, and Scott Trost. *All You Need to Know About the Movie and TV Business.* New York: Simon & Schuster, 1996.

Rickitt, Richard. *Special Effects: The History and Technique.* New York: Watson-Guptil, 2000.

Riley, Christopher. *The Hollywood Standard: The Complete and Authoritative Guide to Script Format and Style.* Studio City, Calif.: Michael Wiese Productions, 2005.

Roberts, Charles. *Digital Video Edition with Final Cut Express: The Real-World Guide to Set Up and Workflow.* Burlington, Mass.: Focal Press, 2003.

Rose, Jay. *Audio Postproduction for Digital Video.* Gilroy, Calif.: CMP Press, 2002.

———. *Producing Great Sound for Digital Video.* 2nd ed. Gilroy, Calif.: CMP Press, 2002.

Rubin, Michael. *Nonlinear—A Field Guide to Digital Video and Film Editing.* 4th ed. Gainesville, Fla.: Triad Publishing, 2000.

Salary Wizard. "Salary Data from Salary.Com, Inc." Available online at http://swz.salary.com/salarywizard or http://salary.monster.com/salarywizard.

Samuelson, David W. *Motion Picture Camera & Lighting Equipment.* 2nd ed. Burlington, Mass.: Focal Press, 1980.

Santiago, David. *Creating 3D Effects for Film, TV, and Games.* Boston: Course Technology PTR, 2004.

Sautter, Carl. *How to Sell Your Screenplay: The Real Rules of Film and Television.* New York: New Chapter Press, 1992

Schreibman, Myrl A. *The Indie Producer's Handbook: Creative Producing from A to Z.* Hollywood, Calif.: ifilm Publishing/Lone Eagle Publishing, 2001.

Seger, Linda. *Making a Good Script Great.* 2nd ed. New York: Samuel French, 1994.

———. *When Women Call the Shots: The Developing Power and Influence of Women in Television and Film.* New York: Henry Holt, 1997.

Seger, Linda, and Edward Jay Whetmore. *From Script to Screen: The Collaborative Art of Filmmaking.* New York: Henry Holt, 1994.

Shook, Frederick. *Television Field Production and Reporting.* 3rd ed. New York: Longman/Addison Wesley, 2000.

Showbiz Labor Guide, 2004/2005. 10th ed. Los Angeles: Entertainment Publishers, 2004.

Singleton, Ralph S., and James A. Conrad. *Filmmaker's Dictionary.* 2nd ed. Hollywood, Calif.: ifilm Publishing/Lone Eagle Publishing, 2000.

SkillSet (Skills for Business). *Jobs in the Film Industry.* Available online at http://www.skillset.org.

Smith, Evan S. *Writing Television Sitcoms.* New York: Perigee Books, 1999.

Stone, Vernon. "Internships in TV and Radio News: Paid and Unpaid." 1995. Available online at http://www.missouri.edu~jourvs/ginterns.html.

———. "Minorities and Women in Television News, 2001." Available online at http://www.missouri.edu/~jourvs/gtvminw.html.

———. "Television and Radio News Careers, 2002." Available online at http://www.missouri.edu/~jourvs/careers8.html.

Stubbs, Liz., and Richard Rodriguez. *Making Independent Films.* New York: Allworth Press, 2000.

Swartz, Charles S. *Understanding Digital CineMass.: A Professional Handbook.* Burlington, Mass.: Focal Press, 2004.

Symes, Peter. *Digital Video Compression.* New York: McGraw-Hill, 2003.

Taub, Eric. *Gaffers, Grips, and Best Boys.* New York: St. Martin's, 1994.

Tibbetts, John C., and James M. Welsh. *The Encyclopedia of Filmmakers.* 2 vols. New York: Facts On File, 2002.

Tozer, E. P. J. *Broadcast Engineer's Reference Book.* Burlington, Mass.: Focal Press, 2004.

Trottier, David. *The Screenwriter's Bible: A Complete Guide to Writing, Formatting, and Selling Your Script.* Los Angeles: Silman-James Press, 1995.

Tucker, Patrick. *Secrets of Screen Acting.* 2nd ed. New York: Routledge, 2003.

Uva, Michael G., and Sabrina Uva. *The Grip Book.* Burlington, Mass.: Focal Press, 1997.

Vaz, Mark Cotta. *The Invisible Art: The Legends of Movie Matte Painting.* San Francisco: Chronicle Books, 2002.

Vinther, Janus. *Special Effects Make-Up.* New York: Routledge, 2003.

Vineyard, Jeremy. *Setting Up Your Shots: Great Camera Moves Every Filmmaker Should Know.* Studio City, Calif.: Michael Wiese Productions, 2000.

Walker, James R., and Douglas A. Ferguson. *The Broadcast Television Industry.* Boston: Allyn & Bacon, 1997.

Walter, Richard. *The Whole Picture: Strategies for Screenwriting Success in the New Hollywood.* New York: Plume Books, 1997.

Weaver, Dan, and Jason Siegel. *Breaking into Television: Proven Advice from Veterans and Interns.* Princeton, N.J.: Peterson's, 1998.

Weiner, Richard. *Webster's New World Dictionary of Media and Communications.* Rev. ed. New York: Macmillan, 1996.

Weston, Judith. *Directing Actors: Creating Memorable Performances for Film and Television.* Studio City, Calif.: Michael Wiese Productions, 1996.

WetFeet.com. "Career Profiles, 2004." Available online at http://wetfeet.com/asp/careerprofiles.

———. "Industry Profiles, 2004." Available online at http://wetfeet.com/asp/industryprofiles.

Weynand, Diana, and Marcus Weise. *How Video Works.* Burlington, Mass.: Focal Press, 2004.

Wharton, Brooke A. *The Writer Got Screwed (But Didn't Have To): A Guide to the Legal and Business Practices of Writing for the Entertainment Industry.* New York: HarperCollins, 1997.

Whitaker, Jerry, and Blair K. Benson. *Standard Handbook of Video and Television Engineering.* 4th ed. New York: McGraw-Hill, 2003.

Whitcomb, Cynthia. *The Writer's Guide to Writing Your Screenplay: How to Write Great Screenplays for Movies and Television.* New York: Watson-Guptil, 2002.

Wiese, Michael. *Producer to Producer: Insider Tip for Entertainment Media.* Studio City, Calif.: Michael Wiese Productions, 1997.

———, and Simon Deke, eds. *Film & Video Budgets.* 2nd ed. Studio City, Calif.: Michael Wiese Productions, 1995.

Wilen, Lydia, and Joan Wilen. *How to See Your Screenplay: A Realistic Guide to Getting a Television or Film Deal.* Garden City Park, N.Y.: Square One Publishers, 2001.

Wolsky, Tom. *Video Production Workshop.* Gilroy, Calif.: CMP Books, 2005.

Wootton, Cliff. *A Practical Guide to Video and Audio Compression: From Sprockets and Rasters to Macro Blocks.* Burlington, Mass.: Focal Press, 2005.

Wright, Steve. *Digital Compositing for Film and Video with CDROM.* Burlington, Mass.: Focal Press, 2001.

Wyatt, Hilary, and Tim Amyes. *Audio Post Production for Television and Film: An Introduction to Technology and Techniques.* 3rd ed. Burlington, Mass.: Focal Press, 2005.

Yager, Fred, and Jan Yager. *Career Opportunities in the Film Industry.* New York: Checkmark Books/Facts On File, 2003.

Yewdall, David Lewis. *Practical Art of Motion Picture Sound.* 2nd ed. Burlington, Mass.: Focal Press, 2003.

Zaza, Tony. *Script Planning: Positioning and Developing Scripts for TV and Film.* Burlington, Mass.: Focal Press, 1993.

Ziegler, Kathleen, Nick Greco, and Tamye Riggs, eds. *MotionGraphics: Film and TV.* New York: Watson-Guptil, 2002.

INDEX

ABOUT THE AUTHORS

ALLAN TAYLOR, a freelance copy editor, indexer, and researcher, comes from a family long involved in the publishing and newspaper fields and, as production manager, has been involved in the computerization of bibliographic databases. He is the coauthor of *Career Opportunities in Writing* and *The Encyclopedia of Ethnic Groups in Hollywood* (both Facts On File) and has created special bibliographic indexes for such volumes as *The Great Spy Pictures, Hollywood Songsters, 101 Things I Don't Know About Art, Questions and Answers About Community Associations,* and *Women Doctors Guide to Health and Healing.*

Mr. Taylor's publishing industry posts include tenures at the R. R. Bowker Company (Bibliographic Services), Engineering Information, Inc. (Production Manager), and Graphic Typesetting Services (Proofreading/Technical Specifications Department Manager). He resides in Los Angeles, California. His Web site is at http://www.tataylor.net.

JAMES ROBERT PARISH, a former entertainment reporter, publicist, and book series editor, is the author of many published biographies and reference books about the entertainment industry, including *Fiasco: A History of Hollywood's Iconic Flops, The American Movies Reference Book, The Complete Actors TV Credits, The Hollywood Songsters, The Hollywood Book of Breakups, The Hollywood Book of Scandals, The Hollywood Book of Death, The RKO Gals, Katharine Hepburn, Whitney Houston, Gus Van Sant,* and *Whoopi Goldberg.* With Allan Taylor he coauthored *Career Opportunities in Writing* and *The Encyclopedia of Ethnic Groups in Hollywood* (both Facts On File) and has written several entries in the Ferguson Young Adult biography series (including Jim Henson, Twyla Tharp, Denzel Washington, Katie Couric, Stan Lee, Halle Berry, Steven Spielberg, Tom Hanks, and Stephen King).

Mr. Parish is a frequent on-camera interviewee on cable and network TV for documentaries on the performing arts both in the United States and in the United Kingdom. He resides in Studio City, California. His Web site is at http://www.jamesrobertparish.com.

DATE DUE

OCT 0 7 2009			
OCT 0 7 REC'D			
GAYLORD			PRINTED IN U.S.A.